VOLUME II

CANADA'S
CONSTITUTION ACT
1982 & AMENDMENTS
A DOCUMENTARY HISTORY

VOLUME II

CANADA'S CONSTITUTION ACT 1982 & AMENDMENTS

A DOCUMENTARY HISTORY

ANNE F. BAYEFSKY

B.A., M.A., LL.B., M.Litt. (Oxon)

COMMON LAW SECTION, UNIVERSITY OF OTTAWA

McGRAW-HILL RYERSON LIMITED

Toronto   Montreal   New York   Auckland   Bogotá   Hamburg   Lisbon   London   Madrid
Mexico   Milan   New Delhi   Paris   San Juan   São Paulo   Singapore   Sydney   Tokyo

V O L U M E II

CANADA'S
CONSTITUTION ACT
1982 & AMENDMENTS
A DOCUMENTARY HISTORY

ISBN 0-07-549731-X

1 2 3 4 5 6 7 8 9 0   D   8 7 6 5 4 3 2 1 0 9

Printed and bound in Canada

For Evelyn and Aba Bayefsky

TABLE OF CONTENTS

VOLUME 1

VOLUME 2

TABLE OF CASES

TABLE OF STATUTES

PREFACE

The Constitution Act 1982 was the product of many years of federal-provincial negotiations and, at certain times, direct public consultation. The patriation agenda varied widely. Sometimes it concerned only a Canadian amending formula; at other times it included a limited charter of rights. On occasion a charter of rights addressed only language rights. In some drafts a charter of rights was to be genuinely entrenched and bypassed only by constitutional amendment. In other drafts the constitutional charter of rights could be avoided by simple legislative majorities. Sometimes amendments affected only the federal Parliament, and the provinces were permitted to opt-in. At other times an opting-in formula applied only to one province. Over the decades the patriation agenda often included a wide range of amendments to the federal-provincial division of powers.

Ultimately, patriation occurred in conjunction with a limited number of constitutional amendments. This book traces the history of those options, embodied in the Constitution Act 1982 and its amendments to date. An examination of the documents reveals the kinds of choices that the provisions of the Act represent. This record is an important tool for understanding our constitution. It permits the lawyer and political scientist to flesh out the meaning of the language from its past forms. Such historical documentation can serve an important part in constitutional scholarship and discussion. The purpose of this collection is to build a foundation for research and legal argument about the Constitution Act 1982 and its amendments.

Such an historical foundation can only be built from the original documents themselves. The material reproduced is therefore unedited. What follows is a chronological tale of the meetings, the correspondence, and the drafts produced during approximately two decades of constitutional negotiation. Although patriation was first seriously considered in the 1920s, a concentrated effort and the resulting volume of material did not emerge until the beginning of the 1960s. It is therefore at this point that the book begins.

The index has been designed to enable the reader to trace the development of a particular provision of the Constitution Act 1982 or amendments, including the Canadian Charter of Rights and Freedoms. For example, when reference is made to a section of the Charter, the index provides a guide to the right referred to therein and then lists the pages in this book where the drafts of that right appear in chronological order.

The sheer volume of material has meant that only those documents that come closest to representing an actual draft or discussion of a draft have been reproduced. In some places, this guideline has been relaxed to permit historical continuity. It should be pointed out, however, that these documents do not tell the whole story. Background papers, reports of committees, minutes of meetings, and many other forms of material surround the constitutional amendment process, and conclusions drawn from the reproduced papers should bear this in mind. Attention should also be given to the authorship of the various documents; documents prepared by government officials, for example, may not have been endorsed by ministers and may therefore not have reflected government policy.

Furthermore, there are other documents that fall within the above-mentioned guidelines but are not available for publication because of their confidential status. In particular, these documents relate to the years 1978–80. All efforts have been made to relate the process of constitutional discussion that occurred during this period.

I would like to thank Ms. Janet Brooks of the Library of Parliament for her assistance and the many students of the University of Ottawa, Common Law Section, who have helped me by their diligent research over the years, particularly J. Anthony VanDuzer, who helped begin this project, and Craig Jenness, who helped complete it.

MAJOR GOVERNMENTAL MEETINGS AND PARLIAMENTARY SESSIONS THAT GAVE RISE TO THE CONSTITUTION ACT 1982

Note: A fold out chart listing the major government meetings and parliamentary sessions which gave rise to the Constitution Act 1982 has been included for your convenience.

Federal-Provincial First Ministers' Conferences

October 14–15, 1964, Ottawa, Ontario
February 5–7, 1968, Ottawa, Ontario
February 10–12, 1969, Ottawa, Ontario
Working Session
June 11–13, 1969, Ottawa, Ontario
December 8–10, 1969, Ottawa, Ontario
Working Sessions
September 14–15, 1970, Ottawa, Ontario
February 8–9, 1971, Ottawa, Ontario
June 14–16, 1971, Victoria, British Columbia
April 9–10, 1975, Ottawa, Ontario
October 30–November 1, 1978, Ottawa, Ontario
February 5–6, 1979, Ottawa, Ontario
September 8–12, 1980, Ottawa, Ontario
November 2–5, 1981, Ottawa, Ontario

Premiers' Conferences

August 18–20, 1976, Edmonton and Banff, Alberta
October 1–2, 1976, Toronto, Ontario
August 18–19, 1977, St. Andrews, New Brunswick
February 22–23, 1978, Montreal, Quebec
August 9–12, 1978, Regina, Saskatchewan
April 16, 1981, Ottawa, Ontario

Committees of Ministers

Conferences of Attorneys General
October 6–7, 1960, Ottawa, Ontario
November 2–3, 1960, Ottawa, Ontario
January 12–13, 1961, Ottawa, Ontario
September 11–12, 1961, Ottawa, Ontario

Committees of Ministers
On Fundamental Rights
May 28–29, 1969, Ottawa, Ontario
November 3–4, 1969, Ottawa, Ontario

On the Judiciary
May 29, 1969, Ottawa, Ontario
November 4, 1969, Ottawa, Ontario

On Official Languages
May 27, 1969, Ottawa, Ontario
November 6, 1969, Ottawa, Ontario
May 25, 1970, Ottawa, Ontario

On the Senate
May 26, 1969, Ottawa, Ontario

Federal-Provincial Meeting of Ministers Responsible for the Constitution
September 26, 1978, Montreal, Quebec

Continuing Committee of Ministers on the Constitution
November 23–25, 1978, Mont St. Marie, Quebec
December 14–16, 1978, Toronto, Ontario
January 22–24, 1979, Vancouver, British Columbia
October 22–23, 1979, Halifax, Nova Scotia
June 17, 1980, Ottawa, Ontario
July 8–11, 1980, Montreal, Quebec
July 14–18, 1980, Toronto, Ontario
July 22–24, 1980, Vancouver, British Columbia
August 26–29, 1980, Ottawa, Ontario

Sub-Committee of Continuing Committee of Ministers on the Constitution and the Leadership of the National Native Organizations
December 3, 1979, Ottawa, Ontario
August 26, 1980, Ottawa, Ontario

Sub-Committee of Continuing Committee of Ministers on the Constitution
August 11–13, 1980, Ottawa, Ontario

Committees of Officials

Meeting of Deputy Attorneys General
November 2–3, 1961, Ottawa, Ontario

Sub-Committee on Fundamental Rights
February 4, 1970, Ottawa, Ontario
March 25, 1970, Ottawa, Ontario
June 1–2, 1970, Ottawa, Ontario
June 29, 1970, Ottawa, Ontario
September 28, 1970, Ottawa, Ontario

Sub-Committee on Official Languages
July 4–5, 1968, Ottawa, Ontario
October 17–18, 1968, Ottawa, Ontario
April 18, 1969, Ottawa, Ontario
October 2–3, 1969, Ottawa, Ontario
April 5–6, 1971, Ottawa, Ontario

Continuing Committee of Officials on the Constitution
May 29–30, 1968, Mont Gabriel, Quebec
July 25–26, 1968, Ottawa, Ontario
September 25–26, 1968, Ottawa, Ontario
November 7–9, 1968, Ottawa, Ontario
December 3–5, 1968, Ottawa, Ontario
April 16–18, 1969, Ottawa, Ontario
May 22–23, 1969, Ottawa, Ontario
September 30–October 1, 1969, Ottawa, Ontario
November 17–19, 1969, Ottawa, Ontario
March 23–24, 1970, Ottawa, Ontario
June 15–17, 1970, Banff, Alberta
August 31–September 1, 1970, Ottawa, Ontario
November 30–December 1, 1970, Ottawa, Ontario
January 20–21, 1971, Ottawa, Ontario
October 11–12, 1978, Ottawa, Ontario
January 11–12, 1979, Ottawa, Ontario
November 15–16, 1979, Toronto, Ontario

Parliamentary Committees

The Special Joint Committee of the Senate and the House of Commons on the Constitution of Canada
Order of Reference of the House of Commons, January 27, 1970
Order of Reference of the Senate, February 17, 1970
First Report to the House of Commons, March 5, 1970
Second Report to the House of Commons, May 20, 1970
Final Report, tabled in House of Commons March 16, 1972

The Special Joint Committee of the Senate and the House of Commons on the Constitution of Canada
Order of Reference, House of Commons, June 27, 1978
Order of Reference, Senate, June 29, 1978
First Report to Parliament, June 30, 1978
Second [and final] Report to Parliament, October 10, 1978

The Special Committee of the Senate on the Constitution
Order of Reference, June 28, 1978

Interim Report, October 10, 1978
First [and final] Report, October 18, 1978

The Special Joint Committee of the Senate and the House of Commons on the Constitution of Canada
Orders of Reference of the House of Commons, October 23, 1980
Orders of Reference of the Senate, November 3, 1980
Report to Parliament, February 13, 1981

House of Commons and Senate Debates

The Constitutional Amendment Bill (Bill C-60), First reading, June 20, 1978

Proposed Resolution for a Joint Address to Her Majesty the Queen Respecting the Constitution of Canada, tabled in the House of Commons and the Senate, October 6, 1980

Proposed Resolution for a Joint Address to Her Majesty the Queen Respecting the Constitution of Canada, moved in the House of Commons, February 17, 1981
Amendments to the Proposed Resolution approved by the House of Commons on April 23, 1981 and by the Senate on April 24, 1981

Proposed Resolution for a Joint Address to Her Majesty the Queen Respecting the Constitution of Canada, as altered by the November 5, 1981 First Ministers' Agreement on the Constitution and tabled in the House of Commons November 20, 1981

Resolution respecting the Constitution of Canada adopted by the House of Commons on December 2, 1981 and adopted by the Senate on December 8, 1981

United Kingdom Houses of Parliament

House of Commons
1st reading, December 22, 1981
2nd reading, February 17, 1982
3rd reading, March 8, 1982

House of Lords
1st reading, March 9, 1982
2nd reading, March 18, 1982
3rd reading, March 25, 1982
Royal Assent, March 29, 1982
Proclaimed in force, April 17, 1982

MAJOR GOVERNMENTAL MEETINGS AND PARLIAMENTARY SESSIONS THAT GAVE RISE TO THE 1983 CONSTITUTIONAL ACCORD

Federal-Provincial First Ministers' Conferences

March 15–16, 1983, Ottawa, Ontario

Committees of Ministers

Federal-Provincial Meetings of Ministers on Aboriginal Constitutional Matters
January 31–February 1, 1983, Ottawa, Ontario
February 28–March 1, 1983, Ottawa, Ontario

Committees of Officials

Federal-Provincial Meetings of Officials on Aboriginal Constitutional Matters
October 14, 1982, Winnipeg, Manitoba
November 17, 1982, Ottawa, Ontario
December 8–9, 1982, Montreal, Quebec
February 15–16, 1983, Ottawa, Ontario

Parliamentary Committees

House of Commons Standing Committee on Indian Affairs and Northern Development
Resolution referred to Committee, June 27, 1983
Report to House of Commons, June 29, 1983

Senate Standing Committee on Legal Development and Constitutional Affairs
Resolution referred to Committee, June 29, 1983
Report to Senate, October 13, 1983

Legislative Assembly Committees

Manitoba Standing Committee on Privileges and Elections
Resolution referred to Committee, August 15, 1983
Report to Legislative Assembly, August 18, 1983

House of Commons and Senate Debates

Resolution tabled in House of Commons, June 27, 1983
Resolution adopted by House of Commons, June 29, 1983
Resolution tabled in Senate, June 27, 1983
Resolution adopted by Senate, November 3, 1983

Provincial Legislative Debates

Alberta
Resolution tabled, June 3, 1983
Resolution adopted, June 3, 1983

British Columbia
Resolution tabled, August 11, 1983
Resolution adopted, October 21, 1983

Manitoba
Resolution tabled, June 27, 1983
Resolution adopted, August 18, 1983

New Brunswick
Resolution tabled, June 22, 1983
Resolution adopted, June 28, 1983

Newfoundland
Resolution tabled, December 1, 1983
Resolution adopted, December 2, 1983

Nova Scotia
Resolution tabled, May 31, 1983
Resolution adopted, May 31, 1983

Ontario
Resolution tabled, October 13, 1983
Resolution adopted, October 18, 1983

Prince Edward Island
Resolution tabled, June 16, 1983
Resolution adopted, June 16, 1983

Saskatchewan
Resolution tabled, November 30, 1983
Resolution adopted, November 30, 1983

Proclaimed in force, June 21, 1984

MAJOR GOVERNMENTAL MEETINGS THAT GAVE RISE TO THE 1987 CONSTITUTIONAL ACCORD*

Federal-Provincial First Ministers' Conferences

November 20-21, 1986, Vancouver, British Columbia
April, 30, 1987, Meech Lake, Quebec
June 2-3, 1987, Ottawa, Ontario

Premiers' Conferences

August 10-12, 1986, Edmonton, Alberta

Committees of Officials

Meeting of Deputy Ministers of Federal-Provincial Relations
March 5-6, 1987, Ottawa, Ontario

* At the time of publication this Constitutional Accord has not become law. In order to do so a resolution authorizing a proclamation to be issued by the Governor General to amend the Constitution of Canada as set out in the Accord must be passed by both Houses of Parliament and all provincial Legislative Assemblies within three years from the adoption of the resolution initiating the amendment procedure (in this case: June 23, 1987—the date the resolution was adopted by the Quebec National Assembly).

VOLUME II

CANADA'S
CONSTITUTION ACT
1982 & AMENDMENTS
A DOCUMENTARY HISTORY

30. The Task Force on Canadian Unity, 1979

A Future Together: Observations and Recommendations, Chapter 9, "Specific Recommendations," January 1979

Catalogue no. CP-32-35/1979

RESPECTING DIVERSITY

LANGUAGE (CHAPTER 5)

1. The principle of the equality of status, rights and privileges of the English and French languages for all purposes declared by the Parliament of Canada, within its sphere of jurisdiction, should be entrenched in the constitution.

   These purposes should include:

   i— The equality of both official languages in the Parliament of Canada;

   ii— the right of members of the public to obtain services from and communicate with the head offices of every department, agency or Crown corporation of the Government of Canada, the central administration in the National Capital Region, and all federal courts in Canada in either of the official languages. Elsewhere, members of the public should be able to obtain services from and communicate with the central administration in both official languages where there is significant demand, and to the extent that it is feasible to provide such services;

   iii— the equality of both official languages as languages of work in the central administration in the National Capital Region, in all federal courts, and in the head offices of every department, agency or Crown corporation of the Government of Canada. Elsewhere, the usual language or languages of work in central institutions should be the language or languages of work normally used in the province in which the central institution is operating. This recommendation is subject to the previous recommendation concerning the languages of service;

   iv— the right of any person to give evidence in the official language of his or her choice in any criminal matter;

   v— the right of every person to have access to radio and television services in both the French and the English languages;

   vi— the availability in both official languages of all printed material intended for general public use.

2. Each provincial legislature should have the right to determine an official language or official languages for that province, within its sphere of jurisdiction.

3. Linguistic rights should be expressed in provincial statutes, which could include:

   i— the entitlement recognized in the statement of the provincial first ministers at Montreal in February 1978: "Each child of a French-speaking or English-speaking minority is entitled to an education in his or her language in the primary or secondary schools in each province, wherever numbers warrant." This right should also be accorded to children of either minority who change their province of residence.

   ii— the right of every person to receive essential health and social services in his or her principal language, be it French or English, wherever numbers warrant.

   iii— the right of an accused in a criminal trial to be tried in his or her principal language, be it French or English, wherever it is feasible.

4. Should all provinces agree on these or any other linguistic rights, these rights should then be entrenched in the constitution.

5. The provinces should review existing methods and procedures for the teaching and learning of both French and English and make greater efforts to improve the availability and quality of instruction in these languages at all levels of education.

THE FIRST CANADIANS (CHAPTER 5)

6. Sections 11 and 12 of the Indian Act should be amended in order that Indian men and women acquire and lose Indian status in exactly the same way.

7. The central government should make greater efforts to promote and protect native languages and cultures, and should more actively facilitate communications between Canada's native peoples and the indigenous people of other countries.

8. i— Both central and provincial authorities should pursue direct discussions with representatives of Canadian Indians, Inuit and Métis, with a view to arriving at mutually acceptable constitutional provisions that would secure the rightful place of native peoples in Canadian society.

   ii— Further, both the central and provincial governments should meet to settle their respective areas of constitutional responsibility in the provision of essential services in the fields of health, social welfare, housing and education to status and non-status Indians, to Inuit, and to Métis on reserves, Crown lands, rural centres and large cities.

9. Both the central and provincial governments, and major voluntary and philanthropic associations, should provide increased funding to native peoples to assist them to undertake research and publish histories of their tribes and communities.

10. Both the public and private sector should make greater efforts to see that native peoples are more adequately represented on boards and commissions, task forces and study groups.

CULTURE (CHAPTER 5)

11. The provinces should:
    i— take the primary role in supporting local and regional cultural and artistic development, particularly by encouraging the participation of the people generally in cultural activities, and by the establishment where they do not exist of provincial arts councils to assist in this process.

    ii— recognize and take more fully into account the impact which their many non-cultural policies and programs have on the cultural development of their societies.

12. The provinces should recognize that education has a Canada-wide dimension by giving greater prominence to Canadian studies, and they should, through a strengthened Council of Ministers of Education, develop ways by which this dimension may be represented more fully in our school systems.

13. The central government and its cultural agencies should concentrate on developing programs of a Canada-wide dimension; they should not seek to enter into domains and pursuits which the provinces can and should perform for themselves.

14. The number of Canada-wide artistic prizes, competitions and cultural activities should be increased for the young people of the country.

15. The public and private sectors of Canada should work in cooperation to increase those youth exchange programs which have demonstrated their capacity to enhance interregional and inter-cultural knowledge among the young people. Also, efforts should be made to extend similar programs to adults.

16. The central government should, in cooperation with the private sector, do its utmost to increase opportunities for low-cost travel in order to enable Canadians who wish to do so to become better acquainted with their country and their fellow-citizens.

17. Steps should be taken to ensure that the products of our varied cultural activities (such as books, recordings, magazines, films and paintings) are more imaginatively and effectively distributed, diffused, or marketed throughout Canada, and in a way that would give them prominence in relation to those from non-Canadian sources.

18. The tax system should be employed more directly in support of the cultural and linguistic development of the country, and consideration should be given to increasing cost allowances and tax write-offs for cultural enterprises.

19. i— The provincial governments should assume the primary responsibility for the support of multiculturalism in Canada, including the funding of ethno-cultural organizations.

    ii— the major ethno-cultural organizations in Canada should attempt to work more closely with the provincial governments to develop ways in which multiculturalism can find most effective expression through provincial initiatives.

    iii— Both the public and the private sectors should make efforts to reflect in their institutions more adequately the cultural diversity of Canada.

UNITY AND THE HEALTH OF THE ECONOMY

GENERAL (CHAPTER 6)

20. Section 121 of the BNA Act should be clarified in order to guarantee more effectively free trade between the provinces for all produce and manufactured goods, and be extended to include services.

21. In addition, government purchasing policies should be based upon considerations of market costs unless specified social and economic objectives would otherwise be served.

22. Impediments to the mobility of persons in the professions, trades and other such occupations should be reduced through the application of widely accepted common standards; and such standards should be set and reviewed periodically by the provincial governments and the appropriate professional bodies in consultation with each other.

23. The constitution should make clear the prohibition of barriers to the interprovincial movement of capital.

24. The annual conference of finance ministers should be used more actively to ensure the coordination of economic stabilization policies, by providing a common assessment of the economy and a better knowledge of the total revenues expenditures and borrowings of the Canadian public sector as a whole.

25. Meetings between the central and provincial governments, and representatives from the private sector should be regularized and integrated under the general supervision of conferences of the first ministers on the economy, to be held every two or three years, with a view to framing and coordinating policies designed to achieve medium and longer-term objectives for the Canadian economy and for its main sectors of activities.

26. With respect to the sharing of Canadian wealth:
    i— the constitution should recognize and entrench the principle of equalizing social and economic opportunities between regions as an objective of the federation, and it should be the responsibility of the central government to maintain a system of equalization payments.
    ii— a program of provincial revenue equalization along the lines of current arrangements should be maintained.
    iii— for the purpose of better balancing provincial resources with the developmental requirements of their economies a new type of equalization program should be developed.

A RESTRUCTURED FEDERALISM

GENERAL (CHAPTER 7)

27. i— There should be a new and distinctive Canadian constitution to meet the present and future needs of all the people of Canada.
    ii— The new constitution should be in the English and French languages, and both texts should be official.

28. The preamble to the constitution should include a declaration that the people of Canada
    i— maintain and reinforce their attachment to democratic institutions, federalism, human rights and the principle of supremacy of the law;
    ii— recognize the historic partnership between English and French-speaking Canadians, and the distinctiveness of Quebec;
    iii— affirm the special place of the native peoples of Canada;
    iv— recognize the richness of the contribution of Canada's other cultural groups;
    v— recognize the diversity among Canada's regions and the need to permit all regional communities to flourish;
    vi— seek the promotion of the social, economic and cultural development and the equality of opportunity for all Canadians in all regions of Canada.

29. A new constitution should recognize two major principles with respect to distribution of powers and to central institutions:
    i— the equality of status of the central and the provincial orders of government;
    ii— the distinctive character of individual provinces.

DISTRIBUTION OF LEGISLATIVE AND EXECUTIVE POWERS (CHAPTER 7)

30. The present distribution of legislative and executive powers should be clarified and adjusted to contemporary needs and realities.

31. The principle roles and responsibilities of the central government should be:
    i— the strengthening of Canadian identity;
    ii— the preservation and enhancement of the integrity of the Canadian state;
    iii— the overriding responsibility for the conduct of international relations;
    iv— the management of Canada-wide economic policy (including monetary policy) and participation in the stimulation of regional economic activity;

v— the establishment of Canada-wide standards, where appropriate; and

vi— the redistribution of income.

32. The principal roles and responsibilities of the provincial governments should be:

   i— the social and cultural well-being and development of their communities;

   ii— provincial economic development, including the exploitation of their natural resources;

   iii— property and civil rights; and

   iv— the management of their territory.

33. In addition to roles and responsibilities defined in the previous recommendation, an essential role and responsibility of the government of Quebec should be the preservation and strengthening of the French heritage in its own territory.

34. A new distribution of powers should, whenever it is desirable or needed in order to fulfil the objectives of dualism and regionalism, recognize the distinctive status of any province or make it possible for a province to acquire such status.

35. i— In a new distribution, the powers allocated to all provincial legislatures should provide the framework which makes it possible for Quebec to fulfil its additional role and responsibility with respect to the French heritage in its own territory.

   ii— In the distribution of powers, provision should be made for the possibility that some provincial governments other than Quebec may wish to assume, now or in the future, some or all of the powers in the cultural domain recommended for Quebec.

   iii— Should the other provinces not wish to avail themselves of such a distribution, powers related to this additional role and responsibility of Quebec should be allocated to Quebec alone.

36. In addition to these objectives, roles and responsibilities, the distribution should take account of the five following considerations:

   i— general and particular concern;

   ii— effectiveness, efficiency and responsiveness;

   iii— common agreement;

   iv— continuity;

   v— overall balance.

37. The use of a list of exclusive powers for Parliament and a list of exclusive powers for provincial legislatures should be retained in a new Canadian constitution.

38. i— Concurrent jurisdiction should be avoided whenever possible through a more precise definition of exclusive powers.

   ii— Wherever powers are concurrent, a federal or provincial paramountcy should be stipulated.

39. The residual power should be assigned to the provincial legislatures.

40. In devising a new distribution of powers, the following steps should be taken:

   i— broad areas of governmental activities should be first identified. Such broad areas might include external affairs, defence, economic policy, transportation, communications, natural resources, administration of justice and law enforcement, the status and rights of citizens, culture, health and welfare, habitat and the environment.

   ii— within each of these broad areas, specific subject matters should be arranged in related groups. Under culture, for example might be grouped legislative powers over: language, education, schools, universities, archives, research, exchanges, copyrights, books, films, arts, leisure, marriage and divorce, property and civil rights.

   iii— jurisdiction with respect to each specific legislative power should then be attributed, exclusively or concurrently, to an order of government according to the criteria established in our previous recommendations. For example, regarding immigration, provincial legislatures should have exclusive jurisdiction with respect to settlement and integration of immigrants; the federal Parliament should have exclusive jurisdiction with respect to deportation of aliens and public safety; jurisdiction should be concurrent with provincial paramountcy with respect to selection criteria and levels of immigration to the province, and with federal paramountcy with respect to the recruitment of immigrants abroad and the admission of refugees.

   iv— areas could be either exclusive, when all powers are attributed exclusively to the same order of government, as in the area of defence, or shared, when some of the powers are attributed exclusively to each of the two orders of government, or concurrently to both.

41. Both the central and provincial governments should be granted equal access to tax sources, with the exception that customs and excise taxes be an exclusive central power. The provincial right to use indirect taxation should be qualified to ensure that the impact of such taxes do not fall upon persons outside the taxing province.

42. i— An emergency power should be assigned expressly

by the constitution to the central government, for both wartime and peacetime.

ii— The wartime emergency power may be invoked in time of real or apprehended war, invasion or insurrection. The peacetime emergency power may be invoked only in highly exceptional circumstances.

iii— The proclamation of any emergency should receive approval of both federal houses, within a specified time limit, to remain in force.

iv— The proclamation should stipulate the reason(s) for the emergency and the intended duration of its application.

v— The Parliament of Canada should stipulate by legislation the powers it needs in cases of emergency; safeguards for provincial powers and for individual rights should vary depending on whether the country is facing a wartime or a peacetime emergency.

43. The power of reservation and the power of disallowance should be abolished.

44. The power to appoint the lieutenant-governor of each province should be vested in the Queen on the advice of the provincial premier.

45. The declaratory power of Parliament should be retained, but its use should be subject to the consent of the province concerned.

46. The spending power of the central government should be retained in matters of federal-provincial programs of interest to the whole of Canada, but its exercise should be subject to ratification by a reconstituted second chamber, and provinces should be granted the right to opt out of any such program, and where appropriate receive fiscal compensation.

FEDERAL-PROVINCIAL RELATIONS AND THE SENATE (CHAPTER 7)

47. The Senate should be abolished and replaced by a new second chamber of the Canadian Parliament to be called the Council of the Federation.

48. i— The Council should be composed of delegations representing the provincial governments and therefore acting under instruction; the provincial delegations could be headed by a delegate of cabinet rank.

ii— The Council should be composed of no more than 60 voting members, to be distributed among provinces roughly in accordance with their respective population up to a maximum of one-fifth of the Council, and with weighting to favour provinces having less than 25 per cent of the country's population. Any province which has at any time had 25 per cent of the population (such as Quebec and Ontario) should be guaranteed one-fifth of the Council seats in perpetuity.

iii— In addition, central government cabinet ministers should be non-voting members so that they have the right to present and defend central government proposals before the Council and its committees.

49. The Council should not have the power to initiate legislation, except in the case of bills proposing constitutional amendments; and its decisions should not be regarded as expressions of confidence or non-confidence, since the government should remain responsible to the House of Commons alone.

50. The scope of the powers of the Council should be the following:

i— legislation and treaties within exclusive federal jurisdiction should not require the approval of the Council.

ii— proposed federal legislation and articles of treaties deemed to belong to the categories of powers described as concurrent with federal paramountcy should be subject to a suspensive veto of short duration by the Council.

iii— proposed federal legislation deemed to belong to the category of powers described as concurrent with provincial paramountcy should be subject to a suspensive veto of a longer duration by the Council, except in the case of measures implementing bilateral agreements between the federal government and one or more provincial governments.

iv— the ratification of treaties, or parts of treaties, which deal with matters within provincial jurisdiction should require the approval of a majority of the provinces in the Council, on the understanding that legislative measures implementing such treaties are to remain within provincial jurisdiction.

v— federal initiatives in areas of provincial jurisdiction that are based on the federal spending power, whether they are to be cost-shared or financed fully from federal funds (with the exception of expenditures related to equalization) should require a two-thirds majority in the Council.

vi— if a province chooses not to participate in a program for which wide provincial consent has been demonstrated, the central government should be required to pay the government of that province a sum equal to the amount it would have cost the central government to implement the program in the province.

vii— a proclamation of a state of emergency, in either peacetime or wartime circumstances, should require, in addition to confirmation by the House of Commons, confirmation by the Council by at least a two-thirds majority.

51. The Council should be used as a forum for the discussion of general proposals and broad orientations arising from conferences of the first ministers on the economy and any other proposals the conference of first ministers may so designate, or any other matters of concern to the members of the Council itself.

52. Federal appointments to the Supreme Court, to major regulatory agencies such as the Canadian Radio-Television Commission, the Canadian Transport Commission and the National Energy Board, and to central institutions such as the Bank of Canada and the Canadian Broadcasting Corporation, should require the approval of the appropriate committee of the Council.

53. To determine the classification of a bill or treaty and hence the powers that the Council may exercise, a permanent committee should be created and be composed of the Speakers and some members from both the House of Commons and the Council.

54. i— The conference of first ministers should be convened annually, unless a simple majority of governments disapprove.

ii— Additionally, first ministers' conferences should be held at the request of any government which secures the agreement of a simple majority of the other ten.

55. A federal-provincial committee on intergovernmental policy issues should be established with a membership of the eleven ministers responsible for intergovernmental affairs.

56. A permanent intergovernmental committee of officials and experts working under the conference of the first ministers should be established to study policy and program duplication on a continuing basis.

57. In order to make federal-provincial relations subject to continuous scrutiny by the legislatures, standing committees should be established in the House of Commons and in all provincial legislatures to review

the activities of the major federal-provincial conferences.

THE SUPREME COURT AND THE JUDICIAL SYSTEM (CHAPTER 7)

58. The existence and independence of the judiciary at both the central and the provincial orders of government should be recognized as a fundamental principle of Canadian federalism and be entrenched in the constitution.

59. i— The existence and composition of the Supreme Court of Canada, and the mode of appointment and removal of its judges, should be entrenched in the constitution.

ii— The Supreme Court should be composed of eleven judges, five of whom are to be chosen from among civil law judges and lawyers, and six from among common law judges and lawyers, having regard, in the latter case, to regional distribution.

iii— The judges of the Supreme Court should be nominated for appointment by the governor in council, following consultation with the attorney general of Quebec with respect to the civil law candidates and with the attorneys general of all other provinces with respect to the common law candidates; the nominations should be ratified by the appropriate committee of the Council of the Federation.

iv— The judges of the Supreme Court should only be removed from office by the governor in council following a joint address of both Houses of Parliament.

v— The chief justice of the Supreme Court should be chosen by the governor in council, for a non-renewable term from among the members of the Court, in alternation between a common law judge and a civil law judge.

60. The Supreme Court should remain a court with general appellate jurisdiction in both federal and provincial law.

61. The Supreme Court should retain its jurisdiction with respect to references, but provincial governments should have the same right as the central government to refer constitutional matters directly to the Supreme Court.

62. The Supreme Court should be divided into three branches, one of provincial jurisdiction which would be subdivided into a Quebec law section and a common law section, one of federal jurisdiction, and one of

constitutional jurisdiction; the constitutional bench should be composed of all members of the Court.

63. Arrangements should be made for the reimbursement of the travelling costs of parties to and from the Supreme Court, whenever the Court is of the opinion that the situation warrants it.

64. All provincial judges should be appointed by the provincial governments concerned, but, with respect to higher court judges, only after consultation with the central government; and Federal Court judges should continue to be appointed by the central government.

CONSTITUTIONAL CHANGE AND ADAPTATION (CHAPTER 7)

65. Articles of the constitution pertaining to:
    — the distribution of legislative and executive powers
    — the constitution of both central houses, the existence and composition of the Supreme Court of Canada, and the method of appointment and removal of its judges
    — the offices of governor general and lieutenant governor
    — the entrenched list of fundamental rights
    — the entrenched linguistic rights
    — the amendment formula
    should be amendable by the following process:
    i— a bill formulating an amendment should be initiated in either the House of Commons or in the Council of the Federation and passed by a majority in the House of Commons and by a majority of votes in the Council;
    ii— ratification of the proposed amendment should be through in a Canada-wide referendum requiring approval by a majority of electors voting in each of four regions constituted by the Atlantic provinces, the province of Quebec, the province of Ontario, and the western provinces and territories; the above list of regions should be modified, if necessary, to include as a separate region any other province that might have, at any point in time, at least 25 per cent of the Canadian population.

66. Parliament should have the power to amend other articles of the constitution, except those concerned with the constitution of the provinces, which should be amendable only by each provincial legislature.

67. A new constitution should recognize the right of the central and provincial government to delegate to each other, by mutual consent, any legislative power, it being understood that such delegation should be subject to periodical revision and be accompanied, where appropriate, by fiscal compensation.

ELECTORAL REFORM AND THE HOUSE OF COMMONS (CHAPTER 7)

68. In order to establish a better balance between the number of votes and the number of seats obtained by each political party in different regions and provinces, the current mode of election to the House of Commons should be modified by introducing an element of proportionality to complement the present simple-majority single-member constituency system.

69. i— The number of members in the House of Commons should be increased by about 60.
    ii— These members should be selected from provincial lists of candidates prepared by the federal parties in advance of a general election, with the seats being distributed between parties on the basis of percentages of popular votes.

70. i— The committee system in the House of Commons should be modified and strengthened.
    ii— The government should make more extensive use of special committees of the House of Commons to conduct in-depth studies of major Canadian issues upon which central government legislation or executive decisions may eventually be required.

INDIVIDUAL COLLECTIVE RIGHTS (CHAPTER 7)

71. The Canadian constitution should entrench a Declaration of Rights.

72. The Declaration of Rights should include the usual political, legal, economic and egalitarian rights.

73. The entrenched collective rights should include the language rights listed in recommendations 1, 2, and 4 and the right of Parliament and provincial legislatures to adopt special measures to benefit native peoples.

74. The basic individual and collective rights on which the central and provincial governments are in agreement should be entrenched in the constitution.

75. In those cases where the central and provincial governments have agreed, additional rights, which contain a clause permitting exceptions where so specified in a statute, should be entrenched in the constitution.

31. Meeting of Officials on the Constitution, Ottawa, Ontario, January 11–12, 1979

Canadian Charter of Rights and Freedoms, Federal Draft, January 8, 1979

Document: 840-153/004

DIVISION III
RIGHTS AND FREEDOMS WITHIN THE CANADIAN FEDERATION

General

Canadian Charter of Rights and Freedoms

5. The provisions of this division, which may be cited as the *Canadian Charter of Rights and Freedoms*, set forth rights and freedoms that, in a free and democratic society, must be assured to the people and that are consistent with Canada's recognition of the standards proclaimed in the *Universal Declaration of Human Rights* and the *International Covenant on Civil and Political Rights*.

Fundamental Freedoms

Fundamental freedoms

6. (1) Everyone has the right to the following fundamental freedoms:
   (a) freedom of conscience and religion;
   (b) freedom of thought, opinion and expression including freedom of the press and other media for the dissemination of news and the expression of opinion and belief; and
   (c) freedom of peaceful assembly and of association.

Justifiable limitations

(2) The manifestation or exercise of the freedoms declared by this section may be made subject only to such limitations as are reasonably justifiable in a free and democratic society in the interests of national security, public safety, order, health or morals or the rights and freedoms of others.

Democratic Rights

Democratic rights of citizens

7. Consistent with the principles of free and democratic elections to the House of Commons and to the legislative assemblies, and of universal suffrage for that purpose, every citizen of Canada shall, without unreasonable distinction or limitation, have the right to vote in an election of members of the House of Commons or of a legislative assembly and to be qualified for membership therein.

Duration of elected legislative bodies

8. (1) Every House of Commons and legislative assembly of a province shall continue for five years, or in the case of a legislative assembly for five or such lesser number of years as is provided for by the constitution of the

province, from the date of the return of the writs for the choosing of its members and no longer, subject to its being sooner dissolved in accordance with law.

Continuation in special circumstances

(2) Notwithstanding subsection (1), in time of real or apprehended war, invasion or insurrection, a House of Commons may be continued by Parliament and a legislative assembly of a province may be continued by the legislature thereof beyond the time limited therefor by or under subsection (1), if such continuation is not opposed by the votes of more than one-third of the members of the House of Commons or the legislative assembly, as the case may be.

Annual sitting of elected legislative bodies

9. There shall be a sitting of Parliament and of each legislature at least once every year and not more than twelve months shall intervene between sittings.

Legal Rights

Legal rights

10. (1) Everyone has the right to life, liberty and security of his or her person and the right not to be deprived thereof except by due process of law, which process encompasses the following:

(a) the right to be secure against unreasonable searches and seizures;

(b) the right to protection against arbitrary or unlawful interference with privacy;

(c) the right not to be arbitrarily detained or imprisoned;

(d) the right on arrest or detention

   (i) to be informed promptly of the reason for the arrest or detention,

   (ii) to be provided with the opportunity to retain and consult counsel without delay, and

   (iii) to the remedy by way of *habeas corpus* for the determination of the validity of his or her detention and for release if the detention is not lawful;

(e) the right as an accused person

   (i) to be informed of the specific charge,

   (ii) to be tried within a reasonable time,

   (iii) to be presumed innocent until proven guilty in a fair and public hearing by an independent and impartial tribunal,

   (iv) not to be denied reasonable bail without just cause having been established, and

   (v) not to be found guilty on account of any act or omission that at the time of the act or omission did not constitute an offence;

(f) the right not to be tried or punished more than once for an offence of which he or she has been finally convicted or acquitted;

(g) the right to the benefit of the lesser punishment where the punishment for an offence of which he or she has been convicted has been varied between the time of commission and the time of conviction;

(h) the right not to be subjected to any cruel or inhuman treatment or punishment;

(i) the right not to give evidence before any court, tribunal, commission, board or other authority, if unreasonably denied counsel or if denied protection against self-crimination or other constitutional safeguard;

(j) the right to the assistance of an interpreter in any proceedings before a court, tribunal, commission, board or other authority, if the party or witness does not understand or speak the language in which the proceedings are conducted; and

(k) the right to a fair hearing in accordance with the principles of fundamental justice for the determination of his or her rights or obligations.

Justifiable derogation

(2) In time of serious public emergency, the existence of which is officially proclaimed through the invocation of the *War Measures Act* or by specific reference to this subsection, the rights mentioned in this section other than the right to life and those mentioned in sub-paragraphs (d) (ii) and (e) (v) and paragraphs (h), (i) and (j) may be derogated from to the extent strictly required by the circumstances of the emergency.

Idem

(3) Nothing in this section shall be interpreted as precluding the enactment of or rendering invalid a law that authorizes the holding of all or part of a proceeding *in camera* in the interests of national security, public safety or order or morality, in the interest of the privacy of one or more of the parties or where, in the opinion of the tribunal, publicity would prejudice the interests of justice.

Non-discrimination Rights

Equality before the law and equal protection of the law

11. (1) Everyone has the right to equality before the law and to equal protection of the law without distinction or restriction other than any distinction or restriction provided by law that is fair and reasonable having regard to the object of the law.

Affirmative action programs

(2) Nothing in this section shall be interpreted as precluding the enactment of or rendering invalid any affirmative action program on behalf of disadvantaged persons or groups.

Mobility Rights

Rights of citizens

12. (1) Every citizen of Canada has the right to enter, remain in and leave Canada.

Rights of citizens and persons lawfully admitted for permanent residence

(2) Every citizen of Canada and every person who has been lawfully admitted to Canada for permanent residence and has not lost the status of a permanent resident has the right

(a) to move and to take up residence in any province or territory, and

(b) to pursue the gaining of a livelihood in any province or territory without distinction based on province or territory of previous residence or domicile.

Justifiable limitations

(3) The rights declared by this section may be made subject only to such limitations as are reasonably justifiable in a free and democratic society in the interests of national security, public safety, order, health or morals or where there exist overriding economic or social considerations.

Property Rights

Property rights

13. (1) Everyone has the right to the use and enjoyment of property, individually or in association with others, and the right not to be deprived thereof except in accordance with law that is fair and just.

Justifiable limitations

(2) Nothing in this section shall be interpreted as precluding the enactment of or rendering invalid laws controlling or restricting the use of property in the public interest or securing against property the payment of taxes or other levies or penalties.

Idem

(3) The rights declared by this section may be made subject only to such limitations in addition to those refered to in subsection (2) as are reasonably justifiable in a free and democratic society in the interests of national security or public safety, order, health or morals.

PROPOSED CHANGES IN THE LANGUAGE AND GENERAL PROVISIONS OF THE CHARTER OF RIGHTS AND FREEDOMS AND IN SECTION 131

C-60 Provisions	Proposed New Provisions
(1) Official Languages and Language Rights	*Official Languages*
13. The English and French languages are the official languages of Canada for all purposes declared by the Parliament of Canada or the legislature of any province, acting within the legislative authority of each respectively.	**14.** (1) English and French are the official languages of Canada, having the status and protection set forth in this Charter.
20. Nothing in sections 13 to 19 shall be held to limit the right of the Parliament of Canada or the legislature of a province, acting within the authority of each respectively pursuant to law, to provide for more languages; and nothing in those sections shall be held to derogate from or diminish any right, based on language, that is assured by virtue of section 9 or 10, or to derogate from or diminish any legal or customary right or privilege acquired or enjoyed either before or after the commencement of this Act with respect to any language that is not English or French.	(2) Nothing in this Charter limits the authority of Parliament or of the legislature of a province to extend the status, protection or use of the English and French languages.
	Language Rights
14. (1) Any individual has the right to use English or French, as he or she may choose, in any of the debates or other proceedings of the Parliament of Canada.	**15.** (1) Everyone has the right to use English or French, as he or she may choose, in any of the debates or other proceedings of Parliament.
(2) Any individual has the right to use English or French, as he or she may choose, in any of the debates or other proceedings of the legislative assembly of any province.	(2) Everyone has the right to use English or French, as he or she may choose, in the debates of the legislative assembly of any province.
15. (1) The statutes and the records and journals of the Parliament of Canada shall be printed and published in English and French.	**16.** (1) The statutes and the records and journals of Parliament shall be printed and published in English and French.

C-60 Provisions	Proposed New Provisions
(2) The statutes and the records and journals of the legislatures of Ontario, Quebec and New Brunswick shall be printed and published in English and French, and all or any of the statutes and the records and journals of the legislature of any other province shall be printed and published in both of those languages or in either of them, accordingly as its legislature may prescribe.	(2) The statutes and the records of the legislatures of Quebec and New Brunswick shall be printed and published in English and French.
(See 131(3)(b))	(3) The records and the journals of the legislature of Ontario, the statutes thereof enacted after such day as is fixed by the legislature and any revision or consolidation of the statutes thereof authorized to have effect after such day as is fixed by the legislature shall be printed and published in English and French.
	(4) The statutes and the records and journals of the legislature of each province not referred to in subsection (2) or (3) shall be printed and published in English and French to the extent practicable accordingly as the legislature of the province prescribes.
(3) Where the statutes of any legislative body described in subsection (1) or (2) are printed and published in English and French, both language versions thereof shall be equally authoritative.	(5) Where the statutes of any legislative body described in any of subsections (1) to (4) are printed and published in English and French, both language versions are equally authoritative.
16. (1) Either English or French may be used by any person in, or in any pleading or process in or any court constituted by the Parliament of Canada.	**17.** (1) Either English or French may be used by any person in, or in any pleading or process in or issuing from, the Supreme Court of Canada or any court constituted by Parliament.
(2) Either English or French may be used by any person in, or in any pleading or process in or issuing from, any court of Ontario, Quebec or New Brunswick.	(2) Either English or French may be used by any person in or in any pleading or process in or issuing from, any court of Ontario, Quebec or New Brunswick as soon as is practicable accordingly as the legislature of each such province respectively prescribes and, in any event, within five years after the time at which this Charter extends to matters coming within the legislative authority of each such province.
	(3) Either English or French may be used by any person in or in any pleading or process in or issuing from, any court of a province not referred to in subsection (2), to the greatest extent possible accordingly as the legislature of the province prescribes.
(3) In proceedings in any court in Canada —in which, in a criminal matter, the court is exercising	(4) In proceedings in any court in Canada relating to an offence

C-60 Provisions	Proposed New Provisions
any criminal jurisdiction conferred on it by or pursuant to an Act of the Parliament of Canada, or — in which, in a matter relating to an offence for which an individual charged with that offence is subject to be imprisoned if he or she is convicted thereof, the court is exercising any jurisdiction conferred on it by or pursuant to an Act of the legislature of any province, any individual giving evidence before the court has the right to be heard in English or French, as he or she may choose, and in being so heard, not to be placed at a disadvantage by not being heard, or being unable to be heard, in the other of those languages.	(a) created by or pursuant to an Act of Parliament, or (b) created by or pursuant to an act of the legislature of a province if the punishment for the offence may be imprisonment, any person giving evidence before the court has the right to be heard in English or French, as he or she may choose, through the services of an interpreter where necessary, and the right not to be placed at a disadvantage in so being heard.

17. Nothing in section 16 shall be held to preclude the application, to or in respect of proceedings in any court described in subsection 16(2), or to or in respect of any proceedings described in subsection 16(3), of such rules for regulating the procedure in any such proceedings, including rules respecting the giving of notice, as may be prescribed by any competent body or authority in that behalf pursuant to law for the effectual execution and working of the provisions of either of those subsections.

18. Nothing in section 17 precludes the application of such rules for regulating procedure as may be prescribed by any competent body or authority for the effectual execution and working of subsections 17(2), (3) and (4).

19. (1) Any member of the public in Canada has the right to use English or French as he or she may choose, in communicating with the head or central office of any department or agency of the executive government of and over Canada, or of any judicial, quasi-judicial or administrative body or Crown corporation established by or pursuant to a law of Canada, wherever that office is located within an area of Canada in which it is determined, in such manner as may be prescribed or authorized by the Parliament of Canada, that a substantial number of persons within the population use that language.

19. (1) Any member of the public in Canada has the right to communicate with and to receive services from any head or central office of an institution of government of Canada in English or French, as he or she may choose, and he or she has the same right with respect to any other principal office of any such institution where that office is located within an area of Canada in which it is determined, in such manner as may be prescribed or authorized by Parliament, that a substantial number of persons within the population use that language.

(2) Any member of the public in any province has the right to use English or French, as he or she may choose, in communicating with any principal office of a department or agency of the executive government of that province, or of a judicial, quasi-judicial or administrative body or Crown corporation established by or pursuant to a law of that province, where that office is located within an area of that province in which it is determined, in such manner as may be prescribed or authorized by the legislature of that province that a substantial number of persons within the population use that language.

(2) Any member of the public in a province has the right to communicate with and to receive services from any head, central or other principal office of an institution of government of the province in English or French, as he or she may choose, to the extent to which and in the areas of the province in which it is determined, in such manner as may be prescribed or authorized by the legislature of the province, that the right should pertain having regard to the practicability and necessity of providing such services.

C-60 Provisions	Proposed New Provisions

20. Nothing in sections 13 to 19 shall be held to limit the right of the Parliament of Canada or the legislature of a province, acting within the authority of each respectively pursuant to law, to provide for more extensive use of both the English and French languages; and nothing in those sections shall be held to derogate from or diminish any right, based on language, that is assured by virtue of section 9 or 10, or to derogate from or diminish any legal or customary right or privilege acquired or enjoyed either before or after the commencement of this Act with respect to any language that is not English or French.

20. Nothing in sections 14 to 19 abrogates or derogates from any legal or customary right or privilege acquired or enjoyed either before or after the commencement of this Act with respect to any language that is not English or French.

21. (1) Where the number of children in any area of a province in respect of whom notice has been given as contemplated by this section, warrants the provision of the facilities required to give effect to the right provided for by this section, any parent who is a citizen of Canada resident within that area and whose primarily spoken language is not that of the numerically larger of the groups comprising those persons resident in that province whose primary languages are either English or French, has the right to have his or her children receive their schooling in the language of basic instruction that is the primarily spoken language of then umerically smaller of those groups, in or by means of facilities that are provided in that area out of public funds and that are suitable and adequate for that purpose.

21. (1) Citizens of Canada resident in a province who are members of an English-speaking or French-speaking minority population of that province have a right to have their children receive their educational instruction in their minority language at the primary and secondary school level wherever the number of children of such citizens resident in an area of the province is sufficient to warrant the provision of minority language education facilities in that area out of public funds.

(2) The exercise by any parent of the right provided for by this section shall be subject to such reasonable requirements respecting the giving of notice by that parent of his or her intended exercise thereof as may be prescribed by the law of the province in which that parent resides.

(2) In each province, the legislature may enact such provisions as are reasonable in the circumstances relating to

(a) the giving of notice by citizens of Canada resident in the province of their desire to exercise the minority language education right conferred by sub-section (1) in respect of their children; and

(3) Nothing in this section shall be held to limit the authority of the legislature of any province to make such provisions as are reasonable for determining, either generally or in any particular case or classes of cases, whether or not the number of children in any area of that province in respect of whom notice has been given as contemplated by this section, warrants the provision of the facilities required to give effect to the right provided for by this section.

(b) the determination of whether or not the number of children of citizens of Canada resident in an area of the province who have given notice as provided is sufficient to warrant the provision of minority language education facilities in that area.

(4) Nothing in this section shall be held to derogate from or diminish any legal or customary right or privilege acquired or enjoyed in any province either before or after the commencement of this Act to have any child receive his or her schooling in the language of basic instruction that is the primarily spoken language of the numerically

C-60 Provisions	Proposed New Provisions

larger of the groups referred to in subsection (1) within that province, or to limit any authority conferred or obligation imposed either before or after that time by the law of that province to require any child, during any period while that child is receiving his or her schooling in any language of basic instruction that is not that primarily spoken language, to be given instruction in the use of that primarily spoken language as part of his or her schooling in that province.

(5) The expression "parent" in this section includes a person standing in the place of a parent.

22. In furtherance of
— the appreciation by Canadians that the preservation of both English and French as the principal spoken languages of Canadians is vital to the prospering of the Canadian federation within the larger North American society, and
— the resolve of Canadians that none of the institutions of government of the Canadian federation, acting within the legislative authority of each individually pursuant to law, should act in such a manner as to affect adversely the preservation of either English or French as the language spoken or otherwise enjoyed by any group of individuals constituting an identifiable and substantial linguistic community in any area of Canada within its jurisdiction,
it is hereby proclaimed that no law made by any such institution after this Charter extends to matters within its legislative authority shall apply or have effect so as to affect adversely the preservation of either English or French as the language spoken or otherwise enjoyed by any such group of individuals.

22. No law enacted by or under the authority of Parliament or a legislature of a province, after this Charter extends to matters within its legislative authority, applies or has effect so as to affect adversely the preservation of either English or French as the language spoken or otherwise enjoyed by any group of persons constituting an identifiable and substantial linguistic community in any area of Canada.

Undeclared Rights

26. Nothing in this Charter shall be held to abrogate, abridge or derogate from any right or freedom not declared by it that may have existed in Canada at the commencement of this Act, including, without limiting the generality of the foregoing, any right or freedom that may have been acquired by any of the native peoples of Canada by virtue of the Royal Proclamation of October 7, 1763.

23. Nothin in this Charter abrogates or derogates from any right or freedom not declared by it that may exist in Canada, including any right or freedom that may pertain to the native peoples of Canada.

(g) Generally Applicable Provisions

23. To the end that full effect may be given to the individual rights and freedoms declared by this Charter,

General

24. To the end that the paramountcy of this Charter be recognized and that full effect be given to the rights and

C-60 Provisions	Proposed New Provisions
it is hereby further proclaimed that, in Canada, no law shall apply or have effect so as to abrogate, abridge or or derogate from any such right or freedom.	freedoms herein declared, any law and any administrative act that is inconsistent with any provision of the Charter is, except as specifically otherwise provided, inoperative and of no force or effect to the extent of the inconsistency.
24. Where no other remedy is available or provided for by law, any individual may, in accordance with the applicable procedure of any court in Canada of competent jurisdiction, request the court to define or enforce any of the individual rights and freedoms declared by this Charter, as they extend or apply to him or her, by means of an injunction or similar relief, accordingly as the circumstances require.	**25.** Where no other effective recourse or remedy is available or provided for by law, anyone whose rights or freedoms as declared by this Charter have been infringed or denied to his or her detriment has the right to apply to a court of competent jurisdiction to obtain such relief or remedy as the court deems appropriate and just in the circumstances.
25. Nothing in this Charter shall be held to prevent such limitations on the exercise or enjoyment of any of the individual rights and freedoms declared by this Charter as are justifiable in a free and democratic society in the interests of public safety or health, the interests of the peace and security of the public, or the interests of the rights and freedoms of others, whether such limitations are imposed by law or by virtue of the construction or application of any law.	No equivalent
27. For greater certainty for the purposes of this Charter, the individual rights and freedoms declared by this Charter are those assured by or by virtue of sections 6 to 10, 14, 16, 19 and 21.	No equivalent
28. A reference in any of sections 10 to 22 to a province shall be construed as including a reference to the Yukon Territory or the Northwest Territories or to the Council or Commissioner in Council thereof, as the case may be.	**26.** A reference in any of sections 7 to 9 and 14 to 22 to a province or to the legislative assembly or legislature of a province shall be construed as including a reference to the Yukon Territory or the Northwest Territories or to the Council or Commissioner in Council thereof, as the case may be.
29. Nothing in this Charter shall be held to confer any legislative authority on any competent body or authority in that behalf in Canada, except as expressly contemplated by this Charter.	**27.** Nothing in this Charter confers any legislative authority on any competent body or authority in that behalf in Canada, except as expressly contemplated by this Charter.

* * * * *

18. Nothing in sections 14 to 17 shall be held to abrogate, abridge or derogate from any right, privilege or obligation with respect to the English and French languages, or either of them, that exists or is continued by virtue of any other provision of the Constitution of Canada.	**131.** (1) Nothing in sections 15 to 18 abrogates or derogates from any right, privilege or obligation with respect to the English and French languages, or either of them, that exists or is continued by virtue of any other provision of the Constitution of Canada.

C-60 Provisions	Proposed New Provisions

131. (1) Until such time as this subsection is repealed by subsection (4), the provisions of the *Canadian Charter of Rights and Freedoms* as enacted by this Act shall be read and construed as extending only to matters coming within the legislative authority of the Parliament of Canada, except as otherwise provided by the legislature of any province acting under the authority conferred on it by the Constitution of Canada.

(2) In order that effect may be given as soon as may be to the extension of the Charter referred to in subsection (1) to matters coming within the legislative authority of the legislatures of all the provinces equally as to matters coming within the legislative authority of the Parliament of Canada, as part of the Constitution of Canada, it is hereby declared and directed that, on and after the commencement of this Act and by virtue of its enactment by the Parliament of Canada, both Houses of the Parliament of Canada shall be deemed to have approved of a resolution for the amendment of the Constitution of Canada in the form and to the effect of the Charter referred to in subsection (1), which resolution may be taken up and dealt with by action as on a joint address or by proclamation, as the case may be, as and when it may lawfully be so taken up and dealt with in accordance with the procedure for such amendment then recognized by accepted usage, if there is then no procedure for that purpose expressly provided for by the Constitution of Canada, or in accordance with the procedure for that purpose expressly so provided for, if there is then such a procedure.

(4) At such time as the resolution deemed by subsection (2) to have been approved by both Houses of the Parliament of Canada has been taken up and dealt with as provided in that subsection and any further action required by law to give effect thereto has been taken,

(2) Until such time as this subsection is repealed by subsection (4), the provisions of the *Canadian Charter of Rights and Freedoms*, in this section referred to as the ''Charter'', shall be read and construed as extending only to matters coming within the legislative authority of Parliament, except as otherwise provided by the legislature of any province acting under the authority conferred on it by the Constitution of Canada.

(3) In order that effect may be given as soon as may be to the extension of the Charter to matters coming within the legislative authority of the legislatures of all the provinces equally as to matters coming within the legislative authority of Parliament as part of the Constitution of Canada, it is hereby declared and directed that, on and after the commencement of this Act and by virtue of its enactment by Parliament, both Houses of Parliament shall be deemed to have approved of a resolution for the amendment of the Constitution of Canada in the form and to the effect of the Charter and, subject to subsection (7), for the repeal of

(a) sections 55 to 57 of the Act of 1867 respecting the reservation of assent to Bills, the disallowance of Acts and the signification of pleasure on Bills reserved, as those sections extended and were applicable immediately before the commencement of this Act to the legislatures of the several provinces by virtue of and in the manner provided in section 9 of the Act of 1867,

(b) sections 85 and 86 of the Act of 1867, section 90 thereof in so far as it relates to the matters provided for in paragraph (a), and section 133 thereof, and

(c) section 23 of the *Manitoba Act, 1870*

which resolution may be taken up and dealt with by action as on a joint address or by proclamation, as the case may be, as and when it may lawfully be so taken up and dealt with in accordance with the procedure for such amendment then recognized by acceptance usage or expressly provided for by the Constitution of Canada.

(4) At such time as the resolution deemed by subsection (3) to have been approved by both Houses of Parliament has been taken up and dealt with as provided in that subsection and any further action required by law to give effect thereto has been taken,

C-60 Provisions	**Proposed New Provisions**

(*a*) subsection (1) of this section is repealed;

(*b*) sections 20, 50, 55 to 57, 85 and 86 of the Act of 1867 are repealed;

(*c*) sections 55 to 57 of the Act of 1867 respecting the reservation of assent to Bills, the disallowance of Acts and the signification of pleasure on Bills reserved, as those sections extended and were applicable immediately before the commencement of this Act to the legislature of the several provinces by virtue of and in the manner provided in section 90 of the Act of 1867, cease to extend and apply thereto, and section 90 is repealed in so far as it relates to the matters provided for in this paragraph; and

(*d*) section 133 of the Act of 1867 and section 23 of the *Manitoba Act, 1870* are repealed.

(3) From and after such time as it is provided by the legislature of any province, acting within the authority conferred on it by the Constitution of Canada, that the provisions of the *Canadian Charter of Rights and Freedoms* as enacted by this Act extend to matters coming within its legislative authority,

(*a*) the provisions of the Act of 1867 respecting the reservation of assent to Bills, the disallowance of Acts and the signification of pleasure on Bills reserved, as those provisions extend and are made applicable to the legislatures of the several provinces by virtue of and in the manner provided in section 90 of the Act of 1867, shall cease to extend and be applicable to the legislature of that province as if they were here repealed or made inapplicable in terms to that province and its legislature; and

(*b*) where that province is Ontario, subsection 15(2) of this Act shall not apply so as to require the printing and publishing in English and French of any statutes of, or any revision or consolidation of statutes authorized by, the legislature of that province except any such statutes enacted after, or any such revision or consolidation authorized to have effect after, such day or days as that legislature shall have fixed therefor.

(a) subsections (1) and (2) are repealed; and

(b) sections 20, 50 and 55 to 57 of the Act of 1867 are repealed.

(5) The legislature of any province, acting within the authority conferred on it by the Constitution of Canada, may at any time provide that the Charter extends to matters coming within its legislative authority

(a) without qualification; or

(b) with the following qualification only: "Section 24 of the *Canadian Charter of Rights and Freedoms* does not apply in respect of the rights declared by sections 10 and 11 thereof where it is expressly declared by an Act of the Legislature that such Act or a specified provision or provisions thereof operate and have force and effect notwithstanding the provisions of the *Canadian Charter of Rights and Freedoms*."

(6) From and after such time as it is provided by the legislature of any province, acting within the authority conferred on it by the Constitution of Canada, that the provisions of the Charter extend to matters coming within its legislative authority, either without qualification or with the qualification referred to in subsection (5), subject to subsection (7), the provisions of the Act of 1867 respecting the reservation of assent to Bills, the disallowance of Acts and the signification of pleasure on Bills reserved, as those provisions extend and are made applicable to the legislatures of the several provinces by virtue of and in the manner provided in section 90 of the Act of 1867, shall cease to extend and be applicable to the legislature of that province as if they were here repealed or made inapplicable in terms to that province and its legislature.

(7) Notwithstanding subsections (3) and (6), where the legislature of a province has provided that the Charter extends to matters coming within its legislative authority with the qualification referred to in subsection (5), the provisions of the Act of 1867 respecting the

C-60 Provisions	**Proposed New Provisions**
	reservation of assent to Bills, the disallowance of Acts and the signification of pleasure on Bills reserved, as those provision extend and are made applicable to the legislatures of the several provinces by virtue of and in the manner provided in section 90 of the Act of 1867, continue to extend and be applicable in respect of provisions enacted by the legislature of that province to the effect that any Act of the legislature of the province or any provision or provisions thereof operate and have force and effect notwithstanding the provisions of the *Canadian Charter of Rights and Freedoms.*
(5) Notwithstanding anything in subsection (1), for the purposes of that subsection the legislative authority of the Parliament of Canada shall be deemed not to extend to the Yukon Territory or the Northwest Territories in relation to any matter provided for in sections 13 to 21 of the *Canadian Charter of Rights and Freedoms* that would not, if those territories were provinces of Canada, come within the legislative authority of Parliament, and in relation to any such matter the reference in subsection (1) to the legislature of any province acting under the authority conferred on it by the Constitution of Canada shall be read as extending to the Commissioner in Council of any territory of Canada acting within the authority which is hereby conferred on the Commissioner in Council by the Parliament of Canada.	(8) Notwithstanding subsection (2), for the purposes of that subsection the legislative authority of Parliament shall be deemed not to extend to the Yukon Territory or the Northwest Territories in relation to any matter provided for in sections 14 to 21 of the Charter that would not, if those territories were provinces, come within the legislative authority of Parliament, and in relation to any such matter the reference in subsection (2) to the legislature of any province acting under the authority conferred on it by the Constitution of Canada shall be read as extending to the Commissioner in Council of any territory of Canada acting within the authority which is hereby conferred on the Commissioner in Council by Parliament.

32. Continuing Committee of Ministers on the Constitution, Vancouver, British Columbia, January 22–24, 1979

(a) Proposed Charter of Rights and Freedoms for Canadians, Ontario Draft

Document: 830-70/042

Note: This document was tabled again at the Federal-Provincial First Ministers' Conference, Ottawa, Ontario, February 5–7, 1979, as "Charter of Rights: Proposed Ontario Draft," Document 800-10/010.

PROPOSED ONTARIO DRAFT FOR DISCUSSION BY FIRST MINISTERS

5. The provisions of this division may be cited as the *Canadian Charter of Rights and Freedoms*.

Fundamental Freedoms

Fundamental freedoms

6. (1) Everyone has the right to the following fundamental freedoms:
(*a*) freedom of conscience and religion;
(*b*) freedom of thought, opinion and expression including freedom in the dissemination of news, opinion and belief; and
(*c*) freedom of peaceful assembly and of association.

Justifiable limitations

(2) The manifestation or exercise of the freedoms declared by this section may be made subject only to such limitations prescribed by law as are reasonably justifiable in a free and democratic society in the interests of national security, public safety, order, health or morals or any rights and freedoms of others.

Democratic Rights

Democratic rights of citizens

7. Consistent with the principles of free and democratic elections to the House of Commons and to the legislative assemblies, and of universal suffrage for that purpose, every citizen of Canada shall, without unreasonable distinction or limitation, have the right to vote in an election of members of the House of Commons or of a legislative assembly and to be qualified for membership therein.

Duration of elected legislative bodies

8. (1) No House of Commons and no legislative assembly of a province shall continue for longer than five years from the date of the return of the writs for the choosing of its members.

Continuation in special circumstances

(2) Notwithstanding subsection (1), in time of real or apprehended war, invasion or insurrection, a House of Commons may be continued by Parliament and a legislative assembly of a province may be continued by the

legislature thereof beyond the time limited therefore by or under subsection (1), if such continuation is not opposed by the votes of more than one-third of the members of the House of Commons or the legislative assembly, as the case may be.

Annual sitting of elected legislative bodies

9. There shall be a sitting of Parliament and of each legislature at least once in every year and not more than twelve months shall intervene between sittings.

Official languages

10. (1) English and French are the official languages of Canada, having the status and protection set forth in this Charter.

(2) Nothing in this Charter limits the authority of Parliament or of the legislature of a province to extend the status protection or use of the English and French languages.

Language rights

11. (1) Everyone has the right to use English or French, as he or she may choose, in any of the debates or other proceedings of Parliament.

(2) Everyone has the right to use English or French, as he or she may choose, in the debates of the legislative assembly of any province.

12. The statutes and the records and journals of Parliament shall be printed and published in English and French and both language versions shall be equally authoritative.

13. (1) Either English or French may be used by any person in, or in any pleading or process in or issuing from, the Supreme Court of Canada or any court constituted by Parliament.

(2) Either English or French may be used by any person in, or in any pleading or process in or issuing from, any court of a province, to the greatest extent possible accordingly as the legislature of the province prescribes.

14. (1) Any member of the public in Canada has the right to communicate with and to receive services from any head or central office of an institution of government of Canada in English or French, as he or she may choose and he or she has the same right with respect to any principal office of any such institution where that office is located within an area of Canada in which it is determined, in such manner as may be prescribed or authorized by Parliament, that a substantial number of persons within the population use that language.

(2) Any member of the public in a province has the right to communicate with and to receive services from any head, central or other principal office of an institution of government of the province in English or French, as he or she may choose, to the extent to which and in the areas of the province in which it is determined, in such manner as may be prescribed or authorized by the legislature of the province that the right should pertain having regard to the practicability and necessity of providing such services.

15. (1) Any person in a province who is a member of an English-speaking or French-speaking minority population of that province has a right to have his or her children receive their educational instruction in their minority language at the primary and secondary school level wherever the number of children of such persons resident in an area of the province is sufficient to warrant the provision of minority language education facilities in that area out of public funds.

(2) In each province, the legislature may enact provisions for the determination of whether or not the number of children of an

English-speaking or French-speaking minority population in an area of the province is sufficient to warrant the provision of minority language education facilities in that area.

16. Nothing in sections 10 to 15 abrogates or derogates from any legal or customary right or privilege acquired or enjoyed either before or after the commencement of this Act with respect to English or French, and any other language in Canada.

Undeclared Rights

17. Nothing in this Charter abrogates or derogates from any right or freedom not declared by it that may exist in Canada, including any right or freedom that may pertain to the native peoples of Canada.

(b) Report of the Continuing Committee of Ministers on the Constitution, Supreme Court Provisions, January 23, 1979

Document: 830-70/037

Summary

1. A consensus agreement was reached at the Mont-Ste-Marie meeting and further refined at the Toronto and Vancouver meetings. The report of the Committee of Officials was considered by Ministers and attached is a draft text of provisions relating to the Supreme Court and the judiciary. This was approved by the Continuing Committee for consideration of First Ministers subject to the reservations spelled out below.

The main elements of the draft provisions are:
— a nine-member court;
— a requirement that the Minister of Justice shall consult with the Attorney General of the appropriate province when making an appointment to the Supreme Court (instead of a requirement of agreement as proposed in Bill C-60);
— a similar consultation requirement to apply to the appointment of provincial, superior, district and county court judges (section 96 judges);
— a requirement that three members of the Court be appointed from the bench or bar of Quebec (a civilian judge of the Federal Court would also qualify);
— a requirement that cases concerning the civil law of Quebec be heard by a special panel of the Court composed (in most circumstances) of a majority of Quebec judges;
— a provision providing for the special appointment of judges to facilitate the holding of trials in the official language of a person's choice, when the person has the

right by law to be heard in the official language of his choice.

General Reservation
2. Quebec expressed a general reservation about the provisions respecting the Supreme Court and reiterated its wishes to see a constitutional court established.

Specific Reservations
3. *Section 3(2)*
British Columbia expressed a specific reservation with respect to section 3(2), which provides that three members of the court shall be appointed from the bench or bar of Quebec. It is British Columbia's position that if there is to be regional representation for Quebec, there should also be representation from other regions on the five-region concept proposed by British Columbia.

4. *Section 4*
Saskatchewan noted that the requirement that the Minister of Justice consult with the Attorney General of the appropriate province before making an appointment to the Supreme Court (section 4) was a much less stringent requirement than that which was part of the Victoria Charter proposals.

5. Quebec expressed a specific reservation with respect to section 6, which provides that a special panel of the Supreme

Court will hear cases involving Quebec civil law issues. Quebec's position is that the Quebec Court of Appeal should be the final court of resort in all civil code cases.

6. *Sections 13 and 15*

Some provinces expressed the view that superior, country and district court judges (section 96 judges) should be appointed by the provincial governments. Section 15 of the draft derives from section 96 of the B.N.A. Act, and would provide for appointment of such judges by the Governor General after consultation by the Minister of Justice with the Attorney General of the appropriate province.

Concern was expressed by almost all provinces that the existing section 101 of the B.N.A. Act which is carried forward in section 13 of the draft text is unacceptable because it allows Parliament to establish a parallel system of federal courts for the administration of federal laws.

It was accepted that these issues could not be adequately canvassed in the time available.

Some provinces wished to see [sections] 14 to 16 of the draft deleted pending further study of these issues. A majority of the provinces agreed that section 14 to 16 should be included, thus establishing a constitutional obligation on the federal Minister of Justice to consult with the Provincial Attorney General respecting section 96 appointments. Such inclusion was, however, made on the understanding that both the above issues would be studied, at an early date, for purposes of further constitutional revision.

XI   THE COURTS AND JUDICIARY [January 17, 1979]

The Supreme Court of Canada

Supreme Court of Canada	**1.** There shall be a general court of appeal for Canada called the Supreme Court of Canada.
Constitution of Supreme Court	**2.** The Supreme Court of Canada shall consist of a chief justice, to be called the Chief Justice of Canada, and eight other judges, who shall be appointed by the Governor General.
Eligibility for appointment	**3.** (1) A person is eligible to be appointed as a judge of the Supreme Court if, after having been admitted to the bar of any province, the person has, for a total period of at least ten years, been a judge of any court in Canada or a barrister or advocate at the bar of any province.
Appointment of judges from Quebec	(2) At least three of the judges of the Supreme Court shall be appointed from among persons who, after having been admitted to the bar of Quebec, have, for a total period of at least ten years, been judges of any court of that province or of a court established by Parliament or advocates at the bar of Quebec.
Procedure on vacancy	**4.** Where a vacancy in the Supreme Court occurs, the Minister of Justice of Canada shall consult with the Attorney General of the province or Attorneys General of the provinces from which the persons being considered for appointment come.
Tenure of office of judges of Supreme Court	**5.** (1) The judges of the Supreme Court hold office during good behaviour until they attain the age of seventy years but are removable by the Governor General on address of the Senate and the House of Commons.
Salaries, allowances and pensions of judges of Supreme Court	(2) The salaries, allowances and pensions of the judges of the Supreme Court shall be fixed and provided by Parliament.
Ultimate appellate jurisdiction of Supreme Court	**6.** The Supreme Court has exclusive ultimate appellate civil and criminal jurisdiction within and for Canada.
Appeals with leave of Supreme Court	**7.** An appeal to the Supreme Court lies with leave of the Supreme Court from any judgment of the highest court of final resort in a province, or a judge thereof, in which judgment can be had in the particular case sought to be appealed to the Supreme Court, where, in the opinion of the Supreme Court, any question involved is one that ought to be decided by it.

Appeals from references by
Lieutenant Governor

8. An appeal to the Supreme Court lies from an opinion pronounced by the highest court in a province on any matter referred to it for hearing and consideration by the Lieutenant Governor in Council of that province.

Additional appeals

9. In addition to any appeal provided for by this division, an appeal to the Supreme Court lies as may be provided by any Act of Parliament.

Laws respecting jurisdiction of
Supreme Court; references of
questions of law or fact

10. Parliament may make laws authorizing the reference of questions of law or fact to the Court and requiring the Court to hear and determine such questions.

Questions relating to
civil law of Quebec

11. Where any case before the Supreme Court involves a question of law relating to the civil law of Quebec and no other question of law, that case shall be heard by a panel of five judges at least three of whom have the qualifications described in section 3 or, with the consent of the parties, by a panel of four judges at least two of whom have those qualifications.

Organization, maintenance and
operation of Supreme Court

12. Parliament may make laws providing for the organization, maintenance and operation of the Supreme Court, and the effectual execution and working of this division and the attainment of its intention and objects including laws providing for the appointment of such ad hoc judges as may be necessary to ensure quorums.

Courts for Better Administration of Laws of Canada

Constitution of courts for better
administration of laws of Canada

13. Parliament may, notwithstanding anything in the Constitution of Canada, from time to time provide for the constitution, organization, maintenance and operation of courts for the better administration of the laws of Canada, but no law providing for the constitution, organization, maintenance or operation of any such court shall derogate from the jurisdiction of the Supreme Court of Canada as a general court of appeal for Canada.

Appointment and Tenure of Office of Judges of Superior, District and County Courts and their Salaries, Allowances and Pensions

Appointment of judges of superior,
district and county courts

14. The Governor General shall appoint the judges of the superior, district and county courts in each province, except those of the courts of probate in Nova Scotia and New Brunswick.

Procedure on vacancy

15. Where a vacancy occurs in the superior, district or county court of a province, the Minister of Justice of Canada shall consult with the Attorney General of the province as to persons being considered for appointment.

Selection of judges appointed by
Governor General

16. The judges of the courts in each province appointed by the Governor General shall be selected from among members of the bar of the province or from among judges who were members of the bar of the province prior to their appointment as judges.

Tenure of office of judges of
superior courts

17. The judges of the superior courts of the provinces hold office during good behaviour until they attain the age of seventy years but are removable by the Governor General on address of the Senate and the House of Commons.

Salaries, allowances and pensions
of judges generally

*18. The salaries, allowances and pensions of the judges of the superior, district and county courts in each province, except the courts of probate in Nova Scotia and New Brunswick, shall be fixed and provided by Parliament.

Deputy judges

19. (1) For the purpose of enabling persons being tried or giving evidence in any superior, district or county court in a province to exercise any right they may have by law to be tried or heard in English or French according to their choice, the Governor in Council may, notwithstanding sections 16 and 17, at the request of the Attorney General and appropriate chief justice of the superior court or chief or senior judge of the district or county courts of that province, appoint any persons who have been judges of a superior, district or county court, of any other province, or any persons who are judges of such a court of any other province with the consent of the Attorney General and appropriate chief justice or chief judge of such province, to be deputy judges of any superior, district or county court in the province on behalf of which the request is made.

Tenure of office of Deputy judges

(2) A deputy judge may be appointed pursuant to this section for any period of time during which period, he or she shall perform such duties as are assigned by the appropriate chief justice or chief judge, and his or her appointment may be terminated at the pleasure of the Governor in Council.

Interpretation

20. For the purposes of this Division, the term "province" includes the Yukon Territory and the Northwest Territories.

(c) Alternative Draft Proposal Suggested by Several Provinces Regarding Communications, January 1979

Cable Distribution

1. In each province the legislature may make laws in relation to cable distribution within the province involving the reception and redistribution of broadcast signals; Parliament may also make laws in relation thereto for each of the provinces.

Relationship between laws of the provinces and laws of Parliament

2. Any law enacted by the legislature of a province pursuant to section 1 shall prevail to the extent of the inconsistency over any law of Parliament enacted thereunder except in the following fields:
the reception and conditions of carriage of broadcast signals,
technical standards relating to the reception and carriage of broadcast signals, and
the national origin of broadcast program content,
in which case any law of Parliament shall prevail to the extent of the inconsistency.

Consultations

3. The government of Canada shall consult the government of the province concerned before Parliament makes a law in relation to cable distribution within that province pursuant to section 1.

Telecommunications undertakings

4. Telecommunications undertakings coming under the jurisdiction of Parliament as well as those coming under the jurisdiction of the legislature of a province and engaging in activities coming under section 1 other than as carriers shall be subject, in so far as such activities are concerned, to the laws enacted under section 1.

Powers continued

5. Except where otherwise expressly provided in [sections] 1 to 4, nothing therein shall derogate from the legislative powers that Parliament and the legislatures of the provinces had immediately before the coming into force of these sections.

(d) Amendments to the Constitution of Canada
(Alberta Draft Proposals)

1. Amendments to the Constitution of Canada may from time to time be made by proclamation by the Governor General under the great seal of Canada when so authorized by resolutions of the Senate and House of Commons and the assent by resolution of the Legislative Assembly in two-thirds of the provinces representing at least fifty per cent of the population of Canada according to the latest general census, provided that if the enactment is one affecting
   (a) the powers of the legislature of a province to make laws,
   (b) the rights or privileges granted or secured by the Constitution of Canada to the legislature or the government of a province,
   (c) the assets or property of a province, or
   (d) the natural resources of a province,
   any Legislative Assembly of a Province which has not approved such enactment and which has expressed its dissent thereto by resolution may continue exclusively to make laws in relation to the subject matters coming within such enactment.

2. Amendments to the Constitution of Canada in relation to any provision that applies to one or more, but not all, of the Provinces may from time to time be made by proclamation issued by the Governor General under the Great Seal of Canada when so authorized by resolutions of the Senate and House of Commons and of the Legislative Assembly of each Province to which an amendment applies.

3. An amendment may be made by proclamation under Section 1 or 2 without a resolution of the Senate authorizing the issue of the proclamation if within ninety days of the passage of a resolution by the House of Commons authorizing its issue the Senate has not passed such a resolution and at any time after the expiration of the ninety days the House of Commons again passes the resolution, but any period when Parliament is prorogued or dissolved shall not be counted in computing the ninety days.

4. The following rules apply to the procedures for amendment described in Sections 1 and 2:
   1) either of these procedures may be initiated by the Senate of the House of Commons or the Legislative Assembly of a Province:

   2) a resolution made for the purposes of this Part may be revoked at any time before the issue of a proclamation authorized by it.

5. The Parliament of Canada may exclusively make laws from time to time amending the Constitution of Canada, in relation to the executive Government of Canada and the Senate and the House of Commons.

6. In each Province the Legislature may exclusively make laws in relation to the amendment from time to time of the Constitution of the Province.

7. Notwithstanding Sections 5 and 6 the following matters may be amended only in accordance with the procedure in Section 1:
   1) the office of the Queen, of the Governor General and of the Lieutenant-Governor:
   2) the requirements of the Constitution of Canada respecting yearly sessions of the Parliament of Canada and the Legislatures:
   3) the maximum period fixed by the Constitution of Canada for the duration of the House of Commons and the Legislative Assemblies:
   4) the powers of the Senate:
   5) the number of members by which a Province is entitled to be represented in the Senate and the residence qualifications of Senators:
   6) the right of a Province to a number of members in the House of Commons not less than the number of Senators representing the Province:
   7) the principles of proportionate representation of the Provinces in the House of Commons prescribed by the Constitution of Canada: and
   8) the use of the English or French language:
      i) No amendments to Section 1 of this Part shall come into force unless it is concurred in by the Parliament of Canada and by the Legislative Assemblies of all the provinces.
      ii) The procedure prescribed in Section 1 of this Part may not be used to make an amendment when there is another provision for making such amendment in the Constitution of Canada but, subject to the limitations contained in subsection (1) of this Section that procedure may nonetheless be used to amend any provision for amending the Constitution.

33. Federal-Provincial First Ministers' Conference, Ottawa, Ontario, February 5–6, 1979

(a) Amending Formula for the Canadian Constitution, Alberta Proposal, Presented by Premier Lougheed

Document: 800–10/023

To Alberta one of the most important items on the agenda for constitutional change is that of an amending formula. At the last Conference in October 1978 the Prime Minister indicated that over the last fifty-one years governments in Canada had failed to resolve this question. We share these concerns and hope that this dilemma can be resolved during this current round of discussions.

Two years ago a resolution was overwhelmingly adopted by the Alberta Legislative Assembly. The resolution reads as follows:

> Be it resolved that the Legislative Assembly of Alberta, while supporting the objective of patriation of the Canadian constitution, reaffirm the fundamental principle of Confederation that all provinces have equal rights within Confederation and hence direct the government that it should not agree to any revised amending formula for the constitution which could allow any existing rights, proprietary interests or jurisdiction to be taken away from any province without the specific concurrence of that province, and that it should refuse to give its support to any patriation prior to obtaining the unanimous consent of all provinces for a proper amending formula.

As one can see, our resolution does not favour the principles contained in the so-called Victoria formula. Our chief criticism of that formula is that it divides Canada into first and second-class provinces and establishes a regional — as opposed to a provincial — concept in the amending process.

The resolution contains two important principles: —
— that all provinces have equal constitutional status; and
— that, with respect to the rights, proprietary interests and jurisdiction of the provinces, neither the federal government nor any other province can determine any particular province's constitutional status.

A number of concerns have been expressed about our position, which I think has been misinterpreted (as recently as in the Task Force Report on National Unity). It has

been suggested that Alberta is seeking a veto; such is not the case. What we have said is that an amending formula should not allow any provincial rights, proprietary interests or jurisdiction to be taken away from any province without the consent of that province. To us there is significant difference between our position and one which establishes a veto for any province.

To Alberta any amending formula must meet certain tests: —

1. The Parliament of Canada must be a participant in all constitutional amendments other than those pertaining to provincial constitutions.
2. All provinces must have an equal say in constitutional amendments affecting existing provincial rights, proprietary interests and jurisdiction.
3. Constitutional amendments affecting existing provincial rights, proprietary interests and jurisdiction should not be imposed on any province not desiring it.
4. Constitutional change must be difficult but not so difficult as to make it impossible. A balance between rigidity and flexibility is essential. Thus any formula must require a high degree of consensus before an amendment can be passed, but no one province should have a veto.
5. A formula must not be based on regional equality but on provincial equality.
6. Given our constitutional development to date it will be necessary to devise more than one method of amending the constitution. It has been recognized to date that Parliament acting alone may amend certain sections of the constitution, or Parliament in concert with one or more provinces may enact an amendment affecting these provinces alone. An example of the latter is the 1930 amendment on natural resources.

After studying this subject very carefully the Government of Alberta has developed a formula which it believes meets the above tests. The Alberta proposal is as follows:

Under the general amending formula, in respect of matters concerning the federal government and all the provinces, amendments could be made by an act of Parliament and the assent by resolution of the Legislative Assembly in two-thirds of the provinces, representing the majority of the population of Canada.

This would be supplemented by a provision that if the enactment is one taking away

(a) the powers of the legislature of a province to make laws,

(b) the rights or privileges granted or secured by the Constitution of Canada to the legislature or the government of a province,

(c) the assets or property of a province, or

(d) the natural resources of a province,

any Legislative Assembly which has not approved such enactment and which has expressed its dissent thereto by resolution may continue exclusively to make laws in relation to the subject matters coming within such enactment.

THE AMENDING FORMULA EXPLAINED

What does the Alberta proposal mean?

1. It establishes a general formula for amending the Constitution of Canada. The formula is two-thirds of the provinces representing fifty per cent of the population. Today two-thirds of the provinces is equal to seven provinces. The population provision means that at least one of the two most populous provinces (Ontario and Quebec) must support any amendment to the constitution. This general formula is the one contained in the 1964 Fulton-Favreau formula.

2. While a general formula is established certain limits as to its application are also established. The limits are that any amendment taking away existing rights, proprietary interests or jurisdiction of provinces may not be imposed on any province opposed to that particular amendment. The limitation does not establish any vetoes, i.e. one province cannot prevent an amendment desired by other provinces in the above areas.

In effect the Alberta proposal provides for a high degree of consensus before any amendment can be passed, i.e. Parliament and seven provinces representing fifty per cent of the population, but leaves those provinces (at most three), not in favour of an amendment which affects existing rights, proprietary interests or jurisdiction, free to continue legislating on a particular subject. It should also be noted that each province is expected to make a decision on any amendment. A province not wishing to have an amendment applied to it must register its dissent. If it fails to do so the amendment would apply to that province once seven provinces had registered their consent. As a result it is expected that every amendment would be debated not only in Parliament but also in every provincial legislature.

The main criticism of the Alberta proposal is that over time different parts of the constitution could be applied differently in Canada. This observation is correct but it overlooks both the constitutional realities and practices of today's federal system.

An examination of the British North America Act of 1867 and its several amendments suggests that individual provinces preferred to preserve certain differences. For example, in the original B.N.A. Act this principle of individual difference is found in Section 94, the uniformity of laws provision; in Section 133 respecting languages; and in Section 119, giving a special financial grant to New Brunswick for ten years. As new provinces were admitted other differences were developed in their terms of union. For example, the wording of Section 93(1) is slightly altered by the wording of Section 17 of the Alberta Act while the wording is different again for Newfoundland. The 1907 amendment on financial grants had special guarantees for British Columbia and Prince Edward Island. In short, since Canada was founded the diversity amongst all provinces has been recognized and accepted.

The 1951 and 1964 amendments giving Parliament authority to legislate for old age pensions and supplementary benefits are also of interest. While Parliament was given authority to legislate it was on condition that "no such law shall affect the operation of any law present or future of a provincial legislature in relation to any such matter". Today as a result of this wording the Canada and Quebec Pension Plans operate side by side, both with equal constitutional validity.

In short, the major operating premise of the Alberta proposal is not without precedent in the Canadian context. The principal benefit of the formula is that it permits constitutional amendment while avoiding the potential rigidity required by unanimity. It protects each and every province by ensuring that their existing jurisdiction, rights and proprietary interests cannot be amended without their consent. It recognizes that diversity can be accommodated within the Canadian federal system. It ensures that an amendment must have wide support throughout the country. On balance we believe that this proposal is the most reasonable and practical one which can be developed at this time.

(b) Report of the Continuing Committee of Ministers on the Constitution to First Ministers: The Amending Formula, "Patriation" of the Constitution, and Delegation of Legislative Authority

Document: 800–10/013

1. AMENDING FORMULA

The Continuing Committee of Ministers on the Constitution discussed the problem of amendment at their meeting at Mont Ste-Marie and at the second meeting in Toronto they agreed that a formula should be developed on the following basis:

(a) there should be a short list of matters requiring unanimity, including amendments relating to provincial ownership of and jurisdiction over natural resources plus the amending formula itself;

(b) all other changes of general concern should require the consent of Parliament and of the legislatures of at least seven provinces comprising at least 85% of the population of Canada; and

(c) changes in the boundaries of provinces should require the consent of the provinces concerned.

In further discussion at the meeting of officials on January 11–12, 1979, several provinces asked that the question of delegation of legislative powers from Parliament to legislatures, or in the reverse direction, should also form a part of the amending procedure as had been the case in the "Fulton-Favreau formula" of 1964. All provinces expressing a view, however, said that delegation should be possible on a "one-to-one" basis (that is from Parliament to one province, or the reverse) rather than being limited to cases where it would involve at least four provinces, as in the case of the Fulton-Favreau formula. These provinces also felt that there should be no constitutional restriction on the sorts of powers that could be delegated.

The meeting of the Continuing Committee of Ministers in Vancouver on January 22–24, 1979, considered a draft formula prepared by the federal government on the above basis. It also considered an alternative formula submitted by the government of Alberta.

2. [*sic*] ALTERNATIVE AMENDING FORMULAE

The following amending formulae are submitted for consideration by the Conference of First Ministers:

(a) *"The Toronto consensus" formula*
The draft formula, prepared by the federal government pursuant to the Toronto consensus, was presented in Vancouver. The formula would require unanimity for amendments relating to the ownership of and legislative jurisdiction in respect of natural resources and also for any amendments of the clause requiring unanimity for those purposes. All other generally entrenched matters could only be amended with the consent of Parliament and the consent of 2/3 of the provinces having at least 85% of the population of Canada.

Although British Columbia preferred a modification of the Victoria formula with British Columbia recognized as a fifth region and using a reconstituted Senate nominated by provincial governments as the forum for the expression of provincial views on amendments, British Columbia indicated that it would find acceptable a modified version of the "Toronto consensus" which would add "language and culture" to the short list of items requiring unanimity for amendment and which would alter the mathematical formula to six or seven provincial legislatures representing 60% of the population of Canada for the amendment of generally entrenched matters. Ontario indicated that it found the "Toronto consensus" formula generally acceptable, although it would like to examine the possibility of adding provisions respecting language, the Supreme Court and the creation of new provinces to the matters subject to the mathematical formula for generally entrenched matters. Furthermore, Ontario felt that 85% might be too high a figure, but that 60%, on the other hand, would be too low.

(b) *The Alberta formula*
This would require the consent of Parliament and of

2/3 of the provinces with at least 50% of the population of Canada for general amendments. However, if an enactment is one taking away

  (i) the powers of a provincial legislature,

 (ii) the rights or privileges of a provincial legislature or government,

(iii) the assets or property of a province, or

(iv) the natural resources of a province,

a legislature which has *not* approved such an enactment and which has expressed its dissent, would continue its exclusive power to make laws for any such subject matter. Newfoundland expressed support for the Alberta formula.

(c) *The Victoria formula*

New Brunswick prefers the "Victoria formula", based on the consent of Parliament and of at least six legislatures distributed among four regions.

(d) *The Fulton-Favreau formula coupled with greater flexibility*

Manitoba indicated that it would prefer a more flexible formula than either the "Toronto consensus" or the Alberta formula and suggested that the Fulton-Favreau formula be taken as a point of departure in elaborating a more flexible formula.

Provisions for the delegation of powers could supplement any of the amending formulae described above.

2. "PATRIATION" OF THE CONSTITUTION

"Patriation" of the Constitution has not been discussed by Ministers. If an amending formula can be agreed upon, "patriation" could be accomplished on the basis contemplated at Victoria in 1971: a formal request by the government of Canada, pursuant to a joint address of the Senate and the House of Commons, for legislation by the British Parliament terminating the power of the British Parliament to legislate with regard to the Constitution of Canada and providing for a proclamation by the Governor General declaring the Constitution to be subject to amendment by the formula agreed upon.

3. DELEGATION OF LEGISLATIVE AUTHORITY

(See Tab S [not reproduced]).

There was a brief discussion in Vancouver on the delegation of legislative authority and general support was expressed for the draft provisions (see Tab S [not reproduced]). Ontario and British Columbia raised points for further clarification and information. It was agreed that the delegation provisions, while not part of the amending formula as such, were closely related to it. Ontario asked whether the words "prior to the enactment thereof" should be added after the word "unless" in s. 2 of the delegation provisions dealing with the consent of a province to the operation in that province of a federal law coming within the legislative jurisdiction of a province. It was explained that the present wording would permit a federal law, agreed to prior to enactment by one province, to be cast in general terms that would allow other provinces to opt-in subsequently. It was agreed, however, that the wording of s. 2 should make clear that one province at least would have to give prior consent before Parliament enacted a law coming within the legislative jurisdiction of a province. British Columbia expressed concern lest Parliament, under s. 3, might agree to allow one province to make laws in the province in relation to a matter coming within the legislative authority of Parliament and then might subsequently refuse to allow other provinces to make laws in respect to the same matter. It was agreed that this matter should be examined.

(c) List of "Best Effort" Draft Proposals, with Joint Government Input, Discussed by First Ministers

Document: 800-010/036

TABLE OF CONTENTS

RESOURCE OWNERSHIP AND INTERPROVINCIAL TRADE

(1) (present Section 92)

(1) Carries forward existing Section 92

Resources

(2) In each province, the legislature may exclusively make laws in relation to
   a) exploration for non-renewable natural resources in the province;
   b) development, exploitation, extraction, conservation and management of non-renewable natural resources in the province, including laws in relation to the rate of primary production therefrom; and
   c) development, exploitation, conservation and management of forestry resources in the province and of sites and facilities in the province for the generation of electrical energy, including laws in relation to the rate of primary production therefrom.

(2) The draft outlines exclusive provincial legislative jurisdiction over certain natural resources and electric energy within the province. These resources have been defined as non-renewable (e.g. crude oil, copper, iron and nickel), forests and electric energy. This section pertains to *legislative* jurisdiction and in no way impairs established *proprietary* rights of provinces over resources whether these resources are renewable or non-renewable.

Export from the province of resource

(3) In each province, the legislature may make laws in relation to the export from the province of the primary production from non-renewable natural resources and forestry resources in the province and the production from facilities in the province for the generation of electrical energy, but such laws may not authorize or provide for prices for production sold for export to another part of Canada that are different from prices authorized or provided for production not sold for export from the province.

(3) Provincial governments are given concurrent legislative authority to pass laws governing the export of the resources referred to above from the province. This legislative capacity is in the sphere of both interprovincial and international trade and commerce. Provincial governments are prohibited from price discrimination between resources consumed in the province and those destined for consumption in other provinces. This new provincial legislative capacity applies to these resources in their raw state and to them in their processed state but does not apply to materials manufactured from them.

Relationship to certain laws of Parliament

(4) Any law enacted by the legislature of a province pursuant to the authority conferred by subsection (3) prevails over a law enacted by Parliament in relation to the regulation of trade and commerce except to the extent that the law so enacted by Parliament,
   a) in the case of a law in relation to the regulation of trade and commerce within Canada, is necessary to serve a compelling national interest that is not merely an aggregate of local interests; or
   b) is a law in relation to the regulation of international trade and commerce.

(4) The effect of this new provincial legislative responsibility over trade and commerce diminishes the scope but does not eliminate the federal government's exclusive authority over trade and commerce. The exercise of the provincial power is subject to two limitations. First, the federal government may legislate for interprovincial trade if there is "compelling national interest". This trigger mechanism may apply to circumstances other than an emergency as established under the peace, order and good government power. Second, federal laws governing international trade prevail over provincial laws in international trade, in effect establishing a concurrent power similar to that for agriculture.

Taxation of resources

(5) In each province, the legislature may make laws in relation to the raising of money by any mode or system of taxation in respect of

a) non-renewable natural resources and forestry resources in the province and the primary production therefrom; and

b) sites and facilities in the province for the generation of electrical energy and the primary production therefrom,

whether or not such production is exported in whole or in part from the province but such laws may not authorize or provide for taxation that differentiates between production exported to another part of Canada and production not exported from the province.

Production from resources

(6) For purposes of this section,

a) production from a non-renewable resource is primary production therefrom if

i) it is in the form in which it exists upon its recovery or severance from its natural state, or

ii) it is a product resulting from processing or refining the resource, and is not a manufactured product or a product resulting from refining crude oil or refining a synthetic equivalent of crude oil; and

b) production from a forestry resource is primary production therefrom if it consists of sawlogs, poles, lumber, wood chips, sawdust or any other primary wood product, or wood pulp, and is not a product manufactured from wood.

Existing Powers

(7) Nothing in subsections (2) to (6) derogates from any powers or rights that a legislature or government of a province had immediately before the coming into force of those subsections.

(5) Provincial powers of taxation are increased to include indirect taxes over the resources outlined in this section — whether these resources are destined in part for export outside the province. These taxes are to apply with equal force both in the province and across the rest of the country.

(6) In determining the scope of provincial legislative powers over resources exported from the province, it became necessary to define the degree to which the resource was processed. It is not intended to extend provincial authority to manufacturing but it is intended to extend it to something beyond its extraction from its natural state. Given the varying resources covered by this section, the wording of this subsection is thought to place the appropriate limitations on provincial powers.

(7) This clause ensures that an existing provincial legislative powers found in s.92 are not impaired by the new section.

LIST OF ALTERNATIVES COVERING THE DISPOSITIONS OF SECTION 109

Option 1	Maintain the status quo, do not carry forward Section 109.
Option 2(a)	
Property in lands, mines, etc.	*"**123.1** All lands, mines, minerals and royalties belonging to any province immediately before this section comes into effect, and all sums then

Note: Numbering is tied in to numbering found in Bill C-60.

due or payable in respect of any such lands, mines, minerals and royalties, belong immediately after this section comes into effect to the province or are then due and payable, subject to any trusts existing in respect thereof and to any interest other than that of the province therein.''

Option 2(b)
Ownership of property

*''**123.1** All property belonging to any province immediately before this section comes into effect, belongs immediately after this section comes into effect to the province, subject to any trusts existing in respect thereof and to any interest other than that of the province therein.''

Option 3
Ownership of property

''**127.1** Nothing in this Act changes the ownership in any property owned by Canada or a province immediately before the coming into force of this Act.''

INDIRECT TAXATION

Taxation within the province by any mode or system of taxation for provincial purposes, except indirect taxation that a) constitutes a tax on the entry into or export from the province or otherwise has effect as a barrier or impediment on interprovincial or international trade, or b) is so imposed that the burden of the tax is passed outside the province.

SUPREME COURT

The Supreme Court of Canada

Supreme Court of Canada

1. There shall be a general court of appeal for Canada called the Supreme Court of Canada.

Constitution of Supreme Court

2. The Supreme Court of Canada shall consist of a chief justice, to be called the Chief Justice of Canada, and eight other judges, who shall be appointed by the Governor General.

Eligibility for appointment

3. (1) A person is eligible to be appointed as a judge of the Supreme Court if, after having been admitted to the bar of any province, the person has, for a total period of at least ten years, been a judge of any court in Canada or a barrister or advocate at the bar of any province.

Appointment of judges from Quebec

(2) At least three of the judges of the Supreme Court shall be appointed from among persons who after having been admitted to the bar of Quebec, have, for a total period of at least ten years, been judges of any court of that province or of a court established by Parliament or advocates at the bar of Quebec.

Procedure on vacancy

4. Where a vacancy in the Supreme Court occurs, the Minister of Justice of Canada shall consult with the Attorney General of the province or Attorneys General of the provinces from which the persons being considered for appointment come.

**Note:* Numbering is tied in to numbering found in Bill C-60.

Tenure of office of judges of
Supreme Court

5. (1) The judges of the Supreme Court hold office during good behaviour until they attain the age of seventy years but are removable by the Governor General on address of the Senate and the House of Commons.

Salaries, allowances and pensions of
judges of Supreme Court

(2) The salaries, allowances and pensions of the judges of the Supreme Court shall be fixed and provided by Parliament.

Ultimate appellate jurisdiction of
Supreme Court

6. The Supreme Court has exclusive ultimate appellate civil and criminal jurisdiction within and for Canada.

Appeals with leave of Supreme
Court

7. An appeal to the Supreme Court lies with leave of the Supreme Court from any judgment of the highest court of final resort in a province, or a judge thereof, in which judgment can be had in the particular case sought to be appealed to the Supreme Court, where, in the opinion of the Supreme Court, any question involved is one that ought to be decided by it.

Appeals from references by
Lieutenant Governor

8. An appeal to the Supreme Court lies from an opinion pronounced by the highest court in a province on any matter referred to it for hearing and consideration by the Lieutenant Governor in Council of that province.

Additional Appeals

9. In addition to any appeal provided for by this division, an appeal to the Supreme Court lies as may be provided by any Act of Parliament.

Laws respecting jurisdiction of
Supreme Court; references of
questions of Law or fact

10. Parliament may make laws authorizing the reference of questions of law or fact to the Court and requiring the Court to hear and determine such questions.

Questions relating to civil law of
Quebec

11. Where any case before the Supreme Court involves a question of law relating to the civil law of Quebec and no other question of law, that case shall be heard by a panel of five judges at least three of whom have the qualifications described in section 3 or, with the consent of the parties, by a panel of four judges at least two of whom have those qualifications.

Organisation, maintenance and
operation of Supreme Court

12. Parliament may make laws providing for the organization, maintenance and operation of the Supreme Court, and the effectual execution and working of this division and the attainment of its intention and objects including laws providing for the appointment of such ad hoc judges as may be necessary to ensure quorums.

Courts for Better Administration of Laws of Canada

Constitution of courts for better
administration of laws of Canada

13. Parliament may, notwithstanding anything in the Constitution of Canada, from time to time provide for the constitution, organization, maintenance and operation of courts for the better administration of the laws of Canada, but no law providing for the constitution, organization, maintenance or operation of any such court shall derogate from the jurisdiction of the Supreme Court of Canada as a general court of appeal for Canada.

*Appointment and Tenure of Office of Judges of Superior, District and County Courts
and their Salaries, Allowances and Pensions*

Appointment of judges of superior,
district and county courts

14. The Governor General shall appoint the judges of the superior, district and county courts in each province, except those of the courts of probate in Nova Scotia and New Brunswick.

Procedure on vacancy

15. Where a vacancy occurs in the superior, district or county court of a province, the Minister of Justice of Canada shall consult with the Attorney General of the province as to persons being considered for appointment.

Selection of judges appointed by Governor General

16. The judges of the courts in each province appointed by the Governor General shall be selected from among members of the bar of the province or from among judges who were members of the bar of the province prior to their appointment as judges.

Tenure of office of judges of superior courts

17. The judges of the superior courts of the provinces hold office during good behaviour until they attain the age of seventy years but are removable by the Governor General on address of the Senate and the House of Commons.

Salaries, allowances and pensions of judges generally

*18. The salaries, allowances and pensions of the judges of the superior, district and county courts in each province, except the courts of probate in Nova Scotia and New Brunswick, shall be fixed and provided by Parliament.

Deputy judges

19. (1) For the purpose of enabling persons being tried or giving evidence in any superior, district or county court in a province to exercise any right they may have by law to be tried or heard in English or French according to their choice, the Governor in Council may, notwithstanding sections 16 and 17, at the request of the Attorney General and appropriate chief justice of the superior court or chief or senior judge of the district or [county] courts of that province, appoint any persons who have been judges of a superior, district or [county] court, of any other province, or any persons who are judges of such a court of any other province with the consent of the Attorney General and appropriate chief justice or chief judge of such province, to be deputy judges of any superior, district or county court in the province on behalf of which the request is made.

Tenure of office of deputy judges

(2) A deputy judge may be appointed pursuant to this section for any period of time during which period, he or she shall perform such duties as are assigned by the appropriate chief justice or chief judge, and his or her appointment may be terminated at the pleasure of the Governor in Council.

Interpretation

20. For the purposes of this Divison, the term "province" includes the Yukon Territory and the Northwest Territories.

FAMILY LAW

1. Repeal head 26 of section 91 — "Marriage and divorce".

2. Repeal head 12 of section 92 — "The solemnization of marriage in the Province" and substitute therefore "Marriage, including the validity of marriage in the Province".

3. Add after section 95 the following section:

"**95A.**(1) The Legislature of each Province may make laws in relation to divorce in the Province, except that Parliament has exclusive authority to make laws in relation to the recognition of divorce decrees granted within or outside Canada, and in relation to the jurisdictional basis upon which a court may entertain an application for divorce.

(2) The Parliament of Canada may make laws in relation to divorce, except that the Legislature of each Province has exclusive authority to make laws in relation to alimony, maintenance, custody and any other corollary to divorce.

(3) Where the Legislature of a Province enacts a law in respect of any of the matters in which it has concurrent authority with the Parliament of Canada under this section, the Parliament of Canada ceases to have authority [in respect of that Province] in all concurrent matters under this section while any such law of the Legislature continues in force."

4. Add to section 96 of the B.N.A. Act the following subsection:

"(2) Notwithstanding that the judges are not appointed under subsection 1, the legislature of a province may confer, or authorize the Lieutenant Governor of the province to confer, concurrently or exclusively, upon any court or division of a court or all or any judges of any court, the judges of which are appointed by the Lieutenant Governor of the province, the jurisdiction of a judge of a superior court of the province in any matters arising out of family relationships, including divorce, annulment of marriage, decrees of validity or nullity of marriage, separation, support, maintenance, adoption, custody, access, affiliation, family property, and rights and obligations among members of a family recognized as such in law''.

5. Add in the transitional provisions of the Act a provision for the continuation of the application of the Divorce Act (Canada) in respect of corollary relief for a period sufficient to allow Provinces to put their legislation in place.

EQUALIZATION AND REGIONAL DEVELOPMENT

''**96**.(1) Without altering the legislative authority of Parliament or of the legislatures or of the rights of any of them with respect to the exercise of their legislative authority, Parliament and the legislatures, together with the Government of Canada and the Governments of the Provinces, are committed to

(a) promoting equal opportunities for the well-being of Canadians;

(b) furthering economic development to reduce disparity in opportunities for social and economic well-being; and,

(c) providing essential public services of reasonable quality to all Canadians.

(2) Parliament and the Government of Canada are further committed to the principle of making equalization payments to provinces that are unable to provide essential public services of reasonable quality without imposing an undue burden of taxation, or to the principle of making arrangements equivalent to equalization payments to meet the commitment specified in Section 96(1)(c).''

(3) The Prime Minister of Canada and the First Ministers of the Provinces shall review together the questions of equalization and regional development at lease once every five years at a meeting convened pursuant to section 97.

SPENDING POWER

LEGISLATIVE TEXT

Renumber section 91 of the B.N.A. Act as subsection 91(1) and add the following:

ALTERNATIVE (2) A

(2) The Parliament of Canada may make laws for the expenditure of money, or for conferring a benefit equivalent to that which would result from the expenditure of money, in relation to any matter not coming within the legislative jurisdiction of Parliament, and not within the concurrent legislative jurisdiction of Parliament and the legislatures where a law of Parliament has paramountcy, subject to such of the following conditions and restrictions as are applicable in any particular case.

ALTERNATIVE (2) B

(2) The Parliament of Canada may make laws for the expenditure of money, or for conferring a benefit equivalent to that which would result from the expenditure of money, subject to such of the following conditions and restrictions as are applicable in any particular case.

(3) A law of Parliament referred to in subsection (2) that provides for payments to all provinces, or for conferring a benefit capable of providing an equivalent to that which would result from payments to them, and that is such that the payments are or the benefit is conditional on expenditures by the provinces or the foregoing of revenue by them, is of no force or effect unless authorized by the governments of a majority of the provinces that have, according to the then latest general census, at least 50% of the population of Canada.

ALTERNATIVE (4) A

(4) A law of Parliament referred to in subsection (3), notwithstanding that it is authorized as provided in that subsection, is of no force or effect unless it provides for payments or benefits to individuals residing in a province that does not accept payments or benefits thereunder that are in amounts determined by or pursuant to a provision of such law.

ALTERNATIVE (4) B

(4) A law of Parliament referred to in subsection (3), notwithstanding that it is authorized as provided in that

subsection, is of no force or effect unless it provides for payments to a province that does not accept payments or benefits in accordance with the general provisions of the law that are equivalent in amount to the payments or benefits that would otherwise have been provided to it under the law.

(5) Subsections (3) and (4) apply whether or not the payments provided or the benefits conferred are provided or conferred on terms or conditions that may vary as between provinces.

(6) A law of Parliament referred to in subsection (2) that provides for payments to individuals or bodies, other than provincial governments, in all provinces and that significantly affects the programs of a province is of no force or effect unless, prior to the enactment thereof, the government of Canada has consulted with the government of each province whose programs would be so affected.

(7) Where the government of Canada is of the opinion that a measure providing for payments as described in subsection (6) that it proposes to introduce for enactment by Parliament will affect the programs of a province, it shall consult with the government of that province before introducing the measure.

(8) A law referred to in subsection (6) shall be deemed not to have the effect therein referred to unless, prior to the enactment of the law, the government of a province has, in writing, advised the government of Canada that, in its opinion, the law will have such an effect.

(9) Where the government of a province has advised the government of Canada as provided in subsection (8) in relation to a particular measure, a copy of the instrument reflecting such advice shall forthwith be laid before Parliament and thereupon no further consideration shall be given to the measure in Parliament for a period of ninety days or such lesser number of days as is agreed to by the government of the province, during which period the government of Canada shall consult with the government of the province in relation to the measure at a meeting convened for that purpose or in such other manner as is agreed upon.

DECLARATORY POWER

1. Amend head 92.10(c) to read as follows:

> "(c) Such works as, although wholly situate within the province, are before or after their execution declared by Parliament to be for the general advantage of Canada, or for the advantage of two or more provinces, for purposes indicated in the declaration."

2. Add new subsections to section 92 which for the purposes of this draft are numbered as follows:

Requirement to consult with respect to use of declaratory power of Parliament

> "**92.** (2) Before Parliament declares any work to be for the general advantage of Canada or for the advantage of two or more provinces
> (a) the government of Canada shall consult with the government of the province or the governments of each of the provinces in which the work is situate; and
> (b) if the consultation under paragraph (a) does not result in an agreement that the work be so declared, the Prime Minister of Canada shall consult the first ministers of the provinces about the proposed declaration at a first ministers' conference.

Declaration on failure on consultation

> (3) Where, after the consultation required by subsection (2), an agreement has not been reached that a work be declared to be for the general advantage of Canada or for the advantage of two or more provinces, a declaration under paragraph 92(1)10(c) shall have effect only for such period not exceeding five years from the effective date of the declaration as is stated in the declaration declaration in respect of the work after the requirements of subsection (2) have again been fulfilled.

Limitation on Declaratory Power
with respect to resources

(4) No declaration under paragraph 92(1)10(c) shall be made by Parliament without the prior consent of the government of the province in which the work to be so declared is situate if it is a work for
    (a) the primary production or initial processing of any non renewable or forestry resource; or
    (b) the generation of electrical energy.

Revocation or Limitation of
declaration

(5) Parliament may revoke any declaration of a work to be a work for the general advantage of Canada or for the advantage of two or more provinces made before or after the coming into force of this section and may limit or, subject to subsections (2) to (4), extend the purposes for which any such declaration had been made.''

(d) Federal Draft Proposals Discussed by First Ministers: Communications, Offshore Resources, and Charter of Rights, February 2, 1979

Document: 800-010/037

[COMMUNICATIONS]

Cable Distribution

1. In each province the legislature may make laws in relation to cable distribution within the province, including the reception and redistribution of broadcast signals; Parliament may also make laws in relation thereto for each of the provinces.

Relationships between laws of the
provinces and laws of Parliament

2. Any law enacted by the legislature of a province pursuant to section 1 shall prevail to the extent of the inconsistency over any law of Parliament enacted thereunder except in relation to Canadian content, Canadian broadcast programs and services, and technical standards, in which case any law of Parliament shall prevail to the extent of the inconsistency.

Consultations

3. The Government of Canada shall consult the government of the province concerned before Parliament makes a law in relation to cable distribution within that province pursuant to section 1.

Telecommunications undertakings

4. Telecommunications undertakings coming under the jurisdiction of Parliament as well as those coming under the jurisdiction of the legislature of a province and engaging in activities coming under section 1 other than as carriers shall be subject, in so far as such activities are concerned, to the laws enacted under section 1.

Powers continued

5. Except where otherwise expressly provided in sections 1 to 4, nothing therein shall derogate from the legislative powers that Parliament and the legislatures of the provinces had immediately before the coming into force of these sections.

[OFFSHORE RESOURCES]

"On the question of Offshore Resources, the revised Constitution should provide concurrent legislative authority for Parliament and the legislatures of coastal provinces concerning the management of the offshore resources, lying adjacent to those provinces, which are within national jurisdiction, but which do not fall within the Provinces or Territories of Canada. This provision would be made without prejudice to the ownership of the resources in question.

Federal powers concerning navigation, international affairs, national defence and so on, would continue to apply as appropriate to the offshore areas. Provision would also be made, however, for the application of various provincial powers, for example, concerning labour relations, to the offshore areas.

In describing the concurrent powers, provision should be made for federal paramountcy concerning international trade, environmental control, and other matters to be determined. Provincial paramountcy should apply to various aspects of associated onshore developments, and to other matters to be determined.

On the important question of the rate of exploration and of production, or more generally the pace of development, there should be federal paramountcy. However, in cases where the provincial government affected disagrees with federal proposals dealing with the rate of production, on the basis of anticipated adverse socioeconomic effects, or adverse effects on the future availability of resources to meet the province's needs, such federal paramountcy would only be exercised in matters of great concern to Canada.

As a necessary complement to such provisions in a revised Constitution, suitable administrative arrangements should be worked out and confirmed in due course by statute, to assure continuing federal and provincial consultation and co-operation in the management and development of the offshore resources."

[CHARTER OF RIGHTS]

COMPARATIVE SUMMARY OF BILL C-60 PROVISIONS AND NEW PROPOSALS

Bill C-60 Provisions	New Draft Proposals
A. *Fundamental Freedoms* 1. Freedom of thought, conscience and religion. 2. Freedom of opinion and expression. 3. Freedom of peaceful assembly and of association. 4. Freedom of press and other media.	A. *Fundamental Freedoms* 1. Freedom of conscience and religion. 2. Freedom of thought, opinion and expression, including freedom of press and other media. 3. Freedom of peaceful assembly and of association.
Limitation Clause	*Limitation Clause*
Those reasonably justifiable in a free and democratic society in interests of — public safety or health — peace and security of public — rights and freedoms of others.	Those prescribed by law as are reasonably justifiable in a free and democratic society in the interests of — national security — public safety, order, health or morals — any rights and freedoms of others.
Override Clause	*Override Clause*
None	None

COMPARATIVE SUMMARY OF BILL C-60 PROVISIONS AND NEW PROPOSALS

B. *Democratic Rights*

1. Principles of universal suffrage and free and democratic elections.
2. Right of citizen to vote and to qualify for election in House of Commons or legislature without discrimination based on race, national or ethnic origin, language, color, religion or sex.
3. Limits on maximum duration of House of Commons and legislatures except in case of national emergency.
4. Requirement for annual sessions of Parliament and legislatures.

Limitation Clause

On first two only: same as under fundamental freedoms.

Override Clause

None

C. *Legal Rights*

1. Right against unreasonable searches and seizures.
2. Right against arbitrary detention, imprisonment or exile.
3. Rights on arrest or detention to be told promptly of reasons therefor, to retain and instruct counsel promptly and to remedy by *habeas corpus*.
4. Right not to testify in any proceedings if denied counsel, protection against self-crimination or other constitutional safeguards.
5. Right to assistance of interpreter in any proceedings.
6. Right to fair hearing when rights of obligations being determined.
7. Right of accused to presumption of innocence.
8. Right of accused to fair and public hearing before impartial tribunal.
9. Right of accused not to be denied bail unfairly.
10. Protection against *ex post facto* offences and punishment.
11. Protection against cruel and unusual punishment or treatment.

B. *Democratic Rights*

1. Consistent with principles of universal suffrage and free and democratic elections, right of citizen to vote and qualify for election in House of Commons or legislature without unreasonable distinction or limitation.
2. Limit on maximum duration of House of Commons and legislatures except in case of national emergency.
3. Requirement for annual sittings of Parliament and legislatures.

Limitation Clause

None, except as built into first two.

Override Clause

None

C. *Legal Rights*

Right to life, liberty and security of person and right not to be deprived thereof except by due process of law, including

1. Right against unreasonable searches and seizures.
2. Right against unreasonable interference with privacy.
3. Right against detention or imprisonment except in accordance with prescribed laws and procedures.
4. Rights on arrest or detention to be told promptly of reasons therefor, to retain and consult counsel promptly and to remedy by *habeas corpus*.
5. Rights as a person charged with a criminal or penal offence
   — to be informed of specific charge,
   — to be tried in reasonable time,
   — to presumption of innocence,
   — to a fair and public hearing before impartial tribunal,
   — not to be denied bail unfairly,
   — to protection against *ex post facto* offences and punishment.
6. Protection against double jeopardy.
7. Benefit of a lesser penalty where law is changed.

COMPARATIVE SUMMARY OF BILL C-60 PROVISIONS AND NEW PROPOSALS

8. Protection against cruel or inhuman treatment or punishment.
9. Right when compelled to give evidence to counsel, to protection against self-crimination and to other constitutional safeguards.
10. Right to assistance of interpreter in any proceedings.
11. Right to fair hearing when rights and obligations being determined.

Limitation Clause

Same as under fundamental freedoms

Limitation Clause

Legal rights, except for right to life, right to counsel, protection against *ex post facto* laws, protection against self-crimination, protection against cruel or inhuman punishment or treatment and right to interpreter, may be overriden in times of serious public emergency. Limits on public proceedings may be placed in normal circumstances.

Override Clause

None

Override Clause

Provinces could opt in with general override power.

D. *Non-Discrimination Rights*

1. Right to equality before the law and to equal protection of the law.
2. Enjoyment of fundamental freedoms, legal rights and mobility rights without discrimination based on race, national or ethnic origin, language, color, religion, age or sex.

D. *Non-Discrimination Rights*

1. Right to equality before the law and to equal protection of the law without distinction or limitation other than one which is provided by law and fair and reasonable having regard to object of law.
2. Exemption of laws which are in furtherance of affirmative action programs even though they may discriminate, as long as discrimination is justifiable.

Limitation Clause

Same as under fundamental freedoms

Limitation Clause

None, except as built in to section.

Override Clause

None

Override Clause

Provinces could opt in with general override power.

E. *Mobility Rights*

1. Right of person not to be arbitrarily exiled from Canada.
2. Right of citizens to take up residence, acquire and hold property and pursue a livelihood, subject to laws of general application, but without discrimination based on province of residence or previous residence.

E. *Mobility Rights*

1. Right of citizen to enter, remain in and leave Canada.
2. Right of citizen or "landed immigrant" to change province of residence or to pursue livelihood in another province, subject to laws of general application, but without discrimination based only on province of present or previous residence.

COMPARATIVE SUMMARY OF BILL C-60 PROVISIONS AND NEW PROPOSALS

Limitation Clause

Same as under fundamental freedoms.

Limitation Clause

Those prescribed by law as are reasonably justifiable in a free and democratic society in the interests of
— national security
— public safety, order, health or morals
— overriding economic or social considerations.

Override Clause

None

Override Clause

None

F. *Property Rights*

1. Right to use and enjoyment of property by individual, and right not to be deprived thereof except in accordance with law.
2. Right to acquire and hold property without discrimination based upon province of residence.

F. *Property Rights*

1. Right to use and enjoyment of property by individuals or groups, and right not to be deprived thereof except in accordance with law that is fair and just.

Limitation Clause

Same as under fundamental freedoms.

Limitation Clause

1. Laws which control or restrict use of property in public interest or for collection of taxes and penalties.
2. Laws which are justifiable in a free and democratic society in the interests of
— national security
— public safety, order, health or morals.

Override Clause

None

Override Clause

None

G. *Language Rights*

1. Power of Parliament and legislatures to declare English and French official languages of Canada for all purposes declared.
2. Power of Parliament and legislatures to provide for more extensive rights to use English and French.
3. Right to use English or French in all debates and other proceedings of Parliament or any legislature.
4. Statutes, records and journals of Parliament and legislatures of Ontario, Quebec and New Brunswick to be printed and published in English and French, both versions equally authoritative. In other provinces, obligation optional with legislatures. In Ontario, date for French publication to be fixed by legislature.

G. *Language Rights*

1. English and French declared official languages of Canada with status and protection set forth in Charter.
2. Power of Parliament and legislatures to extend the status, protection or use of English and French.
3. Right to use English or French in debates and other proceedings of Parliament; same right in debates of legislatures.
4. Statutes, records and journals of Parliament and legislatures of Ontario, Quebec and New Brunswick to be printed and published in English and French, both versions equally authoritative. In other provinces, obligation optional with legislatures with test of "to extent practicable." In Ontario, date for French publication to be fixed by legislature.

COMPARATIVE SUMMARY OF BILL C-60 PROVISIONS AND NEW PROPOSALS

5. Right to use French or English in all court proceedings at federal level and in Ontario, Quebec and New Brunswick.

6. Right of witness to be heard in French or English (without prejudice) in any court in Canada in any criminal proceeding or in any serious provincial penal proceeding.

7. Right of a member of public to communicate in English or French with head or central office of any federal government institution, and with any principal offices thereof in areas designated by Parliament on basis of minority language numbers.

8. Right of member of public to communicate in English or French with principal offices of any provincial government institution in areas designated by provincial legislature on basis of minority language numbers.

9. Preservation of legal or customary rights or privileges re use of languages other than English or French.

10. Rights of minority language (English or French) parents who are Canadian citizens to choose minority language education for their children in areas of province where it is reasonably determined by provincial legislature that numbers of children in any area warrant the provision of necessary facilities out of public funds.

11. Preservation of rights in the future of identifiable English or French language communities to use of French or English.

12. Preservation of existing constitutional rights, privileges or obligations respecting the French and English languages.

13. Repeal of section 133 of *BNA Act* and section 23 of *Manitoba Act* upon entrenchment of Charter.

Limitation Clause

Same as under fundamental freedoms

Override Clause

None

---

5. Right to use French or English in all court proceedings at federal level and in Ontario, Quebec and New Brunswick. But with respect to three provinces, right to be provided as soon as practicable and in any event not later than five years after adoption of Charter. For other provinces, a similar right to greatest extent possible as the legislatures may prescribe.

6. Right of witness to be heard in French or English, through an interpreter where necessary (without prejudice), in any court in Canada in a case involving an offence under federal law or a serious offence under provincial penal law.

7. Right of a member of public to communicate in English or French with head or central office of any federal government institution, and with any principal offices thereof in areas designated by Parliament on basis of minority language numbers.

8. Right of member of public to communicate in English or French with the head, central or principal offices of any provincial government institution, to the extent and in the areas as defined by the provincial legislature on the basis of practicability and necessity for such services.

9. Preservation of legal or customary rights or privileges re use of languages other than English or French.

10. Right of minority language (English or French) parents who are Canadian citizens to choose minority language education for their children in areas of province where it is reasonably determined by provincial legislature that numbers of children in any area warrant the provision of necessary facilities out of public funds.

11. Preservation of rights in the future of identifiable English or French language communities to use of French or English.

12. Preservation of existing constitutional rights, privileges or obligations respecting the French and English languages.

13. Repeal of section 133 of *BNA Act* and section 23 of *Manitoba Act* upon entrenchment of Charter.

Limitation Clause

None

Override Clause

None

COMPARATIVE SUMMARY OF BILL C-60 PROVISIONS AND NEW PROPOSALS

H. *Undeclared Rights*

1. Protection of any undeclared rights existing at time of adoption of Charter, including those of native peoples under Royal Proclamation of 1763.

I. *Enforcement Provisions*

1. Charter provisions to render inoperative any law which is in conflict with its provisions.
2. Where no other remedy exists, courts empowered to grant declaratory, injunctive or similar relief where anyone seeks to have Charter rights defined or enforced.

H. *Undeclared Rights*

1. Protection of any undeclared rights existing at any time, including those that may pertain to native peoples.

I. *Enforcement Provisions*

1. Charter provisions to render inoperative any law or administrative act which is in conflict with its provisions.
2. Where no other effective recourse or remedy exists, courts empowered to grant such relief or remedy for a violation of Charter rights as may be deemed appropriate and just in the circumstances.

34. Continuing Committee of Ministers on the Constitution, Halifax, Nova Scotia, October 22–23, 1979

(a) Rights and Freedoms within the Canadian Federation, Federal Draft, October 17, 1979

Title

Canadian Charter of Rights and Freedoms

1. This section and sections 2 to 23 may be cited as the *Canadian Charter of Rights and Freedoms.*

Fundamental Freedoms

Fundamental freedoms

2. (1) Everyone has the following fundamental freedoms:
(a) freedom of conscience and religion;
(b) freedom of thought, opinion and expression, including freedom in the dissemination of news, opinion and belief; and
(c) freedom of peaceful assembly and of association.

(2) The manifestation or exercise of the freedoms declared by this section may be made subject only to such limitations prescribed by law as are reasonably justifiable in a free and democratic society in the interests of national security, public safety, order, health or morals or the rights and freedoms of others.

Democratic Rights

Democratic rights of citizens

3. Consistent with the principles of free and democratic elections to the House of Commons and to the legislative assemblies, and of universal suffrage for that purpose, every citizen of Canada shall, without unreasonable distinction or limitation, have the right to vote in an election of members of the House of Commons or of a legislative assembly and to be qualified for membership therein.

Duration of elected legislative bodies

4. (1) No House of Commons and no legislative assembly of a province shall continue for longer than five years from the date of the return of the writs for the choosing of its members.

Continuation in special circumstances

(2) Notwithstanding subsection (1), in time of real or apprehended war, invasion or insurrection, a House of Commons may be continued by Parliament and a legislative assembly of a province may be continued by the legislature thereof beyond the time limited therefor by subsection (1), if such continuation is not opposed by the votes of more than one-third of the members of the House of Commons or the legislative assembly, as the case may be.

Annual sitting of elected legislative bodies

5. There shall be a sitting of Parliament and of each legislature at least once in every year and not more than twelve months shall intervene between sittings.

Legal Rights

Legal rights

6. (1) Everyone has the right to life, liberty and security of his or her person and the right not to be deprived thereof except by due process of law, which process encompasses the following:

(a) the right to be secure against unreasonable searches and seizures;

(b) the right to protection against arbitrary or unlawful interference with privacy;

(c) the right not to be detained or imprisoned except on grounds provided by law and in accordance with prescribed procedures;

(d) the right on arrest or detention

  (i) to be informed promptly of the reason for the arrest or detention,

  (ii) to be provided with the opportunity to retain and consult counsel without delay, and

  (iii) to the remedy by way of *habeas corpus* for the determination of the validity of his or her detention and for release if the detention is not lawful;

(e) the right of a person charged with an offence

  (i) to be informed of the specific charge,

  (ii) to be tried within a reasonable time,

  (iii) to be presumed innocent until proven guilty in a fair and public hearing by an independent and impartial tribunal,

  (iv) not to be denied reasonable bail without just cause having been established, and

  (v) not to be found guilty on account of any act or omission that at the time of the act or omission did not constitute an offence;

(f) the right not to be tried or punished more than once for an offence of which he or she has been finally convicted or acquitted;

(g) the right to the benefit of the lesser punishment where the punishment for an offence of which he or she has been convicted has been varied between the time of commission and the time of sentencing;

(h) the right not to be subjected to any cruel or inhuman treatment or punishment;

(i) the right, when compelled to give evidence before any court, tribunal, commission, board or other authority, to counsel, to protection against self-crimination and to any other constitutional safeguard;

(j) the right to the assistance of an interpreter in any proceedings before a court, tribunal, commission, board or other authority, if the party or witness does not understand or speak the language in which the proceedings are conducted; and

(k) the right to a fair hearing in accordance with the principles of fundamental justice for the determination of his or her rights or obligations.

Justifiable derogation

(2) In time of serious public emergency, the existence of which is officially proclaimed by or pursuant to a law enacted to deal with such circumstances or by a law specifically referring to this subsection, the rights mentioned in this section other than the right to life and those mentioned in subparagraphs (1) (d) (ii) and (1) (c) (v) and paragraphs (1) (h), (i) and (j) may be derogated from to the extent strictly required by the circumstances of the emergency.

Idem

(3) Nothing in this section precludes the enactment of or renders invalid a law that authorizes the holding of all or part of a proceeding in camera in the interests of national security, public safety or order or morality, in the interest of the privacy of one or more of the parties or where, in the opinion of the tribunal, publicity would prejudice the interests of justice.

Official Languages

Official languages of Canada

7. (1) English and French are the official languages of Canada, having the status and protection set forth in this Charter.

Authority not limited

(2) Nothing in this Charter limits the authority of Parliament or of the legislature of a province to extend the status, protection or use of the English and French languages.

Language Rights (Federal Level)

Proceedings of Parliament

8. Everyone has the right to use English or French, as he or she may choose, in any of the debates or other proceedings of Parliament.

Statutes and records, etc. of Parliament

9. The statutes and the records and journals of Parliament shall be printed and published in English and French and both language versions are equally authoritative.

Proceedings in courts constituted by Parliament

10. Either English or French may be used by any person in, or in any pleading or process in or issuing from, any court constituted by Parliament.

Communication by public with government of Canada

11. Any member of the public in Canada has the right to communicate with and to receive services from any head or central office of an institution of government of Canada in English or French, as he or she may choose, and he or she has the same right with respect to any other principal office of any such institution when that office is located within an area of Canada in which it is determined, in such manner as may be prescribed or authorized by Parliament, that a substantial number of persons within the population use that language.

Language Rights (Provincial Level)

Proceedings of legislative assemblies

12. Everyone has the right to use English or French, as he or she may choose, in the debates of the legislative assemblies of (named provinces).

Statutes and records, etc. of legislatures

13. (1) The statutes [and the records and journals] of the legislatures of (named provinces) shall be printed and published in English and French and both language versions are equally authoritative.

(2) The statutes [and the records and journals] of the legislatures of each province not referred to in subsection (1) shall be printed and published in English and French to the greatest extent practicable accordingly as the legislature of the province prescribes.

Proceedings in courts of provinces

14. (1) Either English or French may be used by any person in, or in any pleading or process in or issuing from, any court of (named provinces).

Idem

(2) Either English or French may be used by any person in, or in any pleading or process in or issuing from, any court of a province not referred to in subsection (1), to the greatest extent practicable accordingly as the legislature of the province prescribes.

Proceedings in relation to certain offences

(3) In proceedings in any court in Canada relating to an offence
(a) created by or pursuant to an Act of Parliament, or
(b) created by or pursuant to an Act of the legislature of a province if the punishment for the offence may be imprisonment,

any person giving evidence before the court has the right to be heard in English or French, as he or she may choose, through the services of an interpreter where necessary, and the right not to be placed at a disadvantage in so being heard.

Rules for orderly implementation and operation

(4) The legislature of a province may prescribe the date or dates on which the rights provided for by this section are to have effect in all or some parts of the province, and nothing in this section precludes the application of such rules as may be prescribed by any competent body or authority for the orderly implementation and operation of this section.

Communications by public with government of a province

15. Any member of the public in a province has the right to communicate with and to receive services from any head, central or principal office of an institution of government of the province in English or French, as he or she may choose, to the extent to which and in the areas of the province in which it is determined, in such a manner as may be prescribed or authorized by the legislature of the province, that the right should pertain having regard to the practicability and necessity of providing such services.

Language of educational instruction

16. (1) Citizens of Canada in a province who are members of an English-speaking or French-speaking minority population of that province have a right to have their children receive their educational instruction in their minority language at the primary and secondary level wherever the number of children of such citizens resident in an area of the province is sufficient to warrant the provision out of public funds of minority language education facilities in that area.

Provisions for determining where numbers warrant

(2) In each province, the legislature may enact provisions for determining where the number of children of citizens of Canada who are members of an English-speaking or French-speaking minority population in an area is sufficient to warrant the provision out of public funds of minority language education facilities in that area.

Undeclared Rights

Undeclared rights and freedoms

17. Nothing in this Charter abrogates or derogates from any right or freedom not declared by it that may exist in Canada, including any right or freedom that may pertain to the native peoples of Canada.

General

Laws, etc., not to apply so as to abrogate declared rights and freedoms

18. To the end that the paramountcy of this Charter be recognized and that full effect be given to the rights and freedoms herein declared, any law and any administrative act that is inconsistent with any provision of the Charter is, except as specifically otherwise provided in or as authorized by this Charter, inoperative and of no force or effect to the extent of the inconsistency.

Enforcement of declared rights and freedoms

19. Where no other effective recourse or remedy is available or provided for by law, anyone whose rights or freedoms as declared by this Charter have been infringed or denied to his or her detriment has the right to apply to a court of competent jurisdiction to obtain such relief or remedy as the court deems appropriate and just in the circumstances.

Legislative authority not extended

20. Nothing in this Charter confers any legislative authority on any competent body or authority in that behalf in Canada, except as expressly contemplated by this Charter.

| Rights and privileges preserved | **21.** Nothing in sections 8 to 15 abrogates or derogates from any legal or customary right or privilege acquired or enjoyed either before or after the commencement of this Charter with respect to any language that is not English or French. |

| Ibid | **22.** Nothing in sections 8 to 10 and 12 to 14 abrogates or derogates from any right, privilege or obligation with respect to the English and French languages, or either of them, that exists or is continued by virtue of any other provision of the Constitution of Canada.[1] |

| Application of sections 12, 13, and 14 | **23.** A legislature of a province may, by resolution declare that any part of sections 12, 13 and 14 that do not expressly apply to that province shall have application, and therefore such parts shall apply to that province in the same terms as to any province expressly named therein. |

(b) Record of Decisions, October 22–23, 1979

Document: 830-74/017

GENERAL

The meeting was Co-Chaired by the Hon. William H. Jarvis, Minister of State for Federal-Provincial Relations of Canada, and by the Hon. Roy Romanow, Minister of Intergovernmental Affairs of Saskatchewan.

The Conference agreed that initial discussion on the Constitution would refer to the 14 items tabled at the First Ministers' Conference in February 1979, to determine if there were changes in any government's position and whether it would be desirable and feasible to develop a shorter list of important and manageable items for immediate attention and for possible referral to First Ministers at the Conference on December 4th and 5th, 1979.

Ministers agreed that the Co-Chairmen would meet with the press to discuss the meeting in a general way.

AGENDA ITEM 1: DISCUSSIONS OF WHERE MATTERS STAND ON THE CONSTITUTIONAL FRONT

RESOURCE OWNERSHIP AND INTER-PROVINCIAL TRADE — OFFSHORE RESOURCES

The Conference agreed that there was some consensus on the 'best effort' draft proposal from February 1979, al-though various aspects needed further review, including Alberta's concerns about the use of the term "compelling national interest". Ministers also agreed that offshore resources would be reviewed as a sub-item under Resource Ownership and Interprovincial Trade during future discussions which would, among other things, give consideration to the principles referred to in the "Exchange of letters made public — Offshore Mineral Resources" (see Document 830–74/002 [see Annex attached p. 583]). It was emphasized, however, that discussions on 'offshore resources' and 'on-shore resources' should proceed separately, in order that lack of progress in one area would not impede progress in the other.

INDIRECT TAXATION

The Conference confirmed that, as First Ministers had noted in February 1979, there was little interest in pursuing this item further, except in relation to natural resources. No further discussion by Ministers or Officials was required, save in connection with Resource Ownership and Interprovincial Trade.

COMMUNICATIONS

The federal government confirmed that the February draft on cable distribution was still "on the table". The Conference agreed that while this draft on cable distribution

NOTE: [1]This provision has application until such time as specific provisions in the present Constitution may be repealed.

might require certain clarification or refinements (e.g. with respect to the areas of federal paramountcy) the principle reflected in the draft was in the right direction and that the subject should remain on the short list. Reference was also made to the Meeting of Comunications Minsters in Toronto where most provincial ministers agreed that authority over the Licensing and Regulation of cable distribution systems should be provincial and the federal minister agreed that responsibilities in this area should be formally delegated to those provinces who so wish.

THE SENATE

British Columbia and Ontario expressed interest pursuing constitutional discussions on this item; the federal government indicated it would be prepared in time to formalize the position expressed in the Kingston Communiqué.

SUPREME COURT

Discussion was not pursued on this item.

FAMILY LAW

The Conference agreed that there was apparent consensus on the principles of the February "best effort" draft; further discussions by officials would provide an opportunity to resolve reservations expressed by Manitoba, Prince Edward Island and Newfoundland, and to refine the draft.

FISHERIES

The Conference agreed that as federal-provincial consultation directed towards improved administrative cooperation was being pursued among Fisheries Ministers, further discussions in constitutional terms on this item should not take place until a later date. However, any bilateral agreements reached in the meantime that could affect the Constitution should be brought to the CCMC for consideration.

EQUALIZATION AND REGIONAL DEVELOPMENT

The Conference agreed that there should be early continuing discussions on this item; recognition was given to British Columbia's reservations.

CHARTER OF RIGHTS

The Conference agreed that the suggestions made by the federal delegation could form the basis for further discussion. Those suggestions, as contained in the "Bill of Rights — Notes for a Statement by the Honourable William Jarvis" (See Document 830–74/010), were that consideration should be given to the entrenchment of (1) fundamental rights; (2) democratic rights; (3) legal rights; (4) general language rights (with particular regard to language rights protection in areas of federal institution and jurisdiction); and (5) minority language education rights.

Manitoba and British Columbia asked for continued recognition of their previously stated reservations.

SPENDING POWER

The federal government referred to its position in the Kingston Communiqué and suggested the item be the subject of later discussion.

DECLARATORY POWER

Reference was made to the general acceptability of limiting the declaratory power as stated in the "best effort" draft. Some provinces were for the outright abolition of the declaratory power, and others favoured its retention. The federal delegation confirmed that the offer to review past declaration still stood.

THE AMENDING FORMULA, "PATRIATION" OF THE CONSTITUTION AND DELEGATION OF LEGISLATIVE AUTHORITY

British Columbia expressed the view that early patriation of the Constitution, with or without formal agreement on an amending procedure, was of symbolic importance, noting that, in the absence of formal agreement, the current practices and traditions respecting amending procedures would remain in place. Ontario supported this view. The federal delegation agreed that patriation was an important matter, but not necessarily for immediate action. Saskatchewan expressed reservations that without an amending formula, simple patriation might not be the best in the long term interest. Quebec confirmed its traditional position on this item.

MONARCHY

The Conference agreed that no further discussion was required on this item.

ADDITIONAL ISSUES

The federal government suggested that "powers affecting the economy" in areas of major concern be added to the list of items to be reviewed by the CCMC. In this regard, the federal government referred to points raised in the Kingston Communiqué and presented a statement on "Powers Affecting the Economy" — Notes for a Statement by the Honourable William Jarvis, October 21, 1979 (see Document 830–74/008). The Conference agreed that officials would initiate a review that would include:

(i) a clarification of Section 121 of the B.N.A. Act respecting the free movement of goods, services, capital and persons in order to make our common market more effective;

(ii) a clarification of powers pertaining to federal government ability to act in times of economic emergency;

and that officials would consider, in a preliminary way, what other aspects of the question might also be reviewed.

AGENDA ITEM 2: CONSIDERATION OF SPECIFIC CONSTITUTIONAL ITEMS

The Conference agreed that the short list of constitutional items for immediate attention and for possible referral to First Ministers on December 4th and 5th should include the following (the lead government is shown in brackets):
— Resource Ownership and Interprovincial Trade (Alberta)
— Offshore Resources (Newfoundland)
— Communications (Saskatchewan)
— Senate (British Columbia)
— Family Law (Ontario)
— Equalization and Regional Development (Nova Scotia)
— Charter of Rights (Canada)

The Conference established sub-committees of officials, chaired by the "lead" governments, indicated above, to initiate a review of these short list items in preparation for a further meeting of officials on November 15th and 16th in Toronto, following consultation with their respective ministers. The Conference agreed that the Steering Committee of CCMC would meet after the November 15–16 meeting to review reports by officials, and to determine if

a further ministerial meeting was required before the First Ministers' Conference of December 4th and 5th.

The Conference also agreed that the other five items from the February Conference still requiring discussion, i.e.
— The Supreme Court
— Fisheries
— Spending Power
— Declaratory Power
— Patriation and the Amending Formula
should remain on a list of items of "second priority" for attention after discussion in the CCMC in due course.

The Conference further agreed that governments should begin now to consider the question of "Powers affecting the Economy" and that time should be devoted to the November 15–16 meeting of officials to a preliminary discussion of how governments can best prepare for fuller discussions of this item in due course.

REPORTS OF SUB-COMMITTEE CHAIRMAN

RESOURCE OWNERSHIP AND INTERPROVINCIAL TRADE (ALBERTA): — OFFSHORE RESOURCES (NEWFOUNDLAND)

The Committee of Officials was chaired by Alberta and vice-chaired by Newfoundland, with all jurisdictions represented except Prince Edward Island. The Committee reviewed the 'best effort' draft presented to First Ministers in February 1979 and the reservations on this draft as contained in the "Report of the Continuing Committee of Ministers on the Constitution to First Ministers — Resource Ownership and Interprovincial Trade" (See Document 800–010/001). The reservations to the draft remain. Saskatchewan proposed that an alternative to Section 4 (b) of the 'best effort' draft be considered (see Appendix B [p. 585]) and other governments agreed to such consideration being given.

The Committee recommended that difficulties with the "compelling national interest" clause should be reviewed prior to the meeting of officials November 15th and 16th, in Toronto. It was also emphasized that the 'best effort' draft on the declaratory power be read in relation to natural resources, so as not to lose sight of the interrelationship between the two sections.

The Committee determined that the effect on Inuit and Indian land claims in relation to the transfer of jurisdiction for offshore resources required considerable discussion by all governments. Although parallels exist between offshore and onshore resource ownership, with regard to the former, there are the additional questions of international law and the ownership of the seabed. Existing jurisdiction on the onshore should not be diminished by the terms of any agreements reached on the offshore. The Committee recommended that although bilateral discussions should not be precluded, all interested governments should continue to be advised of developments.

COMMUNICATIONS (SASKATCHEWAN)

The Committee of Officials was chaired by Saskatchewan and attended by all governments except New Brunswick and Prince Edward Island. The Committee took note of the federal Minister's statement to the effect that consideration could be given to the four principal aspects of the communications field. Discussion focussed on the February draft on cable distribution. In this regard, the provincial representatives agreed to forward their questions or concerns or proposals for specific wording to the federal representatives in order that more discussion and any necessary changes could be suggested on November 15–16 in Toronto.

SENATE (BRITISH COLUMBIA)

The Committee of Officials was chaired by British Columbia with all governments represented. The Committee agreed to review reform of the Senate in four main areas:
— the role of the Senate;
— the appointment process for Senators;
— the basis of representation in the Senate; and
— the precise powers such an institution would have.
British Columbia would prepare, for distribution, a compilation of proposals on the Senate to assist officials in reviewing their positions prior to November 15th and 16th. All governments agreed to come to the Toronto meeting, prepared to discuss the Senate under these four headings.

FAMILY LAW (ONTARIO)

This Committee of Officials was chaired by Ontario and attended by officials of all jurisdictions except Nova Scotia. Principles of the 'best effort' draft of February 1979 were reviewed in light of the concerns expressed by Newfoundland, Prince Edward Island and Manitoba. While Newfoundland and Prince Edward Island strongly preferred no transfer of divorce jurisdiction, neither would stand in the way of the proposed amendment if there were a con-

census to proceed. Manitoba indicated that it could not accept the proposed transfer of jurisdiction for divorce. In light of this, officials did not proceed to review technical changes in the 'best effort' draft, reporting that the issue for resolution was purely one of policy. The Conference agreed that officials should review the 'best effort' draft, along with the new federal draft (see Appendix A [p. 584]) at the November meeting in Toronto with a view to settling the technical drafting modifications. This might then be considered by the CCMC in December for possible reference.

EQUALIZATION AND REGIONAL DEVELOPMENT (NOVA SCOTIA)

The Conference agreed that the 'best effort' draft should be considered by the Steering Committee and possibly by the CCMC prior to the First Ministers on December 4th and 5th.

CHARTER OF RIGHTS (CANADA)

The Committee of Officials was chaired by the federal government with all jurisdictions, except Prince Edward Island represented. A revised draft, dealing with fundamental freedoms, democratic rights, legal rights, general language rights and minority language education rights, was circulated for discussion purposes by the federal officials and this formed the basis of discussions. The Committee was in general agreement with the provisions respecting fundamental freedoms and democratic rights. A number of provincial representatives indicated a willingness to see some legal rights included if they were confined to criminal and penal matters. Little time was devoted to a review of linguistic rights. The Conference agreed that a further review of these rights would be undertaken by officials on November 15 and 16 and provincial governments were invited to submit their proposals on a charter especially with reference to legal rights and linguistic rights in the provinces.

AGENDA ITEM 3: PLANNING THE HANDLING OF MEETINGS WITH REPRESENTATIVES OF THE NATIVE PEOPLES

Reference was made to ''Process for handling 'Canada's Native Peoples and the Constitution', Notes for a Statement by the Honourable William Jarvis, October 23,

1979'' (See Document 830–74/013). The federal government emphasized that participation in consultations with Native leaders did not constitute a recognition of Native Groups as governments. However, there was a necessity to identify an appropriate process which would allow an effective review of the various issues. The Conference agreed that the Steering Committee of the CCMC would meet with representatives from the Indian, Métis and Inuit national federations in November (following the meeting of officials on November 15th and 16th) to discuss the process for carrying on joint work in regard to the item ''Canada's Native Peoples and the Constitution'' and to have a preliminary discusssion about the subjects that should be considered in that context, so as to report back to ministers before the First Ministers' Conference on December 4th and 5th.

AGENDA ITEM 4: GENERAL DISCUSSION ON THE FUTURE PROGRAM FOR CONSTITUTIONAL STUDY

The federal government indicated that depending upon the progress made by officials, by the Steering Committee of CCMC, by Ministers and by First Ministers it was probable that one or two meetings of the CCMC could be held in the winter or early spring to discuss the following issues particularly:

— Supreme Court;
— Fisheries;
— Spending Power;
— Declaratory Power;
— The Amending Formula, ''Patriation'' of the Constitution and Delegation of Legislative Authority; and
— Powers affecting the Economy.

The Co-Chairman noted that there was close-to-consensus on Family Law (with reservations by Manitoba, and some concerns expressed by Newfoundland and Prince Edward Island) and on Equalization (with reservations by British Columbia); it was also possible that consensus could be realized on Communications and Offshore Resources.

Ontario emphasized the need to develop a complete list of constitutional concerns, including items not previously discussed in detail, such as:

— the creation of new provinces;
— international relations;
— Section 96 of the B.N.A. Act and court issues;
— other aspects of Communications; and,
— institutionalization of First Ministers Conferences; and,

— Constitutional Reform and the Traditional Claims of Quebec — Main Points (see Document 800–10/034).

Saskatchewan and Quebec emphasized their concerns with proceeding by way of bilateral negotiation. Québec referred to the danger of a federal minister presenting to his provincial counterparts an imprecise interpretation of a provincial position. If bilateral negotiations do take place, all provinces should be kept aware of developments.

In this regard Saskatchewan stated that bilateral agreements might encompass principles affecting other provinces. Given that these provinces would be unable to appeal previously signed agreements, such a process would be unacceptable in terms of their constitutional implications.

The federal government responded to these concerns by stating that bilateral consultations, such as those avoiding duplication, would not be seen as a substitute for multilateral consultations. Bilateral consultations could, however, be productive in resolving an issue of concern to a particular province or region.

AGENDA ITEM 5: PREPARATORY DISCUSSIONS FOR DECEMBER FIRST MINSTERS' CONFERENCE

The Conference agree to consider:
— proposed agenda;
— format;
— preparatory work; and,
— other matters.

Any proposals agreed to by Ministers in this regard would be subject to approval by First Ministers.

PROPOSED AGENDA

The federal government referred to the Prime Minister's telex of October 16, 1979, forwarded to all provincial Premiers, suggesting that the agenda for the First Ministers' Conference be as follows:

Item 1: The Economy in General

(a) Short and Medium Term Outlook and Objectives
(b) Federal and Provincial Measures to Improve Economic Performance; and,
(c) Employment Problems of Women;

Item 2: Energy

(a) International and Domestic Outlook;
(b) The New Energy Strategy, (Particularly, Co-Operative Efforts in Conservation, Substitution for Oil, and Development of New Supplies);

Item 3: Increasing the Effectiveness of Governments

(a) Reduction of Duplication of Services; and

(b) Regulatory Reform

Issues of particular interest to Premiers could be raised during discussion on the general items. The agenda had been proposed, based on the hypothesis that the energy pricing issue would be resolved prior to the First Ministers' Conference on December 4th and 5th, 1979.

ECONOMY IN GENERAL

Concern was expressed that the proposed agenda suggested particular discussions on employment problems for women, when other specific problems (such as native and youth employment, grain handling and transportation, monetary policy or inflation) were considered by some provinces to have an even greater priority.

The Conference agreed that all delegations should report on the proposed agenda to their respective First Ministers. If necessary, meetings of officials and of Ministers could be called to confirm the agenda. First Ministers would have to ratify any agenda proposed through this process.

The federal government indicated that the First Ministers' Conference on December 4th and 5th should include discussions on the development of a National Energy Strategy. Alberta indicated they would participate in a major way, on the question of self-sufficiency and the question of substitution for oil. The federal cabinet would be meeting shortly to consider the possibility, proposed by Ontario, of a separate, prior First Ministers' Conference to discuss the energy pricing issue.

INCREASING THE EFFECTIVENESS OF GOVERNMENT

The federal government referred to correspondence from the Prime Minister (dated July 26th, 1979) and the Minister of State for Federal-Provincial Relations, (dated August 7th, 1979) requesting provincial response as to specific priority areas requiring a reduction of duplication and overlap. Quebec expressed concern that the major cause of duplication was due to a lack of clarity in the division of powers in the constitution, therefore requiring a resolution to those constitutional problems. The federal government responded that administrative duplication problems should not be ignored because constitutional problems are yet to be resolved. Quebec also emphasized that any transfer of responsibility from the federal government to the provinces because of duplication, should additionally involve a transfer

of funds. The federal government indicated a willingness to discuss this possibility on a case-by-case basis.

The federal government indicated that a report would be ready for the First Ministers' Conference and expressed the hope that provinces would respond to their request for specific nominations of problem areas as soon as possible. Some provinces suggested that that review in the areas of the environment and the administration of justice were important in the continuing review. The Conference agreed that the Committee on Duplication and Overlap should be mandated to continue its work, and that its reporting relationship to the CCMC should be reconfirmed.

The federal government also indicated that the Interim Report on Regulation from the Economic Council and a federal-provincial committee report would be available for the First Ministers' Conference in December. The possibility of establishing a few pilot task forces to pursue comments in the reports, and to recommend and develop criteria for regulation should be considered.

FORMAT

Ministers agreed that the conference should be "open", but that First Ministers could have the opportunity to meet in private sessions. Opening Statements by First Ministers could be limited to five minutes, with complete texts of the statements tabled for reference by the Conference.

PREPARATORY WORK

The federal government indicated they would attempt to make documentation available to the provinces, and expressed a hope that provinces would discuss with the federal government documentation they would be presenting at the Conference.

Annex to the letter of September 14, 1979, from the Prime Minister of Canada to the Premier of Newfoundland (Document: 830-74/002)

BASIC PRINCIPLES CONCERNING OFFSHORE MINERAL RESOURCES

(1) The Province of Newfoundland should own the mineral resources of the continental margin off its coast insofar as Canada is entitled to exercise sovereign rights over these resources in accordance with international

law. Such ownership should be, to the extent possible, of the same nature as if these resources were located within the boundaries of the Province. The legislative jurisdiction of the Province should, to the extent possible, be the same as for those resources within the boundaries of the Province.

(2) Such ownership of and legislative jurisdiction over off-shore resources by Newfoundland will be consistent with and subject to the division of legislative competence as between Parliament and provincial legislatures under the Constitution of Canada.

(3) Thus the legislative jurisdiction and responsibilities of the Government of Canada in areas such as the protection of the environment, national defence, customs and excise, shipping and navigation, external affairs, the management of international and interprovincial trade and pipelines, will continue.

(4) The above principles will be further confirmed and implemented by the signing of an agreement between the Government of Canada and the Government of Newfoundland and by appropriate legislative action and constitutional change.

APPENDIX A

Draft For Discussion Purposes Only

Family Law

1. Repeal head 26 of section 91 — "Marriage and divorce"
2. Repeal head 12 of section 92 — "The solemnization of marriage in the Province" and substitute therefore "Marriage [,including the validity of marriage,][1] in the Province".
3. Add as one of the legislative authority provisions, the following section:

Divorce

"**00.** (1) The legislature of each province may make laws in relation to divorce in the province and has exclusive authority to make laws in relation to alimony, maintenance, custody and any other relief corollary to divorce.

Idem

(2) Parliament may make laws in relation to divorce and has exclusive authority to make laws in relation to the recognition of divorce decrees granted within or outside Canada and in relation to the jurisdictional basis upon which a court may entertain an application for divorce.

Relationship between laws of provinces and laws of Parliament

(3) Where the legislature of a province enacts a law in relation to any matter over which it has concurrent authority with Parliament under this section, that law prevails in the province over any law of Parliament in relation to that matter to the extent of any inconsistency.

Idem

(4) The legislature of a province may declare that it is assuming authority in relation to all matters over which it has concurrent authority with Parliament under this section and, where the legislature so declares, all laws of Parliament in relation to those matters have no effect in that province while the declaration is in effect.

Power of legislature to confer jurisdiction of superior court judges

00.1 Notwithstanding section 96, the legislature of a province may confer, or authorize the Lieutenant Governor of the province to confer, concurrently or exclusively, upon any court or division of a court or all or any judges of any court, the judges of which are appointed [by the Governor

---

NOTE: [1] It is submitted that the words in the square brackets may narrow rather than extend the head "marriage".

General][1] by the Lieutenant Governor of the Province, [as the Legislature may determine,][1] the jurisdiction of a judge of a superior court of the province in respect of all matters [within the field of family law]."[2]

4. Add as one of the transitional provisions, the following section:

Continuation of existing laws

"**XX.** Except as otherwise provided in this Act, all laws relating to marriage and divorce that are in force in Canada or any province immediately before the coming into effect of this Act continue in force in Canada and that province, respectively, until such time they are repealed, altered or replaced by Parliament or the legislature of the province according to the authority of Parliament or the legislature under this Act."[3]

APPENDIX B

Resources

4(b) is a law in relation to the regulation of international trade and commerce that is necessary to serve a compelling national interest that is not merely an aggregate of local interests or is for the purpose of limiting or imposing restrictions on exports for one or more of the following purposes, namely, ensuring priority of supply of a product or electrical energy for users in Canada, promoting economic activity and development in Canada, and conducting trade or foreign relations with other countries in the interests of Canadians generally.

NOTES: [1] The addition of the words in square brackets would enable a province to confer authority directly on county court judges if so desired.
[2] The words in square brackets reflect the consensus reached at the February First Ministers meeting.
[3] The wording of this general transition section cannot be finalized until the constitutional document is nearly completed.

35. Continuing Committee of Officials on the Constitution, Toronto, Ontario, November 15–16, 1979

(a) Powers Affecting the Economy, Federal Draft, November 8, 1979

Document: 840–177/004

The decision of Ministers at Halifax was that officials initiate a review of "powers affecting the economy" that would include:

(1) discussion of section 121 of the *B.N.A. Act* respecting the free movement of goods, services, capital, and persons in order to make our common market more effective;

(2) a clarification of powers pertaining to the federal government's ability to act in times of economic "emergency"; and

(3) other aspects of powers affecting the economy that might also be reviewed.

(A) FREEDOM OF MOVEMENT OF GOODS, SERVICES, CAPITAL AND PERSONS

While a *de facto* system of free movement very substantially exists at present, the *B.N.A. Act* does not expressly guarantee such. Concern has been expressed in a number or quarters that provincial taxing, spending and regulatory powers have been and can be used to undermine the Canadian common market. There is also concern that some federal actions have had this effect.

The idea that change in the Constitution is desirable in order to guarantee the free flow of capital, goods, services and people is one that has been expressed in a number of forums. The report on the Constitution, prepared for the Canadian Bar Association (Towards a New Canada), 1978, p. 154–55, contains such a proposal. The Report of the Joint Senate-Commons Committee on the Constitution in 1972 suggested an anti-discrimination clause (recommendation 19). The Pepin-Robarts report suggests an expansion of section 121 (recommendation 20) and an amendment to the Constitution making clear that barriers

against the interprovincial movement of capital are prohibited (recommendation 23).

The Second Report of the Ontario Advisory Committee on Confederation (March, 1979), at p. 15, notes:

"Serious consideration should be given to entrenching a "freedom of movement of people, capital, goods and information" provision in the Constitution. Such a provision would have to be carefully drafted to avoid becoming a device for invalidating provincial legislation which may have the incidental effect of imposing a minor impediment to movement."

Bill C-60, the Constitutional Amendment Bill, introduced by the previous government, contained a clause which would have guaranteed citizens certain rights to move, take up residence, aquire property, pursue the gaining of a livelihood anywhere in Canada.

The Pepin-Robarts report suggests that the European Common Market affords more protection to the free flow of capital than does the Canadian Constitution.

The B.N.A. Act does not contain a general guarantee of free movement, although section 121 provides one of a limited nature. Section 121 states:

"All Articles of the Growth, Produce and Manufacture of any one of the Provinces shall from and after the Union be admitted free into each of the other Provinces."

Section 121 applies to goods, but not to people, services or capital. It clearly prohibits the establishment of customs duties on interprovincial trade, but it is not clear that it would prevent *other discriminatory taxing policies* (e.g.: a preferential rate of income tax for investment income received from corporations having their head office in the province). It does not prevent discrimination arising out of the spending or regulatory powers of provinces. Examples of these would be barriers to trade arising out of provincial government procurement policies or provincial standards legislation.

The federal trade and commerce power (section 91(2)), as well as the limitation on provincial taxation powers to the levying of direct taxes within the province (section 92(2)), places some fetters on provincial barriers to free movement between provinces. Some other areas of exclusive federal jurisdiction may play a similar role.

Some of the kinds of issues which remain unexplored in this area are:

(1) whether an expanded section 121 or some other amendment to the Constitution is desirable or necessary to guarantee the free movement of goods, persons, services and capital;

(2) if so, how to define such a guarantee since every impediment to free movement is not necessarily unacceptable; some may arise from what are considered desirable programs, such as subsidies or restrictions on movement for health or safety reasons;

(3) should such apply to the federal as well as the provincial governments?

(B) CLARIFICATION OF FEDERAL POWERS TO ACT IN ECONOMIC EMERGENCIES

Specific concern arises in this area because of the recent decision of the Supreme Court in the *Anti-Inflation* case. The majority of the Court held that Parliament was not entitled to legislate for the general control of prices and wages in times of inflation unless such inflation amounted to an "emergency" or "crisis", or an apprehended "emergency" or "crisis". At the same time, the Court held that the economic situation in 1974–75 amounted to a sufficient emergency. In addition, one member of the Court stated that he would not second-guess a decision by Parliament that an emergency existed, providing a preamble in the statute stated it was passed pursuant to Parliament's "emergency" power. The decision leaves uncertain the scope of federal authority and when it may be applied.

Some may feel that the Court's decision gave too broad an interpretation to what constitutes an emergency. However, it is by no means certain that action could be taken, under that interpretation, to solve critical problems in the economy that might arise in some circumstances. For example, a high rate of inflation might be tolerated for several years without critical damage to the economy. The further persistence of a high rate might, however, be something which the economic life of the country could not stand, and a government in the future should be able to act. Under the present interpretation of emergency, that might not be possible. The kind of issue which could be explored in this area is:

(1) whether there should be an attempt to define more precisely in the Constitution the circumstances in which the federal legislative authority respecting economic "emergencies" might be used.

(C) ASPECTS OF THE DISTRIBUTION OF POWERS RELATING TO THE MANAGEMENT AND DEVELOPMENT OF THE ECONOMY

As we know, legislative authority to deal with many areas of the economy is bifurcated or overlapping. In addition, uncertainties exist in some areas merely because some crucial aspects of the division of powers have not been adequately defined by the courts.

The report on the Constitution, prepared for the Canadian Bar Association (1978), singled out the following as deserving special consideration: the regulation of trade, competition, securities, the monetary system, transportation and telecommunications. The Special Joint Committee on the Senate and the House of Commons (1972) singled out the following: economic policy, trade and commerce, income controls, securities and financial institutions, competition, and foreign ownership.

From a federal point of view, some areas in which we see a need for further examination are: the clarification of powers with respect to foreign borrowing, the extension of section 91(2) to expressly include services and financial transactions, powers respecting competition legislation, and powers respecting the marketing of agricultural products.

(b) Rights and Freedoms within the Canadian Federation, Federal Draft, November 5, 1979

Document: 840-177/005

Title

Canadian Charter of Rights and Freedoms

1. This section and sections 2 to 23 may be cited as the *Canadian Charter of Rights and Freedoms.*

Fundamental Freedoms

Fundamental freedoms

2. (1) Everyone has the following fundamental freedoms:
  (a) freedom of conscience and religion;
  (b) freedom of thought, opinion and expression, including freedom in the dissemination of news, opinion and belief; and
  (c) freedom of peaceful assembly and of association.

(2) The manifestation or exercise of the freedoms declared by this section may be made subject only to such limitations prescribed by law as are reasonably justifiable in a free and democratic society in the interests of the defence of Canada against subversive or hostile acts, public safety, order, health or morals or the rights and freedoms of others.

Democratic Rights

Democratic rights of citizens

3. Consistent with the principles of free and democratic elections to the House of Commons and to the legislative assemblies, and of universal suffrage for that purpose, every citizen of Canada shall, without unreasonable distinction or limitation, have the right to vote in an election of members of the House of Commons or of a legislative assembly and to be qualified for membership therein.

Duration of elected legislative bodies

4. (1) No House of Commons and no legislative assembly of a province shall continue for longer than five years from the date of the return of the writs for the choosing of its members.

Continuation in special circumstances

(2) Notwithstanding subsection (1), in time of real or apprehended war, invasion or insurrection, a House of Commons may be continued by Parliament and a legislative assembly of a province may be continued by the legislature thereof beyond the time limited therefor by subsection (1), if such continuation is not opposed by the votes of more than one-third of the members of the House of Commons or the legislative assembly, as the case may be.

Annual sitting of elected legislative bodies

5. There shall be a sitting of Parliament and of each legislature at least once in every year and not more than twelve months shall intervene between sittings.

Legal Rights

Legal Rights

6. (1) In any criminal or penal matter, proceeding or process, everyone has the right to life, liberty and security of his or her person and the right not to be deprived thereof except by due process of law, which process encompasses the following:

(a) the right to be secure against unreasonable searches and seizures;

(b) the right to protection against arbitrary or unlawful interference with privacy;

(c) the right not to be detained or imprisoned except on grounds provided by law and in accordance with prescribed procedures;

(d) the right on arrest or detention

  (i) to be informed promptly of the reason for the arrest or detention,

  (ii) to be provided with the opportunity to retain and consult counsel without delay, and

  (iii) to the remedy by way of *habeas corpus* for the determination of the validity of his or her detention and for release if the detention is not lawful;

(e) the right of a person charged with an offence

  (i) to be informed of the specific charge,

  (ii) to be tried within a reasonable time,

  (iii) to be presumed innocent until proven guilty in a fair and public hearing by an independent and impartial tribunal,

  (iv) not to be denied reasonable bail without just cause having been established, and

  (v) not to be found guilty on account of any act or omission that at the time of the act or omission did not constitute an offence;

(f) the right not be be tried or punished more than once for an offence of which he or she has been finally convicted or acquitted;

(g) the right to the benefit of the lesser punishment where the punishment for an offence of which he or she has been convicted has been varied between the time of commission and the time of sentencing;

(h) the right not to be subjected to any cruel and inhuman treatment or punishment;

(i) the right, when compelled to give evidence, to counsel, to protection against self-crimination and to any other constitutional safeguard; and

(j) the right to the assistance of an interpreter in proceedings before a court or tribunal, if the accused or witness does not understand or speak the language in which the proceedings are conducted.

Justifiable derogation

(2) In time of serious public emergency, the existence of which is officially proclaimed by or pursuant to a law enacted to deal with such circumstances or by a law specifically referring to this subsection, the rights mentioned in this section other than the right to life and those mentioned in subparagraphs (1)(d)(ii) and (1)(e)(v) and paragraphs (1)(h), (i) and (j) may be derogated from to the extent strictly required by the circumstances of the emergency.

Idem

(3) Nothing in this section precludes the enactment of or renders invalid a law that authorizes the holding of all or part of a proceeding *in camera* in the interests of the defence of Canada against subversive or hostile acts, public order or morality or in the interest of the protection of privacy of one or more of the parties or where publicity would prejudice the interests of justice.

Official Languages

Official languages of Canada

7. (1) English and French are the official languages of Canada, having the status and protection set forth in this Charter.

Authority not limited

(2) Nothing in this Charter limits the authority of Parliament or of the legislature of a province to extend the status, protection or use of the English and French languages.

Language Rights (Federal Level)

Proceedings of Parliament

8. Everyone has the right to use English or French, as he or she may choose, in any of the debates or other proceedings of Parliament.

Statutes and records, etc. of Parliament

9. The statutes and the records and journals of Parliament shall be printed and published in English and French and both language versions are equally authoritative.

Proceedings in courts constituted by Parliament
Communication by public with government of Canada

10. Either English or French may be used by any person in, or in any pleading or process in or issuing from, any court constituted by Parliament.

11. Any member of the public in Canada has the right to communicate with and to receive services from any head or central office of an institution of government of Canada in English or French, as he or she may choose, and he or she has the same right with respect to any other principal office of any such institution when that office is located within an area of Canada in which it is determined, in such manner as may be prescribed or authorized by Parliament, that a substantial number of persons within the population use that language.

Language Rights (Provincial Level)

Proceedings of legislative assemblies

12. Everyone has the right to use English or French, as he or she may choose, in the debates of the legislative assemblies of (named provinces).

Statutes and records, etc. of legislatures

13. (1) The statutes [and the records and journals] of the legislatures of (named provinces) shall be printed and published in English and French and both language versions are equally authoritative.

Idem

(2) The statutes [and the records and journals] of the legislatures of each province not referred to in subsection (1) shall be printed and published in English and French to the greatest extent practicable accordingly as the legislature of the province prescribes.

Proceedings in courts of provinces

14. (1) Either English or French may be used by any person in, or in any pleading or process in or issuing from, any court of (named provinces).

Idem

(2) Either English or French may be used by any person in, or in any pleading or process in or issuing from, any court of a province not referred to in subsection (1), to the greatest extent practicable accordingly as the legislature of the province prescribes.

Proceedings in relation to certain offences

(3) In proceedings in any court in Canada relating to an offence

    (a) created by or pursuant to an Act of Parliament, or

    (b) created by or pursuant to an Act of the legislature of a province if the punishment for the offence may be imprisonment,

any person giving evidence before the court has the right to be heard in English or French, as he or she may choose, through the services of an interpreter where necessary, and the right not to be placed at a disadvantage in so being heard.

Rules for orderly implementation and operation

(4) The legislature of a province may prescribe the date or dates on which the rights provided for by this section are to have effect in all or some parts of the province, and nothing in this section precludes the application of such rules as may be prescribed by any competent body or authority for the orderly implementation and operation of this section.

Communications by public with government of a province

15. Any member of the public in a province has the right to communicate with and to receive services from any head, central or principal office of an institution of government of the province in English or French, as he or she may choose, to the extent to which and in the areas of the province in which it is determined, in such manner as may be prescribed or authorized by the legislature of the province, that the right should pertain having regard to the practicability and necessity of providing such services.

Language of educational instruction

16. (1) Citizens of Canada in a province who are members of an English-speaking or French-speaking minority population of that province have a right to have their children receive their educational instruction in their minority language at the primary and secondary level wherever the number of children of such citizens resident in an area of the province is sufficient to warrant the provision out of public funds of minority language education facilities in that area.

Provisions for determining where numbers warrant

(2) In each province, the legislature may enact provisions for determining where the number of children of citizens of Canada who are members of an English-speaking or French-speaking minority population in an area is sufficient to warrant the provision out of public funds of minority language education facilities in that area.

Undeclared Rights

Undeclared rights and freedoms

17. Nothing in this Charter abrogates or derogates from any right or freedom not declared by it that may exist in Canada, including any right or freedom that may pertain to the native peoples of Canada.

General

Laws, etc., not to apply so as to abrogate declared rights and freedoms

18. To the end that the paramountcy of this Charter be recognized and that full effect be given to the rights and freedoms herein declared, any law and any administrative act that is inconsistent with any provision of the Charter is, except as specifically otherwise provided in or as authorized by this Charter, inoperative and of no force or effect to the extent of the inconsistency.

Enforcement of declared rights and freedoms

19. Where no other effective recourse or remedy is available or provided for by law, anyone whose rights or freedoms as declared by this Charter have been infringed or denied to his or her detriment has the right to apply to a court of competent jurisdiction to obtain such relief or remedy as the court deems appropriate and just in the circumstances.

Legislative authority not extended

20. Nothing in this Charter confers any legislative authority on any competent body or authority in that behalf in Canada, except as expressly contemplated by this Charter.

Rights and privileges preserved

21. Nothing in sections 8 to 15 abrogates or derogates from any legal or customary right or privilege acquired or enjoyed either before or after the commencement of this Charter with respect to any language that is not English or French.

Ibid

22. Nothing in sections 8 to 10 and 12 to 14 abrogates or derogates from any right, privilege or obligation with respect to the English and French languages, or either of them, that exists or is continued by virtue of any other provision of the Constitution of Canada.[1]

NOTE: [1] This provision has application until such time as specific provisions in the present Constitution may be repealed.

Application of sections
12, 13 and 14

23. A legislature of a province may, by resolution, declare that any [parts] of sections 12, 13 and 14 that do not expressly apply to that province shall have application, and thereafter such parts shall apply to that province in the same terms as to any province expressly named therein.

(c) Report of the Sub-Committee of Officials on the Senate

Document: 840-177/011

At the meeting of the Continuing Committee of Ministers held in Halifax on October 22–23, 1979, Ministers established a sub-committee of officials to initiate a review of the subject of the Upper House and constitutional reform in the light of the various proposals that have been made on the subject both by governments and other sources. The sub-committee, under the chairmanship of British Columbia, and on which all governments were represented, met briefly in Halifax to decide upon a work plan and met again for a full day in Toronto on November 15th. This is a report on the work of the sub-committee to date.

The sub-committee first referred to the numerous reports that have already been made both at the officials' and the ministerial level on this subject and attempted to build upon the considerable discussions held to date.

The sub-committee considered, in particular, proposals which have been made public by the Government of British Columbia and proposals, circulated for the information of the sub-committee only, by Ontario and Manitoba, and the proposals of the Task Force on Canadian Unity and the Ontario Advisory Committee.

Discussions centred around a consideration of four vital components of reform of the Upper House, namely, the role which such an institution should perform; its powers; the method of selection of its members; and the basis on which representation in the Upper House should be determined.

There was general agreement that the concerns and aspirations of provincial governments should be better reflected in the central institutions of the Canadian federation. Most delegations indicated that they would be prepared to consider a reconstituted second chamber as a means of achieving this objective.

Although views varied as to the priority to be attached to this subject there was general agreement that discussion of this item should be carried out simultaneously with the examination of the distribution of powers and related issues. It was noted by some provinces that the sub-committee should bear in mind the possible negative impact of a reconstituted Second Chamber on the parliamentary system and First Ministers' Conferences.

A wide-ranging discussion took place on the subject of the powers which a reconstituted Upper House might have and, in particular, the concept of giving such a body special powers on a list of crucial federal-provincial issues (so-called Category A matters). Whereas some provinces expressed support for categorizing the powers of a reconstituted Upper House along these lines, there was no consensus on this approach. It was generally felt that the method of appointment and the basis of representation that might be agreed upon could significantly determine the nature of the powers of the Upper House. Nonetheless there was a consensus that such powers ought not to include an absolute veto.

The present method of appointing Senators was generally recognized to be unsatisfactory. Most provinces that expressed a view favoured all appointments being made by provincial governments although one or two favoured the federal appointment of all or some Senators. The Federal delegation referred to the excerpt in the Kingston communique on this subject. On the question of tenure most delegations favoured a fixed term; others suggested a term corresponding to the life of the provincial government that appointed them.

As to the basis of representation, the options that were discussed ranged from equal representation for each province; representation founded on a regional basis; and representation weighted to give some regard to population differences between provinces. No clear consensus emerged on this issue.

After full discussion it became apparent that the inter-relation between the four vital components of reform is such that it would prove beneficial for the sub-committee now to identify and consider a number of integrated schemes for an Upper House based upon discussions which have been held to date on alternative roles. Accordingly, the sub-committee asked its chairman to prepare a set of such integrated schemes for its consideration and the chairman will be seeking assistance from the representatives of several provincial governments to assist him in this task. The chairman will distribute to each delegation a report on these matters when completed for future consideration by the sub-committee.

Melvin H. Smith
Sub-Committee Chairman

(d) Report of the Sub-Committee on Powers Affecting the Economy, November 16, 1979

Document: 840-177/013

The Sub-Committee met in accordance with the Record of Decision of the meeting in Halifax on October 22–23 of the Continuing Committee of Ministers on the Constitution. That Decision said that "governments should begin now to consider the question of "Powers affecting the Economy" and that time should be devoted at the November 15–16 meeting of officials to a preliminary discussion of how governments can best prepare for fuller discussions of this item in due course."

The Sub-Committee considered a short paper distributed by the federal delegation which suggested that attention be concentrated upon Section 121 of the BNA Act, upon a clarification of federal power to act in times of economic emergency, and upon certain other matters including foreign borrowing.

Some delegations expressed the view that a study of the economic powers was necessary and timely. Others were concerned that concentration on this subject might mean less concentration on other constitutional items already before Ministers.

The view was also expressed that enhancement of the Canadian common market might also be pursued, perhaps as a first step, by means other than constitutional amendment. This could be achieved through the establishment of a formal Federal/Provincial negotiating process leading to intergovernmental agreements.

A number of delegations, including the federal delegation, noted that a clarification of powers in the economic field and constitutional guarantees to protect the integrity of the Canadian common market would be to the advantage of all governments. It was noted that the agreement to study the question in no way implied that only the federal government needed added powers. The federal delegation pointed to difficulties created for all governments by the fact that some of the federal powers are excessively blunt instruments. Others noted the relationship between economic powers on the one hand and the overall distribution of powers on the other.

Attention was drawn by several delegations to the close interconnection between the work proposed in the federal paper and work already under way concerning Resource Ownership and Interprovincial Trade, particularly in regard to anti-discrimination provisions and to a definition of "compelling national interest" or "emergencies".

It was concluded that all delegations would think over the discussion which had taken place and would inform their Ministers. It was agreed that, having had this preliminary discussion among officials on how to go about the work, it would now be for the CCMC to consider priorities for futher work.

It was further agreed that, in the meantime, the Secretariat be asked to distribute pertinent extracts on the subject drawn from various reports bearing on the subject. The federal government also promised to provide general information on arrangements in this field in some other federations.

(e) Report of the Sub-Committee of Officials on a Charter of Rights, November 16, 1979

Document: 840-177/014

I   INTRODUCTION

1. The Sub-Committee of Officials on a Charter of Rights, with representatives from all jurisdictions present, met on November 16 under the chairmanship of the Deputy Attorney General of Canada to consider the provisions of a discussion draft on rights dated November 5, 1979 prepared by federal officials (Document 840-177/005).

2. The discussion draft covered five categories of rights: *fundamental freedoms*, *democratic rights*, *legal rights*, *general language rights* (federal and provincial) and *minority language education rights*, and had been modified to reflect suggestions made at the Halifax meeting to limit the scope of application of legal rights. Discussion first focussed in general terms on the appropriateness of each category of rights for inclusion in a Charter and subsequently turned to a consideration of some specific aspects of the various provisions.

II   POSITIONS ON CATEGORIES OF RIGHTS FOR A CHARTER

3. With respect to *fundamental freedoms* and *democratic rights*, eight provinces indicated general support for inclusion of these categories of rights, subject to further clarification of certain phraseologies. Manitoba maintained its previous position of opposition to any entrenched Charter and Quebec reserved its position.

4. With respect to *legal rights*, five provinces indicated varying degrees of sympathy for inclusion of this category, but all felt that there was need for substantial clarification of the nature and scope of certain rights or of the need for inclusion of some. In addition, some provinces doubted whether the Halifax decision had intended to encompass provincial penal laws. Of the remaining provinces Manitoba maintained its position of opposition to entrenchment, Quebec and B.C. reserved their positions, and Alberta and Saskatchewan were generally opposed to inclusion of this category.

5. On *general language rights*, there was support for inclusion of this category at the *federal level*. At the *provincial level*, however, only New Brunswick and Ontario were favorably disposed to inclusion of this category as drafted (although with reservations as to particular provisions), with Saskatchewan taking the position that if this category were to be included it should be cast in legally binding terms even if only a limited number of provinces would then subscribe. Nova Scotia, Manitoba, Newfoundland, British Columbia and Quebec were opposed to any entrenchment of this category as an area best left to provincial implementation, while Prince Edward Island and Alberta expressed serious doubts on any such entrenchment and reserved their positions.

6. On *minority language education rights*, only Ontario and New Brunswick favoured inclusion of this category although both provinces had concerns respecting the degree, if at all, to which the courts should be involved in enforcing these rights. Prince Edward Island expressed serious doubts on entrenchment and reserved its position. All other provinces felt strongly that this category was one not for entrenchment principally on the ground that the policy and practical considerations involved dictated that it could only be dealt with satisfactorily by provincial laws and practices and not by court enforcement of entrenched rights.

III   SPECIFIC PROVISIONS OF CATEGORIES OF RIGHTS

7. The Sub-Committee reviewed a number of the specific provisions of the discussion draft particularly with respect to legal and linguistic rights. A number of problem areas were identified and some useful suggestions for modifications were made.

8. The Chairman recalled the invitation extended at Halifax by the Minister of Federal-Provincial Relations, Mr. Jarvis, for provinces to submit their proposals and comments on specific provisions of the discussion draft, particularly with respect to legal and linguistic rights as these pertain to provincial jurisdiction. A number of provincial representatives indicated that they would be taking up this invitation in the near future.

(f) Report of the Sub-Committee on Family Law, November 16, 1979

Document: 840-177/016

The Sub-Committee on Family Law met on November 16 with representatives from all governments in attendance. In the absence of Mr. Leal (Ontario), Mr. Tassé (federal) acted as chairman.

Subject to one exception, policy positions were unchanged from those taken at the Halifax CCMC meeting (i.e., Manitoba remained opposed to granting concurrent jurisdiction over divorce to the provinces. Newfoundland and P.E.I., joined by Alberta, had similar concerns but were prepared to agree if a consensus were reached).

The Sub-Committee examined the October 21, 1979 draft circulated by the federal government at the Halifax CCMC meeting. It also considered a revised draft dated November 15, 1979 circulated by Ontario which made certain refinements in the federal draft.

After discussion, a draft was agreed to based on the October 21 draft and incorporating certain aspects of the Ontario draft, as well as suggestions made by other delegations (see detailed Annex attached).

In addition, certain comments of Quebec with respect to the French text were agreed upon.

The meeting noted the reservation of New Brunswick to the wording proposed in s. 3 00.1 with respect to the power of a legislature to confer jurisdiction of Superior Court judges on provincially-appointed judges in respect of matters within the field of family law. New Brunswick would prefer that a qualifying phrase be added to the effect that the field of family law would be "as determined by the legislature of a province".

ANNEX

Section

1 — agreed on federal draft.

2 — agreed on Ontario draft.

3 — 00.(1) — agreed on Ontario draft with last two lines amended to read: "relief corollary to divorce, including maintenance and custody".

00.(2) — agreed on federal draft.

00.(3) — agreed on federal draft.

00.(4) — agreed on federal draft.

00. 1 — agreed on federal draft, changing "all" to "any" in 2nd last line. (Subject to concern of New Brunswick referred to in report.)

4 — agreed on federal draft.

FEDERAL DRAFT, FAMILY LAW
(OCTOBER 21, 1979)

1. Repeal head 26 of section 91 — "Marriage and divorce".

2. Repeal head 12 of section 92 — "The solemnization of marriage in the Province" and substitute therefore "Marriage [including the validity of marriage,][1] in the Province".

3. Add as one of the legislative authority provisions, the following section:

Divorce

"**00.** (1) The legislature of each province may make laws in relation to divorce in the province and has exclusive authority to make laws in relation to alimony, maintenance, custody and any other relief corollary to divorce.

Idem

(2) Parliament may make laws in relation to divorce and has exclusive authority to make laws in relation to the recognition of divorce decrees granted within or outside Canada and in relation to the jurisdictional basis upon which a court may entertain an application for divorce.

NOTE:

[1] It is submitted that the words in square brackets may narrow rather than extend the head "marriage".

Relationship between laws of
provinces and laws of Parliament

(3) Where the legislature of a province enacts a law in relation to any matter over which it has concurrent authority with Parliament under this section, that law prevails in the province over any law of Parliament in relation to that matter to the extent of any inconsistency.

Idem

(4) The legislature of a province may declare that it is assuming authority in relation to all matters over which it has concurrent authority with Parliament under this section and, where the legislature so declares, all laws of Parliament in relation to those matters have no effect in that province while the declaration is in effect.

Power of legislature to confer
jurisdiction of superior court judges

00.1 Notwithstanding section 96, the legislature of a province may confer, or authorize the Lieutenant Governor of the province to confer, concurrently or exclusively, upon any court or division of a court or all or any judges of any court, the judges of which are appointed [by the Governor General or][1] by the Lieutenant Governor of the province, [as the legislature may determine,][1] the jurisdiction of a judge of a superior court of the province in respect of all matters [within the field of family law].''[2]

4. Add as one of the transitional provisions, the following section:

Continuation of existing laws

''**XX**. Except as otherwise provided in this Act, all laws relating to marriage and divorce that are in force in Canada or any province immediately before the coming into effect of this Act continue in force in Canada and that province, respectively, until such time they are repealed, altered or replaced by Parliament or the legislature of the province according to the authority of Parliament or the legislature under this Act.''[3]

ONTARIO REVISED DISCUSSION DRAFT
(NOVEMBER 15, 1979)

(Changes from October 21 [federal] draft are [italicized])

1. Repeal head 26 of section 91 — ''Marriage and divorce''.

2. Repeal head 12 of section 92 — ''The solemnization of marriage in the province'', and substitute ''Marriage in the province''.

3. Add as one of the legislative authority provisions the following section:

Divorce — *provincial authority*

00. (1) The legislature of *a* province may make laws in relation to divorce in the province and has exclusive authority to make laws in relation to maintenance, custody and any other relief corollary to divorce.

Idem — *authority of Parliament*

(2) Parliament may make laws in relation to divorce and has exclusive authority to make laws in relation to the recognition of *divorces* granted within or outside Canada and in relation to the jurisdictional basis upon which a court may entertain an application for divorce.

NOTES:

[1] The addition of the words in square brackets would enable a province to confer authority directly on county court judges if so desired.

[2] The words in square brackets reflect the consensus reached at the February First Ministers' meeting.

[3] The wording of this general transitional section cannot be finalized until the constitutional document is nearly completed.

Paramountcy

(3) Where the legislature of a province enacts a law in relation to any matter over which it has concurrent authority with Parliament under this section, that law prevails* over any law of Parliament in relation to that matter to the extent of any inconsistency.

Idem — *declaration by province*

(4) The legislature of a province may declare that it is assuming authority in relation to all matters over which it has concurrent authority with Parliament under this section and, where the legislature so declares, all laws of Parliament in relation to those matters have no effect in that province while the declaration is in effect.

Jurisdiction of courts in family law

00.1 Notwithstanding section 96, the legislature of a province may confer [or authorize the Lieutenant Governor of the province to confer], concurrently or exclusively, upon *a judge who is or a court whose judges are* appointed* by the Lieutenant Governor of the province,* the jurisdiction of a judge of the superior court of the province in respect of all matters within the field of family law.

4. Add as one of the transitional provisions, the following section:

Continuation of existing laws

"**XX.** Except as otherwise provided in this Act, all laws relating to marriage and divorce that are in force in Canada or any province immediately before the coming into effect of this Act continue in force in Canada and that province, respectively, until such time they are repealed, altered or replaced by Parliament or the legislature of the province according to the authority of Parliament or the legislature under this Act''.

36. *Priorities for a New Canadian Constitution*, Proposed by the Government of Canada June 9, 1980, Tabled in the House of Commons June 10, 1980

The time has come for the Government of Canada and the governments of the provinces to join together in the task of drafting a new Canadian Constitution.

As it enters upon that task, the Government of Canada is dedicated to a full review of all constitutional measures now applying to our federation.

The whole task constitutes a great enterprise and will take time to achieve. Not all of it can be accomplished at once, nor can we wait until all of it is done to demonstrate to the people of Canada that tangible progress is being made.

The Government of Canada believes, therefore, that intensive work should now begin on a list of items of particular priority to the people of Canada and to governments, with the understanding that some or all of these could well become the subject of early adoption as parts of the new Canadian Constitution.

The list of proposed items is this:

A statement of principles

A Charter of Rights, including language rights

A dedication to sharing and/or to equalization: the reduction of regional disparities

The Patriation of the Constitution

Resource ownership and interprovincial trade

Offshore resources

Fisheries

Powers affecting the economy

Communications, including broadcasting

Family law

A new upper house, involving the provinces

The Supreme Court, for the people and for governments

The Government also proposes that the leadership of the Native Peoples continue to be involved in the discussion of constitutional changes which directly affect the Native Peoples, in the context of the joint work on the item "Canada's Native Peoples and the Constitution". In addition, governments would pay special heed to representations from them on the items in the package set out above.

A Statement of Principles for a New Constitution

We, the People of Canada, proudly proclaim that we are and shall always be, with the help of God, a free and self-governing people.

Born of a meeting of the English and French presence on North American soil which had long been the home of our Native Peoples, and enriched by the contribution of millions of people from the four corners of the earth, we have chosen to create a life together which [transcends] the differences of blood relationships, language and religion, and willingly accept the experience of sharing our wealth and cultures, while respecting our diversity.

We have chosen to live together in one [sovereign] country, a true federation, conceived as a constitutional monarchy and founded on democratic principles.

Faithful to our history, and united by a common desire to give new life and strength to our federation, we are resolved to create together a new constitution which:

Shall be conceived and adopted in Canada,

Shall reaffirm the official status of the French and English languages in Canada, and the diversity of cultures within Canadian society,

Shall enshrine our fundamental freedoms, our basic civil, human and language rights, including the right to be educated in one's own language, French or English, where numbers warrant, and the rights of our Native Peoples, and

Shall define the authority of Parliament and of the Legislative Assemblies of our several provinces.

We further declare that our Parliament and provincial Legislatures, our various governments and their agencies shall have no other purpose than to strive for the happiness and fulfillment of each and all of us.

37. Continuing Committee of Ministers on the Constitution, Montreal, Quebec, July 8–11, 1980

(a) Rights and Freedoms within the Canadian Federation, Discussion Draft Tabled by the Delegation of the Government of Canada, July 4, 1980

Document: 830-81/027

Title

Canadian Charter of Rights and Freedoms

1. This section and sections 2 to 23 may be cited as the *Canadian Charter of Rights and Freedoms*.

Fundamental Freedoms

Fundamental freedoms

2. (1) Everyone has the following fundamental freedoms:
(a) freedom of conscience and religion;
(b) freedom of thought, opinion and expression, including freedom in the dissemination of news, opinion and belief; and
(c) freedom of peaceful assembly and of association.

Justifiable limitations

(2) The manifestation or exercise of the freedoms declared by this section may be made subject only to such limitations prescribed by law as are reasonably justifiable in a free and democratic society in the interests of national security, public safety, order, health or morals or the rights and freedoms of others.

Democratic Rights

Democratic rights of citizens

3. Consistent with the principles of free and democratic elections to the House of Commons and to the legislative assemblies, and of universal suffrage for that purpose, every citizen of Canada shall, without unreasonable distinction or limitation, have the right to vote in an election of members of the House of Commons or of a legislative assembly and to be qualified for membership therein.

Duration of elected legislative bodies

4. (1) No House of Commons and no legislative assembly of a province shall continue for longer than five years from the date of the return of the writs for the choosing of its members.

Continuation in special circumstances

(2) Notwithstanding subsection (1), in time or real or apprehended war, invasion or insurrection, a House of Commons may be continued by Parliament and a legislative assembly of a province may be continued by the legislature thereof beyond the time limited therefor by subsection (1), if such continuation is not opposed by the votes of more than one-third of the members of the House of Commons or the legislative assembly, as the case may be.

Annual sitting of elected legislative bodies

5. There shall be a sitting of Parliament and of each legislature at least once in every year and not more than twelve months shall intervene between sittings.

Legal Rights

Legal rights

6. (1) Everyone has the right to life, liberty and security of his or her person and the right not to be deprived thereof except by due process of law, which process encompasses the following:

(a) the right to be secure against unreasonable searches and seizures;

(b) the right to protection against arbitrary or unlawful interference with privacy;

(c) the right not to be detained or imprisoned except on grounds provided by law and in accordance with prescribed procedures;

(d) the right on arrest or detention

(i) to be informed promptly of the reason for the arrest or detention,

(ii) to be provided with the opportunity to retain and consult counsel without delay, and

(iii) to the remedy by way of *habeas corpus* for the determination of the validity of his or her detention and for release if the detention is not lawful;

(e) the right of a person charged with an offence

(i) to be informed of the specific charge,

(ii) to be tried within a reasonable time,

(iii) to be presumed innocent until proven guilty in a fair and public hearing by an independent and impartial tribunal,

(iv) not to be denied reasonable bail without just cause having been established, and

(v) not to be found guilty on account of any act or omission that at the time of the act or omission did not constitute an offence;

(f) the right not to be tried or punished more than once for an offence of which he or she has been finally convicted or acquitted;

(g) the right to the benefit of the lesser punishment where the punishment for an offence of which he or she has been convicted has been varied between the time of commission and the time of sentencing;

(h) the right not to be subjected to any cruel and unusual treatment or punishment;

(i) the right, when compelled to give evidence before any court, tribunal, commission, board or other authority, to counsel, to protection against self-crimination and to any other constitutional safeguard;

(j) the right to the assistance of an interpreter in any proceedings before a court, tribunal, commission, board or other authority, if the party or witness does not understand or speak the language in which the proceedings are conducted.

(2) Everyone has the right to a fair hearing in accordance with the principles of fundamental justice for the determination of his or her rights or obligations.

Justifiable derogation

(3) In time of serious public emergency threatening the life of the country, the existence of which is officially proclaimed by or pursuant to a law enacted to deal with such circumstances or by a law specifically referring to this subsection, the rights mentioned in this section other than the right to life and those mentioned in subparagraphs (1)(d)(i) and (ii) and (1)(e)(i)–(iii) and (v) and paragraphs (1)(f)(g)(h)(i) and (j) may be derogated from to the extent strictly required by the circumstances of the emergency.

Idem

(4) Nothing in this section precludes the enactment of or renders invalid a law that authorizes the holding of all or part of a proceeding *in camera* in the interests of national security, public order or morality or in the interest of the protection of privacy of one or more of the parties or where publicity would prejudice the public interest.

Non-discrimination Rights

Equality before the law and equal protection of the law

7. (1) Everyone has the right to equality before the law and to equal protection of the law without distinction or restriction other than any distinction or restriction provided by law that is fair and reasonable having regard to the object of the law.

Affirmative action programmes

(2) Nothing in this section precludes any programme or activity authorized by or pursuant to law that has as its object the amelioration of conditions of disadvantaged persons or groups.

Mobility Rights

Rights of citizens

8. (1) Every citizen of Canada has the right to enter, remain in and leave Canada.

Rights of citizens and persons lawfully admitted for permanent residence

(2) Every citizen of Canada and every person who has been lawfully admitted to Canada for permanent residence and has not lost the status of a permanent resident has the right

(a) to move to and take up residence in any province or territory, and

(b) to acquire and hold property in, and to pursue the gaining of livelihood in, any province or territory,

subject to any laws of general application in force in that province or territory other than any such laws that discriminate among persons to whom this provision applies primarily on the basis of province or territory of present or previous residence or domicile.

Justifiable limitations

(3) The rights declared by this section may be made subject only to such limitations prescribed by law as are reasonably justifiable in a free and democratic society in the interests of national security, public safety, order, health or morals.

Property Rights

Property rights

9. (1) Everyone has the right to the use and enjoyment of property, individually or in association with others, and the right not to be deprived thereof except in accordance with law and for reasonable compensation.

Justifiable limitations

(2) Nothing in this section precludes the enactment of or renders invalid laws controlling or restricting the use of property in the public interest or securing against property the payment of taxes or duties or other levies or penalties.

Idem

(3) The rights declared by this section may be made subject only to such limitations prescribed by law in addition to those referred to in subsection (2) as are reasonably justifiable in a free and democratic society in the interests of national security or public safety, order, health or morals.

Offical Languages

Official languages of Canada

10. (1) English and French are the official languages of Canada, having the status and protection set forth in this Charter.

Authority not limited

(2) Nothing in this Charter limits the authority of Parliament or of the legislature of a province to extend the status, protection or use of the English and French languages.

Language Rights

Proceedings of Parliament

11. (1) Everyone has the right to use English or French in any of the debates or other proceedings of Parliament.

Debates of legislative assembly

(2) Everyone has the right to use English or French in the debates of the legislative assembly of any province.

Statutes and records, etc., of Parliament

12. (1) The statutes and the records and journals of Parliament shall be printed and published in English and French.

Statutes and records, etc., of certain legislatures

(2) The statutes and the records and journals of the legislatures of Ontario, Quebec, New Brunswick and Manitoba shall be printed and published in English and French.

Idem

(3) The statutes and the records and journals of the legislature of each province not referred to in subsection (2) shall be printed and published in English and French to the greatest extent practicable accordingly as the legislature of the province prescribes.

Both versions of statutes authoritative

(4) Where the statutes of any legislative body described in any of subsections (1) to (3) are printed and published in English and French, both language versions are equally authoritative.

Proceedings in Supreme Court and courts constituted by Parliament

13. (1) Either English or French may be used by any person in, or in any pleading or process in or issuing from, the Supreme Court of Canada or any court constituted by Parliament.

Proceedings in courts of certain provinces

(2) Either English or French may be used by any person in, or in any pleading or process in or issuing from, any court of Ontario, Quebec, New Brunswick and Manitoba.

Idem

(3) Either English or French may be used by any person in, or in any pleading or process in or issuing from, any court of a province not referred to in subsection (2), to the greatest extent practicable accordingly as the legislature of the province prescribes.

Proceedings in relation to certain offences

(4) In proceedings in any court in Canada relating to an offence

(a) created by or pursuant to an Act of Parliament, or

(b) created by or pursuant to an Act of the legislature of a province if the punishment for the offence may be imprisonment,

any person giving evidence before the court has the right to be heard in English or French, through the services of an interpreter where necessary, and the right not to be placed at a disadvantage in so being heard.

Rules for orderly implementation and operation

(5) Nothing in this section precludes the application of such rules as may be prescribed by any competent body or authority for the orderly implementation and operation of this section.

Communication by public with government of Canada

14. (1) Any member of the public in Canada has the right to communicate with and to receive services from any head or central office of an institution of government of Canada in English or French, and has the same right with respect to any other principal office of any such institution where that office is located within an area of Canada in which it is determined, in such manner as may be prescribed or authorized by Parliament, that a substantial number of persons within the population use that language.

Communication by public with government of a province

(2) Any member of the public in a province has the right to communicate with and to receive services from any head, central or other principal office of an institution of government of the province in English or French to the extent to which and in the areas of the province in which it is determined, in such manner as may be prescribed or authorized by the legislature of the province, that the right should pertain having regard to the practicability and necessity of providing such services.

Rights and privileges preserved

15. Nothing in sections 10 to 14 abrogates or derogates from any legal or customary right or privilege acquired or enjoyed either before or after the commencement of this Charter with respect to any language that is not English or French.

Language of educational instruction

16. (1) Citizens of Canada in a province who are members of an English-speaking or French-speaking minority population of that province have a right to have their children receive their education in their minority language at the primary and secondary school level wherever the number of children of such citizens resident in an area of the province is sufficient to warrant the provision out of public funds of minority language education facilities in that area.

Provisions for determining where numbers warrant

(2) In each province, the legislature may, consistent with the right provided in subsection (1), enact provisions for determining whether the number of children of citizens of Canada who are members of an English-speaking or French-speaking minority population in an area of the province is sufficient to warrant the provision out of public funds of minority language education facilities in that area.

Undeclared Rights

Undeclared rights and freedoms

17. Nothing in this Charter abrogates or derogates from any right or freedom not declared by it that may exist in Canada, including any right or freedom that may pertain to the native peoples of Canada.

General

Laws, etc., not to apply so as to abrogate declared rights and freedoms

18. To the end that the paramountcy of this Charter be recognized and that full effect be given to the rights and freedoms herein declared, any law and any administrative act that is inconsistent with any provision of the Charter is, except as specifically otherwise provided in or as authorized by this Charter, inoperative and of no force or effect to the extent of the inconsistency.

Enforcement of declared rights and freedoms

19. Where no other effective recourse or remedy is available or provided for by law, anyone whose rights or freedoms as declared by this Charter have been infringed or denied to his or her detriment has the right to apply to a court of competent jurisdiction to obtain such relief or remedy as the court deems appropriate and just in the circumstances.

Application to territories and territorial institutions

20. A reference in any of sections 3 to 5 and 10 to 16 to a province or to the legislative assembly or legislature of a province includes a reference to the Yukon Territory or the Northwest Territories or to the Council or Commissioner in Council thereof, as the case may be.

Legislative authority not extended

21. Nothing in this Charter confers any legislative authority on any competent body or authority except as expressly provided by this Charter.

Continuation of existing
constitutional provisions

22. Nothing in sections 11 to 13 abrogates or derogates from any right, privilege or obligation with respect to the English and French languages, or either of them, that exists or is continued by virtue of any other provision of the Constitution of Canada.[1]

Application of sections 12 and 13

23. A legislature of a province may, by resolution, declare that any part of sections 12 and 13 that do not expressly apply to that province shall have application, and thereafter such part or parts shall apply to that province in the same terms as to any province expressly named therein.

(b) Charter of Rights and Freedoms, Background Notes, Tabled by the Delegation of the Government of Canada, July 5, 1980

Document: 830-81/028

INTRODUCTION

This paper describes, in summary fashion, each of the rights which have been included in the "discussion draft" of the Charter which the federal delegation tabled at the CCMC meeting today.

Because Canadians are concerned about respect for minority rights, it is important to protect both the language rights of minority groups and fundamental rights, such as freedom of speech. These rights, and others, need to be safeguarded. A Charter of Rights and Freedoms for Canadians should therefore include as wide a range of guarantees as possible.

The discussion draft contains certain changes from earlier drafts. Some of these changes came about as the result of advice and suggestions made by the Special Joint Committee of Parliament in 1978 and by provincial delegations during earlier meetings of the CCMC in 1978 and 1979.

FUNDAMENTAL FREEDOMS AND DEMOCRATIC RIGHTS

(Sections 2–5 of the Discussion Draft of July 4, 1980)

The first group, *Fundamental Freedoms*, includes freedom of conscience and religion, freedom in the dissemination of news and freedom of peaceful assembly. In the proposed Charter, the only limitations allowed on the exercise of these freedoms are those prescribed by law which pertain to such matters as public safety or health, national security or the freedoms of others.

Democratic Rights includes the right to vote in an election of members of the House of Commons or of a legislative assembly and the right to stand for office in either of these institutions. This section of the Charter also limits to five years the time any government may remain in power without "going to the people" and requires that Parliament and provincial legislatures meet at least once in every year.

"Entrenchment" in the constitution would ensure that these rights could not be changed by governments or legislatures without going through the constitutional amendment process. At the First Ministers Conference in February 1979, there was almost complete agreement that these rights should be included in the Charter.

LEGAL RIGHTS

(Section 6 of the Discussion Draft)

Among the many important rights provided for under the draft Charter, each Canadian would be guaranteed the right to life, liberty and security and the right not to be deprived of these "except by due process of law" the major elements of which are listed in the Charter. The proposed Charter enumerates the various considerations which would

---

NOTE:

[1] This provision has application until such time as specific provisions in the present Constitution may be repealed.

guide law enforcement agencies and courts when a person is arrested, detained, tried or punished, or otherwise involved in the legal process. Although many of the rights contained in this section are already available to most Canadians, they are not mandatory and could be changed as the result of the decision of Parliament or, in some cases, of a legislature.

The draft Charter places no limitations on these rights other than in time of "serious public emergency threatening the life of the country". Even under those circumstances, the right to life, the right to be provided with opportunity to retain and consult a lawyer, freedom from cruel or unusual treatment or punishment and many other basic legal rights may not be infringed.

NON-DISCRIMINATION RIGHTS

(Section 7 of the Discussion Draft)

The federal government is proposing that under the Constitution all Canadians, regardless of race, national or ethnic origin, language, color, religion, age, sex, or any other similar grounds, will have the same rights before the law and enjoy the same protection of the law.

Because it has been very difficult to reach an agreement on a complete enumeration of these grounds, the federal "discussion draft" includes a general clause rather than a list.

Non-discrimination rights need to be assured by a clear declaration in the Constitution. Discrimination on any of these grounds can easily occur. The Government of Canada considers the Charter would be seriously deficient if these rights were not covered.

This section contains a provision permitting the use of "affirmative action" programs that are authorized by law to improve the conditions of disadvantaged people or groups of people.

MOBILITY RIGHTS

(Section 8 of the Discussion Draft)

The Mobility Rights contained in the discussion draft of the Charter assure citizens of Canada the constitutional right to enter, remain in and leave the country. Moreover, this section gives all Canadian citizens and permanent residents the right to establish themselves in any province of Canada, and to acquire property and pursue employment in any province of Canada. This section would reduce barriers to mobility of people and their participation in the benefits of Canadian federalism.

What is being proposed in this section is that every Canadian citizen and permanent resident of Canada should enjoy basic rights throughout the country, without discrimination based upon a province of residence or province of birth.

PROPERTY RIGHTS

(Section 9 of the Discussion Draft)

Property Rights and Mobility Rights are the only provisions in the Charter which refer explicitly to economic rights. This section also deals with expropriation and control of property. It would ensure that limitations on these rights could only come about in accordance with law. People would have to be fairly compensated whenever it was necessary to expropriate land or other property.

LANGUAGE RIGHTS

(Sections 10–16 of the Discussion Draft)

Entrenching the language rights of English-speaking and French-speaking Canadians in the Constitution is the best means of
— recognizing the duality of Canadian society,
— being fair and reasonable to all Canadians, wherever they may live,
— ensuring mutual respect for both language groups.

In earlier discussions among governments, it had been generally recognized that it would be desirable to provide language rights. Some governments do, however, have legitimate concerns about their capacity to give full and immediate effect to certain rights. There are also questions about the precise demographic and geographic criteria to apply when determining the circumstances under which certain rights would be practicable. In drafting the language rights provisions of the Charter, the federal government has taken account of these practical concerns.

The federal government and two provinces (Quebec and Manitoba) currently have entrenched provisions on the use of English and French in the *debates*, *statutes*, *records* and *journals* of their legislatures and in *court proceedings*. (Section 133 of the BNA Act and Section 23 of the Manitoba Act.) It is proposed that the other two provinces with large linguistic minorities (Ontario and New Brunswick) should have the same status.

There are also provisions regarding service to the public at both levels of government, and on the use of French or English in criminal proceedings in courts across Canada.

Minority official language education rights, which are covered in Section 16 of the discussion draft, are of special importance.

Great progress has occurred in this area in recent years. The provincial Premiers met in Montreal in 1978. They issued a communiqué on February 23 of that year in which they agreed to the following "principles":

" (i) Each child of the French-speaking or English-speaking minority is entitled to an education in his or her language in the primary or the secondary schools in each province wherever numbers warrant.

(ii) It is understood, due to exclusive jurisdiction of provincial governments in the field of education, and due also to wide cultural and demographic differences, that the implementation of the foregoing principle would be as defined by each province."

The proposal put forward by the federal government in the discussion draft would enable provincial legislatures to determine the numbers of children in any area that would warrant the provision of the necessary facilities. The action taken by most (if not all) provinces in recent years to provide minority language education has removed a practical obstacle to entrenching this right in the Constitution.

UNDECLARED RIGHTS

(Section 17 of the Discussion Paper)

This section provides that, if individuals or groups of Canadians have rights which are not mentioned in this Charter, they will not lose them because they are not "declared" in the Charter. They will continue to be able to enjoy them fully. This provision is particularly relevant to the rights of Canada's native peoples.

The Government of Canada has already indicated that it will be prepared to discuss aboriginal rights and treaty rights (among other important subjects) with the leadership of the three national native organizations when discussions begin, probably later this year, on the constitutional item "Canada's Native Peoples and the Constitution". In the meantime, the leadership of the three national organizations (National Indian Brotherhood, Native Council of Canada, Inuit Committee on National Issues) will be given an opportunity later this summer to meet with a subcommittee of the CCMC to present their views on Constitutional matters, including the Charter of Rights and Freedoms.

(c) Powers Over the Economy: Securing the Canadian Economic Union in the Constitution, Discussion Paper Submitted by the Government of Canada, July 9, 1980

Document: 830-81/036

TABLE OF CONTENTS

1. INTRODUCTION

The purpose of this document is to consider the means whereby the Canadian economic union could be better secured in the Constitution.

An economic union is an entity within which goods, services, labour, capital and enterprise can move freely, that is, without being subject to fiscal and other institutional barriers, and which is endowed with institutions capable of harmonizing the broad internal policies which affect economic development and of implementing common policies with regard to the entity's external economic relations. Moreover, the form which the political institutions of our economic union should take is determined since Canada is, and is destined to remain, a federal state. Accordingly, new constitutional provisions to safeguard and strengthen the Canadian market must take into account the other goals of the Federation, such as the preservation of its linguistic and cultural diversity, and the sharing of income and wealth among citizens and regions.

Canada has achieved a high degree of economic integration over the past century, but the existence and operation of a common market within its territory is not adequately safeguarded in its basic law. The two orders of government have the constitutional authority to restrict in numerous ways the free movement of persons, goods, services, capital and enterprise within the country.

Although the B.N.A. Act does not contain an explicit economic definition of the federation, the following description can be drawn from a number of provisions, as interpreted so far by the courts:

- a customs union, since provincial legislatures are prohibited from levying internal border taxes and Parliament is empowered to establish a common external tariff;
- an imperfect common market for goods — imperfect because Section 121 probably does not prohibit non-tariff barriers to interprovincial trade, and because judicial interpretation has limited the federal trade and commerce power;
- an imperfectly safeguarded common market for capital and enterprise, since provinces can impede the movement of some financial assets and business establishments across interprovincial borders;
- distinct and "protectable" provincial markets for labour and most other services, except in federally regulated industries;
- a highly integrated economic union nonetheless, by virtue of federal jurisdiction over taxation, money and banking, interprovincial trade, commerce and transportation, agriculture, communications, weights and measures, etc.

The Government of Canada is of the view that, of the five broad functional categories suggested in *Powers over The Economy: A Framework for Discussion*, the securing of the economic union should receive priority attention in the process of constitutional renewal. This view is founded on two basic realities.

The first reality is political. To be a citizen of Canada must be dynamic reality rather than a static abstraction, a reality that extends beyond the realm of political and legal institutions to the vital aspects of one's material existence. As the Government of Quebec argued twelve years ago in a proposal on the general aims of the Constitution, "all Canadians must be full citizens, having in principle the same rights, the same responsibilities and the same opportunities for self-fulfillment". To the extent compatible with federalism, this basic equality of all citizens must apply to economic affairs, under provincial law as well as under federal law. Wherever they may have been born or have chosen to reside in the country, Canadians should be free to take up residence, to acquire and hold property, to gain a livelihood, to invest their savings, to sell their products and purchase their supplies in any province or territory of Canada, provided they abide by the laws of general application of that province or territory.

There may be circumstances, of course when the pursuit of other political, social, economic and cultural goals justifies some restriction of the economic freedom of Canadians. But the freest possible access to the national market should be inherent to Canadian citizenship, and therefore secured in the Constitution. Any provincial authority should bear in mind that whenever it discriminates against the residents of other provinces, it exposes its own residents to retaliatory discrimination by the governments of these other provinces; and whenever it seeks to retain the ability to restrict the mobility of other provinces' residents, it simultaneously argues that the freedom of its own residents should be subject to curtailment by nine other governments. As for the federal authority, while it would be imprudent to limit its ability to meet the varying needs and aspirations of different parts of the country in a differentiated way, it should always be aware that such use of its powers can be quite contentious since it inevitably raises difficult problems of interpersonal and interregional equity.

The second reality is economic. It was admirably expressed in A Future Together, the main report of the Task Force on Canadian Unity:

"Our analysis indicates that greater economic benefits should result from increasing levels of integration. Some of these benefits are associated specifically with the integration of regional economic activities into a larger market. For example, larger markets provide a greater scope for the diversification of sectors and specialization, resulting in a better allocation of the factors of production. Competition is enhanced; industries can take advantage of economies of scale; and a larger and more efficient financial sector may be created. Moreover, the availability of a more diversified and broader natural resource base is an important benefit — when the market for one commodity is low it may be counter-balanced by the more favourable position of other commodities.

"Other benefits related to size come into play, particularly when integration takes the form of federal union. We have in mind a variety of aspects related to the efficiency and effectiveness of the larger public sector, such as the economies of scale in the delivery of public goods (for example in national defence), and a greater scope for interregional policy coordination which would take into account programs whose impact could not be restricted to a single region. Also significant is the enhanced capacity of the public sector to raise funds through external borrowings.

"In a federal union the regions can expect their economies to perform better as a result of the movement of labour, capital, goods and services. Other advantages are the greater chance of restraining undue competition among the regions for development projects and the improved leverage of the regions in securing international trade advantages. Finally, as we have noted, a federation allows for interregional transfers of funds through income support measures and adjustment assistance to the regions.

"While such benefits may be difficult to measure precisely, they are nevertheless very real, and they are reflected in the standard of living Canadians have long enjoyed. In a nutshell, integration creates a surplus, because the whole is greater than its parts. And the surplus, using the central government as an instrument can be redistributed so that the strong parts help the weak to the benefit of the whole."

The Task Force also points out that Canada, given its geography, linguistic duality and cultural diversity, cannot be single-minded in its pursuit of economic integration — indeed, no country can afford to be. But it argues that there is still ample scope to increase the "surplus" or benefits arising from the Canadian economic union while keeping attendant costs at a reasonable and acceptable level.

The Federal Government not only shares that view, but considers that there is some urgency in safeguarding and strengthening our economic union, given prevailing trends in the world economy. Technological developments, the internationalization of factors of production, the need to get the benefits of greater economies of scale and specialization of production facilities, have generated considerable pressure for larger markets. There has been continuing liberalization of market access among the main industrialized countries through major tariff reductions. A number of countries have combined their market power through the creation of free trade areas or common markets. These and other developments in the world market place, including the constant emergence of new exporters, have made unavoidable structural adjustments of numerous individual sectors and lines of production within the Canadian economy. These adjustments run the risk of being less effective and costlier if we are unable to exploit fully the potential strength of our national market.

Of particular concern, in this respect, are signs of economic segmentation within Canada which run counter to observed trends in other economic entities. Protectionism among provinces, and weakening of the federal government's ability to promote balanced economic development, can involve significant efficiency losses for Canada as a whole, and hence for each and every one of its parts:

— higher supply costs, fragmentation and stunted growth for firms, and diseconomies of scale which enhance import penetration and reduce the international competitiveness of domestic production;

— diversion of trade to foreign suppliers, when fragmentation results in neither in-province nor out-of-province suppliers being able to service provincial markets on a competitive basis;

— lower incomes and lesser employment opportunities for residents of all provinces;

— higher burdens upon national and provincial taxpayers, due to higher cost of public procurement and lower tax yields.

The converse, of course, applies. The competitiveness of Canadian industry and hence the incomes and employment opportunities of Canadians will be significantly enhanced if we succeed, not only in resisting trends towards segmentation of our domestic market, but in devising new constitutional arrangements which would make closer economic integration possible and compatible with the preservation of our federal system. It should be noted that any increase in the economic surplus generated by the Canadian economic union could only improve our ability to reduce regional economic disparities, provided adequate mechanisms to do so are in place.

The course of Canada's economic development as well as international experience, particularly in the past three decades, should give governments the confidence and the foresight to proceed in this direction, with due care of course, but also with boldness and imagination. Canadians owe much of their current prosperity to the economic union, however imperfect, established 113 years ago by the Fathers of Confederation. Also, the general post-war movement towards freer trade, which is now enshrined in international law, has resulted in enormous productivity and income gains for Canada, regional markets like the European Economic Community, and the world economy as a whole. Economic history and theory points to the benefits that would flow from strengthening and better safeguarding of the Canadian economic union.

In this regard, a survey of relevant provisions of the General Agreement of Tariffs and Trade (GATT), the Treaty of Rome, the constitutions of other federal states and that of Canada may help to bring out some of the deficiencies in the main operating rules of the Canadian economic union. There are, of course, basic differences between the nature, aims and institutions of the Canadian federation and that of a multilateral trade agreement like the GATT, which is based on reciprocity of benefits and a mutual balance of international rights and obligations, or a common market like the EEC, established by a treaty creating a community of sovereign states, and even other federations like the United States, Australia, the Federal Republic of Germany, Switzerland and India, which have their own particular history, geography, social make-up and political traditions. Nevertheless, such comparisons may provide us with useful background and a broad perspective.

* * *

4. THE CANADIAN FEDERATION

Despite judicial pronouncements that section 121 and enumerated federal powers provide evidence that one of the objectives of Confederation was to form "an economic unit of the whole of Canada", it cannot be said that the *B.N.A. Act* establishes explicitly an economic union. Of course, an economic union largely exists; but what degree of economic mobility and integration is constitutionally secured?

4.1   AMBIT OF SECTION 121

Section 121 is the only explicit provision of the *B.N.A. Act* relevant to the flow of goods between provinces. It provides that "All Articles of the Growth, Produce and Manufacture of any one of the Provinces shall, from and after the Union, be admitted free into each of the other Provinces."

Court interpretation has made it clear that section 121 prohibits the imposition of customs duties on the movement of goods between provinces, but it has not been used to preclude non-fiscal impediments to the movement of goods, nor would it seem to prohibit the imposition of other kinds of taxes which might impede the free flow of goods.

There is some indication in the jurisprudence that section 121 might be capable of a broader meaning so as to prevent trade regulations that in essence related to provincial borders. This interpretation stems from Mr. Justice Rand's comments in the case *Murphy v. C.P.R. and A.G. Canada*. Although Mr. Justice Rand's significant departure in interpreting section 121 has been accepted by four of the nine judges of the Supreme Court of Canada in the recent *Reference re Agricultural Products Marketing Act and two other Acts*, it is certainly doubtful under the existing state of authorities that section 121 would be interpreted to prohibit non-tariff barriers on goods. The only certitude is that this section prohibits customs duties affecting interprovincial trade in provincial products. Also, it is to be noted that section 121 has been generally thought to apply equally to Parliament and provincial legislatures, although this is not completely clear. An argument can be made that Parliament's enumerated powers (e.g., taxation and trade and commerce) can override section 121 because those powers are given by the terms of the opening clause of section 91 "notwithstanding anything in this Act". In addition, the decision of the four Justices of the Supreme Court in the aforementioned Agricultural Products Marketing Act Reference indicated that the application of section 121 may be different depending upon whether federal or provincial legislation is involved.

Section 121 has additional shortcomings as a guarantee of free movement. The wording reflects the historical situation that the provinces, which formerly had customs duties, were to abolish such duties on trade with one another. At the same time, the power to enact a uniform tariff against other countries became federal by virtue of section 91(2), 91(3), and 122. The wording overlooks the possibility of taxes on commodities imported from abroad, hence not "of the Growth, Produce or Manufacture of any of the Provinces", as they cross provincial borders. Thus, it is not all products within a province that are to be admitted free. Those originally imported from abroad might be subjected to a provincial tax based on section 92(2) and 92(9). This possibility may be remote since it would be difficult to frame such taxation in a way that did not offend Parliament's trade and commerce power, or that did not constitute indirect taxation.

A more fundamental defect is that the wording of section 121 makes no explicit reference to services, to capital, to enterprise, or to persons. In effect, section 121 is directed to the formation of a customs union, not a common market. This narrow scope is quite explainable in the context of the 1867 *B.N.A. Act* since the framers of that document thought they were conferring on the federal government jurisdiction over all trade and commerce as well as all economic powers necessary for the creation of a highly integrated economic union.

4.2 FEDERAL AND PROVINCIAL LEGISLATIVE JURISDICTION

The Canadian economic union, in fact, has been created more by the allocation to Parliament of certain exclusive powers than by Section 121. Exclusive federal jurisdiction on international and interprovincial trade has meant that in general provincial trade regulations which create direct barriers to the interprovincial movement of goods are *ultra vires*. It is not always easy to detect what forms of legislation do create these barriers, but it is clear, for example, from *A.G. Manitoba v. Manitoba Egg and Poultry Association* that a local board cannot impose quotas on goods entering the local market from an extra-provincial source, and from *Central Canada Potash v. Govt. of Saskatchewan* that provinces cannot regulate the sale-price of goods in the extraprovincial market. Perhaps the most interesting case is that of *Crickard et al. v. A.G., B.C.* where a British Columbia law made it obligatory for each egg imported into the province to bear the name of its country of origin in ink. Since this was a very burdensome operation, the indirect effect of the law was to make it virtually impossible to import eggs into British Columbia. The Act was accordingly declared invalid.

At the same time, of course, the Privy Council's "compartmentalizing" of federal and provincial trade powers and its interpretation that Parliament's authority does not encompass the regulation of "the contracts of a particular business or trade within a province", together with the broad scope of provincial legislative jurisdiction pursuant to a number of headings but most importantly with respect to property and civil rights (92(13)) has meant that there is great capacity for provincial legislation to create barriers to trade. The most recent example, following on the decision in the *Labatt's "Special Lite"* case, is the potential

barriers that can be created by different provincial product standards. In some sense, all exercise of legislative authority can create barriers. Some impediments, however, are more direct and restrictive than others and of a kind more usually classified as non-tariff barriers (i.e., those closely connected with trade).

The federal trade and commerce power may have some inhibiting effect on some kinds of provincial taxing powers. Thus, in the *C.I.G.O.L.* case, the Supreme Court found the Saskatchewan legislation invalid in part on the ground that it was designed to fix the price of oil in the export market and, therefore, constituted the regulation of interprovincial and international trade. However, no decision has declared provincial taxation invalid solely on the ground that it infringed the federal trade and commerce power and, indeed, in most cases it will be difficult to so characterize provincial taxation legislation.

The limiting of provincial taxing powers to direct taxation has been more effective in preventing provincial tax barriers to the free circulation of goods, since it has precluded provinces from imposing customs, excise, export or commodity taxes, which have all been characterized as indirect. However, indirect taxation has received such a narrow construction that the judicial test for direct taxation has been met in a large measure simply by properly drafting the provincial legislation in question. Accordingly, there is considerable scope for provincial taxes which create barriers to trade.

Exclusive federal jurisdiction over interprovincial and international transportation guarantees some aspects of the free movement of goods and people. Thus, it will be recalled that in the *Winner* case the Privy Council denied to New Brunswick the power to regulate the New Brunswick portion of the route of a bus line which originated in the United States and passed through New Brunswick en route to Nova Scotia. This head of jurisdiction, of course, has no relevance to the free movement of capital and only limited relevance to the free movement of persons or services.

The free movement of capital is assured to a large extent by virtue of Parliament's exclusive authority over currency and coinage — 91(14), banking, incorporation of banks and the issue of paper money — 91(15), savings banks 91(16), legal tender — 91(20), and its authority to borrow money on the public credit — 91(4). It is abundantly clear that provincial legislatures could not control the movement of capital by establishing separate monetary systems, currency controls, or banks. However, *de facto* provincial control over near-banks and constitutionally valid control over financial institutions other than banks gives the provinces considerable powers in this field, as does provincial jurisdiction over securities marketing. Whether or not "trade and commerce" includes regulations respecting the flow of capital, as opposed to the flow of commodities, is not clear. It is possible that some restriction of provincial impediments to the flow of capital may arise out of the federal trade and commerce power.

4.3   IMPLICATIONS FOR THE OPERATION OF THE ECONOMIC UNION

In considering the implications of present constitutional law for the operation of the Canadian economic union, two points should be borne in mind. The first is that the ability of governments to restrict economic mobility should be assessed in terms of its potential impact upon the country's future development as well as of its actual impact in the past. The second point concerns the combined and cumulative impact of impediments to economic mobility and interchange: individual measures which may seem by themselves relatively insignificant may lead, when taken together, to significant market fragmentation and efficiency losses.

That there exist today numerous restrictions to economic mobility within Canada, originating in both the federal and provincial domains, should come as a surprise to no one, given the deficiencies and uncertainties of our constitutional framework. An illustrative survey of such restrictions is annexed to this document (Annex A [not reproduced]). It may be useful to review briefly these impediments and related constitutional provisions within the broad framework used to describe the relevant features of the international trading system, the European Economic Community and other federations.

PRINCIPLES AND OBJECTIVES

As noted above, the *B.N.A. Act* does not contain a statement of the principles and objectives of the Canadian economic union. Consequently, rules which are embodied (in different ways and to a varying degree, of course) in the GATT, the Treaty of Rome and the constitutions of other federal states reviewed are not found in Canadian constitutional statutes. Most notable is the absence of any affirmation of the principles of non-discriminatory treatment of goods, services and factors of production, regardless of their province of origin or destination, and of their uniform treatment in provincial taxation and regulations

(what is termed "national treatment" in international law). As a result, legislators and the courts have not always found a clear expression of intent in the application or interpretation of constitutional provisions relevant to the operation and management of the economic union.

GOVERNMENT AIDS AND INCENTIVES

The area of government subsidies and investment incentives in Canada is one without constitutional discipline, the only practical limit imposed upon governments being the cost of their programs to their taxpayers and a measure of common sense. Thus there is little in the Constitution to prevent government subsidies and tax incentives to producers which adversely affect the interests of extra-provincial producers. It is particularly noticeable that the rules established by the Treaty of Rome involve significantly more common discipline in cases of distortions or threats of distortion to internal competitive conditions. Indeed, some of the key operating rules of the GATT Agreement (e.g., serious prejudice, adverse effects) seem to impose more by way of common minimum discipline than there is within the Canadian market. (This does not necessarily mean, however, that they are effectively implemented.) Likewise, it would appear that the constitutions of other federal states contain provisions which may be used to place limitations on the ability of state authorities — and, in the case of Australia, of the federal authority — to grant discriminatory subsidies.

PUBLIC PROCUREMENT

Under existing constitutional arrangements, governments' contracting power is analogous to their spending powers, i.e. unchecked by considerations related to the functioning of the economic union. For example, there is no requirement not to use provincial government purchasing to discriminate against or among out-of-province producers or suppliers, or not to use it to afford protection to their industries. There now exist *preferential and restrictive procurement practices* which are a source of segmentation of the Canadian market, as well as of conflict when these practices favour foreign suppliers over Canadian suppliers from a given province. These government preferences may be implicit or explicit, embodied in laws, regulations or procedures, or be purely a matter of practices. While this is an area where international law, as exemplified by the GATT and the Treaty of Rome, is rather lax, other federal constitutions appear to impose greater discipline in this respect than that of Canada.

TECHNICAL REGULATIONS

Under existing constitutional arrangements, both orders of government have some jurisdiction over consumer and environmental protection, product standards, and technical regulations. There is nothing in the *B.N.A. Act* that enjoins governments to ensure that their measures do not have the effect of creating *unnecessary* obstacles to trade. Similarly there is nothing in the *B.N.A. Act* calling for the *"approximation"* of laws and regulations that affect the functioning of the common market. As a result, the extent to which the technical requirements of economic mobility can be met depends upon the ambit of federal exclusive jurisdiction, or the good will and common sense of provincial authorities. There again, this is an area where international arrangements appear, at least in their intent, to be in advance of Canadian constitutional law, as evidenced by the recently negotiated GATT Agreement on Technical Barriers to Trade, as well as by the relevant provisions of the Treaty of Rome and directives issued pursuant to them.

PUBLIC ENTERPRISES

There is no provision in the Canadian Constitution comparable to the provisions of the Treaty of Rome prohibiting *discrimination by state monopolies* of a commercial character, and stipulating that *rules governing competition* apply equally to private and public enterprises. It should be noted that the other federal constitutions examined make it possible to bring public enterprises under some common market discipline.

COMMODITY TRADE

Under existing constitutional arrangements, legislative authority over marketing of primary commodities is shared between Parliament and provincial legislatures, federal authority in this respect being significantly more limited in Canada than under other federal constitutions.

MOBILITY OF LABOUR

In the absence of any provision in the *B.N.A. Act* affirming the mobility and associated rights of Canadian citizens, the mobility of labour within the economic union is not constitutionally secured. This deficiency is compounded by the lack of any safeguarding of business and professional mobility. In this respect, Canadian constitutional law contrasts sharply with the basic law of all other federal states previously surveyed, as well as with the provisions of the Treaty of Rome.

4.4 AN INSTITUTIONAL PERSPECTIVE

In spite of the deficiencies of the *B.N.A. Act*, the ability of the federal authority to derogate from common market principles is constrained by the fact that Parliament emanates from a national constituency whose support any federal government must preserve in order to remain in office. Thus, discrimination on the basis of province or region of residence, location, origin and destination in federal laws, regulations and practices must be approved by a majority of the people's representatives in the House of Commons, and may therefore be deemed to be in the national interest. Political and public debates, as well as representations regularly made by all provinces on the relative "fairness" or "unfairness" of federal policies and programs, bear witness almost daily to the effectiveness of this constraint.

There is no comparable limitation upon the ability of provincial legislatures to discriminate on the same basis, since they are accountable only to the electorate of a single province. As a result, the effective operation of the Canadian economic union is perhaps unduly sensitive to the precise delineation of powers between the two orders of government, which in turn is largely dependent upon judicial interpretation. Thus, if a judicial decision appears to restrict the authority of Parliament with respect to interprovincial trade, there is automatically a possibility, given the absence of explicit constitutional principles governing the operation of the economic union, that provinces could use their legislative powers in a manner which would segment the Canadian market. Where self-interest governs the use of such powers, the only effective restraint upon provincial ability to do so is fear of retaliatory legislation by other provinces. Obviously, this restraint applies more forcefully to the smaller and economically weaker provinces.

While it must be recognized that enlightened self-interest has largely prevailed so far, one must consider whether this legal void should be allowed to persist. That the possibility of retaliatory discrimination at the provincial level is real has been exemplified recently by Nova Scotia's Bill 61, *An Act Respecting Petroleum Resources* providing under section 26(1)(f) that regulations may be made "respecting the nature and extent of employment of Nova Scotians by holders of petroleum rights and others performing work authorized by a petroleum right". This was largely prompted by Newfoundland's *Petroleum and Natural Gas Act*. Sub-section 124.1 of the regulations pursuant to that act provides that:

> "**124**(1) It is deemed to be a term of every permit or lease that a permittee or lessee shall give preference in his hiring practices to qualified residents of the province and shall purchase goods and services provided from within the province where competitive in terms of fair current market price, quality and delivery."

For the purpose of the above section, residence has been defined to mean residence in the province for three years prior to 1978 or for a period of ten years at any time.

An earlier example of retaliation occurred when the Province of Quebec adopted *The Quebec Construction Industry Labour Relations Act*. This act gives preference in employment to Quebec workers within 13 construction regions. While this measure might have been perfectly legitimate given the particular nature of employment in the construction industry, it had the effect not only of restricting mobility within the province but also of restricting the mobility of workers into Quebec, since no part of contiguous provinces is considered to be within a Quebec construction region. The Ontario Government introduced retaliatory legislation when it proved impossible to amend Quebec's regulations so that Ontario residents might be eligible to apply for classification on the same basis as Quebec workers. However, the legislation was allowed to die on the Order Paper.

A further consequence of this constitutional void may be noted. While the provisions of the *B.N.A. Act* regarding taxation powers and the regulation of trade and commerce limit somewhat the ability of the provinces to erect tax barriers to economic mobility, it leaves considerable scope for discriminatory tax treatment. Until recently, there had been relatively few cases of provinces using their tax systems in this way, but there are indications that this may be changing. For instance, there is legislation in Quebec and British Columbia which provides special tax credits for investment in provincially-domiciled corporations which are not extended for investment in other Canadian corporations. (British Columbia has not yet proclaimed its legislation.) Proliferation of such preferential tax provisions could easily lead to interprovincial competition which would raise provincial tax burdens and constrain the allocation of funds in the Canadian capital market. Moreover, this could aggravate regional economic disparities and raise difficult equity issues, since the more prosperous provinces would obviously have a greater capacity to escalate provincial tax preferences.

4.5 CONSTITUTIONAL PROPOSALS RELATED TO THE CANADIAN ECONOMIC UNION

The constitutional foundation of the Canadian economic union has been the subject of increasing attention in various constitutional studies and reports. Some of the main proposals in this regard are summarized in Annex B [p. 616].

Given the wide range of perspectives and views of the authors and sponsors of these reports, there is a striking degree of convergence in the importance which they attach to the maintenance of the economic union and to its constitutional safeguarding. This is typically sought by means of one or more of the following techniques: the entrenchment of mobility rights as a fundamental right accorded to individuals (or sometime citizens); a more general guarantee of a common market frequently expressed as ensuring the free movement of goods, services and capital; or a better delineation of trade and commerce and related powers.

When safeguarding is sought by the first technique the provision is often formulated to guarantee to individuals the right to settle, to earn a livelihood, to hold property in any province. Sometimes it is framed more generally, as in the report of the Committee on the Constitution of the Canadian Bar Association, as a guarantee that manpower may move freely without discrimination throughout the country. When the second technique is used, a broader range of guarantees are included, usually through revision to section 121 of the *B.N.A. Act*.

The most specific proposals come from the Committee on the Constitution of the Canadian Bar Association, the Task Force on Canadian Unity and the Constitutional Committee of the Quebec Liberal Party. Interestingly, the Committee of the Bar Association uses the terminology of international law to frame its proposal, referring specifically to duties, quantitative restrictions and measures of equivalent effect. The proposal of the Quebec Liberal Party, in addition to the above (with some derogations) would also extend coverage to enterprise, by securing the right of provincially-incorporated firms to do business in another province or to engage in activities under federal jurisdiction, on the condition that they respect provincial and federal laws of general application.

Several of the reports deal specifically with the *trade and commerce* power, and in particular note the direct relationship between this power and the effective functioning of the economic union. Accordingly, the general pattern is support for continued federal jurisdiction in matters of international and interprovincial trade and commerce, and for provincial control over intraprovincial trade and commerce. The Joint Committee of the Senate and the House of Commons (1972) recommended extension of the federal jurisdiction to include the "instrumentalities" of international and interprovincial trade. The Ontario Advisory Committee also seems to envisage extension of the federal jurisdiction, but would subject the exercise of the federal power to consultation with, but not veto by, the provinces through an improved intergovernmental discussion process. The Bar Association Committee would give Parliament additional power to harmonize intraprovincial trade upon a declaration of necessity supported by a 2/3 majority in a reconstituted Upper House. The Quebec Liberal Party's proposal would specify that the federal trade and commerce power extends to standards for products entering into international and interprovincial trade, but would subject federally-initiated marketing plans for agricultural products (both international and interprovincial) to provincial approval through the proposed Federal Council.

In addition, a number of other government activities are generally recognized in the constitutional studies reviewed as bearing on the operation of the economic union. A number of these, such as currency and banking and transportation, are generally considered central to the fulfillment of the economic responsibilities of the federal government. Others, including competition policy and securities regulation, are dealt with in varying ways. For example, The 1972 Report of the Special Joint Committee of the Senate and the House of Commons recommends that for both of these fields there be concurrent powers with federal paramountcy, while the Constitutional Committee of the Quebec Liberal Party and the Ontario Advisory Committee propose that competition be federal and securities provincial.

5. GENERAL APPROACH

In the light of the above observations, the Government of Canada is of the view that there are compelling reasons for securing in the Constitution of Canada the basic operational rules of our economic union and for ensuring that both orders of government abide by these rules. Affirmation of the rights inherent to Canadian citizenship demands it. Prudence and faith in our common destiny require it. Economic theory and experience prescribe it. Precedents, in both international and constitutional law, commend it.

The Federal Government is also of the view that the following considerations should be borne in mind in devising the appropriate means of achieving these goals.

The determination of what rules should be constitutionalized and how this could best be done requires careful consideration. Three complementary techniques could be used:

(i) entrenching in the Constitution the mobility rights of citizens, as well as their right to gain a livelihood and acquire property in any province, regardless of their province of residence or previous residence, subject to laws of general application;

(ii) placing limitations upon the ability of governments to use their legislative and executive powers to impede economic mobility by way of general provisions through the revision and expansion of Section 121 of the *B.N.A. Act*;

(iii) broadening federal powers so that they may encompass all matters which are necessary for economic integration, thus ensuring that the relevant laws and regulations will apply uniformly throughout Canada, or that the "test" of the public interest will be brought to bear upon derogations from uniformity.

Prescriptions which would be too detailed would run the risk of being circumvented, or of preventing governments from adapting their laws and regulations to changing circumstances. Moreover, sweeping general provisions like those of the Australian Constitution, or attribution to the federal authority of virtually all-encompassing jurisdiction, as seems to be the case in the Federal Republic of Germany and India, would not be suitable for Canada.

While theoretical requirements for economic union are an essential reference point, absolute freedom of movement for goods, services and factors of production is neither attainable nor desirable in the real world. Economic efficiency is not the only goal pursued by governments, and the maximization of economic integration does not necessarily lead to a social optimum. Therefore, provisions to secure the Canadian economic union will have to allow governments to pursue other social and *economic* goals, such as redistribution of income and wealth among citizens and the fostering of economic development in lagging areas of the country.

The constitutional securing of absolute economic mobility within Canada would obviously be incompatible with the maintenance of a federal system. The recognition of distinct political entities within the Federation is predicated upon the existence, and continued existence, of different economic, social and cultural aspirations among the various populations they serve. Consequently, provincial legislation and regulations must be capable of variation from province to province, and such variation will inevitably cause some impediments to economic mobility; but these must be kept within the bounds of necessity.

The political dynamics of the Canadian Federation have always required some compromise between the optimal *aménagement* of national markets and the search for an equitable distribution of economic benefits among the various regions of the country. While this is essentially the responsibility of the federal government, it has become customary, under our present constitution, for provincial authorities to use their powers to affect the trade-offs between these two broad goals *within* the territory under their jurisdiction. These trade-offs should continue to be possible.

Trade-offs between these goals are not without cost, however, and the choice of means to implement them is not a matter of indifference. As previously noted, protectionism among provinces is not an economically neutral way of redistributing economic activity among provinces: it can involve significant efficiency losses for Canada as a whole, and hence for each and every one of its parts. It should also be noted that costs can result from injudicious use of the federal government's virtually unrestrained ability, under the present Constitution, to derogate from principles of economic union in areas under its jurisdiction.

A critical requirement to secure constitutionally the Canadian economic union, therefore, is the prohibition of discrimination in relevant laws, regulations and practices on the basis of the province of residence of persons subject to them and of the province of location, origin and destination of the matters they affect, except in special circumstances when such discrimination is deemed in the public interest. This could be achieved by the first and second techniques mentioned above.

Other unwarranted obstacles to economic mobility within Canada should be dealt with through the exercise of federal regulatory powers. In this respect, the strengthening of our economic union may require a better delineation and some broadening of Parliament's jurisdiction over trade and commerce.

Still other undesirable impediments to mobility which may arise from the exercise of federal or provincial jurisdiction would be best dealt with through political and administrative arrangements between the two orders of government, which can be tailored to particular situations and adapted to changing circumstances. Thus, the management of the Canadian economic union has institutional implications which governments should bear in mind in their discussion of other aspects of constitutional renewal, such as intergovernmental relations, legislative delegation and a possible reconstitution of the Senate.

The Federal Government proposes that governments immediately consider how the three complementary techniques mentioned above could be used to better secure in the Constitution the existence and operation of the Canadian economic union, without prejudice to other proposals which they might wish to make at a later stage regarding the division of powers affecting the economy.

6. CONCLUSION

The Government of Canada has little doubt that agreement in principle will be reached on the strengthening and safeguarding the economic union, since all governments are committed to the preservation of the Canadian economic union. Discussions are of course required to determine the full constitutional implications of this fundamental goal, and to establish by what means it could best be achieved. Needless to say, the Federal Government is not wedded to any particular suggestion or proposal advanced in this document, and is prepared to consider alternative views and approaches which other governments may put forward. But it is firmly convinced that any constitutional renewal which did not adequately safeguard the economic foundations of our Federation would fail to meet the expectations of Canadians.

In this respect, there are serious deficiencies in the Constitution of Canada. Our basic law lags behind that of other federations. Our constitutional statutes do not even embody principles enshrined in international law and by which sovereign states have accepted to be bound. The correction of these deficiencies is an essential element of our agenda for change.

Canada is of course much more than an economic union. But Canada's political integrity, cultural development and social progress would be grievously compromised if its governments failed to secure its future economic prosperity. Thus it was that, a century ago, the Fathers of Confederation founded a federal union which enabled all parts of the country to reap the benefits of virtually unprecedented economic growth by world standards. And thus it is today that we, their spiritual heirs and political successors, must review and improve on their considerable accomplishment, so that Canada may successfully meet the economic challenges of the next century.

● ● ●

ANNEX B
SUMMARY OF CONSTITUTIONAL PROPOSALS RELATED TO ECONOMIC MOBILITY WITHIN CANADA*

Proposal	Mobility Rights	Movement of goods, services and capital	Trade and Commerce	Indirect Taxation
1. Working Documents submitted by the Quebec Delegation to the Continuing Committee of Officials on the Constitution, July 1968	Unrestricted movement of persons within the Union should be guaranteed by the Constitution	Unrestricted movement of goods within the Union should be guaranteed by the Constitution	International trade should be an exclusive federal power	Allow indirect taxation by provinces, with the exception of customs revenue
2. Special Joint Committee of the Senate and of the House Commons, 1972			Parliament should have exclusive jurisdiction over international and interprovincial trade, including the instrumentalities of such power. Intraprovincial trade should remain with the provinces	Allow provincial indirect taxation except that it should not impede international and interprovincial trade and not fall on persons resident in other provinces
3. Canada West Foundation: Update, March, 1978				Allow provinces indirect taxation within the province for provincial purposes. Assumes federal trade and commerce power would prevent provinces from establishing customs duties
4. The Constitutional Amendment Bill, June, 1978	Right to move and take up residence in any province and to equal protection of the law regardless of place of residence Right to acquire property and to pursue gaining of a livelihood in any province			

	Mobility	Goods and services	Trade and commerce	Taxation
5. British Columbia's Constitutional Proposal, September, 1978				Provincial access to indirect taxation except customs and excise taxes. However, every effort must be made to prevent such taxes from creating artificial economic barriers in restraint of commerce
6. Harmony in Diversity: Alberta Government, October, 1978			Federal powers over trade and commerce should not render ineffective provincial jurisdiction and control over their natural resources	Allow provinces access to indirect taxes, except customs duties
7. Committee on the Constitution, The Canadian Bar Association, 1978	That manpower may move freely without discrimination throughout the country	Goods, services and capital in any province shall be admitted to each of the other provinces free of duties, quantitative restrictions or measures of equivalent effect except as may be necessary for health and safety	Federal Parliament have exclusive jurisdiction to regulate interprovincial and international commerce and the provinces have exclusive jurisdiction to regulate intraprovincial commerce. Federal Parliament should have power to harmonize intraprovincial trade upon a declaration of necessity but only after obtaining a 2/3 majority in the reconstituted Upper House	Allow provinces indirect taxation except customs duties and taxes which have a tendency to be automatically passed to persons outside the province Neither the federal Parliament nor provinces should be able to levy taxes which create barriers to interprovincial trade

*Note: In addition to the four general categories of provisions directly related to economic mobility listed in the table, a number of other government activities are recognized in constitutional reports as bearing on the nature of the economic union. These include matters such as currency and banking, the external tariff, competition policy, securities regulation and transportation.

ANNEX B (contd.)

Proposal	Mobility Rights	Movement of goods, services and capital	Trade and Commerce	Indirect Taxation
8. Task Force on Canadian Unity, February, 1979	Impediments to mobility of persons in professions, trades etc. should be reduced by application of widely accepted common standards	Guarantee more effectively free trade between the provinces for produce, manufactured goods and services Procurement policies should be based on market costs unless specified social and economic objectives would be otherwise served Prohibit barriers to interprovincial movement of capital		Allow provinces indirect taxation except customs and excise taxes. Provincial indirect taxes should not fall on persons outside the province
9. Ontario's Second Report of the Advisory Committee on Confederation, March, 1979		Entrench a "freedom of movement of people, capital, goods and information" in the Constitution. Provision should be carefully drafted so as not to invalidate provincial legislation with an incidental and minor effect on movement	Federal primacy in interprovincial and international trade subject to consultation with, but not any veto by, the provinces	Provincial access to all modes of taxation, subject to the proviso that no provincial tax shall be imposed on residents of another province

10. Constitutional Committee of the Quebec Liberal Party, 1980	Right of each Canadian to settle anywhere and to enjoy rights identical to those of the citizens of the province where he settles	Guarantee the free circulation of goods and capital subject to provincial right to (a) adopt general laws of a non-discriminatory nature (b) regulate investments of certain financial institutions (c) pass laws relative to health, public safety and professions A provincial company should be allowed to do business in another province subject to respecting laws of general application	Central jurisdiction over international and interprovincial trade, including the standardizing of products destined for such trade	Allow provinces indirect taxation except tariffs and customs duties Imposition by provinces of tariff measures in any form whatsoever should be prohibited

Note: In addition to the four general categories of provisions directly related to economic mobility listed in the table, a number of other government activities are recognized in constitutional reports as bearing on the nature of the economic union. These include matters such as currency and banking, the external tariff, competition policy, securities regulation and transportation.

(d) Report to Ministers of the Sub-Committee of Officials on Equalization, July 9, 1980

Document: 830-81/056

The Committee heard the three changes to the Best Efforts Draft proposed by the Government of Quebec.

The changes are as follows:—

1) the deletion from Section 96(1)(b) of the best efforts draft of the words "for social and economic well-being";

2) the word "province" in 96(2) of the draft would be changed to "provincial governments" so that the section would read "Making equalization payments to provincial governments . . .";

3) the deletion of the last clause of Section 96(2) beginning with the words "or to the principle . . ."

The proposed changes received the support of all provinces except British Columbia which reserved its position. Some noted that these changes may make it more difficult to meet the reservations of British Columbia.

Since changes were being suggested, other provinces took the occasion to propose further changes, more particularly with respect to Section 96(2) of the best efforts draft.

Manitoba and Saskatchewan proposed that Section 96(2) be re-worded to read:—

"Parliament and the Government of Canada are further committed to the principle of making equalization payments to ensure that provincial governments have sufficient revenues to provide reasonably comparable levels of public services at reasonably comparable levels of taxation."

These changes as proposed by Manitoba and Saskatchewan were also supported by Prince Edward Island, New Brunswick, Nova Scotia and Quebec; Newfoundland and Ontario reserved their positions, and British Columbia, Alberta, and the Federal Government were opposed.

Gérard Veilleux
Chairman

DRAFT PROPOSAL DISCUSSED BY FIRST MINISTERS

Equalization and Regional Developments

"**96.**(1) Without altering the legislative authority of Parliament or of the legislatures or of the rights of any of them with respect to the exercise of their legislative authority, Parliament and the legislatures, together with the Government of Canada and the Governments of the Provinces, are committed to

(a) promoting equal opportunities for the well-being of Canadians;

(b) furthering economic development to reduce disparity in opportunities for social and economic well-being; and,

(c) providing essential public services of reasonable quality to all Canadians.

(2) Parliament and the Government of Canada are further committed to the principle of making equalization payments to provinces that are unable to provide essential public services of reasonable quality without imposing an undue burden of taxation, or to the principle of making arrangements equivalent to equalization payments to meet the commitment specified in Section 96(1)(c)."

(3) The Prime Minister of Canada and the First Ministers of the Provinces shall review together the questions of equalization and regional development at least once every five years at a meeting convened pursuant to section 97.

38. Continuing Committee of Ministers on the Constitution, Toronto, Ontario, July 14–18, 1980

(a) Powers Over the Economy: Options Submitted for Consideration by the Government of Canada to Safeguard the Canadian Economic Union in the Constitution

Document: 830-82/077

In a Discussion Paper submitted to the Continuing Committee of Ministers on the Constitution on July 9, 1980[1], the Government of Canada outlined three techniques which could be used to safeguard the Canadian economic union in the Constitution:

(i) entrenching the mobility rights of citizens in the proposed Charter of Rights;

(ii) subjecting the exercise of legislative and executive powers to the provisions of a revised Section 121 of the *B.N.A. Act*;

(iii) clarifying and, to a limited extent, broadening the federal trade and commerce power.

Federal proposals regarding mobility rights of citizens are contained in Section 8 of the proposed *Canadian Charter of Rights and Freedoms* tabled on July 10, 1980. A copy of that section is attached. Legislative drafts tabled today, and also attached, outline a manner in which the other two techniques might be implemented.

A NEW SECTION 121

The existing Section 121 of the *B.N.A. Act* prohibits only the imposition of border taxes (e.g., customs duties) within Canada. Therefore, it establishes only a customs union and does not constitute an adequate foundation for the Canadian economic union.

The new draft submitted for consideration by the federal government would secure in the Constitution an essential operating principle for economic union, namely the principle of non-discrimination in law or practice on the basis of the province of residence of persons, and the province of origin or destination of goods, services and capital. The draft would apply to both orders of government, not only to the provinces.

The new Section 121 would not seek to prohibit all possible impediments to economic mobility, since the federal government recognizes that the Canadian Federation has other goals — political, social, cultural, as well as economic — the pursuit of which must not be restricted by too sweeping provisions regarding economic mobility. Accordingly, the suggested legislative text would provide for exceptions, so that the principle of non-discrimination would be applied in a flexible manner.

Thus, the new provisions would not prevent affirmative action programs, regional development policies, industrial incentives, income redistribution, etc. For example, it would be absurd that the Constitution should prevent the federal government from introducing measures such as the National Oil Policy put in place in the early 1960's, to facilitate the development of Western Canada's oil resources while allowing Quebec and the Atlantic provinces to obtain lower priced oil from foreign sources. Similarly, provincial governments should not be prevented from implementing differentiated policies and programs to meet the special needs of various areas and communities within a province.

THE TRADE AND COMMERCE POWER

In general terms, the federal trade and commerce power has been interpreted as applying only to international and interprovincial movement of goods. It is not certain to what extent it applies to services and capital. The suggested draft of Section 91(2) of the *B.N.A. Act* annexed to

---

[1]*Powers Over the Economy: Securing the Canadian Economic Union in the Constitution*, July 9, 1980, CCMC Document 830–81/036.

this document and submitted for consideration would make clear that the federal trade and commerce power does apply to such matters. The draft would also provide for the regulation of competition and product standards throughout Canada to the extent reasonably necessary for the operation of the Canadian economic union.

The Government of Canada is not wedded to the particular options it has advanced for safeguarding the Canadian economic union in the Constitution and is prepared to consider other options which may be put forward. But it is convinced that the constitutional safeguarding of the Canadian economic union must be achieved.

ANNEX A
MOBILITY RIGHTS
(Extract from Canadian Charter of Rights and Freedoms)

Rights of citizens	**8.** (1) Every citizen of Canada has the right to enter, remain in and leave Canada.

Rights of citizens and persons lawfully admitted for permanent residence	(2) Every citizen of Canada and every person who has been lawfully admitted to Canada for permanent residence and has not lost the status of a permanent resident has the right
	    (a) to move to and take up residence in any province or territory, and
	    (b) to acquire and hold property in, and to pursue the gaining of a livelihood in, any province or territory,
	subject to any laws of general application in force in that province or territory other than any such laws that discriminate among persons to whom this provision applies primarily on the basis of province or territory of present or previous residence or domicile.

Justifiable limitations	(3) The rights declared by this section may be made subject only to such limitations prescribed by law as are reasonably justifiable in a free and democratic society in the interests of national security, public safety, order, health or morals.

ANNEX B
DRAFT (JULY 16, 1980)

Canadian economic union	**121.** (1) Neither Canada nor a province shall by law or practice discriminate in a manner that unduly impedes the operation of the Canadian economic union, directly or indirectly, on the basis of the province or territory of residence or former residence of a person, on the basis of the province or territory of origin or destination of goods, services or capital or on the basis of the province or territory into which or from which goods, services or capital are imported or exported.
Derogation	(2) Nothing in subsection (1) renders invalid a law of Parliament or of a legislature enacted in the interests of public safety, order, health or morals.
Idem	(3) Nothing in subsection (1) renders invalid a law of Parliament enacted pursuant to the principles of equalization and regional development to which Parliament and the legislatures are committed or declared by Parliament to be in an overriding national interest or enacted pursuant to an international obligation undertaken by Canada.
Customs union	(4) Nothing in subsection (2) or (3) renders valid a law of Parliament or a legislature that impedes the admission free into any province of goods, services or capital originating in or imported into any other province or territory.

ANNEX C
DRAFT (JULY 6, 1980)

91. 2. The regulation of trade and commerce in goods, services and capital.

2.1. The regulation of competition throughout Canada and the establishment of product standards applicable throughout Canada where such regulation or such standards are reasonably necessary for the operation of the Canadian economic union.

ANNEX D
EXPLANATORY NOTES (JULY 16, 1980)

SECTION 121

Section 121 of the *British North America Act, 1867* provides:

> "All Articles of the Growth, Produce, or Manufacture of any one of the Provinces shall, from and after the Union, be admitted free into each of the other Provinces."

This section only applies to the interprovincial movement of goods, and only those originating in a province of Canada. It is not clear that it prohibits barriers other than interprovincial customs duties.

The new subsection 121 (1) would expand this section to prevent federal and provincial governments creating barriers to interprovincial trade either by law or through discriminatory practices. Discrimination would be clearly prevented not only with respect to the movement of goods but also with respect to the provision of services and with respect to the investment, transfer or disposition of capital. It would also cover barriers other than tariff barriers, if they would "unduly" impede movement. (That is, measures that might have minor effects on free movement would not be prevented.)

Subsection (2) allows both Parliament and the provincial legislatures to enact legislation restricting free movement where such legislation is required for purposes of public safety, public order, public health or public morals. Such restrictions to be valid would have to be imposed by statute and not merely be effected through administrative practices.

Subsection (3) allows Parliament to enact legislation restricting free movement where required to serve regional development purposes including the making of equalization payments or in order to fulfill an international obligation.

In addition, Parliament can restrict free movement where it determines this to be necessary to serve an overriding national interest, but it would have to state expressly in its legislation the interest being served.

Subsection (4) provides that derogations may not create customs barriers at provincial borders. This preserves the present prohibition in section 121 against interprovincial customs barriers with respect to goods and ensures that it applies to services and capital as well.

SECTION 91

Section 91 of the *British North American Act, 1867* provides:

> "It shall be lawful for the Queen, by and with the Advice and Consent of the Senate and House of Commons, to make Laws for the Peace, Order, and good Government of Canada, in relation to all Matters not coming within the Classes of Subjects by this Act assigned exclusively to the Legislatures of the Provinces; and for greater Certainty, but not so as to restrict the Generality of the foregoing Terms of this Section, it is hereby declared that (notwithstanding anything in this Act) the exclusive Legislative Authority of the Parliament of Canada extends to all Matters coming within the Classes of Subjects next hereinafter enumerated; that is to say, —
>
> . . . .
>
> 2. The Regulation of Trade and Commerce."

The new head of federal power 91 2 would make it completely clear that federal jurisdiction over trade and commerce includes the regulation of services and capital as well as of physical commodities.

The new head 2.1 is designed to remedy two specific gaps in existing federal authority over trade and commerce. This provision would make it clear that Parliament can legislate to regulate competition and it would enable Parliament to regulate product standards to the extent necessary for the operation of the Canadian economic union. While Parliament regulates competition now, it does so through the exercise of its jurisdiction over criminal law.

The amended section would give Parliament direct authority in this regard. Two recent decisions of the Supreme Court of Canada have brought into serious question the authority of Parliament to establish minimum food standards applicable to products sold across the country, particularly with respect to that portion of such products sold in the province of production. The proposed amendment would clarify Parliament's authority with respect to products standards generally where some of the product is sold outside the province of production.

(b) Report of the Committee of Officials on the Preamble/Principles of a Constitution

Document: 830-82/013

The Committee, established on July 9 by the CCMC, met on July 15 and 16, 1980. All governments were represented.

The Chairman, an official of the Government of Canada, referring to the opening statement on this item by the Hon. Jean Chretien at the CCMC's plenary session on July 9, proposed that the meeting discuss what subjects or items should be covered in a preamble to a new Constitution. He stressed that the meeting would not be intended to do any drafting at this time or, indeed, to consider any drafts.

Representatives from some provinces indicated that they were prepared to proceed on this basis. Most provincial representatives, however, expressed the view that, in the absence of Ministerial direction, it would be premature to suggest subjects for possible inclusion in a Preamble until there was a clearer view of the likely scope of constitutional change. Some of those representatives were of the view that no sustained work would be feasible in regard to the Preamble until the changes to be made to the Constitution were virtually or fully agreed.

After discussion there was a general understanding that items might be listed for possible inclusion in a preamble or in a statement of aims for use in the event that either a preamble or statement were proceeded with.

On this basis, the following themes or subjects were suggested by representatives of one or more governments.

A — *Framework or Organizing Themes*

1. Statement of who we are as people

2. Statement of values we hold in common

3. Statement of institutions and rights we have, or would have, to express and protect these values.

B — *Specific Subjects*

1. The notion that the "people" are involved in the process, perhaps even a principal source of sovereignty, e.g. "we, the people of Canada . . ."
"we, the diverse peoples of Canada . . ."
(It was noted that this would be a significant departure from the preamble to the BNA Act.)

2. References to the origins of the people (Historical and possibly specific)

(There was also a view that there should be no precise historical references to origins, on the grounds that these inevitably invited recrimination and criticism.)

3. References to the descendants of the original peoples (or to the native peoples)

4. The idea of "nations" or "communities"
(Opposition was also expressed to references to "nations".)

5. Self-determination of provinces
(There was also a recommendation that there be no such reference.)

6. Dualism in Canada
(There was also an explicit recommendation that dualism not be referred to.)

7. Reference to the help or protection of the Almighty

8. Reference to the confidence with which we face the future

9. Reference to the diversity of Canada, of its people and of its cultures

10. Reference to the goals of harmony among Canadians, and of the unity of Canada

11. References to theme of conservation, to the careful stewardship of natural resources and to the development of human skills.
(Strong concern was also voiced in regard to the nature of possible references to resources.)

12. References to the physical beauty, magnitude and diversity of Canada

13. References to the protection of the natural environment, in trust for future generations

14. Reference to the rule of law and to justice

15. In regard to rights and freedoms:
    a) a specific reference to the Universal Declaration of Human Rights
    b) the dignity and worth of individuals
    c) freedoms, including free association and other basic civil, human and language rights
    d) non-discrimination and equality of sex, race, colour and creed
    e) if a Charter of Rights and Freedoms is entrenched

in the Constitution, the references to rights should be brief or confined to a reference to the Charter itself; if there were no entrenchment, views ranged from the suggestion that the references should be more extensive to the recommendation that there be no references.

(N.B. There was also a view that at this stage "freedom" should not be listed.)

16. References to federalism, the federation and/or the federal system — possibly extensive

17. Reference to constitutional monarchy

18. Reference to the Parliamentary system and institutions

19. Reference to democracy or democratic system or institutions
(A caution was also expressed in regard to "democracy" as a misleading concept.)

20. References to sharing of wealth, riches and cultures
(A caution was expressed with regard to the sharing of wealth and riches.)

21. References to equity — equalization — and the suggestion that such references could be brief if a provision in regard to equalization were included in the Constitution

22. Reference to the Canadian Economic Union, or Common Market, to economic co-operation or solidarity

23. Reference to Canada's international role and responsibilities, e.g. in regard to peace and justice
(There was also a view that there should be no such reference)

24. No reference, or implied and explicit references to Patriation of the Constitution.

25. Reference to French and English as official languages of Canada

26. Reference to provinces, to regions and to the Government of Canada

27. References to the similarity in principle of the Canadian and United Kingdom constitutions (cf. Preamble of the BNA Act)

In suggesting items for this list, it was understood that the participants were not assigning agreed weights or priorities to or among the items, or indeed agreeing to the inclusion of any particular item mentioned in an eventual preamble or statement of aims.

Some participants were opposed to "inspirational" preambles and others were against lengthy preambles. Others favoured the idea of an inspirational preamble.

Concern was expressed by some representatives as to the use to which a preamble might be put by the courts.

At the request of some provincial representatives, copies of the federal draft statement of principles of June 10, 1980 and of the Preamble and Statement of Aims in Bill C-60 were made available. In addition, the Ontario representatives distributed a "staff discussion draft" of a Preamble, dated 1980.

N.R.J. Gwyn,
Chairman

NRJG/cd

(c) Report of the Committee of Officials on the Senate, July 17, 1980

Document: 830-82/017

The Committee of Officials on the Senate met twice on July 16th and once again on July 17. The Committee had for consideration a Ministerial Document entitled "Points of a Senate Consensus". A copy of the Document is annexed to this Report.

The Committee decided to proceed on the basis of the Ministerial Document according to which there is a need for a new second chamber (Point 1) and that it not be an elected body (Point 2). It was agreed that debate should focus initially on Point 6 (power to ratify certain federal actions and the possibility of establishing a category of suspensive powers).

During discussion of Point 6, it became apparent that several of the various delegations held views that were based upon distinct approaches to the question of Upper House reform; that the approaches were quite different; and that the different approaches were all compatible with the broad lines of the "Points of a Senate Consensus".

Four distinct "models" for Upper House reform were isolated for the purposes of discussion. The four "models" were based upon a consideration of what should be the principal purposes of an "Upper House" in the Canadian federation.

Model I

According to this model, the traditional function of the Upper House of providing review for all or most legislation emanating from the Commons should be maintained, with powers of absolute or suspensive veto, but the members of the Upper House should be appointed solely, primarily or on a 50% basis by the provinces. Members appointed by the provinces would be representatives of the provinces, but they would not be delegates voting on instruction by provincial governments.

Model II

According to this model, the "Upper House" should be an institution for ratifying federal action, dealing only with a limited list of specified matters of shared federal-provincial concern. Voting members would be solely or primarily provincial delegates voting on government instruction. Such an institution would not have the additional general power to review legislation within federal jurisdiction, but could have an advisory function.

Model III

This model would combine the main features of Model I and Model II. Membership would be provided solely, primarily or on a 50% basis by provincial governments, and each provincial delegation would include a Cabinet Minister. On a limited list of specified matters of shared federal-provincial concern, each provincial Cabinet Minister would cast a block vote for the province. On all other matters subject to Upper House review, members would be free to vote as they saw fit.

Model IV

During discussion, a fourth approach emerged for consideration. This approach would involve two distinct institutions: a version of Model I to serve as the new Upper House and a version of Model II to serve as a new intergovernmental institution.

In discussion, some governments noted that a final position on the new Upper House would be related to any redistribution of powers.

The Committee agreed that, in Vancouver, it would address itself to matters such as method of selection, representation and powers.

The Committee draws to the attention of Ministers that three of the four models identify a function of general review, and three of the four models identify a function of ratification of federal action on a limited list of specified matters of shared federal-provincial concern.

The Committee seeks instruction from Ministers as to whether they wish only one or both of these functions to be performed by a new or reconstituted body or bodies.

Edward Greathed
Chairman

Attachment

APPENDIX A
COMMITTEE REPORT
MINISTERIAL DOCUMENT
POINTS OF A SENATE CONSENSUS

In private discussion, the Ministers arrived at the following points of a Senate consensus:

1. on the need for a new second chamber.
2. that the new second chamber not be an elected body.
3. that it be composed of provincial representatives but that consideration be given to the possibility of federal representatives at the same time that the role and powers of the second chamber are discussed.
4. that on representation:
   a) a majority wanted equal representation on a province by province basis
   b) some wanted a weighted representation based on an undetermined number per region, using four regions as a basis
   c) one province wanted equal representation from five regions
   d) two reserved their position.
5. that the new upper chamber could possibly, but not necessarily, be a substitute for some of the regular federal-provincial mechanisms.
6. that the new chamber have the power to ratify federal actions in such areas as:
   a) declaratory power
   b) federal spending power
   c) amendments to the Constitution
   d) other powers as contained in the British Columbia proposal

   and, that there was a willingness to discuss further the establishment of another category of suspensive powers.

This consensus is to be used as a basis for discussion, after governments have given it further consideration.

(d) Report of the Committee of Officials on Fisheries, July 17, 1980

Document: 830-82/016

The Committee has heard and discussed the positions expressed by each of the governments and tried to develop consensus, particularly on three aspects of the legislative jurisdiction concerning fisheries. The "modus operandi" was to have both federal-provincial and interprovincial meetings.

Regarding the *inland fisheries*, the representatives of the ten provincial governments agreed that there should be "exclusive provincial jurisdiction in the matter of inland fisheries except for "diadromous"* species where there would be concurrent jurisdiction, with federal paramountcy for international relations and quotas to provinces."

Regarding *marine plants and sedentary species*, the representatives of the ten provincial governments agreed that there should be "exclusive provincial jurisdiction over aquaculture in tidal and non tidal zones, marine plants and sedentary species such as oysters, clams and mussels. However, the discussion of the delineation of the seaward extension for provincial responsibility has not been completed.

On these two questions, the federal representatives stated "a willingness to consider a transfer of constitutional powers to the provinces in the field of inland fisheries subject to an exception with respect to salmon and other "diadromous" species and appropriate provision for the protection of the environment and native rights. Similarly constitutional change could be considered with respect to aquaculture and selected estuarine and inter tidal species."

Regarding the *sea coast fisheries*, a variety of positions have been expressed by governments. In response to an expression by the federal side of a willingness "to consider proposals which have achieved a broad inter-provincial consensus", the provincial delegates have devoted a considerable portion of the time to defining the degree of the consensus which exists. It is possible to report that most of the provinces support the fundamental proposition that there should be a concurrent jurisdiction in this area.

Particular attention was paid to an examination of the proposal of Newfoundland for concurrent jurisdiction with federal or provincial paramountcy for different aspects of the question. Three provinces have expressed an objection to certain aspects of this proposal. These are coastal provinces. Two of them want concurrent powers with a federal paramountcy while the other province does not favour concurrent powers but prefers to see exclusive federal jurisdiction.

On this matter, the federal representatives indicated that they intend to recommend to federal ministers that they consult with fishermen and the fishing industry on any consensus among the provinces for constitutional change.

With respect to sea coast fisheries, the federal position was, "that no change in legislative jurisdiction is necessary or desirable, having regard in particular to the realities of the fishery, and the interprovincial and international aspects of fisheries management. In the federal view, concurrent legislative jurisdiction would introduce unnecessary complexity into the field, would not necessarily achieve the objective of improved federal-provincial cooperation, and would not be in the best interests of fishermen or fish processors. However, noting that many provinces had expressed a desire for more meaningful consultative procedures, the federal delegation indicated that it was prepared to consider legal mechanisms achieving this objective. It appeared to the federal delegation that there was a wide variety of proposals from the various provinces and that no consensus on a specific approach with respect to coastal fisheries had developed."

The Committee recommends that it continue its deliberations in Vancouver next week.

A number of papers presented to the Committee are appended.

NEWFOUNDLAND SUGGESTED B.N.A. ACT AMENDMENT ON FISHERIES, JULY, 1980

Document: 830-81/022

(a) Section 91(12) of the British North America Act should be repealed.

---

* diadromous species — species such as salmon and eels which spend part of their life cycle in both fresh and salt water

(b) The enactment of a separate section in the British North America Act in the following terms:

"**95A.** (1) With respect to fish stocks adjacent to each province (as defined in subsection (5) below), the Legislature may make laws relative to the sea coast (and inland)* fisheries but any law covering those matters set out in subsection (3) shall have effect in and for the province so long as they are not repugnant to any Act of the Parliament of Canada made under subsection (2).

(2) The Parliament of Canada may make laws relative to the sea coast (and inland)* fisheries but any law covering those matters set out in subsection (4) shall have effect in and for any or all of the provinces so long as they are not repugnant to any Act of the Legislature of a province made under subsection (1).

(3) The matters referred to in subsection (1) are:
(a) fixing standards for and implementing different areas of scientific and other forms of research;
(b) fixing parameters for the total allowable catch for stocks;
(c) the allocation of quotas to foreign countries and the licensing of foreign vessels, subject to 4 (a) below;
(d) inspection for export;
(e) conservation of fish stocks;
(f) matters incidental or pertaining to the foregoing.

(4) The matters referred to in sub-section (2) are:
(a) fixing the level of catch within the parameters referred to in subsection (3)(b) and the issuance of quotas up to the level so fixed, including a cumulative quota to the government of Canada for allocation by it to foreign countries;
(b) licensing of fishing vessels other than foreign vessels taking fish from the residual quota;
(c) all matters not referred to in this sub-section and sub-section (3).

5. (a) The delineation of the fish stocks adjacent to each Province shall, as between Provinces which traditionally have fished these stocks, be determined by agreement between the Provinces in accordance with equitable principles taking account of all relevant information relating to traditional fishing patterns.

(b) If no agreement can be reached within a reasonable period of time, the Provinces concerned shall refer the particular matter in dispute for expeditious and final determination by a Review Board equitably constituted by the said Provinces based upon the fishing patterns referred to in paragraph (a).

* Possible deletion

NEWFOUNDLAND SUGGESTED B.N.A. ACT AMENDMENT ON FISHERIES, JULY, 1980

Document: 830-82/008

EXPLANATORY NOTES TO DOCUMENT 830-81/022 [see above]

Section 4 (a) Management of the fishery would continue on a stock and species basis. Fishermen would be licenced by their respective province to fish the provincial quota of any stock allocated to that province.

Section 4 (b) Should a province decide not to fish its quota in any given year, it may upon the advice of the provinces involved license vessels from other provinces to fish its residual quota.

Harvesting plans would be developed jointly between the provinces involved where more than one province has an allocation from a fish stock. In case of failure to agree, the matter would be referred to the Review Board.

PRINCE EDWARD ISLAND POSITION ON FISHERIES

Document: 830-82/011

Position — Put fisheries into Section 95 as a concurrent jurisdictional area.

Rationale — 1. To acknowledge the legitimate provincial role in fisheries without losing the benefit of common regulation from the Federal level.
2. To encourage meaningful joint consultations.
3. Is based on established constitutional practice.

Prince Edward Island recognizes that the subject of fisheries is one which by its very nature extends beyond the interests of a single province. It therefore requires a strong federal authority in allocating quotas, licensing participation etc. There is no question then that the federal government ought to enjoy legislative paramountcy over areas of common concern between the provinces.

However, since the provinces have a strong interest in most of these matters, especially as they relate to fisheries development and marketing, a role must be recognized for provincial action in this area provided it is not repugnant to laws of the Parliament of Canada. Since we think a definitive list of *exclusive* jurisdictional areas would be difficult to arrive at and since concurrency already exists in our constitution in agriculture and immigration under section 95, we would argue that fisheries should be similarly treated.

We think that there should be enshrined in the Constitution a Federal obligation to protect the fisheries and an equitable right of access by coastal Provinces as a matter of principle.

(e) Report of the Sub-Committee on Family Law, July 17, 1980

Document: 830-82/018

Your sub-committee has met in three sessions during the course of this week and has been working from the "Best Effort" draft.

Our concern in the most recent round of discussions of your officials has been to come to grips with the perceived problems inherent in the draft with respect to the enforcement of maintenance and custody orders in the event, contemplated by the draft, that legislative jurisdiction in these matters be passed to the provinces exclusively.

Our discussions were focussed around a position paper submitted by the Manitoba delegation and supported by the Prince Edward Island delegation which, in result, would be a rejection of the "Best Effort" draft on two essential points. The Manitoba position is best summarized by their wording of two recommendations in the following form:

1. The present federal jurisdiction with respect to divorce be retained.

2. Federal jurisdiction be expanded with additional concurrent and paramount jurisdiction to deal with the monitoring and enforcement of all custody and maintenance orders issued pursuant to either federal or provincial legislation.

By a vote of nine to two, with Manitoba and Prince Edward Island contra, your officials have rejected the Manitoba proposals, 1 and 2, and have reaffirmed their support of the "Best Effort" draft approach.

Although arriving at this position, your officials are keenly aware of the criticisms that have been levied against the perceived implications of the "Best Effort" draft in the area of custody and maintenance order enforcement. We are also aware of the deficiencies under the existing law, of enforcement, both at the federal and provincial level. Consequently, we devoted considerable time to exploring the possibility of devising another solution to the enforcement problem. In the time available we were not able to complete our task and beg leave to be permitted to pursue this matter in the meeting to be reconvened in Vancouver next week.

The Manitoba paper also recommends that:

3. Provincial jurisdiction be expanded to appoint judges with jurisdiction to deal with all matters that relate to Family Law to facilitate the establishment of a Unified Family Court system.

The officials of all eleven jurisdictions support the adoption of proposal 3.

At the request of the federal officials your sub-committee was asked to consider the possibility and advisability of amending "Best Effort" draft in order to reserve to Parliament exclusive jurisdiction to make laws in relation to the recognition of decrees effecting nullity of marriage (including annulment) and in relation to the jurisdictional basis upon which a court may entertain the application. On this complex issue, there was considerable discussion and no resolution. Your sub-committee begs leave to have the opportunity to continue discussions in Vancouver.

All of which is respectfully submitted.

H. Allan Leal
Chairman

39. Continuing Committee of Ministers on the Constitution, Vancouver, British Columbia, July 22–24, 1980

(a) Report of the Sub-Committee of Officials on Equalization, July 23, 1980

Document: 830-83/008

I — OVERVIEW DISCUSSION

The sub-committee of officials on Equalization met on July 9, 1980. The sub-committee heard the three changes to the February 1979 'Best Efforts Draft' proposed by the Government of Quebec.

The changes are as follows: —

a) the deletion from Section 96(1)(b) of the best efforts draft of the words "for social and economic well-being";

b) the word "province" in 96(2) of the draft would be changed to "provincial governments" so that the section would read "Making equalization payments to provincial governments . . .";

c) the deletion of the last clause of Section 96(2) beginning with the words "or to the principle . . ."

Some noted that these changes may make it more difficult to meet the reservations of British Columbia.

Since changes were being suggested, other provinces took the occasion to propose further modifications, more particularly with respect to Section 96(2) of the best efforts draft. Manitoba and Saskatchewan proposed that Section 96(2) be re-worded to read: —

"Parliament and the Government of Canada are further committed to the principle of making equalization payments to ensure that provincial governments have sufficient revenues to provide reasonably comparable levels of public services at reasonably comparable levels of taxation."

[Following] is a tabular presentation of the three versions of the February 1979 'Best Efforts Draft' currently on the table. The changes to the original draft proposed by the governments of Quebec, Manitoba and Saskatchewan are sidelined.

II — ISSUE FOR MINISTERIAL CONSIDERATION

The issue before Ministers is to decide which draft:

a) the February 1979 'Best Efforts Draft'; or

b) the February 1979 'Best Efforts Draft' as amended by Quebec; or

c) the February 1979 'Best Efforts Draft' incorporating the Quebec changes plus the further modifications suggested by Manitoba and Saskatchewan;

obtain the consensus of the Conference.

Gérard Veilleux
Chairman

Equalization and Regional Development

February 1979 Best Efforts Draft	*Government of Quebec Proposal*	*Governments of Manitoba and Saskatchewan Proposal (including Quebec's Proposal)*
96(1) Without altering the legislative authority of Parliament or of the legislatures or of the rights of any of them with respect to the exercise of their legislative authority, Parliament and the legislatures, together with the Government of Canada and the Governments of the Provinces, are committed to	96(1) Without altering the legislative authority of Parliament or of the legislatures or of the rights of any of them with respect to the exercise of their legislative authority, Parliament and the legislatures, together with the Government of Canada and the Governments of the Provinces, are committed to	96(1) Without altering the legislative authority of Parliament or of the legislatures or of the rights of any of them with respect to the exercise of their legislative authority, Parliament and the legislatures, together with the Government of Canada and the Governments of the Provinces, are committed to
(a) promoting equal opportunities for the well-being of Canadians;	(a) promoting equal opportunities for the well-being of Canadians;	(a) promoting equal opportunities for the well-being of Canadians;
(b) furthering economic development to reduce disparity in opportunities for social and economic well-being; and	(b) furthering economic development to reduce disparity in opportunities; and,	(b) furthering economic development to reduce disparity in opportunities; and
(c) providing essential public services of reasonable quality to all Canadians.	(c) providing essential public services of reasonable quality to all Canadians.	(c) providing essential public services of reasonable quality to all Canadians.
(2) Parliament and the Government of Canada are further committed to the principle of making equalization payments to provinces that are unable to provide essential public services of reasonable quality without imposing an undue burden of taxation, or to the principle of making arrangements equivalent to equalization payments to meet the commitment specified in Section 96(1)(c).	(2) Parliament and the Government of Canada are further committed to the principle of making equalization payments to provincial governments that are unable to provide essential public services of reasonable quality without imposing an undue burden of taxation.	(2) Parliament and the Government of Canada are further committed to the principle of making equalization payments to ensure that provincial governments have sufficient revenues to provide reasonably comparable levels of public services at reasonably comparable levels of taxation.
(3) The Prime Minister of Canada and the First Ministers of the Provinces shall review together the questions of equalization and regional development at least once every five years at a meeting convened pursuant to section 97.	(3) The Prime Minister of Canada and the First Ministers of the Provinces shall review together the questions of equalization and regional development at least once every five years at a meeting convened pursuant to section 97.	(3) The Prime Minister of Canada and the First Ministers of the Provinces shall review together the questions of equalization and regional development at least once every five years at a meeting convened pursuant to section 97.

(b) Report of the Sub-Committee on Family Law, July 24, 1980

Document: 830-83/009

Your sub-committee met on Wednesday, July 23, 1980 for a limited period of time only since there is a substantial overlap in the personnel comprising this sub-committee and those on the Supreme Court and the Charter of Rights sub-committees.

We considered the two items carried over on our agenda from the Toronto meeting last week. After further discussion, the delegates from the several jurisdictions were asked to indicate whether they favoured the principle of the proposal advanced by the delegates of Canada that the best efforts draft should be amended to provide that the federal Parliament be given exclusive legislative authority to prescribe the basis for recognition of decrees of annulment and declarations of nullity and to establish the basis of jurisdiction of the courts granting these decrees. [Federal proposal follows.]

Seven provinces and the delegates of the federal administration voted in favour of the adoption of the principle. The delegates of Quebec and Ontario were opposed. No vote was recorded for New Brunswick. Presumably this matter can now be referred for drafting.

Your sub-committee resumed its search for a solution to the perceived problem of more expeditious and effective enforcement of maintenance and custody orders. Due to the lack of time for a full discussion, the delegates indicated they were not prepared to vote upon this issue and the matter was tabled.

All of which is respectfully submitted.

H. Allan Leal
Chairman

FAMILY LAW
FEDERAL PROPOSAL ON NULLITY JURISDICTION AND RECOGNITION (JULY 19, 1980)

1. The federal proposal is that the "best efforts" draft be amended to retain for Parliament exclusive authority with respect to the recognition of nullity decrees and the jurisdictional basis upon which they are granted. It would include decrees with respect to both void and voidable marriages.

2. The proposal would parallel for nullity what is done with respect to divorce in the February 1979 "best efforts" draft. It would not however affect the substantive grounds for nullity which would, under the "best efforts" draft, be exclusively provincial. Under the federal proposal any legislation by Parliament dealing with grounds would be struck down by the courts as trenching upon exclusive provincial jurisdiction in this area.

3. The proposal is made for the same reasons that the "best efforts" draft retains federal power over divorce jurisdiction and the recognition of divorce decreers, i.e., to prevent "limping" marriages, where parties are considered to be married in one province and not in another, and to prevent "forum shopping" by parties. The purpose is to ensure to the greatest extent possible that, where a court of a province with which the parties are connected pronounces on the status of the parties, the pronouncement will be recognized by sister provinces and therefore have full effect throughout Canada.

4. The recognition of nullity decrees is at present governed by the judge-made rules of conflict of laws, rather than by legislation. That could continue to be the case under this proposal. Under the "best efforts" draft however, with exclusive power over marriage proposed for the provinces it would be possible for barriers to be erected against the recognition of sister province decrees upon any basis. For example:

a) It would be open for a province to legislate that its courts shall refuse to recognize a nullity decree that had been granted on the basis of grounds that were unacceptable to the legislating province.

b) Given the uncertainty as to the precise boundary between divorce and nullity (e.g. s. 4(1)(d) of the present Divorce Act) it might also be possible for decrees, otherwise thought to be subject to divorce recognition rules, to be made under provincial nullity laws, and thereby running the risk of non-recognition in other provinces.

5. If such problems were to arise, under the proposed amendment Parliament would have the authority to legislate to remedy the situation and ensure recognition of the decrees of courts of sister provinces. This would probably take the form of specifying some appropriate factor or factors connecting the person or persons involved with the province in which the decree is sought.

(c) Report on the Supreme Court

Document: 830-83/010

AREAS OF AGREEMENT OR NEAR AGREEMENT

1. There is agreement or near agreement on most aspects of the Supreme Court. There was wide ranging support for the proposition that the Supreme Court should reflect the principle of dualism arising from our two systems of law. Saskatchewan and Alberta expressed their willingness to discuss the notion of a separate constitutional court should this matter be raised again. This is reflected particularly in the proposals which were discussed concerning the composition of the Court and the alternate appointment of Chief Justices discussed below. All delegations agreed that the Supreme Court should be entrenched in the Constitution.

2. As a reaction to Quebec's proposal for a 5 judge constitutional panel, Manitoba put forward the suggestion that the *court be increased to 11 members*, 5 being appointed from Quebec, 6 from other provinces. General support developed for this with all but three delegations expressing agreement. Alberta reserved its position. Nova Scotia also reserved its position, expressing concern in regard to an 11 member court, 5 with civil law training, sitting on common law cases. Saskatchewan also expressed some concern in this respect. British Columbia expressed opposition and put forward a proposal that the court be increased to 11 members, 4 being appointed from Quebec.

The Manitoba compromise would obviate the need for a special Quebec civil law bench. With 5 civil law judges on the court, there can be no doubt that civil law cases will be heard by a panel comprised mostly or entirely of civil law judges.

3. There is general support for the *principle of alternating the post of Chief Justice* between civil law and common law appointees and for *entrenching* this in the Constitution. British Columbia reserved on the entrenchment of the principle. Manitoba expressed opposition. There is considerable support for the proposal that the Chief Justice should hold that post for a fixed term of seven years. Alberta and Saskatchewan reserved on this issue. Manitoba expressed opposition.

4. There appears to be a consensus that there should be an *equality of access* to the Supreme Court so that both the federal and provincial governments would have equal ability to refer constitutional questions directly to the Court.

Manitoba and Saskatchewan expressed the view that references on constitutional issues should not be made directly to the Supreme Court but in all instances should go first to a lower court, that is, to the provincial court of appeal or to the Federal Court of Appeal depending upon whether the reference was initiated by a provincial or the federal government.

5. As far as the *jurisdiction of the Court* is concerned, it was agreed to adopt the "best efforts" draft with some modifications to lessen the rigidity of that text. Additional changes to the text would be required depending upon the decisions made on the issues noted elsewhere in this report.

6. A number of jurisdiction (6) agreed that the best efforts draft should be made more flexible to allow Parliament *to provide* for the *salaries*, allowances, and pensions of the judges of the Supreme Court by means other than through an Act of Parliament, for example, by order in council.

MATTERS REQUIRING FURTHER DISCUSSION

1. PROCEDURE FOR APPOINTMENT

On Tuesday Ministers referred to officials the question of the appointment procedure for Supreme Court judges. The [following] committee report, marked Appendix A, indicates that considerable consensus exists, at the officials level, on both this issue and on an appropriate deadlock breaking mechanism. These items could be reported to First Ministers as areas of agreement or near agreement if Ministers so wish.

The appointment procedure which seems to have received general support is a two step process whereby the federal Minister of Justice would consult with all provincial Attorneys General when a vacancy occurred or was about to occur on the court. The second step would require agreement on the candidate selected by the federal Attorney General and the provincial Attorney General of the province from which the appointee came.

A "deadlock breaking" mechanism suggested by Manitoba whereby the Chief Justice of the Supreme Court would join with the federal Minister of Justice and the provincial Attorney General in question to constitute a committee to resolve the deadlock has received the support of 9 delegations. While Saskatchewan supports this proposal it would also support the earlier Victoria proposal. New Brunswick supports the Victoria proposal but is also of the view that a deadlock breaking mechanism is not appropriate. Quebec is of the view that a deadlock breaking mechanism is not necessary but would find Manitoba's proposal acceptable. British Columbia reserved its position.

2. SECTION 96 OF THE B.N.A. ACT

There was a brief discussion of the issues respecting section 96 of the B.N.A. Act. Simply stated, all jurisdictions agree that court interpretations of section 96 (which empowers the Governor General to appoint provincial superior, district and county court judges) have created serious restrictions on the ability of provinces to confer effective powers on administrative tribunals and provincially appointed judges in a number of areas where such jurisdiction would be desirable, e.g., family law. In addition, several provinces view federal appointment of section 96 judges as an anachronism and inconsistent with responsibility for administration of Justice in the provinces.

Two principal approaches to dealing with these matters were discussed: repealing section 96 to permit provincial appointment of these judges, and amending section 96 to enable provinces to confer superior court jurisdiction on provincial tribunals and judges in appropriate cases. It was recognized that under either approach a number of serious policy issues will require consideration this being more so the case in looking at repeal as opposed to amendment of section 96.

Quebec, Ontario, Alberta and Saskatchewan feel strongly that the proper approach to dealing with this matter is to transfer the appointment power over section 96 judges to the provinces wishing to have such power. All other provinces feel that the appointment power should remain federal (although some would not oppose transfer of the power to provinces wishing it and some wish consultation on appointment), but that consideration should be given to amending section 96 to permit provinces to confer some superior court jurisdiction on provincial administrative/tribunals and judges.

If Ministers agree, the foregoing matters will be pursued by the sub-committee during the August meeting of Ministers.

OVERVIEW COMMENTS

The most significant development with respect to discussion on the Supreme Court is the support which has developed for the idea that some aspects of dualism should be reflected in the Supreme Court provisions. The support focusses on the fact that there are two legal systems in Canada and on the understanding that different approaches to resolving legal problems therefore arise.

APPENDIX A
REPORT OF THE SUB-COMMITTEE ON THE SUPREME COURT (JULY 23, 1980)

1. Officials of all governments met on Tuesday to discuss further the issue of an appointment procedure for Justices of the Supreme Court.

2. As a result of these discussions a 2-step procedure has emerged the essential elements of which are:

Step 1 — The Minister of Justice of Canada is to consult with all 10 provincial Attorneys General when a vacancy on the Court is to be filled. Provincial Attorneys General may submit names of candidates.

Step 2 — The Minister of Justice of Canada and the Attorney General of the province in question must agree on the candidate selected.

3. In view of the "agreement" requirement in Step 2, the matter of a deadlock-breaking mechanism was discussed. Three options for such a mechanism were identified:

(a) — the Victoria Charter formulation but with specified time periods significantly shortened — Saskatchewan and New Brunswick expressed support for this mechanism;

(b) — the Manitoba proposal whereby the Chief Justice of the Court, the Minister of Justice of Canada, and the Attorney General in question would constitute a committee to resolve the deadlock by majority decision — Saskatchewan, Newfoundland, Ontario, Alberta, Prince Edward Island, Manitoba, Quebec, Nova Scotia and the federal government expressed support for this mechanism;

(c) — no mechanism — the rationale for this option is that the deadlock is a political problem which should be resolved politically — New Brunswick and Quebec supported this position. British Columbia also tended to this position although it reserved on the matter.

It is to be noted that several provinces (Saskatchewan, Quebec and New Brunswick) have expressed support for more than one option.

(d) Report on the Preamble/Principles of a Constitution, July 24, 1980

Document: 830-83/011

On July 23, the CCMC discussed the Report of the Committee of Officials (CICS document 830-82/013, dated July 16).

Several delegations suggested a preamble which was inspirational in character. Concern was expressed by some delegations about the possibility that a preamble to the Constitution might be used by the courts to interpret other parts of the Constitution. It was also noted that the preamble might not be used by the courts to interpret other parts of the Constitution unless the meaning of those parts was unclear. It was decided that this matter be reviewed at the next meeting of the CCMC at the end of August.

Ministers then had an exchange of views on 22 of the 27 items listed in the Officials Committee Report (items 1–19 inclusive, and 25–27). A few of these items received very little support, while several others were regarded by most delegations as being suitable subjects for inclusion in a preamble. No decisions were reached on the inclusion or exclusion of any particular item.

In the course of discussions, many important matters were touched upon. These included, among other things, reference to Canada as a constitutional monarchy, reference to Quebec as a distinct society and mainstay of French Canada, reference to Quebec's commitment to federalism to which it freely adhered, and consideration of the need to find a suitable means of expressing Canadian duality, especially linguistic duality.

Ministers decided to reflect on the exchange of views and to take into account the various considerations that had been voiced. They further decided to return to the subject during the next meeting of the CCMC at the end of August. It was anticipated that by that time some delegations might have new drafts of a preamble or statement of principles to present to the Conference. At that stage the Committee of Officials would meet again for preliminary discussion of any new drafts that might be available.

(e) Report of the Sub-Committee on Patriation/Amending Formula, July 24, 1980

Document: 830-83/013

SUMMARY

I AMENDING FORMULA

AREAS OF CONSENSUS

1. CATEGORIES OF AMENDMENT

The Sub-committee agreed that:

a) amendments to provisions which concern Parliament and all the provinces can only be made according to a procedure which permits the involvement of Parliament and all the provinces.

b) amendments affecting one or more but not all of the provinces can only be made with the approval of Parliament and the Legislatures of the provinces concerned.

c) amendments to the constitution of a province, with certain specified exceptions such as the office of the Lieutenant Governor, can only be made by the Legislature of the province.

d) amendments to subject matters applying to Parliament exclusively can only be made by Parliament acting alone. The Sub-committee noted that, as under section 91(1) of the BNA Act, there were various matters which could fall under this category but which should be made subject to a general amending formula. These matters should be reviewed by the Sub-committee.

2. PROVINCIAL BOUNDARIES

The Sub-committee agreed that procedures for changes to provincial boundaries should be explicitly provided for in any amending formula. It was also agreed that changes to provincial boundaries can only be made according to the procedure for amendments affecting one or more but not all of the provinces, i.e., requiring the approval of the provinces affected.

3. UNANIMITY

Unanimity was considered too rigid and unworkable for purposes of a general amending formula.

ISSUES FOR DIRECTION

1. SPECIAL PROTECTIONS IN THE AMENDING FORMULA

a) Should the general amending formula make special arrangements in respect of the amendment of certain matters or subjects?

b) If so, what should be the nature of these special arrangements?

c) What matters should be included in these special arrangements?

2. APPROVALS PROCEDURE (THE FORMULA)

a) Should each province have equal status or should one or more provinces have a veto?

b) If one or more provinces have vetos, should the amending formula be based on a regional concept or on a mathematical formula with a high population requirement?

c) If on the other hand, each province is to have equal status, what should the amending formula be?

d) In what forum should constitutional amendments be approved by provinces?

II DELEGATION

AREAS OF CONSENSUS

1. PRINCIPLE OF DELEGATION

All governments agreed that the principle of delegating legislative authority should be incorporated in a revised Constitution. However, Quebec expressed reservations on the concept of delegation of powers through any mechanism other than a proper amending formula. While Quebec is ready to study proposals of legislative delegation and to recognize the objectives of greater flexibility being sought through delegation, it was mentioned that the practical consequences of such delegation may lead to actual situations, regarding the exercise of legislative powers, which would not have been possible or permitted through an amending formula.

2. ONE-TO-ONE DELEGATION

The Sub-committee agreed that delegation should be on a one-to-one basis, from Parliament to any legislature, or vice-versa.

3. SCOPE OF AUTHORITY TO BE DELEGATED

The Sub-committee agreed that the scope of authority to be delegated should include the power to legislate in relation to any matter, subject or class of subjects.

4. FINANCIAL RESPONSIBILITY

Financial responsibility for the administration of the authority being delegated would be determined as an aspect of delegation on a case-by-case basis.

ISSUE FOR DIRECTION

PROVINCIAL ACCESS TO DELEGATION

Concern was expressed by two Provinces lest Parliament might agree to allow one province to make laws in the province in relation to a matter coming within the legislative authority of Parliament and then might subsequently refuse to delegate to other provinces the power to make laws in respect to the same matter. On the other hand the flexibility inherent in delegation would be reduced if Parliament was obliged to grant to any province what it had granted to others.

I. AMENDING FORMULA

A. OVERVIEW OF DISCUSSION

- The Sub-committee focussed on the Alberta amending formula proposal tabled at the First Ministers' Conference in February 1979 (see Appendix A) [*supra*, p. 555], proposals tabled at the First Ministers' Conference in October 1978 (see appendix B [*infra*, p. 640]).
- The Sub-committee noted that the draft text submitted by Alberta and the principles underlying that text were

based on a resolution passed by the Alberta Legislature in 1976.

- Quebec stated that in its view, discussion of the amending formula should await agreement on other aspects of constitutional change, particularly the distribution of powers.
- The federal representatives indicated that they could support any general formula that provided an effective combination of stability and flexibility, that was broadly acceptable to the provinces, and that resulted in a generally uniform constitutional regime for all provinces.
- The major portion of the Sub-committee's time was spent on considering the special protections in the Alberta proposal for amendments to the legislative powers/rights and privileges/property and assets/and natural resources of a province; and, on the implications of permitting any province to prevent the application to itself of any amendment with regard to these matters without its consent, (the "opting out" process). The Sub-committee then discussed whether such special protections should be restricted to a more limited range of matters, and whether in these circumstances unanimous approval or "opting out" should be used.
- The Sub-committee believes that with some additional clarification of technical issues and political direction on the issues identified below, it might be possible to develop an amending formula acceptable to many governments.

B. AREAS OF CONSENSUS

1. CATEGORIES OF AMENDMENT

The Sub-committee agreed that:
a) amendments to provisions which concern Parliament and all the provinces can only be made according to a procedure which permits the involvement of Parliament and all the provinces.
b) amendments affecting one or more but not all of the provinces can only be made with the approval of Parliament and the Legislatures of the provinces concerned.
c) amendments to the constitution of a province, with certain specified exceptions such as the office of the Lieutenant Governor, can only be made by the Legislature of the province.
d) amendments to subject matters applying to Parliament exclusively can only be made by Parliament acting alone. The Sub-committee noted that, as under section 91(1) of the BNA Act, there were various matters which could fall under this category but which should be made

subject to a general amending formula. These matters should be reviewed by the Sub-committee.

2. PROVINCIAL BOUNDARIES

The Sub-committee agreed that procedures for changes to provincial boundaries should be explicitly provided for in any amending formula. It was also agreed that changes to provincial boundaries can only be made according to the procedure for amendments affecting one or more but not all of the provinces, i.e., requiring the approval of the provinces affected.

3. UNANIMITY

Unanimity was considered too rigid and unworkable for purposes of a general amending formula.

C. ISSUES FOR DIRECTION

1. SPECIAL PROTECTIONS IN THE AMENDING FORMULA

a) Should the general amending formula make special arrangements in respect of the amendment of certain matters or subjects?

The Committee discussed the possibility of having the amendment of some matters dealt with differently from others. Note was made that the Fulton-Favreau and the Toronto consensus formulas both distinguished between some matters amendable only through unanimous consent and other matters which would be amended through a less rigid procedure. The Alberta proposal makes special provision for a certain category of matters, amendments to which could not be imposed upon a dissenting province.

The general view was that making such special arrangements for the amendment of certain matters was a useful approach, depending however, on which matters were singled out for special protection.

b) If so, what should be the nature of these special arrangements?

The Committee concluded that there were essentially two possibilities in this regard:

    (1) the amending procedure could require *unanimity* for a limited list of matters; or

    (2) it could specify that certain amendments would not

take effect in a province or provinces which dissented to the amendment in question.

c) What matters should be included in these special arrangements?

The Committee examined the following options:

. . . *The Alberta proposal*

(i) Amendments affecting matters relating to:

    a/ the powers of the legislature of a province to make laws;

    b/ the rights and privileges granted or secured by the Constitution of Canada to the legislature or the government of a province;

    c/ the assets or property of a province;

    d/ natural resources of a province.

would have no force or effect in a province which dissented to the amendment in question.

(ii) the amendment of the part of the amending procedure which made this special arrangement would require unanimity.

. . . *Alternative approach*

(i) amendments affecting matters related to:

    a/ the powers of a province to make laws in relation to natural resources;

    b/ the rights and privileges granted or secured by the Constitution of Canada to the legislature or the government of a province;

    c/ the assets or property of a province

               OR

    provincial ownership of natural resources in a province

               OR

    proprietary rights of a province

would have no force or effect in a province which dissented to the amendment in question,

               OR

would require unanimous approval to take effect.

(ii) unanimity would be required for the amendment of this part of the amending formula.

. . . *"Toronto consensus" formulation*

(i) unanimity would be required for amendments relating to:

    a/ provincial ownership and jurisdiction over natural resources;

b/ this provision of the amending formula.

There was a general consensus that whatever the formulation provided, the amendment of the procedure for changes in provincial boundaries (requiring the consent of Parliament and the province(s) affected) should also require unanimity.

2. APPROVALS PROCEDURE (THE FORMULA)

a) Should each province have equal status or should one or more provinces have a veto?

Some provinces thought that no one province should have a veto since this offends the principle of the equality of all provinces. Quebec wants to have a veto but is prepared to consider the Alberta amending proposal as a possible alternative approach. Certain provinces suggested that if one province has a veto, then they may also require a veto.

b) If one or more provinces have vetos, should the amending formula be based:

   (i) on a regional concept and, if so, how many regions should there be (Victoria charter — 4 regions; B.C. proposal — 5 regions)

   OR

   (ii) on a mathematical formula with a high population percentage requirement, and if so:
   - should the mathematical formula be expressed as a ratio (e.g. 2/3 of the provinces) or as an absolute number (e.g. 7 provinces).
   - what should the population requirement be (e.g. X provinces with 85% of the population, X provinces with 80% of the population, X provinces including every province with 10% of the population etc.)

c) If on the other hand, each province is to have equal status, what should the amending formula be?

   The Committee identified two possible formulas:
   (i) 2/3 (or 7 provinces) with 50% of the population;
   (ii) 2/3 (or 7 provinces) with 60% of the population.

d) In what forum should constitutional amendments be approved by provinces?

   British Columbia proposed that amendments be approved by a reconstituted Upper House representing the provinces with provincial delegations voting on instruction.

   Most other governments agreed that amendments be made by way of legislative resolutions.

II. DELEGATION OF LEGISLATIVE AUTHORITY

A. OVERVIEW

The Sub-committee discussed the federal draft on Delegation of Legislative Authority (February, 1979) and the report of the same date of the CCMC to First Ministers. A revised federal draft [follows] (see appendix C) which is still under review.

B. AREAS OF CONSENSUS

1. PRINCIPLE OF DELEGATION

All governments agreed that the principle of delegating legislative authority should be incorporated in a revised Constitution. However, Quebec expressed reservations on the concept of delegation of powers through any mechanism other than a proper amending formula. While Quebec is ready to study proposals of legislative delegation and to recognize the objectives of greater flexibility being sought through delegation, it was mentioned that the practical consequences of such delegation may lead to actual situations, regarding the exercise of legislative powers, which would not have been possible or permitted through an amending formula.

2. ONE-TO-ONE DELEGATION

The Sub-committee agreed that delegation should be on a one-to-one basis, from Parliament to any legislature, or vice-versa.

3. SCOPE OF AUTHORITY TO BE DELEGATED

The Sub-committee agreed that the scope of authority to be delegated should include the power to legislate in relation to any matter, subject or class of subjects.

4. FINANCIAL RESPONSIBILITY

Financial responsibility for the administration of the authority being delegated would be determined as an aspect of delegation on a case-by-case basis.

C. ISSUES FOR DIRECTION

PROVINCIAL ACCESS TO DELEGATION

Concern was expressed by two provinces lest Parliament might agree to delegate to one province the power to make laws in the province in relation to a matter coming within the legislative authority of Parliament and then might subsequently refuse to delegate to other provinces the power to make laws in respect to the same matter. On the other hand the flexibility inherent in delegation would be reduced if Parliament were obliged to grant to any province what it had granted to others.

APPENDIX B
BRITISH COLUMBIA PROPOSAL, NOVEMBER 1, 1978

Document: 800-8/012 (page 18)

[Tabled at Federal-Provincial First Ministers' Conference, Ottawa, Ontario, October 30–November 1, 1978.]

SUMMARY OF PROPOSALS

The Government of British Columbia makes the following proposals concerning the process of constitutional amendment in Canada:

(1) The constitutional amendment process should be one that is *exclusively Canadian*.

(2) Subject matters of concern to only the provincial legislature should be amendable by the provincial legislatures acting unilaterally.

(3) Subject matters of concern to only Parliament should be amendable by Parliament acting unilaterally. Careful attention should be focused on the identification of these matters to exclude some which may be said to be included in this category — for example, the Senate and the Supreme Court of Canada — do not in fact affect only Parliament but rather have a significant impact on the provinces as well.

(4) Subject matters of concern only to Parliament and some, but not all, of the provincial legislatures should be amendable by those governments concerned.

(5) Subject matters of concern to Parliament and all the provincial legislatures should be amendable by the affirmative votes of the House of Commons, the Atlantic Region, Quebec, Ontario, the Prairie Region, and the Pacific Region.

(6) The forum for aggregating the five regional votes required for constitutional amendments should be the Senate, provided that it is reformed along the lines suggested by British Columbia. (*See* Paper No. 3: "Reform of the Canadian Senate.")

(7) If the Senate is not reformed along these lines then the forum for aggregating the five regional votes required for constitutional amendments should be the respective provincial legislatures.

In conclusion, the Government of British Columbia believes that the amending formula in any constitution, particularly federal constitutions, must be a happy balance of flexibility and stability — flexibility to permit the constitution to keep abreast of contemporary needs, stability to provide some measure of constitutional certainty to governors and the governed alike. British Columbia's proposals seek to strike that balance.

APPENDIX C
FEDERAL DRAFT PROPOSAL, JULY 23, 1980

DELEGATION OF LEGISLATIVE AUTHORITY

Delegation to Parliament

XX. (1) Notwithstanding anything in the Constitution of Canada, Parliament may make laws in relation to any matter, subject or class of subjects coming within the legislative jurisdiction of a province.

Consent of provincial legislature

(2) No law may be enacted by Parliament under subsection (1) unless, prior to the enactment thereof, the legislature of at least one province has consented to the enactment of such a law by Parliament.

Idem

(3) No law enacted under subsection (1) has effect in any province unless the legislature of that province has consented to the operation of such a law in that province.

Delegation to legislature of a province	(4) Notwithstanding anything in the Constitution of Canada, the legislature of a province may make laws in the province in relation to any matter, subject or class of subjects coming within the legislative jurisdiction of Parliament.
Consent of Parliament	(5) No law may be enacted by a province under subsection (4) unless, prior to the enactment thereof, Parliament has consented to the enactment of such a law by the legislature of that province.
Extent of Consent	(6) A consent given under this section may relate to any matter, subject or class of subjects.
Enforcement	(7) Parliament or the legislature of a province may make laws for enforcing any law made by it under this section.
Revocation of consent	(8) A consent given under this section may at any time be revoked, and
	(a) if a consent given under subsection (3) is revoked, any law made by Parliament to which the consent relates that is operative in the province in which the consent is revoked thereupon ceases to have effect in that province; and
	(b) if a consent given under subsection (5) is revoked, any law made by the legislature of a province to which the consent relates thereupon ceases to have effect.
Repeal of law by Parliament	(9) Parliament may appeal any law made by it under this section, insofar as it is part of the law of one or more provinces, but the repeal does not affect the operation of that law in any province to which the repeal does not relate.
Repeal of law by provincial legislature	(10) The legislature of a province may repeal any law made by it under this section.

(f) Report of the Committee of Officials on Fisheries, July 24, 1980

Document: 830-83/014

The Committee continued its work using the "modus operandi" established in Toronto, i.e. to hold both federal-provincial and interprovincial meetings. From this process it was possible to develop draft formulations for consideration by governments for amendment to the BNA Act regarding fisheries jurisdiction.

In summary, *agreement or near agreement* is possible regarding *inland fisheries, marine plants and sedentary species.* The essential issues requiring resolution concern:

—jurisdiction over diadromous species, and
—provisions for fish habitat and native peoples' fisheries

Regarding *sea coast fisheries,* a provincial text has been produced, which officials, except as noted below, believe susceptible to promoting a broad provincial consensus. This text contemplates concurrent jurisdiction. The federal representatives maintain a position based on exclusive federal jurisdiction. This essential issue remains to be resolved.

A. INLAND FISHERIES, MARINE PLANTS AND SEDENTARY SPECIES

Regarding the *inland fisheries, marine plants and sedentary species* the Committee has produced a "best efforts" draft, which appears as Appendix 1 to this report. The first paragraph of the best effort has been supported by the provincial members of the Committee. The draft includes alternative formulations dealing with diadromous species. In advancing this draft(s) the Committee wishes to draw the attention fo Ministers to the fact that the alternative formulations regarding diadromous species reflect approaches based on concurrent jurisdiction with limited federal paramountcy and exclusive federal jurisdiction.

With the exception of one coastal province, the provinces have indicated their support for either Option "A" or for an exclusive provincial jurisdiction on diadromous species in non-tidal waters.

With either approach, it will be necessary in the preparation of a final text to negotiate and define more precisely a number of terms appearing in the text. These are noted in Appendix 1.

Federal representatives have also noted the necessity to make provision for the protection of fish habitat and native peoples' fisheries as well as the prevention of fish diseases. It is not clear, at this time, whether all of these matters require reference in this section or whether they are covered by other sections of the BNA Act.

Finally, the Committee would wish it to be understood that its advancing this text(s) as a "best efforts" draft does not reflect unanimous support by all governments.

B. SEA COAST FISHERIES

Regarding the *sea coast fisheries*, it has been possible to develop a "best efforts" draft based on a revision of the Newfoundland proposal which provincial officials, two coastal provinces excepted, consider worthy of consideration by governments as a basis for consensus. This draft appears as Appendix II to this report. Federal representatives continue to oppose this approach maintaining it is unworkable.

Federal representatives developed further the concept of considering legal mechanisms aimed at achieving meaningful consultation with the provinces and enunciated a number of policy issues which might be included in a mandatory consultation enactment. They further undertook, in advance of the meetings scheduled for August 25 to produce and circulate a document which would detail the concept of the federal proposal and provide a specific legal formulation. Such a formulation would have particular application to the sea coast fishery but may have implications for other fisheries as well. Federal representatives indicated that this proposal would be in the context of exclusive federal jurisdiction over sea coast fisheries.

APPENDIX I
AMENDMENT REGARDING INLAND FISHERIES, MARINE PLANTS AND SENDENTARY SPECIES

92.1 (1) The Legislature of each province may exclusively make laws in relation to:

a) inland fisheries in the non tidal waters of the province;

b) marine and aquatic plants[1] in the non tidal waters of the province and in tidal waters in or adjacent to the province;[2]

c) sedentary species in tidal waters in or adjacent to the province;

d) aquaculture within the province and in tidal waters or adjacent to the province that is not included in either a), b) or c);

A (2) Notwithstanding paragraph 1(a) the Parliament of Canada may make laws in relation to the determination of total allowable catches for diadromous species in non tidal waters and their allocation between provinces and any such law shall be paramount.

OR

B (2) Notwithstanding paragraph 1(a) the Parliament of Canada may exclusively make laws in relation to sea coast and inland fisheries for diadromous species.

Comment

(1) While these matters are not reflected in the draft, the Federal government would wish provision to be made for the protection of the fish habitat and native people's fisheries, as well as the prevention of fish diseases.

APPENDIX II
AMENDMENT REGARDING SEA COAST FISHERIES

(a) Section 91(12) of the British North America Act would be repealed.

(b) A separate section in the British North America Act, in the following terms, would be enacted.

---

[1] Participants to the committee agree that aquaculture, marine plants, sedentary species and diadromous species should be defined either by a generic description or a list of exclusion or inclusion. Diadromous species means species which spawn in fresh water and migrate to sea or spawn at sea migrate into fresh water.

[2] There is an option to delineate the jurisdiction area by indicating a mileage from the ordinary low water mark or by a reference only to adjacent waters for both marine plants and sedentary species and aquaculture.

95A. (1) With respect to fish stocks adjacent to each province (as defined in subsection (5) below), the Legislature may make laws relative to the sea coast fisheries but any law covering those matters set out in subsection (3) shall have effect in and for the province so long as they are not repugnant to any Act of the Parliament of Canada made under subsection (2).

(2) The Parliament of Canada may make laws relative to the sea coast fisheries but any law covering those matters set out in subsection (4) shall have effect in and for any or all of the provinces so long as they are not repugnant to any Act of the Legislature of a province made under subsection (1).

(3) The matters referred to in subsection (1) are:

(a) fixing parameters for the total allowable catch for stocks;

(b) the allocation of quotas to foreign countries and the licensing of foreign vessels;

(c) conservation of fish stocks.

(4) The matters referred to in subsection (2) are:

(a) fixing the level of catch within the parameters referred to in subsection (3) (a) and the issuance of quotas up to the level so fixed;

(b) licensing of fishing vessels other than foreign vessels taking fish from the residual quota;

(c) all matters not referred to in this subsection and subsection (3).

5. (a) The allocation of the fish stocks adjacent to each Province shall be determined by agreement between the Provinces in accordance with equitable principles taking account of all relevant information including traditional fishing patterns.

(b) If no agreement can be reached within a reasonable period of time, the Provinces concerned shall refer the particular matter in dispute for expeditious arbitration.

(g) Report to Ministers from the Sub-Committee of Officials on Offshore Resources, July 24, 1980

Document: 830-83/015

The Continuing Committee of Ministers on the Constitution determined on July 15 that a sub-committee of officials should meet to carry out the following mandate:

"To report to he Ministers on possible options for resolution of the offshore resources issue under the following headings:
1. Ownership
2. Concurrent jurisdiction
3. Administrative arrangements between governments"

The Committee was chaired by New Brunswick and was attended by representatives of all governments.

I. AREAS OF AGREEMENT AND DISAGREEMENT

There is a fundamental disagreement between the federal and provincial governments on the issue of ownership of offshore mineral resources.

All provinces agreed that offshore resources should be treated in a manner consistent with constitutional provisions for resources onshore. The federal government does not agree with this approach, but federal representatives fully recognized that coastal provinces should have an important role in making decisions concerning offshore resources.

II. APPROACHES TO RESOLUTION OF THE ISSUE

The Committee identified a number of possible options:

1. *Ownership*
   a) A determination of ownership by clear constitutional recognition.
   b) Extension of the onshore resource regime to offshore resources.
2. *Concurrent Jurisdiction*
   Determination of paramountcy is the key to any system of concurrent jurisdiction. Two alternatives were identified, one with greater provincial and one with greater federal control.

3. *Administrative Arrangements*

This option sets aside the ownership question. The 1977 Memorandum of Understanding, and improvements in decision-making and revenue sharing were discussed in anticipation of the forthcoming federal proposal.

The Committee noted however that, at this juncture, no government prefers concurrency, and most provinces have stated that administrative arrangements are not an acceptable alternative to a constitutional solution.

III. OVERVIEW OF DISCUSSIONS

It was acknowledged by the members of the Committee that the three headings were not mutually exclusive. For example, various types of administrative arrangements could be required depending on how the ownership and jurisdiction questions might be resolved. Many provincial representatives indicated however that they could not foresee an acceptable solution based solely on administrative arrangements.

The Committee proceeded to identify possible options for resolution of the offshore question as follows.

1. OWNERSHIP

A. CONSTITUTIONAL RECOGNITION

If provincial ownership of offshore resources were to be constitutionally recognized, it was identified that this could be expressed in a number of ways: one possible method of expressing this (as proposed by Newfoundland) could be by (a) a new Section 109 (Appendix I) and (b) a parallel amendment to Section 92 (Appendix II), because ownership and jurisdiction are not synonymous. British Columbia put forward a modified draft of the Newfoundland amendment.

An alternative method of conferring ownership on provinces has been identified by British Columbia. This could be achieved by extension of the boundaries of the provinces seaward to the extent of the Canadian territorial sea by action of federal and provincial legislatures as prescribed under existing Section 3 of the British North America Act (1871). It was suggested that extension of provincial rights over the continental shelf beyond the limits of the territorial sea might be achieved similarly or by constitutional amendment. It was noted however that this extension of provincial boundaries would result in the recognition of more than mineral rights, but that it would not include ownership of other than things attached to the seabed such as marine plants and sedentary species.

The Newfoundland approach was preferred as a legal technique.

The kind of legislative and constitutional regime that would be consistent with provincial ownership is illustrated in the table [on the following page].

B. EXTENSION OF ONSHORE RESOURCE REGIME TO OFFSHORE RESOURCES

If the ownership question is set aside without explicit constitutional resolution, any scheme of shared legislative responsibility would require constitutional amendment to grant the coastal provinces the power to:

(a) extend provincial laws offshore;

(b) make laws concerning the management and regulation of offshore minerals;

(c) treat the offshore as part of the province for tax purposes (subject to the principles applied to onshore resources);

(d) levy indirect taxes to the degree necessary to replace royalties and other revenues normally incident to ownership (subject to the principles applied to onshore resources).

The distribution of responsibilities under this option could also be illustrated by the table under 1A.

2. CONCURRENT JURISDICTION

The Committee considered the possibility of basing constitutional arrangements on concurrent jurisdiction, recognizing that, at this juncture, no government prefers such an approach. The examination served to clarify the potential complexities of such arrangements.

The Committee noted that under concurrent jurisdiction, the question of ownership would be put aside, and decisions would be required in order to determine which order of government should have jurisdiction, paramount or exclusive, on a broad series of specific matters which are usually associated with resource development.

In order to help Ministers consider this alternative, the Committee developed an *illustrative* list of matters on which decisions would be required. Two points should be borne in mind in connection with the list below. First, it does not include matters over which there is at present no doubt concerning exclusive federal jurisdiction (e.g., defence).

Second, in most cases, the items on the list do not represent possible heads of power. The illustrative list is as follows:

a) Allocation of rights (permits and licences)
b) Rate of exploration and production
c) Pace of development
d) Price setting
e) Fiscal powers (taxes, royalties and rentals, government participation)
f) Marketing
g) Spin-offs
h) Operating regulations
i) Environmental protection
j) Safety
k) Labour relations
l) Manpower training, etc.
m) Property and Civil Rights
n) Interprovincial trade
o) International treaty obligations

The Committee recognized that a number of these represented normal governmental activities onshore, such as manpower training, labour relations and so on, which cover many fields in addition to resource development. The handling of these matters could be examined on their merits, no matter what regime was chosen for the offshore. The Memorandum of Agreement of 1977 between Canada and the Maritime provinces had contemplated the application of various kinds of provincial legislation to the offshore.

The Committee also noted, however, that the first 8 subject headings (a to h) dealt directly with offshore development.

If "concurrent jurisdiction" were to be adopted as the system for handling the offshore, both orders of government would wish to have authority to legislate under each of these headings. For each such heading there would also have to be a determination of which government would be paramount.

Illustrative Distribution of Responsibilities

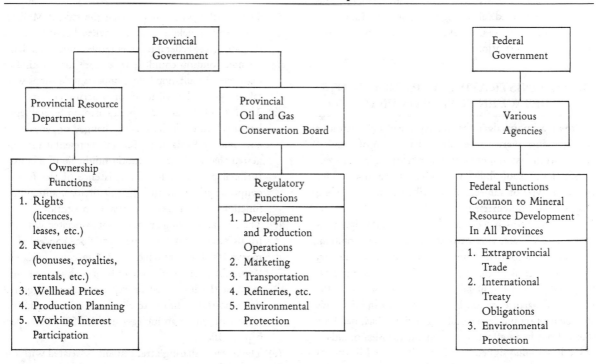

Notes:
1. All revenues, except federal taxes, go to the coastal province.
2. The foregoing division of legislative powers is subject to whatever determination is made with respect to onshore resources.
3. Some provinces object to the allocation of extraprovincial trade and international treaty obligations exclusively to the federal government. Similarly, the federal government does not agree with all the exclusive powers assigned to provinces.

In examining the question of paramountcy, the Committee recognized that there could be a very great number of combinations, if some headings were to be under federal paramountcy, and others under provincial. Further combinations could be produced by a blending of concurrency and exclusivity. It was noted, however, that there were *two distinct ways* of handling paramountcy which would tend to lead to quite different regimes, sufficiently different that the Committee recognized them as separate alternatives.

The first alternative would say, for each assignment of paramountcy, something like this — "the province shall be paramount except in specified circumstances where the federal government may overrule or take the final decision". This alternative would tend to result in provinces mounting their own offshore administrations, with the federal government in a monitoring role.

The second alternative would say, for each assignment of paramountcy, something like this — "the federal government shall be paramount, but in certain specified circumstances where the provinces are particularly concerned, shall act only when some 'stringent' conditions are met". This alternative, given federal willingness to share decision making with the provinces, would tend to produce a jointly-mounted administration.

3. ADMINISTRATIVE ARRANGEMENTS BETWEEN GOVERNMENTS

It was acknowledged that if a regime of administrative arrangements were to be adopted in place of explicit constitutional statements on ownership or concurrent jurisdiction, responsibility would have to be allocated for the same type of subjects as described in the preceding section under concurrency.

Most provinces stated that administrative arrangements are not an acceptable alternative to a constitutional solution.

While no confirmation was available from federal representatives as to the final form which an administrative arrangement might take, it was confirmed that the point of departure would be the kind of administrative arrangement set out in the draft legislation which had been worked out in an effort to implement the Memorandum of Understanding signed in 1977 by the Prime Minister of Canada and the Premiers of Nova Scotia, New Brunswick and Prince Edward Island.

The draft legislation had provided for a Maritime Offshore Resources Board (MORB), with one member appointed by each of the three provinces, and three by the Government of Canada. The Chairman and Vice-Chairman would have been elected by the members, one coming from the provincial side and one from the federal. All major decisions pertaining to the exploration and development of the offshore were to have been taken by the Board. Day-to-day administration would have been in the hands of a resource-management agency operated as a branch of the Department of Energy, Mines and Resources and that agency would have carried out the Board's direction. In cases where the Board did not agree, a designated federal Minister would have taken the decision. A similar arrangement would have been available to other coastal provinces, singly or in groups.

At the Committee's meeting of July 22, federal representatives acknowledged that provinces had a number of criticisms of these arrangements. They sought the reaction of the provinces to a number of possible solutions which governments, including the federal government, might wish to think about in devising new arrangements.

Some of the problems and possible ways of solving them which were tentatively explored, were these:

(a) The MORB would have given the federal Minister final decision-making authority when Board members did not agree. Federal representatives suggested that a possible solution could lie in a more formal kind of high level consultation before important decisions were taken against the wishes of provincial members;

(b) The MORB would have been based on federal legislation which could have been changed or repealed at any time by Parliament. Federal representatives suggested that a possible solution might lie in a constitutional provision for the existence of the Board, coupled perhaps with a listing of its major policy functions in an annex to a new Constitution;

(c) The revenue-sharing arrangement associated with the MORB called for the coastal province concerned to receive 100% of "provincial type" revenues inside the "administration lines" and 75% of such revenues seaward of the lines. Federal representatives suggested that a possible solution to provincial criticisms in this respect might be an increase in this 75% share, perhaps to 100%;

(d) The revenue-sharing arrangement associated with the MORB left in federal hands the final decisions on how much revenue would be shareable, with the possibility that this revenue could be kept deliberately low. Federal representatives indicated that a possible solution could perhaps lie in the adoption of a principle by the governments concerned under which it would be agreed that the revenue-raising system would be devised in such a way as to capture a high proportion of the economic rent from each offshore mineral resource, in a comparable manner to the approach followed by the western provinces in respect of their own land-based resources.

Federal representatives noted that the ideas in (c) and (d) above would have to be subject, at any point in time, to the then existing system of fiscal equalization, and to any possible system of resource revenue sharing — either or both of which would apply to offshore revenues in the same way as to onshore revenues. They would also be contingent on a clearly defined concept of revenues eligible for sharing. Federal representatives indicated that this definition would exclude direct administrative costs incurred by the federal government and federal contributions to the international community.

Federal representatives also noted that any improved administrative arrangement would be available on a bilateral basis if any province so wished.

Provincial representatives stated that while revenue is an important concern, the main criticism of the 1977 Memorandum of Agreement related to the lack of decision making authority for the province. The sub-committee noted that other theoretical models could vest the provinces with such authority, including final decision making.

Provincial representatives emphasized that their major concern is to establish provincial control of offshore resource development in order to protect and enhance their social, economic and physical environment. This stand is based on the fundamental proposition that the necessary sensitivity to the inevitable social and economic impact of mineral resource development is highest at the provincial level. Therefore such impact is managed best by provincial governments.

Federal representatives stressed that administrative arrangements could be designed to ensure a major role for the coastal provinces and to ensure sensitivity in decision-making to social and economic impacts.

The federal government is committed to bringing forward a proposal on administrative arrangements.

APPENDIX I
OFFSHORE RESOURCES DRAFT, JULY 17, 1980

PROPRIETARY RIGHTS

109.1 All lands, mines, minerals and royalties within and arising from the seabed and subsoil of internal waters, the territorial sea and the continental shelf* adjacent or appurtenant to any province and all economic or proprietary rights in the non-renewable natural resources thereof, (and all rights to produce energy from the water, current, tides and winds)** shall belong to the adjacent province.

109.2(1) The delimitation of the area adjacent or appurtenant to each Province shall as between adjacent or opposite Provinces, be that area within lines drawn by agreement in accordance with principles of international law.

109.2(2) If no agreement can be reached within a reasonable period of time, the Provinces concerned shall resort to arbitration, one member of the Arbitration Board being chosen by each Province, and one other or two others in the case of an even number either by agreement of the members of the Board or failing agreement by the Chief Justice of the Supreme Court of Canada.

APPENDIX II
OFFSHORE RESOURCES: LEGISLATIVE JURISDICTION, JULY 17, 1980 (ADDITION TO BEST EFFORTS DRAFT ON RESOURCE OWNERSHIP)

PROPOSED REVISION — SECTION 92

92 (8) For purposes of this section "Province" includes the non-renewable natural resources of the seabed and subsoil of internal waters, the territorial sea and the continental

---

* The continental shelf referred to here includes the shelf, slope and rise to the limit of jurisdiction as determined from time to time by international law. The definition of the continental shelf currently in use by the Law of the Sea Conference is attached as Appendix III.

** Possible inclusion

shelf* adjacent or appurtenant to any province (and all rights of energy production from the water, currents, tides and winds.**)

APPENDIX III
PART VI. CONTINENTAL SHELF

ARTICLE 76
DEFINITION OF
THE CONTINENTAL SHELF

1. The continental shelf of a coastal State comprises the sea-bed and subsoil of the submarine areas that extend beyond its territorial sea throughout the natural prolongation of its land territory to the outer edge of the continental margin, or to a distance of 200 nautical miles from the baselines from which the breadth of the territorial sea is measured where the outer edge of the continental margin does not extend up to that distance.

2. The continental shelf of a coastal State shall not extend beyond the limits provided for in paragraphs 4 to 6.

3. The continental margin comprises the submerged prolongation of the land mass of the coastal State, and consists of the sea-bed and subsoil of the shelf, the slope and the rise. It does not include the deep ocean floor with its oceanic ridges or the subsoil thereof.

4. (a) For the purposes of this Convention, the coastal State shall establish the outer edge of the continental margin wherever the margin extends beyond 200 nautical miles from the baselines from which the breadth of the territorial sea is measured, by either:

(i) A line delineated in accordance with paragraph 7 by reference to the outermost fixed points at each of which the thickness of sedimentary rocks is at least 1 per cent of the shortest distance from such point to the foot of the continental slope; or,

(ii) A line delineated in accordance with paragraph 7 by reference to fixed points not more than 60 nautical miles from the foot of the continental slope.

(b) In the absence of evidence to the contrary, the foot of the continental slope shall be determined as the point of maximum change in the gradient at its base.

5. The fixed points comprising the line of the outer limits of the continental shelf on the sea-bed, drawn in accordance with paragraph 4 (a) (i) and (ii), either shall not exceed 350 nautical miles from the baselines from which the breadth of the territorial sea is measured or shall not exceed 100 nautical miles from the 2,500 metre isobath, which is a line connecting the depth of 2,500 metres.

6. Notwithstanding the provisions of paragraph 5, on submarine ridges, the outer limit of the continental shelf shall not exceed 350 nautical miles from the baselines from which the breadth of the territorial sea is measured. This paragraph does not apply to submarine elevations that are natural components of the continental margin, such as its plateaux, rises, caps, banks and spurs.

7. The coastal State shall delineate the seaward boundary of its continental shelf where that shelf extends beyond 200 nautical miles from the baselines from which the breadth of the territorial sea is measured by straight lines not exceeding 60 nautical miles in length, connecting fixed points, such points to be defined by co-ordinates of latitude and longitude.

8. Information on the limits of the continental shelf beyond the 200 nautical mile exclusive economic zone shall be submitted by the coastal State to the Commission on the Limits of the Continental Shelf set up under annex II on the basis of equitable geographical representation. The Commission shall make recommendations to coastal States on matters related to the establishment of the outer limits of their continental shelf. The limits of the shelf established by a coastal State taking into account these recommendations shall be final and binding.

9. The coastal State shall deposit with the Secretary-General of the United Nations charts and relevant information, including geodetic data, permanently describing the outer limits of its continental shelf. The Secretary-General shall give due publicity thereto.

10. The provisions of this article are without prejudice to the question of delimitation of the continental shelf between adjacent or opposite States.

---

* The continental shelf referred to here includes the shelf, slope and rise to the limit of jurisdiction as determined from time to time by international law.
** Possible inclusion

(h) Third Report of the Committee of Officials on Communications, July 24, 1980

Document: 830-83/016

As directed by Ministers, the Committee discussed the following specific issues concerning telecommunications carriers and cable distribution:

a. *Carriers*   Officials explored means of defining appropriate federal power over interprovincial aspects of telecommunications carriers.

b. *Cable Distribution*   The two most recent drafts were reviewed and pros and cons identified.

CARRIERS

ITEMS OF AGREEMENT

All governments agreed that there should be provincial jurisdiction over the intra provincial aspects of telecommunications carriers. All governments further agreed that there is a national dimension to the interprovincial aspects of telecommunications carriers and that constitutional recognition of this dimension is necessary.

All governments agreed that it would be appropriate to consider means of accommodating these roles.

ISSUES TO BE RESOLVED

On the instruction of Ministers, the Committee developed a proposal designed to accommodate both federal and provincial concerns which would without prejudice to the position stated by the federal Minister at Montreal (CICS document #830-81/008) and the position of any other government.

The proposal is based on concurrent powers over the interprovincial aspects of carriers with general provincial paramountcy except in certain defined areas which would be subject to federal paramountcy.

As illustrative of areas reflecting the national dimension of telecommunications carriage and which could be sub-

ject to federal paramountcy under this approach, officials suggested the following for purposes of discussion:

(1) general management of the technical aspects of the radio frequency spectrum;

(2) the use of telecommunications and telecommunications systems for maritime and aeronautical communications, defence or in national emergency;

(3) satellite communications;

(4) national and international carriers, e.g. CNCP Telecommunications, Teleglobe, Telesat Canada.

The ten provinces agreed to follow an approach based on concurrency over the interprovincial aspects of telecommunications carriers with general provincial paramountcy and federal paramountcy over specific areas. DO MINISTERS WISH THE COMMITTEE TO PREPARE A DRAFT AMENDMENT, IN TIME FOR CONSIDERATION BY MINISTERS AT THEIR NEXT MEETING, BASED UPON THE PROPOSAL OUTLINED ABOVE?

CABLE DISTRIBUTION

ITEMS OF AGREEMENT

All governments agreed that there is a role for both orders of government in cable distribution. More precisely they agree that there should be concurrent jurisdiction with provincial paramountcy except for certain areas to be defined which would be subject to federal paramountcy.

ISSUES TO BE RESOLVED

Following the direction of Ministers, the Committee prepared a list of pros and cons of both the Vancouver draft and the federal draft tabled at the First Ministers' Conference in February, 1979. These [follow] as Annex "A".

All provinces but one supported the provincial consensus draft developed at Vancouver in January, 1979 which would provide for provincial jurisdiction over non-broadcast services, both programming and non-programming and federal paramountcy over the broadcast component. No province supported the February draft which would involve federal paramountcy over the provision of all programming services by whatever technical means.

Officials note that in the discussion of Ministers there was general agreement that each order of government should have jurisdiction over some content on cable. IN VIEW OF THIS, DO MINISTERS WISH THE COMMITTEE TO PREPARE A "BEST EFFORT" DRAFT, FOR THE NEXT MEETING OF THE CCMC, BASED UPON THE VANCOUVER DRAFT? ALTERNATIVELY, SOME OTHER APPROACH, AS DIRECTED BY MINISTERS, COULD BE FOLLOWED.

Ontario officials noted that these discussions would likely be more productive if federal officials were provided with clear direction on the areas of content over which the federal government is prepared to admit provincial paramountcy and if provincial officials were provided with clear direction on the extent to which they are prepared to admit federal paramountcy over non-broadcast services.

BROADCASTING

In order to complete the tasks assigned to it by Ministers, the Committee could not devote time to a full discussion of the field of broadcasting. A majority of governments nevertheless wish to draw to the attention of Ministers three possible approaches to a division of constitutional authority over broadcasting.

The first of these is a continuation of the present constitutional arrangement, namely exclusive federal jurisdiction over all aspects of broadcasting.

A second option, supported by a number of provinces is based on a system of concurrent or shared jurisdiction. In this approach provincial primacy would include the authority to licence and regulate broadcasting undertakings located within a province. Areas of federal primacy would include national broadcasting sources (CBC, CTV) as well as general management of the technical aspects of the radio frequency spectrum.

A final approach, favoured by some provinces, is again based on shared jurisdiction, perhaps expressed in terms of concurrency within the field. This approach assumes overall federal primacy, except in certain areas subject to provincial powers. These areas would include at least educational broadcasting and provincial laws of general application in areas of provincial jurisdictional competence, e.g., commercial advertising.

Most provinces continue to believe that further work developing the latter two options would be productive in terms of defining the provincial role in the field of broadcasting.

Provinces consider that any further work in developing the latter two options is dependent on a decision by Ministers on whether Provinces can assume some constitutional role in the authorization and regulation of programming undertakings and services.

OVERVIEW OF THE DISCUSSION

While the Committee has identified certain areas of agreement, there are fundamental areas of disagreement which remain unresolved. Ministers are advised that these areas of disagreement must be resolved to ensure that any future work of officials will be productive.

ANNEX A

THE VANCOUVER DRAFT

Pros	Cons
1. Would give Provinces a full role in the regulation of some programming services (i.e. closed circuit), as a means of stimulating local identities and of ensuring the provision of local news, information and entertainment.	1. Would give federal government no role in closed-circuit. Access of national program production to closed-circuit would not be guaranteed. Advertising revenues which are vital to Canadian program production would be affected and impact unfavourably on the national program production capability.

Pros	Cons
2. Would permit the Provinces to stimulate Canadian program production on cable. Would permit Provinces to encourage the development of diverse, specialized services for subscribers to meet local and community needs (e.g. children's channels).	2. Could deny access to closed-circuit of Canadian program production. Also limits federal responsibility to Canadian content-like regulation without positive action for program stimulation for cable distribution.
3. Would permit the federal government to stimulate Canadian program production through the CBC and through the regulation of all broadcasting.	3. These means already exist and have not been so far considered as proper and sufficient means to achieve these objectives.
4. Would permit the federal government to stimulate Canadian program production through its general copyright powers (by which it could require cable operators to compensate program producers) and through its taxation powers (such as the Capital Cost Allowance which has revived the film industry) and through the spending power to stimulate Canadian cultural development generally.	4. While this is important as a protective measure, it must be coupled with a positive ability to ensure continued stimulation of the Canadian production industry. This proposal would seriously undermine the Canadian production industry.
5. Would give the federal government the authority to regulate the importation of foreign stations into Canada for distribution over cable.	5. The wording as presently contained in the objective must be clarified if this is the intent. Could give the federal government authority to restrict the freedom of choice of broadcast programming available to individuals.
6. Would give the federal government the authority to ensure that all Canadian television stations—both English and French—were distributed by all cable systems on a *mandatory* and on a *priority* basis.	6. Limits jurisdiction ove technical standards and thereby may restrict orderly technical development of the cable industry in Canada especially with respect to interconnection and closed-circuit.
7. Would give the federal government authority to ensure high technical quality of cable-distributed Canadian broadcast signals.	7. Does not recognize the important interrelationships and similarities between broadcast and non-broadcast services, e.g. signal carriage priorities, advertising, etc. Non-programming can have serious spillover effects on the programming area.
8. Provides for a clear distinction as well as a clear allocation of authority between broadcast and non-broadcast components of cable and, thus, allows for clear lines of accountability to the public.	8. Although the objective is commendable it should not be done at the expense of the total service.
9. Would provide for single tier regulation, and, thus, be preferable from point of view of public and industry.	9. The status quo provides for single tier regulation. Any provincial involvement in cable implies two tier.
10. Would ensure that all financial and hardware aspects of cable are regulated so as to fit local and community requirements.	

THE FEBRUARY DRAFT

Pros	Cons
1. Limits federal paramountcy to matters properly of broadcasting concern and provides concurrent and residual powers over matters properly within cable distribution, thus striking a proper balance between both legitimate interests.	1. Scope of federal paramountcy could nullify provincial regulation of cable.
2. Would extend federal authority to systems operating in a wholly closed-circuit basis within a province.	2. Would extend federal authority to systems operating on a wholly closed-circuit basis within a province.
3. Allows protection and stimulation of Canadian program production capability by ensuring a paramount authority over all programming services with a significant role by provinces in matters of concern to them. Ensures access to all cable systems by Canadian production in both official languages.	3. Perpetuates the ''single system'' concept which requires federal paramountcy over *all* programming services.
4. Provides concurrent jurisdiction and thus ensures a major role for the province.	4. Would not permit Provinces to play full role in the regulation of any programming services. They, thus, would lack the tools necessary to stimulate local identities and to ensure the provision of local news, information and entertainment.
5. Would provide a federal role in resource allocation in order to support national program production.	5. Could place Provinces in the position of having to implement federal policies, with which they may disagree. For example, Provinces might have to increase subscriber rates to accommodate a federal levy on cable subscribers for the support of program production.
6. Involves the federal government in the economic regulation of cable keeping in mind national, social and cultural objectives. National priorities can apply to all cable systems without denying provincial priorities.	6. Involves the federal government in the economic regulation of cable. Federal priorities could, thus, distort provincial priorities in such matters as service quality and extension of cable service. For example, a ban on advertising on the community channel could impede its full development, and could lead to the demise, or prevent the inauguration, of such a service. Or, a ban on all commercial sponsorship could require Provinces to subsidize heavily the provision of educational channels. Would permit the federal government to ban advertising on closed-circuit channels.
7. Scope of federal paramountcy ensures that advertising revenues are not syphoned off such that the Canadian production industry is further endangered, not to mention the impact on the viability of individual broadcasters.	7. Would effect a hazy split between areas of federal and provincial paramountcy thus obscuring accountability to the public.

Pros	Cons
8. Won't permit the development of national technical standards for the distribution of cable television which would benefit equipment suppliers, cable operators and users.	**8.** Would lead to two-tier regulation — which would result in conflict, duplication and increased costs.
9. See answer in point 1.	**9.** Would give the federal government authority to set technical standards which could frustrate provincial policies governing the ownership and technical arrangements respecting cable distribution hardware.
10. See answer in point 8.	**10.** Would lead to a fedeal regulatory role in closed circuit cable services of a purely local nature (e.g. meter-reading, security service, etc.).
11. Would ensure a federal regulatory role in closed-circuit cable services not of a purely local nature.	

(i) Report of the Committee of Officials on a New Second Chamber, July 24, 1980

Document: 830-83/017

BACKGROUND

Ministers met on July 22 to discuss a new second chamber and to provide directions for further work by the Committee of Officials. The Chairman of the Committee gave an oral report on the conclusions reached by Ministers on the basis of the ministerial document "Points of a Senate Consensus" (Montreal) and the Report of the Committee of Officials on the Senate (Toronto; July 17, 1980) [*supra*, p. 625].

After discussion, Ministers asked the Committee:

(a) as a first step, to study the desirability of creating an institution for ratifying federal action, dealing only with a limited list of specified matters of shared federal-provincial concern, and whose voting members would be solely provincial delegates voting on government instruction;

(b) as a second step, to look at the desirability of a wide role of review of House of Commons legislation for a new second chamber whose members would be appointed solely or primarily by the provinces;

(c) to enquire into the desirability of having both of the functions in (a) and (b) dealt with in one new institution or of having two separate institutions for those functions;

(d) to examine the issue of the basis of representation (whether there should be equality of representation by province or region or a weighted formula); and

(e) to consider whether the new body or bodies should make special provision for handling matters related to "dualism".

A. AN INSTITUTION FOR RATIFYING CERTAIN FEDERAL ACTIONS

Under section (a) of the ministerial directives, the Committee examined the desirability of creating a new institution for ratifying federal action on a limited list of specified matters of federal-provincial concern.

(i) *Role of the new institution*

There was a general view in the Committee that the principal role of the new institution should be that of providing a "national consensus" on a short list of "crucial" matters of special concern to the provinces where the federal authorities may now act alone.

(ii) *Matters requiring ratification by the new institution*

There was a general view that the following matters be subject to the requirement of ratification by the new institution:
— the exercise of the declaratory power;
— the exercise of the spending power in areas of provincial jurisdiction;
— the exercise of the emergency power (after the fact in certain cases);
— federal legislation to be administered by the provinces.

The Committee also retained for further examination other matters which might be added to the list if other means of handling them could not be found:
— approval of appointments to certain federal boards and commissions;
— matters which have or might emerge in the overall process or constitutional review which Ministers deem appropriate.

The Committee considered the following matters for action by the new institution, but the general view was that they not be included on the present list:
— constitutional amendments;
— the delegation of legislative authority;
— approval of appointments to the Supreme Court;
— a role in treaty-making in areas of provincial jurisdiction.

(iii) *Method of selection of members of the new institution*

The general view was that members be appointed by provincial governments and vote on instruction by their provincial government. Such members may or may not be provincial Cabinet Ministers. It was noted that there should be no prohibition against dual membership in a legislature and in the new institution. There was a general view that there should be provision for non-voting participation by federal government spokesmen.

(iv) *Tenure*

It was agreed that appointments to the new institution should be at the pleasure of the Lieutenant-Governor in Council.

(v) *Basis of representation*

Seven provinces expressed a preference for equality of representation by provinces, although three of them would accept a compromise weighted formula. Two provinces preferred a weighted formula approach based on population and/or other considerations, but one would accept equality if that were the general view. One preferred equality of representation for five regions but would consider a weighted formula. The federal view was that this was a matter in the first instance for the provinces to determine.

(vi) *Voting procedures*

It was generally agreed that members would cast a bloc vote by province on instruction by their provincial government. There was a general view that ratification should require a majority or 2/3 vote, the choice of which, in the view of some provinces, would depend on the basis of representation selected. These criteria might be varied for issues related to dualism.

B. A NEW SECOND CHAMBER FOR THE REVIEW OF FEDERAL BILLS

Consideration of this matter was carried out under the terms of section (b) of the directives given by Ministers.

(i) *Powers*

There was general agreement that the new second chamber should have the power to review all federal legislation except for appropriations bills and those matters covered under the institution described above in section A. It was also generally agreed that a new second chamber having the review role would only exercise a short suspensive veto of, say, 90 days which could be overridden by a repassage in the House of Commons requiring only one reading and a simple majority.

(ii) *Voting procedures*

All members would be free agents and would not vote on instruction.

(iii) *Basis of representation*

A majority of provinces expressed a preference for equality of representation, but two could move to a compromise weighted formula. Two preferred a weighted formula based on population and/or other considerations. One preferred equality for five regions but would consider a compromise weighted formula. Manitoba provided the following proposal for compromise weighted formula:
— the Yukon and NWT: 2 each;
— P.E.I.: 4;

— N.S., N.B., Newfoundland, Manitoba and Saskatchewan: 8 each;
— Alberta: 10;
— B.C.: 12;
— Ontario and Quebec: 16 each.

(iv) *Appointments*

It was agreed that appointments should be for a fixed period of, say, 8 years, to ensure independence, and that the duration of the initial appointments should be staggered. Whether members could be reappointed was judged to be a matter requiring further consideration. On whether there should be a mix of federal and provincial appointments or provincial appointments only, views were mixed. The federal government proposed that 50% of the members should be federally appointed and 50% provincially. Two provinces shared this view. The majority of provinces favoured provincial appointments only, but a number were willing to consider a minority proportion of federal appointments. It was suggested by one province that consideration could be given to having 75% of the members appointed by provinces and 25% appointed federally.

C. ONE INSTITUTION OR TWO?

There were divergent views on whether the two distinct functions of ratification and review should be handled by one institution or two. If they were combined in one institution, there would be two sorts of members (government delegates and free agents) who would have different rights and powers. Provincial delegates alone would debate and vote on matters for ratification. Both delegates and free agents would debate bills under legislative review.

Arguments in favour of having both functions handled by one institution were:

— there would be a highly beneficial cross-fertilization between the delegates and the free agents if they sat in one House;
— in any given year, the number of issues requiring ratification would be limited and might not provide enough business to keep members of the new institution fully occupied if they did not also have to consider questions arising under the review function;
— creation of two separate institutions rather than one might be criticized by the public as creating one more level of "bureaucracy";
— there would be significant cost savings on support services by having both functions handled by one institution.

Arguments in favour of having the two functions handled by two separate institutions were:

— a single institution might lead to undue confusion for the public on the operations of government;
— the participation of those provincial delegates who are Cabinet Ministers in the deliberation of bills under legislative review would be time consuming and could conflict with their other responsibilities;
— if provincial delegates were accorded voting privileges and were to participate in debate on bills under legislative review, this would alter the balance of the voting structure and would distort the careful distinctions made between the two separate functions to be served;
— it would be inappropriate for provincial Cabinet Ministers to participate in a general review of legislation solely under federal jurisdiction.

There was no agreement on whether there should be one or two institutions.

D. DUALISM

Both Quebec and Ontario had suggested a dualist function for the new institution(s) or for a special committee thereof. During discussion, the following points emerged:

(i) there was general sympathy for accommodating the dualism concept;
(ii) there was general willingness to examine proposals respecting language and linguistic measures;
(iii) there was concern about expanding the proposals to include "culture" because of the problems of defining such a concept;
(iv) it was felt that the mechanisms for dealing with dualism could only be properly discussed when a more concrete idea of the scope of the dualism proposal has been developed and a clearer picture of the new institution(s) has emerged;
(v) until mechanisms had been proposed for examination, it was felt to be premature to discuss whether francophone insterests under the dualism principle could best be safeguarded by Quebec members of a new second chamber, by francophone members of a new second chamber or in some other way.

It was suggested that Ontario and Quebec should prepare more precise proposals for consideration by the Committee at the August meeting of the CCMC. All other governments were invited to submit any ideas they might have to Ontario and Quebec.

SUMMARY

On the basis of this examination of the ministerial objectives, guidance is requested on the following questions:

1. Should a new institution(s) deal with one or both functions of ratification and review?
2. In the event that it is decided that both functions would be desirable, should there be one institution combining two distinct functions and procedures or two separate institutions?

3. What should be the basis of provincial representation and the degree of federal participation in either of the two functions?
4. What should be the voting procedure for either of the two functions?

Respectfully submitted on behalf of the Committee,

Edward D. Greathed
Chairman

(j) Report of the Committee on Natural Resources, Interprovincial Trade, and Powers Over the Economy

Document: 830-83/018

The Committee on Natural Resources, Interprovincial Trade and Powers over the Economy met on July 22, 23 and 24. All governments were represented. The Chairman began by outlining the Committee's mandate, as determined by the Ministers at the meeting in Toronto on July 17. The Ministers had directed the Committee to examine the paper entitled "Powers Over the Economy: Options Submitted for Consideration by the Government of Canada to Safeguard the Canadian Economic Union in the Constitution" (Document No. 830-82/007) which included drafts on revised Section 121, revisions to Section 91(2) and part 8 of the proposed Charter of Rights pertaining to mobility of citizens. In addition the Ministers directed the Committee to examine other drafts which might be forthcoming from other governments.

The Chairman indicated that, based on the officials' discussion on July 17, there did not appear to be a consensus on: (i) the nature and magnitude of the problem with respect to powers over the economy; (ii) the solutions (techniques) which might be adopted to solve the perceived problem; and (iii) the rationale for the linkage between the discussion on the topic of "Powers Over the Economy" and other aspects of the constitutional discussions, in particular natural resources.

The Committee began its deliberations by a detailed study and analysis of the federal government's proposed revisions to Section 121. (These are annexed to this report as Appendix I [*supra*, pp. 621–623]). The federal government outlined the purpose and intent of the revisions stating that it wished to minimize economic discrimination within Canada based on provincial or territorial boundaries. This would not constitute an absolute prohibition of differentiated social and economic policies of governments. The Committee accepted the goal of furthering and maintaining the objectives of an economic union. The Committee's discussion on Section 121 appeared to polarize around which technique was more appropriate to maintain and further the objectives of the economic union, the expansion of Section 121 or a statement of principles coupled with a commitment to consultation amongst governments.

The Committee then addressed itself to the prohibitions found in Section 121(1). After some discussion it was agreed that Section 121(1) is not intended to apply so as to prohibit provincial legislation or policies having intraprovincial application but not discriminatory on the basis of the *province* of residence, origin or destination. Although such legislation or policies might be "discriminatory" *within* a province, it would not be discriminatory in the sense intended by Section 121(1).

In addition, the Committee agreed that governments would need to have some powers to legislate in ways that are discriminatory in the sense intended by Section 121(1). The Committee then addressed itself to the derogations therefrom found in Section 121(2) and (3).

In addition to the discussion on derogations considerable time was spent on the scope and meaning of specific words within the text, in particular the words "practice" and "unduly impedes". Some provinces expressed concern over the potential role of the courts in interpreting this section.

In addition to the material presented by the Government of Canada various other documents were submitted to the Committee for its consideration. These were: —

(1) A.E. Safarian, "Ten Markets or One?" (Ontario Economic Council)
(2) Ontario's Document No. 830-83/012 (See Appendix I A)
(3) Quebec's Document No. 830-83/006
(4) Saskatchewan's Document Nos. 830-83/003, 830-83/004, 830-83/005 and Saskatchewan's analysis of Document No. 830-82/007

The Ontario proposal for a revised Section 121, which concentrated on the intent rather than the effect of legislation and practice, was then discussed. Although the Ontario draft explicitly added a proposal for an exception for intra-provincial regional development programs, several provincial delegates thought that the Ontario proposal went further than the Government of Canada proposal because of the elimination of the "undue" test.

The Government of Saskatchewan paper (Document No. 830-83/003) was then discussed. It proposed an alternative technique with respect to constitutional revision of the subject "Powers Over the Economy".

Following the discussion of the two provincial papers the Committee focussed its attention once more on the concept of derogation from the principle outlined in Section 121(1). Several provinces expressed concern and disagreement with Section 121(3). Specifically they were concerned that Section 121(3) enhanced federal legislative powers while provincial governments were being required to curtail their legislative powers. Committee members noted that Section 121(3) had three separate provisions for continued federal legislative activity: (i) equalization and regional development; (ii) laws declared by Parliament to be in an overriding national interest; and (iii) laws enacted pursuant to an international obligation undertaken by Canada. Federal representatives assured the provinces that this wording was not intended to add to federal legislative powers and that rewording of the clause to clarify this point might be favourable considered. However, some provinces thought that this part should be extended to include provincial legislatures which should also be authorized to establish an "Overriding provincial interest".

Federal representatives disagreed believing that this defeated the very purpose of a revised Section 121.

Nova Scotia raised the possibility and desirability of including in the Constitution a specific list of derogations from the general prohibitions on discrimination contained in revised Section 121 and offered a specific list.

The concept of a specific list of derogations precipitated a discussion on how and where to draw the line. If the list were too great the general principle would be destroyed; if the list were too short many accepted existing provincial policies could be nullified. One solution proposed was to develop derogations based on a proposal contained in the Pepin-Robarts Report. The report stated: — "Similarly, we think preferential provincial purchasing policies should be permitted only in those cases where the province requires them to alleviate acute economic hardship. We further suggest that the justification for such practices and the time they are expected to last should be specified and should be agreed to by other provinces." (Page 71) To some provinces this did not go far enough.

There was no agreement on how to define and limit the derogations. Some provinces were concerned that the wording of the new section should give clear guidance to the courts in interpreting it. Other governments wished to reduce the role of the courts by finding other ways of resolving disputes. It was stated by some governments that disputes with respect to discrimination should be resolved by the political process. This process could include First Ministers' Conferences or a revised second Chamber. It was further suggested that if the political process could not resolve the matter then there could be ultimate recourse to the courts.

An alternative "technique" to promote and maintain the economic union was proposed by Saskatchewan (Appendix II). Saskatchewan drew attention to the parallel between its proposal and the "best efforts" draft on equalization. Following a brief discussion which focussed on the lack of judicial enforceability of the commitments of all governments contained in the proposal, the officials agreed to forward it to the Ministers for their further consideration.

REVISIONS TO SECTION 91(2)

The Committee discussed changes proposed by the federal government to Section 91(2), trade and commerce (see

Appendix III [*supra*, p. 623]). Discussion focussed on three subject matters:

1. federal legislative powers over product standards;
2. federal legislative powers over competition policy; and
3. incorporation of the words "goods, services and capital" under the trade and commerce power.

1. PRODUCT STANDARDS

As a result of the decisions by the Supreme Court in the "Lite" beer and Dominion Stores cases, the Government of Canada has concern that its legislative powers over uniform product standards have been significantly curtailed. This concern related to the differentiation in powers to set standards for products originating and consumed within a province and those being exported from the province in either interprovincial or international trade.

The discussion focused on

(a) the need for a constitutional amendment to solve this problem as opposed to other techniques such as inter-governmental agreements, delegation, adoption of federal standards by provinces or letting market forces prevail;

(b) the implications of such an amendment on existing provincial legislative powers such as occupational health and safety and higher standards for certain products; and

(c) the possibility of derogations from the federal standards in the case of products produced and consumed primarily within a particular province. Nova Scotia tabled an alternative draft which advanced this concept (see Appendix IV).

2. COMPETITION POLICY

The federal government outlined the difficulties it faced in incorporating and enforcing competition policy under criminal law power. It advanced the argument that a different grant of power under the head of trade and commerce was preferable. To a great extent the discussion focussed on the following questions:

(a) Would this separate head under 91(2) add to or merely clarify federal legislative powers?

No conclusive answer was established.

(b) What would the effect be on existing provincial legislative powers to regulate areas such as professions, utilities, marketing of agricultural products, liquor, insurance companies and provincial Crown corporations?

Again no definitive view emerged.

3. SECTION 91(3) — TRADE AND COMMERCE

The federal government argued that there was a need to clarify its legislative powers over trade and commerce and that, while a substantial body of opinion believed the existing section included services and capital, it was desirable to incorporate these words to avoid any possible doubts.

The discussion focussed on whether the addition of these words increased or clarified federal powers. Specific items of concern to the provinces included the effect upon credit unions, language policy, government borrowing, securities and professions. It was noted that there are ways of drafting reference to "services and capital" to minimize the risk of a judicial extension of the trade and commerce power.

SUMMARY

In summary, the Committee's discussion focussed on two basic techniques to maintain the economic union. If the one advanced by the Government of Canada were pursued there appeared to be general agreement on the following:

1. The principles of the economic union should somehow be described.
2. Provincial governments should be permitted to discriminate within the province for regional development purposes provided such discrimination did not have an extra-provincial effect.
3. Some derogations from the general principles of the economic union should be provided for.

The Saskatchewan technique also recognized the need for an outline of the principles for an economic union. In this respect the two techniques, despite wording differences, were coming to grips with the same issue. The substantial difference was how best to safeguard the operation of the economic union.

NATURAL RESOURCES

There was a brief discussion on this topic. Part of the discussion was devoted to an explanation of the evolution of the 1979 "best efforts" draft. This included some of the reservations and concerns which various governments have with respect to matters such as: the definition of natural resources, compelling national interest, the linkage between provincial legislative powers over natural resources and federal powers over trade and commerce, indirect taxation and resources.

Because certain sections of the "best efforts" draft considered critical by some provinces were not acceptable to the Government of Canada, the Government of Alberta proposed, for discussion purposes, an alternative technique to limit federal powers over trade and commerce as this power affected natural resources (see Appendix V).

This led to a discussion as to whether or not the Government of Canada was prepared to consider limitations to its legislative powers over trade and commerce and to admit provinces to powers over the export of resources. While the federal government did not present a position it indicated that it was prepared to listen to what the provinces said with respect to this topic. It indicated that it continued to place priority on powers over the economy and a greater commitment on the part of the provinces to the economic union. It also indicated that it might consider subjecting the use of the declaratory power to review by a reformed Senate. This was supported by some provinces.

The Committee requests further ministerial direction with respect to the topic of natural resources and interprovincial trade.

APPENDIX IA
ONTARIO'S DISCUSSION PROPOSALS CONCERNING RESOURCES AND POWERS OVER THE ECONOMY, JULY 24, 1980

Document: 830-83/012

Economic Principles

1. Ontario submits for discussion a proposed set of principles defining the nature and implementation of a Canadian Economic Union.
2. These principles could be inserted in the Constitution to serve as an introductory section preceeding Section 121, or, as part of a General Statement of Principles.
3. Ontario's proposal is that these principles be made effective through a revised Section 121.

Section 121

4. A proposed revision by Ontario to the federal draft of Section 121 [follows].
5. It aims to remove the new concept of "unduly" in referring to impediments to the Canadian Economic Union and brings the intent within established constitutional doctrine.

6. It permits intra provincial discrimination to reduce substantial economic disparities among sub-regions of a province, and adds a derogation relating to the protection of culture.

ONTARIO DISCUSSION PROPOSAL ON PRINCIPLES OF THE ECONOMIC UNION

1. The Government of Canada and the governments of the provinces jointly agree that the best economic and social interests of the people of Canada are to be promoted through the continuation and strengthening of the Canadian Economic Union in all parts of Canada.
2. The aims of the Canadian Economic Union are to foster and encourage through its laws and practices:
   (a) equality of economic opportunity of persons residing in all provinces and of persons residing in sub-regions of a province;
   (b) freedom of movement of people, goods, services and capital throughout Canada and the reduction and avoidance of impediments to that freedom;
   (c) harmonization between governments of policies and practices relating to trade and commerce in order to promote national and regional economic growth;
   (d) harmonization between governments of fiscal policies to stabilize and promote national and regional economic growth;
   (e) rationalization by governments of the administration of public services so as to reduce and avoid overlap, duplication and waste.
3. Towards the achievement of these aims, the Government of Canada and the governments of the provinces commit themselves to the ongoing, systematic and co-operative review of the operation of the Canadian Economic Union.

FURTHER DISCUSSION DRAFT SECTION 121 — ONTARIO JULY 23, 1980

121 (1) Canada is constituted an economic union within which all persons, goods, services, and capital may move freely and without discrimination based on province or territory of residence, or former residence, or origin or of destination in Canada.

(2) Parliament or a legislature shall not enact a law in relation to the establishment or the authorization of discrimination or to the adoption of discriminatory practices contrary to subsection (1).

(3) Nothing in subsection (2) renders invalid a law of Parliament or the legislature that would otherwise be valid if it is enacted in relation to the protection of culture, public safety, order, health or morals.

(4) Nothing in subsection (2) renders invalid a law of Parliament that would otherwise be valid if it is enacted.

(a) In accordance with the principles of equalization or regional development recognized in this Constitution;

(b) in relation to a matter that is declared by Parliament in the enactment to have an overriding national interest; or

(c) to perform an international obligation of Canada.

(5) Nothing in subsection (2) renders invalid a law of a legislature that would otherwise be valid if it is directed at the reduction of substantial economic disparities between regions wholly within the province.

(6) Nothing in subsections (3) (4) or (5) renders valid a law of Parliament or a legislature that impedes the admission free into any province of goods, services or capital originating in or imported into any other province or territory.

APPENDIX II
THE CANADIAN ECONOMIC UNION

DRAFT — FOR DISCUSSION PURPOSES ONLY — SASKATCHEWAN, JULY 23, 1980.

Document: 830-83/004

121. Without altering the legislative or other authority of Parliament or the legislatures or of the Government of Canada or the governments of the Provinces or the rights of any of them with respect to the exercise of their respective legislative or other authority:

(a) Parliament and the legislatures, together with the Government of Canada and the governments of the Provinces, are committed to

(i) the maintenance and enhancement of the Canadian economic union,

(ii) the movement throughout Canada of persons, goods, services and capital without discrimination by Canada or any Province, by law or practice, in a manner that unjustifiably impedes the operation of the Canadian economic union, and

(iii) the harmonization of federal and provincial laws,

policies, and practices that affect the Canadian economic union; and

(b) pursuant to the commitments specified in clause (a), the Government of Canada and the governments of the Provinces are committed to the ongoing, systematic and co-operative review by them of the operation of the Canadian economic union.

APPENDIX IV
NOVA SCOTIA SUGGESTED RE-DRAFT OF SECTION 91(2.1)

91. (2.1) The regulation of competition throughout Canada.

(2.2) The establishment of reasonable minimum product standards in Canada or in the various provinces or regions thereof; but any law of the legislature of a province concerning standards for products substantially produced and consumed within the province and which does not contravene Section 121 shall have paramountcy over a law of Canada passed pursuant to this subsection.

COMMENTS ON CHANGES FROM FEDERAL DRAFT

(a) "reasonable minimum" product standards — new.

(b) drops the requirement of being "reasonably necessary" for the operation of the Canadian economic union.

(c) excludes products in intraprovincial trade only, where the province chooses to legislate.

(d) provincial legislation would be subject to the tests of Section 121 — i.e., it could not discriminate in a way that "unduly impedes" the economic union, except for the reasons spelled out in the derogations.

APPENDIX V
ALBERTA DRAFT, JULY 23, 1980

THE TRADE UNION AND COMMERCE POWER

91. 2. The regulation of trade and commerce, but not including natural resources and the primary production therefrom.

(k) Report by the Sub-Committee of Officials on a Charter of Rights, July 24, 1980

Document: 830-83/019

1. A sub-committee of officials representing all eleven governments and under the chairmanship of Roger Tassé met on July 22, 23 and 24 in Vancouver to examine the several issues on an entrenched Charter of Rights which had been referred to them by Ministers, namely

   (a) review the federal discussion draft of July 4, 1980 to consider how entrenchment of its provisions might impact on provincial legislative powers, having particular regard to the legal and practical implications of the proposed legal rights;

   (b) consider changes that would clarify and improve the language of the draft;

   (c) consider the possibility and desirability of entrenching the Canadian Bill of Rights rather than the proposed Charter;

   (d) consider the possibility of entrenching a Charter of Rights at the federal level only initially, thus permitting provinces to assess the impact of entrenched rights; and

   (e) consider the practicability of including an override (non-obstante) clause in an entrenched Charter, thus allowing jurisdictions to enact laws that would expressly supersede particular rights.

Note: Manitoba does not agree that the sub-committee was asked to review the language of the draft other than to examine its impact on legislative powers of the provinces, and does not agree that the sub-committee was asked to consider entrenchment of the Canadian Bill of Rights, but was asked to consider the possibility of amending the Bill of Rights as a means of extending the protection of freedoms at the federal level.

2. *Items (a) and (b)* (impact and language of proposed Charter provisions) were addressed together, it is being understood that discussion on these and other items were *without prejudice to any province's position on the principle of entrenchment itself.* This will be a matter for further ministerial consideration in light of this report.

3. On each of the categories of rights, a number of concerns were identified by officials both as to the meaning of certain expressions in the text and as to the impli-

cations for the exercise of legislative powers if rights were entrenched. The discussions brought forward numerous suggestions for modifications and improvements which will be given further consideration in attempting to prepare a revised text for review at the August meeting of Ministers, assuming that it be the wish of Ministers.

4. What follows with respect to each of the categories of rights and related matters is not an exhaustive description of all issues discussed, but simply an attempt to encapsulate some of the major concerns that were identified and the general views that were expressed.

5. *Fundamental Freedoms (Section 2):* Concerns were expressed here respecting such matters as:

   — would freedom of religion interfere with existing confessional school rights, tax exemptions for religious institutions and qualifications for performing marriages?

   — would freedom of expression preclude laws regulating advertising?

   — should freedom of the press and other media be made clearer?

On none of these was there strong feeling that major modifications were essential; only that further reflection was needed in drafting specific provisions.

6. *Democratic Rights (Sections 3–5):* There was general agreement that these rights and their manner of expresssion were acceptable, subject to dropping the preambular clause to section 3. Manitoba, however, would not wish to leave to the courts determination of what limitations on the right to vote were reasonable.

7. *Legal Rights (Section 6):* Detailed discussion on this category produced a substantial number of serious concerns and reservations respecting both the specific language of the rights and the limits that would be imposed on existing legislative powers and administrative procedures and practices (both federal and provincial) if all proposed rights were entrenched.

   One major concern related to the problems that would arise if all the rights applied not only to criminal and penal proceedings but to civil and administrative matters as well. On this point, a substantial majority of jurisdictions favoured limiting virtually all rights to criminal and penal matters and proceedings; this concern extended to a fair hearing in all cases where rights and obligations are being determined. A substantial majority favoured leaving protection in this area to legislation and common law.

Other concerns included:
— the consequences of possibly importing American jurisprudence relating to due process of law and non-admissibility of illegally obtained evidence. On this latter point it was agreed that we should not import the U.S. exclusionary rule nor should we permit a rule admitting all illegally obtained evidence. Rather, the rule should be one falling somewhere in between. As to the method of ensuring this result, it was agreed that the views of the Task Force on Evidence should be sought before any decision is taken respecting appropriate Charter wording;
— the dangers of leaving to courts the determination of "reasonable" standards for application of such rights as those relating to search, seizure and privacy;
— the difficulties that could arise by permitting a right to counsel whenever one is compelled to give evidence;

In general, a number of useful suggestions were made for modifications in the provisions of this category of rights which will be given further consideration.

8. *Non-Discrimination Rights (Section 7):* It was recognized that entrenching this category would create a very substantial limitation on existing legislative powers in an area where rights are evolving, and would leave to the courts broad powers to judge social values. There were also concerns about the wording of the draft proposals which would require further consideration in any redraft. Seven jurisdictions opposed including this category, with the others inclined to its inclusion if appropriate wording can be found.

9. *Mobility Rights (Section 8):* Apart from the first section (right of citizens to enter, remain in and leave Canada) on which most were agreed, a number of concerns were expressed about the substantial impact some of these provisions would have on provincial laws (economic and social), especially the property and employment rights. About one-half favoured inclusion of a right to move and take up residence but there was little provincial support for property and employment rights. Quebec strongly opposes any entrenchment of this category of rights.

10. *Property Rights (Section 9):* Concerns were expressed here both on the meaning of some of the provisions and on the substantive provisions as they would affect provincial

laws or legislative powers. In particular, serious doubts were voiced about the wisdom of allowing courts to determine what is reasonable compensation for property taken. A large majority of jurisdictions felt that this category should not be included although some of these were sympathetic to the principle involved.

10. a. *Limitation Clauses:* On several occasions during discussion of the foregoing rights, concerns were expressed about the scope and meaning of the limitation clauses found in various sections. As one possible means of overcoming this problem federal representatives suggested that consideration be given to an opening clause in the Charter that would indicate that none of the rights and freedoms were absolutes but must be balanced against the interests of an organized free and democratic society operating under the rule of law. This could eliminate the need for any specific limitation clauses. This proposal was not favourably received by most provinces that responded to it.

11. *Official Languages (Section 10):* (*Note*: On all language provisions of the draft Charter the representative of Quebec abstained from discussion and the Manitoba representative reserved on that province's position.) Suggestions were made for amendments to this section: one would have deleted all but the provision that "English and French are the official languages of Canada"; the other would have accepted this amendment but retained the provisions of section 10(2) allowing greater legislative protection for language use. A majority favoured retaining the section as is. On the question of entrenching section 10, four favoured, two opposed and two reserved.

12. *Language Rights (Sections 11–16)*
(1) *Section 11:* On use of both languages in Parliament 8 were in favour; and on use of both languages in legislatures four were in favour, four opposed.
(2) *Section 12:* With respect to statutes in both languages, 8 were in favour of the federal level, with only New Brunswick affirmative on this as a *binding* obligation for that province. As for those six provinces where the extent of the obligation would be left to their legislatures, five were in favour and one opposed. Seven provinces favoured the principle of both versions of the statutes being authoritative, one opposed.
(3) *Section 13:* On the use of both languages in the courts, 8 agreed to this at the federal level. Ontario opposed a *binding* obligation for that province, while New Brunswick favoured it for itself. As for the six provinces where the extent of the right is for determination by the legislatures, three provinces were in favour (one suggesting this rule should apply for *all* provinces), one opposed and two

reserved. On the question of ensuring a witness to give evidence in either language in criminal and serious penal proceedings, a number of concerns were expressed about the language of the provision and its possible conflict with Criminal Code provisions on language of trials. Two provinces opposed inclusion of the right in any form, and two reserved. Four favoured its inclusion, with an amendment which would delete reference to the witness not being disadvantaged in testifying in his own language. One province abstained.

(4) *Section 14:* On services to the public in both languages at the federal level, there was agreement on this although some provinces would object if it extended to RCMP contract services to the provinces. On services at the provincial level, three provinces were in favour with another three possibly in favour as long as no legal obligation was implied. Two provinces were opposed.

(5) *Section 15:* Seven provinces were agreed on the preservation of third language rights in addition to French and English, one opposed.

(6) *Section 16:* Some concerns were expressed on the draft proposals for minority language education rights, particularly with respect to the extent to which the courts could review the scope of a province's discretion in determining where numbers warrant. Other concerns expressed related to the practical problems that could arise in provinces with two or more separate school systems if provisions for schools along linguistic lines were superimposed. An amendment to delete the test for the validity of provincial action implementing minority language education rights in section 16(2) (''consistent with the right provided in subsection (1)'') received support of three provinces with other provinces reserving their position. Concerning acceptance of the principle contained in section 16, four jurisdictions approved, two opposed and three abstained.

13. *Undeclared Rights (Section 17):* Concerns identified in this provision related to the courts inventing new rights, possible conflicts between specified and unspecified rights and the singling out for special attention of native peoples' terms of clarification of intent and content. On the acceptability of the principle in this section and on the exclusion of a reference to native rights, two provinces favoured the principle with native rights deleted, three provinces opposed the section in any form and four provinces reserved their position, two of whom would delete reference to native rights in any case.

14. *Paramountcy of Charter Rights (Section 18):* One province opposed inclusion of this provision which would render inoperative any law or administrative act conflicting with a Charter right. Several other provinces felt that no position could be taken on the acceptability of this provision until the specific rights to be included in an entrenched Charter were determined. Others indicated that if there is going to be an entrenched Charter, then a provision along the lines of this section is required.

15. *Remedies for Violations of Rights (Section 19):* Views were somewhat divided on the possible problems inherent in the wording of this provision which specifies the power of courts to grant appropriate remedies for breaches of rights where no other effective remedy or recourse exists. However, no jurisdiction appeared to disagree with the need to provide for remedies. One concern, generally shared, was that remedies should also exist for apprehended as well as actual breaches. As to whether invoking section 19 remedies should be conditioned on the absence of other effective recourses, some felt it should, while other jurisdictions took the opposite view. One province believed that court enforcement might be appropriate for certain types of rights but not others.

16. *Application of Charter to Territories (Section 20):* There were only two minor technical drafting changes proposed for this section.

17. *No Extension of Legislative Powers (Section 21):* This provision, which is designed to ensure that the Charter makes no change in the distribution of legislative powers, created doubts for some provinces as to its need. Three felt it should be deleted, two favoured its retention, one was indifferent and four reserved.

17. [sic] *Protection of Existing Language Guarantees (Section 22):* There was some provincial concern on this provision as to when the repeal of existing language guarantees in Quebec and Manitoba would take place. On the suggestion that the appropriate time would be when the Charter language rights are entrenched for these two jurisdictions, four jurisdictions agreed and five reserved their position. Quebec and Manitoba also noted concerns they have with the existing wording of the language guarantees in the B.N.A. Act and the Manitoba Act, in light of the *Blaikie* case. This matter will require further consideration.

18. *Opting-in to Language Guarantees (Section 23):* Manitoba proposed that this provision be amended to permit a province that opts into the more stringent language guarantees of the Charter to opt out subsequently. Four jurisdictions favoured this approach while five were opposed and one abstained.

19. The sub-committee next turned to *item (c) of the mandate*, an examination of the question of possible entrenchment of the Canadian Bill of Rights. However, due to differing views of the sub-committee's mandate on this matter, it was put over pending clarification by Ministers as to what was intended on this subject.

20. The sub-committee then turned to *item (e) of its mandate*, namely the practicability of including an override clause in an entrenched Charter. There was only time for a general canvassing of preliminary views on this matter but most jurisdictions felt that, if it were possible to fashion a suitable override clause, this could perhaps be an acceptable approach to dealing with an entrenched Charter. However, further discussion will be required to test the viability of this proposition.

Roger Tassé
Chairman

(I) Co-Chairman's Summary of Consensus Reached by Ministers on Committee Reports, July 7–24, 1980

Document: 830-83/022

1) Equalization

Ministers received the report of the officials' committee on Equalization (Tab 1 [*supra*, p. 630]), chaired by Gérard Veilleux.

There was some discussion of the three alternatives in the Committee Report. No clear consensus emerged, although there was considerable support for Option B (The February, 1979 Best Efforts Draft, as amended by Quebec).

It was noted that British Columbia supports the broad principles as set down in section 91 (1), (a) (b) and (c) of the Best Efforts Draft (including the amended versions), but does not support the entrenchment of an equalization formula in the constitution.

2) Family Law

Ministers received the report of the officials' committee on Family Law (Tab 2 [*supra*, p. 632]), chaired by Allan Leal.

It was agreed that the committee should meet again,
1) to continue its effort to achieve a solution to the problem of effective enforcement of maintenance and custody orders; and
2) to begin the drafting of an amendment "to provide that the federal Parliament be given exclusive legislative authority to prescribe the basis for recognition of decrees of annulment and declarations of nullity and to establish the basis of jurisdiction of the courts granting these decrees."

3) Supreme Court

Ministers received the report of the officials' committee on the Supreme Court (Tab 3 [*supra*, p. 633]), chaired by Roger Tassé.

In response to a suggestion by the provincial co-chairman, the committee chairman noted that pending further political direction, there was not much more the committee could do on the question of a deadlock-breaking mechanism.

4) Offshore Resources

Ministers received the report of the officials' committee on Offshore Resources (Tab 4 [*supra*, p. 643]), chaired by Donald Dennison.

The provincial co-chairman noted that governments were awaiting the federal paper on new administrative arrangements. It was agreed that this issue required further political direction.

5) Communications

Ministers received the officials' committee report on Communications (Tab 5 [*supra*, p. 649]), chaired by Philippe Doré.

In response to requests for direction put to the ministers in the report, ministers issued the following instructions:

(1) that the committee proceed with the preparation of a draft amendment, in time for consideration by minis-

ters at their next meeting, based upon the principle of concurrency over the interprovincial aspects of telecommunications carriers with general provincial paramountcy and federal paramountcy over specific areas.

(2) that on the subject of cable, the committee proceed with the preparation of a "best effort" draft, for the next meeting of the CCMC, based upon the Vancouver draft.

(3) that the committee proceed with the further development of options contained in the committee report with a view to proposing options for ministers' consideration which would define a provincial role in broadcasting.

6) Fisheries

Ministers received the report of the officials' committee on Fisheries (Tab 6 [*supra*, p. 641]), chaired by John Fitzgerald.

7) Patriation/Amending Formula

Ministers received the report of the officials' committee on Patriation/Amending Formula (Tab 7 [*supra*, p. 636]), chaired by Gary Posen.

The provincial co-chairman suggested that those provinces with technical questions regarding the Alberta proposals should submit them in writing to Alberta, along with copies to the other governments, and that Alberta should provide written responses, again with copies to other governments.

8) Preamble/Principles of a Constitution

Ministers received a summary of their discussion, prepared by the officials' committee on Preamble/Principles of a Constitution chaired by Nicholas Gwyn (Tab 8 [*supra*, p. 635], as revised to reflect ministers' discussions).

9) Senate

Ministers received a report (Tab 9 [*supra*, p. 653]), from the officials' committee on the Senate, chaired by Edward Greathed.

10) Charter of Rights

Ministers received a report (Tab 10 [*supra*, p. 661]), from the officials' committee on the Charter of Rights, chaired by Roger Tassé.

It was agreed that the committee should meet again to consider the Diefenbaker Bill of Rights in the context of Manitoba's clarification of the ministers' mandate to the committee: whether the Bill of Rights could have a status greater than that of an ordinary statute but short of constitutional entrenchment.

11) Natural Resources, Interprovincial Trade, and Powers over the Economy

Ministers received a report (Tab 11 [*supra*, p. 656]) from the officials' committee on Natural Resources and and Powers over the Economy, chaired by Peter Meekison.

It was agreed that the committee should meet prior to the next CCMC session to consider the option of concurrency with federal paramountcy with respect to trade in resources, as well as the Best Efforts Draft.

12) Final Business

Ministers agreed to empower the two co-chairmen to meet at an early date and draft a workplan for the August CCMC meeting. This workplan would be sent to ministers for their comments.

Ministers agreed that the CCMC be convened Tuesday, August 26. The Secretariat was instructed to keep Saturday of that week open in case it was required. Ottawa was confirmed as the location.

Ministers agreed to leave the arrangements for a meeting with native representatives to the co-chairmen, who in turn would inform them of the arrangements.

40. Sub-Committee Meeting of Continuing Committee of Ministers on the Constitution, August 11–13, 1980

(a) Report of the Sub-Committee on Family Law, August 12, 1980

Document: 840-195/002 (R)

Your sub-committee met on Monday, August 11, 1980 with delegates from all provincial jurisdictions and the federal administration in attendance.

Your sub-committee renewed its search for a solution to the perceived problem of more expeditious and effective enforcement of maintenance and custody orders. We are pleased to report that we have arrived at a solution which we recommend for consideration by Ministers which embodies three principles as follows:

(i) that maintenance and custody orders made anywhere in Canada have legal effect throughout Canada;

(ii) that these orders may be enforced throughout Canada by the single expedient of registration;

(iii) that provision be made for the provinces to make laws providing for the variation and non-enforcement of orders by reason of a change in circumstances and for the non-enforcement of orders on grounds of public policy or lack of due process of law.

The recommended text embodying these principles [follows] as Appendix "A".

The vote to accept this draft was 8 in favour of the resolution with three jurisdictions abstaining. The delegate of Manitoba supported the first two principles and reserved on the third.

All of which is respectfully submitted.

H. Allan Leal
Chairman

APPENDIX A

x. An order for maintenance or custody made in Canada has legal effect throughout Canada.

xx. An order referred to in section x made in any province may be registered in any other province in a court of competent jurisdiction and shall be enforced in like manner as an order of that court.

xxx. The legislatures of the provinces may make laws to give effect to the provisions of sections x and xx including laws providing for the variation and non-enforcement of orders by reason of a change in circumstances and for the non-enforcement of orders on grounds of public policy or lack of due process of laws.

FAMILY LAW: PROPOSED CONSTITUTIONAL TEXT (AUGUST 12, 1980)

95A The Legislature of each province may make laws in relation to marriage in the province, including the validity of marriage in the province, except that Parliament has exclusive authority to make laws in relation to the recognition of a declaration that a marriage is void whether granted within or outside Canada, and in relation to the jurisdictional basis upon which a court may entertain an application for a declaration that a marriage is void.

(b) Report of the Sub-Committee of Officials on Communications, August 13, 1980

Document: 840-195/004

As directed by Ministers, the Sub-Committee met in Toronto on August 12 and 13th.

British Columbia tabled a Document: 840-195/003 suggesting an integrated approach to the four sectors of communications. The proposal however was not discussed.

TELECOMMUNICATIONS CARRIERS

The Sub-Committee first discussed briefly the draft on telecommunications carriers set out in the Vancouver report 830-83/016 [*supra*, p. 649]. Discussions centered on the following points: the Federal heads of paramountcy concerning "maritime communications", "satellite communications" and "national and international carriers". Some provinces felt that the heads of jurisdiction should be restricted in maritime matters to "communications relating to navigation" and in "satellite communications" to exclude earth stations. They also felt that Federal jurisdiction should apply to "overseas telecommunications" instead of "national and international carriers".

Provinces recognized a need for a conflict resolution mechanism in interprovincial aspects of telecommunications carriers. They suggested the following models:
a) adding a new head of Federal paramountcy
b) adding a new clause providing for a role for either a federal-provincial agency, an interprovincial agency, or a reformed Senate.

Provinces stated that pending an indication from the federal government as to areas of federal paramountcy sought, the proposal on telecommunications carriers set out in the Vancouver report 830-83/016 would represent a "best efforts" draft subject to the above concerns.

Saskatchewan tabled a list of Questions to Federal Officials on telecommunications carriers.

BROADCASTING

There was an initial discussion on broadcasting where some provinces restated and elucidated their positions for Federal officials. Then Provinces met among themselves with a view to developing a common approach to this area.

Federal officials stated that it would be desirable for provinces to achieve a degree of consensus in the area of broadcasting as they have in the areas of telecommunications carriers and cable in order to assist the discussions in the entire field of communications. At the request of the federal government, some provinces restated their views of the local and regional dimensions of broadcasting.

In response to a request from the provinces, federal officials noted that they were not able to change their position on broadcasting. The provinces perceived the federal position to be based exclusively on the "single-system" concept. Federal officials expressed however, their readiness to consider alternative proposals, without prejudice, as instructed by Ministers in Vancouver.

With the agreement of the Committee, the provincial delegations met to formulate a provincial concensus draft on broadcasting. On reconvening, the Chairman reported that the provincial discussions extended to the entire field of communications and that no document resulted from this meeting although there was a full and productive discussion. Areas of agreement were identified and all provinces agreed that further discussions would be useful.

(c) Provincial Consensus Draft on Communications, August 13, 1980

Document: 830-84/012

(1) In each province the Legislature may make laws in relation to telecommunication works and undertakings in the province notwithstanding that such works and undertakings connect the province with any other or others of the provinces, extend beyond the limits of the province, or emit signals originating in the province beyond the province, or receive or distribute in the province signals originating outside the province.

(2) The Parliament of Canada may make laws in relation to telecommunication works and undertakings mentioned in sub-section (1) other than works and undertakings wholly situate within a province.

(3) No law enacted by the Legislature of a province or the Parliament of Canada under this section shall in its pith and substance be directed to the disruption of the free flow of information.

(4) Any law enacted by the Legislature of a province under sub-section (1) prevails over a law enacted by Parliament under sub-section (2) except a law of Parliament in relation to:

(a) matters of a technical nature respecting management of the radio frequency spectrum;

(b) the space segment of communication satellites;

(c) regulation of Canadian broadcasting transmitting network undertakings that extend to four or more provinces, including the re-distribution of these signals by other telecommunications undertakings;

(d) foreign broadcast signals;

(e) the use of telecommunication works and undertakings for aeronautics, radio-navigation, defence, or in national emergencies.

(5) In the event that the laws of two or more provinces conflict so as to disrupt the free flow of information, one of the provinces may petition the Parliament of Canada to enact a law to resolve the specific conflict and such law shall prevail.

(d) Ontario Draft, Powers Over the Economy, from the Report of the Committee on Natural Resources, Interprovincial Trade, and Powers Over the Economy, August 13, 1980

Document: 840-195/005

s. 121(1) It is hereby declared that Canada is an economic union and

(a) every citizen of Canada and every person lawfully admitted to Canada for permanent residence has the right,

(i) to move to and reside in any province or territory,

(ii) to pursue the gaining of a livelihood in any province or territory without discrimination based on residence or former residence, and

(b) all goods, services and capital may move freely and without discrimination within Canada based on the province or territory of origin or destination.

(2) Neither Parliament nor a legislature may enact a law that in its pith and substance is inconsistent with subsection 1.

41. Continuing Committee of Ministers on the Constitution, Ottawa, Ontario, August 26–29, 1980

(a) The Canadian Charter of Rights and Freedoms, Federal Draft, August 22, 1980

Document: 830-84/004

Canadian Charter of Rights and Freedoms

1. The *Canadian Charter of Rights and Freedoms* recognizes the following rights and freedoms subject only to such reasonable limits as are generally accepted in a free and democratic society.

Fundamental Freedoms

Fundamental freedoms

2. Everyone has the following fundamental freedoms:
(*a*) freedom of conscience and religion;
(*b*) freedom of thought, belief, opinion, and expression, including freedom of the press and other media; and
(*c*) freedom of peaceful assembly and of association.

Democratic Rights

Democratic rights of citizens

3. Every citizen of Canada has, without unreasonable distinction or limitation, the right to vote in an election of members of the House of Commons or of a legislative assembly and to be qualified for membership therein.

Duration of elected legislative bodies

4. (1) No House of Commons and no legislative assembly shall continue for longer than five years from the date of the return of the writs for the election of its members.

Continuation in special circumstances

(2) In time of real or apprehended war, invasion or insurrection, a House of Commons may be continued by Parliament and a legislative assembly may be continued by the legislature beyond the period of five years, if such continuation is not opposed by the votes of more than one-third of the members of the House of Commons or the legislative assembly, as the case may be.

Annual sitting of legislative bodies

5. There shall be a sitting of Parliament and of each legislature at least once in every year and not more than twelve months shall intervene between sittings.

Legal Rights

Life, liberty and security of person

6. Everyone has the right to life, liberty and security of the person and the right not to be deprived thereof except by due process of law.

Search and seizure

7. Everyone has the right to be secure against unreasonable search and seizure.

Detention or imprisonment

8. Everyone has the right not to be arbitrarily detained or imprisoned.

Invasion of privacy

9. Everyone has the right to be secure against arbitrary invasion of privacy.

Arrest or detention

10. Everyone has the right on arrest or detention
   (a) to be informed promptly of the reasons therefor;
   (b) to retain and instruct counsel without delay; and
   (c) to the remedy by way of *habeas corpus* for the determination of the validity of the detention and for release if the detention is not lawful.

Proceedings against accused in criminal and penal matters

11. Anyone charged with an offence has the right
   (a) to be informed promptly of the specific offence;
   (b) to be tried within a reasonable time;
   (c) to be presumed innocent until proven guilty according to law in fair and public hearing by an independent and impartial tribunal;
   (d) not to be denied reasonable bail without just cause;
   (e) not to be found guilty on account of any act or omission that at the time of the act or omission did not constitute an offence;
   (f) not to be tried or punished more than once for an offence of which he or she has been finally convicted or acquitted; and
   (g) to the benefit of the lesser punishment where the punishment for an offence of which he or she has been convicted has been varied between the time of commission and the time of sentencing.

Treatment or punishment

12. Everyone has the right not to be subjected to any cruel and unusual treatment or punishment.

Self-crimination

13. A witness has the right when compelled to testify not to have any evidence so given used against him or her in any subsequent proceedings, except a prosecution for perjury or the giving of contradictory evidence.

Counsel

14. A witness has the right not to be compelled to testify if denied the right to consult counsel.

Interpreter

15. A party or witness has the right to the assistance of an interpreter if that person does not understand or speak the language in which the proceedings are conducted.

Mobility Rights*

Rights of citizens

16. (1) Every citizen of Canada has the right to enter, remain in and leave Canada.

Rights of citizens and permanent residents

(2) Every citizen of Canada and every person who has the status of a permanent resident has the right
   (a) to move to and take up residence in any province; and
   (b) to acquire and hold property in, and to pursue the gaining of a livelihood in any province.

Limitation

(3) The rights specified in subsection (2) are subject to any laws or practices of general application in force in a province other than those that discriminate among persons primarily on the basis of province of present or previous residence.

Non-discrimination Rights

Equality before the law and equal protection of the law

17. (1) Everyone has the right to equality before law and to equal protection of the law without discrimination because of race, national or ethnic origin, colour, religion, age or sex.

(*This section is subject to revision in light of discussions in the "Powers over the Economy" committee respecting amendments to section 121 of the *BNA Act*.)

Affirmative action programmes

(2) This section does not preclude any programme or activity that has as its object the amelioration of conditions of disadvantaged persons or groups.

Official Languages

Official languages of Canada

18. (1) English and French are the official languages of Canada and have equality of status and equal rights and privileges as to their use in all institutions of the Parliament and Government of Canada (*)

Status of languages and extension thereof

(2) In addition, English and French have the status set forth in this Charter, which does not limit the authority of Parliament or a legislature to extend the status or use of the two languages or either of them.

Language Rights

Proceedings of Parliament

19. (1) Everyone has the right to use English or French in any debates and other proceedings of Parliament.

Debates of legislatures

(2) Everyone has the right to use English or French in the debates of the legislature of any province.

Statutes, etc. of Parliament

20. (1) The statutes, records and journals of Parliament shall be printed and published in English and French.

Statutes, etc. of certain legislatures

(2) The statutes, records and journals of the legislatures of Ontario, Quebec, New Brunswick and Manitoba shall be printed and published in English and French.

Idem

(3) The statutes, records and journals of the legislature of each province not referred to in subsection (2) shall be printed and published in English and French to the greatest extent practicable accordingly as the legislature of the province prescribes.

Both versions of satutes authoritative

(4) Where the statutes of Parliament or a provincial legislature are printed and published in English and French, both language versions are equally authoritative.

Proceedings in Supreme Court and courts established by Parliament

21. (1) Either English or French may be used by any person in, or in any pleading or process in or issuing from, the Supreme Court of Canada or any court established by Parliament.

Proceedings in courts of certain provinces

(2) Either English or French may be used by any person in, or in any pleading or process in or issuing from, any court of Ontario, Quebec, New Brunswick or Manitoba.

Idem

(3) Either English or French may be used by any person in, or in any pleading or process in or issuing from, any court of a province not referred to in subsection (2), to the greatest extent practicable accordingly as the legislature prescribes.

Rules for orderly implementation and adaption

(4) Nothing in this section precludes the making of such rules by any competent body or authority for the orderly implementation and operation of this section.

Communications by public with government of Canada

22. (1) Any member of the public in Canada has the right to communicate with and to receive services from any head or central office of an institution of the Parliament or Government of Canada in English or French, and has the same right with respect to any other office of any such institution where that office is located within an area of Canada in which it is

---

(*New Brunswick may wish special provision added respecting status of English and French in that province.)

determined, in such manner as may be prescribed or authorized by Parliament, that a substantial number of persons within the population use that language.

Communications by public with government of a province

(2) Any member of the public in a province has the right to communicate with and to receive services from any head, central or principal office of an institution of the legislature or government of the province in English or French to the greatest extent practicable accordingly as the legislature prescribes. (*)

Rights and privileges preserved

23. Nothing in sections 18 to 22 abrogates or derogates from any legal or customary right or privilege acquired or enjoyed either before or after the commencement of this Charter with respect to any language that is not English or French.

Language of educational instruction

24. (1) Citizens of Canada in a province who are members of an English-speaking or French-speaking minority population of that province have a right to have their children receive their education in their minority language at the primary and secondary school level wherever the number of children of such citizens resident in an area of the province is sufficient to warrant the provision out of public funds of minority language education facilities in that area.

Provisions for determining where numbers warrant

(2) In each province, the legislature may, consistent with the right provided in subsection (1), enact provisions for determining whether the number of children of citizens of Canada who are members of an English-speaking or French-speaking minority population in an area of the province is sufficient to warrant the provision out of public funds of minority language education facilities in that area.

Undeclared Rights

Undeclared rights and freedoms

25. The enumeration in this Charter of certain rights and freedoms shall not be construed to exclude, or to derogate from, any other rights or freedoms that may exist in Canada, including any rights or freedoms that may pertain to the native peoples of Canada.

General

Laws, etc. not to apply so as to abrogate declared rights and freedoms

26. Any law, order, regulation or rule that authorizes, forbids or regulates any activity or conduct in a manner inconsistent with this Charter is, to the extent of such inconsistency, inoperative and of no force or effect.

Enforcement of declared rights and freedoms

27. Where no other legal recourse or remedy is available, anyone whose rights or freedoms as declared by this Charter have been infringed or denied to his or her detriment has the right to apply to a court of competent jurisdiction to obtain relief or remedy by way of declaration, injunction, damages or penalty, as may be appropriate and just in the circumstances.

Application to territories and territorial institutions

28. A reference in this Charter to a province or to the legislative assembly or legislature of a province shall be deemed to include a reference to the Yukon Territory or the Northwest Territories or to the appropriate legislative authroity thereof, as the case may be.

Legislative authority not extended

29. Nothing in this Charter confers any legislative power on any body or authority except as expressly provided by this Charter.

(*New Brunswick may wish special provision added respecting language of services to the public.)

Continuation of existing
constitutional provisions

30. Nothing in sections 19 to 21 abrogates or derogates from any right, privilege or obligation with respect to the English and French languages, or either of them, that exists or is continued by virtue of any provision of the Constitution of Canada.(*)

Application of sections 20 and 21

31. A legislature of a province to which subsections 20(2) and 21(2) do not expressly apply may declare that one or both of those subsections shall have application, and therefore any such provision shall apply to that province in the same terms as to any province expressly named therein.

REVISED FEDERAL DRAFT ON MOBILITY RIGHTS, AUGUST 22, 1980

Rights of citizens to move

16.(1) Every citizen of Canada has the right to enter, remain in and leave Canada.

Rights of persons in Canada to move, etc.

(2) Everyone in Canada has the right
  (a) to move to and take up residence in any province; and
  (b) to acquire and hold property in, and pursue the gaining of a livelihood in, any province.

Limitations

(3) The rights specified in subsection (2) are subject to
  (a) any laws or practices of general application in force in a province other than those that discriminate among persons primarily on the basis of province of present or previous residence, and
  (b) any other laws referred to in subsections (4) or (5) of section 121 of the *British North America Act.*

(b) Tabular Comparison of Charter of Rights Drafts, August 22, 1980

Summary of Provisions — July 4, 1980 Draft	Summary of Provisions — August 22, 1980 Draft
Section 1 — Title	**Section 1 — Recognized Rights and Limits**
1. To be entitled "Canadian Charter of Rights and Freedoms".	1. Rights and freedoms recognized subject only to reasonable limits generally accepted in free and democratic society.
Section 2 — Fundamental Freedoms	**Section 2 — Fundamental Freedoms**
2. (1) (a) Freedom of conscience and religion. (b) Freedom of thought, opinion and expression, including freedom to disseminate news, opinion and belief.	2. (1)(a) Freedom of conscience and religion. (b) Freedom of thought, belief, opinion and expression, including freedom of press and other media.

(*Transitional provisions will be required for repeal of these provisions at an appropriate time.)

(*c*) Freedom of peaceful assembly and of association.

Limitation Clause

(2) Those prescribed by law as are reasonably justifiable in a free and democratic society in interests of
— national security
— public safety, order, health or morals
— rights and freedoms of others.

Section 3-5 — Democratic Rights

3. Principles of universal suffrage and free democratic elections affirmed.

Right of citizens to vote and to qualify for election to House of Commons or legislature without unreasonable distinction or limitation.

4. (1) Limits on maximum duration of House of Commons and legislatures (5 years)
(2) except in case of national emergency.

5. Requirement for annual sittings of Parliament and legislatures.

Section 6 — Legal Rights

6. (1) Right to life, liberty and security of person and right not to be deprived thereof except by due process of law which encompasses:
(*a*) right against unreasonable searches and seizures.
(*b*) right against arbitrary or unlawful interference with privacy;
(*c*) right against detention or imprisonment except on lawful grounds and prescribed procedures;
(*d*) right on arrest or detention
   (i) to be told promptly of reason;
   (ii) to be provided with the opportunity to retain and consult counsel promptly; and
   (iii) to remedy of *habeas corpus*:
(*e*) right when charged with offence
   (i) to know specific charge,
   (ii) to be tried within reasonable time,
   (iii) to presumption of innocence, to a fair and public hearing before impartial tribunal,
   (iv) not to be denied reasonable bail unfairly,
   (v) to protection against *ex post facto* offences and punishment;

(*c*) Freedom of peaceful assembly and of association.

Limitation Clause

Deleted

Section 3-5 — Democratic Rights

3. Deleted

Right of citizens to vote and to qualify for election to House of Commons or legislature without unreasonable distinction or limitation.

4. (1) Limits on maximum duration of House of Commons and legislatures (5 years)
(2) except in case of national emergency.

5. Requirement for annual sittings of Parliament and legislatures.

Section 6-15 — Legal Rights

6. Right to life, liberty and security of person and right not to be deprived thereof except by due process of law.
7. Right against unreasonable search and seizure.
9. Right against arbitrary invasion of privacy.
8. Right against arbitrary detention or imprisonment.
10. Right on arrest or detention
(*a*) to be told promptly of reasons therefor;
(*b*) to retain and instruct counsel without delay; and
(*c*) to remedy of *habeas corpus*.
11. Right when charged with offence
(*a*) to be informed promptly of specific charge;
(*b*) to be tried within reasonable time;
(*c*) to presumption of innocence until proven guilty according to law in fair and public hearing before impartial tribunal;
(*d*) not to be denied reasonable bail unfairly;
(*e*) to protection against *ex post facto* offences and punishment;

(*f*) protection against double jeopardy;

(*g*) benefit of lesser penalty where law is changed before sentencing;

(*h*) protection against cruel and unusual treatment or punishment;

(*i*) right when compelled to testify to benefit of counsel, to protection against self-incrimination and to other constitutional safeguards;

(*j*) right of party or witness to assistance of interpreter in any proceedings.

(2) Right to fair hearing when rights or obligations being determined.

Limitation Clauses

(3) In times of serious public emergency threatening life of country limits strictly required by circumstances may be placed on right to liberty and security, right against unreasonable searches and seizures, right against arbitrary interference with privacy, right against unauthorized detention or imprisonment, right to *habeas corpus*, right to reasonable bail, and right to fair hearing for determination of rights and obligations, but all other rights protected.

(4) Right to legal proceedings in public may be curtailed in interests of
— national security or public
— public order or morality
— protection of individual privacy.

Section 7 — Non-Discrimination Rights

7. (1) Right to equality before the law and equal protection of the law without unreasonable and unfair distinction or restriction.

Limitation Clause

(2) Those limits provided by fair and reasonable test.

Those programs or activities designed for "affirmative action" on behalf of disadvantaged persons or groups.

Section 8 — Mobility Rights

8. (1) Right of citizen to enter, remain in and leave Canada.

(*f*) to protection against double jeopardy;

(*g*) to benefit of lesser penalty where law is changed before sentencing.

12. Protection against cruel and unusual treatment or punishment.

13. Right of witness compelled to testify not to have evidence used against him in subsequent proceedings, except prosecution for perjury or giving contradictory evidence.

14. Right of witness not to be compelled to testify if denied right to consult counsel.

15. Right of party or witness to assistance of interpreter in any proceedings.

Deleted.

Limitation Clauses

Deleted.

Deleted.

Section 17 — Non-Discrimination Rights

17. (1) Right to equality before the law and equal protection of the law without discrimination because of race, national or ethnic origin, colour, religion, age or sex.

Exception

(2) Those programs or activities designed for "affirmative action" on behalf of disadvantaged persons or groups.

Section 16 — Mobility Rights

16. (1) Right of citizen to enter, remain in and leave Canada.

(2) Right of citizen or permanent resident to
  (a) move to and take up residence
  (b) acquire and hold property, and pursue a livelihood, in any province or territory subject to laws of general application but without discrimination based on place of residence or previous residence.

(2) Right of citizen or permanent resident to
  (a) move to and take up residence
  (b) acquire and hold property, and pursue a livelihood in any province or territory.

(3) Rights subject to laws or practices of general application but without discrimination based on place of residence or previous residence.

Limitation Clause

(3) Those prescribed by law as are reasonably justifiable in a free and democratic society in the interests of
  — national security
  — public safety, order, health or morals.

Limitation Clause

Deleted.

Section 9 — Property Rights

9. (1) Right to use and enjoyment of property, individually or collectively, and right not to be deprived thereof except in accordance with law and for reasonable compensation.

Property Rights

Deleted.

Limitation Clause

(2) Those which control or restrict use of property in public interest or to secure payment of taxes, duties or penalties;

(3) Those prescribed by law as are reasonably justifiable in a free and democratic society in the interest of
  — national security
  — public safety, order, health or morals.

Section 10 — Official Languages

10. (1) English and French official languages of Canada with status and protection specified in Charter.

(2) Power of Parliament and legislatures to provide more extensive rights for French and English.

Section 18 — Official Languages

18. (1) English and French official languages of Canada with status, rights and privileges re use in all federal institutions.

(2) English and French have status provided in Charter which may be extended by Parliament or legislatures.

Section 11-16 — Language Rights

11. (1) Right to use English or French in all debates and proceedings of Parliament.

(2) Right to use English or French in debates of legislatures of all provinces.

12. (1) Statutes, records and journals of Parliament to be in English and French.

Sections 19-24 — Language Rights

19. (1) Right to use English or French in all debates and proceedings of Parliament.

(2) Right to use English or French in debates of legislatures of all provinces.

20. (1) Statutes, records and journals of Parliament to be in English and French.

(2) Statutes, records and journals of legislatures of Ontario, Quebec, New Brunswick and Manitoba to be in English and French.

(3) For other provinces not referred to in (2) the same requirement to greatest extent practicable as determined by the legislatures.

(4) Where the statutes are published as per subsection (1) to (3) both versions of statutes are equally authoritative.

13. (1) Right to use English or French in all proceedings of federally constituted courts.

    (2) Right to use English or French in all proceedings of courts in Ontario, Quebec, New Brunswick and Manitoba.

    (3) Right to use English or French in courts of other provinces not referred to in (2) to greatest extent practicable as determined by the legislatures.

    (4) Right of witness to be heard in English or French, through interpreter where necessary, in any court in Canada in any criminal or serious provincial penal procedings.

    (5) Power to make rules for the orderly implementation and operation of language rights in the courts.

14. (1) Right of public to communicate with and receive services in English or French from head or central office of any federal government institution, and from any other principal office in areas determined by Parliament on basis of minority language numbers.

    (2) Right of public to communicate with and receive services in English or French from any head, central or principal office of a provincial government institution in areas of provinces where legislatures determine practicability and necessity of providing such services.

15. Preservation of legal and customary rights or privileges for use of languages other than French or English.

16. (1) Right of minority language (English or French speaking) parents who are Canadian citizens to choose minority language education for their children in any areas of province where numbers warrant.

---

(2) Statutes, records and journals of legislatures of Ontario, Quebec, New Brunswick and Manitoba to be in English and French.

(3) For other provinces not referred to in (2) the same requirement to greatest extent practicable as determined by the legislatures.

(4) Where the statutes are printed and published in both languages, both versions are equally authoritative.

21. (1) Right to use English or French in all proceedings of federally constituted courts.

    (2) Right to use English or French in all proceedings of courts in Ontario, Quebec, New Brunswick and Manitoba.

    (3) Right to use English or French in courts of other provinces not referred to in (2) to greatest extent practicable as determined by the legislatures.

    Deleted.

    (4) Power to make rules for the orderly implementation and operation of language rights in the courts.

22. (1) Right of public to communicate with and receive services in English or French from head or central office of any federal government institution, and from any other office in areas determined by Parliament on basis of minority language numbers.

    (2) Right of public to communicate with and receive services in English or French from any head, central or principal office of a provincial government institution to greatest extent practicable as determined by the legislature.

23. Preservation of legal and customary rights or privileges for use of languages other than French or English.

24. (1) Right of minority language (English or French speaking) parents who are Canadian citizens to choose minority language education for their children in any areas of province where numbers warrant.

(2) Legislatures may enact rules, consistent with this right, for determining sufficiency of numbers.

Section 17 — Undeclared Rights

17. Preservation of any rights not specifically mentioned in Charter including those that may pertain to native peoples.

Sections 18-23 — General

18. Charter rights to render inoperative any law or administrative act which is in conflict with Charter provisions.

19. Where no other effective recourse or remedy exists, courts are empowered to grant such relief or remedy for a violation of Charter rights as may be deemed appropriate and just.

20. Charter provisions made applicable to Territories.

21. Legislative authority is not affected except as expressly provided by the Charter.

22. Preservation of existing constitutional provisions respecting French and English languages until Charter provisions are effective.

23. Power of other provinces to entrench same language rights as Ontario, Quebec, New Brunswick and Manitoba respecting statutes and courts.

(2) Legislatures may enact rules, consistent with this right, for determining sufficiency of numbers.

Section 25 — Undeclared Rights

25. Preservation of any rights not specifically mentioned in Charter including those that may pertain to native peoples.

Sections 26-31 — General

26. Charter rights to render inoperative any law, order, rule or regulation that authorizes, forbids or regulates activities or conduct in manner inconsistent with Charter.

27. Where no other effective recourse or remedy exists, courts are empowered to grant remedy by way of declaration, injunction, damages or penalty for a violation of Charter rights.

28. Charter provisions made applicable to Territories.

29. Legislative authority is not affected except as expressly provided by the Charter.

30. Preservation of existing constitutional provisions repsecting French and English languages until Charter provisions are effective.

31. Power of other provinces to entrench same language rights as Ontario, Quebec, New Brunswick and Manitoba respecting statutes and courts.

(c) The Canadian Charter of Rights and Freedoms, Provincial Proposal (In the Event That There Is Going to be Entrenchment), August 28, 1980

Annex to Document: 830-84/031

Canadian Charter of
Rights and Freedoms

    1. The *Canadian Charter of Rights and Freedoms* recognizes the following rights and freedoms subject only to such reasonable limits as are generally accepted in a free society living under a parliamentary democracy.
    (*a*) freedom of religion;

(*b*) freedom of thought, belief, opinion, and expression, including freedom of the press and other media; and

(*c*) freedom of peaceful assembly and of association.

Democratic Rights

Democratic rights of citizens

3. Every citizen of Canada has, without unreasonable distinction or limitation, the right to vote in an election of members of the House of Commons or of a legislative assembly and to be qualified for membership therein.

Duration of elected legislative bodies

4. (1) No House of Commons and no legislative assembly shall continue for longer than five years from the date of the return of the writs for the election of its members.

Continuation in special circumstances

(2) In time of real or apprehended war, invasion or insurrection, a House of Commons may be continued by Parliament and a legislative assembly may be continued by the legislature beyond the period of five years, if such continuation is not opposed by the votes of more than one-third of the members of the House of Commons or the legislative assembly, as the case may be.

Annual sitting of legislative bodies

5. There shall be a sitting of Parliament and of each legislature at least once in every year and not more than twelve months shall intervene between sittings.

Legal Rights

Search and seizure

6. Everyone has the right to be secure against search and seizure except on grounds provided by law and in accordance with prescribed procedures.

Detention or imprisonment

7. Everyone has the right not to be detained or imprisoned except on grounds provided by law and in accordance with prescribed procedures.

Arrest or detention

8. Everyone has the right on arrest or detention

(*a*) to be informed promptly of the reasons therefor;

(*b*) to retain and instruct counsel without delay; and

(*c*) to the remedy by way of *habeas corpus* for the determination of the validity of the detention and for release if the detention is not lawful.

Proceedings against accused in criminal and penal matters
*

9. Anyone charged with an offence has the right

(*a*) to be informed promptly of the specific offence;

(*b*) to be tried within a reasonable time;

(*c*) to be presumed innocent until proven guilty according to law in a fair and public hearing by an independent and impartial tribunal;

(*d*) not to be denied pre-trial release except on grounds provided by law and in accordance with prescribed procedures;

(*e*) not to be found guilty on account of any act or omission that at the time of the act or omission did not constitute an offence;

(*f*) not to be tried or punished more than once for an offence of which he or she has been finally convicted or acquitted; and

(*g*) to the benefit of the lesser punishment where the punishment for an offence of which he or she has been convicted has been varied between the time of commission and the time of sentencing.

Treatment or punishment

10. Everyone has the right not to be subjected to any cruel and unusual punishment.

---

*The Provinces (officials) were split 5-5 on the inclusion of this provision — see concordance.

Self-incrimination
**

11. A witness has the right when compelled to testify not to have any evidence so given used against him or her in any subsequent proceedings, except a prosecution for perjury or the giving of contradictory evidence.

Interpreter

12. A party or witness has the right to the assistance of an interpreter if that person does not understand or speak the language in which the proceedings are conducted.

***

***

Mobility Rights

The Provinces (officials) suggested that the whole issue of Mobility Rights, if in the constitution, should be elsewhere than in the Charter of Rights.

****

Official Language and Language Rights

(Sections 18–24 and 30 and 31 of the Federal August 22, 1980 Draft would be sections 13–21 if included in this document.)

****

Provincial officials have not made any *joint* proposal with respect to these subject matters prior to further discussion by the Minister of the Federal Draft Proposals.

General

Laws, etc. not to apply so as to abrogate declared rights and freedoms
Admissibility of Evidence

22.(*a*) Any law, order, regulation or rule that authorizes, forbids or regulates any activity or conduct in a manner inconsistent with this Charter is, to the extent of such inconsistency, inoperative and of no force or effect.

(*b*) Nothing in this Charter affects the admissibility of evidence or the ability of Parliament or a legislature to legislate thereon.

Application to territories and territorial institutions

23. A reference in this Charter to a province or to the legislative assembly or legislature of a province shall be deemed to include a reference to the Yukon Territory or the Northwest Territories or to the appropriate legislative authority thereof, as the case may be.

Legislative authority not extended

24. Nothing in this Charter confers any legislative power on any body or authority except as expressly provided by this Charter.

(d) Charter of Rights, Report to Ministers by Sub-Committee of Officials, August 29, 1980

Document: 830-84/031

1. Since its report of July 24, 1980 to Ministers, the sub-committee of officials has met this week to consider:
   (a) a revised federal discussion draft Charter dated August 22, 1980;
   (b) a provincial proposal dated August 28, 1980 for modifications and deletions in the federal discussion draft;
   (c) the practicability of including an override (non-obstante) clause in an entrenched Charter; and
   (d) the possibility of strengthening the Canadian Bill of Rights as an alternative to an entrenched Charter.

2. As before discussion on these items proceeded *without prejudice to any province's position on the principle of entrenchment itself,* it being felt that this was a matter for ministerial consideration in light of this report.

**The Provinces (officials) suggested that consideration of the inclusion of this provision or any other provision dealing with this subject matter be deferred pending the report of the Evidence Task Force.

Federal Discussion Draft of August 22, 1980

3. This draft was prepared in light of concerns of provincial officials noted in the earlier report and sought to cover in particular the following points:

— to remove the specific grounds for limiting rights by specifying in section 1 that all rights are subject to generally accepted reasonable limits,

— to clarify and limit the scope of legal rights,

— to ensure that courts could not exclude improperly obtained evidence on that ground alone,

— to contain the scope of non-discrimination rights,

— to eliminate the category of property rights,

— to allow for some restrictions on mobility rights[1],

— to eliminate the right of witnesses in criminal and penal proceedings to give evidence in English or French as they choose.

In addition, officials of Ontario and Manitoba were invited to consider a delay provision for the implementation of the language rights provisions respecting statutes (five years) and courts (ten years).

4. Following examination of the revised draft, officials of most provinces remained concerned about both the scope of rights covered by the draft and by the language of many of its provisions. To respond to these concerns, provincial officials met and prepared a joint provincial proposal for a Charter in the event one was to be entrenched. This was subsequently reviewed with federal officials.

Provincial Proposal for a Charter, August 28, 1980

5. The changes which this proposal would make in the federal draft are set out in a tabular comparison of Charter of Rights drafts annexed hereto and carry the unanimous support of provincial officials except as otherwise indicated in the table.

6. The principal changes may be summarized as follows:

— several of the legal rights would be deleted,

— other of the remaining legal rights would be qualified by a "lawful grounds and prescribed procedures" test rather than a "reasonable or non-arbitrary" test,

— any reference to non-discrimination rights would be deleted,

— mobility rights, if included in the Constitution, would not be in the Charter,

— any reference to undeclared rights would be deleted,

— the remedies section for breach of rights would be deleted, and

— the paramountcy of Charter rights provision would be qualified to ensure that admissibility of evidence rules would not be superseded.

7. Provincial officials did not make any *joint* proposal on official languages and language rights, feeling that further discussion by Ministers of the federal draft provisions was required on this matter.

8. Federal officials indicated in response to the joint provincial proposals that a number of changes advanced would be given close consideration in a re-examination of the federal draft. With respect to some of the others, serious doubts were expressed about the acceptability of proposed changes and deletions.

Legislative Override Clause

9. Some consideration was given to the possible inclusion in an entrenched Charter of an override clause whereby a legislative body could expressly provide that a law would operate notwithstanding a Charter right. While some doubt was voiced about the desirability of including such a provision, there was general agreement that further consideration should be given this matter.

10. One mechanism that was discussed, in the event it is decided that an override clause is necessary (and this could depend on the ultimate scope and wording of an entrenched Charter), is a requirement that any law enacted under an override provision be adopted by a 60% majority of the legislative body and that any such law would expire after a specified time period, e.g., five years unless repealed earlier. There was no discussion of the particular categories of rights to which any override clause might apply.

Strengthening Canadian Bill of Rights

11. As an alternative to entrenching a Charter, some consideration was given to the possibility of strengthening the Canadian Bill of Rights by making it a clear statement of effective rights rather than an interpretive statute. In discussion of this matter, it was noted by federal officials that this would not be seen as a viable approach to protecting basic rights since it

— would apply only at the federal level,

— would not cover the range of rights contemplated

---

[1]A revised draft on mobility rights was tabled by federal officials to correspond with amendments being proposed to Section 121 of the *BNA Act*.
  A copy is annexed to the federal draft Charter of August 22, 1980.

in the federal draft, particularly language rights, and
— would not guarantee common basic rights to persons throughout Canada.

Issues for Ministers

12. In light of the foregoing summary, the following issues arise for consideration and determination by Ministers:

(1) Should there be an entrenched Charter of Rights?
(2) If so, which categories of rights should be included from among the following categories:
   (*a*) fundamental freedoms
   (*b*) democratic rights
   (*c*) legal rights (including the scope of such rights)
   (*d*) non-discrimination rights

(*e*) mobility rights
(*f*) language rights at the federal level
(*g*) language rights at the provincial level
(*h*) minority language education rights?
(3) Should inclusion of an override clause along the lines described above be contemplated?
13. Annexed hereto are the following documents:
(1) Provincial Tabular Comparison of Charter Drafts
(2) Provincial Proposal for a Charter, August 28, 1980 [*supra*, p. 678].
(3) Federal Discussion Draft of Charter, August 22, 1980 [*supra*, p. 669].

Roger Tassé
Chairman

TABULAR COMPARISON OF CHARTER OF RIGHTS DRAFTS

Summary of Provisions — July 4, 1980 Draft	Summary of Provisions — August 22, 1980 Draft	Provincial Proposal (In the Event that There is Going to be Entrenchment) — August 28, 1980 Draft
Section 1 — Title	**Section 1 — Recognized Rights and Limits**	**Section 1**
1. To be entitled "Canadian Charter of Rights and Freedoms".	1. Rights and freedoms recognized subject only to reasonable limits generally accepted in free and democratic society.	Rights and freedoms recognized subject only to reasonable limits generally accepted in a free society living under a parliamentary democracy. (unanimous)
Section 2 — Fundamental Freedoms	**Section 2 — Fundamental Freedoms**	**Section 2 — Fundamental Freedoms**
2. (1) (*a*) Freedom of conscience and religion.	2. (1) (*a*) Freedom of conscience and religion.	2. (1) (*a*) Freedom of religion (unanimous)
(*b*) Freedom of thought, opinion and expression, including freedom to disseminate news, opinion and belief.	(*b*) Freedom of thought, belief, opinion and expression, including freedom of press and other media.	(*b*) As in August 22 Draft (unanimous)
(*c*) Freedom of peaceful assembly and of association.	(*c*) Freedom of peaceful assembly and of association.	(*c*) As in August 22 Draft (unanimous)

Summary of Provisions — July 4, 1980 Draft	Summary of Provisions — August 22, 1980 Draft	Provincial Proposal (In the Event that There is Going to be Entrenchment) — August 28, 1980 Draft

Limitation Clause

Limitation Clause

(2) Those prescribed by law as are reasonably justifiable in a free and democratic society in interests of
— national security
— public safety, order, health or morals
— rights and freedoms of others.

Deleted

Section 3-5 — Democratic Rights

Section 3-5 — Democratic Rights

Section 3-5 — Democratic Rights

3. Principles of universal suffrage and free democratic elections affirmed.

3. Deleted

Right of citizens to vote and to qualify for election to House of Commons or legislature without unreasonable distinction or limitation.

Right of citizens to vote and to qualify for election to House of Commons or legislature without unreasonable distinction or limitation.

Agree with August 22 draft

4. (1) Limits on maximum duration of House of Commons and legislatures (5 years)
   (2) except in case of national emergency.

4. (1) Limits on maximum duration of House of Commons and legislatures (5 years)
   (2) except in case of national emergency.

5. Requirement for annual sittings of Parliament and legislatures.

5. Requirement for annual sittings of Parliament and legislatures.

Section 6 — Legal Rights

Section 6-15 — Legal Rights

Section 6-15 — Legal Rights

6. (1) Right to life, liberty and security of person and right not to be deprived thereof except by due process of law which encompasses:
   (*a*) right against unreasonable searches and seizures.

6. Right to life, liberty and security of person and right not to be deprived thereof except by due process of law.

6. Delete (unanimous)

7. Right against unreasonable searches and seizures.

7. Right against search and seizure except on lawful grounds and in accordance with prescribed procedures
   (N.B. & Newfoundland dissented and would prefer the federal August 22 draft).

(*b*) right against arbitrary or unlawful interference with privacy;

9. Right against arbitrary invasion of privacy.

9. Delete (N.B. dissenting if Federal August 22 draft applied only to federal legislation)

Summary of Provisions — July 4, 1980 Draft	Summary of Provisions — August 22, 1980 Draft	Provincial Proposal (In the Event that There is Going to be Entrenchment) — August 28, 1980 Draft
(c) right against detention or imprisonment except on lawful grounds and prescribed procedures;	8. Right against arbitrary detention or imprisonment.	8. Agree with July 4 draft (unanimous)
(d) right on arrest or detention (i) to be told promptly of reason; (ii) to be provided with the opportunity to retain and consult counsel promptly; and (iii) to remedy of *habeas corpus*;	10. Right on arrest or detention (a) to be told promptly of reasons therefor; (b) to retain and instruct counsel without delay; and (c) to remedy of *habeas corpus*.	10. Agree with August 22 draft (unanimous)
(e) right when charged with offence (i) to know specific charge, (ii) to be tried within reasonable time, (iii) to presumption of innocence, to a fair and public hearing before impartial tribunal, (iv) not to be denied reasonable bail unfairly, (v) to protection against *ex post facto* offences and punishment;	11. Right when charged with offence (a) to be informed promptly of specific charge; (b) to be tried within reasonable time; (c) to presumption of innocence until proven guilty according to law in fair and public hearing before impartial tribunal; (d) not to be denied reasonable bail unfairly, (e) to protection against *ex post facto* offences and punishment;	11. (a) Agree with August 22 draft (unanimous) (b) Delete — Man., Alta., P.E.I., Ont., Sask. Agree to August 22 — B.C., N.B., Nfld., Que., N.S. (c) Agree with August 22 draft (unanimous) (d) Right not to be denied pre-trial release except on lawful grounds and in accordance with prescribed procedures (unanimous) (e) Agree with August 22 draft (unanimous)
(f) protection against double jeopardy; (g) benefit of lesser penalty where law is changed before sentencing; (h) protection against cruel and unusual treatment or punishment;	(f) to protection against double jeopardy; (g) to benefit of lesser penalty where law is changed before sentencing. 12. Protection against cruel and unusual treatment or punishment.	(f) Agree with August 22 draft (unanimous) (g) Agree with August 22 draft (unanimous) 12. Delete words "treatment or" but otherwise agree with August 22 draft (unanimous)

Summary of Provisions — July 4, 1980 Draft	Summary of Provisions — August 22, 1980 Draft	Provincial Proposal (In the Event that There is Going to be Entrenchment) — August 28, 1980 Draft
(*i*) right when compelled to testify to benefit of counsel, to protection against self-incrimination and to other constitutional safeguards;	13. Right when compelled to testify not to have evidence used against him in subsequent proceedings, except prosecution for perjury or giving contradictory evidence.	13. Defer and reword after report from Evidence Task Force (unanimous)
(*j*) right of party or witness to assistance of interpreter in any proceedings.	14. Right of witness not to be compelled to testify if denied right to consult counsel.	14. Delete (unanimous)
	15. Right of party or witness to assistance of interpreter in any proceedings.	15. Agree with August 22 draft (unanimous)
(2) Right to fair hearing when rights or obligations being determined.	Deleted.	

Limitation Clauses | **Limitation Clauses**

| (3) In times of serious public emergency threatening life of country limits strictly required by circumstances may be placed on right to liberty and security, right against unreasonable searches and seizures, right against arbitrary interference with privacy, right against unauthorized detention or imprisonment, right to *habeas corpus*, right to reasonable bail, and right to fair hearing for determination of rights and obligations, but all other rights protected. | Deleted. | |
| (4) Right to legal proceedings in public may be curtailed in interests of
— national security or public
— public order or morality
— protection of individual privacy. | Deleted. | |

Summary of Provisions — July 4, 1980 Draft	Summary of Provisions — August 22, 1980 Draft	Provincial Proposal (In the Event that There is Going to be Entrenchment) — August 28, 1980 Draft

Section 7 — Non-Discrimination Rights

7. (1) Right to equality before the law and equal protection of the law without unreasonable and unfair distinction or restriction.

Limitation Clause

(2) Those limits provided by fair and reasonable test.

Those programs or activities designed for "affirmative action" on behalf of disadvantaged persons or groups.

Section 8 — Mobility Rights

8. (1) Right of citizen to enter, remain in and leave Canada.

(2) Right of citizen or permanent resident to
(a) move to and take up residence
(b) acquire and hold property, and

pursue a livelihood, in any province or territory subject to laws of general application but without discrimination based on place of residence or previous residence.

Limitation Clause

(3) Those prescribed by law as are reasonably justifiable in a free and democratic society in the interests of
— national security
— public safety, order, health or morals.

Section 17 — Non-Discrimination Rights

17. (1) Right to equality before the law and equal protection of the law without discrimination because of race, national or ethnic origin, colour, religion, age or sex.

Exception

(2) Those programs or activities designed for "affirmative action" on behalf of disadvantaged persons or groups.

Section 16 — Mobility Rights

16. (1) Right of citizen to enter, remain in and leave Canada.

(2) Right of citizen or permanent resident to
(a) move to and take up residence
(b) acquire and hold property, and

pursue a livelihood, in any province or territory

(3) Rights subject to laws or practices of general application but without discrimination based on place of residence or previous residence.

Limitation Clause

Deleted.

Section 17 — Non-Discrimination Rights

17. Delete (N.B. dissented because it favours the principle but does not support current wording.)

Section 16 — Mobility Rights

Whole issue, if in the constitution, should be elsewhere than in Charter of Rights (unanimous)

Summary of Provisions — July 4, 1980 Draft	Summary of Provisions — August 22, 1980 Draft	Provincial Proposal (In the Event that There is Going to be Entrenchment) — August 28, 1980 Draft

Section 9 — Property Rights

9. (1) Right to use and enjoyment of property, individually or collectively, and right not to be deprived thereof except in accordance with law and for reasonable compensation.

Limitation Clause

(2) Those which control or restrict use of property in public interest or to secure payment of taxes, duties or penalties;

(3) Those prescribed by law as are reasonably justifiable in a free and democratic society in the interest of
— national security
— public safety, order, health or morals.

Property Rights

Deleted.

Section 10 — Official Languages

10. (1) English and French official languages of Canada with status and protection specified in Charter.

(2) Power of Parliament and legislatures to provide more extensive rights for French and English.

Section 18 — Official Languages

18. (1) English and French official languages of Canada with equal status, rights and privileges re use in all federal institutions.

(2) English and French have status provided in Charter which may be extended by Parliament or legislatures.

Section 11-16 — Language Rights

11. (1) Right to use English or French in all debates and proceedings of Parliament.

(2) Right to use English or French in debates of legislatures of all provinces.

Sections 19-24 — Language Rights

19. (1) Right to use English or French in all debates and proceedings of Parliament.

(2) Right to use English or French in debates of legislatures of all provinces.

Summary of Provisions — July 4, 1980 Draft	Summary of Provisions — August 22, 1980 Draft	Provincial Proposal (In the Event that There is Going to be Entrenchment) — August 28, 1980 Draft
12. (1) Statutes, records and journals of Parliament to be in English and French.	20. (1) Statutes, records and journals of Parliament to be in English and French.	
(2) Statutes, records and journals of legislatures of Ontario, Quebec, New Brunswick and Manitoba to be in English and French.	(2) Statutes, records and journals of legislatures of Ontario, Quebec, New Brunswick and Manitoba to be in English and French.	
(3) For other provinces not referred to in (2) the same requirement to greatest extent practicable as determined by the legislatures.	(3) For other provinces not referred to in (2) the same requirement to greatest extent practicable as determined by the legislatures.	
(4) Where the statutes are published as per subsections (1) to (3) both versions of statutes are equally authoritative.	(4) Where the statutes are printed and published in both languages, both versions are equally authoritative.	
13. (1) Right to use English or French in all proceedings of federally constituted courts.	21. (1) Right to use English or French in all proceedings of federally constituted courts.	
(2) Right to use English or French in all proceedings of courts in Ontario, Quebec, New Brunswick and Manitoba.	(2) Right to use English or French in all proceedings of courts in Ontario, Quebec, New Brunswick and Manitoba.	
(3) Right to use English or French in courts of other provinces not referred to in (2) to greatest extent practicable as determined by the legislatures.	(3) Right to use English or French in courts of other provinces not referred to in (2) to greatest extent practicable as determined by the legislatures.	
(4) Right of witness to be heard in English or French, through interpreter where necessary, in any court in Canada in any criminal or serious provincial penal proceedings.	Deleted.	

Summary of Provisions — July 4, 1980 Draft	Summary of Provisions — August 22, 1980 Draft	Provincial Proposal (In the Event that There is Going to be Entrenchment) — August 28, 1980 Draft
(5) Power to make rules for the orderly implementation and operation of language rights in the courts.	(4) Power to make rules for the orderly implementation and operation of language rights in the courts.	
14. (1) Right of public to communicate with and receive services in English or French from head or central office of any federal government institution, and from any other principal office in areas determined by Parliament on basis of minority language numbers.	22. (1) Right of public to communicate with and receive services in English or French from head or central office of any federal government institution, and from any other office in areas determined by Parliament on basis of minority language numbers.	
(2) Right of public to communicate with and receive services in English or French from any head, central or principal office of a provincial government institution in areas of provinces where legislatures determine practicability and necessity of providing such services.	(2) Right of public to communicate with and receive services in English or French from any head, central or principal office of a provincial government institution to greatest extent practicable as determined by the legislature.	
15. Preservation of legal and customary rights or privileges for use of languages other than French or English.	23. Preservation of legal and customary rights or privileges for use of languages other than French or English.	
16. (1) Right of minority language (English or French speaking) parents who are Canadian citizens to choose minority language education for their children in any areas of province where numbers warrant.	24. (1) Right of minority language (English or French speaking) parents who are Canadian citizens to choose minority language education for their children in any areas of province where numbers warrant.	
(2) Legislatures may enact rules, consistent with this right, for determining sufficiency of numbers.	(2) Legislatures may enact rules, consistent with this right, for determining sufficiency of numbers.	

Summary of Provisions — July 4, 1980 Draft	Summary of Provisions — August 22, 1980 Draft	Provincial Proposal (In the Event that There is Going to be Entrenchment) — August 28, 1980 Draft
Section 17 — Undeclared Rights	**Section 25 — Undeclared Rights**	**Section 25 — Undeclared Rights**
17. Preservation of any rights not specifically mentioned in Charter including those that may pertain to native peoples.	25. Preservation of any rights not specifically mentioned in Charter including those that may pertain to native peoples.	Delete (unanimous)
Sections 18-23 — General	**Sections 26-31 — General**	**Section 26**
18. Charter rights to render inoperative any law or administrative act which is in conflict with Charter provisions.	26. Charter rights to render inoperative any law, order, rule or regulation that authorizes, forbids or regulates activities or conduct in manner inconsistent with Charter.	(a) Agree with August 22 draft and add (b) nothing in this Charter affects the admissibility of evidence or the ability of Parliament or a Legislature to legislate thereon. (unanimous)
19. Where no other effective recourse or remedy exists, courts are empowered to grant such relief or remedy for a violation of Charter rights as may be deemed appropriate and just.	27. Where no other legal recourse or remedy exists, courts are empowered to grant remedy by way of declaration, injunction, damages or penalty for a violation of Charter rights.	27. Delete (unanimous)
20. Charter provisions made applicable to Territories.	28. Charter provisions made applicable to Territories	28. Agree with August 22 draft (unanimous)
21. Legislative authority is not affected except as expressly provided by the Charter.	29. Legislative authority is not affected except as expressly provided by the Charter.	29. Agree with August 22 draft (unanimous)
22. Preservation of existing constitutional provisions respecting French and English languages until Charter provisions are effective.	30. Preservation of existing constitutional provisions respecting French and English languages until Charter provisions are effective.	
23. Power of other provinces to entrench same language rights as Ontario, Quebec, New Brunswick and Manitoba respecting statutes and courts.	31. Power of other provinces to entrench same language rights as Ontario, Quebec, New Brunswick and Manitoba respecting statutes and courts.	

(e) Powers Over the Economy, Amended Federal Approach, August 21, 1980

Three changes have been made, in the [following] draft, to the federal proposal for a new section 121.

First, the references to "capital" have been deleted. This has been done in order to eliminate the impact on provincial policies relating to matters such as provincial monopolies, application of provincial funds or mandatory shares in mineral development ventures. This deletion of references to "capital" does not, however, eliminate the other problems arising from provincial laws and practices that relate to people, goods and services, particularly with respect to the export from the province of natural resource production and possible price/supply discrimination.

Second, a new provincial "derogation" clause, subsection (4), has been added. This would allow a provincial legislature to declare that a law or practice is in an "overriding provincial interest" and thereby avoid the prohibition contained in subsection (1). Federal officials have said that such an override is not appropriate for a province because some of the persons adversely affected by the otherwise prohibited laws and practices would be outside the provinces and, by that fact, would be non-participants in the political process that would lead up to the making of such a declaration. They claim, of course, that the converse is the case for a declaration by Parliament because all Canadians are represented there.

The only answer to that objection is that there may be certain non-tariff-barriers that arise from provincial policy imperatives and that provinces should be able to create through deliberate choice, a choice which is theirs and not subject to judicial review.

Third, the new subsection (5) provides for a two stage enforcement mechanism: the courts make their determination with regard to any law or practice, and then the matter is referred to the new upper chamber. The upper chamber would then have a year in which it could consider the matter. If, in that year, it disapproved the law or practice, it would be inoperative from the time of the disapproval. Of course, the chamber could approve it, or could fail to consider it, in which cases, the law or practice would continue to operate. This approach has the advantage of bifurcating the enforcement mechanism to allow both judicial and political review of the matter in question. Its disadvantage lies in the respective power position of the various governments in the new upper chamber, a matter that is not yet settled.

These three modications to the federal proposals could be made alternatively or cumulatively.

AMENDED FEDERAL APPROACH

Canadian economic union	**121.** (1) Neither Canada nor a province shall by law or practice discriminate in a manner that unduly impedes the operation of the Canadian economic union, directly or indirectly, on the basis of the province or territory of residence or former residence of a person, on the basis of the province or territory or origin or destination of goods or services or on the basis of the province or territory into which or from which goods or services are imported or exported.
Derogation	(2) Nothing in subsection (1) renders invalid a law of Parliament of a legislature enacted in the interests of public safety, order, health or morals.
Idem	(3) Nothing in subsection (1) renders invalid a law of Parliament enacted pursuant to the principles of equalization and regional development to which Parliament and the legislatures are committed or declared by Parliament to be in an overriding national interest or enacted pursuant to an international obligation undertaken by Canada.
Idem	(4) Nothing in subsection (1) renders invalid a law or practice of a province that has been declared by a law enacted by the legislature of the province to be in a compelling provincial interest.

Review

(5) Where a law or practice of Canda or of a province is declared by final judgment of a court of competent jurisdiction to be contrary to subsection (1), the law or practice shall be referred by Canada or the province, as the case may be, to the (new upper chamber) as soon as practicable for its consideration, and, if within one year of the referral, the (new upper chamber) disapproves the law or practice, the law or practice is inoperative from the time of the disapproval.

Customs union

(6) Nothing in subsection (2), (3) or (4) renders valid a law of Parliament or a legislature that impedes the admission free into any province of goods or services originating in or imported into any other province or territory.

(f) Economic Union, Federal Draft, August 26, 1980

Document: 830-84/008

Canadian economic union

121. (1) Canada is constituted an economic union within which all persons may move without discrimination based on province or territory of residence or former residence and within which all goods, services and capital may move without discrimination based on province or territory of origin or entry into Canada or of destination or export from Canada.

Non-discrimination

(2) Neither Canada nor a province shall by law or practice discriminate in a manner that contravenes the principle expressed in subsection (1).

Derogation

(3) Subsection (2) does not render invalid a law of Parliament or a legislature enacted in the interests of public safety, order, health or morals.

Idem

(4) Subsection (2) does not render invalid a law of Parliament enacted
   (*a*) in accordance with the principles of equalization and regional development recognized in section — — ; or
   (*b*) in relation to a matter that is declared by Parliament in the enactment to be of an overriding national interest.

Idem

(5) Subsection (2) does not render invalid a law of a legislature enacted in relation to the reduction of substantial economic disparities between regions wholly within a province that does not discriminate to a greater degree against persons resident or formerly resident outside the province or against goods, services or capital from outside the province than it does against persons resident or goods, services or capital from a region within the province.

Customs union continued

(6) Nothing in subsection (3), (4) or (5) renders valid a law of Parliament or a legislature that impedes the admission free into any province of goods, services or capital originating in or imported into any other province or territory.

Legislative authority not extended

(7) Nothing in this section confers any legislative authority on Parliament or a legislature.

— Section 121 is repealed.

---

1. Add to section 91 the following heads of jurisdiction immediately following head 91.2:

2.1 Competition
2.2 The establishment of product standards throughout Canada.

2. Add to section 91 the following new subsections:

(2) The authority of Parliament to make laws in relation to the regulation of trade and commerce extends to the making of laws in relation to the regulation of trade and commerce in goods, services and capital.

(3) The authority conferred on Parliament by heads 91(2.1) and 91(2.2) does not render invalid a law enacted by a legislature that is not in conflict with a law of Parliament enacted under either of those heads.

(g) Resource Ownership and Interprovincial Trade, Federal Draft, August 22, 1980

Document: 830-84/009

(1) (present Section 92)

Resources

(2) For greater certainty, in each province, the legislature may exclusively make laws in relation to

    (*a*) exploration for non-renewable natural resources in the province;

    (*b*) development, exploitation, extraction, conservation and management of non-renewable natural resources in the province, including laws in relation to the rate of primary production therefrom; and

    (*c*) development, exploitation, conservation and management of forestry resources in the province and of sites and facilities in the province for the generation of electrical energy, including laws in relation to the rate of primary production from such forestry resources and of production from such sites and facilities for the generation of electrical power.

Export from the province of resource

(3) In each province, the legislature may make laws in relation to the export from the province to another part of Canada of the primary production from non-renewable natural resources and forestry resources in the province and the production from facilities in the province for the generation of electrical energy.

Relationship to certain laws of Parliament

(4) Nothing in subsection (3) derogates from the authority of Parliament to enact laws in relation to the matters referred to in that subsection, and where such a law of Parliament and a law of a province conflict, the law of Parliament prevails to the extent of the conflict.

(1) Carries forward existing Section 92

(2) The draft outlines exclusive provincial legislative jurisdiction over certain natural resources and electric energy within the province. These resources have been defined as non-renewable (e.g.: crude oil, copper, iron and nickel), forests and electric energy. This section pertains to *legislative* jurisdiction and in no way impairs established *proprietary* rights of provinces over resources whether these resources are renewable or non-renewable.

(3) Provincial governments are given concurrent legislative authority to pass laws governing the export of the resources referred to above from the province to another part of Canada. This new provincial legislative capacity applies to these resources in their raw state and to them in their processed state but does not apply to materials manufactured from them.

(4) The effect of this new provincial legislative responsibility over interprovincial trade and commerce does not eliminate the federal government's authority. In effect a concurrent power similar to that for agriculture is established. Thus, a federal law will prevail over a provincial law in the case of conflict between the two.

Taxation of resources

(5) In each province, the legislature may make laws in relation to the raising of money by any mode or system of taxation in respect of

a) non-renewable natural resources and forestry resources in the province and the primary production therefrom; and

b) sites and facilities in the province for the generation of electrical energy and the production therefrom,

whether or not such production is exported in whole or in part from the province but such laws may not authorize or provide for taxation that differentiates between production exported to another part of Canada and production not exported from the province.

Production from resources

(6) The expression ''primary production'' has the meaning assigned by the Sixth Schedule.

Existing powers

(7) Nothing in subsections (2) to (6) derogates from any powers or rights that a legislature or government of a province had immediately before the coming into force of those subsections.

(5) Provincial powers of taxation are increased to include indirect taxes over the resources outlined in this section — whether these resources are destined in part for export outside the province. These taxes are to apply with equal force both in the province and across the rest of the country.

THE SIXTH SCHEDULE

For the purposes of section 92,

a) production from a non-renewable resource is primary production therefrom if

i) it is in the form in which it exists upon its recovery or severance from its natural state, or

ii) it is a product resulting from processing or refining the resource, and is not a manufactured product resulting from refining crude oil, refining upgraded heavy crude oil, refining gases or liquids derived from coal, or refining a synthetic equivalent of crude oil; and

b) production from a forestry resource is primary production therefrom if it consists of sawlogs, poles, lumber, wood chips, sawdust or any other primary wood product, or wood pulp, and is not a product manufactured from wood.

In determining the scope of provincial legislative powers over resources exported from the province, it became necessary to define the degree to which the resource was processed. It is not intended to extend provincial authority to manufacturing but it is intended to extend it to something beyond its extraction from its natural state. Given the varying resources covered by this section, this definition is thought to achieve the appropriate delineation of powers.

(h) Offshore Resources: A Constitutional Proposal by the Federal Government, August 26, 1980

Document: 830-84/007

I. SHARING OF OFFSHORE RESOURCE REVENUES

1. *Provincial and Federal Sales*

It is proposed that a coastal province receive 100 per cent of offshore resource revenues each year at least until it becomes a "have" province. Beyond that point, a coastal province would share an increasing proportion of its offshore resource revenues with all Canadians. A formula to implement this principle might be based on a sliding scale of per capita revenues derived from offshore resources. Up to a certain maximum per capita, the province would still retain 100 per cent of the revenues, *even if it had become, or already were, a "have" province*. After that, the provincial share would decrease progressively, depending on the level of its per capita resource revenues.

2. *Definition of Revenues to be Shared*

Shared revenues would include royalties, fees, rentals and payments for exploration or development rights, in other words, all those types of levy on natural resources that are primarily provincial in Western Canada.

The governments concerned would adopt a principle according to which the offshore revenue-raising system would be devised in such a way as to capture a high proportion of the economic rent from offshore mineral resources, in a manner comparable to the approach followed by the Western provinces in respect of their own resources.

Shared revenues would not include revenues from federal taxes such as the corporation income tax and federal sales and excise taxes. In calculating revenues to be shared, deductions would be made for federal contributions to the international community that may result from the Law of the Sea Conference, and for direct administrative costs borne by the federal government. Finally, the then-prevailing system of equalization would apply to offshore resource revenues.

II. LEGISLATION

It is proposed that "normal" federal and provincial legislation would apply to offshore mineral resource matters. Federal legislation implementing the national energy policy would apply.

III. MANAGEMENT OF OFFSHORE MINERAL RESOURCES

It is proposed that bilateral joint bodies be created to manage offshore resource exploitation. Day-to-day administration would be done under their responsibility. The joint bodies might each be composed of three provincial representatives, three federal representatives, and a neutral chairman to be selected by both parties.

The federal government recognizes the very legitimate concerns of the coastal provinces concerning the on-shore socio-economic impacts of offshore resource exploitation. At the same time, it must be recognized that there is a legitimate national interest in the pace of development of offshore resources, in view of Canada's energy goals. For those reasons, it is proposed that the joint bodies would be required to respond to these provincial concerns up to the point where the national interest would be affected, in which case it would prevail.

A joint body would serve as the policy advisor to both governments represented on it, and would be responsible for offshore mineral resource management on the basis of the relevant federal or provincial legislation. This would mean that industry would normally be able to deal with only one agency concerning offshore resource matters, off the coast of each province.

The joint bodies would also provide a forum for the necessary federal-provincial consultation.

IV. CONSTITUTIONAL CONFIRMATION

It is proposed that the offshore resources arrangement be confirmed in the new Constitution. This could be done by mentioning the joint bodies in the text or by some other mechanism, such as the delegation of federal legislative authority to the provinces where necessary to provide for the applicability of provincial legislation under the terms of the proposal.

(i) Communications, Federal Draft, August 26, 1980

Document: 830-84/010

1. Section 91 of the B.N.A. Act would be amended by adding the four following paragraphs:

> **91.** (*w*) The frequency spectrum including technical aspects only of frequency assignment.
>
> (*x*) Interprovincial and international telecommunications services and the technical aspects of telecommunications.
>
> (*y*) Telecommunications works and undertakings transmitting by broadcasting and telecommunications works and undertaking, other than carrier works and undertakings, providing programming or other services beyond the limits of a province.
>
> (*z*) The regulation and distribution, including distribution in priority to all other signals through all or any telecommunications undertakings in a province, of a national program service as defined from time to time by Parliament, and the regulation and distribution of non-Canadian programming.

2. Section 92 of the B.N.A. Act would be amended by adding the two following paragraphs:

> **92.** (*y*) Telecommunications carrier works and undertakings in the province other than:
> - (*a*) national and international telecommunications carriers;
> - (*b*) space and satellite telecommunications carriers including related earth stations;
> - (*c*) carriage on all or any telecommunications carriers in the province of telecommunications for a national purpose.
>
> (*z*) Telecommunications works and undertakings providing programming or other services in the province and not within the jurisdiction of Parliament by virtue of class (*y*) of section 91.

3. A provision to the following effect would be added:

Communications Consultations —

> The Government of Canada and the governments of the provinces shall consult together at least once in every year, bilaterally or on a regional or national basis, on the formulation, co-ordination and implementation of laws, policies, programmes and practices respecting communications.

(j) Delegation of Legislative Authority, Federal Draft, August 28, 1980

Document: 830-84/027

Delegation to Parliament

(1) Notwithstanding anything in the Constitution of Canada, Parliament may make laws in relation to any legislative jurisdiction of a province.

Consent of provincial legislature

(2) No law may be enacted by Parliament under subsection (1) unless, prior to the enactment thereof, the legislature of at least one province has consented to the enactment of such a law by Parliament.

Idem

(3) No law enacted under subsection (1) has effect in any province unless the legislature of that province has consented to the operation of such a law in that province.

Delegation to legislature of a province	(4) Notwithstanding anything in the Constitution of Canada, the legislature of a province may make laws in the province in relation to any matter or class of subjects coming within the legislative jurisdiction of Parliament.
Consent of Parliament	(5) No law may be enacted by a province under subsection (4) unless, prior to the enactment thereof, Parliament has consented to the enactment of such a law by the legislature of that province.
Extent of consent	(6) A consent given under this section may be general or specific, may relate to any law or to the enactment of laws in relation to any matter of class of subjects and may include the authority to amend such law or laws.
Enforcement	(7) Parliament or the legislature of a province may make laws for enforcing any law made by it under this section.
Revocation of consent	(8) A consent given under this section may at any time be revoked.
Effect of revocation of consent	(9) Where a consent given under subsection (3) is revoked any law made by Parliament to which the consent relates that is operative in the province in which the consent is revoked thereupon ceases to have effect in that province.
Idem	(10) Where a consent given under subsection (5) is revoked, any law made by the legislature of a province to which the consent relates thereupon ceases to have effect.
Repeal of law by Parliament	(11) Parliament may repeal any law made by it under this section, insofar as it is part of the law of one or more provinces, but the repeal does not affect the operation of that law in any province to which the repeal does not relate.
Repeal of law by provincial legislature	(12) The legislature of a province may repeal any law made by it under this section.

(k) Fisheries: A Constitutional Proposal Submitted by the Government of Canada to the Continuing Committee of Ministers on the Constitution: Mandatory Consultation on Fisheries, August 22, 1980

Document: 830-84/014

PLEASE NOTE   December 1983

The federal government has asked that this document be read subject to the following caveats:

a) the federal offers contained in the document were subject to agreement being reached on several items involved in the negotiations at the time, and the document must therefore be read in this context; and,

b) the proposals contained in the document do not represent continuing offers by the federal government.

1. Constitutional Confirmation of the Principle

Recognizing that the provinces have an interest in fisheries management because of (a) the impact of fisheries on local communities and (b) the constitutional jurisdiction of the provinces over closely related matters including fish processing and infrastructure, the federal government proposes that there be a constitutional provision establishing the principle of mandatory consultation. For example:

Fisheries Consultation

"**97.1** The Minister of the government of Canada responsible for fisheries and a minister designated by each provincial government shall consult together at least once in every year, either bilaterally or on a regional basis, on the formulation, coordination and implementation of policies and programmes of the government of Canada respecting fisheries and provincial policies and programmes significantly affecting fisheries.''

2. The Mechanism

The procedures for consultation would be spelled out in more detail in federal-provincial agreements, which might be signed in conjunction with the enactment of new constitutional legislation. These agreements could be bilateral, regional or national as desired. They could be given the structure of a formal agreement; alternatively they could be concluded more simply by way of an exchange of ministerial correspondence.

The use of agreements for this purpose would, of course, provide for more flexibility than would a series of detailed constitutional provisions. This format would permit province by province variations, and would allow for periodic revision in the light of experience. The agreements should therefore be concluded either for a fixed term, or with provision for termination after a specified period upon advance notice by any party.

The agreements, if concluded on a multilateral basis, might establish an institutional framework for consultation such as a ''Committee'' or ''Council''. Alternatively, the procedures could be put on a more informal basis by simply providing for periodic meetings.

The agreements could establish procedures and requirements for consultation not only at the ministerial level pursuant to the proposed constitutional provision, but at the official level as well.

The agreements would list the particular subjects on which consultation would be required; such as, on a purely illustrative basis:

(a) Annual total allowable catches and fishing regulations (in the case of salmon, annual expectations and escapement targets);

(b) Allocations between groups of fishermen (i.e., between relatively homogeneous sets of fishing enterprises, relative to size of vessel, type of gear and base of operation);

(c) Fishermen and fishing vessel licensing régimes (including fees);

(d) Processing plant licensing and certification régimes (including fees);

(e) Provincial infrastructure support programmes;

(f) Programmes of financial assistance and economic development in the fisheries sector (including loan boards);

(g) Fish Habitat;

(h) International negotiations; and

(i) Foreign investment in the fisheries sector.

Finally, governments may wish to consider whether such agreements might appropriately include the specification of agreed fisheries management principles of a very general character.

(I) A Preamble to the Constitution, Federal Proposals

Document: 830-84/015

I. Considering the evolutionary nature of Canadian constitutional change, and the need for continuity, the Government of Canada believes much of the present preamble of the BNA Act (''Whereas the provinces'' through ''interests of the British Empire'') should be incorporated into the new *preamble* with the following changes:

1. its language should be modernized where appropriate;

2. listing of the provinces should be ordered alphabetically in order to demonstrate that there are no ''junior'' provinces;

3. reference should be added that the provinces are *freely* united in the federation;

4. mention should be retained of the Crown, but as the Crown *of Canada* (rather than of the U.K.);

5. the constitution should be described as similar in principle to the *present* constitution *of Canada* (rather than to that of the U.K.);

6. reference should be added to Canada's sovereignty and independence; and,

7. the present clause which refers to promoting ''the interests of the British Empire'' should be replaced with a clause which refers to promoting the freedom and well-being of Canadians.

II. To the new preamble should then be added a *statement of the fundamental aims of the Canadian constitution*. The Government of Canada believes this statement should be brief and basic — in the sense that each item included be both "timeless" enough and general enough to reflect within itself the many different concerns and priorities of different groups, and different generations, of Canadians.

A. The government of Canada believes that virtually all the major concerns voiced at the CCMC's ministerial discussions in Vancouver on the preamble can be reflected within the following brief list of broad and basic aims:

1. the guarantee of fundamental rights and freedoms;
2. the democratic foundation of laws and political institutions on the will and consent of the people;
3. the achievement of greater social justice, equality of economic opportunity and cultural security;
4. the desire of Canada to contribute internationally to the attainment of these aims by others.

B. In addition to this short list of general aims, the Government of Canada considers that the new constitution also needs to contain explicit statements of the following:

1. Canada's permanent national commitment to the endurance and self-fulfillment of the distinct French-speaking society centered in though not confined to Québec;
2. Canada's commitment to overcome unacceptable regional disparities through equalization; and,
3. the rights of the native peoples.

The Government of Canada believes that of these items, B.2 and B.3 should not be explicitly included in the preamble, because they can best be stated in specific sections of the new constitution dealing with equalization and, later on, native rights.

In contrast, the constitution will deal with item B.1 in various ways under a number of different heads (e.g. official languages, Supreme Court, amending formula). This is one of the reasons that the Government of Canada holds the view that item B.1 should be stated explicitly in the preamble.

(m) Report of the Sub-Committee of Officials on Patriation and the Amending Formula, August 28, 1980

Document: 830-84/027

A. AMENDING FORMULA

The Sub-Committee reviewed the amending formula proposal submitted by the Government of Alberta. A number of suggestions were made for technical improvements to the proposal and these have been incorporated into the draft.

Two issues of substance were considered; their resolution will require guidance from Ministers. They are the financial effects of amendments, and amendments which by their nature must apply universally. A brief description of these issues and some options for dealing with them are set out in the commentary on the Alberta draft.

B. DELEGATION OF LEGISLATIVE AUTHORITY

The Sub-Committee confirmed the agreement in principle by all governments that delegation of legislative authority should be provided for in the constitution.

— Such delegation should be on a one-to-one basis (from Parliament to any legislature, or vice-versa)
— The scope of authority to be delegated should include the power to enact specific laws, or the power to enact laws in relation to matters or classes of subjects.
— There should be no provision in the constitution with regard to financial responsibility for the administration of the authority being delegated. This should be determined on a case by case basis.

Two concerns were raised; one general, one specific.

— Quebec expressed some reservations with regard to the concept, lest this mechanism become the real means for revising the constitution in practical terms, rather than the amending formula.
— Two provinces suggested that Parliament be obliged to delegate to any other province what is has agreed to delegate to one.

The Sub-Committee recommends that the federal draft dated August 28 be put forward as a best-effort draft, on the understanding that further technical refinements may be necessary.

G.S. Posen, Chairman

AMENDMENTS TO THE CONSTITUTION OF CANADA

DRAFT	COMMENTARY

1. Amendments to the Constitution of Canada may from time to time be made by proclamation issued by the Governor General under the Great Seal of Canada when so authorized by resolutions of the Senate and House of Commons and the assent by resolution of the Legislative Assembly in two-thirds of the provinces representing at least fifty percent of the population of Canada according to the latest general census, *but any amendment affecting*
   (a) the powers of the legislature of a province to make laws,
   (b) the rights or privileges granted or secured by the Constitution of Canada to the legislature or the government of a province,
   (c) the assets or property of a province, or
   (d) the natural resources of a province,
   shall have no effect in any province whose Legislative Assembly has expressed its dissent thereto by resolution prior to the issue of the proclamation, until such time as that Assembly may withdraw its dissent and approve such amendment by resolution.

- drafting improvement

- drafting improvement

- new provision for legislative assemblies to "opt in" to an amendment already in effect.

Financial implications
It was recognized that the formula, which permits provinces to opt out of amendments, will result in situations with potential important financial implications for all governments. Three ways of dealing with this problem were considered:
- add to the formula the principle that if a province dissents from an amendment, it should not be penalized financially compared with provinces that have approved the amendment.
- add to the formula the obligation that First Ministers or Finance Ministers review the financial implications of any proposed amendment.
- make no provision constitutionally; deal with this issue on a case-by-case basis; leave its solution to the political process.

DRAFT	COMMENTARY
2. A proclamation shall not be issued under section 1 before the expiry of one year from the adoption of the resolution initiating the amendment procedure thereunder, unless the legislative assembly in each province has previously adopted a resolution of assent or dissent.	• new provision to allow legislative assemblies one year to act before any amendment to be proclaimed e.g., if a particular legislature is not in session when the seventh province has given its assent to a proposed amendment that legislature should be allowed to reconvene and express a dissent and thus opt out within this one year period before Parliament acts to proclaim the amendment. • however, if all legislative assemblies have acted on the proposed amendment (either assent or dissent) before the expiry of one year, the amendment can be proclaimed earlier.
3. Amendments to the Constitution of Canada in relation to any provision that applies to one or more, but not all, of the Provinces *including any such amendment made to provincial boundaries* may from time to time be made by proclamation issued by the Governor General under the Great Seal of Canada when so authorized by resolutions of the Senate and House of Commons and the assent by resolution of the Legislative Assembly of each Province to which an amendment applies.	• explicit provision for amendment of provincial boundaries by this section.
4. An amendment may be made by proclamation under *section 1, 3 or 9* without a resolution of the Senate authorizing the issue of the proclamation if within ninety days of the passage of a resolution by the House of Commons authorizing its issue the Senate has not passed such a resolution and at any time after the expiration of the ninety days the House of Commons again passes the resolution, but any period when Parliament is prorogued or dissolved shall not be counted in computing the ninety days.	• technical drafting improvement
5. The following rules apply to the procedures for amendment described in sections 1, 3 and 9 (1) either of these procedures may be initiated by the Senate or the House of Commons or the Legislative Assembly of a Province, (2) a resolution of authorization or assent made for the purposes of this Part may be revoked at any time before the issue of a proclamation authorized or assented to by it, (3) *a resolution of dissent made for the purposes of this Part may be revoked at any time before or after the issue of a proclamation.*	• technical improvement
6. The Parliament of Canada may exclusively make laws from time to time amending the Constitution	

DRAFT

of Canada, in relation to the executive Government of Canada and the Senate and House of Commons.

7. In each Province the Legislature may exclusively make laws in relation to the amendment from time to time of the Constitution of the Province.

8. Notwithstanding sections 6 and 7, the following matters may be amended only in accordance with the procedure in section 1:
    (1) the office of the Queen, of the Governor General and of the Lieutenant-Governor,
    (2) the requirements of the Constitution of Canada respecting yearly sessions of the Parliament of Canada and the Legislatures,
    (3) the maximum period fixed by the Constitution of Canada for the duration of the House of Commons and the Legislative Assemblies,
    (4) the powers of the Senate,
    (5) the number of members by which a Province is entitled to be represented in the Senate and the residence qualifications of Senators.
    (6) the right of a Province to a number of members in the House of Commons not less than the number of Senators representing the Province,
    (7) the principles of Proportionate representation of the Provinces in the House of Commons prescribed by the Constitution of Canada, and
    (8) the use of the English or French language.

COMMENTARY

UNIVERSAL APPLICABILITY
- It was noted that a number of the items identified under this provision, although relating to the rights and privileges of the legislature or government of a province, must, by their very nature, apply cross the country. *The opting out feature in section 1, therefore, cannot be applied to them.*
- — Examples of such items are:
  — Supreme Court of Canada
  — a new upper house
  — Charter of rights
  — use of English or French language
  — section 121
  — section 125 — immunity of Crown land and property from taxation
- With no opting out on this range of items, the general amending formula (Parliament plus 2/3 of the provinces with 50% of the population) might make amendments too easy to obtain
  — Furthermore, it provides no special protection to Quebec on items concerning language/culture and dualism.
- Therefore, should the general formula be altered a) to make it more difficult to approve amendments on such items, b) to provide special protection for Quebec on specific items of this nature?
- Options considered:
  —require that these items be amended only by unanimous agreement (inherent protection for Quebec and all others)
  —use a higher population requirement, e.g., 80%, (inherent protection for Quebec and some others)
  —identify linguistic/cultural or dualism items and require that Quebec be among the 2/3 of the provinces with 50% of population approving amendments in this regard; all other items would require only 2/3 of provinces with 50% of population
  —no special provisions or formulas; eliminate opting out for these items; go with 2/3 and 50% population.

DRAFT	COMMENTARY

DRAFT

9. (1) No amendment to section 1 of this Part, this section, or *to any provision in the Constitution with respect to the procedure for altering provincial boundaries shall* come into force unless it is authorized in by resolutions of the Senate and House of Commons and assented to by resolution of the Legislative Assemblies of all the provinces.

(2) The procedure prescribed in section o of this Part may not be used to make an amendment when there is another provision for making such amendment in the Constitution of Canada but, subject to the limitations contained in subsection (1) of this section that procedure may nonetheless be used to amend any provision for amending the Constitution.

10. The enactments set out in the Schedule shall continue as law in Canada and as such shall, together with this Act, collectively be known as the Constitution of Canada, and amendments thereto shall henceforth be made only according to the authority contained therein.

COMMENTARY

• addition to make consistent with change in section 3.

• technical improvement; will require Schedule similar to that in Victoria Charter setting out those statutes to be included in the Constitution of Canada.

APPENDIX: REFERENDA AS AN APPEAL PROCEDURE

The federal delegation raised informally the possibility of supplementing the Alberta formula with referenda as an "appeal procedure" under certain circumstances. For example, if the ten provinces were to adopt a proposed amendment of general application and Parliament rejected it or failed to consider it during the 12 month period for ratification by legislative bodies, 3% of the electorate of Canada at the time of the previous federal general election could, by petition, require that a referendum be held throughout Canada. If the amendment were supported by a majority of the electors voting, the amendment would be adopted and become binding on Canada.

Similarly, if Parliament and the legislatures of seven or more, but not all provinces, adopted an amendment during the 12 month period for ratification by legislative bodies,

in any province whose legislature had expressed its dissent, 3% of the electorate in that province at the time of the previous provincial general election could, by petition, require that a referendum be held in that province. If the amendment were supported by a majority of the electors voting, it would become binding on that province.

There was no support among the provinces for the use of referenda as an appeal procedure against negative action by a legislative assembly or Parliament. The objection was raised that if electors could appeal negative action (or lack of action) through a referendum, one should also permit electors the possibility of overruling positive action by Parliament or the provinces.

It was agreed that the concept was a new one in the context of the CCMC, that most governments did not have the mandate to adopt a position and that, in any event, there was little interest on the part of the provinces in pursuing the matter. The federal government asked, nonetheless, that the concept be recorded.

42. Federal-Provincial First Ministers' Conference, Ottawa, Ontario, September 8–12, 1980

(a) The Canadian Charter of Rights and Freedoms, Revised Discussion Draft, Federal, September 3, 1980

Document: 800-14/064

Rights and freedoms in Canada

1. The *Canadian Charter of Rights and Freedoms* recognizes the following rights and freedoms subject only to such reasonable limits as are generally accepted in a free and democratic society with a parliamentary system of government.

Fundamental freedoms

Fundamental freedoms

2. Everyone has the following fundamental freedoms:
(*a*) freedom of conscience and religion;
(*b*) freedom of thought, belief, opinion and expression, including freedom of the press and other media; and
(*c*) freedom of peaceful assembly and of association.

Democratic Rights

Democratic rights of citizens

3. Every citizen of Canada has, without unreasonable distinction or limitation, the right to vote in an election of members of the House of Commons or of a legislative assembly and to be qualified for membership therein.

Duration of elected legislative bodies

4. (1) No House of Commons and no legislative assembly shall continue for longer than five years from the date of the return of the writs for the election of its members.

Continuation in special circumstances

(2) In time of real or apprehended war, invasion or insurrection, a House of Commons may be continued by Parliament and a legislative assembly may be continued by the legislature beyond the period of five years, if such continuation is not opposed by the votes of more than one-third of the members of the House of Commons or the legislative assembly, as the case may be.

Annual sitting of legislative bodies

5. There shall be a sitting of Parliament and of each legislature at least once in every year and not more than twelve months shall intervene between sittings.

Legal Rights

Life, liberty and security of person

6. Everyone has the right to life, liberty and security of the person and right not to be deprived thereof except in accordance with the principles of fundamental justice.

Search and seizure

7. Everyone has the right to be secure against unreasonable search and seizure.

Detention or imprisonment

8. Everyone has the right not to be arbitrarily detained or imprisoned.

Arrest or detention

9. Everyone has the right on arrest or detention

(*a*) to be informed promptly of the reasons therefor;

(*b*) to retain and instruct counsel without delay; and

(*c*) to the remedy by way of *habeas corpus* for the determination of the validity of the detention and for release if the detention is not lawful.

Proceedings against accused in criminal and penal matters

10. Anyone charged with an offence has the right

(*a*) to be informed promptly of the specific offence;

(*b*) to be tried within a reasonable time;

(*c*) to be presumed innocent until proven guilty according to law in a fair and public hearing by an independent and impartial tribunal;

(*d*) not to be denied reasonable bail without just cause;

(*e*) not to be found guilty on account of any act or omission that at the time of the act or omission did not constitute an offence;

(*f*) not to be tried or punished more than once for an offence of which he or she has been finally convicted or acquitted; and

(*g*) to the benefit of the lesser punishment where the punishment for an offence of which he or she has been convicted has been varied between the time of commission and the time of sentencing.

Treatment or punishment

11. Everyone has the right not to be subjected to any cruel and unusual treatment or punishment.

Self-crimination

12. A witness has the right when compelled to testify not to have any evidence so given used to incriminate him or her in any subsequent proceedings, except a prosecution for perjury or for the giving of contradictory evidence.

Interpreter

13. A party [or] witness has the right to the assistance of an interpreter if that person does not understand or speak the language in which the proceedings are conducted.

Mobility Rights

Rights of citizens to move

14. (1) Every citizen of Canada has the right to enter, remain in and leave Canada.

Rights of persons in Canada to move, etc.

(2) Everyone in Canada has the right

(a) to move to and take up residence in any province; and

(b) to acquire and hold property in, and to pursue the gaining of a livelihood in any province.

Limitations

(3) The rights specified in subsection (2) are subject to

(a) any laws or practices of general application in force in a province other than those that discriminate among persons primarily on the basis of province of present or previous residence, and

(b) any other laws referred to in subsections (4) or (5) of section 121 of the *British North America Act*.

Non-discrimination Rights

Equality before the law and equal protection of the law

15. (1) Everyone has the right to equality before the law and to equal protection of the law without discrimination because of race, national or ethnic origin, colour, religion, age or sex.

Affirmative action programmes

(2) This section does not preclude any programme or activity that has as its object the amelioration of conditions of disadvantaged persons or groups.

Official Languages

Official languages of Canada

16. **(1)** English and French are the official languages of Canada and have equality of status and equal rights and privileges as to their use in all institutions of the Parliament and Government of Canada.

Status of languages and extension thereof

(2) In addition, English and French have the status set forth in this Charter, which does not limit the authority of Parliament or a legislature to extend the status or use of the two languages or either of them.

Language Rights

Proceedings of Parliament

17. **(1)** Everyone has the right to use English or French in any debates and other proceedings of Parliament.

Debate of legislatures

(2) Everyone has the right to use English or French in the debates of the legislature of any province.

Statutes, etc. of certain legislatures

18. **(1)** The statutes, records and journals of Parliament shall be printed and published in English and French.

Statutes, etc. of certain legislatures

(2) The statutes, records and journals of the legislatures of Ontario, Quebec, New Brunswick and Manitoba shall be printed and published in English and French.

Idem

(3) The statutes, records and journals of the legislatures of each province not referred to in subsection (2) shall be printed and published in English and French to the greatest extent practicable accordingly as the legislature of the province prescribes.

Both versions of statutes authoritative

(4) Where the statutes of Parliament or a provincial legislature are printed and published in English and French, both language versions are equally authoritative.

Proceedings in Supreme Court and courts established by Paliament

19. **(1)** Either English or French may be used by any person in, or in any pleading or process in or issuing from, the Supreme Court of Canada or any court established by Parliament.

Proceedings in courts of certain provinces

(2) Either English or French may be used by any person in, or in any pleading or process in or issuing from, any court of Ontario, Quebec, New Brunswick or Manitoba.

Idem

(3) Either English or French may be used by any person in, or in any pleading or process in or issuing from, any court of a province not referred to in subsection (2), to the greatest extent practicable accordingly as the legislature prescribes.

Rules for orderly implementation and operation

(4) Nothing in this section precludes the making of such rules by any competent body or authority for the orderly implementation and operation of this section.

Communications by public with government of Canada

20. **(1)** Any member of the public in Canada has the right to communicate with and to receive available services from any head or central office of an institution of the Parliament or Government of Canada in English or French, and has the same right with respect to any other office of any such institution where that office is located within an area of Canada in which it is determined, in such manner as may be prescribed or authorized by Parliament, that a substantial number of persons within the population use that language.

Communications by public with government of a province

(2) Any member of the public in a province has the right to communicate with and to receive available services from any head, central or principal office of an institution of the legislature or government of the province in English or French to the greatest extent practicable accordingly as the legislature prescribes.

Rights and privileges preserved

21. Nothing in sections 16 to 20 abrogates or derogates from any legal or customary right or privilege acquired or enjoyed either before or after the commencement of this Charter with respect to any language that is not English or French.

Language of educational instruction

22. (1) Citizens of Canada in a province who are members of an English-speaking or French-speaking minority population of that province have a right to have their children receive their education in their minority language at the primary and secondary school levels wherever the number of children of such citizens resident in an area of the province is sufficient to warrant the provision out of public funds of minority language educational facilities in that area.

Provisions for determining where numbers warrant

(2) In each province, the legislature may, consistent with the right provided in subsection (1), enact provisions for determining whether the number of children of citizens of Canada who are members of an English-speaking or French-speaking minority population in an area of the province is sufficient to warrant the provision out of public funds of minority language educational facilities in that area.

Undeclared Rights

Undeclared rights and freedoms

23. The enumeration in this Charter of certain rights and freedoms shall not be construed to deny the existence of any other rights or freedoms that may exist in Canada, including any rights or freedoms that may pertain to the native peoples of Canada.

General

Laws, etc. not to apply so as to derogate from declared rights and freedoms

24. Any law, order, regulation or rule that is inconsistent with the provisions of this Charter is, to the extent of such inconsistency, inoperative and of no force or effect.

Laws respecting evidence

25. No provision of this Charter other than section 12 affects the laws respecting the admissibility of evidence in any proceedings or the authority of Parliament or a legislature to make laws in relation thereto.

Application to territories and territorial institutions

26. A reference in this Chapter to a province or to the legislative assembly or legislature of a province shall be deemed to include a reference to the Yukon Territory or the Northwest Territories or to the appropriate legislative authority thereof, as the case may be.

Legislative authority not extended

27. Nothing in this Charter confers any legislative power on any body or authority except as expressly provided by this Charter.

Continuation of existing constitutional provisions

28. Nothing in sections 17 to 19 abrogates or derogates from any right, privilege or obligation with respect to the English and French languages, or either of them, that exists or is continued by virtue of any other provisions of the Constitution of Canada.(*)

(*Transitional provisions will be required for repeal of these provisions at an appropriate time.)

Application of certain language rights

29. A legislature of a province to which subsections 18(2) and 19(2) do not expressly apply may declare that one or both of those subsections shall have application, and thereafter any such provision shall apply to that province in the same terms as to any province expressly named therein.

(b) Charter of Rights and Freedoms, Commentary on Revised Discussion Draft, Federal, September 3, 1980

Document: 800-14/069

The revised discussion draft contains the following changes from the August 22, 1980 draft, tabled at the August 25, 1980 CCMC meeting:

MODIFICATIONS

Section 1 — The Canadian Charter of Rights and Freedoms recognizes the following rights and freedoms subject only to such reasonable limits as are generally accepted in a free and democratic society.

has been changed to:

The Canadian Charter of Rights and Freedoms recognizes the following rights and freedoms subject only to such reasonable limits as are generally accepted in a free and democratic society *with a parliamentary system of government.*

Section 6 — Everyone has the right to life, liberty and security of the person and the right not to be deprived thereof except by due process of law.

has been changed to:

Everyone has the right to life, liberty and security of the person and right not to be deprived thereof except *in accordance with the principles of fundamental justice.*

Section 12 — A witness has the right when compelled to testify not to have any evidence so given used against him or her in any subsequent proceedings, except a prosecution for perjury or the giving of contradictory evidence.

has been changed to:

A witness has the right when compelled to testify not to have any evidence so given used *to incriminate* him or her in any subsequent proceedings, except a prosecution for perjury or for the giving of contradictory evidence.

Section 14 — (1) Every citizen of Canada has the right to enter, remain in and leave Canada.

(2) Every citizen of Canada and every person who has the status of a permanent resident has the right

(*a*) to move to and take up residence in any province; and

(*b*) to acquire and hold property in, and to pursue the gaining of a livelihood in any province.

(3) The rights specified in subsection (2) are subject to any laws or practices of general application in force in a province other than those that discriminate among persons primarily on the basis of province of present or previous residence.

has been changed to:

(1) Every citizen of Canada has the right to enter, remain in and leave Canada.

(2) *Everyone in Canada has the right*

(*a*) to move to and take up residence in any province; and

(*b*) to acquire and hold property in, and to pursue the gaining of a livelihood in any province.

(3) The rights specified in subsection (2) are subject to

(a) any laws or practices of general application in force in a province other than those that discriminate among persons primarily on the basis of province of present or previous residence, and

(b) *any other laws referred to in subsections (4) or (5) of section 121 of the British North America Act.*

Section 23 — The enumeration in this Charter of certain rights and freedoms shall not be construed to exclude, or to derogate from, any other rights or freedoms that may exist in Canada, including any rights or freedoms that may pertain to the native peoples of Canada.

has been changed to:

The enumeration in this Chapter of certain rights and freedoms shall not be construed *to deny the existence of* any other rights or freedoms that may exist in Canada, including any rights or freedoms that may pertain to the native peoples of Canada.

Section 24 — Any law, order, regulation or rule that authorizes, forbids or regulates any activity or conduct in a manner inconsistent with this Charter is, to the extent of such inconsistency, inoperative and of no force or effect.

has been changed to:

Any law, order, regulation or rule that *is*

inconsistent with the provisions of this Charter is, to the extent of such inconsistency, inoperative and of no force or effect.

DELETIONS

Everyone has the right to be secure against arbitrary invasion of privacy.

A witness has the right not to be compelled to testify if denied the right to consult counsel.

Where no other legal resource or remedy is available, anyone whose rights or freedoms as declared by this Charter have been infringed or denied to his or her detriment has the right to apply to a court of competent jurisdiction to obtain relief or remedy by way of declaration, injunction, damages or penalty, as may be appropriate and just in the circumstances.

ADDITIONS

Section 25 — No provision of this Charter other than section 12 affects the laws respecting the admissibility of evidence in any proceedings or the authority of Parliament or a legislature to make laws in relation thereto.

(c) Report of the Continuing Committee of Ministers on the Constitution to First Ministers: Charter of Rights

Document: 800-14/009

I. ISSUES FOR RESOLUTION BY FIRST MINISTERS

1. Should there be an entrenched Charter of Rights?
2. If there is to be an entrenched Charter, which of the following categories of rights should be included?

(a) fundamental freedoms
(b) democratic rights
(c) legal rights
(d) non-discrimination rights
(e) mobility rights
(f) language rights at the federal level

(g) language rights at the provincial level

(h) minority language education rights

3. If there is to be an entrenched Charter, should an override clause be included to enable enactment of laws expressly overriding entrenched rights, and if so, to what categories of rights might an override apply?

II. BACKGROUND

1. Ministers considered a report from a Sub-Committee of Officials dated August 29 which is attached hereto [*supra*, p. 680] in which are set out their deliberations on the possible contents of an entrenched Charter and related matters. As noted in that report, the officials' discussions were without prejudice to the position of any province on the principle of entrenchment itself. Manitoba and Alberta in particular emphasized that the attached report and the annexes thereto do not in any way reflect a commitment by the governments of those provinces to entrenching any rights. Some others shared this view. The annex to the report [*supra*, p. 678] entitled "Provincial Proposal (In the Event that there is Going to be Entrenchment)" should be read subject to the foregoing qualifications.

2. In considering the report, Ministers did not discuss in any detail the issues outlined above. A poll was taken on the issue of the principle of entrenchment. The Governments of Canada, New Brunswick, Newfoundland and Ontario supported this principle. Ontario and Newfoundland indicated that an entrenched Charter should be limited in scope. The Governments of Nova Scotia, Quebec, Manitoba, Prince Edward Island, British Columbia, Alberta and Saskatchewan were opposed to entrenchment of rights.

3. In light of the position taken on the principle of entrenchment, Ministers decided that it would not be productive to canvass positions of governments on the other issues set out above.

(d) Report of the Continuing Committee of Ministers on the Constitution to First Ministers: Resource Ownership and Interprovincial Trade

Document: 800-14/001

ISSUES FOR THE FIRST MINISTERS' CONSIDERATION

(1) Should the proposed concurrent power with respect to export of resources* from the province extend to interprovincial trade only or should it extend to international trade as well?

(2) Are the provisions on federal paramountcy found in subsection (4) of the attached draft appropriate or should federal jurisdiction be more limited in the area of interprovincial trade and commerce?

(3) Are the non-discrimination provisions necessary if section 121 (the economic union) is revised?

(4) Should the non-discrimination provisions in subsection (3.1) of the attached draft extend to discrimination between the province of production and other provinces?

(5) Should uranium and thorium be specifically identified in the schedule?

(6) Should the underlined portion in subsection (2) be retained?

COMMENT

The federal government advised the Ministers that the 1979 "best efforts" draft (see Appendix II [*supra*, p. 559]) was no longer acceptable. They proposed an alternative draft which

(a) confirmed provincial ownership of resources;

---

*As used in this paper resources means non-renewable natural resources, forestry products, and electricity.

(b) incorporated a clause with respect to indirect taxation; and

(c) incorporated a concurrent power with federal paramountcy with respect to trade and commerce as it affects the export to other provinces of non-renewable natural resources, forestry products and electricity.

The [following] draft (Appendix I) represents the federal draft as modified by discussions.

The Ministers' discussion focussed on the following matters:

(1) Should provincial legislative powers over trade and commerce in the area of non-renewable natural resources, forestry and electricity be extended to include international trade as well as interprovincial trade?

While no agreement was reached the draft that is submitted to First Ministers (Appendix I) recognizes the need for some role for provinces in the area of international trade and commerce. The federal government has reserved its position on this question.

(2) The relationship between exclusive provincial powers over resources, including provincial laws affecting export from the province, and the federal government's powers over trade and commerce was the subject of considerable debate. The federal government is prepared to extend to provinces authority to make laws affecting the export of resources from the provinces in the area of interprovincial trade and commerce provided that no such law is contrary to federal legislation. This is a new concurrent legislative power similar to that for agriculture. This is a departure from the 1979 "best efforts" draft which had established a "compelling

national interest" test as the federal override clause. Some provinces prefer the "compelling national interest" test to federal paramountcy. Alberta believes that the federal override should be confined to a strictly defined "emergency" power.

(3) The Ministers agreed that there should be no discrimination in price and supply on resources exported by the province to other parts of Canada. In other words, subject to transportation cost differences, other parts of Canada should be treated equally with respect to price and the supply of resources. There was no agreement, however, whether the supplying province should be able to make a distinction for its own residents in price and supply, as opposed to those outside the province.

(4) Should the definition of natural resources include all resources and not be limited to non-renewable, forestry, and electricity?

(5) While the declaratory power was not one of the twelve items identified by First Ministers for discussion, the Ministers recognized the interrelationship between that federal power and their discussion on natural resources. They recommend that some attention be given to this power when the First Ministers are considering the subject matters of resources and a reformed Upper House.

(6) Two provinces remain concerned that the indirect tax provisions for a province to levy indirect taxes in the area of non-renewable natural resources is too broad.

After discussion [of] the draft attached as Appendix I a majority or provinces indicated a preference for the 1979 "best efforts" draft which is attached as Appendix II [*supra*, p. 559].

APPENDIX I
RESOURCE OWNERSHIP AND INTERPROVINCIAL TRADE
(Federal Draft as Modified by Discussions)

---

(1) (present Section 92)

Resources

(2) In each province the legislation may exclusively make laws in relation to
  (a) exploration for non-renewable natural resources in the province;
  (b) development, conservation and management of non-renewable natural resources and forestry

(1) Carries forward existing Section 92.

(2) The draft outlines exclusive provincial legislative jurisdiction over certain natural resources and electric energy within the provinces. These resources have been defined as non-renewable (e.g.: crude oil, copper, iron and nickel), forests and electric energy. This section pertains to *legislative* jurisdiction and in

resources in the province, including laws in relation to the rate of primary production therefrom; and

(c) development, conservation and management of sites and facilities in the province for the generation and production of electrical energy.

and such legislation shall not be invalid merely because part or all of the product may enter interprovincial or international trade.

Export from the Province of Resource

(3) In each province the legislature may make laws
   (a) in relation to the export from the province to another part of Canada of the primary production from non-renewable resources and forestry resources in the province and the production from facilities in the province for the generation of electrical energy; and

   (b) in relation to the export of such production from the province to other countries but not including (to be determined).

(3.1) *No law authorized under subsection (3) may provide for discrimination in prices or in supplies exported to another part of Canada.*

Relationship to Certain Laws of Parliament

(4) Nothing in subsection (3) derogates from the authority of Parliament to enact laws in relation to the matters referred to in that subsection, and where such a law of Parliament and a law of a province conflict, the law of Parliament prevails to the extent of the conflict.

Taxation of Resources

(5) In each province the legislature may make laws in

---

no way impairs established *proprietary* rights of provinces over resources whether these resources are renewable or non-renewable.

British Columbia has concerns over the definition of resources and would prefer to see the term "natural resources".

This inclusion is designed to safeguard otherwise valid provincial laws from being declared ultra vires for affecting trade and commerce and would prevent compulsion of export of resources from provinces.

The Government of Canada (i) does not find such a provision acceptable and (ii) does not think a section to prevent federal legislation compelling exports from the province to be necessary.

(3) All governments agree with paragraph (a).

Subject to appropriate drafting, all provinces agree that they should have some jurisdiction in the area of international trade beyond the authority to enter into contracts but short of full concurrency. The Government reserves its position.

(3.1) This clause prohibits discrimination on exports from the province.

Ontario believes that this prohibition should extend to discrimination between the province of production and other provinces.

(4) The effect of this new provincial legislative responsibility over trade and commerce does not eliminate the federal government's authority. In effect a concurrent power similar to that for agriculture is established. Thus, a federal law will prevail over a provincial law in the case of conflict between the two.

(5) Provincial powers of taxation are increased to include

relation to the raising of money by any mode or system of taxation in respect of

(a) non-renewable natural resources and forestry resources in the province and the primary production therefrom; and

(b) sites and facilities in the province for the generation of electrical energy and the production therefrom,

whether or not such production is exported in whole or in part from the province but such laws may not authorize or provide for taxation that differentiates between production exported to another part of Canada and production not exported form the province.

Production from Resources

(6) The expression "primary production" has the meaning assigned by the Sixth Schedule.

Existing Powers

(7) Nothing in subsections (2) to (6) derogates from any powers or rights that a legislature or government of a province had immediately before the coming into force of those subsections.

The Sixth Schedule

For the purpose of section 92,

(a) production from a non-renewable resource is primary production therefrom if

(i) it is in the form in which it exists upon its recovery or severance from its natural state, or

(ii) it is a product resulting from processing or refining the resource, and is not a manufactured product or a product resulting from refining crude oil, refining upgraded heavy crude oil, refining gases or liquids derived from coal or refining a synthetic equivalent of crude oil; and

(b) production from a forestry resource is primary production therefrom if it consists of sawlogs, poles, lumber, wood chips, sawdust or any other primary wood product, or wood pulp, and is not a product manufactured from wood.

indirect taxes over the resources outlined in this section — whether these resources are destined in part for export outside the province. These taxes are to apply with equal force both in the province and across the rest of the country.

Ontario and Prince Edward Island have reservations concerning the section on taxation, believing it to be too broad.

In determining the scope of provincial legislative powers over resources exported from the province, it became necessary to define the degree to which the resource was processed. It is not intended to extend provincial authority to manufacturing but it is intended to extend it to something beyond its extraction from its natural state. Given the varying resources covered by this section, this definition is thought to achieve the appropriate delineation of powers.

This change includes upgraded heavy crude oil and coal liquids and gases in primary production.

(c) "non-renewable natural resources" includes uranium and thorium.

This ensures uranium and thorium are included in non-renewable resources.

The Government of Canada considers this neither necessary nor acceptable.

(e) Report of the Continuing Committee of Ministers on the Constitution to First Ministers: Communications

Document: 800-14/002

The Ministers studied two drafts. The federal draft is based on exclusive jurisdiction for both orders of government and provides for federal-provincial consultation.

The provincial draft supported by ten governments, is based on virtually total concurrency with each level of government being paramount in some areas. It enshrines the principle of prevention of disruption of the "free flow of information". It also provides a mechanism for the resolution of conflicts of provincial laws where such conflicts in fact disrupt the free flow of information, irrespective of intention, by way of federal legislation enacted pursuant to the petition of a province.

FREQUENCY SPECTRUM

The federal draft provides for exclusive Federal jurisdiction over the spectrum. The intent of the draft is that the federal government would discharge its responsibility in a way that will not frustrate provincial jurisdiction over provincial undertakings. It was recognized that the language of the draft is inadequate for this purpose. The provincial draft provides for concurrency over the spectrum with federal paramountcy over matters of a technical nature respecting management of the radio frequency spectrum; the draft provides for provincial paramountcy over other matters which are considered to be of a nontechnical nature.

BROADCASTING

The federal draft provides for exclusive federal jurisdiction in this area.

The provincial draft provides for full concurrency with

federal paramountcy over broadcast network undertakings extending to four or more provinces and foreign broadcast signals and residual provincial paramountcy.

CABLE

The federal draft provides for exclusive federal jurisdiction over national cable undertakings operating as national carriers and cable works and undertakings that provide programming or other services beyond the limits of a province. The federal draft also provides for exclusive provincial jurisdiction over cable undertakings in the province involving off-air or closed circuit systems, subject to exclusive federal jurisdiction over distribution of a national program service as defined from time to time by Parliament, carriage of telecommunications 'for a national purpose' and technical standards and non-Canadian programming.

The provincial draft provides for exclusive provincial jurisdiction over closed circuit cable undertakings wholly situate within the province and concurrency with provincial paramountcy over other cable undertakings. The draft provides for federal paramountcy over the redistribution of broadcast signals that extend to four or more provinces and foreign broadcast signals on cable undertakings.

CARRIERS

The federal draft provides for exclusive federal jurisdiction over national carriers and space and satellite carriers including earth stations. It also provides for priority carriage of telecommunications 'for a national purpose' on provincial undertakings. The draft provides for exclusive provincial jurisdiction over carrier works and undertakings in the province, except for exclusive federal jurisdiction in interprovincial and international telecommunications services, interconnection, networking, rates and charges as well as technical standards and priority carriage 'for a national purpose', technical standards and earth stations.

The provincial draft provides for exclusive provincial jurisdiction over works and undertakings wholly situate within the province. It provides for concurrent jurisdiction with provincial paramountcy over other works and undertakings subject to federal paramountcy over the space segment of communications satellites and the use of telecommunications works and undertakings for aeronautics, radio-navigation, defence, and national emergencies.

ISSUES FOR CONSIDERATION BY FIRST MINISTERS

Spectrum: *The issue* is how to frame the federal jurisdiction in this area so as not to interfere with jurisdiction conferred to provinces in the field of communications.

Broadcasting: *The issue* is whether broadcasting should remain exclusively within federal jurisdiction (as per federal draft — copy attached) or whether the field should be concurrent with federal paramountcy over national networks (as per provincial draft — copy attached) and residual provincial paramountcy.

Cable: Both proposals provide for provincial jurisdiction in cable systems. *The issue* is the extent of involvement of each order of government in this area.

Carriers: *The issue* is whether there should be exclusive federal jurisdiction or concurrent jurisdiction with provincial paramountcy in interprovincial and international carriage.

Technical Standards: *The issue* is whether there should be exclusive federal jurisdiction over all technical aspects of telecommunications.

FEDERAL DRAFT ON COMMUNICATIONS

1. Section 91 of the B.N.A. Act would be amended by adding the four following paragraphs:

91. (*w*) The frequency spectrum including technical aspects only of frequency assignment.

(*x*) Interprovincial and international telecommunications services and the technical aspects of telecommunications.

(*y*) Telecommunications works and undertakings transmitting by broadcasting and telecommunications works and undertaking, other than carrier works and undertakings, providing programming or other services beyond the limits of a province.

(*z*) The regulation and distribution, including distribution in priority to all other signals through all or any telecommunications undertakings in a province, of a national program service as defined from time to time by Parliament, and the regulation and distribution of non-Canadian programming.

2. Section 92 of the B.N.A. Act would be amended by adding the two following paragraphs:

92. (*y*) Telecommunications carrier works and undertakings in the province other than:
   (*a*) national and international telecommunications carriers;
   (*b*) space and satellite telecommunications carriers including related earth stations;
   (*c*) carriage on all or any telecommunications carriers in the province of telecommunications for a national purpose.

(*z*) Telecommunications works and undertakings providing programming or other services in the province and not within the jurisdiction of Parliament by virtue of class (*y*) of section 91.

3. A provision to the following effect would be added:

Communications Consultations

The Government of Canada and the governments of the provinces shall consult together at least once in every year, bilaterally or on a regional or national basis, on the formulation, co-ordination and implementation of laws, policies, programmes and practices respecting communications.

BEST EFFORTS DRAFT: COMMUNICATIONS

(1) In each province the Legislature may make laws in relation to telecommunications works and undertakings in the province notwithstanding that such works and undertakings connect the province with any other or others of the provinces, extend beyond the limits of the province, or emit signals originating in the province beyond the province, or receive or distribute in the province signals originating outside the province.

(2) The Parliament of Canada may make laws in relation to telecommunications works and undertakings mentioned in sub-section (1) other than works and undertakings wholly situate within a province.

(3) No law enacted by the Legislature of a province or the Parliament of Canada under this section shall in its pith and substance be directed to the disruption of the free flow of information.

(4) Any law enacted by the Legislature of a province under sub-section (1) prevails over a law enacted by Parliament under sub-section (2) except a law of Parliament in relation to:

(a) matters of a technical nature respecting management of the radio frequency spectrum;

(b) the space segment of communication satellites;

(c) regulation of Canadian broadcasting trasmitting network undertakings that extend to four or more provinces, including the re-distribution of their signals by other telecommunications undertakings;

(d) foreign broadcast signals, including the redistribution of these signals by other telecommunications undertakings;

(e) the use of telecommunications works and undertakings for aeronautics, radio-navigation, defence, or in national emergencies.

(5) In the event that the laws of two or more provinces conflict so as to disrupt the free flow of information, one of the provinces may petition the Parliament of Canada to enact a law to resolve the specific conflict and such a law shall prevail.

(f) Report of the Continuing Committee of Ministers on the Constitution to First Ministers: New Upper House, Involving the Provinces

Document: 800-14/003

Explanatory Note

The following proposal, which is submitted as a preliminary draft, is presented to the First Ministers as a first step towards the broader and urgent question of second chamber reform to which Ministers are committed.

During the course of its discussions on this whole subject, Ministers identified two sets of functions in second chamber reform:

1. The ratifying of federal action on a limited list of specified matters of joint federal-provincial concern; and

2. A general parliamentary review function involving a suspensive veto.

This led to the consideration of such issues as whether a new institution should deal with one or both; the functions of ratification and review; whether these functions would be performed by one combined institution or two separate institutions; the basis of provincial representation and the degree of federal participation; the appropriate voting procedure for each function.

In considering these issues it became clear that a final resolution of all these, because of their complexity rather than because of fundamental disagreements among Ministers, could not be completed in the time available. Ministers were, however, able to explore in detail the ratification function and arrive at specific proposals for that aspect.

The proposal submitted to the First Ministers at this time sets forth an interim institutional framework for dealing with the first of these functions.

There remains for the next stage of constitutional discussions the development of the institutional framework for the second of these functions and their interrelationship.

BEST EFFORTS DRAFT: COUNCIL OF THE PROVINCES

Council established	**1.** There shall be a body to be called the Council of the Provinces.
Membership	**2.** The Council shall have thirty (30) members.
Appointment	**3.** The Lieutenant Governor in Council of each province shall appoint three members to the Council.
Head of delegation	**4.** The Lieutenant Governor in Council of each province shall designate one member to be the head of that province's delegation.
Tenure of members	**5.** Each member holds office at the pleasure of the Lieutenant-Governor in Council of his respective province.

Qualifications

    6. (*a*) A member of a provincial legislative assembly may also be a member of the Council.

        (*b*) Subject to (a) the legislative assembly of a province may prescribe the qualifications for its members to the Council.

Federal government spokesmen

    7. The federal Cabinet may designate any person or persons, including federal Cabinet ministers, who shall be entitled to appear in and speak to any matter coming before the Council.

Votes

    8. (*a*) Each province shall have one vote on every matter before the Council.

        (*b*) The vote of each province shall be cast by the head of that province's delegation or his designate.

Ratification

    9. (*a*) Unless otherwise specified herein, the ratification of any matter coming before the Council requires a two-thirds majority of the votes cast.

        (*b*) Unless otherwise specified herein the failure of legislation or an appointment to receive the required majority means that the legislation or appointment shall not take effect.

        (*c*) Legislation on which the Council has made no decision within ninety days from the time of referral shall be deemed to be ratified unless an extension of the time is made by the federal government. Appointments on which the Council has made no decision within thirty days from the time of referral shall be deemed to be ratified.

Powers

    10. Matters coming within the following classes shall be referred to the Council for its consideration, debate and disposition according to section 9, namely

        (*a*) The exercise by the Parliament of Canada of the declaratory power pursuant to section 92(10)(*c*).

        (*b*) (i) Laws of the Parliament of Canada initiating general conditional grants to the provinces in relation to matters within exclusive[1] provincial jurisdiction[2]

           (ii) [3]

---

[1] Ministers were unable to conclude whether this provision should be limited to areas of exclusive provincial jurisdiction or made broader.

[2] Ministers recognize the necessity, at some stage, of further ministerial or First Ministerial determination of what if any fiscal equivalent should be available to non-participating provincial governments.

[3] At the request of Quebec the following clause was also considered, but Ministers did not reach a conclusion: "Laws of the Parliament of Canada initiating payments to classes of individuals or institutions in relation to matters within exclusive provincial jurisdiction."

(c) (i) Laws of the Parliament of Canada made pursuant to the opening words of Section 91 or actions of the Government of Canada pursuant thereto, which have the effect of suspending in whole or in part the normal distribution of legislative powers between the Parliament of Canada and the legislatures of one or more of the provinces, except in cases where there is a state of real or apprehended war, invasion or insurrection.

(ii) Any measure taken to deal with real or apprehended insurrection will become inoperative fifteen days after having been proclaimed unless it is ratified by the Council.

(d) Laws of the Parliament of Canada, or sections thereof, which are to be administered by provincial governments.

(e) Approval of appointments to the managing bodies of such federal boards, commissions or agencies, as are determined from time to time by the Conference of First Ministers, to have significant interest to all or some of the provinces.[4]

(f) Other matters which have emerged or might emerge in the overall process of constitutional review which Ministers or First Ministers deem appropriate.

Dualism   **11.** In the case of any matter coming before the Council which is in relation to the French language or French culture the ratification of the Council would require that the two-thirds majority prescribed by section 9(a) include the affirmative vote of Quebec.[5]

Procedure   **12.** (a) The Council shall have power to determine its own procedure.

(b) A simple majority only shall be necessary for the establishing of any rules of procedure.

(g) Report of the Continuing Committee of Ministers on the Constitution to First Ministers: Supreme Court

Document: 800-14/004

Areas of Agreement

The following appear to be matters on which there is agreement:
— the Supreme Court be entrenched in the Constitution;
— judges to hold office during good behaviour until retirement age but the age of retirement be reduced from seventy-five to seventy years;
— provincial governments as well as the federal government have the right to make references directly to the Supreme Court;
— there be a guaranteed right to appeal constitutional issues to the Supreme Court with the leave of that Court; in the case of appeals from references made by a provincial government to its Court of Appeals or references made by the federal government to the

---

[4] There was some discussion as to whether, as an alternative, a list of specific subject areas such as energy, communications, tariffs, monetary policy and transportation should be specified.

[5] Ministers also examined the alternative of a weighted vote on this aspect but did not reach a conclusion. Ministers also recognized the fundamental definitional problem attached to the word "culture".

Federal Court leave off the Supreme Court would not be required;

— the Minister of Justice should consult with the provincial Attorneys General before Parliament enacts any law respecting those aspects of the Supreme Court not entrenched in the Constitution.

These are reflected in the attached draft text.

The following issues need to be focussed upon by Ministers.

1. Composition and Role

The Committee notes that there was broad acceptance of the proposition that the Supreme Court should reflect the principle of dualism arising from our two systems of law. There is less agreement, however, on the precise means by which this should be accomplished.

The proposal which is supported by a majority of governments is an eleven-man court composed of six common law judges and five civil law judges. Most of those supporting this proposal expressed the view that while it was not their preferred position, they were willing to support the proposal to accommodate Quebec's particular interests. A draft text of such a proposal [follows] as Appendix A.

A proposal which would provide for an eleven-man court, seven common law judges and four civil law judges was also discussed. There was less support for this proposal. The lack of approval in most instances was related to the aforementioned concern to accommodate Quebec's interest.

A thirteen-man court, composed of eight common law judges as proposed by Nova Scotia was also discussed. Nova Scotia's proposals in this regard, together with its proposals for an eleven-man court, [follow] as Appendix B.

A proposal tabled by British Columbia, which also involves an eleven-man court, seven common law and four civil law judges was discussed. A copy of that proposal [follows] as Appendix C with a notation thereon respecting an amendment subsequently suggested by British Columbia.

Issue: Should the Supreme Court be composed of eleven judges, with six common law and five civil law judges? If not, how many judges should there be and how should the court be structured?

2. Entrenchment of Principle of Alternating Chief Justice

Another issue related to the principle of dualism is that of entrenching the principle of alternate appointments of common law and civil law Chief Justices in the Constitution.

Issue: Should the alternate appointment of Chief Justices from among the common law and civil law members be entrenched in the Constitution?

3. Appointment Procedure

It is generally agreed that the appointment procedure should require the federal Minister of Justice to *consult with all provincial Attorneys General* when a vacancy is to be filled and to obtain the *consent* of the Attorney General of the province from which the appointee comes. An unresolved issue arising out of this, however, is the requirement for a *deadlock-breaking mechanism* to provide for cases in which the Minister of Justice and the Attorney General fail to agree.

Issue: Which of the following options is appropriate to deal with the situation where the federal Minister of Justice and the provincial Attorney General fail to agree on appointment:

(1) a variation of the Victoria Charter formulation to allow provinces to also nominate candidates for consideration by the nominating council, but with specified time periods significantly shortened; (a copy of the relevant provisions of the Victoria Charter [follows] as Appendix D)?

(2) a provision requiring the Chief Justice to join with the federal Minister of Justice and the provincial Attorney General to decide the matter?

(3) a provision requiring the federal Minister of Justice and the provincial Attorney General to choose a third person to join with them to decide the matter and if they are unable to agree the Chief Justice to choose such third person?

(4) no mechanism?

4. Appointment of Superior, District and County Court Judges (section 96)

At the Ottawa CCMC meeting nine provinces supported the following proposition:

1) that a province may appoint the judges of its Superior, District, and County Courts and where it exercises that power, the provisions of s.96 of the B.N.A. Act would not be applicable to the province; and

2) that the constitution:

(a) guarantee the existence of a superior court of general jurisdiction in each province;

(b) guarantee the independence of the members of such courts;

(c) enable a province to establish bodies to administer the application of its laws;

(*d*) enshrine the power of judicial review in the superior court of general jurisdiction; and

(*e*) provide that there shall not be a dual system of courts.

The representative of Manitoba while in favour of the principles in para. (2) favoured the retention of the federal appointing power.

The federal Minister of Justice stated that, while he recognized the difficulties caused by the judicial interpretation of s.96 for provinces attempting to create administrative bodies, he did not believe that it was necessary to change the whole judicial system in Canada in order to solve that problem. In his view, the matter required further consideration.

Issue: Should section 96 be repealed in accordance with the proposal outlined above?

APPENDIX A
BEST EFFORTS DRAFT PROPOSAL

The Supreme Court of Canada

Supreme Court of Canada

1. There shall be a general court of appeal for Canada called the Supreme Court of Canada.

Constitution of Court

2. The Supreme Court of Canada shall consist of eleven judges, who shall be appointed by the Governor General.

Eligibility for appointment

3. (1) A person is eligible to be appointed as a judge of the Supreme Court if, after having been admitted to the bar of any province, the person has, for a total period of at least ten years, been a judge of any court in Canada or a member of the bar of any province.

Appointment of judges from Quebec

(2) Five of the judges of the Supreme Court shall be appointed from among persons who, after having been admitted to the bar of Quebec, have, for a total period of at least ten years, been judges of any court of that province or of a court established by Parliament or members of the bar of Quebec.

Designation of Chief Justice of Canada

4. (1) A chief justice, to be called the Chief Justice of Canada, shall be designated by the Governor General.

Alternate designation

(2) The Chief Justice of Canada shall be designated for a single term, alternatively, from among the judges apponted under subsection 3(2) and from among the other judges of the Supreme Court.

Term of office

(3) The term of office of a judge as Chief Justice of Canada expires seven years after the designation has effect or upon the judge attaining the age of retirement, whichever first occurs.

Procedure on vacancy in Court

5. (1) Where a vacancy in the Supreme Court occurs, the Minister of Justice of Canada shall consult with the Attorneys General of all of the provinces and shall seek the consent of the Attorney General of *the* province *of the* person being considered for appointment as to the appointment of that person.

Procedure where no consent

(2) Where consent is not forthcoming, the Minister of Justice of Canada and the appropriate provincial Attorney General shall, together with (a person chosen by them or if they do not agree a person chosen by) the Chief Justice of Canada, determine the person to be recommended for appointment.

Tenure of office of judges of court

6. (1) The judges of the Supreme Court hold office during good behaviour until they attain the age of seventy years but are removable by the Governor General on address of the Senate and the House of Commons.

Salaries, allowances and pensions of judges

(2) Parliament shall provide for the salaries, allowances and pensions of the judges of the Supreme Court.

Ultimate appellate jurisdiction of Court	**7.** The Supreme Court has exclusive ultimate appellate civil and criminal jurisdiction.
Appeals with leave of Court	**8.** An appeal to the Supreme Court lies with leave of the Supreme Court from any judgment of the highest court in a province, or a judge thereof, in which judgment can be had in the particular case sought to be appealed to the Supreme Court, where any question involved raises a constitutional issue.
Appeals from Governor *General* in Council references	**9.** An appeal to the Supreme Court lies from an opinion pronounced by the highest court established by Parliament on any constitutional question referred to it by the Governor *General* in Council.
Direct references by Governor *General* in Council	**10.** Parliament may make laws authorizing the Governor *General* in Council to refer questions of law or fact directly to the Supreme Court.
Appeals from provincial references	**11.** An appeal to the Supreme Court lies from an opinion pronounced by the highest court in a province on any constitutional question referred to it by the Lieutenant Governor in Council of the province.
Direct provincial references	**12.** The legislature of a province may make laws authorizing the Lieutenant Governor in Council to refer *questions of law or fact* directly to the Supreme Court.
Additional appeals	**13.** In addition to any appeal provided for by this Act, an appeal to the Supreme Court lies as may be provided by Parliament.
Organization, maintenance and operation of Court	**14.** Parliament may make laws providing for the organization, maintenance and operation of the Supreme Court, and the effective executive and working of this division and the attainment of its intention and objects.
Consultation	**15.** The Minister of Justice of Canada shall consult with the Attorneys General of the provinces in respect of proposals for laws referred to in sections 13 and 14.

Transitional

Continuation of Supreme Court of Canada	**XX.** (1) The court existing immediately before the commencement of this Act under the name of the Supreme Court of Canada is continued as provided in this Act.
Continuation in office of judges	(2) The Chief Justice of Canada and other judges of the Supreme Court of Canada shall continue in office as though appointed and designated in the manner provided in this Act except that they shall hold office *as judges and Chief Justice* until attaining the age of seventy-five years.
Continuation of laws	(3) Until otherwise provided pursuant to this Act, all laws respecting the Supreme Court of Canada and the judges thereof that were in force immediately before the commencement of this Act shall continue, subject to this Act.

APPENDIX B
NOVA SCOTIA DISCUSSION PAPER: SUPREME COURT OF CANADA

WHEREAS:

1) There exists in Canada two legal regimes, i.e. civil law regime in the province of Quebec and common law regimes in all the other provinces; and

2) The workload of the Supreme Court has increased and may be expected to increase substantially as a result of the proposed changes in the jurisdiction of the court (e.g. right of provinces to make direct references) and the proposed constitutional changes in the B.N.A. Act (e.g. inclusion of charter of rights, etc.) and

3) The practice has been to select the members of the court from the regions of Canada subject to the statutory requirement that three members come from the civil law regime of Quebec; and

4) Judges from the civil law regime should exercise the appellate jurisdiction of the court in civil cases from Quebec and vice versa in respect to civil cases from the common law provinces; and

5) That constitutional questions or issues coming before the court should be decided by a composition of the members of the court which reflect the two legal civil regimes of Canada;

THEREFORE:

Proposal #1

(a) The Supreme Court be increased from 9 members to 13 members to be appointed as follows:
   — 5 members from the civil law province of Quebec
   — 3 members from the common law province of Ontario
   — 3 members from the common law provinces of Manitoba, Saskatchewan, Alberta, British Columbia
   — 2 members from the common law provinces of New Brunswick, Nova Scotia, Prince Edward Island, Newfoundland;

(b) Civil law appeals not involving constitutional issues be heard by a panel of the court comprising all or a majority of civil law appointed members of the court,

(c) Common law appeals not involving constitutional issues be heard by a panel of the court comprising all or a majority of common law appointed members of the court,

(d) Constitutional questions or appeal raising constitutional issues be heard by *either*
   — an 11 member panel comprising 6 common law appointed judges and 5 civil law appointed judges,
   or
   — a 7 member panel comprising 4 common law appointed judges and 3 civil law appointed judges as the Chief Justice considers appropriate

OR

Proposal #2

(a) The Supreme Court be increased from 9 members to 11 members to be appointed as follows:
   — 4 members from the civil law province of Quebec,
   — 3 members from the common law province of Ontario
   — 2 members from the common law provinces of Manitoba, Saskatchewan, Alberta, British Columbia

   — 2 members from the common law provinces of New Brunswick, Nova Scotia, Prince Edward Island, Newfoundland,

(b) Civil law appeals not involving constitutional issues be heard by a panel of the court comprising a majority of civil law appointed members of the court.

(c) Common law appeals not involving constitutional issues be heard by a panel of the court comprising a majority of common law appointed members of the court.

(d) Constitutional questions or appeal raising constitutional issues be heard by *either*
   — a 9 member panel comprising 5 common law appointed judges and 4 civil law appointed judges
   or
   — a 7 member panel comprising 4 common law appointed judges and 3 civil law appointed judges as the Chief Justice considers appropriate.

APPENDIX C
SUPREME COURT OF CANADA: B.C. PROPOSAL, AUGUST 26, 1980

When the Supreme Court of Canada becomes an instrument of the Constitution as the final adjudicator of national legal issues, it will symbolize to Canadians a new era in the life of the Court. If the Constitutional proposals meet with the approval of all governments, it will mark the end of an era where the Court has been viewed by some as an emanation of just the central government.

British Columbia, therefore, views the Court as an important element in the reform of the Canadian Constitution and one which must be the subject of Continuing indepth consideration in the remaining three weeks.

We make the following proposal which we believe will meet the needs of all Canadians in forming the basis of an agreement on the court.

We propose that the Court consist of eleven Justices whose selection will be determined in the following way:

(a) Justices of the Supreme Court shall be appointed by the Governor in Council upon the recommendation of a Council of Canadian Attorneys-General; this Council will be made up of the Attorney-General of Canada and the Attorney-General of each province;

(b) Nominations of Justices by the Council will be initiated by the Attorney-General or Attorneys-General from the appropriate nominating area identified by the Council;

(c) To reflect the legal duality of the Canadian nation four Justices shall be nominated by the Attorney-General of Quebec;

(d) To reflect the diversity of the nation, Justices shall be chosen to ensure that the Court reflects the collective experience and background knowledge of all parts of Canada. Representation shall come from all areas of Canada as was attempted in the Federal Bill C-60; a model which British Columbia can accept.

This proposal ensures an immediate additional seat for both the civil and common law jurisdictions. With the changes in the Court which are forthcoming, the Council of Attorneys General will be able to meet regularly and begin the process of deciding how to best reflect Canada's duality and diversity through court appointments.

Note: British Columbia agreed to consider an amendment to the above saying that a nominating council be constituted to select the area from which the judge will come and then the appointment would be made by the Attorney General of the appropriate province and the Attorney General of Canada with a deadlock to be resolved by the Council of Attorneys General.

APPENDIX D
VICTORIA CHARTER — DEADLOCK BREAKING MECHANISM

Art. 29. Where after the lapse of ninety days from the day a vacancy arises in the Supreme Court of Canada, the Attorney General of Canada and the Attorney General of a Province have not reached agreement on a person to be appointed to fill the vacancy, the Attorney General of Canada may inform the Attorney General of the appropriate Province in writing that he proposes to convene a nominating council to recommend an appointment.

Art. 30. Within thirty days of the day when the Attorney General of Canada has written the Attorney General of the Province that he proposes to convene a nominating council, the Attorney General of the Province may inform the Attorney General of Canada in writing that he selects either of the following types of nominating councils:

(1) a nominating council consisting of the following members: the Attorney General of Canada or his nominee and the Attorneys General of the Provinces or their nominees;

(2) a nominating council consisting of the following members: the Attorney General of Canada or his nominee, the Attorney General of the appropriate Province or his nominee and a Chairman to be selected by the two Attorneys General, and if within six months from the expiration of the thirty days they cannot agree on a Chairman, then the Chief Justice of the appropriate Province, or if he is unable to act, the next senior Judge of his court, shall name a Chairman;

and if the Attorney General of the Province fails to make a selection within the thirty days above referred to, the Attorney General of Canada may select the person to be appointed.

Art. 31. When a nominating council has been created, the Attorney General of Canada shall submit the names of not less than three qualified persons to it about whom he has sought the agreement of the Attorney General of the appropriate Province to the appointment, and the nominating council shall recommend therefrom a person for appointment to the Supreme Court of Canada; a majority of the members of a council constitutes a quorum, and a recommendation of the majority of the members at a meeting constitutes a recommendation of the council.

(h) Report of the Continuing Committee of Ministers on the Constitution to First Ministers: Family Law

Document: 800-14/005

The matter of the transfer to the provinces of legislative competence to enact laws in relation to the whole or any part of marriage and divorce was included in the twelve items to be addressed by the Continuing Committee of Ministers.

At an early stage of our deliberations a consensus

emerged favouring the following principles:

i. that legislative jurisdiction concerning marriage, including the validity of marriages, be transferred to the provinces;

ii. that legislative jurisdiction to prescribe grounds for divorce be transferred to those provinces wishing to avail themselves of this power and that for the remainder of the provinces Parliament retain this power;

iii. that in order to prevent a marriage being valid in one province but invalid in another and to prevent parties from resorting to courts in a jurisdiction with which they have no reasonable connection, Parliament should retain exclusive authority to establish rules for the recognition of divorces, whether granted inside or outside Canada, and to establish the basis for jurisdiction of courts granting this relief in Canada;

iv. that the provinces be given exclusive legislative competence with respect to relief ancillary to the granting of divorce i.e. maintenance and custody;

v. that the present section 96 of the British North America Act be amended to provide that the provinces be enabled to confer jurisdiction in all family law matters on courts established or on judges appointed by provincial administrations.

At the request of the delegates of the federal delegation ministers were asked to consider reserving to Parliament the same powers with respect to recognition of declarations of nullity and the jurisdiction of the courts to grant them as would apply to divorce. The provincial consensus supports this principle.

In addition concern has been expressed both inside and outside this Conference that the transfer of legislative competence to the provinces in relation to maintenance and custody would jeopardize the enforcement of these orders on a national scale. Ministers moved to eliminate or blunt this possibility by proposing that such orders have binding effect on a national basis wherever made in the country; and by providing for the registration and enforcement of these orders in all courts of competent jurisdiction in all provinces irrespective of the province in which the order is made. The powers to vary orders by reason of change of circumstance and the power to decline to enforce an order which offends public policy or which was granted without regard to due process of law are made subject to the power of provincial reservation.

The text reflecting these proposals is appended hereto as [Best Efforts Draft].

Manitoba and Prince Edward Island support the principles set forth in Sections 3, 4 and 6 and reject the balance of the proposals.

The Province of Alberta reserves on the proposed transfer to the provinces of legislative jurisdiction in relation to divorce.

BEST EFFORTS DRAFT: FAMILY LAW

1. Repeal head 26 of section 91 — "Marriage and divorce".
2. Repeal head 12 of section 92 — "The Solemnization of Marriage in the Province".
3. Add as new legislative authority provisions, the following sections:

Marriage jurisdiction

"1. The legislature of each province may make laws in relation to marriage in the province, including the validity of marriage in the province, except that Parliament has exclusive authority to make laws in relation to the recognition of a declaration that a marriage is void, whether granted within or outside Canada, and in relation to the jurisdictional basis upon which a court may entertain an application for a declaration that a marriage is void.

Divorce — provincial jurisdiction

2. (1) The legislature of each province may make laws in relation to divorce in the province and has exclusive authority to make laws in relation to relief ancillary thereto.

Divorce jurisdiction of Parliament

(2) Parliament may make laws in relation to divorce and has exclusive authority to make laws in relation to the recognition of divorces, whether granted within or outside Canada, and in relation to the jurisdictional basis upon which a court may entertain an application for a divorce.

Relationship between laws of provinces and laws of Parliament

(3) Where the legislature of a province enacts a law in relation to any matter over which it has concurrent authority with Parliament under this section, that law prevails in the province over any law of Parliament in relation to that matter to the extent of any inconsistency.

Declaration assuming authority

(4) The legislature of each province may declare that it is assuming authority in relation to all matters over which it has concurrent authority with Parliament under this section and, where the legislature so declares, notwithstanding subsection 3, all laws of Parliament in relation to those matters have no effect in that province while the declaration is in effect.

Effect of Order

3. An order for maintenance or custody made in Canada has legal effect throughout Canada.

Registration and enforcement of order

4. An order referred to in section 3 made in any province or territory may be registered in any other province or territory in a court of competent jurisdiction and shall be enforced in like manner as an order of that court.

Authority to make laws

5. The legislatures of the provinces may make laws to give effect to the provisions of sections 3 and 4 and may make laws providing for the variation and non-enforcement of orders by reason of a change in circumstances and, in addition, for the non-enforcement of orders on grounds of public policy or lack of due process of law.

Power of legislature to confer jurisdiction of superior court judges

6. Notwithstanding section (96), the legislature of each province may confer, or authorize the Lieutenant Governor of the province to confer, concurrently or exclusively, upon any court or division of a court or all or any judges of any court, the judges of which are appointed by the Governor General or by the Lieutenant Governor of the province, as the legislature may determine, the jurisdiction of a judge of a superior court of the province in respect of any matters within the field of family law."

4. Add as one of the transitional provisions, the following section:

Continuation of existing laws

"**XX.** Except as otherwise provided in this Act, all laws relating to marriage and divorce that are in force in Canada or any province immediately before the coming into effect of this Act continue in force in Canada and that province, respectively, until such time as they are repealed, altered or replaced by Parliament or the legislature of the province according to the authority of Parliament or the legislature under this Act.''*

(i) Report of the Sub-Committee on Family Law

Document: 800-14/080

At the request of the Chairman of the Conference the sub-committee on Family Law of the Continuing Committee of Ministers on the Constitution was reconvened for the purpose of considering what amendments might be made to section 5 of the "best efforts" draft in order to attract a fuller consensus on these provisions.

The sub-committee met on three occasions and it now appears that the delegates of the Government of Canada

---

*Note: The wording of this general transitional section will need to be finalized later.

and all provincial administrations except that of Manitoba are now agreed that section 5 of the ''best efforts'' draft is acceptable.

The further deliberations of your sub-committee have confirmed that Manitoba remains opposed to both the transfer of divorce jurisdiction and the present text of section 5 of the ''best efforts'' draft. Manitoba indicated it would be willing to accept a revised text of section 5 which would restrict the power of the provincial legislatures to make laws with respect to the variation of orders where there is a change in circumstances.

Prince Edward Island has joined the consensus in adopting the provisions of the present section 5 but remains opposed to the transfer of divorce jurisdiction to the provinces.

All of which is respectfully submitted.

[Best Efforts Draft]

Authority to make laws

5. The legislature of the provinces may make laws to give effect to the provisions of sections 3 and 4 and may make laws respecting the variation and enforcement of orders in the provinces where there is a change in circumstances.

(j) Report of the Continuing Committee of Ministers on the Constitution to First Ministers: Fisheries

Document: 800-14/006

ISSUES FOR CONSIDERATION BY FIRST MINISTERS

The Ministers believe that the following issues require the consideration of First Ministers:

INLAND FISHERIES, MARINE PLANTS, AQUACULTURE AND SEDENTARY SPECIES

1. Should the federal government continue to exercise exclusive jurisdiction over all aspects of inland fisheries for an anadromous species (e.g. salmon)?
2. It is necessary for conservation purposes for the federal government to continue to exercise exclusive jurisdiction over marine plants?
3. To what extent is it necessary for the federal government to exercise jurisdiction for the protection of fish habitat?
4. What is the appropriate way for provision to be made for native peoples' fisheries?

SEA COAST FISHERIES

1. Should there be concurrent jurisdiction over sea coast fisheries or should exclusive federal jurisdiction continue?

GENERAL

1. Regardless of possible changes in jurisdiction, is it appropriate to make constitutional provision for mandatory consultation in fisheries matters?

OVERVIEW DISCUSSION

Regarding *inland fisheries, aquaculture, marine plants* and *sedentary species* two formulations for amendment of the British North America Act have emerged.

The first, supported by nine provinces, would make these matters subject to exclusive provincial jurisdiction. Most provinces would accept that the Government of Canada would retain a paramountcy regarding certain matters related to the conservation of anadromous fish stocks.

The second, supported by the Government of Canada and Nova Scotia, would make inland fisheries, acquaculture and sedentary species matters subject to exclusive provincial jurisdiction except that the Government of Canada would retain exclusive jurisdiction over anadromous species. The Government of Canada would also wish provision to be made, regarding protection of fish habitat in interprovincial and international waterways, waters frequented by anadromous species, and provision for native peoples' fisheries. The Government of Canada would also maintain exclusive jurisdiction over marine plants.

The alternative formulations appear as Appendix I.

A draft of a new section 92.1, prepared by the federal government, was tabled for discussion purposes. This draft incorporates (with minor variation) the formulations to which reference is made above and also includes formulations which attempt to meet the previously expressed concerns of the Government of Canada regarding protection of fish habitat and provision for native peoples' fisheries.

Ministers reviewed these draft formulations and some provinces found unacceptable the formulation for the protection of fish habitat. All provinces expressed the desire to seek further advice regarding the formulation providing for native peoples' fisheries before commenting.

A copy of the federal proposal [follows] (Appendix III) for the information of First Ministers.

Regarding *sea coast* fisheries, nine provinces support the fundamental proposition that there should be, at least, concurrent jurisdiction in this area.

The Government of Canada and Nova Scotia maintain that this area should remain under exclusive federal jurisdiction. The 'best efforts' draft of Vancouver (830-83/014) remains, in the opinion of most provincial ministers, susceptible to promoting the broad provincial consensus, which the federal government indicated in the Toronto meetings, necessary for consideration of the proposal by the federal government.

This draft appears as Appendix II [*supra*, p. 641].

Ministers also considered the federal proposal concerning mandatory consultation in fisheries. The federal government explained that this proposal should be considered as a response to expressions of provincial concern regarding the adequacy of existing consultative mechanisms. As such, it could be included in any disposition made on the question of fisheries jurisdiction. The proposal does not intend to address that question. Most provinces, while supporting the necessity for consultation, indicated that the proposal, by itself, could not be considered an acceptable response to the proposals advanced by provinces regarding fisheries jurisdiction.

APPENDIX I: BEST EFFORTS DRAFT

AMENDMENT:
ALTERNATIVE FORMULATIONS REGARDING INLAND FISHERIES, MARINE PLANTS AND SEDENTARY SPECIES

Supported by Nine Provinces	**Supported by Federal Government and One Coastal Province**
92.1 (1) The Legislature of each province may exclusively make laws in relation to:	The Legislature of each province may exclusively make laws in relation to:
(a) inland fisheries in the non tidal waters of the province;	(a) inland fisheries in the non-tidal waters in the province.
(b) marine and aquatic plants[1] in the non tidal waters of the province and in tidal waters in or adjacent to the province[1];	
(c) sedentary species in tidal waters in or adjacent to the province;	(c) sedentary species in tidal waters in or adjacent to the province;

---

1. Requires definition.

(*d*) aquaculture within the province and in tidal waters or adjacent to the province that is not included in either (*a*), (*b*) or (*c*);

(2) Notwithstanding paragraph 1(*a*) the Parliament of Canada may make laws in relation to the determination of total allowable catches for andromous species in non tidal waters and their allocation between provinces and any such law shall be paramount.

(*d*) aquaculture within the province and in tidal waters or adjacent to the province that is not included in either (*a*) or (*c*);

Notwithstanding paragraph 1(*a*) the Parliament of Canada may exclusively make laws in relation to sea coast and inland fisheries for andromous species.

Comment

(1) The Federal government would also wish provision to be made for the protection of the fish habitat and native people's fisheries.

APPENDIX III: DRAFT AMENDMENT TO SECTION 92.1

SUBMITTED BY THE FEDERAL GOVERNMENT

1. Class 12 of section 91 of the *British North America Act, 1867*, as amended, is repealed and the following substituted therefor:

"**12.** Sea coast fisheries except those assigned exclusively to the legislatures of the provinces by subsection 92.1(1)."

2. The said Act is further amended by adding thereto immediately after section 92 thereof the following heading and sections:

Fisheries powers of provinces

"**92.1** (1) The legislature of a province may exclusively make laws in relation to
(*a*) fisheries in waters within the province other than tidal waters;
(*b*) sedentary species in waters within or adjacent to the provinces; and
(*c*) aquaculture within or adjacent to the province.

Exception for anadromous species

(2) Notwithstanding paragraph (1)(*a*), Parliament may exclusively make laws in relation to sea coast and inland fisheries for anadromous stocks that migrate to sea.

Protection, etc. of fish habitat

(3) Notwithstanding subsection (1), Parliament may make laws for the protection and enhancement of fish habitat in all tidal waters and in:
(*a*) the waters of lakes, rivers and canals extending beyond the limits of any one province; and
(*b*) inland waters that provide a spawning ground or habitat for anadromous stocks that migrate to sea.

Paramountcy

(4) A law made under subsection (2) or (3) prevails over a law made under subsection (1) to the extent of any inconsistency.

Definitions

(5) In subsection (1),

"Aquaculture"

"Sedentary species"

"adjacent to the province"

Indian fishing rights

Limitation

Other rights

Fisheries consultation

"aquaculture" means operations in which fish or other marine or aquatic organisms are raised for harvest in an artificially enclosed space;

"sedentary species" means marine animals which, at the harvestable stage, either are immobile on or under the seabed or are unable to move except in constant physical contact with the seabed or the subsoil, but for greater certainty does not include crabs, lobsters or scallops;

"adjacent to the province" means [geographical limits to be determined re sedementary species and aquaculture).

92.2(1) Indians have the right to fish for food throughout the year for their personal and community use, both in the province in which they reside and in any other area to which an Indian treaty applicable to them applies, on all unoccupied Crown lands and on any other lands to which they may have a right of access, subject to provincial conservation laws that are reasonably necessary to secure to them a continuing supply of fish for this purpose.

(2) Subsection (1) does not apply where the right described therein has been expressly surrendered by treaty.

(3) Nothing in subsection (1) derogates from or diminishes any other right enjoyed by Indians, whether under treaty or otherwise."

xx The minister of the government of Canada responsible for fisheries and a minister designated by each provincial government shall consult together at least once in every year, either bilaterally or on a regional basis, on the formulation, coordination and implementation of policies and programmes of the government of Canada respecting fisheries and provincial policies and programmes significantly affecting fisheries.

xxx The Schedule to the *British North America Act, 1930* is amended by:

(*a*) in portion (1) relating to Manitoba, deleting section 10 thereof and deleting in section 13 the words "and fish" and "and fishing" wherever they appear therein;

(*b*) in portion (2) relating to Alberta, deleting section 9 thereof and deleting in section 12 the words "and fish" and "and fishing" wherever they appear therein; and

(*c*) in portion (3) relating to Saskatchewan, deleting section 9 thereof and deleting in section 12 the words "and fish" and "and fishing" wherever they appear therein.

(k) Report of the Continuing Committee of Ministers on the Constitution to First Ministers: Offshore Resources

Document: 800-14/007

ISSUES FOR CONSIDERATION BY FIRST MINISTERS

Ministers suggest that there are two options for consideration by First Ministers:

(1) Constitutional recognition of provincial ownership with the same rights, privileges and responsibilities as pertain with onshore resources.

(2) Adoption of administrative arrangements which might be designed to confer on provinces all or most of the advantages of ownership.

OVERVIEW OF DISCUSSION

There is a fundamental disagreement between the federal and provincial governments on the issue of ownership of offshore mineral resources.

All provinces agree that offshore resources should be treated in a manner consistent with constitutional provisions for resources onshore. The federal government does not agree with this approach, but fully recognizes that coastal provinces should have an important role in making decisions concerning offshore resources.

Three routes to resolution of the offshore resources issue have been considered:

(*a*) recognition of provincial ownership

(*b*) systems of concurrent jurisdiction, and

(*c*) administrative arrangements.

(a) Recognition of Provincial Ownership

If provincial ownership of offshore resources were to be constitutionally recognized, this could be expressed in a number of ways. One possible method could be by (a) a new Section 92 (Appendix I [*supra*, p. 647]) and (b) a parallel amendment to Section 92 (Appendix II [*supra*, p. 647]), because ownership and jurisdiction are not synonomous.

An alternative method of conferring ownership on provinces is extension of provincial boundaries seaward to the extent of the territorial sea by action of federal and provincial legislatures as prescribed under existing Section 3 of the British North America Act (1871). It was suggested that extension of provincial rights over the continental shelf beyond the limits of the territorial sea might be achieved similarly or by constitutional amendment.

Illustrative Distribution of Responsibilities

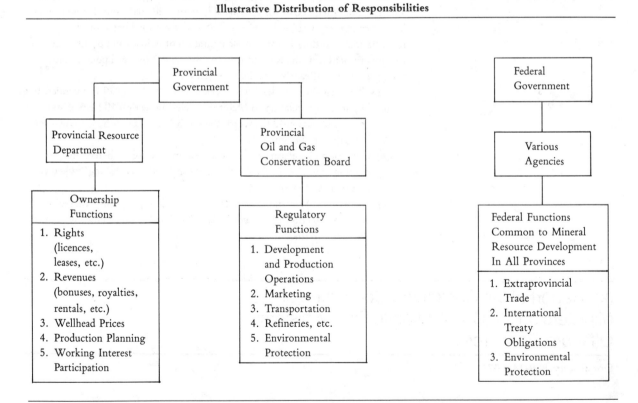

Notes:

1. All revenues, except federal taxes, go to the coastal province.
2. The foregoing division of legislative powers is subject to whatever determination is made with respect to onshore resources.
3. Some provinces object to the allocation of extraprovincial trade and international treaty obligations exclusively to the federal government. Similarly, the federal government does not agree with all the exclusive powers assigned to provinces.

The first approach was preferred as a legal technique.

The kind of legislative and constitutional regime that would be consistent with provincial ownership is illustrated in the table [on the previous page].

(b) Systems of Concurrent Jurisdiction

No government considers a system of concurrent jurisdiction to be a preferable solution.

(c) Administrative Arrangements

At the August 26–29 meeting of the CCMC, the federal government tabled a proposal on administrative arrangements, which would be confirmed in the Constitution. A copy of the federal proposal is attached as Appendix III. [See *supra*, p. 695.] Its main features can be summarized as follows:

(a) *Revenue Sharing*: a coastal province would receive 100% of offshore resource revenues such as royalties, fees, rentals and payments for exploration or development rights, until it became a "have" province; beyond that point, a province would receive a decreasing proportion of these revenues. The federal proposal includes a principle under which the offshore revenue raising system would be designed to capture a high proportion of the economic rent, comparable to the approach of the Western Provinces;

(b) *Legislation*: federal legislation implementing the national energy policy would apply;

(c) *Management*: bilateral joint bodies would be responsible for overall management of the offshore, including day-to-day administration, and would be composed of three provincial representatives, three federal representatives, and a neutral chairman. On pace of development, the joint bodies would be required to respond to provincial concerns, up to the point where the national interest would be affected, in which case it would prevail;

(d) *Constitutional Confirmation*: a way would be found to provide constitutional confirmation of the proposal.

The major concerns raised by the Provinces centred on the following points:

(1) *Revenues:* some provinces were concerned that the term used in the federal proposal "100% of offshore resource revenues", is misleading since a considerable portion of the economic rent from resources, whether onshore or offshore, does not flow to the provinces, but goes to the Federal Government through corporation income taxes, federal sales and excise taxes, and export taxes. Moreover, the value of the rights awarded to Petro Canada are not accounted for in the revenue sharing arrangement, and such working interest participation is considered to be an important source of provincial revenues.

Some provinces noted that the term "have" province is not defined, and that there are various ways in which this could be done with differing impacts.

On a more fundamental basis, provinces stated that the federal revenue sharing proposal did not meet the principle of equality of treatment for all resources. Such sharing of revenue is accomplished better through broad-based mechanisms such as federal taxation and equalization.

(2) *Management and Control:* There was general concern by the coastal provinces over their lack of real power to manage and control offshore resource development, given the fact that federal resource management legislation would generally obtain. The provinces agreed that real provincial management and control of offshore mineral resources and more crucial to them than is the simple question of revenues.

Again, the coastal provinces objected to the treatment of the offshore resources in a manner which was not consistent with the treatment of resources onshore with regard to the extent of the control and exercise of over-riding federal powers related to national interest and national energy policy.

In summary, no province indicated approval for the federal proposal as presently defined.

However, there was indication from some coastal provinces that if an arrangement could be devised conferring to provinces benefits and control equivalent to those traditionally enjoyed with regard to onshore resources, such a solution may constitute a satisfactory alternative to ownership.

It was noted that the term "ownership" comprises a large number of rights. It is the allocation of these rights among governments which is important. Some of the chief rights, in so far as natural resources are concerned are:

— control of pace of development and rate of production
— the right to a fair economic return
— the right to government participation
— regulation of operations.

(I) Report of the Continuing Committee of Ministers on the Constitution to First Ministers: Equalization

Document: 800-14/008

Attached is a tabular presentation of the three drafts on equalization considered by Ministers.

ISSUES FOR CONSIDERATION BY FIRST MINISTERS

First Ministers are to decide:
1) Which of the following drafts:
   (a) the Government of Quebec proposal, which provides that payments are to be made to provincial governments; or
   (b) the Governments of Manitoba and Saskatchewan

proposal, which, while incorporating the Quebec proposal, provides more specifically that such payments will ensure that provincial governments have sufficient revenue to provide reasonably comparable levels of public services at a reasonably comparable levels of taxation; or
   (c) the Government of British Columbia proposal supports the principle of providing essential public services of reasonable quality to all Canadians, but without specifying a particular method of achieving this objective;
is acceptable to the Conference.
2) Whether the draft should contain (section 3) a requirement for the First Ministers to meet every five years.

BEST EFFORTS DRAFT
EQUALIZATION AND REGIONAL DEVELOPMENT

Government of Quebec Proposal	Governments of Manitoba and Saskatchewan Proposal (including Quebec's Proposal)	Government of British Columbia Proposal
96(1) Without altering the legislative authority of Parliament or of the legislatures or of the rights of any of them with respect to the exercise of their legislative authority, Parliament and the legislatures, together with the Government of Canada and the Governments of the Provinces, are committed to (a) promoting equal opportunities for the well-being of Canadians; (b) furthering economic development to reduce disparity in opportunities; and, (c) providing essential public services of reasonable quality to all Canadians.	**96**(1) Without altering the legislative authority of Parliament or of the legislatures or of the rights of any of them with respect to the exercise of their legislative authority, Parliament and the legislatures, together with the Government of Canada and the Governments of the Provinces, are committed to (a) promoting equal opportunities for the well-being of Canadians; (b) furthering economic development to reduce disparity in opportunities; and, (c) providing essential public services of reasonable quality to all Canadians.	**96**(1) Without altering the legislative authority of Parliament or of the legislatures or of the rights of any of them with respect to the exercise of their legislative authority, Parliament and the legislatures, together with the Government of Canada and the Governments of the Provinces, are committed to (a) promoting equal opportunities for the well-being of Canadians; (b) furthering economic development to reduce disparity in opportunities; and, (c) providing essential public services of reasonable quality to all Canadians.

(2) Parliament and the Government of Canada are further committed to the principle of making equalization payments to provincial governments that are unable to provide essential public services of reasonable quality without imposing an undue burden of taxation.

(3) The Prime Minister of Canada and the First Ministers of the Provinces shall review together the questions of equalization and regional development at least once every five years.

(2) Parliament and the Government of Canada are further committed to the principle of making equalization payments to ensure that provincial governments have sufficient revenues to provide reasonably comparable levels of public services at reasonably comparable levels of taxation.

(3) The Prime Minister of Canada and the First Ministers of the Provinces shall review together the questions of equalization and regional development at least once every five years.

(2) Parliament and the Government of Canada are committed to taking such measures as are appropriate to ensure that provinces are able to provide the essential public services referred to in S.96(1)(c) without imposing an undue burden of provincial taxation.

(3) The Prime Minister of Canada and the First Ministers of the Provinces shall review together the question and principles of such measures at least once every five years.

(m) Report of the Continuing Committee of Ministers on the Constitution to First Ministers: Patriation and the Amending Formula

Document: 800-14/010

A. AMENDING FORMULA

- Ministers generally support the basic elements of an amending formula proposal submitted by Alberta to the Conference of First Ministers in February 1979.
- Quebec noted that while willing to consider this subject, it believed that no decisions should be taken on it until the discussions on the distribution of powers were successfully completed.
- The Alberta proposal provides for general amendments to be made with the assent of Parliament and 2/3 of the provinces with at least 50% of the population. However, if the amendment is one affecting —
  - (a) the powers of the legislature of a province to make laws;
  - (b) the rights and privileges granted or secured by the Constitution to the legislature or government of a province;
  - (c) the assets or property of a province; or,
  - (d) the natural resources of a province

  then up to 3 provinces can dissent from it and the amendment will not apply to them (this procedure has been termed "opting-out").

- Ministerial discussions disclosed two issues of substance with regard to the Alberta formula. These issues are:
  - how to deal with amendments which by their nature must apply across Canada therefore cannot be subject to opting-out;
  - whether constitutional provision should be made for the financial implications of amendments.

ISSUES FOR CONSIDERATION BY FIRST MINISTERS

1. UNIVERSAL APPLICABILITY

- It was noted that a number of the items identified under section 8 of the Alberta draft and other items, although relating to the rights and privileges of the legislature of government of a province, must, by their very nature, apply across the country. *The opting-out feature in section 1(2), therefore, cannot be applied to them.*
- Examples of such items are:
  - Supreme Court of Canada
  - a new upper house
  - charter of rights

— use of English or French language

— section 121

— section 125 — immunity of Crown land and property from taxation

- With no opting out on items of this nature, the general amending formula (2/3 of the provinces with 50% of the population) would apply. It was suggested that:

  (*a*) some amendments would be too easy to obtain, e.g., when considered in relation to entrenched language rights;

  (*b*) amendments of particular concern to a province could be made without that province's approval, e.g., the right of a province to a number of members in the House of Commons not less than the number of Senators representing the province is of particular concern to Prince Edward Island; amendments concerning language/culture and dualism could be passed without Quebec's assent.

- The options considered by Ministers for resolving the problem of how to deal with items that by their nature do not lend themselves to the opting out process were:

  (*a*) *Unanimity* — provides inherent protection for Quebec and all others;

  (*b*) *Higher population requirement* — for example, 2/3 of the provinces with at least *80%* of the population of Canada — provides inherent protection for Quebec and Ontario;

  (*c*) *Quebec assent requirement* — identify particular linguistic/cultural and dualism items and require that Quebec be included among the 2/3 of the provinces approving such amendments;

  (*d*) *Assent of province concerned* — identify items of particular concern to a province and require that that province be among the 2/3 of the provinces approving such an amendment.

- Ministers suggested that one way of handling this problem would be to identify all items that could not be subject to opting out, and to see if they could be categorized under some or all of the options. It was agreed that this possible means of solution should be brought to the attention of First Ministers.

2. FINANCIAL EFFECTS

- It was recognized that the formula, which permits provinces to opt out of amendments, will result in situations with potential important financial implications for all governments. Three alternatives for dealing with this problem are suggested for consideration by First Ministers:

  (*a*) add to the formula the principle that if a province dissents from an amendment, it should not be penalized financially compared with provinces that have approved the amendment, or

  (*b*) add to the formula the obligation that First Ministers or Finance Ministers review the financial implications of any proposed amendment, or

  (*c*) make no provision constitutionally; deal with these issue on a case-by-case basis; leave its solution to the political process.

B. DELEGATION OF LEGISLATIVE AUTHORITY

- All governments have agreed in principle that delegation of legislative authority should be provided for in the constitution.

  — Quebec, however, noted that it wishes to examine this proposal more carefully in relation to the amending formula proposal which has been developed.

- The major elements of such delegation are:

  — it would be on a one-to-one basis (from Parliament to any legislature, or vice versa);

  — its scope should include the power to enact specific laws, or the power to enact laws in relation to any matters or classes of subjects.

- A best-effort draft is submitted for approval in principle by First Ministers.

  — further technical refinements to this draft may be necessary;

  — two provinces have suggested that the draft be amended to oblige Parliament to delegate to any other province what it has agreed to delegate to one.

BEST EFFORTS DRAFT AMENDMENTS TO THE CONSTITUTION OF CANADA

1. (1) Amendments to the Constitution of Canada may from time to time be made by proclamation issued by the Governor General under the Great Seal of Canada when so authorized by resolutions of the Senate and House of Commons and the assent by resolution of the Legislative Assembly in two-thirds of the provinces representing at

least fifty percent of the population of Canada according to the latest general census.

(2) Any amendment made under sub-section (1) affecting:

(a) the powers of the legislature of a province to make laws,

(b) the rights or privileges granted or secured by the Constitution of Canada to the legislature or the government of a province,

(c) the assets or property of a province, or

(d) the natural resources of a province,

shall have no effect in any province whose Legislative Assembly has expressed its dissent thereto by resolution prior to the issue of the proclamation, until such time as that Assembly may withdraw its dissent and approve such amendment by resolution.

2. A proclamation shall not be issued under Section 1 before the expiry of one year from the adoption of the resolution initiating the amendment procedure thereunder, unless the legislative assembly in each province has previously adopted a resolution of assent or dissent.

3. Amendments to the Constitution of Canada in relation to any provision that applies to one or more, but not all, of the Provinces including any such amendment made to provincial boundaries may from time to time be made by proclamation issued by the Governor General under the Great Seal of Canada when so authorized by resolutions of the Senate and House of Commons and the assent by resolution of the Legislative Assembly of each Province to which an amendment applies.

4. An amendment may be made by proclamation under section 1, 3 or 9 without a resolution of the Senate authorizing the issue of the proclamation if within ninety days of the passage of a resolution by the House of Commons authorizing its issue the Senate has not passed such a resolution and at any time after the expiration of the ninety days the House of Commons again passes the resolution, but any period when Parliament is prorogued or dissolved shall not be counted in computing the ninety days.

5. The following rules apply to the procedures for amendment described in sections 1, 3 and 9

(1) either of these procedures may be initiated by the Senate or the House of Commons or the Legislative Assembly of a Province,

(2) a resolution of authorization or assent made for the purposes of this Part may be revoked at any time before the issue of a proclamation authorized or assented to by it,

(3) a resolution of dissent made for the purposes of this Part may be revoked at any time before or after the issue of a proclamation.

6. The Parliament of Canada may exclusively make laws from time to time amending the Constitution of Canada, in relation to the executive Government of Canada and the Senate and House of Commons.

7. In each Province the Legislature may exclusively make laws in relation to the amendment from time to time of the Constitution of the Province.

8. Notwithstanding sections 6 and 7, the following matters may be amended only in accordance with the procedure in section 1(1):

(1) the office of the Queen, of the Governor General and of the Lieutenant-Governor,

(2) the requirements of the Constitution of Canada respecting yearly sessions of the Parliament of Canada and the Legislatures,

(3) the maximum period fixed by the Constitution of Canada for the duration of the House of Commons and the Legislative Assemblies,

(4) the powers of the Senate,

(5) the number of members by which a Province is entitled to be represented in the Senate and the residence qualifications of Senators.

(6) the right of a Province to a number of members in the House of Commons not less than the number of Senators representing the Province,

(7) the principles of Proportionate representation of the Provinces in the House of Commons prescribed by the Constitution of Canada, and

(8) the use of the English or French language.

9. (1) No amendment to section 1 of this Part, this section, or to any provision in the Constitution with respect to the procedure for altering provincial boundaries shall come into force unless it is authorized in by resolutions of the Senate and House of Commons and assented to by resolution of the Legislative Assemblies of all the provinces.

(2) The procedure prescribed in section o of this Part may not be used to make an amendment when there is another provision for making such amendment in the Constitution of Canada but, subject to the limitations contained in subsection (1) of this section that procedure may nonetheless be used to amend any provision for amending the Constitution.

10. The enactments set out in the Schedule shall continue as law in Canada and as such shall, together with this Act, collectively be known as the Constitution of Canada, and amendments thereto shall henceforth be made only according to the authority contained therein.

BEST EFFORTS DRAFT
DELEGATION OF LEGISLATIVE AUTHORITY

Delegation to Parliament

(1) Notwithstanding anything in the Constitution of Canada, Parliament may make laws in relation to any matter or class of subjects coming within the legislative jurisdiction of a province.

Consent of provincial legislature

(2) No law may be enacted by Parliament under subsection (1) unless, prior to the enactment thereof, the legislature of at least one province has consented to the enactment of such a law by Parliament.

Idem

(3) No law enacted under subsection (1) has effect in any province unless the legislature of that province has consented to the operation of such a law in that province.

Delegation to legislature of a province

(4) Notwithstanding anything in the Constitution of Canada, the legislature of a province may make laws in the province in relation to any matter or class of subjects coming within the legislative jurisdiction of Parliament.

Consent of Parliament

(5) No law may be enacted by a province under subsection (4) unless, prior to the enactment thereof, Parliament has consented to the enactment of such a law by the legislature of that province.

Extent of consent

(6) A consent given under this section may be general or specific, may relate to any law or to the enactment of laws in relation to any matter of class of subjects and may include the authority to amend such laws or laws.

Enforcement

(7) Parliament or the legislature of a province may make laws for enforcing any law made by it under this section.

Revocation of consent

(8) A consent given under this section may at any time be revoked.

Effect of revocation of consent

(9) Where a consent given under subsection (3) is revoked any law made by Parliament to which the consent relates that is operative in the province in which the consent is revoked thereupon ceases to have effect in that province.

Idem

(10) Where a consent given under subsection (5) is revoked, any law made by the legislature of a province to which the consent relates thereupon ceases to have effect.

Repeal of law by Parliament

(11) Parliament may repeal any law made by it under this section, insofar as it is part of the law of one or more provinces, but the repeal does not affect the operation of that law in any province to which the repeal does not relate.

Repeal of law by provincial legislature

(12) The legislature of a province may repeal any law made by it under this section.

(n) Report of the Continuing Committee of Ministers on the Constitution to First Ministers: The Powers Over the Economy, *A*. The Economic Union (Section 121)

Document: 800-14/011

The Ministers reviewed various proposals and alternatives to further and maintain the objectives of an economic union.

ISSUES FOR THE FIRST MINISTERS' CONSIDERATION

(1) Do governments accept provisions in the Constitution to safeguard the economic union?

(2) Do governments think that the principles contained therein should be enforceable?

(3) If there is agreement that enforceability is necessary then how should such enforceability be reflected within the Constitution?

    (*a*) Should it be by recourse to the courts?

    (*b*) Should it be through reference to a political mechanism such as a new Upper House (Council of the Provinces) or a First Ministers' Conference?

    (*c*) Should it be by some combination of (a) and (b) above — courts and a political mechanism?

(4) To what extent should there be provision for derogations from the principles of the economic union?

COMMENTS

Discussion focussed on two distinct alternatives on how the economic union should be furthered and maintained.

The first alternative focussed on the position advanced by the federal government which wished to minimize economic discrimination within Canada based on provincial or territorial boundaries. In its draft the federal government did not propose an absolute prohibition, recognizing there were differentiated social and economic policies of governments. Three different approaches are attached reflecting different ways of enforcing the objectives of the economic union. For the purposes of discussion the approaches have been identified as

    (*a*) the "unduly impedes" test (Draft 1)

    (*b*) the "non-discrimination" test (Draft 2)

    (*c*) the "pith and substance" test (Draft 3)

The second alternative (Draft 4) discussed by the Ministers and accepted by a majority of provinces was a statement of economic principles in the Constitution which does not limit federal and provincial legislative authority. It is similar in approach to the equalization draft. In addition the second alternative contains a statement committing governments to the ongoing systematic and co-operative review by them of the operation of the Canadian economic union.

The Ministers discussed various alternatives for referring derogations to a political body. Depending upon the form and responsibilities of a new Upper House (Council of the Provinces), provincial derogations might be referred to it for consideration. Such a review could take place after the courts had examined a particular law or practice and found it to be in contravention to the principles found in section 121. Another proposal was suggested which would permit provinces to submit specific derogations to a revised Upper Chamber prior to their enactment. Another alternative would be to have First Ministers' Conferences discuss and possibly rule on provincial derogations.

DRAFT 1: ECONOMIC UNION [FEDERAL]

121. (1) Neither Canada nor a province shall by law or practice discriminate in a manner that unduly impedes the operation of the Canadian economic union on the basis of the province or territory of residence or former residence of a person, on the basis of the province or territory of origin or destination of goods, services or capital or on the basis of the province or territory into which or from which goods, services or capital are imported or exported.

    (2) Nothing in subsection (1) renders invalid a law of Parliament or of a legislature enacted in the interests of public safety, order, health or morals.

121. (1) This is based on the original draft presented by the Government of Canada. Concern was expressed by provinces over the "unduly impedes" test as creating uncertainty, thereby leaving too much discretion to the courts.

    Some provinces expressed concern over the inclusion of the word "practice".

    (2) Derogation

(3) Subsection (1) does not render invalid a law of Parliament enacted

    (*a*) in accordance with the principles of equalization and regional development recognized in section   ; or

    (*b*) in relation to a matter that is declared by Parliament in the enactment to be of an overriding national interest.

(4) Subsection (1) does not render invalid a law of a legislature

    (*a*) providing for reasonable residency requirements as a qualification for the receipt of publicly provided goods or services

    (*b*) enacted in relation to the reduction of economic disparities between regions wholly within a province that does not discriminate to a greater degree against persons resident or formerly resident outside the province or against goods, services or capital from outside the province than it does against persons resident or goods, services or capital from a region within the province.

(5) Nothing in subsection (2) or (3) renders valid a law of Parliament or a legislature that impedes the admission free into any province of goods, services or capital originating in or imported into any other province or territory.

(6) Nothing in this section confers any legislative authority on Parliament or a legislature.

(7) A law or practice of Parliament or a legislature that is found inconsistent with subsection (1) by final judgment of a court of competent jurisdiction shall stand and be deemed to be valid and operative, unless repealed or rescinded, for six months after the date of the judgment during which time the (New Second Chamber) shall consider the law and if the (New Second Chamber) ratifies the law or practice as being desirable public policy notwithstanding that it is inconsistent with subsection (1), the law shall continue to stand thereafter.

(3) Federal derogation

Saskatchewan suggests ratification by the upper house.

(4) Provincial derogation.

The Government of Canada agrees with the objectives of (*a*) but reserves its position on the drafting.

Whether (*b*) is necessary in light of subsections (1) and (2) is not certain.

Depending on the type of adjudication process, some provinces wished to see a broader area of derogations.

Saskatchewan proposed two further derogations relating to monopolies owned and operated by the province and the export from the province of government-owned capital.

Nova Scotia suggests a derogation which would recognize the special case of have-not provinces.

(7) This subsection provides for a mechanism whereby laws or practices considered by individuals and/or other governments to be discriminatory could be reviewed by a political body after a court had found them to be in contravention of subsection (1).

DRAFT 2: ECONOMIC UNION [FEDERAL]

121. (1) Canada is an economic union within which all persons may move without discrimination based on province or territory of residence or former residence and within which all goods, services and capital may move without discrimination based on province or territory of origin or entry into Canada or of destination within or of export from Canada.

(2) Neither Canada nor a province shall by law or practice contravene the principle expressed in subsection (1).

Remainder of this Draft as in Draft 1.

121. (1) This draft is based on a draft presented by the Government of Canada on August 26 and was designed to overcome provincial concerns. Most provinces feel that while this subsection diminishes the discretion of the court, it does not give sufficient latitude for reasonable derogations from the principles contained within the subsection.

(2) The concern expressed above may be overcome by reinserting the unduly impedes test in subsection (2).

DRAFT 3: ECONOMIC UNION (ONTARIO PROPOSAL)

121. (1) It is hereby declared that Canada is an economic union and
   (*a*) every citizen of Canada and every person lawfully admitted to Canada for permanent residence has the right,
      (i) to move to and reside in any province or territory,
      (ii) to pursue the gaining of a livelihood in any province or territory without discrimination based on residence or former residence,
      (iii) to acquire and hold property in any province or territory in Canada, and
   (*b*) all goods, services and capital may move freely and without discrimination within Canada based on the province or territory of origin or destination.

(2) Neither Parliament nor a legislature may enact a law that in its pith and substance is inconsistent with subsection (1).

(2) The "pith and substance" clause is thought by Ontario to provide a more accurate judicial test than "unduly impedes" or other such phrases and would effectively replace most of the specific derogations contained in the other drafts.

(3) Neither the Government of Canada nor of a province shall engage in any practice that is intended to operate in a manner that is inconsistent with subsection (1).

This Draft can be Extended by the Process Envisaged in Subsection (7) of Draft 1.

DRAFT 4: ECONOMIC UNION (SASKATCHEWAN PROPOSAL)

121. (1) Without altering the legislative or other authority of Parliament or the legislatures or of the Government of Canada or the governments of the Provinces or the rights of any of them with respect to the exercise of their respective legislative or other authority:

(*a*) Parliament and the legislatures, together with the Government of Canada and the governments of the Provinces, are committed to
  (i) the maintenance and enhancement of the Canadian economic union,

  (ii) the movement throughout Canada of persons, goods, services and capital without discrimination by Canada or any Province, by law or practice, in a manner that unjustifiably impedes the operation of the Canadian economic union, and
  (iii) the harmonization of federal and provincial laws, policies, and practices that affect the Canadian economic union; and

(*b*) pursuant to the commitments specified in clause (a), the Government of Canada and the governments of the Provinces are committed to the ongoing, systematic and co-operative review by them of the operation of the Canadian economic union.

(o) Report of the Continuing Committee of Ministers on the Constitution to First Ministers: The Powers Over the Economy, *B.* Trade and Commerce (Section 91(2))

Document: 800-14/012

The Ministers discussed amendments proposed by the federal government to Section 91(2).

ISSUES FOR THE FIRST MINISTERS' CONSIDERATION

(1) Should a new head of power over competition be added to section 91?

(2) Should a new head of power over product standards be added to section 91?

(3) If the answer is yes to questions 1 or 2, what is the best means of preserving provincial legislation not in conflict with federal legislation under this new head?

(4) Should the ambit of the federal trade and commerce power be clarified to ensure that services and capital are included?

COMMENTS

The new head "competition" was proposed by the federal government because of the difficulties it has experienced in incorporating and enforcing competition policy under criminal law power. There was no agreement as to the possible effects such a head would have on existing provincial legislative powers to regulate professions, insurance companies and the marketing of agricultural products, etc.

The federal government proposed a new head of power for product standards because of its concern that its legislative powers over uniform product standards have been significantly curtailed as a result of recent Supreme Court decisions.

The federal government argued that, while a substantial body of opinion believes existing section 91(2), trade and commerce, includes services and capital, it was desirable to incorporate these words in the Constitution to clarify its legislative powers, thereby eliminating any doubts.

The attached draft was developed

(1) to preserve section 91(2) in its present form to maintain existing jurisprudence; and

(2) to establish new concurrent powers with federal paramountcy over

   (*a*) competition; and

   (*b*) product standards.

SUGGESTED FEDERAL DRAFT

1. Add to section 91 the following heads of jurisdiction immediately following head 91.2:

   2.1 Competition

While some provinces recognized the usefulness of a civil head of power to regulate competition, most still express concern over the possible effect of this change on existing provincial jurisdiction.

   2.2 The establishment of products standards throughout Canada

While it was recognized that recent court decisions have placed federal jurisdiction in jeopardy, some provinces expressed concern that the proposed modification, in spite of subsection (3) below, might restrict provincial ability to establish standards for products circulating essentially within a province, or standards at a level different from national ones.

2. Add to section 91 the following new subsections:

   (2) For greater certainty, "regulation of trade and commerce" in subsection (1) includes the regulation of trade and commerce in goods, services and capital.

There is no agreement on this proposal. Provinces either take the view that it is not necessary, or that its effects on existing provincial jurisdiction must be more carefully assessed before they can form a view on the matter. To meet this concern, some suggested that the words "For greater certainty" be added at the beginning.

   (3) The authority conferred on Parliament by heads 91 (2.1) and 91 (2.2) does not render invalid a law enacted by a legislature that is not in conflict with a law of Parliament enacted under either of those heads.

(p) Report of the Continuing Committee of Ministers on the Constitution to First Ministers: The Preamble

Document: 800-14/013

On August 29, Ministers discussed the Report of the Committee of Officials on the Preamble (CICS Document 830-84/033).

They decided to present the attached draft of a preamble and statement of purpose of the Constitution for the consideration of First Ministers.

Manitoba suggested that the CCMC record its support for a preamble that is as brief and simple as possible.

It was also suggested that a draft of the preamble not be made public until First Ministers had had an opportunity to review the attached draft together privately.

If First Ministers agree to a preamble and statement of purpose, the CCMC recommends that there be an understanding that there will be further opportunity to receive suggestions for stylistic changes and that these should be communicated to the CCMC officials committee.

ISSUES FOR CONSIDERATION

The draft contains two sets of passages that have been placed in [parentheses], indicating that the CCMC did not reach a final decision on the particular form of words to recommend to the First Ministers Conference.

The principal issues which require decision by First Ministers are:

1. *With regard to lines 1–5*, which of the five alternative versions set out in the draft should be adopted for the preamble? If none, which of these should be modified for inclusion?
2. *With regard to lines 17 and 18*, which of the two alternative proposals should be adopted?
3. After the choices have been made in respect of 1 and 2, is the draft acceptable?

BEST EFFORTS DRAFT PREAMBLE AND STATEMENT OF PURPOSE OF THE CONSTITUTION

(*a*) *Federal Government*:

1   (In accordance with the will of the citizens of Canada,

the Government of Canada and the Governments of 2
the Provinces of Canada have expressed their intention 3
to remain freely united in a federation, as a sovereign 4
and independent country, under the Crown of Canada) 5

. . .

(*b*) *British Columbia*:

  (i) (The will of Canadians is that the Provinces of 1
      Canada choose to remain freely united in a fede- 2
      ration with a federal government, 3
      as a sovereign and independent country, 4
      under the Crown of Canada) . . . 5

  (ii) (It is the will of Canadians that Canada remain 1
       united as a federation, as a sovereign and inde- 2
       pendent country, under the Crown of Canada) . . . 3

(*c*) *Manitoba*:

(It is the will of Canadians to remain freely united in a 1
federation of provinces, as a sovereign and independent 2
country, under the Crown of Canada, with a federal 3
(central) government) . . . 4

(*d*) *Quebec*:

(In accordance with the will of Canadians, the Provinces 1
of Canada choose to remain freely united in a federation, 2
as a sovereign and independent country, under the 3
Crown of Canada (all of which meets with the approval 4
of the federal government)) . . . 5

with a Constitution similar in principle to that which has 6
been in effect in Canada. 7

THE FUNDAMENTAL PURPOSE of the Federation (Con- 8
stitution) is to preserve and promote freedom, justice and 9
well-being for all Canadians, by: 10

PROTECTING individual and collective rights, including 11
those of the native people;* 12
ENSURING that laws and political institutions are 13
founded on the will and consent of the people; 14
FOSTERING economic opportunity, and the security and 15
fulfillment of Canada's diverse cultures; 16
(RECOGNIZING the distinct French-speaking society 17
centred in though not confined to Quebec;) 18
(RECOGNIZING the distinctive character of Québec soci- 17
ety with its French-speaking majority;) 18
CONTRIBUTING to the freedom and well-being of all 19
mankind. 20

---

* This phrase is subject to acceptance by the native leadership.

43. *Proposed Resolution for Joint Address to Her Majesty the Queen Respecting the Constitution of Canada*, Tabled in the House of Commons and the Senate, October 6, 1980

Catalogue no. YC3-321/5-57

TABLE OF CONTENTS

INTRODUCTION

●●●

In the explanatory notes that follow, a number of abbreviations have been used to facilitate reading and to avoid repetition.

1. References to "the B.N.A. Act" are references to the *British North America Act, 1867*, as amended.

2. The *Constitution Act, 1980*, being Schedule B to the *Canada Act*, is referred to as Schedule B.

3. The *Canadian Charter of Rights and Freedoms*, which is set out as Part I of the *Constitution Act, 1980*, is referred to as the Charter.

4. Sections are indicated to be "new" if they do not now appear in the written Constitution (i.e. the B.N.A. Act, 1867, as amended, or any subsequent constitutional enactment).

(1) In some cases, a "new" provision is substantially already law as an unwritten constitutional or legal principle (e.g. some aspects of the rights and freedoms contained in the Charter).

(2) In other cases, "new" measure is derived from a non-constitutional statute, such as the *Canadian Bill of Rights*, referred to herein as the Bill of Rights.

If a "new" provision would replace another statutory provision, the explanatory note states the source from which it is derived.

5. Some sections are indicated as being present sections "modified". The term "modified" is used where a change from a present section is not so extensive as to warrant the description "new" but where a new idea is introduced into the present provision or where the modification is made for technical rather than substantive reasons.

EXPLANATORY NOTES

Resolution: The proposed Resolution describes the historical position of Canada which has made it necessary for certain amendments to the Canadian Constitution to be enacted by the United Kingdom Parliament, the present status of Canada as an independent state and the desire for change that has led the Senate and House of Commons to put forward the resolution.

The Address to the Queen: The Address is similar to previous Addresses to the Monarch and asks Her Majesty to lay the *Canada Act* before the Parliament of the United Kingdom for enactment.

CANADA ACT

Preamble: The preamble to the *Canada Act* recites the action taken in Canada that makes it appropriate for the United Kingdom Parliament to enact the proposed Act.

Proposed Resolution for a Joint Address to Her Majesty the Queen respecting the Constitution of Canada

WHEREAS in the past certain amendments to the Constitution of Canada have been made by the Parliament of the United Kingdom at the request and with the consent of Canada;

AND WHEREAS it is in accord with the status of Canada as an independent state that Canadians be able to amend their Constitution in Canada in all respects;

AND WHEREAS it is also desirable to provide in the Constitution of Canada for the recognition of certain fundamental rights and freedoms and to make other amendments to that Constitution.

NOW THEREFORE the Senate and the House of Commons, in Parliament assembled, resolve that a respectful address be presented to Her Majesty the Queen in the following words:

To the Queen's Most Excellent Majesty:
Most Gracious Sovereign:

We, Your Majesty's loyal subjects, the Senate and the House of Commons of Canada in Parliament assembled, respectfully approach Your Majesty, requesting that you may graciously be pleased to cause to be laid before the Parliament of the United Kingdom a measure containing the recitals and clauses hereinafter set forth:

An Act to amend the Constitution of Canada

Whereas Canada has requested and consented to the enactment of an Act of the Parliament of the United Kingdom to give effect to the provisions hereinafter set forth and the Senate and the

EXPLANATORY NOTES

House of Commons of Canada in Parliament assembled have submitted an address to Her Majesty requesting that Her Majesty may graciously be pleased to cause a Bill to be laid before the Parliament of the United Kingdom for that purpose.

Be it therefore enacted by the Queen's Most Excellent Majesty, by and with the advice and consent of the Lords Spiritual and Temporal, and Commons, in this present Parliament assembled, and by the authority of the same, as follows:

Enacting Clause: This is the form used in enacting United Kingdom laws.

1. Section 1 would enact the *Constitution Act, 1980* set out in Schedule B. The Act, except the general amending procedure, would come into force on proclamation by the Governor General. (See sections 29, 57 and 58 of Schedule B.)

2. Section 2 would re-enact, in modified form, section 4 of the *Statute of Westminster, 1931*. By reason of this section and the repeal, in so far as they relate to Canada, of section 4 and subsection 7(1) of that statute in item 16 of Schedule I to Schedule B, the United Kingdom Parliament would no longer be deemed to have authority to make laws for Canada.

3. This section would, for the first time in respect of a United Kingdom Act applicable to Canada, give equal authority to the English and French versions of the Act. The French version of the Act, so far as it is not contained in Schedule B, is set out in Schedule A because laws of the United Kingdom are only enacted in English.

4. The short title of the Act would be the *Canada Act.*

1. The *Constitution Act, 1980* set out in Schedule B to this Act is hereby enacted for and shall have the force of law in Canada and shall come into force as provided in that Act.   *Constitution Act, 1980* enacted

2. No Act of the Parliament of the United Kingdom passed after the *Constitution Act, 1980* comes into force shall extend to Canada as part of its law.   Parliament of United Kingdom not to legislate for Canada

3. So far as it is not contained in Schedule B, the French version of this Act is set out in Schedule A to this Act and has the same authority in Canada as the English version thereof.   French version

4. This Act may be cited as the *Canada Act.*   Short title

SCHEDULE B

CONSTITUTION ACT, 1980

CONSTITUTION ACT, 1980

PART I

PART I

CANADIAN CHARTER OF RIGHTS AND FREEDOMS

Sections 1-30. The Charter. At present, a number of rights and freedoms are provided for by law. At the federal level, they are found in such statutes as the *Canadian Bill of Rights,* the *Canadian Human Rights Act,* the *Official Languages Act* and the *Criminal Code.* At the provincial level, laws have been enacted relating to such matters as non-discrimination, political and legal rights and,

Guarantee of Rights and Freedoms

1. The *Canadian Charter of Rights and Freedoms* guarantees the rights and freedoms set out in it subject only to such reasonable limits as are   Rights and Freedoms in Canada

EXPLANATORY NOTES

in a few instances, language rights. However, with few and limited exceptions, the rights and freedoms are not constitutionally guaranteed. What protection has been legislated yesterday can be removed or limited by another enactment tomorrow. The entrenchment of the rights contained in this Charter would place those rights beyond the ordinary reach of Parliament or a single provincial legislature.

The Charter would assure basic protection with respect to several categories of rights and freedoms, some of which are drawn from existing federal and provincial laws and some of which are new. The Charter provides for the following categories of rights: fundamental freedoms, democratic rights, mobility rights, legal rights, nondiscrimination rights and language rights. The language rights relate to the use of English and French at the federal level in legislative proceedings, statutes and courts and in the provision by federal institutions of services to the public. In addition, certain rights to minority language educational instruction in each province and territory would be recognized.

1. New. Section 1 expresses a constitutional guarantee of the rights and freedoms set out in the Charter while at the same time acknowledging that such rights may be subject to reasonable limits traditionally recognized by the courts in a democratic society with a parliamentary system of government.

2. Section 2 declares the fundamental freedoms of all people in Canada. They are, with some modifications, essentially the freedoms now found in section 1 of the Bill of Rights. In section 2

(a) freedom of "religion" is expanded to include "conscience".

(b) freedom of "thought", etc., enlarges the prior freedom of "speech" to encompass not only the right to express one's views but also the right to hold those views. It includes freedom of the press and modernizes that concept by expressly including other media of information.

(c) freedom of "peaceful assembly", etc., adds the qualification 'peaceful" to the prior freedom.

Sections 3-5. These sections declare certain rights that are fundamental to the continued existence of a free and democratic parliamentary system.

generally accepted in a free and democratic society with a parliamentary system of government.

Fundamental Freedoms

2. Everyone has the following fundamental freedoms:

(a) freedom of conscience and religion;

(b) freedom of thought, belief, opinion and expresssion, including freedom of the press and other media of information; and

(c) freedom of peaceful assembly and of association.

Fundamental freedoms

Democratic Rights

3. Every citizen of Canada has, without unreasonable distinction or limitation, the right to vote in an election of members of the House of Commons or of a legislative assembly and to be qualified for membership therein.

Democratic rights of citizens

4. (1) No House of Commons and no legislative assembly shall continue for longer than five years from the date fixed for the return of the writs at a general election of its members.

Duration of elected legislative bodies

(2) In time of real or apprehended war, invasion or insurrection, a House of Commons may be continued by Parliament and a legislative assembly may be continued by the legislature beyond five years if such continuation is not opposed by the votes of more than one-third of the members of the House of Commons or the legislative assembly, as the case may be.

Continuation in special circumstances

EXPLANATORY NOTES

3. New. Section 3 would ensure the right of citizens to vote and become members of legislative bodies.

4. Section 4 would modify section 50 of the B.N.A. Act and similar provisions in provincial constitutions in respect of the duration of the House of Commons and the legislative assemblies and would combine the substance of those provisions with part of section 91, class 1 of the B.N.A. Act. It would guarantee federal and provincial elections at least once every five years (except in time of real or apprehended war, invasion or insurrection). (Section 91, class 1 would be repealed by section 51 of Schedule B.)

5. Section 5 would modify section 20 of the B.N.A. Act and similar provisions in provincial constitutions in respect of sittings of Parliament and the legislatures. It would require at least one sitting of those bodies every twelve months. (For repeals, see items 1(2) and 2(2) of Schedule I to Schedule B.)

6. Section 6 would recognize three rights. The first right is that of a citizen to enter, remain in and leave Canada. The other rights are those of a citizen or permanent resident, firstly, to move to and to take up residence in any province and, secondly, to seek a livelihood in any province, without discrimination based on provincial boundaries. These last two rights would be subject to the same general laws as are applicable to residents of that province (e.g. laws respecting the payment of taxes and terms and conditions of employment) and to laws specifying reasonable residence requirements for newcomers as a condition for receiving public social services.

Sections 7-14. These sections set out basic legal rights in Canada. Some of these rights are now recognized in the Bill of Rights and others would be recognized for the first time in this Act. Of the latter, some now find expression in the *International Covenant on Civil and Political Rights* (the U.N. Covenant) to which Canada became a party in 1976. All rights would have immediate application except for the non-discrimination rights which would begin to apply three years later. (See the explanatory note for section 29.)

7. This provision derives from section 1 of the Bill of Rights with some modification in wording.

5. There shall be a sitting of Parliament and of each legislature at least once every twelve months.

> Annual sitting of legislative bodies

Mobility Rights

6. (1) Every citizen of Canada has the right to enter, remain in and leave Canada.

> Rights of citizens to move

(2) Every citizen of Canada and every person who has the status of a permanent resident of Canada has the right

> Rights to move and gain livelihood

(*a*) to move to and take up residence in any province; and

(*b*) to pursue the gaining of a livelihood in any province.

(3) The rights specified in subsection (2) are subject to

> Limitation

(*a*) any laws or practices of general application in force in a province other than those that discriminate among persons primarily on the basis of province of present or previous residence; and

(*b*) any laws providing for reasonable residency requirements as a qualification for the receipt of publicly provided social services.

Legal Rights

7. Everyone has the right to life, liberty and security of the person and the right not to be deprived thereof except in accordance with the principles of fundamental justice.

> Life, liberty and security of person

8. Everyone has the right not to be subjected to search or seizure except on grounds, and in accordance with procedures, established by law.

> Search or seizure

9. Everyone has the right not to be detained or imprisoned except on grounds, and in accordance with procedures, established by law.

> Detention or imprisonment

10. Everyone has the right on arrest or detention

> Arrest or detention

(*a*) to be informed promptly of the reasons therefor;

EXPLANATORY NOTES

8. New. This provision derives in part from the U.N. Covenant.

9. This provision derives from paragraph 2(*a*) of the Bill of Rights.

10. The provisions on arrest and detention are in essence the same as those set out in paragraph 2(*c*) of the Bill of Rights.

11. Paragraphs 11(*c*) and (*d*) would assure rights of an accused in criminal and penal proceedings at present found in paragraphs 2(*e*) and (*f*) of the Bill of Rights. Paragraphs 11(*a*), (*b*), (*e*), (*f*) and (*g*) would assure new rights of an accused in such proceedings and are drawn from similar provisions now found in the U.N. Covenant.

12. This provision derives from paragraph 2(*b*) of the Bill of Rights.

13. The protection against self-crimination is an elaboration of the right now provided in paragraph 2(*d*) of the Bill of Rights.

14. This provision derives from paragraph 2(*g*) of the Bill of Rights.

15. The guarantee of the right to equality before the law and to the equal protection of the law without discrimination based on race, national or ethnic origin, colour, religion, age or sex derives essentially from section 1 of the Bill of Rights

---

(*b*) to retain and instruct counsel without delay; and

(*c*) to have the validity of the detention determined by way of *habeas corpus* and to be released if the detention is not lawful.

11. Anyone charged with an offence has the right

    Proceedings in criminal and penal matters

(*a*) to be informed promptly of the specific offence;

(*b*) to be tried within a reasonable time;

(*c*) to be presumed innocent until proven guilty according to law in a fair and public hearing by an independent and impartial tribunal;

(*d*) not to be denied reasonable bail except on grounds, and in accordance with procedures, established by law;

(*e*) not to be found guilty on account of any act or omission that at the time of the act or omission did not constitute an offence;

(*f*) not to be tried or punished more than once for an offence of which he or she has been finally convicted or acquitted; and

(*g*) to the benefit of the lesser punishment where the punishment for an offence of which he or she has been convicted has been varied between the time of commission and the time of sentencing.

12. Everyone has the right not to be subjected to any cruel and unusual treatment or punishment.

    Treatment or punishment

13. A witness has the right when compelled to testify not to have any incriminating evidence so given used to incriminate him or her in any other proceedings, except a prosecution for perjury or for the giving of contradictory evidence.

    Self-crimination

14. A party or witness in any proceedings who does not understand or speak the language in which the proceedings are conducted has the right to the assistance of an interpreter.

    Interpreter

Non-discrimination Rights

15. (1) Everyone has the right to equality before the law and to the equal protection of the law without discrimination because of race, national or ethnic origin, colour, religion, age or sex.

    Equality before the law and equal protection of the law

EXPLANATORY NOTES

except for ethnic origin and age which are new. Subsection (2) would ensure that "affirmative action" programs for disadvantaged groups will not be prohibited even though such programs may discriminate among persons. Section 15 would not have application until three years after the coming into force of this Act. (See the explanatory note for section 29.)

Sections 16-22. These sections would give constitutional equality of status to English and French and recognize language rights at the federal level.

16. (1) New. Subsection 16(1) declares English and French to be the official languages of Canada and would recognize their equality of status and use in all institutions of the Parliament and government of Canada. It derives from section 2 of the *Official Languages Act* of Canada.

(2) New. Subsection (2) anticipates legislation by Parliament and the legislatures to extend the status of English and French beyond that specified in the Charter.

17. The right to use English and French in debates of Parliament is provided for in section 133 of the B.N.A. Act. The Charter would extend the right to cover other proceedings (e.g. Parliamentary committees).

18. The requirement in section 18 to print and publish federal statutes, etc., in English and French derives from section 133 of the B.N.A. Act. The section would also ensure that both language versions are equally authoritative.

19. This section would confirm the right to use both English and French in all courts established by Parliament. It derives from section 133 of the B.N.A. Act.

20. Section 20 would assure to members of the public the right, in specified circumstances, to use either English or French in communications with, and in receiving services from, institutions of the Parliament and government of Canada. The section derives in part from sections 9 and 10 of the *Official Languages Act* of Canada.

(2) This section does not preclude any law, program or activity that has as its object the amelioration of conditions of disadvantaged persons or groups. | Affirmative action programs

Official Languages of Canada

16. (1) English and French are the official languages of Canada and have equality of status and equal rights and privileges as to their use in all institutions of the Parliament and government of Canada. | Official languages of Canada

(2) Nothing in this Charter limits the authority of Parliament or a legislature to extend the status or use of English and French or either of those languages. | Extension of status and use

17. Everyone has the right to use English or French in any debates and other proceedings of Parliament. | Proceedings of Parliament

18. The statutes, records and journals of Parliament shall be printed and published in English and French and both language versions are equally authoritative. | Parliamentary statutes and records

19. Either English or French may be used by any person in, or in any pleading in or process issuing from, any court established by Parliament. | Proceedings in courts established by Parliament

20. Any member of the public in Canada has the right to communicate with, and to receive available services from, any head or central office of an institution of the Parliament or government of Canada in English or French, as he or she may choose, and has the same right with respect to any other office of any such institution where that office is located within an area of Canada in which it is determined, in such manner as may be prescribed or authorized by Parliament, that a substantial number of persons within the population use that language. | Communications by public with federal institutions

EXPLANATORY NOTES

21. By section 21, existing language protection provided for by the present constitution (e.g. the protection set out in section 133 of the B.N.A. Act and section 23 of the *Manitoba Act, 1870*) would be continued.

22. New. This section would preserve existing rights and privileges relating to languages other than English and French.

23. New. Subsection (1) would establish a right for Canadian citizens whose first language learned and still understood is English or French to have their children educated in that language. Subsection (2) would enable citizens who move from one province to another to have their children educated in English or French if any of their children started their studies in that language. In both cases, the right would be subject to there being a sufficient number of students in a given area to warrant the provision in that area of minority language educational facilities.

24. New. Section 24 would make it clear that the Charter is not intended to affect any rights and freedoms not specified in it, including those of the native peoples.

Sections 25-30. These sections are all new and would provide guidance as to how the rights and freedoms guaranteed by the Charter would apply.

21. Nothing in sections 16 to 20 abrogates or derogates from any right, privilege or obligation with respect to the English and French languages, or either of them, that exists or is continued by virtue of any other provision of the Constitution of Canada.

Continuation of existing constitutional provisions

22. Nothing in sections 16 to 20 abrogates or derogates from any legal or customary right or privilege acquired or enjoyed either before or after the coming into force of this Charter with respect to any language that is not English or French.

Rights and privileges preserved

Minority Language Educational Rights

23. (1) Citizens of Canada whose first language learned and understood is that of the English or French linguistic minority population of the province in which they reside have the right to have their children receive their primary and secondary school instruction in that minority language if they reside in an area of the province in which the number of children of such citizens is sufficient to warrant the provision out of public funds of minority language educational facilities in that area.

Language of instruction

(2) Where a citizen of Canada changes residence from one province to another and, prior to the change, any child of that citizen has been receiving his or her primary or secondary school instruction in either English or French, that citizen has the right to have any or all of his or her children receive their primary and secondary school instruction in that same language if the number of children of citizens resident in the area of the province to which the citizen has moved, who have a right recognized by this section, is sufficient to warrant the provision out of public funds of minority language educational facilities in that area.

Continuity of language of instruction

Undeclared Rights and Freedoms

24. The guarantee in this Charter of certain rights and freedoms shall not be construed as denying the existence of any other rights or freedoms that exist in Canada, including any rights or freedoms that pertain to the native peoples of Canada.

Undeclared rights and freedoms

EXPLANATORY NOTES

25. Section 25 provides that any law that is inconsistent with the Charter is inoperative to the extent of the inconsistency. This would establish the supremacy of the Charter over all other laws.

26. Section 26 would make it clear that no provision of the Charter other than the section respecting self-crimination (section 13) would affect existing or future laws respecting the admissibility of evidence.

27. This section makes it clear that the Charter, where relevant, would apply in its entirety to the Yukon Territory and the Northwest Territories.

28. The Charter would not extend any legislative powers.

29. On coming into force, the Charter would be entrenched in the Constitution and, except for the non-discrimination rights contained in section 15, would have immediate application. Section 15 would not have application for three years in order to permit Parliament and the provincial legislatures to make consequential amendments to other legislation. The Charter could only be amended under sections 36 and 50.

30. New. This section would give the Charter the title *Canadian Charter of Rights and Freedoms*.

PART II

31. (1) New. Subsection (1) would affirm the commitment by Parliament and the provincial legislatures to promote equal opportunities, further economic development and provide essential public services.

General

25. Any law that is inconsistent with the provisions of this Charter is, to the extent of such inconsistency, inoperative and of no force or effect.

> Primacy of Charter

26. No provision of this Charter, other than section 13, affects the laws respecting the admissibility of evidence in any proceedings or the authority of Parliament or a legislature to make laws in relation thereto.

> Laws respecting evidence

27. A reference in this Charter to a province or to the legislative assembly or legislature of a province shall be deemed to include a reference to the Yukon Territory and the Northwest Territories, or to the appropriate legislative authority thereof, as the case may be.

> Application to territories and territorial authorities

28. Nothing in this Charter extends the legislative powers of any body or authority.

> Legislative powers not extended

Application of Charter

29. (1) This charter applies

(*a*) to the Parliament and government of Canada and to all matters within the authority of Parliament including all matters relating to the Yukon Territory and Northwest Territories; and

(*b*) to the legislature and government of each province and to all matters within the authority of the legislature of each province.

(2) Notwithstanding subsection (1), section 15 shall not have application until three years after this Act, except Part V, comes into force.

> Application of Charter

Citation

30. This Part may be cited as the *Canadian Charter of Rights and Freedoms*.

> Citation

PART II

EQUALIZATION AND REGIONAL DISPARITIES

31. (1) Without altering the legislative authority of Parliament or of the provincial legislatures, or the rights of any of them with respect to the exercise of their legislative authority, Parliament and the legislatures, together with the

> Commitment to promote equal opportunities

EXPLANATORY NOTES

(2) New. Subsection (2) would affirm the commitment of the Parliament and government of Canada to take measures to ensure the provision of essential public services at reasonable levels of provincial taxation.

PART III

32. This section would introduce a new obligation for federal-provincial discussions on the Constitution. A constitutional conference of first ministers would be convened annually until a general procedure for amending the Constitution of Canada comes into force under Part V.

PART IV

Sections 33-40. New. These sections would provide an interim procedure for amending the Constitution that would apply until such time as a general procedure comes into force. Part IV would also provide a mechanism whereby the Senate and House of Commons and the provincial legislative assemblies could choose to adopt the general amending procedure set out in Part V or some other amending procedure prior to the day on which the procedure set out in Part V would come into force automatically (i.e. two years after the rest of the Act comes into force). Finally it would provide that, in the event of a lack of agreement as to an appropriate general amending procedure, upon provincial request the people would, by means of a referendum, choose between

government of Canada and the provincial governments, are committed to

(a) promoting equal opportunities for the well-being of Canadians;

(b) furthering economic development to reduce disparity in opportunities; and

(c) providing essential public services of reasonable quality to all Canadians.

(2) Parliament and the government of Canada are committed to taking such measures as are appropriate to ensure that provinces are able to provide the essential public services referred to in paragraph (1)(c) without imposing an undue burden of povincial taxation.

Commitment respecting essential public services

PART III

CONSTITUTIONAL CONFERENCES

32. Until Part V comes into force, constitutional conference composed of the Prime Minister of Canada and the first ministers of the provinces shall be convened by the Prime Minister of Canada at least once in every year unless, in any year, a majority of those composing the conference decide that it shall not be held.

Constitutional conferences

PART IV

INTERIM AMENDING PROCEDURE AND RULES FOR ITS REPLACEMENT

33. Until Part V comes into force, an amendment to the Constitution of Canada may be made by proclamation issued by the Governor General under the Great Seal of Canada where so authorized by resolutions of the Senate and House of Commons and by the legislative assembly or government of each province.

Interim procedure for amending Constitution of Canada

34. Until Part V comes into force, an amendment to the Constitution of Canada in relation to any provision that applies to one or more, but not all, provinces may be made by proclamation issued by the Governor General under the Great Seal of Canada where so authorized by resolutions of the Senate and House of Commons and by the legislative assembly or government of each province to which the amendment applies.

Amendment of provisions relating to some but not all provinces

EXPLANATORY NOTES

a procedure proposed by the government of Canada and one proposed by the provinces.

33. This section sets out the general rule that, in the interim period, constitutional amendments would require the unanimous consent of both Houses of Parliament and the legislative assemblies or governments of all provinces.

34. This section provides a special rule whereby some amendments that would not apply to all provinces, such as the Terms of Union with certain provinces, could be made where authorized by both Houses of Parliament and the legislative assemblies of the provinces concerned.

35. The interim amending procedure could be initiated by the Senate, the House of Commons or a provincial legislative assembly or government. An authorization could be withdrawn before the amendment becomes law.

36. This section would provide a limitation on the use of the interim amending procedure. If there is another procedure for amending the Constitution, such as section 91, class 1 or section 92, class 1 of the B.N.A. Act, during the interim period it would apply rather than the unanimity rules set out in sections 33 and 34.

37. The interim amending procedure would be replaced by the general amending procedure, with or without amendments, two years after the rest of the Act comes into force or earlier if unanimous agreement is reached. If agreement is not reached and the provinces propose another procedure, the interim procedure would remain in effect until after a referendum is held under section 38.

38. Section 38 provides that if eight or more provinces having eighty per cent of the population of all provinces wish to propose an alternative general amending procedure they could do so within two years after the rest of the Act comes into force. A referendum would then have to be held within a further two year period to decide whether the procedure proposed by the provinces or the procedure set out in paragraph 41(1)(*b*) (or another procedure proposed by the government of Canada) should be adopted as the general procedure for amending the Constitution.

35. (1) The procedures for amendment described in sections 33 and 34 may be initiated either by the Senate or House of Commons or by the legislative assembly or government of a province.

(2) A resolution made or other authorization given for the purposes of this Part may be revoked at any time before the issue of a proclamation authorized by it.

36. Sections 33 and 34 do not apply to an amendment to the Constitution of Canada where there is another provision in the Constitution for making the amendment, but the procedure prescribed by section 33 shall be used to amend the *Canadian Charter of Rights and Freedoms* and any provision for amending the Constitution, including this section, and may be used in making a general consolidation and revision of the Constitution.

Rules applicable to amendment procedures

Idem

Limitation on use of interim amending procedure

37. Part V shall come into force.

(*a*) with or without amendment, on such day as may be fixed by proclamation issued pursuant to the procedure prescribed by section 33, or

(*b*) on the day that is two years after the day this Act, except Part V, comes into force,

whichever is the earlier day but, if a referendum is required to be held under subsection 38(3), Part V shall come into force as provided in section 39.

38. (1) The governments or legislative assemblies of eight or more provinces that have, according to the then latest general census, combined populations of at least eighty per cent of the population of all the provinces may make a single proposal to substitute for paragraph 41(1)(*b*) such alternative as they consider appropriate.

(2) One copy of an alternative proposed under subsection (1) may be deposited with the Chief Electoral Officer of Canada by each proposing province within two years after this Act, except Part V, comes into force but, prior to the expiration of that period, any province that has deposited a copy may withdraw that copy.

Coming into force of Part V

Provincial alternative procedure

Procedure for perfecting alternative

EXPLANATORY NOTES

(3) Where copies of an alternative have been filed as provided by subsection (2) and, on the day that is two years after this Act, except Part V, comes into force, at least eight copies remain filed by provinces that have, according to the then latest general census, combined populations of at least eighty per cent of the population of all the provinces, the government of Canada shall cause a referendum to be held within two years after that day to determine whether

(*a*) paragraph 41(1)(*b*) or any alternative thereto proposed by the government of Canada by depositing a copy thereof with the Chief Electoral Officer at least ninety days prior to the day on which the referendum is held, or

(*b*) the alternative proposed by the provinces, shall be adopted.

Referendum

39. Where a referendum is held, Part V, with any amendments necessary to reflect the choice of the voters, would come into force on proclamation issued within six months after the referendum.

39. Where a referendum is held under subsection 38(3), a proclamation under the Great Seal of Canada shall be issued within six months after the date of the referendum bringing Part V into force with such modifications, if any, as are necessary to incorporate the proposal approved by a majority of the persons voting at the referendum and with such other changes as are reasonably consequential on the incorporation of that proposal.

Coming into force of Part V where referendum held

40. Section 40 would authorize the making of rules for the holding of a referendum and would ensure the right of citizens to vote in a referendum.

40. (1) Subject to subsection (2), Parliament may make laws respecting the rules applicable to the holding of a referendum under subsection 38(3).

Rules for referendum

(2) Every citizen of Canada has, without unreasonable distinction or limitation, the right to vote in a referendum held under subsection 38(3).

Right to vote

PART V

PART V

PROCEDURE FOR AMENDING CONSTITUTION OF CANADA

*Sections 41-51.*New. These sections would provide a general procedure whereby the Constitution of Canada could be amended in Canada. Under the procedure, amendments would be made by proclamation issued by the Governor General after specified prior authorization has been obtained. Except where otherwise indicated, the procedure derives from the proposed *Canadian Constitutional Charter, 1971,* known as the Victoria Charter. As set out in Part IV, the general amending procedure would come into force after the

41.(1) An amendment to the Constitution of Canada may be made by proclamation issued by the Governor General under the Great Seal of Canada where so authorized by

(*a*) resolutions of the Senate and House of Commons; and

(*b*) resolutions of the legislative assemblies of at least a majority of the provinces that includes.

(i) every province that at any time before the issue of the proclamation had, according to any previous general census, a popu-

General procedure for amending Constitution of Canada

EXPLANATORY NOTES

other provisions of the *Canada Act*. This would leave time for further discussion and for possible agreed changes in the procedure to be made before it has effect. (For coming into force, see also section 58.)

41. The proposed general procedure for amending most constitutional provisions, other than those that relate only to Parliament, the federal executive government or provincial constitutions and those for which the Constitution provides another amending procedure, derives from the Victoria Charter and is set out in subsection 41(1). For an amendment to be made under the general procedure, it would be necessary to have the approval of the Senate and House of Commons and the legislative assemblies of at least six provinces representing all regions of Canada. (See subsection 41(2) for definitions.)

42. This provision, which is not found in earlier proposals, would permit an amendment to the Constitution to be made upon authorization by a national referendum initiated by the government of Canada. For an amendment to be authorized by a referendum, a double majority would be needed; a majority of all votes cast and a majority of the votes cast in six or more provinces representing all regions of Canada.

43. This section provides a special rule whereby amendments that would not apply to all provinces, such as Terms of Union with certain provinces, could be made upon authorization by the Senate and House of Commons and the provinces concerned.

44. Where the Senate does not approve a constitutional amendment approved by the House of Commons, the amendment could nevertheless be made if, after a delay period, the House of Commons approves the amendment a second time.

lation of at least twenty-five per cent of the population of Canada,

(ii) at least two of the Atlantic provinces that have, according to the then latest general census, combined populations of at least fifty per cent of the population of all the Atlantic provinces, and

(iii) at least two of the Western provinces that have, according to the then latest general census, combined populations of at least fifty per cent of the population of all the Western provinces.

(2) In this section,   *Definitions*

"Atlantic provinces" means the provinces of Nova Scotia, New Brunswick, Prince Edward Island and Newfoundland;   *"Atlantic provinces"*

"Western provinces" means the provinces of Manitoba, British Columbia, Saskatchewan and Alberta.   *"Western provinces"*

42. (1) An amendment to the Constitution of Canada may be made by proclamation issued by the Governor General under the Great Seal of Canada where so authorized by a referendum held throughout Canada under subsection (2) at which   *Amendment authorized by referendum*

(*a*) a majority of persons voting thereat, and

(*b*) a majority of persons voting thereat in each of the provinces, resolutions of the legislative assemblies of which would be sufficient, together with resolutions of the Senate and House of Commons, to authorize the issue of a proclamation under subsection 41(1).

have approved the making of the amendment.

(2) A referendum referred to in subsection (1) shall be held where directed by proclamation issued by the Governor General under the Great Seal of Canada authorized by resolutions of the Senate and House of Commons.   *Authorization of referendum*

43. An amendment to the Constitution of Canada in relation to any provision that applies to one or more, but not all, provinces may be made by proclamation issued by the Governor General under the Great Seal of Canada where so authorized by resolutions of the Senate and House of Commons and of the legislative assembly of each province to which the amendment applies.   *Amendment of provisions relating to some but not all provinces*

44. An amendment to the Constitution of Canada may be made by proclamation under subsection 41(1) or section 43 without a resolution of the Senate authorizing the issue of the proclamation if, within ninety days after the passage by   *Amendments without Senate resolutions*

EXPLANATORY NOTES

the House of Commons of a resolution authorizing its issue, the Senate has not passed such a resolution and if, at any time after the expiration of those ninety days, the House of Commons again passes the resolution, but any period when Parliament is prorogued or dissolved shall not be counted in computing those ninety days.

45. The procedures for amendment set out in sections 41 and 43 could be initiated at the national or provincial level. An authorization could be withdrawn prior to the making of the authorized amendment.

45. (1) The procedures for amendment described in subsection 41(1) and section 43 may be initiated either by the Senate or House of Commons or by the legislative assembly of a province.

Rules applicable to amendment procedures

(2) A resolution made for the purposes of this Part may be revoked at any time before the issue of a proclamation authorized by it.

Idem

46. This section would authorize the making of rules for the holding of a referendum and would ensure the right of citizens to vote in a referendum.

46. (1) Subject to subsection (2), Parliament may make laws respecting the rules applicable to the holding of a referendum under section 42.

Rules for referendum

(2) Every citizen of Canada has, without unreasonable distinction or limitation, the right to vote in a referendum held under section 42.

Right to vote

47. This section would make it clear that the general procedure for amendment does not apply where the Constitution contains another procedure for making an amendment such as the procedure set out in section 48 or 49. (But see also section 50.)

47. The procedures prescribed by section 41, 42 or 43 do not apply to an amendment to the Constitution of Canada where there is another provision in the Constitution for making the amendment, but the procedures prescribed by section 41 or 42 shall nevertheless be used to amend any provision for amending the Constitution, including this section, and section 41 may be used in making a general consolidation or revision of the Constitution.

Limitation on use of general amending formula

48. This section, together with section 50, would clarify and limit the existing power of Parliament pursuant to section 91, class 1 of the B.N.A. Act to amend the Constitution and that class would be repealed when Part V comes into force. (See also section 51.)

48. Subject to section 50, Parliament may exclusively make laws amending the Constitution of Canada in relation to the executive government of Canada or the Senate or House of Commons.

Amendments by Parliament

49. This section, together with paragraph 50 (a), would define the power of the provinces to amend their own constitutions. It would replace section 92, class 1 of the B.N.A. Act, which would be repealed when Part V comes into force. (See also section 51.)

49. Subject to section 50, the legislature of each province may exclusively make laws amending the constitution of the province.

Amendments by provincial legislatures

50. Section 50 would make it clear that certain provisions of particular importance in the Constitution, or that might appear to come within another amending procedure, could only be amended under the procedure set out in section 41 or 42 which involves either both Houses of Parliament and the provincial legislative assemblies or a national referendum. For example, just

50. An amendment to the Constitution of Canada in relation to the following matters may be made only in accordance with a procedure prescribed by section 41 or 42:

(a) the office of the Queen, the Governor General and the Lieutenant Governor of a province;

(b) the *Canadian Charter of Rights and Freedoms*;

Matters requiring amendment under general formula

EXPLANATORY NOTES

as at present, a province could not change the office of Lieutenant Governor under its power to amend the provincial constitution. Similarly, Parliament could not alter the role of the Governor General under its power to amend the Constitution in relation to the executive government of Canada. These changes could only be made under the general amending procedure.

(*c*) the commitments relating to equalization and regional disparities set out in section 31;

(*d*) the powers of the Senate;

(*e*) the number of members by which a province is entitled to be represented in the Senate and the residence qualifications of Senators;

(*f*) the right of a province to a number of members in the House of Commons not less than the number of Senators representing the province; and

(*g*) the principles of proportionate representation of the provinces in the House of Commons prescribed by the Constitution of Canada.

51. When Part V comes into force, two provisions of the B.N.A. Act that contain authority to amend the Constitution would be repealed together with the provisions of this Act respecting interim amendments and annual constitutional conferences.

51. Class 1 of section 91 and class 1 of section 92 of the *Constitution Act, 1867* (formerly named the *British North America Act, 1867*), the *British North America (No. 2) Act, 1949*, referred to in item 21 of Schedule I to this Act and Parts III and IV of this Act are repealed.

Consequential amendments

PART VI

PART VI

GENERAL

52. (1) New. This subsection would specify for the first time that certain constitutional Acts and Orders are to be included in the expression "Constitution of Canada". These documents are listed in Schedule I to Schedule B. The subsection does not exclude other Acts and Orders from also being a part of the Constitution.

(2) New. Subsection 52(2) expresses the general rule that amendments to the Constitution may henceforth only be made by the Canadian procedure provided in the Constitution.

53. New. This section would repeal or amend various Acts and Orders forming the Constitution of Canada consequential on the adoption of the *Canada Act,* would rename the British North America Acts to be Constitution Acts and modernize certain other titles of constitutional documents. It would also continue those Acts and Orders as law in Canada, whether or not they are repealed as law in the United Kingdom, and amend other enactments by reference to reflect the new titles.

52. (1) The Constitution of Canada includes

(*a*) the *Canada Act;*

(*b*) the Acts and orders referred to in Schedule I; and

(*c*) any amendment to any Act or order referred to in paragraph (*a*) or (*b*).

Constitution of Canada

(2) Amendments to the Constitution of Canada shall be made only in accordance with the authority contained in the Constitution of Canada.

Amendments to Constitution of Canada

53. (1) The enactments referred to in Column I of Schedule I are hereby repealed, or amended to the extent indicated in Column II thereof, and, unless repealed, shall continue as law in Canada under the names set out in Column III thereof.

Repeals and new names

(2) Every enactment, except the *Canada Act,* that refers to an enactment referred to in Schedule I by the name in Column I thereof is hereby amended by substituting for that name the corresponding name in Column III thereof, and any British North America Act not referred to in Schedule I may be cited as the *Constitution Act* followed by the year and number, if any, of its enactment.

Consequential amendments

EXPLANATORY NOTES

54. New. Many of the documents composing the Constitution of Canada were enacted by the United Kingdom Parliament, which enacted them only in English. While unofficial French versions appear in the Statutes of Canada, they do not have legal status. This section would provide for the enactment of official French versions of those documents.

55-56. Where any part of the Constitution of Canada is enacted in English and French, both language versions would be equally authoritative, as would both language versions of Schedule B.

57-58. Schedule B would come into force on proclamation except for Part V which would come into force as set out in sections 33 to 40.

59. This section would provide a short title for Schedule B.

54. A French version of the portions of the Constitution of Canada referred to in Schedule I shall be prepared by the Minister of Justice of Canada as expeditiously as possible and, when any portion thereof sufficient to warrant action being taken has been so prepared, it shall be put forward for enactment by proclamation issued by the Governor General under the Great Seal of Canada pursuant to the procedure then applicable to an amendment of the same provisions of the Constitution of Canada.

French version of Constitution of Canada

55. Where any portion of the Constitution of Canada has been or is enacted in English and French or where a French version of any portion of the Constitution is enacted pursuant to section 54, the English and French versions of that portion of the Constitution are equally authoritative.

English and French versions

56. The English and French versions of this Act are equally authoritative.

English and French versions

57. Subject to section 58, this Act shall come into force on a day to be fixed by proclamation issued by the Governor General under the Great Seal of Canada.

Commencement

58. Part V shall come into force as provided in Part IV.

Exception respecting amending formula

59. This Schedule may be cited as the *Constitution Act, 1980* and the Constitution Acts, 1867 to 1975 (No. 2) and this Act may be cited together as the *Constitution Acts, 1867 to 1980*.

Citations

SCHEDULE I TO THE CONSTITUTION ACT, 1980
MODERNIZATION OF THE CONSTITUTION

Item	Column I Act Affected	Column II Amendment	Column III New Name
1.	British North America Act, 1867, 30-31 Vict., c. 3 (U.K.)	(1) Section 1 is repealed and the following substituted therefor: "1. This Act may be cited as the *Constitution Act, 1867*." (2) Section 20 is repealed.	Constitution Act, 1867
2.	An Act to amend and continue the Act 32-33 Victoria chapter 3; and to establish and provide	(1) The long title is repealed and the following substituted therefor: "*Manitoba Act, 1970*".	Manitoba Act, 1870

Item	Column I Act Affected	Column II Amendment	Column III New Name
	for the Government of the Province of Manitoba, 1870, 33 Vict., c. 3 (Can.)	(2) Section 20 is repealed.	
3.	Order of Her Majesty in Council admitting British Columbia into the Union, dated the 16th day of May, 1871.		British Columbia Terms of Union
4.	British North America Act, 1871, 34-35 Vict., c. 28 (U.K.)	Section 1 is repealed and the following substituted therefor: "1. This Act may be cited as the *Constitution Act, 1871*."	Constitution Act, 1871
5.	Order of Her Majesty in Council admitting Prince Edward Island into the Union, dated the 26th day of June, 1873.		Prince Edward Island Terms of Union
6.	Parliament of Canada Act, 1875, 38-39 Vict., c. 38 (U.K.)		Parliament of Canada Act, 1875
7.	Order of Her Majesty in Council admitting all British possessions and Territories in North America and islands adjacent thereto into the Union, dated the 31st day of July, 1880.		Adjacent Territories Order
8.	British North America Act, 1886, 49-50 Vict., c. 35 (U.K.)	Section 3 is replaced and the following substituted therefor: "3. This Act may be cited as the *Constitution Act, 1886*."	Constitution Act, 1886
9.	Canada (Ontario Boundary) Act, 1889, 52–53 Vict., c. 28 (U.K.)		Canada (Ontario Boundary) Act, 1889
10.	Canadian Speaker (Appointment of Deputy) Act, 1895, 2nd Sess., 59 Vict., c. 3 (U.K.)	The Act is repealed.	
11.	The Alberta Act, 1905, 4–5 Edw. VII, c. 3 (Can.)		Alberta Act
12.	The Saskatchewan Act, 1905, 4–5 Edw. VII, c. 42 (Can.)		Saskatchewan Act

Item	Column I Act Affected	Column II Amendment	Column III New Name
13.	British North America Act, 1907, 7 Edw. VII, c. 11 (U.K.)	Section 2 is repealed and the following substituted therefor: "2. This Act may be cited as the *Constitution Act, 1907.*"	Constitution Act, 1907
14.	British North America Act, 1915, 5–6 Geo. V, c. 45 (U.K.)	Section 3 is repealed and the following substituted therefor: "3. This Act may be cited as the *Constitution Act, 1915.*"	Constitution Act, 1915
15.	British North America Act, 1930, 20-21 Geo. V, c. 26 (U.K.)	Section 3 is repealed and the following substituted therefor: "3. This Act may be cited as the *Constitution Act, 1930.*"	Constitution Act, 1930
16.	Statute of Westminster, 1931, 22 Geo. V, c. 4 (U.K.)	In so far as they apply to Canada, (*a*) The expression "and Newfoundland" in section 1 and subsection 10(3) is repealed; (*b*) section 4 is repealed; and (*c*) subsection 7(1) is repealed.	Statute of Westminster, 1931
17.	British North America Act, 1940, 3–4 Geo. VI, c. 36 (U.K.)	Section 2 is repealed and the following substituted therefor: "2. This Act may be cited as the *Constitution Act, 1940.*"	Constitution Act, 1940
18.	British North America Act, 1943, 6–7 Geo. VI, c. 30 (U.K.)	The Act is repealed.	
19.	British North America Act, 1946, 9–10 Geo. VI, c. 63 (U.K.)	The Act is repealed.	
20.	British North America Act, 1949, 12–13 Geo. VI, c. 22 (U.K.)	Section 3 is repealed and the following substituted therefor: "3. This Act may be cited as the *Newfoundland Act.*"	Newfoundland Act
21.	British North America (No. 2) Act, 1949, 13 Geo. VI, c. 81 (U.K.)	The Act is repealed. (effective when section 51 of the *Constitution Act, 1980* comes into force)	
22.	British North America Act, 1951, 14–15 Geo. VI, c. 32 (U.K.)	The Act is repealed.	

Item	Column I Act Affected	Column II Amendment	Column III New Name
23.	British North America Act, 1952, 1 Eliz. II, c. 15 (Can.)	The Act is repealed.	
24.	British North America Act, 1960, 9 Eliz. II, c. 2 (U.K.)	Section 2 is repealed and the following substituted therefor: "2. This Act may be cited as the *Constitution Act, 1960*."	Constitution Act, 1960
25.	British North America Act, 1964, 12–13 Eliz. II, c. 73 (U.K.)	Section 2 is repealed and the following substituted therefor: "2. This Act may be cited as the *Constitution Act, 1964*."	Constitution Act, 1964
26.	British North America Act, 1965, 14 Eliz. II, c. 4, Part I (Can.)	Section 2 is repealed and the following substituted therefor: "2. This Part may be cited as the *Constitution Act, 1965*."	Constitution Act, 1965
27.	British North America Act, 1974, 23 Eliz. II, c. 13, Part I (Can.)	Section 3, as amended by 25–26 Eliz. II, c. 28, s. 38(1) (Can.) is repealed and the following substituted therefor: "3. This Part may be cited as the *Constitution Act, 1974*."	Constitution Act, 1974
28.	British North America Act, 1975, 23–24 Eliz. II, c. 28, Part 1 (Can.)	Section 3, as amended by 25–26 Eliz. II, c. 28, s. 31 (Can.) is repealed and the following substituted therefor: "3. This Part may be cited as the *Constitution Act (No. 1), 1975*."	Constitution Act (No. 1), 1975
29.	British North America Act, (No. 2), 1975, 23–24 Eliz. II, c. 53 (Can.)	Section 3 is repealed and the following substituted therefor: "3. This Act may be cited as the *Constitution Act (No. 2), 1975*."	Constitution Act (No. 2), 1975

44. The Special Joint Committee of the Senate and of the House of Commons on the Constitution of Canada, 1980–81

(a) Orders of Reference of the House of Commons, October 23, October 28, November 13, December 2, 1980, and February 4, 1981, from *Minutes of Proceedings and Evidence*, Issue 57, p. 42, February 13, 1981

Thursday, October 23, 1980

RESOLVED, — That a Special Joint Committee of the Senate and of the House of Commons be appointed to consider and report upon the document entitled "Proposed Resolution for a Joint Address to Her Majesty the Queen respecting the Constitution of Canada" published by the Government on October 2, 1980, and to recommend in their report whether or not such an Address, with such amendments as the Committee considers necessary, should be presented by both Houses of Parliament to Her Majesty the Queen;

That 15 Members of the House of Commons to be designated no later than three sitting days after the adoption of this motion be members on the part of this House of the Special Joint Committee;

That the Committee have power to appoint from among its Members such sub-committees as may be deemed advisable and necessary and to delegate to such sub-committees all or any of their powers except the power to report directly to the House;

That the Committee have power to sit during sittings and adjournments of the House of Commons;

That the Committee have power to send for persons, papers and records, and to examine witnesses and to print such papers and evidence from day to day as may be ordered by the Committee;

That the Committee submit their report not later than December 9, 1980;

That the quorum of the Committee be 12 members, whenever a vote, resolution or other decision is taken, so long as both Houses are represented and that the Joint Chairmen be authorized to hold meetings, to receive evidence and authorize the printing thereof, when 6 members are present so long as both Houses are represented; and

That a Message be sent to the Senate requesting that House to unite with this House for the above purpose, and to select, if the Senate deems it to be advisable, Members to act on the proposed Special Joint Committee.

Tuesday, October 28, 1980

ORDERED, — That the members designated to serve on the part of this House on the Special Joint Committee to consider a proposed address to Her Majesty the Queen concerning the Constitution of Canada be: Mr. Beatty, Mr. Bockstael, Miss Campbell, Mr. Corbin, Mr. Crombie, Mr. Epp, Mr. Fraser, Mr. Henderson, Mr. Irwin, Mr. Joyal, Mr. Knowles, Mr. Lapierre, Mr. Mackasey, Mr. McGrath and Mr. Nystrom; and that a message be sent to the Senate to acquaint their honours thereof.

Thursday, November 13, 1980

ORDERED, — That, further to the resolution of this House of January 25, 1977, as subsequently implemented, this House approves the television and radio broadcasting of the proceedings of the Special Joint Committee on the Constitution on the basis of the same principles and practice, *mutatis mutandis,* governing the broadcasting of the proceedings of the House of Commons, including the concept of "electronic Hansard", provided that any subcommittee of the said Committee, shall not be broadcast by television, but shall be broadcast by radio, except the subcommittee on Agenda, which shall not be broadcast;

That it be an instruction to the Committee that it undertake the aforementioned action as soon as physically possible without disturbing the proceedings of the Committee now undertaken or planned;

That it be an instruction to the Committee that all decisions concerning the implementation of this Order shall be taken only by the Committee's subcommittee on Agenda; and

ORDERED, — That a Message be sent to the Senate asking Their Honours to unite with this House in the aforementioned actions.

Tuesday, December 2, 1980

ORDERED, — That the Order of Reference creating the Special Joint Committee on the Constitution of Canada be amended by deleting the words "December 9, 1980" and substituting therefor the words "February 6, 1981"; and

That a Message be sent to the Senate to acquaint Their Honours thereof and to invite them to join with this House in the aforementioned action.

Wednesday, February 4, 1981

ORDERED, — That, notwithstanding any previous Order, the Special Joint Committee on the Constitution of Canada shall complete its work and make its final report not later than February 13, 1981; and

That a Message be sent to the Senate to acquaint Their Honours thereof.

ATTEST

C.B. Koester
The Clerk of the House of Commons

(b) Orders of Reference of the Senate, November 3, November 5, November 13, December 2, 1980, and February 5, 1981, from *Minutes of Proceedings and Evidence*, Issue 57, p. 40, February 13, 1981

Extract from the Minutes of the Proceedings of the Senate, November 3, 1980:

"The Senate resumed the debate on the motion of the Honourable Senator Perrault, P.C., seconded by the Honourable Senator Frith:

That the Senate do unite with the House of Commons in the appointment of a Special Joint Committee to consider the report upon the document entitled "Proposed Resolution for a Joint Address to Her Majesty the Queen respecting the Constitution of Canada" published by the Government on October 2, 1980, and to recommend in their report whether or not such an Address, with such amendments as the Committee considers necessary, should be presented by both Houses of Parliament to Her Majesty the Queen;

That ten Members of the Senate, to be designated at a later date, act on behalf of the Senate as members of the Special Joint Committee;

That the Committee have power to appoint from among its members such sub-committees as may be deemed advisable and necessary and to delegate to such sub-committees all or any of their powers except the power to report directly to the Senate;

That the Committee have power to sit during sittings adjournments of the Senate;

That the Committee have power to send for persons, papers and records, and to examine witnesses and to print such papers and evidence from day to day as may be ordered by the Committee;

That the Committee submit their report not later than December 9, 1980;

That the quorum of the Committee be twelve members, whenever a vote, resolution or other decision is taken, so long as both Houses are represented and that the Joint Chairmen be authorized to hold meetings, to receive evidence and authorize the printing thereof, when six members are present so long as both Houses are represented; and

That a Message be sent to the House of Commons to inform that House accordingly.

. . .

So it was resolved in the affirmative.''

Extract from the Minutes of the Proceedings of the Senate, November 5, 1980:

''In amendment,
The Honourable Senator Frith moved, seconded by the Honourable Senator Petten:

. . .

''That the following Senators be appointed to act on behalf of the Senate on the said Special Joint Committee, namely, the Honourable Senators Asselin, Austin, Connolly, Goldenberg, Hays, Lamontagne, Lucier, Petten, Roblin and Tremblay; and''.

. . .

The Question then being put on the motion as amended of the Honourable Senator Frith, seconded by the Honourable Senator Perrault, P.C., it was —
resolved in the affirmative.''

Extract from the Minutes of the Proceedings of the Senate, November 13, 1980;

''With leave of the Senate,
The Honourable Senator Frith moved, seconded by the Honourable Senator McIlraith, P.C.:

That the Senate do unite with the House of Commons in approving the television and radio broadcasting of the proceedings of the Special Joint Committee on the Constitution of Canada on the basis of the same principles and practice, *mutatis mutandis*, governing the broadcasting of the proceedings of the House of Commons, including the concept of ''electronic Hansard'', provided that any subcommittee of the said Committee, shall not be broadcast by television, but shall be broadcast by radio, except the Subcommittee on Agenda, which shall not be broadcast;

That it be an instruction to the Committee that it undertake the aforementioned action as soon as physi-

cally possible without disturbing the proceedings of the Committee now undertaken or planned;

That it be an instruction to the Committee that all decisions concerning the implementation of this Order shall be taken only by the Committee's Subcommittee on Agenda; and

That a Message be sent to the House of Commons to inform that House accordingly.

The question being put on the motion, it was —
resolved in the affirmative.''

Extract from the Minutes of the Proceedings of the Senate, December 2, 1980:

''With leave of the Senate,
The Honourable Senator Frith moved, seconded by the Honourable Senator Roblin, P.C.:

That the Senate joined with the House of Commons in amending the Order of Reference creating the Special Joint Committee on the Constitution of Canada by deleting the words ''December 9, 1980'' and substituting therefor the words ''February 6, 1981''; and

That a Message be sent to the House of Commons to acquaint that House accordingly.

After debate, and
The question being put on the motion, it was —
resolved in the affirmative.''

Extract from the Minutes of the Proceedings of the Senate, February 5, 1981:

''With leave of the Senate,
The Honourable Senator Perrault, P.C. moved, seconded by the Honourable Senator Frith:

That, notwithstanding any previous Order, the Special Joint Committee on the Constitution of Canada shall complete its work and make its final report no later than February 13, 1981; and

That a Message be sent to the House of Commons to acquaint that House accordingly.

After debate, and
The question being put on the motion, it was —
resolved in the affirmative.''

Robert Fortier
The Clerk of the Senate

(c) Consolidation of Proposed Resolution and Possible Amendments as Placed Before the Special Joint Committee by the Minister of Justice, January 12, 1981

PROPOSED RESOLUTION AS TABLED OCTOBER 6, 1980

Proposed Resolution for a Joint Address to Her Majesty the Queen respecting the Constitution of Canada

WHEREAS in the past certain amendments to the Constitution of Canada have been made by the Parliament of the United Kingdom at the request and with the consent of Canada;

AND WHEREAS it is in accord with the status of Canada as an independent state that Canadians be able to amend their Constitution in Canada in all respects;

AND WHEREAS it is also desirable to provide in the Constitution of Canada for the recognition of certain fundamental rights and freedoms and to make other amendments to that Constitution.

NOW THEREFORE the Senate and the House of Commons, in Parliament assembled, resolve that a respectful address be presented to Her Majesty the Queen in the following words:

To the Queen's Most Excellent Majesty:
Most Gracious Sovereign;

We, Your Majesty's loyal subjects, the Senate and the House of Commons of Canada in Parliament assembled, respectfully approach Your Majesty, requesting that you may graciously be pleased to cause to be laid before the Parliament of the United Kingdom a measure containing the recitals and clauses hereinafter set forth:

An Act to amend the Constitution of Canada

Whereas Canada has requested and consented to the enactment of an Act of the Parliament of

RESOLUTION WITH POSSIBLE AMENDMENTS

Proposed Resolution for a Joint Address to Her Majesty the Queen respecting the Constitution of Canada

WHEREAS in the past certain amendments to the Constitution of Canada have been made by the Parliament of the United Kingdom at the request and with the consent of Canada;

AND WHEREAS it is in accord with the status of Canada as an independent state that Canadians be able to amend their Constitution in Canada in all respects;

AND WHEREAS it is also desirable to provide in the Constitution of Canada for the recognition of certain fundamental rights and freedoms and to make other amendments to that Constitution.

NOW THEREFORE the Senate and the House of Commons, in Parliament assembled, resolve that a respectful address be presented to Her Majesty the Queen in the following words:

To the Queen's Most Excellent Majesty:
Most Gracious Sovereign:

We, Your Majesty's loyal subjects, the Senate and the House of Commons of Canada in Parliament assembled, respectfully approach Your Majesty, requesting that you may graciously be pleased to cause to be laid before the Parliament of the United Kingdom a measure containing the recitals and clauses hereinafter set forth:

An Act to give effect to a request by the Senate and House of Commons of Canada

Whereas Canada has requested and consented to the enactment of an Act of the Parliament of

PROPOSED RESOLUTION

the United Kingdom to give effect to the provisions hereinafter set forth and the Senate and the House of Commons of Canada in Parliament assembled have submitted an address to Her Majesty requesting that Her Majesty may graciously be pleased to cause a Bill to be laid before the Parliament of the United Kingdom for that purpose.

Be it therefore enacted by the Queen's Most Excellent Majesty, by and with the advice and consent of the Lords Spiritual and Temporal, and Commons, in this present Parliament assembled, and by the authority of the same, as follows:

Constitution Act, 1980 enacted

1. The *Constitution Act, 1980* set out in Schedule B to this Act is hereby enacted for and shall have the force of law in Canada and shall come into force as provided in that Act.

Parliament of United Kingdom not to legislate for Canada

2. No Act of the Parliament of the United Kingdom passed after the *Constitution Act, 1980* comes into force shall extend to Canada as part of its law.

French version

3. So far as it is not contained in Schedule B, the French version of this Act is set out in Schedule A to this Act and has the same authority in Canada as the English version thereof.

Short title

4. This Act may be cited as the *Canada Act*.

SCHEDULE B

CONSTITUTION ACT, 1980

PART I

CANADIAN CHARTER OF RIGHTS AND FREEDOMS

Guarantee of Rights and Freedoms

Rights and Freedoms in Canada

1. The *Canadian Charter of Rights and Freedoms* guarantees the rights and freedoms set out in it subject only to such reasonable limits as are generally accepted in a free and democratic society with a parliamentary system of government.

Fundamental Freedoms

Fundamental freedoms

2. Everyone has the following fundamental freedoms:
(*a*) freedom of conscience and religion;
(*b*) freedom of thought, belief, opinion and expression, including freedom of the press and other media of information; and

POSSIBLE AMENDMENTS

the United Kingdom to give effect to the provisions hereinafter set forth and the Senate and the House of Commons of Canada in Parliament assembled have submitted an address to Her Majesty requesting that Her Majesty may graciously be pleased to cause a Bill to be laid before the Parliament of the United Kingdom for that purpose.

Be it therefore enacted by the Queen's Most Excellent Majesty, by and with the advice and consent of the Lords Spiritual and Temporal, and Commons, in this present Parliament assembled, and by the authority of the same, as follows:

Constitution Act, 1981 enacted

1. The *Constitution Act, 1981* set out in Schedule B to this Act is hereby enacted for and shall have the force of law in Canada and shall come into force as provided in that Act.

Parliament of United Kingdom not to legislate for Canada French version

2. No Act of the Parliament of the United Kingdom passed after the *Constitution Act, 1981* comes into force shall extend to Canada as part of its law.

3. So far as it is not contained in Schedule B, the French version of this Act is set out in Schedule A to this Act and has the same authority in Canada as the English version thereof.

Short title

4. This Act may be cited as the *Canada Act*.

SCHEDULE B

CONSTITUTION ACT, 1981

PART I

CANADIAN CHARTER OF RIGHTS AND FREEDOMS

Guarantee of Rights and Freedoms

Rights and freedoms in Canada

1. The *Canadian Charter of Rights and Freedoms* guarantees the rights and freedoms set out in it subject only to such reasonable limits prescribed by law as can be demonstrably justified in a free and democratic society.

Fundamental Freedoms

Fundamental freedoms

2. Everyone has the following fundamental freedoms:
(*a*) freedom of conscience and religion;
(*b*) freedom of thought, belief, opinion and expression, including freedom of the press and other media of information;

PROPOSED RESOLUTION	POSSIBLE AMENDMENTS
(*c*) freedom of peaceful assembly and of association.	(*c*) freedom of peaceful assembly; and (*d*) <u>freedom</u> of association.

PROPOSED RESOLUTION

(*c*) freedom of peaceful assembly and of association.

Democratic Rights

Democratic rights of citizens

3. Every citizen of Canada has, without unreasonable distinction or limitation, the right to vote in an election of members of the House of Commons or of a legislative assembly and to be qualified for membership therein.

Duration of elected legislative bodies

4. (1) No House of Commons and no legislative assembly shall continue for longer than five years from the date fixed for the return of the writs at a general election of its members.

Continuation in special circumstances

(2) In time of real or apprehended war, invasion or insurrection, a House of Commons may be continued by Parliament and a legislative assembly may be continued by the legislature beyond five years if such continuation is not opposed by the votes of more than one-third of the members of the House of Commons or the legislative assembly, as the case may be.

Annual sitting of legislative bodies

5. There shall be a sitting of Parliament and of each legislature at least once every twelve months.

Mobility Rights

Rights of citizens to move

6. (1) Every citizen of Canada has the right to enter, remain in and leave Canada.

Rights to move and gain livelihood

(2) Every citizen of Canada and every person who has the status of a permanent resident of Canada has the right

(*a*) to move to and take up residence in any province; and

(*b*) to pursue the gaining of a livelihood in any province.

Limitation

(3) The rights specified in subsection (2) are subject to

(*a*) any laws or practices of general application in force in a province other than those that discriminate among persons primarily on the basis of province of present or previous residence; and

(*b*) any laws providing for reasonable residency requirements as a qualification for the receipt of publicly provided social services.

Legal Rights

Life, liberty and security of person

7. Everyone has the right to life, liberty and security of the person and the right not to be deprived thereof except in accordance with the principles of fundamental justice.

POSSIBLE AMENDMENTS

(*c*) freedom of peaceful assembly; and

(*d*) <u>freedom</u> of association.

Democratic Rights

Democratic rights of citizens

3. Every citizen of Canada has, without unreasonable distinction or limitation, the right to vote in an election of members of the House of Commons or of a legislative assembly and to be qualified for membership therein.

Maximum duration of legislative bodies

4. (1) No House of Commons and no legislative assembly shall continue for longer than five years from the date fixed for the return of the writs at a general election of its members.

Continuation in special circumstances

(2) In time of real or apprehended war, invasion or insurrection, a House of Commons may be continued by Parliament and a legislative assembly may be continued by the legislature beyond five years if such continuation [is] not opposed by the votes of more than one-third of the members of the House of Commons or the legislative assembly, as the case may be.

Annual sitting of legislative bodies

5. There shall be a sitting of Parliament and of each legislature at least once every twelve months.

Mobility Rights

Mobility of citizens

6. (1) Every citizen of Canada has the right to enter, remain in and leave Canada.

Rights to move and gain livelihood

(2) Every citizen of Canada and every person who has the status of a permanent resident of Canada has the right

(*a*) to move to and take up residence in any province; and

(*b*) to pursue the gaining of a livelihood in any province.

Limitation

(3) The rights specified in subsection (2) are subject to

(*a*) any laws or practices of general application in force in a province other than those that discriminate among persons primarily on the basis of province of present or previous residence; and

(*b*) any laws providing for reasonable residency requirements as a qualification for the receipt of publicly provided social services.

Legal Rights

Life, liberty and security of person

7. Everyone has the right to life, liberty and security of the person and the right not to be deprived thereof except in accordance with the principles of fundamental justice.

PROPOSED RESOLUTION	POSSIBLE AMENDMENTS

Search or seizure
8. Everyone has the right not to be subjected to search or seizure except on grounds, and in accordance with procedures, established by law.

Search and seizure
8. Everyone has the right to be secure against unreasonable search and seizure.

Detention or imprisonment
9. Everyone has the right not to be detained or imprisoned except on grounds, and in accordance with procedures, established by law.

Detention or imprisonment
9. Everyone has the right not to be arbitrarily detained or imprisoned.

Arrest or detention
10. Everyone has the right on arrest or detention

(a) to be informed promptly of the reasons therefor;

(b) to retain and instruct counsel without delay; and

(c) to have the validity of the detention determined by way of *habeas corpus* and to be released if the detention is not lawful.

Arrest or detention
10. Everyone has the right on arrest or detention

(a) to be informed promptly of the reasons therefor;

(b) to retain and instruct counsel without delay and to be informed of that right; and

(c) to have the validity of the detention determined by way of *habeas corpus* and to be released if the detention is not lawful.

Proceedings in criminal and penal matters
11. Anyone charged with an offence has the right

(a) to be informed promptly of the specific offence;

(b) to be tried within a reasonable time;

(c) to be presumed innocent until proven guilty according to law in a fair and public hearing by an independent and impartial tribunal;

(d) not to be denied reasonable bail except on grounds, and in accordance with procedures, established by law;

(e) not to be found guilty on account of any act or omission that at the time of the act or omission did not constitute an offence;

(f) not to be tried or punished more than once for an offence of which he or she has been finally convicted or acquitted; and

(g) to the benefit of the lesser punishment where the punishment for an offence of which he or she has been convicted has been varied between the time of commission and the time of sentencing.

Proceedings in criminal and penal matters
11. Any person charged with an offence has the right

(a) to be informed promptly of the specific offence;

(b) to be tried within a reasonable time;

(c) not to be compelled to be a witness in proceedings against that person in respect of the offence;

(d) to be presumed innocent until proven guilty according to law in a fair and public hearing by an independent and impartial tribunal;

(e) not to be denied reasonable bail without just cause;

(f) except in the case of an offence under military law tried before a military tribunal, to the benefit of trial by jury where the maximum punishment for the offence is imprisonment for five years or a more severe punishment;

(g) not to be found guilty on account of any act or omission that at the time of the act or omission did not constitute an offence under Canadian or international law;

(h) if finally convicted or acquitted of the offence in Canada, not to be tried for it again and, if so convicted, not to be punished for it more than once; and

(i) if convicted of the offence and if the punishment for the offence has been varied between the time of comission and the time of sentencing, to the benefit of the lesser punishment.

Treatment or punishment
12. Everyone has the right not to be subjected to any cruel and unusual treatment or punishment.

Treatment or punishment
12. Everyone has the right not to be subjected to any cruel and unusual treatment or punishment.

Self-crimination
13. A witness has the right when compelled to testify not to have any incriminating

Self-crimination
13. A witness who testifies in any proceedings has the right not to have any

PROPOSED RESOLUTION	POSSIBLE AMENDMENTS

evidence so given used to incriminate him or her in any other proceedings, except a prosecution for perjury or for the giving of contradictory evidence.

incriminating evidence so given used to incriminate that witness in any other proceedings, except in a prosecution for perjury or for the giving of contradictory evidence.

Interpreter

14. A party or witness in any proceedings who does not understand or speak the language in which the proceedings are conducted has the right to the assistance of an interpreter.

Interpreter

14. A party or witness in any proceedings who does not understand or speak the language in which the proceedings are conducted has the right to the assistance of an interpreter.

Non-discrimination Rights

Equality Rights

Equality before the law and equal protection of the law

15. (1) Everyone has the right to equality before the law and to the equal protection of the law without discrimination because of race, national or ethnic origin, colour, religion, age or sex.

Equality before and under the law and equal protection and benefit of the law

15. (1) Every individual is equal before and under the law and has the right to the equal protection and equal benefit of the law without discrimination and, in particular, without discrimination based on race, national or ethnic origin, colour, religion, sex or age.

Affirmative action program

(2) This section does not preclude any law, program or activity that has as its object the amelioration of conditions of disadvantaged persons or groups.

Affirmative action programs

(2) Subsection (1) does not preclude any law, program or activity that has as its object the amelioration of conditions of disadvantaged individuals or groups including those that are disadvantaged because of race, national or ethnic origin, colour, religion, sex or age.

Official Languages of Canada

Official Languages of Canada

Official languages of Canada

16. (1) English and French are the official languages of Canada and have equality of status and equal rights and privileges as to their use in all institutions of the Parliament and government of Canada.

Official languages of Canada

16. (1) English and French are the official languages of Canada and have equality of status and equal rights and privileges as to their use in all institutions of the Parliament and government of Canada.

Official languages of New Brunswick

(2) English and French are the official languages of New Brunswick and have equality of status and equal rights and privileges as to their use in all institutions of the legislature and government of New Brunswick.

Extension of status and use

(2) Nothing in this Charter limits the authority of Parliament or a legislature to extend the status or use of English and French or either of those languages.

Extension of status and use

(3) Nothing in this Charter limits the authority of Parliament or a legislature to advance the equality of status or use of English and French.

Proceedings of Parliament

17. Everyone has the right to use English or French in any debates and other proceedings of Parliament.

Proceedings of Parliament

17. (1) Everyone has the right to use English or French in any debates and other proceedings of Parliament.

Proceedings of New Brunswick legislature

(2) Everyone has the right to use English or French in any debates and other proceedings of the legislature of New Brunswick.

Parliamentary statutes and records

18. The statutes, records and journals of Parliament shall be printed and published in English and French and both language versions are equally authoritative.

Parliamentary statutes and records

18. (1) The statutes, records and journals of Parliament shall be printed and published in English and French and both language versions are equally authoritative.

New Brunswick statutes and records

(2) The statutes, records and journals of the legislature of New Brunswick shall be printed and published in English and French and both language versions are equally authoritative.

PROPOSED RESOLUTION

POSSIBLE AMENDMENTS

Proceedings in courts established by Parliament

19. Either English or French may be used by any person in, or in any pleading in or process issuing from, any court established by Parliament.

Proceedings in courts established by Parliament

19. (1) Either English or French may be used by any person in, or in any pleading in or process issuing from, any court established by Parliament.

Proceedings in New Brunswick courts

(2) Either English or French may be used by any person in, or in any pleading in or process issuing from, any court of New Brunswick.

Communications by public with federal institutions

20. Any member of the public in Canada has the right to communicate with, and to receive available services from, any head or central office of an institution of the Parliament or government of Canada in English or French, as he or she may choose, and has the same right with respect to any other office of any such institution where that office is located within an area of Canada in which it is determined, in such manner as may be prescribed or authorized by Parliament, that a substantial number of persons within the population use that language.

Communications by public with federal institutions

20. (1) Any member of the public in Canada has the right to communicate with, and to receive available services from, any head or central office of an institution of the Parliament or government of Canada in English or French, and has the same right with respect to any other office of any such institution where

(*a*) there is a significant demand for communications with and services from that office in such language; or

(*b*) due to the nature of the office, it is reasonable that communications with and services from that office be available in both English and French.

Communications by public with New Brunswick institutions

(2) Any member of the public in New Brunswick has the right to communicate with, and to receive available services from, any office of an institution of the legislature or government of New Brunswick in English or French.

Continuation of existing constitutional provisions

21. Nothing in sections 16 to 20 abrogates or derogates from any right, privilege or obligation with respect to the English and French languages, or either of them, that exists or is continued by virtue of any other provision of the Constitution of Canada.

Continuation of existing constitutional provisions

21. Nothing in sections 16 to 20 abrogates or derogates from any right, privilege or obligation with respect to the English and French languages, or either of them, that exists or is continued by virtue of any other provision of the Constitution of Canada.

Rights and privileges preserved

22. Nothing in sections 16 to 20 abrogates or derogates from any legal or customary right or privilege acquired or enjoyed either before or after the coming into force of this Charter with respect to any language that is not English or French.

Rights and privileges preserved

22. Nothing in sections 16 to 20 abrogates or derogates from any legal or customary right or privilege acquired or enjoyed either before or after the coming into force of this Charter with respect to any language that is not English or French.

Minority Language Educational Rights

Minority Language Educational Rights

Language of instruction

23. (1) Citizens of Canada whose first language learned and still understood is that of the English or French linguistic minority population of the province in which they reside have the right to have their children receive their primary and secondary school instruction in that minority language if they reside in an areas of the province in which the number of children of such citizens is sufficient to warrant the provision out of public funds of minority language educational facilities in that area.

Language of instruction

23. (1) Citizens of Canada

(*a*) whose first language learned and still understood is that of the English or French linguistic minority population of the province in which they reside, or

(*b*) who have received their primary school instruction in Canada in English or French and reside in a province where the language in which they received that instruction is the language of the English or French linguistic minority population of the province,

have the right to have their children receive primary and secondary school instruction in that language in that province.

PROPOSED RESOLUTION	POSSIBLE AMENDMENTS
Continuity of language of instruction (2) Where a citizen of Canada changes residence from one province to another and, prior to the change, any child of that citizen has been receiving his or her primary or secondary school instruction in either English or French, that citizen has the right to have any or all of his or her children receive their primary and secondary school instruction in that same language if the number of children of citizens resident in the area of the province to which the citizen has moved, who have a right recognized by this section, is sufficient to warrant the provision out of public funds of minority language educational facilities in that area.	**Continuity of language instruction** (2) Citizens of Canada of whom any child has received or is receiving primary or secondary school instruction in English or French in Canada, have the right to have all their children receive primary and secondary school instruction in the same language. **Application where numbers warrant** (3) The right of citizens of Canada under this section to have their children receive primary and secondary school instruction in the language of the English or French linguistic minority population of a province applies where they reside in an area of the province in which the number of children of citizens who have such a right is sufficient to warrant the provision out of public funds of minority language instruction in that area.

Undeclared Rights and Freedoms

Enforcement

Undeclared rights and freedoms **24.** The guarantee in this Charter of certain rights and freedoms shall not be construed as denying the existence of any other rights or freedoms that exist in Canada, including any rights or freedoms that pertain to the native peoples of Canada.	**Enforcement of guaranteed rights and freedoms** **24.** Anyone whose rights or freedoms, as guaranteed by this Charter, have been infringed or denied may apply to a court of competent jurisdiction to obtain such remedy as the court considers appropriate and just in the circumstances.

General

General

Primacy of Charter **25.** Any law that is inconsistent with the provisions of this Charter is, to the extent of such inconsistency, inoperative and of no force or effect.	**Rights and freedoms not affected by Charter** **25.** The guarantee in this Charter of certain rights and freedoms shall not be construed as denying the existence of (*a*) any aboriginal, treaty or other rights or freedoms that may pertain to the aboriginal peoples of Canada including any right or freedom that may have been recognized by the Royal Proclamation of October 7, 1763; or (*b*) any other rights or freedoms that may exist in Canada.
Laws respecting evidence **26.** No provision of this Charter, other than section 13, affects the laws respecting the admissibility of evidence in any proceedings or the authority of Parliament or a legislature to make laws in relation thereto.	**Interpretation of Charter** **26.** This Charter shall be interpreted in a manner consistent with the preservation and enhancement of the multicultural heritage of Canadians.
Application to territories and territorial authorities **27.** A reference in this Charter to a province or to the legislative assembly or legislature of a province shall be deemed to include a reference to the Yukon Territory and the Northwest Territories, or to the appropriate legislative authority thereof, as the case may be.	**Application to territories and territorial authorities** **27.** A reference in this Charter to a province or to the legislative assembly or legislature of a province shall be deemed to include a reference to the Yukon Territory and the Northwest Territories, or to the appropriate legislative authority thereof, as the case may be.
Legislative powers not extended **28.** Nothing in this Charter extends the legislative powers of any body or authority.	**Legislative powers not extended** **28.** Nothing in this Charter extends the legislative powers of any body or authority.

PROPOSED RESOLUTION	POSSIBLE AMENDMENTS
Application of Charter	*Application of Charter*

Application of Charter

29. (1) This Charter applies

(*a*) to the Parliament and government of Canada and to all matters within the authority of Parliament including all matters relating to the Yukon Territory and Northwest Territories; and

(*b*) to the legislature and government of each province and to all matters within the authority of the legislature of each province.

Exception

(2) Notwithstanding subsection (1), section 15 shall not have application until three years after this Act, except Part V, comes into force.

Application of Charter

29. (1) This Charter applies

(*a*) to the Parliament and government of Canada and to all matters within the authority of Parliament including all matters relating to the Yukon Territory and Northwest Territories; and

(*b*) to the legislature and government of each province and to all matters within the authority of the legislature of each province.

Exception

(2) Notwithstanding subsection (1), section 15 shall not have application until three years after this Act, except Part V, comes into force.

Citation

Citation

30. This Part may be cited as the *Canadian Charter of Rights and Freedoms.*

Citation

Citation

30. This Part may be cited as the *Canadian Charter of Rights and Freedoms.*

PART II

EQUALIZATION AND REGIONAL DISPARITIES

PART II

EQUALIZATION AND REGIONAL DISPARITIES

Commitment to promote equal opportunities

31. (1) Without altering the legislative authority of Parliament or of the provincial legislatures, or the rights of any of them with respect to the exercise of their legislative authority, Parliament and the legislatures, together with the government of Canada and the provincial governments, are committed to

(*a*) promoting equal opportunities for the well-being of Canadians;

(*b*) furthering economic development to reduce disparity in opportunities; and

(*c*) providing essential public services of reasonable quality to all Canadians.

Commitment respecting essential public services

(2) Parliament and the government of Canada are committed to taking such measures as are appropriate to ensure that provinces are able to provide the essential public services referred to in paragraph (1)(*c*) without imposing an undue burden of provincial taxation.

Commitment to promote equal opportunities

31. (1) Without altering the legislative authority of Parliament or of the provincial legislatures, or the rights of any of them with respect to the exercise of their legislative authority, Parliament and the legislatures, together with the government of Canada and the provincial governments, are committed to

(*a*) promoting equal opportunities for the well-being of Canadians;

(*b*) furthering economic development to reduce disparity in opportunities; and

(*c*) providing essential public services of reasonable quality to all Canadians.

Commitment respecting public services

(2) Parliament and the government of Canada are committed to the principle of making equalization payments to ensure that provincial governments have sufficient revenues to provide reasonably comparable levels of public services at reasonably comparable levels of taxation.

PART III

CONSTITUTIONAL CONFERENCES

PART III

CONSTITUTIONAL CONFERENCES

Constitutional conferences

32. Until Part V comes into force, a constitutional conference composed of the Prime Minister of Canada and the first ministers of the provinces shall be convened by the Prime Minister of Canada at least once in every year unless, in

Constitutional conferences

32. Until Part V comes into force, a constitutional conference composed of the Prime Minister of Canada and the first ministers of the provinces shall be convened by the Prime Minister of Canada at least once in every year unless, in

PROPOSED RESOLUTION	POSSIBLE AMENDMENTS

any year, a majority of those composing the conference decide that it shall not be held.

PART IV

INTERIM AMENDING PROCEDURE AND
RULES FOR ITS REPLACEMENT

Interim procedure for amending Constitution of Canada

33. Until Part V comes into force, an amendment to the Constitution of Canada may be made by proclamation issued by the Governor General under the Great Seal of Canada where so authorized by resolutions of the Senate and House of Commons and by the legislative assembly or government of each province.

Amendment of provisions relating to some but not all provinces

34. Until Part V comes into force, an amendment to the Constitution of Canada in relation to any provision that applies to one or more, but not all, provinces may be made by proclamation issued by the Governor General under the Great Seal of Canada where so authorized by resolutions of the Senate and House of Commons and by the legislative assembly or government of each province to which the amendment applies.

Rules applicable to amendment procedures

35. (1) The procedures for amendment described in sections 33 and 34 may be initiated either by the Senate or House of Commons or by the legislative assembly or government of a province.

Idem

(2) A resolution made or other authorization given for the purposes of this Part may be revoked at any time before the issue of a proclamation authorized by it.

Limitation on use of interim amending procedure

36. Sections 33 and 34 do not apply to an amendment to the Constitution of Canada where there is another provision in the Constitution for making the amendment, but the procedure prescribed by section 33 shall be used to amend the *Canadian Charter of Rights and Freedoms* and any provision for amending the Constitution, including this section, and may be used in making a general consolidation and revision of the Constitution.

Coming into force of Part V

37. Part V shall come into force

(*a*) with or without amendment, on such day as may be fixed by proclamation issued pursuant to the procedure prescribed by section 33, or

(*b*) on the day that is two years after the day this Act, except Part V, comes into force, whichever is the earlier day but, if a referendum is required to be held under subsection 38(3), Part V shall come into force as provided in section 39.

---

any year, a majority of those composing the conference decide that it shall not be held.

PART IV

INTERIM AMENDING PROCEDURE AND
RULES FOR ITS REPLACEMENT

Interim procedure for amending Constitution of Canada

33. Until Part V comes into force, an amendment to the Constitution of Canada may be made by proclamation issued by the Governor General under the Great Seal of Canada where so authorized by resolutions of the Senate and House of Commons and by the legislative assembly or government of each province

Amendment of provisions relating to some but not all provinces

34. Until Part V comes into force, an amendment to the Constitution of Canada in relation to any provision that applies to one or more, but not all, provinces may be made by proclamation issued by the Governor General under the Great Seal of Canada where so authorized by resolutions of the Senate and House of Commons and by the legislative assembly or government of each province to which the amendment applies.

Rules applicable to amendment procedures

35. (1) The procedures for amendment described in sections 33 and 34 may be initiated either by the Senate or House of Commons or by the legislative assembly or government of a province.

Idem

(2) A resolution made or other authorization given for the purposes of this Part may be revoked at any time before the issue of a proclamation authorized by it.

Limitation on use of interim amendment procedure

36. Sections 33 and 34 do not apply to an amendment to the Constitution of Canada where there is another provision in the Constitution for making the amendment, but the procedure prescribed by section 33 shall be used to amend the *Canadian Charter of Rights and Freedoms* and any provision for amending the Constitution, including this section.

Coming into force of Part V

37. Part V shall come into force

(*a*) with or without amendment, on such day as may be fixed by proclamation issued pursuant to the procedure prescribed by section 33, or

(*b*) on the day that is two years after the day this Act, except Part V, comes into force, whichever is the earlier day but, if a referendum is required to be held under subsection 38(3), Part V shall come into force as provided in section 39.

PROPOSED RESOLUTION

Provincial alternative procedure

38. (1) The governments or legislative assemblies of eight or more provinces that have, according to the then latest general census, combined populations of at least eighty per cent of the population of all the provinces may make a single proposal to substitute for paragraph 41(1)(*b*) such alternative as they consider appropriate.

Procedure for perfecting alternative

(2) One copy of an alternative proposed under subsection (1) may be deposited with the Chief Electoral Officer of Canada by each proposing province within two years after this Act, except Part V, comes into force but, prior to the expiration of that period, any province that has deposited a copy may withdraw that copy.

Referendum

(3) Where copies of an alternative have been filed as provided by subsection (2) and, on the day that is two years after this Act, except Part V, comes into force, at least eight copies remain filed by provinces that have, according to the then latest general census, combined populations of at least eighty per cent of the population of all the provinces, the government of Canada shall cause a referendum to be held within two years after that day to determine whether

(*a*) paragraph 41(1)(*b*) or any alternative thereto proposed by the government of Canada by depositing a copy thereof with the Chief Electoral Officer at least ninety days prior to the day on which the referendum is held, or

(*b*) the alternative proposed by the provinces, shall be adopted.

Coming into force of Part V where referendum held

39. Where a referendum is held under subsection 38(3), a proclamation under the Great Seal of Canada shall be issued within six months after the date of the referendum bringing Part V into force with such modifications, if any, as are necessary to incorporate the proposal approved by a majority of the persons voting at the referendum and with such other changes as are reasonably consequential on the incorporation of that proposal.

Rules for referendum

40. (1) Subject to subsection (2), Parliament may make laws respecting the rules applicable to the holding of a referendum under subsection 38(3).

Right to vote

(2) Every citizen of Canada has, without unreasonable distinction or limitation, the right to vote in a referendum held under subsection 38(3).

POSSIBLE AMENDMENTS

Provincial alternative procedure

38. (1) The legislative assemblies of seven or more provinces that have, according to the then latest general census, combined populations of at least eighty per cent of the population of all the provinces may make a single proposal to substitute for paragraph 41(1)(*b*) such alternative as they consider appropriate.

Procedure for perfecting alternative

(2) One copy of an alternative proposed under subsection (1) may be deposited with the Chief Electoral Officer of Canada by each proposing province within two years after this Act, except Part V, comes into force but, prior to the expiration of that period, any province that has deposited a copy may withdraw that copy.

Referendum

(3) Where copies of an alternative have been deposited as provided by subsection (2) and, on the day that is two years after this Act, except Part V, comes into force, at least seven copies remain deposited by provinces that have, according to the then latest general census, combined populations of at least eighty per cent of the population of all the provinces, the government of Canada shall cause a referendum to be held within two years after that day to determine whether

(*a*) paragraph 41(1)(*b*) or any alternative thereto approved by Parliament and deposited with the Chief Electoral Officer at least ninety days prior to the day on which the referendum is held, or

(*b*) the alternative proposed by the provinces, shall be adopted.

Coming into force of Part V where Referendum held

39. Where a referendum is held under subsection 38(3), a proclamation under the Great Seal of Canada shall be issued within six months after the date of the referendum bringing Part V into force with such modifications, if any, as are necessary to incorporate the proposal approved by a majority of the persons voting at the referendum and with such other changes as are reasonably consequential on the incorporation of that proposal.

Right to vote

40. (1) Every citizen of Canada has, without unreasonable distinction or limitation, the right to vote in a referendum held under subsection 38(3).

Establishment of Referendum Rules Commission

(2) If a referendum is required to be held under subsection 38(3), a Referendum Rules Commission shall forthwith be established by commission issued under the Great Seal of Canada consisting of

PROPOSED RESOLUTION	POSSIBLE AMENDMENTS

<table>
<tr><td></td><td>

(*a*) the Chief Electoral Officer of Canada, who shall be chairman of the Commission;

(*b*) a person appointed by the Governor General in Council; and

(*c*) a person appointed by the Governor General in Council

　(i) on the recommendation of the governments of a majority of provinces, or

　(ii) if the governments of a majority of provinces do not recommend a candidate within thirty days after the Chief Electoral Officer of Canada requests such a recommendation, on the recommendation of the Chief Justice of Canada from among persons recommended by the governments of the provinces within thirty days after the expiration of the first mentioned thirty day period or, if none are so recommended, from among such persons as the Chief Justice considers qualified.
</td></tr>
<tr><td>Duty of Commission</td><td>

(3) A Referendum Rules Commission shall cause rules for the holding of a referendum under subsection 38(3) approved by a majority of the Commission to be laid before Parliament within sixty days after the Commission is established or, if Parliament is not then sitting, on any of the first ten days thereafter that Parliament is sitting.
</td></tr>
<tr><td>Rules for referendum</td><td>

(4) Subject to subsection (1) and taking into consideration any rules approved by a Referendum Rules Commission in accordance with subsection (3), Parliament may enact laws respecting the rules applicable to the holding of a referendum under subsection 38(3).
</td></tr>
<tr><td>Proclamation</td><td>

(5) If Parliament does not enact laws respecting the rules applicable to the holding of a referendum within sixty days after receipt of a recommendation from a Referendum Rules Commission under subsection (4), the rules recommended by the Commission shall forthwith be brought into force by proclamation issued by the Governor General under the Great Seal of Canada.
</td></tr>
<tr><td>Computation of period</td><td>

(6) Any period when Parliament is prorogued or dissolved shall not be counted in computing the sixty day period referred to in subsection (5).
</td></tr>
<tr><td>Rules to have force of law</td><td>

(7) Subject to subsection (1), rules made under this section have the force of law and prevail over other laws made under the Constitution of Canada to the extent of any inconsistency.
</td></tr>
</table>

PROPOSED RESOLUTION

PART V

PROCEDURE FOR AMENDING
CONSTITUTION OF CANADA

General
procedure for
amending
Constitution
of Canada

41. (1) An amendment to the Constitution of Canada may be made by proclamation issued by the Governor General under the Great Seal of Canada where so authorized by

(*a*) resolutions of the Senate and House of Commons, and

(*b*) resolutions of the legislative assemblies of at least a majority of the provinces that includes

(i) every province that at any time before the issue of the proclamation had, according to any previous general census, a population of at least twenty-five per cent of the population of Canada,

(ii) at least two of the Atlantic provinces that have, according to the then latest general census, combined populations of at least fifty per cent of the population of all the Atlantic provinces, and

(iii) at least two of the Western provinces that have, according to the then latest general census, combined populations of at least fifty per cent of the population of all the Western provinces.

Definitions
"Atlantic
provinces"

(2) In this section,

"Atlantic provinces" means the provinces of Nova Scotia, New Brunswick, Prince Edward Island and Newfoundland;

"Western
provinces"

"Western provinces" means the provinces of Manitoba, British Columbia, Saskatchewan and Alberta.

Amendment
authorized by
referendum

42. (1) An amendment to the Constitution of Canada may be made by proclamation issued by the Governor General under the Great Seal of Canada where so authorized by a referendum held throughout Canada under subsection (2) at which

(*a*) a majority of persons voting thereat, and

(*b*) a majority of persons voting thereat in each of the provinces, resolutions of the legislative assemblies of which would be sufficient, together with resolutions of the Senate and House of Commons, to authorize the issue of a proclamation under subsection 41(1).

have approved the making of the amendment.

Authorization of
referendum

(2) A referendum referred to in subsection (1) shall be held where directed by proclamation issued by the Governor General under the Great

POSSIBLE AMENDMENTS

PART V

PROCEDURE FOR AMENDING
CONSTITUTION OF CANADA

General
procedure for
amending
Constitution
of Canada

41. (1) An amendment to the Constitution of Canada may be made by proclamation issued by the Governor General under the Great Seal of Canada where so authorized by

(*a*) resolutions of the Senate and House of Commons; and

(*b*) resolutions of the legislative assemblies of at least a majority of the provinces that includes

(i) every province that at any time before the issue of the proclamation had, according to any previous general census, a population of at least twenty-five per cent of the population of Canada,

(ii) two <u>or more</u> of the Atlantic provinces, and

(iii) two <u>or more</u> of the Western provinces that have <u>in the aggregate</u>, according to the then latest general census, a population of at least fifty per cent of the population of all of the Western provinces.

Definitions
"Atlantic
provinces"

(2) In this section,

"Atlantic provinces" means the provinces of Nova Scotia, New Brunswick, Prince Edward Island and Newfoundland;

"Western
provinces"

"Western provinces" means the provinces of Manitoba, British Columbia, Saskatchewan and Alberta.

Amendment
authorized by
referendum

42. (1) An amendment to the Constitution of Canada may be made by proclamation issued by the Governor General under the Great Seal of Canada where so authorized by a referendum held throughout Canada under subsection (2) at which

(*a*) a majority of persons voting thereat, and

(*b*) a majority of persons voting thereat in each of the provinces, resolutions of the legislative assemblies of which would be sufficient, together with resolutions of the Senate and House of Commons, to authorize the issue of a proclamation under subsection 41(1),

have approved the making of the amendment.

Authorization of
Referendum

(2) A referendum referred to in subsection (1) shall be held where directed by proclamation issued by the Governor General under the Great

PROPOSED RESOLUTION	POSSIBLE AMENDMENTS

Seal of Canada <u>authorized by resolutions of the</u> Senate and House of Commons.

Seal of Canada, <u>which proclamation may be issued where</u>

> (*a*) an amendment to the Constitution of Canada has been authorized under paragraph 41(1)(*a*) by resolutions of the Senate and House of Commons;
>
> (*b*) the requirements of paragraph 41(1)(*b*) in respect of the proposed amendment have not been satisfied within twelve months after the passage of the resolutions of the Senate and House of Commons; and
>
> (*c*) the issue of the proclamation has been authorized by the Governor General in Council.

Time limit for referendum

(3) A proclamation issued under subsection (2) in respect of a referendum shall provide for the referendum to be held within two years after the expiration of the twelve month period referred to in paragraph (*b*) of that subsection.

Amendment of provisions relating to some but not all provinces

43. An amendment to the Constitution of Canada in relation to any provision that applies to one or more, but not all, provinces may be made by proclamation issued by the Governor General under the Great Seal of Canada where so authorized by resolutions of the Senate and House of Commons and of the legislative assembly of each province to which the amendment applies.

Amendment of provisions relating to some but not all provinces

43. An amendment to the Constitution of Canada in relation to any provision that applies to one or more, but not all, provinces may be made by proclamation issued by the Governor General under the Great Seal of Canada where so authorized by resolutions of the Senate and House of Commons and of the legislative assembly of each province to which the amendment applies.

Amendments without Senate resolution

44. An amendment to the Constitution of Canada may be made by proclamation under subsection 41(1) or section 43 without a resolution of the Senate authorizing the issue of the proclamation if, within <u>ninety</u> days after the passage by the House of Commons of a resolution authorizing its issue, the Senate has not passed such a resolution and if, at any time after the expiration of those <u>ninety</u> days, the House of Commons again passes the resolution, <u>but any</u> period when Parliament is prorogued or dissolved shall not be counted in computing <u>those ninety</u> days.

Amendments without Senate resolution

44. (1) An amendment to the Constitution of Canada may be made by proclamation under subsection 41(1) or section 43, <u>as appropriate,</u> without a resolution of the Senate authorizing the issue of the proclamation if, within <u>one hundred and eighty</u> days after the passage by the House of Commons of a resolution authorizing its issue, the Senate has not passed such a resolution and if, at any time after the expiration of those <u>one hundred and eighty</u> days, the House of Commons again passes the resolution.

Computation of period

(2) Any period when Parliament is prorogued or dissolved shall not be counted in computing <u>the one hundred and eighty day period referred to in subsection (1).</u>

Rules applicable to amendment procedures

45. (1) The procedures for amendment described in subsection 41(1) and section 43 may be initiated either by the Senate or House of Commons or by the legislative assembly of a province.

Rules applicable to amendment procedures

45. (1) The procedures for amendment described in subsection 41(1) and section 43 may be initiated either by the Senate or House of Commons or by the legislative assembly of a province.

Idem

(2) A resolution made for the purposes of this Part may be revoked at any time before the issue of a proclamation authorized by it.

Idem

(2) A resolution made for the purposes of this Part may be revoked at any time before the issue of a proclamation authorized by it.

Rules for referendum

46. (1) Subject to subsection (2), Parliament may make laws respecting the rules applicable

Right to vote

46. (1) Every citizen of Canada has, without unreasonable distinction or limitation,

PROPOSED RESOLUTION	POSSIBLE AMENDMENTS

PROPOSED RESOLUTION

to the holding of a referendum under section 42.

Right to vote

(2) Every citizen of Canada has, without unreasonable distinction or limitation, the right to vote in a referendum held under section 42.

POSSIBLE AMENDMENTS

the right to vote in a referendum held under section 42.

Establishment of Referendum Rules Commission

(2) Where a referendum is to be held under section 42, a Referendum Rules Commission shall forthwith be established by commission issued under the Great Seal of Canada consisting of

(*a*) the Chief Electoral Officer of Canada, who shall be chairman of the Commission;

(*b*) a person appointed by the Governor General in Council; and

(*c*) a person appointed by the Governor General in Council

(i) on the recommendation of the governments of a majority of provinces, or

(ii) if the governments of a majority of provinces do not recommend a candidate within thirty days after the Chief Electoral Officer of Canada requests such a recommendation, on the recommendation of the Chief Justice of Canada from among persons recommended by the governments of the provinces within thirty days after the expiration of the first mentioned thirty day period or, if none are so recommended, from among such persons as the Chief Justice considers qualified.

Duty of Commission

(3) A Referendum Rules Commission shall cause rules for the holding of a referendum under section 42 approved by a majority of the Commission to be laid before Parliament within sixty days after the Commission is established or, if Parliament is not then sitting, on any of the first ten days thereafter that Parliament is sitting.

Rules for referendum

(4) Subject to subsection (1) and taking into consideration any rules approved by a Referendum Rules Commission in accordance with subsection (3), Parliament may enact laws respecting the rules applicable to the holding of a referendum under section 42.

Proclamation

(5) If Parliament does not enact laws respecting the rules applicable to the holding of a referendum within sixty days after receipt of a recommendation from a Referendum Rules Commission under subsection (4), the rules recommended by the Commission shall forthwith be brought into force by proclamation issued by the Governor General under the Great Seal of Canada.

Computation of period

(6) Any period when Parliament is prorogued or dissolved shall not be counted in computing the sixty day period referred to in subsection (5).

PROPOSED RESOLUTION	POSSIBLE AMENDMENTS

Rules to have force of law

(7) Subject to subsection (1), rules made under this section have the force of law and prevail over other laws made under the Constitution of Canada to the extent of any inconsistency.

Limitation on use of general amending formula

47. The procedures prescribed by section 41, 42 or 43 do not apply to an amendment to the Constitution of Canada where there is another provision in the Constitution for making the amendment, but the procedures prescribed by section 41 or 42 shall nevertheless be used to amend any provision for amending the Constitution, including this section, and section 41 may be used in making a general consolidation or revision of the Constitution.

Limitation on use of general amendment procedure

47. (1) The procedures prescribed by section 41, 42 or 43 do not apply to an amendment to the Constitution of Canada where there is another provision in the Constitution for making the amendment, but the procedures prescribed by section 41 or 42 shall, nevertheless, be used to amend any provision for amending the Constitution, including this section.

Idem

(2) The procedures prescribed by section 41 or 42 do not apply in respect of an amendment referred to in section 43.

Amendments by Parliament

48. Subject to section 50, Parliament may exclusively make laws amending the Constitution of Canada in relation to the executive government of Canada or the Senate or House of Commons.

Amendments by provincial legislatures

49. Subject to section 50, the legislature of each province may exclusively make laws amending the constitution of the province.

Matters requiring amendment under general formula

50. An amendment to the Constitution of Canada in relation to the following matters may be made only in accordance with a procedure prescribed by section 41 or 42:

(a) the office of the Queen, the Governor General and the Lieutenant Governor of a province;

(b) the *Canadian Charter of Rights and Freedoms*;

(c) the commitments relating to equalization and regional disparities set out in section 31;

(d) the powers of the Senate;

(e) the number of members by which a province is entitled to be represented in the Senate and the residence qualifications of Senators;

(f) the right of a province to a number of members in the House of Commons not less than the number of Senators representing the province; and

(g) the principles of proportionate representation of the provinces in the House of Commons prescribed by the Constitution of Canada.

Consequential amendments

51. Class 1 of section 91 and class 1 of section 92 of the *Constitution Act, 1867* (formerly named the *British North America Act, 1867*), the *British North America (No. 2) Act, 1949*, referred to in item 21 of Schedule I to this Act and Parts III and IV of this Act are repealed.

48. Subject to section 50 Parliament may exclusively make laws amending the Constitution of Canada in relation to the executive government of Canada or the Senate or House of Commons.

49. Subject to section 50 the legislature of each province may exclusively make laws amending the constitution of the province.

50. An amendment to the Constitution of Canada in relation to the following matters may be made only in accordance with a procedure prescribed by section 41 or 42:

(a) the office of the Queen, the Governor General and the Lieutenant Governor of a province;

(b) the *Canadian Charter of Rights and Freedoms*;

(c) the commitments relating to equalization and regional disparities set out in section 31;

(d) the powers of the Senate;

(e) the number of members by which a province is entitled to be represented in the Senate and the residence qualifications of Senators;

(f) the right of a province to a number of members in the House of Commons not less than the number of Senators representing the province; and

(g) the principles of proportionate representation of the provinces in the House of Commons prescribed by the Constitution of Canada.

51. Class 1 of section 91 and class 1 of section 92 of the *Constitution Act, 1867* (formerly named the *British North America Act, 1867*), the *British North America (No. 2) Act, 1949*, referred to in item 22 of Schedule I to this Act and Parts III and IV of this Act are repealed.

PROPOSED RESOLUTION	POSSIBLE AMENDMENTS
PART VI	PART VI
GENERAL	GENERAL

<table>
<tr><td>

Constitution of Canada

52. (1) The Constitution of Canada includes

(a) the *Canada Act*;

(b) the Acts and orders referred to in Schedule I; and

(c) any amendment to any Act or order referred to in paragraph (a) or (b).

Amendments to Constitution of Canada

(2) Amendments to the Constitution of Canada shall be made only in accordance with the authority contained in the Constitution of Canada.

Repeals and new names

53.(1) The enactments referred to in Column I of Schedule I are hereby repealed, or amended to the extent indicated in Column II thereof, and, unless repealed, shall continue as law in Canada under the names set out in Column III thereof.

Consequential amendments

(2) Every enactment, except the *Canada Act*, that refers to an enactment referred to in Schedule I by the name in Column I thereof is hereby amended by substituting for that name the corresponding name in Column III thereof, and any British North America Act not referred to in Schedule I may be cited as the *Constitution Act* followed by the year and number, if any, of its enactment.

French version of Constitution of Canada

54. A French version of the portions of the Constitution of Canada referred to in Schedule I shall be prepared by the Minister of Justice of Canada as expeditiously as possible and, when any portion thereof sufficient to warrant action being taken has been so prepared, it shall be put forward for enactment by proclamation issued by the Governor General under the Great Seal of Canada pursuant to the procedure then applicable to an amendment of the same provisions of the Constitution of Canada.

English and French versions

55. Where any portion of the Constitution of Canada has been or is enacted in English and French or where a French version of any portion of the Constitution is enacted pursuant to section 54, the English and French versions of that portion of the Constitution are equally authoritative.

English and French versions

56. The English and French versions of this Act are equally authoritative.

</td><td>

Primacy of Constitution of Canada

52. (1) The Constitution of Canada is the supreme law of Canada, and any law that is inconsistent with the provisions of the Constitution is, to the extent of the inconsistency, of no force or effect.

Constitution of Canada

(2) The Constitution of Canada includes

(a) the *Canada Act*;

(b) the Acts and orders referred to in Schedule I; and

(c) any amendment to any Act or order referred to in paragraph (a) or (b).

Amendments to Constitution of Canada

(3) Amendments to the Constitution of Canada shall be made only in accordance with the authority contained in the Constitution of Canada.

Repeals and new names

53. (1) The enactments referred to in Column I of Schedule I are hereby repealed or amended to the extent indicated in Column II thereof and, unless repealed, shall continue as law in Canada under the names set out in Column III thereof.

Consequential amendments

(2) Every enactment, except the *Canada Act*, that refers to an enactment referred to in Schedule I by the name in Column I thereof is hereby amended by substituting for that name the corresponding name in Column III thereof, and any British North America Act not referred to in Schedule I may be cited as the *Constitution Act* followed by the year and number, if any, of its enactment.

French version of Constitution of Canada

54. A French version of the portions of the Constitution of Canada referred to in Schedule I shall be prepared by the Minister of Justice of Canada as expeditiously as possible and, when any portion thereof sufficient to warrant action being taken has been so prepared, it shall be put forward for enactment by proclamation issued by the Governor General under the Great Seal of Canada pursuant to the procedure then applicable to an amendment of the same provisions of the Constitution of Canada.

English and French versions

55. Where any portion of the Constitution of Canada has been or is enacted in English and French or where a French version of any portion of the Constitution is enacted pursuant to section 54, the English and French versions of that portion of the Constitution are equally authoritative.

English and French versions

56. The English and French versions of this Act are equally authoritative.

</td></tr>
</table>

PROPOSED RESOLUTION		POSSIBLE AMENDMENTS	

Commencement	**57.** Subject to section 58, this Act shall come into force on a day to be fixed by proclamation issued by the Governor General under the Great Seal of Canada.	Commencement	**57.** Subject to section 58, this Act shall come into force on a day to be fixed by proclamation issued by the Governor General under the Great Seal of Canada.
Exception respecting amending formula	**58.** Part V shall come into force as provided in Part IV.	Exception respecting amending procedure	**58.** Part V shall come into force as provided in Part IV.
Citations	**59.** This Schedule may be cited as the *Constitution Act, 1980* and the Constitution Acts, 1867 to 1975 (No. 2) and this Act may be cited together as the *Constitution Acts, 1867 to 1980*.	Short Title and citations	**59.** This Schedule may be cited as the *Constitution Act, 1981* and the Constitution Acts 1867 to 1975 (No. 2) and this Act may be cited together as the *Constitution Acts, 1867 to 1981*.

SCHEDULE I TO THE CONSTITUTION ACT, 1981
MODERNIZATION OF THE CONSTITUTION

Item	Column I Act Affected	Column II Amendment	Column III New Name
1.	British North America Act, 1867, 30-31 Vict., c. 3 (U.K.)	(1) Section 1 is repealed and the following is substituted therefor: "1. This Act may be cited as the *Constitution Act, 1867.*" (2) Section 20 is repealed.	Constitution Act, 1867
2.	An Act to amend and continue the Act 32–33 Victoria chapter 3; and to establish and provide for the Government of the Province of Manitoba, 1870, 33 Vict., 3 (Can.)	(1) The long title is repealed and the following substituted therefor: "*Manitoba Act, 1870.*" (2) Section 20 is repealed.	Manitoba Act, 1870
3.	Order of Her Majesty in Council Admitting Rupert's Land and the North-Western Territory into the union dated the 23rd day of June, 1870		Rupert's Land and North-Western Territory Order
4.	Order of Her Majesty in Council admitting British Columbia into the Union, dated the 16th day of May, 1871.		British Columbia Terms of Union
5.	British North America Act, 1871, 34–35 Vict., c. 28 (U.K.)	Section 1 is repealed and the following substituted therefor: "1. This Act may be cited as the *Constitution Act, 1871.*"	Constitution Act, 1871

Item	Act Affected	Amendment	New Name
6.	Order of Her Majesty in Council admitting Prince Edward Island into the Union, dated the 26th day of June, 1873.		Prince Edward Island Terms of Union
7.	Parliament of Canada Act, 1875, 38–39 Vict., c. 38 (U.K.)		Parliament of Canada Act, 1875
8.	Order of Her Majesty in Council admitting all British possessions and Territories in North America and islands adjacent thereto into the Union, dated the 31st day of July, 1880.		Adjacent Territories Order
9.	British North America Act, 1886, 49–50 Vict., c. 35 (U.K.)	Section 3 is repealed and the following substituted therefor: "3. This Act may be cited as the *Constitution Act, 1886*."	Constitution Act, 1886
10.	Canada (Ontario Boundary) Act, 1889, 52–53 Vict., c. 28 (U.K.)		Canada (Ontario Boundary) Act, 1889
11.	Canadian Speaker (Appointment of Deputy) Act, 1895, 2nd Sess., 59 Vict., c. 3 (U.K.)	The Act is repealed.	
12.	The Alberta Act, 1905, 4–5 Edw. VII, c. 3 (U.K.)		Alberta Act
13.	The Saskatchewan Act, 1905, 4–5 Edw. VII, c. 42 (Can.)		Saskatchewan Act
14.	British North America Act, 1907, 7 Edw. VII, c. 11 (U.K.)	Section 2 is repealed and the following substituted therefor: "2. This Act may be cited as the *Constitution Act, 1907*."	Constitution Act, 1907
15.	British North America Act, 1915, 5–6 Geo. V, c. 45 (U.K.)	Section 3 is repealed and the following substituted therefor: "3. This Act may be cited as the *Constitution Act, 1915*."	Constitution Act, 1915
16.	British North America Act, 1930, 20–21 Geo. V, c. 26 (U.K.)	Section 3 is repealed and the following substituted therefor: "3. This Act may be cited as the *Constitution Act, 1930*."	Constitution Act, 1930

Item	Act Affected	Amendment	New Name
17.	Statute of Westminster, 1931, 22 Geo. V, c. 4 (U.K.)	In so far as they apply to Canada, (*a*) the expression "and New-foundland" in section 1 and sub-section 10(3) is repealed; (*b*) section 4 is repealed; and (*c*) subsection 7(1) is repealed.	Statute of Westminster, 1931
18.	British North America Act, 1940, 3–4 Geo. VI, c. 36 (U.K.)	Section 2 is repealed and the following substituted therefor: "2. This Act may be cited as the *Constitution Act, 1940.*"	Constitution Act, 1940
19.	British North America Act, 1943, 6–7 Geo. VI, c. 30 (U.K.)	The Act is repealed.	
20.	British North America Act, 1946, 9–10 Geo. VI, c. 63 (U.K.)	The Act is repealed.	
21.	British North America Act, 1949, 12–13 Geo. VI, c. 22 (U.K.)	Section 3 is repealed and the following substituted therefor: "3. This Act may be cited as the *Newfoundland Act.*"	Newfoundland Act
22.	British North America (No. 2) Act, 1949, 13 Geo. VI, c. 81 (U.K.)	The Act is repealed. (effective when section 51 of the *Constitution Act, 1980* comes into force)	
23.	British North America Act, 1951, 14–15 Geo. VI, c. 32 (U.K.)	The Act is repealed.	
24.	British North America Act, 1952, I Eliz. II, c. 15 (Can.)	The Act is repealed.	
25.	British North America Act, 1960, 9 Eliz. II, c. 2 (U.K.)	Section 2 is repealed and the following substituted therefor: "2. This Act may be cited as the *Constitution Act, 1960.*"	Constitution Act, 1960
26.	British North America Act, 1964, 12–13 Eliz. II, c. 73 (U.K.)	Section 2 is repealed and the following substituted therefor: "2. This Act may be cited as the *Constitution Act, 1964.*"	Constitution Act, 1964
27.	British North America Act, 1965, 14 Eliz. II, c. 4, Part I (Can.)	Section 2 is repealed and the following substituted therefor: "2. This Part may be cited as the *Constitution Act, 1965.*"	Constitution Act, 1965

Item	Act Affected	Amendment	New Name
28.	British North America Act, 1974, 23 Eliz. II, c. 13, Part I (Can.)	Section 3, as amended by 25–26 Eliz. II, c. 28, s. 38(1) (Can.) is repealed and the following substituted therefor: "3. This Part may be cited as the *Constitution Act, 1974*."	Constitution Act, 1974
29.	British North America Act, 1975, 23–24 Eliz. II, c. 28, Part I (Can.)	Section 3, as amended by 25–26 Eliz. II, c. 28, s. 31 (Can.) is repealed and the following substituted therefor: "3. This Part may be cited as the *Constitution Act (No. 1), 1975*."	Constitution Act (No. 1), 1975
30.	British North America Act, (No. 2), 1975, 23–24 Eliz. II, c. 53 (Can.)	Section 3 is repealed and the following substituted therefor: "3. This Act may be cited as the *Constitution Act (No. 2), 1975*."	Constitution Act (No. 2), 1975

(d) Report to Parliament and Proposed Resolution for a Joint Address to Her Majesty the Queen Respecting the Constitution of Canada, as Amended by the Committee, from *Minutes of Proceedings and Evidence*, Issue 57, pp. 2–37, February 13, 1981

SPECIAL JOINT COMMITTEE OF THE SENATE AND OF THE HOUSE OF COMMONS ON THE CONSTITUTION OF CANADA

Joint Chairmen:
　Senator Harry Hays, P.C.
　Serge Joyal, M.P.

Representing the Senate:

Senators:

Martial Asselin	H. Carl Goldenberg
Jack Austin	Maurice Lamontagne
John J. Connoly	

Representing the House of Commons:

Messrs.

Perrin Beatty	Robert Bockstael

Coline Campbell (Miss)	Jake Epp
Eymard G. Corbin	John A. Fraser
David Crombie	George Henderson
	(Quorum 12)

Richard Prégent
Paul Bélisle
Joint Clerks of the Committee

Other Senators and Members who served on the Committee:

Senators:

Willie Adams	Ernest G. Cottreau
Margaret Anderson	Richard Donahoe
James Balfour	C. William Doody
Louis Philippe Beaubien	Jacques Flynn
Rhéal Bélisle	Royce Frith
Martha P. Bielish	Louis de G. Giguère
Florence B. Bird	Allister Grosart
Peter Bosa	Joseph Philippe Guay

Stanley Haidasz
Paul C. Lafond
Renaude Lapointe

Fernand Leblanc
P. Derek Lewis

And Members:

Warren Allmand	Jesse Flis
Vic Althouse	Girve Fretz
Doug Anguish	Benno Friesen
George Baker	Jim Fulton
Walter Baker	Jean-Robert Gauthier
Les Benjamin	Rosaire Gendron
David Berger	Pierre Gimaïel
Derek Blackburn	René Gingras
Bill Blaikie	Lorne Greenaway
Garnet M. Bloomfield	Bert Hargrave
John Bosley	Maurice Harquail
Herb Breau	Jim Hawkes
Edward Broadbent	Céline Hervieux-Payette
Pat Carney	Ray Hnatyshyn
J. Ray Chénier	Bruce Halliday
Eva Côté	Stan Hovdebo
Vince Dantzer	Peter Ittinuar
Roland de Corneille	Pauline Jewett
Simon de Jong	Cyril Keeper
Yves Demers	David Kilgour
Walter Dinsdale	Thérèse Killens
Rolland Dion	Fred King
Maurice A. Dionne	John Kushner
Jean-Guy Dubois	Claude-André Lachance
Louis Duclos	Mike Landers
Denis Ethier	Peter Lang

REPORT TO PARLIAMENT

Friday, February 13, 1981

The Special Joint Committee of the Senate and the House of Commons on the Constitution of Canada has the honour to report as follows:

ORDERS OF REFERENCE

The Special Joint Committee of the Senate and the House of Commons on the Constitution of Canada was established pursuant to Orders of Reference adopted on October 23, 1980 by the House of Commons and on November 3, 1980 by the Senate. The Orders of Reference read in part as follows:

"That a Special Joint Committee of the Senate and of the House of Commons be appointed to consider and report upon the document entitled "Proposed Resolution for a Joint Address to Her Majesty the Queen respecting the Constitution of Canada" published by the Government on October 2, 1980, and to recommend in their report whether or not such an Address, with such amendments as the Committee considers necessary, should be presented by both House of Parliament to Her Majesty the Queen;"

Additional Orders of Reference were issued by both Houses. The complete text of all Orders of Reference is set out in Appendix A [not reproduced].

INTRODUCTION

The Committee's report is divided into four main parts. Part I is entitled "Organization of Committee's Work" and describes the Committee's activities. Part II is entitled "Summary of Evidence" and outlines the evidence presented by governments, groups and individuals. Part III describes the Committee's response to the submissions received by it. Part IV sets out the Committee's recommendation to the Senate and the House of Commons.

I. ORGANIZATION OF COMMITTEE'S WORK

1. INITIAL ACTION

The Committee commenced sitting on November 6, 1980. By advertisements published in the major daily newspapers throughout Canada, the Committee asked for written submissions and indicated that witnesses would be invited to appear.

Beginning on Monday, November 17, 1980, pursuant to further Orders of both Houses, the sittings of the Committee were broadcast on television and radio on a regular basis.

2. OUTLINE OF ACTIVITIES

The work of the Committee fell into four phases. On November 7, the Minister of Justice, the Honourable Jean Chrétien, the first witness, made his opening statement. On November 12, and 13, he was examined by Committee members. From November 14 to January 9, witnesses representing groups. January 12, the Minister of Justice returned for the "clause by clause" consideration which continued until February 9. Thereupon, the committee proceeded *in camera* to prepare this Report.

The Committee was composed of 25 members of whom 10 were from the Senate and 15 from the House of Commons. There were 15 members of the Liberal Party, 8 members of the Progressive Conservative Party and 2 members of the New Democratic Party. A substantial number of other Senators and members of the House of Commons participated in the work of the Committee at one time or another as indicated on the inside front cover of Issue No. 57 of the Minutes of Proceedings and Evidence of the Committee. The Committee held 106 meetings on 56 sitting days for a total of 267 sitting hours. The Minister of Justice, Mr. Chrétien, appeared as a witness 39 times and the acting Minister, the Honourable Robert Kaplan, appeared on his behalf 9 times. Clause by clause consideration occupied 90.5 hours.

The resources of both Houses of Parliament and the Library of Parliament, as well as those of the Department of Justice, the Federal-Provincial Relations Office and other government departments, the Prime Minister's Office and the Parliamentary Centre for Foreign Affairs and Foreign Trade, were directed to the facilitation of the work of the Committee.

3. PARTICIPATION BY GOVERNMENTS, GROUPS AND INDIVIDUALS

As of February 2, 1981, 914 individuals and 294 groups had sent letters, telegrams and briefs to the Committee. Of those that expressed a wish to appear before the Committee, the Premiers of Nova Scotia, New Brunswick, Prince Edward Island and Saskatchewan, representatives of the governments of the Yukon Territory and the Northwest Territories and 104 groups and individuals attended as witnesses. The groups represented a broad cross section of Canadian Society. A list of those who were invited to give evidence as witnesses is attached as Appendix B [not reproduced]. A list of those who had, as of February 2, 1981, made written submissions to the Committee is attached as Appendix C [not reproduced]. The complete text of the oral evidence may be found in Issues 1 to 56 of the Minutes of Proceedings and Evidence of the Committee.

II. SUMMARY OF EVIDENCE

The Research Branch of the Library of Parliament prepared a statistical account of the 962 briefs, letters and telegrams sent to the Committee prior to December 31, 1980, the last date for the receipt of such submissions. Specific comments on the proposed Resolution as a whole, on any of the major issues raised thereby or on any clauses contained therein, were categorized in tabular form. This account is set out as Appendix D [not reproduced]. Written submissions received after December 31, 1980 were made available to Committee members but are not reflected in Appendix D.

III. RESPONSE TO SUBMISSIONS AND EVIDENCE

On January 12, 1981, the Minister of Justice, on behalf of the government presented to the Committee a consolidation containing a number of suggested amendments to the proposed Resolution. The Progressive Conservative and New Democratic Parties thereupon responded with amendments both to the original resolution and to the consolidation. The government proposed 58 amendments of which 58 were approved; the Progressive Conservative Party proposed 22 amendments of which 7 were approved; and the New Democratic Party proposed 43 amendments of which 2 were approved.

IV. RECOMMENDATIONS

Your Committee has considered the document entitled "Proposed Resolution for a Joint Address to Her Majesty the Queen respecting the Constitution of Canada" published by the Government on October 2, 1980 and, in particular, has considered what amendments were necessary to the Address contained in the document, and whether or not the Address as amended by the Committee should be presented on behalf of both Houses of Parliament to Her Majesty the Queen.

Your Committee recommends that the Government propose to the Senate and the House of Commons for adoption a Resolution for an Address to Her Majesty the Queen respecting the Constitution of Canada, and that such Resolution be the "Proposed Resolution for a Joint Address to Her Majesty the Queen respecting the Constitution of Canada" published by the Government on October 2, 1980, as amended and approved by this Committee; and that, upon its adoption by the Senate and the House of Commons, the Address be presented to Her Majesty the Queen.

PROPOSED RESOLUTION FOR A JOINT ADDRESS TO HER MAJESTY THE QUEEN RESPECTING THE CONSTITUTION OF CANADA, AS AMENDED BY THE COMMITTEE

[Moved in the House of Commons, February 17, 1981, by the Honourable Jean Chrétien, Minister of Justice.]

WHEREAS in the past certain amendments to the Constitution of Canada have been made by the Parliament of the United Kingdom at the request and with the consent of Canada;

AND WHEREAS it is in accord with the status of Canada as an independent state that Canadians be able to amend their Constitution in Canada in all respects;

AND WHEREAS it is also desirable to provide in the Constitution of Canada for the recognition of certain fundamental rights and freedoms and to make other amendments to that Constitution;

NOW THEREFORE the Senate and the House of Commons, in Parliament assembled, resolve that a respectful address be presented to Her Majesty the Queen in the following words:

To the Queen's Most Excellent Majesty:
Most Gracious Sovereign:

We, Your Majesty's loyal subjects, the Senate and the House of Commons of Canada in Parliament assembled, respectfully approach Your Majesty, requesting that you may graciously be pleased to cause to be laid before the Parliament of the United Kingdom a measure containing the recitals and clauses hereinafter set forth:

An Act to amend the Constitution of Canada

Whereas Canada has requested and consented to the enactment of an Act of the Parliament of the United Kingdom to give effect to the provisions hereinafter set forth and the Senate and the House of Commons of Canada in Parliament assembled have submitted an address to Her Majesty requesting that Her Majesty may graciously be pleased to cause a Bill to be laid before the Parliament of the United Kingdom for that purpose.

Be it therefore enacted by the Queen's Most Excellent Majesty, by and with the advice and consent of the Lords Spiritual and Temporal, and Commons, in this present Parliament assembled, and by the authority of the same, as follows:

Constitution Act, 1981 enacted

1. The *Constitution Act, 1981* set out in Schedule B to this Act is hereby enacted for and shall have the force of law in Canada and shall come into force as provided in that Act.

Termination of power to legislate for Canada

2. No Act of the Parliament of the United Kingdom passed after the *Constitution Act, 1981* comes into force shall extend to Canada as part of its law.

French version

3. So far as it is not contained in Schedule B, the French version of this Act is set out in Schedule A to this Act and has the same authority in Canada as the English version thereof.

Short title

4. This Act may be cited as the *Canada Act*.

SCHEDULE B

CONSTITUTION ACT, 1981

PART I

CANADIAN CHARTER OF RIGHTS AND FREEDOMS

Guarantee of Rights and Freedoms

Rights and freedoms in Canada

1. The *Canadian Charter of Rights and Freedoms* guarantees the rights and freedoms set out in it subject only to such reasonable limits prescribed by law as can be demonstrably justified in a free and democratic society.

Fundamental Freedoms

Fundamental freedoms

2. Everyone has the following fundamental freedoms:

(*a*) freedom of conscience and religion;

(*b*) freedom of thought, belief, opinion and expression, including freedom of the press and other media of communication;

(*c*) freedom of peaceful assembly; and

(*d*) freedom of association.

Democratic Rights

Democratic rights of citizens

3. Every citizen of Canada has the right to vote in an election of members of the House of Commons or of a legislative assembly and to be qualified for membership therein.

Maximum duration of legislative bodies

4. (1) No House of Commons and no legislative assembly shall continue for longer than five years from the date fixed for the return of the writs at a general election of its members.

Continuation in special circumstances

(2) In time of real or apprehended war, invasion or insurrection, a House of Commons may be continued by Parliament and a legislative assembly may be continued by the legislature beyond five years if such continuation is not opposed by the votes of more than one-third of the members of the House of Commons or the legislative assembly, as the case may be.

Annual sitting of legislative bodies

5. There shall be a sitting of Parliament and of each legislature at least once every twelve months.

Mobility Rights

Mobility of citizens

6. (1) Every citizen of Canada has the right to enter, remain in and leave Canada.

Rights to move and gain livelihood

(2) Every citizen of Canada and every person who has the status of permanent resident of Canada has the right

(*a*) to move to and take up residence in any province; and

(*b*) to pursue the gaining of a livelihood in any province.

Limitation

(3) The rights specified in subsection (2) are subject to

(*a*) any laws or practices of general application in force in a province other than those that discriminate among persons primarily on the basis of province of present or previous residence; and

(b) any laws providing for reasonable residency requirements as a qualification for the receipt of publicly provided social services.

Legal Rights

Life, liberty and security of person

7. Everyone has the right to life, liberty and security of the person and the right not to be deprived thereof except in accordance with the principles of fundamental justice.

Search or seizure

8. Everyone has the right to be secure against unreasonable search or seizure.

Detention or imprisonment

9. Everyone has the right not to be arbitrarily detained or imprisoned.

Arrest or detention

10. Everyone has the right on arrest or detention

(a) to be informed promptly of the reasons therefor;

(b) to retain and instruct counsel without delay and to be informed of that right; and

(c) to have the validity of the detention determined by way of *habeas corpus* and to be released if the detention is not lawful.

Proceedings in criminal and penal matters

11. Any person charged with an offence has the right

(a) to be informed without unreasonable delay of the specific offence;

(b) to be tried within a reasonable time;

(c) not to be compelled to be a witness in proceedings against that person in respect of the offence;

(d) to be presumed innocent until proven guilty according to law in a fair and public hearing by an independent and impartial tribunal;

(e) not to be denied reasonable bail without just cause;

(f) except in the case of an offence under military law tried before a military tribunal, to the benefit of trial by jury where the maximum punishment for the offence is imprisonment for five years or a more severe punishment;

(g) not to be found guilty on account of any act or omission unless, at the time of the act or omission, it constituted an offence under Canadian or international law or was criminal according to the general principles of law recognized by the community of nations;

(h) if finally acquitted of the offence, not to be tried for it again and, if finally found guilty and punished for the offence, not to be tried or punished for it again; and

(i) if found guilty of the offence and if the punishment for the offence has been varied between the time of commission and the time of sentencing, to the benefit of the lesser punishment.

Treatment or punishment

12. Everyone has the right not to be subjected to any cruel and unusual treatment or punishment.

Self-crimination

13. A witness who testifies in any proceedings has the right not to have any incriminating evidence so given used to incriminate that witness in any other proceedings, except in a prosecution for perjury or for the giving of contradictory evidence.

Interpreter

14. A party or witness in any proceedings who does not understand or speak the language in which the proceedings are conducted or who is deaf has the right to the assistance of an interpreter.

Equality Rights

Equality before and under law and equal protection and benefit of law

15. (1) Every individual is equal before and under the law and has the right to the equal protection and equal benefit of the law without discrimination and, in particular, without discrimination based on race, national or ethnic origin, colour, religion, sex, age or mental or physical disability.

Affirmative action programs

(2) Subsection (1) does not preclude any law, program or activity that has as its object the amelioration of conditions of disadvantaged individuals or groups including those that are disadvantaged because of race, national or ethnic origin, colour, religion, sex, age or mental or physical disability.

Official Languages of Canada

Official languages of Canada

16. (1) English and French are the official languages of Canada and have equality of status and equal rights and privileges as to their use in all institutions of the Parliament and government of Canada.

Official languages of New Brunswick

(2) English and French are the official languages of New Brunswick and have equality of status and equal rights and privileges as to their use in all institutions of the legislature and government of New Brunswick.

Advancement of status and use

(3) Nothing in this Charter limits the authority of Parliament or a legislature to advance the equality of status or use of English and French.

Proceedings of Parliament

17. (1) Everyone has the right to use English or French in any debates and other proceedings of Parliament.

Proceedings of New Brunswick legislature

(2) Everyone has the right to use English or French in any debates and other proceedings of the legislature of New Brunswick.

Parliamentary statutes and records

18. (1) The statutes, records and journals of Parliament shall be printed and published in English and French and both language versions are equally authoritative.

New Brunswick statutes and records

(2) The statutes, records and journals of the legislature of New Brunswick shall be printed and published in English and French and both language versions are equally authoritative.

Proceedings in courts established by Parliament

19. (1) Either English or French may be used by any person in, or in any pleading in or process issuing from, any court established by Parliament.

Proceedings in New Brunswick courts

(2) Either English or French may be used by any person in, or in any pleading in or process issuing from, any court of New Brunswick.

Communications by public with federal institutions

20. (1) Any member of the public in Canada has the right to communicate with, and to receive available services from, any head or central office of an institution of the Parliament or government of Canada in English or French, and has the same right with respect to any other office of any such institution where

(*a*) there is a significant demand for communications with and services from that office in such language; or

(*b*) due to the nature of the office, it is reasonable that communications with and services from that office be available in both English and French.

Communications by public with New Brunswick institutions

(2) Any member of the public in New Brunswick has the right to communicate with, and to receive available services from, any office of an institution of the legislature or government of New Brunswick in English or French.

Continuation of existing constitutional provisions

21. Nothing in sections 16 to 20 abrogates or derogates from any right, privilege or obligation with respect to the English and French languages, or either of them, that exists or is continued by virtue of any other provision of the Constitution of Canada.

Rights and privileges preserved

22. Nothing in sections 16 to 20 abrogates or derogates from any legal or customary right or privilege acquired or enjoyed either before or after the coming into force of this Charter with respect to any language that is not English or French.

Minority Language Educational Rights

Language of instruction

23. (1) Citizens of Canada

(*a*) whose first language learned and still understood is that of the English or French linguistic minority population of the province in which they reside, or

(*b*) who have received their primary school instruction in Canada in English or French and reside in a province where the language in which they received that instruction is the language of the English or French linguistic minority population of the province,

have the right to have their children receive primary and secondary school instruction in that language in that province.

Continuity of language instruction

(2) Citizens of Canada of whom any child has received or is receiving primary or secondary school instruction in English or French in Canada, have the right to have all their children receive primary and secondary school instruction in the same language.

Application where numbers warrant

(3) The right of citizens of Canada under subsections (1) and (2) to have their children receive primary and secondary school instruction in the language of the English or French linguistic minority population of a province

(*a*) applies wherever in the province the number of children of citizens who have such a right is sufficient to warrant the provision to them out of public funds of minority language instruction; and

(*b*) includes, where the number of those children so warrants, the right to have them receive that instruction in minority language educational facilities provided out of public funds.

Enforcement

Enforcement of guaranteed rights and freedoms

24. (1) Anyone whose rights or freedoms, as guaranteed by this Charter, have been infringed or denied may apply to a court of competent jurisdiction to obtain such remedy as the court considers appropriate and just in the circumstances.

Exclusion of evidence bringing administration of justice into disrepute

(2) Where, in proceedings under subsection (1), a court concludes that evidence was obtained in a manner that infringed or denied any rights or freedoms guaranteed by this Charter, the evidence shall be excluded if it is established that, having regard to all the circumstances, the admission of it in the proceedings would bring the administration of justice into disrepute.

General

Aboriginal rights and freedoms not affected by Charter

25. The guarantee in this Charter of certain rights and freedoms shall not be construed so as to abrogate or derogate from any aboriginal, treaty or other rights or freedoms that pertain to the aboriginal peoples of Canada including

(*a*) any rights or freedoms that have been recognized by the Royal Proclamation of October 7, 1763; and

(*b*) any rights or freedoms that may be acquired by the aboriginal peoples of Canada by way of land claims settlement.

Other rights and freedoms not affected by Charter

26. The guarantee in this Charter of certain rights and freedoms shall not be construed as denying the existence of any other rights or freedoms that exist in Canada.

Multicultural heritage

27. This Charter shall be interpreted in a manner consistent with the preservation and enhancement of the multicultural heritage of Canadians.

Rights respecting certain schools preserved

28. Nothing in this Charter abrogates or derogates from any rights or privileges guaranteed by or under the Constitution of Canada, in respect of denominational, separate or dissentient schools.

Application to territories and territorial authorities

29. A reference in this Charter to a province or to the legislative assembly or legislature of a province shall be deemed to include a reference to the Yukon Territory and the Northwest Territories, or to the appropriate legislative authority thereof, as the case may be.

Legislative powers not extended

30. Nothing in this Charter extends the legislative powers of any body or authority.

Application of Charter

Application of Charter

31. (1) This Charter applies

(*a*) to the Parliament and government of Canada and to all matters within the authority of Parliament including all matters relating to the Yukon Territory and Northwest Territories; and

(*b*) to the legislature and government of each province and to all matters within the authority of the legislature of each province.

Exception

(2) Notwithstanding subsection (1), section 15 shall not have effect until three years after this Act, except Part VI, comes into force.

Citation

Citation

32. This Part may be cited as the *Canadian Charter of Rights and Freedoms*.

PART II
RIGHTS OF THE ABORIGINAL PEOPLES OF CANADA

Recognition of aboriginal and treaty rights

33. (1) The aboriginal and treaty rights of the aboriginal peoples of Canada are hereby recognized and affirmed.

Definition of "aboriginal peoples of Canada"

(2) In this Act, "aboriginal peoples of Canada" includes the Indian, Inuit and Métis peoples of Canada.

PART III
EQUALIZATION AND REGIONAL DISPARITIES

Commitment to promote equal opportunities

34. (1) Without altering the legislative authority of Parliament or of the provincial legislatures, or the rights of any of them with respect to the exercise of their legislative authority, Parliament and the legislatures, together with the government of Canada and the provincial governments, are committed to

(*a*) promoting equal opportunities for the well-being of Canadians;

(*b*) furthering economic development to reduce disparity in opportunities; and

(*c*) providing essential public services of reasonable quality to all Canadians.

Commitment respecting public services

(2) Parliament and the government of Canada are committed to the principle of making equalization payments to ensure that provincial governments have sufficient revenues to provide reasonably comparable levels of public services at reasonably comparable levels of taxation.

PART IV
CONSTITUTIONAL CONFERENCES

Constitutional conferences

35. (1) Until Part VI comes into force, a constitutional conference composed of the Prime Minister of Canada and the first ministers of the provinces shall be convened by the Prime Minister of Canada at least once in every year.

Participation of aboriginal peoples

(2) A conference convened under subsection (1) shall have included in its agenda an item respecting constitutional matters that directly affect the aboriginal peoples of Canada, including the identification and definition of the rights of those peoples to be included in the Constitution of Canada, and the Prime Minister of Canada shall invite representatives of those peoples to participate in the discussions on that item.

Participation of territories

(3) The Prime Minister of Canada shall invite elected representatives of the governments of the Yukon Territory and the Northwest Territories to participate in the discussions on any item on the agenda of a conference convened under subsection (1) that, in the opinion of the Prime Minister, directly affects the Yukon Territory and the Northwest Territories.

PART V

INTERIM AMENDMENT PROCEDURE AND RULES FOR ITS REPLACEMENT

Interim procedure for amending Constitution of Canada

36. Until Part VI comes into force, an amendment to the Constitution of Canada may be made by proclamation issued by the Governor General under the Great Seal of Canada where so authorized by resolutions of the Senate and House of Commons and by the legislative assembly or government of each province.

Amendment of provisions relating to some but not all provinces

37. Until Part VI comes into force, an amendment to the Constitution of Canada in relation to any provision that applies to one or more, but not all, provinces may be made by proclamation issued by the Governor General under the Great Seal of Canada where so authorized by resolutions of the Senate and House of Commons and by the legislative assembly or government of each province to which the amendment applies.

Amendments respecting certain language rights

38. (1) Notwithstanding section 40, an amendment to the Constitution of Canada

(*a*) adding a province as a province named in subsection 16(2), 17(2), 18(2), 19(2) or 20(2), or

(*b*) otherwise providing for any or all of the rights guaranteed or obligations imposed by any of those subsections to have application in a province to the extent and under the conditions stated in the amendment, may be made by proclamation issued by the Governor General under the Great Seal of Canada where so authorized by resolutions of the Senate and House of Commons and the legislative assembly of the province to which the amendment applies.

Initiation of amendment procedure

(2) The procedure for amendment prescribed by subsection (1) may be initiated only by the legislative assembly of the province to which the amendment applies.

Initiation of amendment procedures

39. (1) The procedures for amendment prescribed by sections 36 and 37 may be initiated either by the Senate or House of Commons or by the legislative assembly or government of a province.

Revocation of authorization

(2) A resolution made or other authorization given for the purposes of this Part may be revoked at any time before the issue of a proclamation authorized by it.

Limitation on use of interim amendment procedure

40. Sections 36 and 37 do not apply to an amendment to the Constitution of Canada where there is another provision in the Constitution for making the amendment, but the procedure prescribed by section 36 shall be used to amend the *Canadian Charter of Rights and Freedoms* and any provision for amending the Constitution, including this section.

Coming into force of Part VI

41. Part VI shall come into force

(*a*) with or without amendment, on such day as may be fixed by proclamation issued pursuant to the procedure prescribed by section 36, or

(*b*) on the day that is two years after the day this Act, except Part VI, comes into force,

whichever is the earlier day but, if a referendum is required to be held under subsection 42(3), Part VI shall come into force as provided in section 43.

Provincial alternative procedure

42. (1) The legislative assemblies of seven or more provinces that have, according to the then latest general census, combined populations of at least eighty per cent of the population of all the provinces may make a single proposal to substitute for paragraph 45(1)(*b*) such alternative as they consider appropriate.

Procedure for perfecting alternative

(2) One copy of an alternative proposed under subsection (1) may be deposited with the Chief Electoral Officer of Canada by each proposing province within two years after this Act, except Part VI, comes into force but, prior to the expiration of that period, any province that has deposited a copy may withdraw that copy.

Referendum

(3) Where copies of an alternative have been deposited as provided by subsection (2) and, on the day that is two years after this Act, except Part VI, comes into force, at least seven copies remain deposited by provinces that have, according to the then latest general census, combined populations of at least eighty per cent of the population of all the provinces, the government of Canada shall cause a referendum to be held within two years after that day to determine whether

(*a*) paragraph 45(1)(*b*) or any alternative thereto approved by resolutions of the Senate and House of Commons and deposited with the Chief Electoral Officer at least ninety days prior to the day on which the referendum is held, or

(*b*) the alternative proposed by the provinces,

shall be adopted.

Coming into force of Part VI where referendum held

43. Where a referendum is held under subsection 42(3), a proclamation under the Great Seal of Canada shall be issued within six months after the date of the referendum bringing Part VI into force with such modifications, if any, as are necessary to incorporate the proposal approved by a majority of the persons voting at the referendum and with such other changes as are reasonably consequential on the incorporation of that proposal.

Right to vote

44. (1) Every citizen of Canada has, subject only to such reasonable limits prescribed by law as can be demonstrably justified in a free and democratic society, the right to vote in a referendum held under subsection 42(3).

Establishment of Referendum Rules Commission

(2) If a referendum is required to be held under subsection 42(3), a Referendum Rules Commission shall forthwith be established by commission issued under the Great Seal of Canada consisting of

(*a*) the Chief Electoral Officer of Canada, who shall be chairman of the Commission;

(*b*) a person appointed by the Governor General in Council; and

(*c*) a person appointed by the Governor General in Council

(i) on the recommendation of the governments of a majority of the provinces, or

(ii) if the governments of a majority of the provinces do not recommend a candidate within thirty days after the Chief Electoral Officer of Canada requests such a recommendation, on the recommendation of the Chief Justice of Canada from among persons recommended by the governments of the provinces within thirty days after the expiration of the first mentioned thirty day period or, if none are so recommended, from among such persons as the Chief Justice considers qualified.

Duty of Commission

(3) A Referendum Rules Commission shall cause rules for the holding of a referendum under subsection 42(3) approved by a majority of the Commission to be laid before Parliament within sixty days after the Commission is established or, if Parliament is not then sitting, on any of the first ten days next thereafter that Parliament is sitting.

Rules for referendum

(4) Subject to subsection (1) and taking into consideration any rules approved by a Referendum Rules Commission in accordance with subsection (3), Parliament may enact laws respecting the rules applicable to the holding of a referendum under subsection 42(3).

Proclamation

(5) If Parliament does not enact laws under subsection (4) respecting the rules applicable to the holding of a referendum within sixty days after receipt of a recommendation from a Referendum Rules Commission, the rules recommended by the Commission shall forthwith be brought into force by proclamation issued by the Governor General under the Great Seal of Canada.

Computation of period

(6) Any period when Parliament is prorogued or dissolved shall not be counted in computing the sixty day period referred to in subsection (5).

Rules to have force of law

(7) Subject to subsection (1), rules made under this section have the force of law and prevail over other laws made under the Constitution of Canada to the extent of any inconsistency.

PART VI

PROCEDURE FOR AMENDING CONSTITUTION OF CANADA

General procedure for amending Constitution of Canada

45. (1) An amendment to the Constitution of Canada may be made by proclamation issued by the Governor General under the Great Seal of Canada where so authorized by

(*a*) resolutions of the Senate and House of Commons; and

(*b*) resolutions of the legislative assemblies of at least a majority of the provinces that includes

(i) every province that at any time before the issue of the proclamation had, according to any previous general census, a population of at least twenty-five per cent of the population of Canada,

(ii) two or more of the Atlantic provinces, and

(iii) two or more of the Western provinces that have in the aggregate, according to the then latest general census, a population of at least fifty per cent of the population of all of the Western provinces.

Definitions
"Atlantic provinces"

(2) In this section,

"Atlantic provinces" means the provinces of Nova Scotia, New Brunswick, Prince Edward Island and Newfoundland;

"Western provinces"

"Western provinces" means the provinces of Manitoba, British Columbia, Saskatchewan and Alberta.

Amendment authorized by referendum

46. (1) An amendment to the Constitution of Canada may be made by proclamation issued by the Governor General under the Great Seal of Canada where so authorized by a referendum held throughout Canada under subsection (2) at which

(*a*) a majority of persons voting thereat, and

(*b*) a majority of persons voting thereat in each of the provinces, resolutions of the legislative assemblies of which would be sufficient, together with resolutions of the Senate and House of Commons, to authorize the issue of a proclamation under subsection 45(1),

have approved the making of the amendment.

Authorization of referendum

(2) A referendum referred to in subsection (1) shall be held where directed by proclamation issued by the Governor General under the Great Seal of Canada, which proclamation may be issued where

(*a*) an amendment to the Constitution of Canada has been authorized under paragraph 45(1)(*a*) by resolutions of the Senate and House of Commons;

(*b*) the requirements of paragraph 45(1)(*b*) in respect of the proposed amendment have not been satisfied within twelve months after the passage of the resolutions of the Senate and House of Commons; and

(*c*) the issue of the proclamation has been authorized by the Governor General in Council.

Time limit for referendum

(3) A proclamation issued under subsection (2) in respect of a referendum shall provide for the referendum to be held within two years after the expiration of the twelve month period referred to in paragraph (*b*) of that subsection.

Amendment of provisions relating to some but not all provinces

47. An amendment to the Constitution of Canada in relation to any provision that applies to one or more, but not all, provinces may be made by proclamation issued by the Governor General under the Great Seal of Canada where so authorized by resolutions of the Senate and House of Commons and of the legislative assembly of each province to which the amendment applies.

Amendments respecting certain language rights

48. (1) Notwithstanding section 54, an amendment to the Constitution of Canada

(*a*) adding a province as a province named in subsection 16(2), 17(2), 18(2), 19(2) or 20(2), or

(*b*) otherwise providing for any or all of the rights guaranteed or obligations imposed by any of those subsections to have application in a province to the extent and under the conditions stated in the amendment,

may be made by proclamation issued by the Governor General under the Great Seal of Canada where so authorized by resolutions of the Senate and House of Commons and the legislative assembly of the province to which the amendment applies.

Initiation of amendment procedure

(2) The procedure for amendment prescribed by subsection (1) may be initiated only by the legislative assembly of the province to which the amendment applies.

Initiation of amendment procedures

49. (1) The procedures for amendment prescribed by subsection 45(1) and section 47 may be initiated either by the Senate or House of Commons or by the legislative assembly of a province.

Revocation of authorization

(2) A resolution made for the purposes of this Part may be revoked at any time before the issue of a proclamation authorized by it.

Right to vote

50. (1) Every citizen of Canada has, subject only to such reasonable limits prescribed by law as can be demonstrably justified in a free and democratic society, the right to vote in a referendum held under section 46.

Establishment of Referendum Rules Commission

(2) Where a referendum is to be held under section 46, a Referendum Rules Commission shall forthwith be established by commission issued under the Great Seal of Canada consisting of

(*a*) the Chief Electoral Officer of Canada, who shall be chairman of the Commission;

(*b*) a person appointed by the Governor General in Council; and

(*c*) a person appointed by the Governor General in Council

(i) on the recommendation of the governments of a majority of the provinces, or

(ii) if the governments of a majority of the provinces do not recommend a candidate within thirty days after the Chief Electoral Officer of Canada requests such a recommendation, on the recommendation of the Chief Justice of Canada from among persons recommended by the governments of the provinces within thirty days after the expiration of the first mentioned thirty day period or, if none are so recommended, from among such persons as the Chief Justice considers qualified.

Duty of Commission

(3) A Referendum Rules Commission shall cause rules for the holding of a referendum under section 46 approved by a majority of the Commission to be laid before Parliament within sixty days after the Commission is established or, if Parliament is not then sitting, on any of the first ten days next thereafter that Parliament is sitting.

Rules for referendum

(4) Subject to subsection (1) and taking into consideration any rules approved by a Referendum Rules Commission in accordance with subsection (3), Parliament may enact laws respecting the rules applicable to the holding of a referendum under section 46.

Proclamation

(5) If Parliament does not enact laws under subsection (4) respecting the rules applicable to the holding of a referendum within sixty days after receipt of a recommendation from a Referendum Rules Commission, the rules recommended by the Commission shall forthwith be brought into force by proclamation issued by the Governor General under the Great Seal of Canada.

Computation of period

(6) Any period when Parliament is prorogued or dissolved shall not be counted in computing the sixty day period referred to in subsection (5).

Rules to have force of law

(7) Subject to subsection (1), rules made under this section have the force of law and prevail over other laws made under the Constitution of Canada to the extent of any inconsistency.

Limitation on use of general amendment procedure

51. (1) The procedures prescribed by section 45, 46 or 47 do not apply to an amendment to the Constitution of Canada where there is another provision in the Constitution for making the amendment, but the procedures prescribed by section 45 or 46 shall, nevertheless, be used to amend any provision for amending the Constitution, including this section.

Idem

(2) The procedures prescribed by section 45 or 46 do not apply in respect of an amendment referred to in section 47.

Amendments by Parliament

52. Subject to section 54, Parliament may exclusively make laws amending the Constitution of Canada in relation to the executive government of Canada or the Senate or House of Commons.

Amendments by provincial legislatures

53. Subject to section 54, the legislature of each province may exclusively make laws amending the constitution of the province.

Matters requiring amendment under general amendment procedure

54. An amendment to the Constitution of Canada in relation to the following matters may be made only in accordance with a procedure prescribed by section 45 or 46:

(*a*) the office of the Queen, the Governor General and the Lieutenant Governor of a province;

(b) the *Canadian Charter of Rights and Freedoms*;

(c) the commitments relating to equalization and regional disparities set out in section 34;

(d) the powers of the Senate;

(e) the number of members by which a province is entitled to be represented in the Senate;

(f) the method of selecting Senators and the residence qualifications of Senators;

(g) the right of a province to a number of members in the House of Commons not less than the number of Senators representing the province; and

(h) the principles of proportionate representation of the provinces in the House of Commons prescribed by the Constitution of Canada.

Consequential amendments

55. (1) Class 1 of section 91 and class 1 of section 92 of the *Constitution Act, 1867* (formerly named the *British North America Act, 1867*), the *British North America (No. 2) Act, 1949*, referred to in item 22 of Schedule I to this Act and Parts IV and V of this Act are repealed.

Idem

(2) When Parts IV and V of this Act are repealed, this section may be repealed and this Act may be renumbered, consequential upon the repeal of those Parts and this section, by proclamation issued by the Governor General under the Great Seal of Canada.

PART VII

AMENDMENT TO THE CONSTITUTION ACT, 1867

Amendment to *Constitution Act, 1867*

56. (1) The *Constitution Act, 1867* (formerly named the *British North America Act, 1867*) is amended by adding thereto, immediately after section 92 thereof, the following heading and section:

"Non-Renewable Natural Resources, Forestry Resources and Electrical Energy

Laws respecting non-renewable natural resources, forestry resources and electrical energy

92A. (1) In each province, the legislature may exclusively make laws in relation to

(a) exploration for non-renewable natural resources in the province;

(b) development, conservation and management of non-renewable natural resources and forestry resources in the province, including laws in relation to the rate of primary production therefrom; and

(c) development, conservation and management of sites and facilities in the province for the generation and production of electrical energy.

Export from provinces of resources

(2) In each province, the legislature may make laws in relation to the export from the province to another part of Canada of the primary production from non-renewable natural resources and forestry resources in the province and the production from facilities in the province for the generation of electrical energy, but such laws may not authorize or provide for discrimination in prices or in supplies exported to another part of Canada.

Authority of Parliament

(3) Nothing in subsection (2) derogates from the authority of Parliament to enact laws in relation to the matters referred to in that subsection and, where such a law of Parliament and a law of a province conflict, the law of Parliament prevails to the extent of the conflict.

Taxation of resources

(4) In each province, the legislature may make laws in relation to the raising of money by any mode or system of taxation in respect of

(*a*) non-renewable natural resources and forestry resources in the province and the primary production therefrom, and

(*b*) sites and facilities in the province for the generation of electrical energy and the production therefrom,

whether or not such production is exported in whole or in part from the province, but such laws may not authorize or provide for taxation that differentiates between production exported to another part of Canada and production not exported from the province.

"Primary production"

(5) The expression "primary production" has the meaning assigned by the Sixth Schedule.

Existing powers or rights

(6) Nothing in subsections (1) to (5) derogates from any powers or rights that a legislature or government of a province had immediately before the coming into force of this section."

Idem

57. The said Act is further amended by adding thereto the following Schedule:

"THE SIXTH SCHEDULE

Primary Production from Non-Renewable Natural Resources and Forestry Resources

1. For the purposes of section 92A of this Act,

(*a*) production from a non-renewable natural resource is primary production therefrom if

(i) it is in the form in which it exists upon its recovery or severance from its natural state, or

(ii) it is a product resulting from processing or refining the resource, and is not a manufactured product or a product resulting from refining crude oil, refining upgraded heavy crude oil, refining gases or liquids derived from coal or refining a synthetic equivalent of crude oil; and

(*b*) production from a forestry resource is primary production therefrom if it consists of sawlogs, poles, lumber, wood chips, sawdust or any other primary wood product, or wood pulp, and is not a product manufactured from wood."

PART VIII

GENERAL

Primacy of Constitution of Canada

58. (1) The Constitution of Canada is the supreme law of Canada, and any law that is inconsistent with the provisions of the Constitution is, to the extent of the inconsistency, of no force or effect.

Constitution of Canada

(2) The Constitution of Canada includes

(*a*) the *Canada Act;*

(*b*) the Acts and orders referred to in Schedule I; and

(*c*) any amendment to any Act or order referred to in paragraph (*a*) or (*b*).

Amendments to Constitution of Canada

(3) Amendments to the Constitution of Canada shall be made only in accordance with the authority contained in the Constitution of Canada.

Repeals and new names

59. (1) The enactments referred to in Column I of Schedule I are hereby repealed or amended to the extent indicated in Column II thereof and, unless repealed, shall continue as law in Canada under the names set out in Column III thereof.

Consequential amendments

(2) Every enactment, except the *Canada Act*, that refers to an enactment referred to in Schedule I by the name in Column I thereof is hereby amended

by substituting for that name the corresponding name in Column III thereof, and any British North America Act not referred to in Schedule I may be cited as the *Constitution Act* followed by the year and number, if any, of its enactment.

French version of Constitution of Canada

60. A French version of the portions of the Constitution of Canada referred to in Schedule I shall be prepared by the Minister of Justice of Canada as expeditiously as possible and, when any portion thereof sufficient to warrant action being taken has been so prepared, it shall be put forward for enactment by proclamation issued by the Governor General under the Great Seal of Canada pursuant to the procedure then applicable to an amendment of the same provisions of the Constitution of Canada.

English and French versions of certain constitutional texts

61. Where any portion of the Constitution of Canada has been or is enacted in English and French or where a French version of any portion of the Constitution is enacted pursuant to section 60, the English and French versions of that portion of the Constitution are equally authoritative.

English and French versions of this Act

62. The English and French versions of this Act are equally authoritative.

Commencement

63. Subject to section 64, this Act shall come into force on a day to be fixed by proclamation issued by the Governor General under the Great Seal of Canada.

Exception

64. Part VI shall come into force as provided in Part V.

Short title and citations

65. This Schedule may be cited as the *Constitution Act, 1981*, and the Constitution Acts 1867 to 1975 (No. 2) and this Act may be cited together as the *Constitution Acts, 1867 to 1981*.

SCHEDULE I TO THE CONSTITUTION ACT, 1981
MODERNIZATION OF THE CONSTITUTION

Item	Column I Act Affected	Column II Amendment	Column III New Name
1.	British North America Act, 1867, 30-31 Vict., c. 3 (U.K.)	(1) Section 1 is repealed and the following substituted therefor: "1. This Act may be cited as the *Constitution Act, 1867*." (2) Section 20 is repealed.	Constitution Act, 1867
2.	An Act to amend and continue the Act 32-33 Victoria chapter 3; and to establish and provide for the Government of the Province of Manitoba, 1870, 33 Vict., c. 3 (Can.)	(1) The long title is repealed and the following substituted therefor: "*Manitoba Act, 1870*." (2) Section 20 is repealed.	Manitoba Act, 1870
3.	Order of Her Majesty in Council admitting Rupert's Land and the North-Western Territory into the union, dated the 23rd day of June, 1870.		Rupert's Land and North-Western Territory Order

Item	Act Affected	Amendment	New Name
4.	Order of Her Majesty in Council admitting British Columbia into the Union, dated the 16th day of May, 1871.		British Columbia Terms of Union
5.	British North America Act, 1871, 34-35 Vict., c. 28 (U.K.)	Section 1 is repealed and the following substituted therefor: "1. This Act may be cited as the *Constitution Act, 1871*."	Constitution Act, 1871
6.	Order of Her Majesty in Council admitting Prince Edward Island into the Union, dated the 26th day of June, 1873.		Prince Edward Island Terms of Union
7.	Parliament of Canada Act, 1875, 38-39 Vict., c. 38 (U.K.)		Parliament of Canada Act, 1875
8.	Order of Her Majesty in Council admitting all British possessions and Territories in North America and islands adjacent thereto into the Union, dated the 31st day of July, 1880.		Adjacent Territories Order
9.	British North America Act, 1886, 49-50 Vict., c. 35 (U.K.)	Section 3 is repealed and the following substituted therefor: "3. This Act may be cited as the *Constitution Act, 1886*."	Constitution Act, 1886
10.	Canada (Ontario Boundary) Act, 1889, 52-53 Vict., c. 28 (U.K.)		Canada (Ontario Boundary) Act, 1889
11.	Canadian Speaker (Appointment of Deputy) Act, 1895, 2nd Sess., 59 Vict., c. 3 (U.K.)	The Act is repealed.	
12.	The Alberta Act, 1905, 4-5 Edw. VII, c. 3 (Can.)		Alberta Act
13.	The Saskatchewan Act, 1905, 4-5 Edw. VII, c. 42 (Can.)		Saskatchewan Act

Item	Act Affected	Amendment	New Name
14.	British North America Act, 1907, 7 Edw. VII, c. 11 (U.K.)	Section 2 is repealed and the following substituted therefor: "2. This Act may be cited as the *Constitution Act, 1907.*"	Constitution Act, 1907
15.	British North America Act, 1915, 5-6 Geo. V, c. 45 (U.K.)	Section 3 is repealed and the following substituted therefor: "3. This Act may be cited as the *Constitution Act, 1915.*"	Constitution Act, 1915
16.	British North America Act, 1930, 20-21 Geo. V, c. 26 (U.K.)	Section 3 is repealed and the following substituted therefor: "3. This Act may be cited as the *Constitution Act, 1930.*"	Constitution Act, 1930
17.	Statute of Westminster, 1931, 22 Geo. V, c. 4 (U.K.)	In so far as they apply to Canada, (*a*) section 4 is repealed; and (*b*) subsection 7(1) is repealed.	Statute of Westminster, 1931
18.	British North America Act, 1940, 3-4 Geo. VI, c. 36 (U.K.)	Section 2 is repealed and the following substituted therefor: "2. This Act may be cited as the *Constitution Act, 1940.*"	Constitution Act, 1940
19.	British North America Act, 1943, 6-7 Geo. VI, c. 30 (U.K.)	The Act is repealed.	
20.	British North America Act, 1946, 9-10 Geo. VI, c. 63 (U.K.)	The Act is repealed.	
21.	British North America Act, 1949, 12-13 Geo. VI, c. 22 (U.K.)	Section 3 is repealed and the following substituted therefor: "3. This Act may be cited as the *Newfoundland Act.*"	Newfoundland Act
22.	British North America (No. 2) Act, 1949, 13 Geo. VI, c. 81 (U.K.)	The Act is repealed (effective when section 55 of the *Constitution Act, 1981* comes into force)	
23.	British North America Act, 1951, 14-15 Geo. VI, c. 32 (U.K.)	The Act is repealed.	
24.	British North America Act, 1952, 1 Eliz. II, c. 15 (Can.)	The Act is repealed.	

Item	Act Affected	Amendment	New Name
25.	British North America Act, 1960, 9 Eliz. II, c. 2 (U.K.)	Section 2 is repealed and the following substituted therefor: "2. This Act may be cited as the *Constitution Act, 1960*."	Constitution Act, 1960
26.	British North America Act, 1964, 12-13 Eliz. II, c. 73 (U.K.)	Section 2 is repealed and the following substituted therefor: "2. This Act may be cited as the *Constitution Act, 1964*."	Constitution Act, 1964
27.	British North America Act, 1965, 14 Eliz. II, c. 4, Part I (Can.)	Section 2 is repealed and the following substituted therefor: "2. This Part may be cited as the *Constitution Act, 1965*."	Constitution Act, 1965
28.	British North America Act, 1974, 23 Eliz. II, c. 13, Part I (Can.)	Section 3, as amended by 25-26 Eliz. II, c. 28, s. 38(1) (Can.) is repealed and the following substituted therefor: "3. This Part may be cited as the *Constitution Act, 1974*."	Constitution Act, 1974
29.	British North America Act, 1975, 23-24 Eliz. II, c. 28, Part I (Can.)	Section 3, as amended by 25-26 Eliz. II, c. 28, s. 31 (Can.) is repealed and the following substituted therefor: "3. This Part may be cited as the *Constitution Act (No. 1), 1975*."	Constitution Act (No. 1), 1975
30.	British North America Act (No. 2), 1975, 23-24 Eliz. II, c. 53 (Can.)	Section 3 is repealed and the following substituted therefor: "3. This Act may be cited as the *Constitution Act (No. 2), 1975*."	Constitution Act (No. 2), 1975

45. Premiers' Conference, Ottawa, Ontario, April 16, 1981

(a) News Release, April 16, 1981

Document: 850-19/001

Ottawa — Premiers from eight Canadian provinces today signed a new and historic Canadian patriation plan including an amending formula for the constitution.

Alberta, British Columbia, Manitoba, Newfoundland, Nova Scotia, Prince Edward Island, Quebec and Saskatchewan were signatories to the "Constitutional Accord: Canadian Patriation Plan".

It calls for patriation of the constitution and, as part of the patriation plan, acceptance of an amending formula that would ensure all future amendments are made in Canada.

In the constitutional accord the signing provinces agree to:
* patriate rapidly the Constitution of Canada;
* adopt a new amending formula for the Canadian Constitution;
* enter into intensive constitutional negotiations during a three-year period based on the new amending formula; and
* discontinue all court action on this matter.

The Canadian patriation plan is conditional upon the Government of Canada withdrawing the proposed joint address on the constitution.

Under the Canadian patriation plan the United Kingdom parliament would end its trusteeship over the British North America Act without damaging its historically fine relationship with Canada.

The new amending formula combines flexibility and stability; this is a principal feature of the accord.

Under the formula, all amendments to the constitution must have approval of the Canadian parliament, except those related to the internal constitution of a province.

Most amendments would require legislative approval of two-thirds of the provinces (seven) representing at least 50 per cent of the population of the ten provinces. This establishes legal equality amongst all provinces.

When an amendment diminishes a province's rights, privileges, or powers, an individual province may choose to retain these rights, privileges and powers by obtaining the approval of a majority vote of the total number of members of its legislature; and such a province would then receive adequate financial compensation.

For a limited number of important matters including those relating to the Crown, parliamentary representation, language and the composition of the Supreme Court, the consent of all provincial legislatures would be required.

This amending formula is demonstrably preferable for all Canadians to that proposed by the federal government because it:
* recognizes the equality of provinces within Canada.
* avoids the need for a referendum to choose an amending formula or as a method of amending the constitution.
* removes the absolute veto power that the federal government proposes to give the senate over constitutional reform, including senate reform.

The premiers agreed that together with the federal government an agenda for constitutional change could be immediately drawn up. This would include all the subjects that were discussed during last summer's constitutional conferences.

The eight premiers pointed out that their agreement on the Canadian constitution shows clearly and positively that significant constitutional progress is possible when all parties approach the issue with sincerity and goodwill.

The premiers are prepared to go forward with this plan before their respective Legislatures upon acceptance by the Prime Minister of Canada.

By working together, the federal and provincial governments now have an opportunity to make a modern, made-in-Canada constitution, the premiers said.

Details of the accord and amending formula are being sent simultaneously to the prime minister and the premiers of Ontario and New Brunswick for their active consideration.

The eight premiers are now waiting for the prime minister to call a constitutional conference.

(b) Constitutional Accord: Canadian Patriation Plan, April 16, 1981

Document: 850-19/002

WHEREAS Canada is a mature and independent country with a federal system of government,

AND WHEREAS the Parliament of the United Kingdom has retained, at the request of the Parliament of Canada and with the approval of the Provinces, residual power to amend certain parts of the British North America Acts upon receiving a proper request from Canada,

AND WHEREAS it is fitting and proper for the Constitution of Canada to be amendable in all respects by action taken wholly within Canada,

AND WHEREAS the full exercise of the sovereignty of Canada requires a Canadian amending procedure in keeping with the federal nature of Canada,

NOW THEREFORE, the Governments subscribing to this Accord agree as follows:

1. To patriate the Constitution of Canada by taking the necessary steps through the Parliament of Canada and the Legislatures of the Provinces;
2. To accept, as part of patriation, the amending formula attached to this Accord as the formula for making all future amendments to the Constitution of Canada;
3. To embark upon an intensive three-year period of constitutional renewal based on the new amending formula and without delay to determine an agenda following acceptance of this Accord; and
4. To discontinue court proceedings now pending in Canada relative to the proposed Joint Address on the Constitution now before Parliament.

The Canadian Patriation Plan is conditional upon the Government of Canada withdrawing the proposed Joint Address on the Constitution now before Parliament and subscribing to this Accord.

The Provinces of New Brunswick and Ontario are invited to sign this Accord.

Dated at Ottawa this 16th day of April, 1981.

Signed on behalf of the under-mentioned Governments, to be followed by ratification by the respective Legislatures or National Assembly. [*Note*: Document is not signed.]

ALBERTA
Peter Lougheed, Premier

BRITISH COLUMBIA
William R. Bennett, Premier

MANITOBA
Sterling R. Lyon, Premier

NEWFOUNDLAND
Brian A. Peckford, Premier

NOVA SCOTIA
John M. Buchanan, Premier

PRINCE EDWARD ISLAND
J. Angus MacLean, Premier

QUÉBEC
René Lévesque, Premier

SASKATCHEWAN
Allan E. Blakeney, Premier

(c) Amending Formula for the Constitution of Canada and Delegation of Legislative Authority: Text and Explanatory Notes, April 16, 1981

Document: 850-19/004

PART A
AMENDING FORMULA FOR THE CONSTITUTION OF CANADA

EXPLANATORY NOTES

GENERAL COMMENT

The amending formula which is part of the Canadian patriation plan agreed to by eight governments in Ottawa on April 16, 1981, is the result of intensive discussions among the governments of Alberta, British Columbia, Manitoba, Newfoundland, Nova Scotia, Prince Edward Island, Quebec and Saskatchewan.

In developing the formula several important principles were recognized:

1. All amendments to the Constitution of Canada, except those related to the internal constitution of the provinces, require the agreement of the Parliament of Canada.

2. Any formula must recognize the constitutional equality of provinces as equal partners in Confederation.

3. Any amending formula must protect the diversity of Canada.

4. Any constitutional amendment taking away an existing provincial area of jurisdiction or proprietary right should not be imposed on any province not desiring it.

5. Any amending formula must strike a balance between stability and flexibility.

6. Some amendments are of such fundamental importance to the country that all eleven governments must agree.

During discussions, it was recognized that more than one method of amending the Constitution would be necessary. Accordingly, this formula contains different methods depending on the nature of the amendment.

The eleven sections described as "Part A—Amending Formula for the Constitution of Canada" are designed to contain a full and complete procedure for the future amendment of the Constitution of Canada in all respects. The provisions contained in Part A would replace both the limited amending formulas now contained in sections 91(1) and 92(1) of the B.N.A. Act as well as the United Kingdom Parliament's residual responsibility for amending certain aspects of the Canadian Constitution.

This amending formula would apply not only to the B.N.A. Act, 1867, and amendments made to it since that date, but also to the other parts of the Constitution of Canada, including the constitutional statutes and Orders-in-Council which relate to the entry into Canada of particular provinces, for example, The Manitoba Act, 1870, the Terms of Union admitting British Columbia in 1871, and Prince Edward Island in 1873, The Alberta Act, 1905, The Saskatchewan Act, 1905, and the Terms of Union with Newfoundland, 1949.

This amending formula is clearly preferable to the one proposed by the federal government for a number of reasons: 1) it recognizes the constitutional equality of each of Canada's provinces; 2) it gives the Senate only a suspensive rather than an absolute veto over constitutional amendment; 3) it omits the referendum provision opposed by many as being inappropriate to the Canadian federal system.

PART A

Amending Formula for the Constitution of Canada	Explanatory Notes
1. (1) Amendments to the Constitution of Canada may be made by proclamation issued by the Governor General under the Great Seal of Canada when so authorized by:	1. (1) This provision is known as the general amending formula. It would apply to all amendments to the Constitution of Canada unless another method of amendment is specifically provided for elsewhere in Part A.

Amending Formula for the Constitution of Canada	**Explanatory Notes**

(*a*) resolutions of the Senate and House of Commons; and

(*b*) resolutions of the Legislative Assemblies of at least two-thirds of the provinces that have in the aggregate, according to the latest decennial census, at least fifty per cent of the population of all of the provinces

This provision requires that an amendment be supported by the Parliament of Canada and by at least seven provincial Legislatures representing at least 50% of the total population of all of the provinces.

(2) Any amendment made under subsection (1) derogating from the legislative powers, the proprietary rights or any other rights or privileges of the Legislature or government of a province shall require a resolution supported by a vote of a majority of the Members of each of the Senate, of the House of Commons, and of the requisite number of Legislative Assemblies.

(2) Any amendment which diminishes provincial rights or powers must be supported by a majority of the actual membership of each of the Senate, the House of Commons, and the requisite number of Legislatures.

(3) Any amendment made under subsection (1) derogating from the legislative powers, the proprietary rights, or any other rights or privileges of the Legislature or government of a Province shall not have effect in any province whose Legislative Assembly has expressed its dissent thereto by resolution supported by a majority of the Members prior to the issue of the proclamation, provided, however, that Legislative Assembly, by resolution supported by a majority of the Members, may subsequently withdraw its dissent and approve the amendment.

(3) If an amendment, proposed under the general amending formula, would diminish the existing legislative powers, proprietary rights or any other rights or privileges of provincial Legislatures or governments, a province has two decisions to make:

(*a*) whether or not to approve the amendment, and

(*b*) if the amendment is approved under subsection (1), whether to retain its existing powers, rights or privileges by dissenting from its application within that province.

In this case, the Legislature of the province would have to express its dissent by adopting a Resolution supported by a majority of the total number of members of the Assembly. Such a procedure is commonly designated an "opting-out" provision.

A province wishing to use this "opting-out" procedure must do so before the proclamation making the amendment is issued. Also the opting-out provision applies only where the proposed amendment derogates from, or diminishes, the legislative powers, proprietary rights or any other rights and privileges of the Legislature or government of a province. Proprietary rights includes natural resources and assets. Broadly speaking, those powers, rights and privileges are assigned to the provinces by sections 92, 93 and 109 of the British North America Act.

Amending Formula for the Constitution of Canada	Explanatory Notes

In summary, no single province should be able to block an amendment desired by at least seven other provinces and the federal government. Conversely, that particular province would not be required to have this kind of amendment apply to it if it found the amendment to be unacceptable.

2. (1) No proclamation shall issue under section 1 before the expiry of one year from the date of the passage of the resolution initiating the amendment procedure, unless the Legislative Assembly of every province has previously adopted a resolution of assent or dissent.

2. (1) This provision ensures that a proposed amendment cannot come into force before one year has expired from the time of initiation unless all provinces have expressed their views by resolution prior to that time, and the necessary consents have been obtained. Thus, no amendment can be made until all Legislatures have had an opportunity to debate the proposed amendment.

(2) No proclamation shall issue under section 1 after the expiry of three years from the date of the passage of the resolution initiating the amendment procedure.

(2) This provision ensures that a proposed amendment must gain the requisite level of support within a reasonable length of time from initiation or it will lapse.

(3) Subject to this section, the Government of Canada shall advise the Governor General to issue a proclamation forthwith upon the passage of the requisite resolutions under this Part.

(3) This provision ensures that a proposed amendment, enjoying the requisite level of support, is proclaimed.

3. In the event that a province dissents from an amendment conferring legislative jurisdiction on Parliament, the Government of Canada shall provide reasonable compensation to the government of that province, taking into account the per capita costs to exercise that jurisdiction in the provinces which have approved the amendment.

3. If a province dissents under section 1(2) from a constitutional amendment that confers legislative jurisdiction on Parliament, then this provision requires the Government of Canada to provide reasonable compensation to the government of that province. Such compensation would take into account the per capita costs incurred by the federal government in those provinces where the federal jurisdiction is exercised.

This provision is designed to prevent a taxpayer, resident in a province to which the amendment does not apply, from paying twice: first, in his or her federal tax bill and second, to the province which continues to exercise the jurisdiction.

4. Amendments to the Constitution of Canada in relation to any provision that applies to one or more, but not all, of the provinces, including any alteration to boundaries between provinces or the use of the English or the French language within that province may be made only by proclamation issued by the Governor General under the Great Seal

4. The purpose of this provision is to allow the Parliament of Canada and the Legislature of a province or provinces to amend the Constitution in relation to any provision that applies to one or more but not all, of the provinces. Such an amendment would only require the approval of the provincial Legislatures affected and Parliament. Instances of

Amending Formula for the Constitution of Canada

Explanatory Notes

of Canada when so authorized by resolutions of the Senate and House of Commons and the Legislative Assembly of every province to which the amendment applies.

matters falling within that category are, for example, the provisions of the Manitoba Act, the Terms of Union of Prince Edward Island and British Columbia, The Saskatchewan Act, The Alberta Act, and the Terms of Union with Newfoundland. This provision ensures that any such amendment has the consent of the affected province or provinces.

Alterations to boundaries between provinces would also be dealt with under this section and could be made by the approval of the Legislatures of those provinces affected and the Parliament of Canada.

Any amendments to the Constitution in relation to the use of the English or French language within a province could be made by resolution of the Legislature of the province affected and the federal Parliament. This provision would apply to those portions of section 133 of the B.N.A. Act which relate to the province of Quebec and those language provisions of the Manitoba Act which apply to Manitoba. This provision could make section 133 applicable to a province where it does not apply now but which wishes it to be applicable therein.

5. An amendment may be made without a resolution of the Senate authorizing the issue of the proclamation if, within one hundred and eighty days after the passage by the House of Commons of a resolution authorizing its issue, the Senate has not passed such a resolution and if, after the expiration of those one hundred and eighty days, the House of Commons again passed the resolution, but any period when Parliament is dissolved shall not be counted in computing the one hundred and eighty days.

5. Under this provision, the Senate of Canada will have only a suspensive veto over constitutional amendments. If the Senate refuses or fails to authorize the issue of a proclamation within one hundred and eighty days of the House of Commons passing a resolution authorizing its issue, the amendment may still proceed provided the matter is again submitted to and passed by the House of Commons.

6. (1) The procedures for amendment may be initiated by the Senate, by the House of Commons, or by the Legislative Assembly of a province.

6. (1) Self-explanatory.

   (2) A resolution authorizing an amendment may be revoked at any time before the issue of a proclamation.

   (2) This section permits either of the Houses of Parliament or any Legislature to revoke an affirmative resolution before the proclamation implementing the proposed amendment is issued. However, once the proclamation is issued, an affirmative resolution may not be revoked.

   (3) A resolution of dissent may be revoked at any time before or after the issue of a proclamation.

   (3) This provision allows a resolution disapproving a proposed amendment to be revoked at any

Amending Formula for the Constitution of Canada	Explanatory Notes
	time either before or after the issue of a proclamation. This is designed to allow provinces which have dissented from an amendment to revoke their dissent subsequently and be subject to the amendment.
7. Subject to sections 9 and 10, Parliament may exclusively make laws amending the Constitution of Canada in relation to the executive government of Canada or the Senate and House of Commons.	7. This provision allows Parliament, acting alone, to amend those parts of the Constitution of Canada that relate solely to the operation of the executive government of Canada at the federal level or to the Senate or House of Commons. Some aspects of certain institutions important for maintaining the federal-provincial balance, such as the Senate and the Supreme Court, are excluded from this provision and are covered in sections 9 and 10. This provision is intended to replace section 91(1) of the B.N.A. Act.
8. Subject to section 9, the Legislature of each province may exclusively make laws amending the constitution of the province.	8. This provision allows the Legislature of a province, acting alone, to amend the provincial Constitution and is intended to replace section 92(1) of the B.N.A. Act. Exceptions to this provision include the office of the Lieutenant-Governor.
9. Amendments to the Constitution of Canada in relation to the following matters may be made only by proclamation issued by the Governor General under the Great Seal of Canada when authorized by resolutions of the Senate and House of Commons and of the Legislative Assemblies of all of the provinces:	9. This section recognizes that some matters are of such fundamental importance that amendments in relation to them should require the consent of all the provincial Legislatures and Parliament.
(a) the office of the Queen, of the Governor General or of the Lieutenant Governor;	(a) Self-explanatory.
(b) the right of a province to a number of members in the House of Commons not less than the number of Senators representing the province at the time this provision comes into force;	(b) This clause relates to the protection provided to provinces under section 51 A of the B.N.A. Act.
(c) the use of the English or French language except with respect to section 4;	(c) This clause would require any changes to the Constitution related to the use of the English or French language either within the institutions of the federal government or nationwide to require the unanimous approval of Parliament and all the Legislatures.
(d) the composition of the Supreme Court of Canada;	(d) This clause would ensure that the Supreme Court of Canada is comprised of judges a proportion of whom are drawn from the Bar or Bench of Quebec and are, therefore, trained in the civil law. Other aspects of the Supreme Court of Canada are dealt with in section 10.

Amending Formula for the Constitution of Canada	**Explanatory Notes**

(e) an amendment to any of the provisions of this Part.

(e) This clause provides that any amendment to the amending formula itself requires unanimous approval of Parliament and all of the provincial Legislatures.

10. Amendments to the Constitution of Canada in relation to the following matters shall be made in accordance with the provisions of section 1 (1) of this Part and sections 1 (2) and 1 (3) shall not apply:

10. Amendments to the Constitution in respect of the matters listed in section 10 may be achieved if approved by 1) the House of Commons and Senate of Canada and 2) at least seven provinces having, in the aggregate, at least 50% of the total population of all the provinces according to the latest decennial census. The types of amendments listed in this section are not subject to provincial non-application and, therefore, apply nationwide.

(a) the principle of proportionate representation of the provinces in the House of Commons;

(a) Self-explanatory.

(b) the powers of the Senate and the method of selection of members thereto;

(b) Self-explanatory.

(c) the number of members by which a province is entitled to be represented in the Senate and the residence qualifications of Senators;

(c) Self-explanatory.

(d) the Supreme Court of Canada, except with respect to clause *(d)* of section 9.

(d) This clause refers to all amendments relating to the Supreme Court of Canada except the composition of the Court which is dealt with in section 9, clause *(d)*. The Supreme Court of Canada is established by a law of Parliament under section 101 of the B.N.A. Act and not by the Constitution itself. This clause anticipates constitutional amendments relating to the Court. Such amendments would apply nationwide.

(e) the extension of existing provinces into the Territories;

(e) and *(f)* The alteration of boundaries between provinces is dealt with in section 4. The extension of existing provinces or the establishment of new provinces are dealt with in clauses *(e)* and *(f)*.

(f) notwithstanding any other law or practice, the establishment of new provinces;

(g) an amendment to any of the provisions of Part B.

(g) This clause deals with amendments to the delegation of legislative authority provisions contained in Part B.

11. A constitutional conference composed of the Prime Minister of Canada and the First Ministers of the provinces shall be convened by the Prime Minister of Canada within fifteen years of the enactment of this Part to review the provisions for the amendment of the Constitution of Canada.

11. This section provides that the First Ministers of Canada shall meet within fifteen years to review the amending formula itself. This is a minimum requirement and does not preclude other constitutional conferences.

PART B
DELEGATION OF LEGISLATIVE AUTHORITY

EXPLANATORY NOTES

GENERAL COMMENTS

Part B allows for the delegation of legislative authority from one order of government to the other, something which is not now provided for in the B.N.A. Act. Delegation of legislative authority would add considerable flexibility to Canada's constitutional arrangements and could reduce the duplication of administrative services.

This Part would permit the Parliament of Canada to consent to the making of a provincial law in an area of federal responsibility. Conversely, it would permit one or more provinces to consent to the making of a federal law in an area of provincial responsibility. There is also provision for the consents to relate to all laws in relation to a particular matter of jurisdiction, as distinct from a particular statute. In the event of delegation, financial compensation is payable to the governments exercising delegated power.

Delegation could conceivably be used to test the effect of transferring responsibility for a certain jurisdictional area before proceeding in a more general way through the amending formula itself. Finally, a delegation of power may be revoked upon two years' notice.

PART B

Delegation of Legislative Authority	Explanatory Notes
1. Notwithstanding anything in the Constitution of Canada, Parliament may make laws in relation to a matter coming within the legislative jurisdiction of a province, if prior to the enactment, the Legislature of at least one province has consented to the operation of such a statute in that province.	1. This section permits one or more provinces to consent to Parliament enacting a law in an area of provincial jurisdiction.
2. A statute passed pursuant to section 1 shall not have effect in any province unless the Legislature of that province has consented to its operation.	2. Statutes passed by the federal Parliament pursuant to section 1 only have effect in those provinces that have consented to their operation.
3. The Legislature of a province may make laws in the province in relation to a matter coming within the legislative jurisdiction of Parliament, if, prior to the enactment, Parliament has consented to the enactment of such a statute by the Legislature of that province.	3. This is the converse of section 1. It permits Parliament to consent to one or more provinces enacting a law in an area of federal jurisdiction.
4. A consent given under this Part may relate to a specific statute or to all laws in relation to a particular matter.	4. This section provides that the delegation may be in respect to either a whole matter of constitutional jurisdiction or merely a specific statute.
5. A consent given under this Part may be revoked upon giving two years' notice, and (a) if the consent was given under section 1, any law made by Parliament to which the consent relates shall thereupon cease to have effect in the province revoking the consent, but the revocation of the consent does not affect the operation of that law in any other province;	5. This section allows for the delegation of authority to be revoked provided two years' notice is given. After the two years, the law ceases to have force and effect within those jurisdictions that have revoked the consent. In the case of a delegation to the Parliament of Canada by several provinces, the federal law ceases to have effect only in those provinces which have revoked the consent.

(*b*) if the consent was given under section 3, any law made by the Legislature of a province to which the consent relates shall thereupon cease to have effect.

6. In the event of a delegation of legislative authority from Parliament to the Legislature of a province, the Government of Canada shall provide reasonable compensation to the government of that province, taking into account the per capita costs to exercise that jurisdiction.

7. In the event of a delegation of legislative authority from the Legislature of a province to Parliament, the government of the province shall provide reasonable compensation to the Government of Canada, taking into account the per capita costs to exercise that jurisdiction.

6. and 7. These are reciprocal sections which would provide that the order of government that acquires the right to pass a law through the delegation process is entitled to be provided with reasonable compensation from the other order of government for the exercise of that jurisdiction. The definition of reasonable compensation must take into account the per capita costs of exercising that jurisdiction.

46. House of Commons and Senate Debates, February–May, 1981

(a) Amendments to the Proposed Resolution for a Joint Address to Her Majesty the Queen Respecting the Constitution of Canada, as Moved in the House of Commons and the Senate*

HOUSE OF COMMONS

Debates, Tuesday, February 17, 1981

Mr. Epp, seconded by Mr. Baker (Nepean — Carleton), moved in amendment thereto, — That the motion be amended in Schedule B of the proposed resolution by deleting Clause 46, and by making all necessary changes to the Schedule consequential thereto.   p. 7388

April 23, 1981

And the question being put on the amendment, it was negatived on the following division:
(Yeas, 98; Nays, 170) p. 9469

Debates, Thursday, April 23, 1981

Mr. Knowles, seconded by Mr. Ittinuar, moved in amendment thereto, — That the proposed *Constitution Act, 1981* be amended by

(*a*) adding immediately after line 40 on page 9 the following section:

"28. Notwithstanding anything in this Charter, the rights and freedoms referred to in it are guaranteed equally to male and female persons.";

(*b*) renumbering the subsequent clauses accordingly;

(*c*) adding to clause 54 immediately after line 20 on page 20 the following paragraph:

"(*c*) the rights of the aboriginal peoples of Canada set out in Part II;"; and

(*d*) relettering paragraphs (*c*) to (*h*) of clause 54 as paragraphs (*d*) to (*i*).

And the question being put on the amendment, it was agreed to on the following division:
(Yeas, 265; Nays, Nil) pp. 9470–1

Debates, Thursday, April 23, 1981

Mr. Baker (Nepean — Carleton), seconded by Mr. Clark (Yellowhead), moved in amendment thereto, — That Motion Number 36 in the name of the Minister of Justice, be amended as follows:

(*a*) by deleting Clause 1 of Part I and substituting the following therefor:

1. Affirming that
   (*a*) the Canadian nation is founded upon principles that acknowledge the supremacy of God, the dignity and worth of the human person and the position of the family in a society of free individuals and free institutions, and
   (*b*) individuals and institutions remain free only when freedom is founded upon respect for moral and spiritual values and the rule of law,
the *Canadian Charter of Rights and Freedoms* guarantees the rights and freedoms set out in it subject only to such reasonable limits prescribed by law as can be demonstrably justified in a free and democratic society."

(*b*) by deleting Clause 7 of Part I and substituting the following therefor:

"7. Everyone has the right to life, liberty, security of the person and enjoyment of property and the right not to be deprived thereof except in accordance with the principles of fundamental justice."

(*c*) by adding after Clause 27 of Part I the following new Clause:

---

* Compiled by Janet Brooks, Bibliographies and Compilations Section, Information and Reference Branch, Library of Parliament, Ottawa.

"28. Notwithstanding anything in this Charter, the rights and freedoms set out in it are guaranteed equally to male and female persons."

(*d*) by adding after new Clause 28 of Part I the following new Clause:

"29. Nothing in this Charter affects the authority of Parliament to legislate in respect of abortion and capital punishment."

(*e*) by deleting Clause 35 of Part IV and substituting the following therefor:

"35. (1) No later than two months after the coming into force of this Act, the Prime Minister of Canada and the first ministers of the provinces shall constitute a permanent conference to be designated the "Constitutional Conference of Canada" hereinafter referred to as the "Conference".

(2) The Conference shall examine all Canadian constitutional laws and propose amendments necessary for the development of the Canadian federation.

(3) A Conference convened under subsection (1) shall have included in its agenda an item respecting constitutional matters that directly affect the aboriginal peoples of Canada, including the identification and definition of the rights of those peoples to be included in the Constitution of Canada and the Prime Minister of Canada shall invite representatives of those peoples to participate in the discussions on that item.

(4) The Prime Minister of Canada shall invite elected representatives of the governments of the Yukon Territory and the Northwest Territories to participate in the discussions on any item on the agenda of a Conference convened under subsection (1) that, in the opinion of the Prime Minister, directly affects the Yukon Territory and the Northwest Territories.

(5) The Conference shall meet at least twice each year.

(6) The Conference shall be assisted by the Continuing Committee of Ministers on the Constitution."

(*f*) by deleting Part V.

(*g*) by deleting Clause 45 of Part VI and substituting the following therefor:

45. (1) An amendment to the Constitution of Canada may be made by proclamation issued by the Governor General under the Great Seal of Canada where so authorized by

(*a*) resolutions of the Senate and House of Commons; and

(*b*) resolutions of the legislative assemblies of at least two-thirds of the provinces that have in the aggregate, according to the then latest decennial census, at least fifty per cent of the population of all the provinces.

(2) Any amendment made under subsection (1) derogating from the legislative powers, the proprietary rights or any other rights or privileges of the legislature or government of a province shall require a resolution supported by a vote of a majority of the members of each of the Senate, of the House of Commons, and of the requisite number of legislative assemblies.

(3) Any amendment made under subsection (1) derogating from the legislative powers, the proprietary rights or any other rights or privileges of the legislature or government of a province shall not have effect, financially or otherwise, in and for any province whose legislative assembly has expressed its dissent thereto by resolution supported by a majority of the members prior to the issue of the proclamation, provided, however, that the legislative assembly, by resolution supported by a majority of the members, may subsequently withdraw its dissent and approve the amendment.

(4) The provisions of subsections (2) and (3) do not apply to the *Canadian Charter of Rights and Freedoms*."

(*h*) by adding after Clause 48 of Part VI the following new Clause:

"49. An amendment to the Constitution of Canada may be made by proclamation under section 45 or section 47, as appropriate, without a resolution of the Senate authorizing the issue of the proclamation if, within one hundred and eighty days after the passage by the House of Commons of a resolution authorizing its issue, the Senate has not passed such a resolution and if, at any time after the expiration of those one hundred and eighty days, the House of Commons again passes the resolution."

(*i*) by deleting Clause 49 of Part VI and substituting the following therefor:

"49. (1) The procedures for amendment prescribed by subsection 45(1) and section 47 may be initiated by either the Senate or House of Commons or by the legislative assembly of a province.

(2) A resolution authorizing an amendment made for the purposes of this Part may be revoked at any time before the issue of a proclamation.

(3) A resolution of dissent made for the purposes of this Part may be revoked at any time before or after the issue of a proclamation."

(*j*) by deleting Clause 54 of Part VI and substituting the following therefor:

"54. An amendment to the Constitution of Canada in relation to the following matters may be made only in accordance with the procedure prescribed by section 45(1):

(*a*) The Canadian Charter of Rights and Freedoms;

(*b*) the commitments relating to equalization and regional disparities set out in section 34;

(*c*) the powers of the Senate;

(*d*) the number of members by which a province is entitled to be represented in the Senate;

(*e*) the method of selecting Senators and the residence qualifications of Senators; and

(*f*) the principles of proportionate representation of the provinces in the House of Commons prescribed by the Constitution of Canada.''

(*k*) by adding after Clause 4 of Part VI the following new Clause:

"55. An amendment to the Constitution of Canada in relation to the following matters may be made only by proclamation issued by the Governor General under the Great Seal of Canada where so authorized by resolutions of the Senate and the House of Commons and by the legislative assembly of each province.

(*a*) the office of the Queen, the Governor General and the Lieutenant Governor of a province;

(*b*) The right of a province to a number of members in the House of Commons not less than the numbers of Senators representing the province; and

(*c*) any of the provisions of this Part.''

and

(*l*) by deleting Clause 63 of Part VIII and substituting the following therefor:

"63. (1) This Act, or any provision thereof, shall come into force on a day or days to be fixed by proclamations to be issued by the Governor General under the Great Seal of Canada where so authorized no later than July 1, 1983 by resolutions of the legislative assemblies of at least two-thirds of the provinces that have in the aggregate, according to the then latest decennial census, a population of at least fifty per cent of all the provinces.

(2) A resolution made for the purposes of this section may be revoked before the issue of a proclamation authorized by it.''

And the question being put on the amendment, it was negatived on the following division:
(Yeas, 93; Nays, 175) pp. 9471–3

Debates, Thursday, April 23, 1981

Mr. Pinard, seconded by Mr. Chrétien, moved in amendment thereto, — That the proposed *Constitution Act, 1981* be amended

(*a*) by adding immediately after the heading ''CANADIAN CHARTER OF RIGHTS AND FREEDOMS'' on page 3, the following:

"Whereas Canada is founded upon principles that recognize the supremacy of God and the rule of law;''

(*b*) by striking out in clause 11 of the French version, line 36 on page 5 and substituting the following:

"déclaré coupable et puni;''

(*c*) by striking out subclause 33(1) of the French version at lines 27 to 29 on page 10 and substituting the following:

"33. (1) Les droits, ancestraux ou issus de traités, des peuples autochtones du Canada sont, par les présentes, confirmés.''

(*d*) by striking out in subclause 45(1), lines 20 to 24 on page 16 and substituting the following:

"inces''.

And the question being put on the amendment, it was agreed to on the following division:
(Yeas, 173; Nays, 94) p. 9473

. . .

SENATE

Debates, Thursday, March 26, 1981

In amendment, the *Honourable Senator Yuzyk* moved, seconded by the Honourable Senator Tremblay, that the motion be amended in Schedule B of the resolution by inserting immediately after Clause 28 the following:

"28.1 Notwithstanding anything in this Charter, the rights and freedoms set out herein are guaranteed equally to men and women.''   p. 2177

April 24, 1981

The motion in amendment of the Honourable Senator Yuzyk, seconded by the Honourable Senator Tremblay, was withdrawn.   p. 2381

Debates, Friday, April 24, 1981

In amendment, the *Honourable Senator Perrault*, P.C., moved, seconded by the Honourable Senator Frith, that the motion be amended in Schedule B of the resolution as follows:

(*a*) by adding, immediately after the heading ''CANADIAN CHARTER OF RIHTS AND FREEDOMS'' on page 3, the following:

"Whereas Canada is founded upon principles that recognize the supremacy of God and the rule of law.''

(*b*) by striking out, in clause 11 of the French version, line 36 on page 5 and substituting the following:

"déclaré coupable et puni;''

(*c*) by adding, immediately after line 40 on page 9, the following clause:

"28. Notwithstanding anything in this Charter, the rights and freedoms referred to in it are guaranteed equally to male and female persons."

(*d*) by renumbering the subsequent clauses accordingly

(*e*) by striking out subclause 33(1) of the French version at lines 27 and 29 on page 10 and substituting the following:

"33. (1) Les droits, ancestraux ou issus de traités, des peuples autochtones du Canada sont, par les présentes, confirmés."

(*f*) by striking out, in subclause 45(1), lines 20 to 24 on page 16 and substituting the following:

"inces."

(*g*) by adding to clause 54, immediately after line 20 on page 20, the following paragraph:

"(c) the rights of the aboriginal peoples of Canada set out in Part II;"

(*h*) by relettering paragraphs (c) to (h) of clause 54 as paragraphs (d) to (i).

The question being put on the motion in amendment of the Honourable Senator Perrault, P.C., seconded by the Honourable Senator Frith,

The Senate divided and the names being called they were taken down.

(Yeas, 46; Nays, Nil) pp. 2364–2379
So it was resolved in the affirmative.

Debates, Friday, April 24, 1981

In amendment, the *Honourable Senator Flynn*, P.C., moved, seconded by the Honourable Senator Roblin, P.C., that the proposed Constitution Act, 1981, be amended as follows:

1. (*a*) by adding to Clause 16 of Part 1, immediately after line 32 on page 6 the following:

"(3) English and French are the official languages of Ontario and have equality of status and equal rights and privileges as to their use in all institutions of the legislature and government of Ontario;"

(*b*) by renumbering subsection (3) as subsection (4).

2. By adding to Clause 17 of Part I, immediately after line 3 on page 7 the following:

"(3) Everyone has the right to use English or French in any debates and other proceedings of the legislature of Ontario."

3. by adding to Clause 18 of Part I, immediately after line 12 on page 7 the following:

"(3) The statutes, records and journals of the legislature of Ontario shall be printed and published in English and French and both language versions are equally authoritative.".

4. by adding to Clause 19 of Part I, immediately after line 20 on page 7 the following:

"(3) Either English or French may be used by any person in, or in any pleading in or process issuing from, any court of Ontario."

5. by deleting Clause 63 of Part VIII and substituting the following therefor:

"63. (1) This Act, or any provision thereof, shall come into force on a day or days to be fixed by proclamation to be issued by the Governor General under the Great Seal of Canada where so authorized by resolutions of the legislative assemblies of at least two-thirds of the provinces that have in the aggregate, according to the then latest decennial census, a population of at least fifty per cent of all the provinces.

(2) A resolution made for the purposes of this section may be revoked before the issue of a proclamation authorized by it."

The question being put on the motion in amendment of the Honourable Senator Flynn, P.C., seconded by the Honourable Senator Roblin, P.C.

The Senate divided and the names being called they were taken down.

(Yeas, 21; Nays, 44) pp. 2366–2380
So it was resolved in the negative.

Debates, Tuesday, May 19, 1981
THE CONSTITUTION
MOTION FOR AN ADDRESS TO HER MAJESTY THE QUEEN — PROPOSED OPPOSITION AMENDMENTS OF FRIDAY, APRIL 24, 1981, PRINTED AS APPENDIX

The Hon. the Speaker: Honourable senators, before proceeding further I should like to make a brief statement.

During the last sitting of the Senate, on Friday, April 24, 1981, the *Honourable Senator Flynn*, P.C. intended to move certain amendments to the motion that an Address be presented to Her Majesty the Queen respecting the Constitution of Canada. Those amendments were not moved, but, as indicated on page 2372 of *Debates of the Senate*, it was agreed that they should be included in Senator Flynn's speech.

Through inadvertence, those amendments did not appear in the *Debates* of that day, and it is now suggested that they be printed as an appendix to today's proceedings.

Is this procedure agreeable to honourable senators?

Hon. Senators: Agreed.

APPENDIX "A"
(*See p. 2383*) [not reproduced]

THE CONSTITUTION

MOTION FOR AN ADDRESS TO HER MAJESTY THE QUEEN
PROPOSED OPPOSITION AMENDMENTS OF
FRIDAY, APRIL 24, 1981

That the proposed Constitution Act, 1981, be amended as follows:

A. by deleting Clause 1 of Part 1 and substituting the following therefor:

"1. Affirming that
(*a*) The Canadian nation is founded upon principles that acknowledge the supremacy of God, the dignity and worth of the human person and the position of the family in a society of free individuals and free institutions, and
(*b*) individuals and institutions remain free only when freedom is founded upon respect for moral and spiritual values and the rule of law,
the Canadian Charter of Rights and Freedoms guarantees the rights and freedoms set out in it subject only to such reasonable limits prescribed by law as can be demonstrably justified in a free and democratic society."

B. by deleting Clause 7 of Part I and substituting the following therefor:

"7. Everyone has the right to life, liberty, security of the person and enjoyment of property and the right not to be deprived thereof except in accordance with the principles of fundamental justice."

C. by adding after Clause 27 of Part I the following new Clause:

"28. Notwithstanding anything in this Charter, the rights and freedoms set out in it are guaranteed equally to male and female persons."

D. by adding after new Clause 28 of Part I the following new clause:

"29. Nothing in this Charter affects the authority of Parliament to legislate in respect of abortion and capital punishment."

That the proposed Constitution Act, 1981, be amended as follows:

by deleting Clause 35 of Part IV and substituting the following therefor:

"35. (1) No later than two months after the coming into force of this Act, the Prime Minister of Canada and the first ministers of the provinces shall constitute a permanent conference to be designated the "Constitutional Conference of Canada" hereinafter referred to as the "Conference".

(2) The Conference shall examine all Canadian constitutional laws and propose amendments necessary for the development of the Canadian federation.

(3) A Conference convened under subsection (1) shall have included in its agenda an item respecting constitutional matters that directly affect the aboriginal peoples of Canada, including the identification and definition of the rights of those peoples to be included in the Constitution of Canada and the Prime Minister shall invite representatives of those peoples to participate in the discussions on that item.

(4) The Prime Minister of Canada shall invite elected representatives of the governments of the Yukon Territory and the Northwest Territories to participate in the discussions on any item on the agenda of a Conference convened under subsection (1) that, in the opinion of the Prime Minister, directly affects the Yukon Territory and the Northwest Territories.

(5) The Conference shall meet at least twice each year.

(6) The Conference shall be assisted by the Continuing Committee of Ministers on the Constitution."

That the proposed Constitution Act, 1981, be amended as follows:

A. by deleting Clause 45 of Part VI and substituting the following therefor:

"45. (1) An amendment to the Constitution of Canada may be made by proclamation issued by the Governor General under the Great Seal of Canada where so authorized by
(*a*) resolutions of the Senate and House of Commons; and
(*b*) resolutions of the legislative assemblies of at least two-thirds of the provinces that have in the aggregate, according to the then latest decennial census, at least fifty per cent of the population of all the provinces.

(2) Any amendment made under subsection (1) derogating from the legislative powers, the proprietary rights or any other rights or privileges of the legislature or government of a province shall require a resolution supported by a vote of a majority of the members of each of

the Senate, of the House of Commons, and of the requisite number of legislative assemblies.

(3) Any amendment made under subsection (1) derogating from the legislative powers, the proprietary rights or any other rights or privileges of the legislature or government of a province shall not have effect, financially or otherwise, in and for any province whose legislative assembly has expressed its dissent thereto by resolution supported by a majority of the members prior to the issue of the proclamation, provided, however, that the legislative assembly, by resolution supported by a majority of the members, may subsequently withdraw its dissent and approve the amendment.

(4) The provisions of subsection (2) and (3) do not apply to the Canadian Charter of Rights and Freedoms.''

B. by deleting Clause 46 of Part VI

C. by adding after Clause 48 of Part VI the following new Clause:

''49. An amendment to the Constitution of Canada may be made by proclamation under section 45 or section 47, as appropriate, without a resolution of the Senate authorizing the issue of the proclamation if, within one hundred and eighty days after the passage by the House of Commons of a resolution authorizing its issue, the Senate has not passed such a resolution and if, at any time after the expiration of those one hundred and eighty days, the House of Commons passes the resolution.''

D. by deleting Clause 49 of Part VI and substituting the following therefor:

''49.(1) The procedures for amending prescribed by subsection 45(1) and section 47 may be initiated by either the Senate or House of Commons or by the legislative assembly of a province.

(2) A resolution authorizing an amendment made for the purposes of this Part may be revoked at any time before the issue of a proclamation.

(3) A resolution of dissent made for the purposes of this Part may be revoked at any time before or after the issue of a proclamation.''

E. by deleting Clause 54 of Part VI and substituting the following therefor:

''54. An amendment to the Constitution of Canada in relation to the following matters may be made only in accordance with the procedure prescribed by section 45(1):
(*a*) The Canadian Charter of Rights and Freedoms;
(*b*) the commitments relating to equalization and regional disparities set out in section 34;
(*c*) the powers of the Senate;
(*d*) the number of members by which a province is entitled to be represented in the Senate;

(*e*) the method of selecting Senators and the residence qualifications of Senators; and
(*f*) the principles of proportionate representation of the provinces in the House of Commons prescribed by the Constitution of Canada.''

F. by adding after Clause 54 of Part VI the following new Clause:

''55. An amendment to the Constitution of Canada in relation to the following matters may be made only by proclamation issued by the Governor General under the Great Seal of Canada where so authorized by resolutions of the Senate and the House of Commons and by the legislative assembly of each province:
(*a*) the office of the Queen, the Governor General and the Lieutenant Governor of a province;
(*b*) The right of a province to a number of members in the House of Commons not less than the members of Senators representing the province;
(*c*) any of the provisions of this Part; and
(*d*) clauses 16 to 22, inclusive, of Part I.''

G. by deleting Part V.

That the proposed Constitution Act, 1981, be amended as follows:

by deleting Clause 63 of Part VIII and substituting the following therefor:

''63.(1) This Act, or any provision thereof, shall come into force on a day or days to be fixed by proclamation to be issued by the Governor General under the Great Seal of Canada where so authorized by resolutions of the legislative assemblies of at least two-thirds of the provinces that have in the aggregate, according to the then latest decennial census, a population of at least fifty per cent of all the provinces.

(2) A resolution made for the purposes of this section may be revoked before the issue of a proclamation authorized by it.''

That the proposed Constitution Act, 1981, be amended as follows:

1.(*a*) by adding to Clause 16 of Part I, immediately after line 32 on page 6 the following:

''(3) English and French are the official languages of Ontario and have equality of status and equal rights and privileges as to their use in all institutions of the legislature and government of Ontario;''

(*b*) by renumbering subsection (3) as subsection (4).

2. By adding to Clause 17 of Part I, immediately after line 3 on page 7 the following:

"(3) Everyone has the right to use English or French in any debates and other proceedings of the legislature of Ontario."

3. by adding to Clause 18 of Part I, immediately after line 12 on page 7 the following:

"(3) The statutes, records and journals of the legislature of Ontario shall be printed and published in English

and French and both language versions are equally authoritative."

4. by adding to Clause 19 of Part I, immediately after line 20 on page 7 the following:

"(3) Either English or French may be used by any person in, or in any pleading in or process issuing from, any court of Ontario." pp. 2398–9

(b) *The Canadian Constitution 1981*: Consolidation of Proposed Constitutional Resolution Tabled by the Minister of Justice in the House of Commons on February 13, 1981, with the Amendments Approved by the House of Commons on April 23, 1981, and by the Senate on April 24, 1981

Catalogue no. X2-321/2

THAT, WHEREAS in the past certain amendments to the Constitution of Canada have been made by the Parliament of the United Kingdom at the request and with the consent of Canada;

AND WHEREAS it is in accord with the status of Canada as an independent state that Canadians be able to amend their Constitution in Canada in all respects;

AND WHEREAS it is also desirable to provide in the Constitution of Canada for the recognition of certain fundamental rights and freedoms and to make other amendments to that Constitution;

A respectful address be presented to Her Majesty the Queen in the following words:

To the Queen's Most Excellent Majesty:
Most Gracious Sovereign:

We, Your Majesty's loyal subjects, the House of Commons of Canada in Parliament assembled, respectfully approach Your Majesty, requesting that you may graciously be pleased

to cause to be laid before the Parliament of the United Kingdom a measure containing the recitals and clauses hereinafter set forth:

An Act to give effect to a request by the Senate and House of Commons of Canada

Whereas Canada has requested and and consented to the enactment of an Act of the Parliament of the United Kingdom to give effect to the provisions hereinafter set forth and the Senate and the House of Commons of Canada in Parliament assembled have submitted an address to Her Majesty requesting that Her Majesty may graciously be pleased to cause a Bill to be laid before the Parliament of the United Kingdom for that purpose.

Be it therefore enacted by the Queen's Most Excellent Majesty, by and with the advice and consent of the Lords Spiritual and Temporal, and Commons, in this present Parliament assembled, and by the authority of the same, as follows:

Constitution Act, 1981 enacted	**1.** The *Constitution Act, 1981* set out in Schedule B to this Act is hereby enacted for and shall have the force of law in Canada and shall come into force as provided in that Act.
Termination of power to legislate for Canada	**2.** No Act of the Parliament of the United Kingdom passed after the *Constitution Act, 1981* comes into force shall extend to Canada as part of its law.
French version	**3.** So far as it is not contained in Schedule B, the French version of this Act is set out in Schedule A to this Act and has the same authority in Canada as the English version thereof.
Short title	**4.** This Act may be cited as the *Canada Act.*

CONSTITUTION ACT, 1981

PART I, SCHEDULE B
CANADIAN CHARTER OF RIGHTS AND FREEDOMS

Whereas Canada is founded upon principles that recognize the supremacy of God and the rule of law:

Guarantee of Rights and Freedoms

Rights and freedoms in Canada

1. The *Canadian Charter of Rights and Freedoms* guarantees the rights and freedoms set out in it subject only to such reasonable limits prescribed by law as can be demonstrably justified in a free and democratic society.

Fundamental Freedoms

Fundamental freedoms

2. Everyone has the following fundamental freedoms:
(*a*) freedom of conscience and religion;
(*b*) freedom of thought, belief, opinion and expression, including freedom of the press and other media of communication;
(*c*) freedom of peaceful assembly; and
(*d*) freedom of association.

Democratic Rights

Democratic rights of citizens

3. Every citizen of Canada has the right to vote in an election of members of the House of Commons or of a legislative assembly and to be qualified for membership therein.

Maximum duration of legislative bodies

4. (1) No House of Commons and no legislative assembly shall continue for longer than five years from the date fixed for the return of the writs at a general election of its members.

Continuation in special circumstances

(2) In time of real or apprehended war, invasion or insurrection, a House of Commons may be continued by Parliament and a legislative assembly may be continued by the legislature beyond five years if such continuation is not opposed by the votes of more than one-third of the members of the House of Commons or the legislative assembly, as the case may be.

Annual sitting of legislative bodies

5. There shall be a sitting of Parliament and of each legislature at least once every twelve months.

Mobility Rights

Mobility of citizens

6. (1) Every citizen of Canada has the right to enter, remain in and leave Canada.

Rights to move and gain livelihood

(2) Every citizen of Canada and every person who has the status of a permanent resident of Canada has the right

(*a*) to move to and take up residence in any province; and

(*b*) to pursue the gaining of a livelihood in any province.

Limitation

(3) The rights specified in subsection (2) are subject to

(*a*) any laws or practices of general application in force in a province other than those that discriminate among persons primarily on the basis of province of present or previous residence; and

(*b*) any laws providing for reasonable residency requirements as a qualification for the receipt of publicly provided social services.

Legal Rights

Life, liberty and security of person

7. Everyone has the right to life, liberty and security of the person and the right not to be deprived thereof except in accordance with the principles of fundamental justice.

Search or seizure

8. Everyone has the right to be secure against unreasonable search or seizure.

Detention or imprisonment

9. Everyone has the right not to be arbitrarily detained or imprisoned.

Arrest or detention

10. Everyone has the right on arrest or detention

(*a*) to be informed promptly of the reasons therefor;

(*b*) to retain and instruct counsel without delay and to be informed of that right; and

(*c*) to have the validity of the detention determined by way of *habeas corpus* and to be released if the detention is not lawful.

Proceedings in criminal and penal matters

11. Any person charged with an offence has the right

(*a*) to be informed without unreasonable delay of the specific offence;

(*b*) to be tried within a reasonable time;

(*c*) not to be compelled to be a witness in proceedings against that person in respect of the offence;

(*d*) to be presumed innocent until proven guilty according to law in a fair and public hearing by an independent and impartial tribunal;

(*e*) not to be denied reasonable bail without just cause;

(*f*) except in the case of an offence under military law tried before a military tribunal, to the benefit of trial by jury where the maximum punishment for the offence is imprisonment for five years or a more severe punishment;

(*g*) not to be found guilty on account of any act or omission unless, at the time of the act or omission, it constituted an offence under Canadian or international law or was criminal according to the general principles of law recognized by the community of nations;

(*h*) if finally acquitted of the offence, not to be tried for it again and, if finally found guilty and punished for the offence, not to be tried or punished for it again; and

(*i*) if found guilty of the offence and if the punishment for the offence has been varied between the time of commission and the time of sentencing, to the benefit of the lesser punishment.

Treatment or punishment

12. Everyone has the right not to be subjected to any cruel and unusual treatment or punishment.

Self-crimination

13. A witness who testifies in any proceedings has the right not to have any incriminating evidence so given used to incriminate that witness in any other proceedings, except in a prosecution for perjury or for the giving of contradictory evidence.

Interpreter

14. A party or witness in any proceedings who does not understand or speak the language in which the proceedings are conducted or who is deaf has the right to the assistance of an interpreter.

Equality Rights

Equality before and under law and equal protection and benefit of law

15. (1) Every individual is equal before and under the law and has the right to the equal protection and equal benefit of the law without discrimination and, in particular, without discrimination based on race, national or ethnic origin, colour, religion, sex, age or mental or physical disability.

Affirmative action programs

(2) Subsection (1) does not preclude any law, program or activity that has as its object the amelioration of conditions of disadvantaged individuals or groups including those that are disadvantaged because of race, national or ethnic origin, colour, religion, sex, age or mental or physical disability.

Official Languages of Canada

Official languages of Canada

16. (1) English and French are the official languages of Canada and have equality of status and equal rights and privileges as to their use in all institutions of the Parliament and government of Canada.

Official languages of New Brunswick

(2) English and French are the official languages of New Brunswick and have equality of status and equal rights and privileges as to their use in all institutions of the legislature and government of New Brunswick.

Advancement of status and use

(3) Nothing in this Charter limits the authority of Parliament or a legislature to advance the equality of status or use of English and French.

Proceedings of Parliament

17. (1) Everyone has the right to use English or French in any debates and other proceedings of Parliament.

Proceedings of New Brunswick legislature

(2) Everyone has the right to use English or French in any debates and other proceedings of the legislature of New Brunswick.

Parliamentary statutes and records

18. (1) The statutes, records and journals of Parliament shall be printed and published in English and French and both language versions are equally authoritative.

New Brunswick statutes and records

(2) The statutes, records and journals of the legislature of New Brunswick shall be printed and published in English and French and both language versions are equally authoritative.

Proceedings in courts established by Parliament

19. (1) Either English or French may be used by any person in, or in any pleading in or process issuing from, any court established by Parliament.

Proceedings in New Brunswick courts

(2) Either English or French may be used by any person in, or in any pleading in or process issuing from, any court of New Brunswick.

Communications by public with federal institutions

20. (1) Any member of the public in Canada has the right to communicate with, and to receive available services from, any head or central office of an institution of the Parliament or government of Canada in English or French, and has the same right with respect to any other office of any such institution where

(*a*) there is a significant demand for communications with and services from that office in such language; or

(*b*) due to the nature of the office, it is reasonable that communications with and services from that office be available in both English and French.

Communications by public with New Brunswick institutions

(2) Any member of the public in New Brunswick has the right to communicate with, and to receive available services from, any office of an institution of the legislature or government of New Brunswick in English or French.

Continuation of existing constitutional provisions

21. Nothing in sections 16 to 20 abrogates or derogates from any right, privilege or obligation with respect to the English and French languages, or either of them, that exists or is continued by virtue of any other provision of the Constitution of Canada.

Rights and privileges preserved

22. Nothing in sections 16 to 20 abrogates or derogates from any legal or customary right or privilege acquired or enjoyed either before or after the coming into force of this Charter with respect to any language that is not English or French.

Minority Language Educational Rights

Language of instruction

23. (1) Citizens of Canada
(a) whose first language learned and still understood is that of the English or French linguistic minority population of the province in which they reside, or
(b) who have received their primary school instruction in Canada in English or French and reside in a province where the language in which they received that instruction is the language of the English or French linguistic minority population of the province,
have the right to have their children receive primary and secondary school instruction in that language in that province.

Continuity of language instruction

(2) Citizens of Canada of whom any child has received or is receiving primary or secondary school instruction in English or French in Canada have the right to have all their children receive primary and secondary school instruction in the same language.

Application where numbers warrant

(3) The right of citizens of Canada under subsections (1) and (2) to have their children receive primary and secondary school instruction in the language of the English or French linguistic minority population of a province
(a) applies wherever in the province the number of children of citizens who have such a right is sufficient to warrant the provision to them out of public funds of minority language; and
(b) includes, where the number of those children so warrants, the right to have them receive that instruction in minority language educational facilities provided out of public funds.

Enforcement

Enforcement of guaranteed rights and freedoms

24. (1) Anyone whose rights or freedoms, as guaranteed by this Charter, have been infringed or denied may apply to a court of competent jurisdiction to obtain such remedy as the court considers appropriate and just in the circumstances.

Exclusion of evidence bringing administration of justice into disrepute

(2) Where, in proceedings under subsection (1), a court concludes that evidence was obtained in a manner that infringed or denied any rights or freedoms guaranteed by this Charter, the evidence shall be excluded if it is established that, having regard to all the circumstances, the admission of it in the proceedings would bring the administration of justice into disrepute.

General

Aboriginal rights and freedoms not affected by Charter

25. The guarantee in this Charter of certain rights and freedoms shall not be construed so as to abrogate or derogate from any aboriginal, treaty or other rights or freedoms that pertain to the aboriginal peoples of Canada including

(*a*) any rights or freedoms that have been recognized by the Royal Proclamation of October 7, 1763; and

(*b*) any rights or freedoms that may be acquired by the aboriginal peoples of Canada by way of land claims settlement.

Other rights and freedoms not affected by Charter

26. The guarantee in this Charter of certain rights and freedoms shall not be construed as denying the existence of any other rights or freedoms that exist in Canada.

Multicultural heritage

27. This Charter shall be interpreted in a manner consistent with the preservation and enhancement of the multicultural heritage of Canadians.

Rights guaranteed equally to both sexes

28. Notwithstanding anything in this Charter, the rights and freedoms referred to in it are guaranteed equally to male and female persons.

Rights respecting certain schools preserved

29. Nothing in this Charter abrogates or derogates from any rights or privileges guaranteed by or under the Constitution of Canada in respect of denominational, separate or dissentient schools.

Application to territories and territorial authorities

30. A reference in this Charter to a province or to the legislative assembly or legislature of a province shall be deemed to include a reference to the Yukon Territory and the Northwest Territories, or to the appropriate legislative authority thereof, as the case may be.

Legislative powers not extended

31. Nothing in this Charter extends the legislative powers of any body or authority.

Application of Charter

Application of Charter

32. (1) This Charter applies

(*a*) to the Parliament and government of Canada and to all matters within the authority of Parliament including all matters relating to the Yukon Territory and Northwest Territories; and

(*b*) to the legislature and government of each province and to all matters within the authority of the legislature of each province.

Exception

(2) Notwithstanding subsection (1), section 15 shall not have effect until three years after this Act, except Part VI, comes into force.

Citation

Citation

33. This Part may be cited as the *Canadian Charter of Rights and Freedoms*.

PART II
RIGHTS OF THE ABORIGINAL PEOPLES OF CANADA

Recognition of aboriginal and treaty rights

Definition of "aboriginal peoples of Canada"

34. (1) The aboriginal and treaty rights of the aboriginal peoples of Canada are hereby recognized and affirmed.

(2) In this Act, "aboriginal peoples of Canada" includes the Indian, Inuit and Métis peoples of Canada.

PART III
EQUALIZATION AND REGIONAL DISPARITIES

Commitment to promote equal opportunities

35. (1) Without altering the legislative authority of Parliament or of the provincial legislatures, or the rights of any of them with respect to the exercise of their legislative authority, Parliament and the legislatures, together with the government of Canada and the provincial governments, are committed to

(*a*) promoting equal opportunities for the well-being of Canadians;

(*b*) furthering economic development to reduce disparity in opportunities; and

(*c*) providing essential public services of reasonable quality to all Canadians.

Commitment respecting public services

(2) Parliament and the government of Canada are committed to the principle of making equalization payments to ensure that provincial governments have sufficient revenues to provide reasonably comparable levels of public services at reasonably comparable levels of taxation.

PART IV
CONSTITUTIONAL CONFERENCES

Constitutional conferences

36. (1) Until Part VI comes into force, a constitutional conference composed of the Prime Minister of Canada and the first ministers of the provinces shall be convened by the Prime Minister of Canada at least once in every year.

Participation of aboriginal peoples

(2) A conference convened under subsection (1) shall have included in its agenda an item respecting constitutional matters that directly affect the aboriginal peoples of Canada, including the identification and definition of the rights of those peoples to be included in the Constitution of Canada, and the Prime Minister of Canada shall invite representatives of those peoples to participate in the discussions on that item.

Participation of territories

(3) The Prime Minister of Canada shall invite elected representatives of the governments of the Yukon Territory and the Northwest Territories to participate in the discussions on any item on the agenda of a conference convened under subsection (1) that, in the opinion of the Prime Minister, directly affects the Yukon Territory and the Northwest Territories.

PART V
INTERIM AMENDMENT PROCEDURE AND RULES FOR ITS REPLACEMENT

Interim procedure for amending Constitution of Canada

37. Until Part VI comes into force, an amendment to the Constitution of Canada may be made by proclamation issued by the Governor General under the Great Seal of Canada where so authorized by resolutions of the Senate and House of Commons and by the legislative assembly or government of each province.

Amendment of provisions relating to some but not all provinces

38. Until Part VI comes into force, an amendment to the Constitution of Canada in relation to any provision that applies to one or more, but not all, provinces may be made by proclamation issued by the Governor General under the Great Seal of Canada where so authorized by resolutions of the Senate and House of Commons and by the legislative assembly or government of each province to which the amendment applies.

Amendments respecting certain language rights

39. (1) Notwithstanding section 41, an amendment to the Constitution of Canada

(*a*) adding a province as a province named in subsection 16(2), 17(2), 18(2), 19(2) or 20(2), or

(*b*) otherwise providing for any or all of the rights guaranteed or obligations imposed by any of those subsections to have application in a province to the extent and under the conditions stated in the amendment,

may be made by proclamation issued by the Governor General under the Great Seal of Canada where so authorized by resolutions of the Senate and House of Commons and the legislative assembly of the province to which the amendment applies.

Initiation of amendment procedure

(2) The procedure for amendment prescribed by subsection (1) may be initiated only by the legislative assembly of the province to which the amendment applies.

Initiation of amendment procedures

40. (1) The procedures for amendment prescribed by sections 37 and 38 may be initiated either by the Senate or House of Commons or by the legislative assembly or government of a province.

Revocation of authorization

(2) A resolution made or other authorization given for the purposes of this Part may be revoked at any time before the issue of a proclamation authorized by it.

Limitation on use of interim amendment procedure

41. Sections 37 and 38 do not apply to an amendment to the Constitution of Canada where there is another provision in the Constitution for making the amendment, but the procedure prescribed by section 37 shall be used to amend the *Canadian Charter of Rights and Freedoms* and any provision for amending the Constitution, including this section.

Coming into force of Part VI

42. Part VI shall come into force

(*a*) with or without amendment, on such day as may be fixed by proclamation issued pursuant to the procedure prescribed by section 37, or

(*b*) on the day that is two years after the day this Act, except Part VI, comes into force,

whichever is the earlier day but, if a referendum is required to be held under subsection 43(3), Part VI shall come into force as provided in section 44.

Provincial alternative procedure

43. (1) The legislative assemblies of seven or more provinces that have, according to the then latest general census, combined populations of at least eighty per cent of the population of all the provinces may make a single proposal to substitute for paragraph 46(1)(*b*) such alternative as they consider appropriate.

Procedure for perfecting alternative

(2) One copy of an alternative proposed under subsection (1) may be deposited with the Chief Electoral Officer of Canada by each proposing province within two years after this Act, except Part VI, comes into force but, prior to the expiration of that period, any province that has deposited a copy may withdraw that copy.

Referendum

(3) Where copies of an alternative have been deposited as provided by subsection (2) and, on the day that is two years after this Act, except Part VI, comes into force, at least seven copies remain deposited by provinces that have, according to the then latest general census, combined populations of at

least eighty per cent of the population of all the provinces, the government of Canada shall cause a referendum to be held within two years after that day to determine whether

(a) paragraph 46(1)(b) or any alternative thereto approved by resolutions of the Senate and House of Commons and deposited with the Chief Electoral Officer at least ninety days prior to the day on which the referendum is held, or

(b) the alternative proposed by the provinces,

shall be adopted.

Coming into force of Part VI where referendum held

44. Where a referendum is held under subsection 43(3), a proclamation under the Great Seal of Canada shall be issued within six months after the date of the referendum bringing Part VI into force with such modifications, if any, as are necessary to incorporate the proposal approved by a majority of the persons voting at the referendum and with such other changes as are reasonably consequential on the incorporation of that proposal.

Right to vote

45. (1) Every citizen of Canada has, subject only to such reasonable limits prescribed by law as can be demonstrably justified in a free and democratic society, the right to vote in a referendum held under subsection 43(3).

Establishment of Referendum Rules Commission

(2) If a referendum is required to be held under subsection 43(3), a Referendum Rules Commission shall forthwith be established by commission issued under the Great Seal of Canada consisting of

(a) the Chief Electoral Officer of Canada, who shall be chairman of the Commission;

(b) a person appointed by the Governor General in Council; and

(c) a person appointed by the Governor General in Council

(i) on the recommendation of the governments of a majority of the provinces, or

(ii) if the governments of a majority of the provinces do not recommend a candidate within thirty days after the Chief Electoral Officer of Canada requests such a recommendation, on the recommendation of the Chief Justice of Canada from among persons recommended by the governments of the provinces within thirty days after the expiration of the first mentioned thirty day period or, if none are so recommended, from among such persons as the Chief Justice considers qualified.

Duty of Commission

(3) A Referendum Rules Commission shall cause rules for the holding of a referendum under subsection 43(3) approved by a majority of the Commission to be laid before Parliament within sixty days after the Commission is established or, if Parliament is not then sitting, on any of the first ten days next thereafter that Parliament is sitting.

Rules for referendum

(4) Subject to subsection (1) and taking into consideration any rules approved by a Referendum Rules Commission in accordance with subsection (3), Parliament may enact laws respecting the rules applicable to the holding of a referendum under subsection 43(3).

Proclamation

(5) If Parliament does not enact laws under subsection (4) respecting the rules applicable to the holding of a referendum within sixty days after receipt of a recommendation from a Referendum Rules Commission, the rules recommended by the Commission shall forthwith be brought into force by proclamation issued by the Governor General under the Great Seal of Canada.

Computation of period

(6) Any period when Parliament is prorogued or dissolved shall not be counted in computing the sixty day period referred to in subsection (5).

Rules to have force of law

(7) Subject to subsection (1), rules made under this section have the force of law and prevail over other laws made under the Constitution of Canada to the extent of any inconsistency.

PART VI
PROCEDURE FOR AMENDING CONSTITUTION OF CANADA

General procedure for amending Constitution of Canada

46. (1) An amendment to the Constitution of Canada may be made by proclamation issued by the Governor General under the Great Seal of Canada where so authorized by

(*a*) resolutions of the Senate and House of Commons; and

(*b*) resolutions of the legislative assemblies of at least a majority of the provinces that includes

(i) every province that at any time before the issue of the proclamation had, according to any previous general census, a population of at least twenty-five per cent of the population of Canada,

(ii) two or more of the Atlantic provinces, and

(iii) two or more of the Western provinces.

Definitions
"Atlantic provinces"

(2) In this section,

"Atlantic provinces" means the provinces of Nova Scotia, New Brunswick, Prince Edward Island and Newfoundland;

"Western provinces"

"Western provinces" means the provinces of Manitoba, British Columbia, Saskatchewan and Alberta.

Amendment authorized by referendum

47. (1) An amendment to the Constitution of Canada may be made by proclamation issued by the Governor General under the Great Seal of Canada where so authorized by a referendum held throughout Canada under subsection (2) at which

(*a*) a majority of persons voting thereat, and

(*b*) a majority of persons voting thereat in each of the provinces, resolutions of the legislative assemblies of which would be sufficient, together with resolutions of the Senate and House of Commons, to authorize the issue of a proclamation under subsection 46(1),

have approved the making of the amendment.

Authorization of referendum

(2) A referendum referred to in subsection (1) shall be held where directed by proclamation issued by the Governor General under the Great Seal of Canada, which proclamation may be issued where

(*a*) an amendment to the Constitution of Canada has been authorized under paragraph 46(1)(*a*) by resolutions of the Senate and House of Commons;

(*b*) the requirements of paragraph 46(1)(*b*) in respect of the proposed amendment have not been satisfied within twelve months after the passage of the resolutions of the Senate and House of Commons; and

(*c*) the issue of the proclamation has been authorized by the Governor General in Council.

Time limit for referendum

(3) A proclamation issued under subsection (2) in respect of a referendum shall provide for the referendum to be held within two years after the expiration of the twelve month period referred to in paragraph (*b*) of that subsection.

Amendment of provisions relating to some but not all provinces

48. An amendment to the Constitution of Canada in relation to any provision that applies to one or more, but not all, provinces may be made by proclamation issued by the Governor General under the Great Seal of Canada where so authorized by resolutions of the Senate and House of Commons and of the legislative assembly of each province to which the amendment applies.

Amendments respecting certain language rights

49. (1) Notwithstanding section 55, an amendment to the Constitution of Canada

(*a*) adding a province as a province named in subsection 16(2), 17(2), 18(2), 19(2) or 20(2), or

(*b*) otherwise providing for any or all of the rights guaranteed or obligations imposed by any of those subsections to have application in a province to the extent and under the conditions stated in the amendment,

may be made by proclamation issued by the Governor General under the Great Seal of Canada where so authorized by resolutions of the Senate and House of Commons and the legislative assembly of the province to which the amendment applies.

Initiation of amendment procedure

(2) The procedure for amendment prescribed by subsection (1) may be initiated only by the legislative assembly of the province to which the amendment applies.

Initiation of amendment procedures

50. (1) The procedures for amendment prescribed by subsection 46(1) and section 48 may be initiated either by the Senate or House of Commons or by the legislative assembly of a province.

Revocation of authorization

(2) A resolution made for the purposes of this Part may be revoked at any time before the issue of a proclamation authorized by it.

Right to vote

51. (1) Every citizen of Canada has, subject only to such reasonable limits prescribed by law as can be demonstrably justified in a free and democratic society, the right to vote in a referendum held under section 47.

Establishment of Referendum Rules Commission

(2) Where a referendum is to be held under section 47, a Referendum Rules Commission shall forthwith be established by commission issued under the Great Seal of Canada consisting of

(*a*) the Chief Electoral Officer of Canada, who shall be chairman of the Commission;

(*b*) a person appointed by the Governor General in Council; and

(*c*) a person appointed by the Governor General in Council

(i) on the recommendation of the governments of a majority of the provinces, or

(ii) if the governments of a majority of the provinces do not recommend a candidate within thirty days after the Chief Electoral Officer of Canada requests such a recommendation, on the recommendation of the Chief Justice of Canada from among persons recommended by the governments of the provinces within thirty days after the expiration of the first mentioned thirty day period or, if none are so recommended, from among such persons as the Chief Justice considers qualified.

Duty of Commission

(3) A Referendum Rules Commission shall cause rules for the holding of a referendum under section 47 approved by a majority of the Commission to be laid before Parliament within sixty days after the Commission is established or, if Parliament is not then sitting, on any of the first ten days next thereafter that Parliament is sitting.

Rules for referendum

(4) Subject to subsection (1) and taking into consideration any rules approved by a Referendum Rules Commission in accordance with subsection (3), Parliament may enact laws respecting the rules applicable to the holding of a referendum under section 47.

Proclamation

(5) If Parliament does not enact laws under subsection (4) respecting the rules applicable to the holding of a referendum within sixty days after receipt of a recommendation from a Referendum Rules Commission, the rules recommended by the Commission shall forthwith be brought into force by proclamation issued by the Governor General under the Great Seal of Canada.

Computation of period

(6) Any period when Parliament is prorogued or dissolved shall not be counted in computing the sixty day period referred to in subsection (5).

Rules to have force of law

(7) Subject to subsection (1), rules made under this section have the force of law and prevail over other laws made under the Constitution of Canada to the extent of any inconsistency.

Limitation on use of general amendment procedure

52. (1) The procedures prescribed by section 46, 47 or 48 do not apply to an amendment to the Constitution of Canada where there is another provision in the Constitution for making the amendment, but the procedures prescribed by section 46 or 47 shall, nevertheless, be used to amend any provision for amending the Constitution, including this section.

Idem

(2) The procedures prescribed by section 46 or 47 do not apply in respect of an amendment referred to in section 48.

Amendments by Parliament

53. Subject to section 55, Parliament may exclusively make laws amending the Constitution of Canada in relation to the executive government of Canada or the Senate or House of Commons.

Amendments by provincial legislatures

54. Subject to section 55, the legislature of each province may exclusively make laws amending the constitution of the province.

Matters requiring amendment under general amendment procedure

55. An amendment to the Constitution of Canada in relation to the following matters may be made only in accordance with a procedure prescribed by section 46 or 47:

(*a*) the office of the Queen, the Governor General and the Lieutenant Governor of a province;

(*b*) the *Canadian Charter of Rights and Freedoms*;

(*c*) the rights of the aboriginal peoples of Canada set out in Part II;

(*d*) the commitments relating to equalization and regional disparities set out in section 35;

(*e*) the powers of the Senate;

(*f*) the number of members by which a province is entitled to be represented in the Senate;

(*g*) the method of selecting Senators and the residence qualifications of Senators;

(*h*) the right of a province to a number of members in the House of Commons not less than the number of Senators representing the province; and

(*i*) the principles of proportionate representation of the provinces in the House of Commons prescribed by the Constitution of Canada.

Consequential amendments

56. (1) Class 1 of section 91 and class 1 of section 92 of the *Constitution Act, 1867* (formerly named the *British North America Act, 1867*), the *British North America (No. 2) Act, 1949*, referred to in item 22 of Schedule I to this Act and Parts IV and V of this Act are repealed.

Idem

(2) When Parts IV and V of this Act are repealed, this section may be repealed and this Act may be renumbered, consequential upon the repeal of those Parts and this section, by proclamation issued by the Governor General under the Great Seal of Canada.

PART VII
AMENDMENT TO THE CONSTITUTION ACT, 1867

Amendment to *Constitution Act, 1867*

57. The *Constitution Act, 1867* (formerly named the *British North America Act, 1867*) is amended by adding thereto, immediately after section 92 thereof, the following heading and section:

"Non-Renewable Natural Resources, Forestry Resources and Electrical Energy

Laws respecting non-renewable natural resources, forestry resources and electrical energy

92A. (1) In each province, the legislature may exclusively make laws in relation to

(*a*) exploration for non-renewable natural resources in the province;

(*b*) development, conservation and management of non-renewable natural resources and forestry resources in the province, including laws in relation to the rate of primary production therefrom; and

(*c*) development, conservation and management of sites and facilities in the province for the generation and production of electrical energy.

Export from provinces of resources

(2) In each province, the legislature may make laws in relation to the export from the province to another part of Canada of the primary production from non-renewable natural resources and forestry resources in the province and the production from facilities in the province for the generation of electrical energy, but such laws may not authorize or provide for discrimination in prices or in supplies exported to another part of Canada.

Authority of Parliament

(3) Nothing in subsection (2) derogates from the authority of Parliament to enact laws in relation to the matters referred to in that subsection and, where such a law of Parliament and a law of a province conflict, the law of Parliament prevails to the extent of the conflict.

Taxation of resources

(4) In each province, the legislature may make laws in relation to the raising of money by any mode or system of taxation in respect of

(*a*) non-renewable natural resources and forestry resources in the province and the primary production therefrom, and

(*b*) sites and facilities in the province for the generation of electrical energy and the production therefrom,

whether or not such production is exported in whole or in part from the province, but such laws may not authorize or provide for taxation that differentiates between production exported to another part of Canada and production not exported from the province.

"Primary production"

(5) The expression "primary production" has the meaning assigned by the Sixth Schedule.

Existing powers or rights

(6) Nothing in subsections (1) to (5) derogates from any powers or rights that a legislature or government of a province had immediately before the coming into force of this section."

Idem

58. The said Act is further amended by adding thereto the following Schedule:

"THE SIXTH SCHEDULE

Primary Production from Non-Renewable Natural Resources and Forestry Resources

1. For the purposes of section 92A of this Act,

(*a*) production from a non-renewable natural resource is primary production therefrom if

(i) it is in the form in which it exists upon its recovery or severance from its natural state, or

(ii) it is a product resulting from processing or refining the resource, and is not a manufactured product or a product resulting from refining crude oil, refining upgraded heavy crude oil, refining gases or liquids derived from coal or refining a synthetic equivalent of crude oil; and

(b) production from a forestry resource is primary production therefrom if it consists of sawlogs, poles, lumber, wood chips, sawdust or any other primary wood product, or wood pulp, and is not a product manufactured from wood.''

PART VIII
GENERAL

Primacy of Constitution of Canada

59. (1) The Constitution of Canada is the supreme law of Canada, and any law that is inconsistent with the provisions of the Constitution is, to the extent of the inconsistency, of no force or effect.

Constitution of Canada

(2) The Constitution of Canada includes

(a) the *Canada Act*;

(b) the Acts and orders referred to in Schedule I; and

(c) any amendment to any Act or order referred to in paragraph (a) or (b).

Amendments to Constitution of Canada

(3) Amendments to the Constitution of Canada shall be made only in accordance with the authority contained in the Constitution of Canada.

Repeals and new names

60. (1) The enactments referred to in Column I of Schedule I are hereby repealed or amended to the extent indicated in Column II thereof and, unless repealed, shall continue as law in Canada under the names set out in Column III thereof.

Consequential amendments

(2) Every enactment, except the *Canada Act*, that refers to an enactment referred to in Schedule I by the name in Column I thereof is hereby amended by substituting for that name the corresponding name in Column III thereof, and any British North America Act not referred to in Schedule I may be cited as the *Constitution Act* followed by the year and number, if any, of its enactment.

French version of Constitution of Canada

61. A French version of the portions of the Constitution of Canada referred to in Schedule I shall be prepared by the Minister of Justice of Canada as expeditiously as possible and, when any portion thereof sufficient to warrant action being taken has been so prepared, it shall be put forward for enactment by proclamation issued by the Governor General under the Great Seal of Canada pursuant to the procedure then applicable to an amendment of the same provisions of the Constitution of Canada.

English and French versions of certain constitutional texts

62. Where any portion of the Constitution of Canada has been or is enacted in English and French or where a French version of any portion of the Constitution is enacted pursuant to section 61, the English and French versions of that portion of the Constitution are equally authoritative.

English and French versions of this Act

63. The English and French versions of this Act are equally authoritative.

Commencement

64. Subject to section 65, this Act shall come into force on a day to be fixed by proclamation issued by the Governor General under the Great Seal of Canada.

Exception 65. Part VI shall come into force as provided in Part V.

Short title and citations 66. This Schedule may be cited as the *Constitution Act, 1981*, and the Constitution Acts 1867 to 1975 (No. 2) and this Act may be cited together as the *Constitution Acts, 1867 to 1981*.

SCHEDULE I TO THE CONSTITUTION ACT, 1981
MODERNIZATION OF THE CONSTITUTION

Item	Column I Act Affected	Column II Amendment	Column III New Name
1.	British North America Act, 1867, 30–31 Vict., c. 3 (U.K.)	(1) Section 1 is repealed and the following substituted therefor: "1. This Act may be cited as the *Constitution Act, 1867*." (2) Section 20 is repealed.	Constitution Act, 1867
2.	An Act to amend and continue the Act 32–33 Victoria chapter 3; and to establish and provide for the Government of the Province of Manitoba, 1870, 33 Vict., c. 3 (Can.)	(1) The long title is repealed and the following substituted therefor: "*Manitoba Act, 1870*." (2) Section 20 is repealed.	Manitoba Act, 1870
3.	Order of Her Majesty in Council admitting Rupert's Land and the North-Western Territory into the union, dated the 23rd day of June, 1870.		Rupert's Land and North-Western Territory Order
4.	Order of Her Majesty in Council admitting British Columbia into the Union, dated the 16th day of May, 1871.		British Columbia Terms of Union
5.	British North America Act, 1871, 34–35 Vict., c. 28 (U.K.)	Section 1 is repealed and the following substituted therefor: "1. This Act may be cited as the *Constitution Act, 1871*."	Constitution Act, 1871
6.	Order of Her Majesty in Council admitting Prince Edward Island into the Union, dated the 26th day of June, 1873.		Prince Edward Island Terms of Union
7.	Parliament of Canada Act, 1875, 38–39 Vict., c. 38 (U.K.)		Parliament of Canada Act, 1875
8.	Order of Her Majesty in Council admitting all British		Adjacent Territories Order

Item	Act Affected	Amendment	New Name
	possessions and Territories in North America and islands adjacent thereto into the Union, dated the 31st day of July, 1880.		
9.	British North America Act, 1886, 49–50 Vict., c. 35 (U.K.)	Section 3 is repealed and the following substituted therefor: "3. This Act may be cited as the *Constitution Act, 1886*."	Constitution Act, 1886
10.	Canada (Ontario Boundary) Act, 1889, 52–53 Vict., c. 28 (U.K.)		Canada (Ontario Boundary) Act, 1889
11.	Canadian Speaker (Appointment of Deputy) Act, 1895, 2nd Sess., 59 Vict., c. 3 (U.K.)	The Act is repealed.	
12.	The Alberta Act, 1905, 4–5 Edw. VII, c. 3 (Can.)		Alberta Act
13.	The Saskatchewan Act, 1905 4–5 Edw. VII, c. 42 (Can.)		Saskatchewan Act
14.	British North America Act, 1907, 7 Edw. VII, c. 11 (U.K.)	Section 2 is repealed and the following substituted therefor: "2. This Act may be cited as the *Constitution Act, 1907*."	Constitution Act, 1907
15.	British North America Act, 1915, 5–6 Geo. V, c. 45 (U.K.)	Section 3 is repealed and the following substituted therefor: "3. This Act may be cited as the *Constitution Act, 1915*."	Constitution Act, 1915
16.	British North America Act, 1930, 20–21 Geo. V, c. 26	Section 3 is repealed and the following substituted therefor: "3. This Act may be cited as the *Constitution Act, 1930*."	Constitution Act, 1930
17.	Statute of Westminster, 1931, 22 Geo. V, c. 4 (U.K.)	In so far as they apply to Canada, (*a*) section 4 is repealed; and (*b*) subsection 7(1) is repealed.	Statute of Westminster, 1931
18.	British North America Act, 1940, 3–4 Geo. VI, c. 36 (U.K.)	Section 2 is repealed and the following substituted therefor: "2. This Act may be cited as the *Constitution Act, 1940*."	Constitution Act, 1940
19.	British North America Act, 1943, 6–7 Geo. VI, c. 30 (U.K.)	The Act is repealed.	
20.	British North America Act, 1946, 9–10 Geo. VI, c. 63 (U.K.)	The Act is repealed.	

Item	Act Affected	Amendment	New Name
21.	British North America Act, 1949, 12–13 Geo. VI, c. 22 (U.K.)	Section 3 is repealed and the following substituted therefor: "3. This Act may be cited as the *Newfoundland Act*."	Newfoundland Act
22.	British North America (No. 2) Act, 1949, 13 Geo. VI, c. 81 (U.K.)	The Act is repealed. (effective when section 56 of the *Constitution Act, 1981* comes into force)	
23.	British North America Act, 1951, 14–15 Geo. VI, c. 32 (U.K.)	The Act is repealed.	
24.	British North America Act, 1952, 1 Eliz. II, c. 15 (Can.)	The Act is repealed.	
25.	British North America Act, 1960, 9 Eliz. II, c. 2 (U.K.)	Section 2 is repealed and the following substituted therefor: "2. This Act may be cited as the *Constitution Act, 1960*."	Constitution Act, 1960
26.	British North America Act, 1964, 12–13 Eliz. II, c. 73 (U.K.)	Section 2 is repealed and the following substituted therefor: "2. This Act may be cited as the *Constitution Act, 1964*."	Constitution Act, 1964
27.	British North America Act, 1965, 14 Eliz. II, c. 4, Part I (Can.)	Section 2 is repealed and the following substituted therefor: "2. This Part may be cited as the *Constitution Act, 1965*."	Constitution Act, 1965
28.	British North America Act, 1974, 23 Eliz. II, c. 13, Part I (Can.)	Section 3, as amended by 25–26 Eliz. II, c. 28, s. 38(1) (Can.) is repealed and the following substituted therefor: "3. This Part may be cited as the *Constitution Act, 1974*."	Constitution Act, 1974
29.	British North America Act, 1975, 23–24 Eliz. II, c. 28, Part I (Can.)	Section 3, as amended by 25–26 Eliz. II, c. 28, s. 31 (Can.) is repealed and the following substituted therefor: "3. This Part may be cited as the *Constitution Act (No. 1), 1975*."	Constitution Act (No. 1), 1975
30.	British North America Act (No. 2), 1975, 23–24 Eliz. II, c. 53 (Can.)	Section 3 is repealed and the following substituted therefor: "3. This Act may be cited as the *Constitution Act (No. 2), 1975*."	Constitution Act (No. 2), 1975

47. Reference re Amendment of the Constitution of Canada (Nos. 1, 2, and 3) (1981), 125 D.L.R. (3d) 1 (S.C.C.)

Supreme Court of Canada, Laskin C.J.C., Martland, Ritchie, Dickson, Beetz, Estey, McIntyre, Chouinard and Lamer JJ. September 28, 1981.

Constitutional law — Amendments to Constitution of Canada — Proposed Resolution for Joint Address to the Queen respecting Constitution of Canada — Whether provincial powers, rights or privileges or federal-provincial relationships affected — Whether constitutional convention requiring agreement of Provinces before seeking such amendments — Whether agreement of Provinces to such amendments required as a matter of law — Whether Terms of Union between Newfoundland and Canada can be amended pursuant to proposed Resolution without consent of Government, Legislature or majority of people of Newfoundland.

On appeals to the Supreme Court of Canada from the answers given by the Manitoba, Newfoundland, and Quebec Courts of Appeal on References of certain questions to those Courts made by the respective Governments of those three Provinces, the following questions were asked and answers given as indicated:

ON THE APPEALS FROM THE MANITOBA AND NEWFOUNDLAND COURTS OF APPEAL

"1. If the amendments to the Constitution of Canada sought in the 'Proposed Resolution for a Joint Address to Her Majesty the Queen respecting the Constitution of Canada', or any of them, were enacted, would federal-provincial relationships or the powers, rights or privileges granted or secured by the Constitution of Canada to the provinces, their legislatures or governments be affected and if so, in what respect or respects?"

Answer by all members of the Court: Yes.

"2. Is it a constitutional convention that the House of Commons and Senate of Canada will not request Her Majesty the Queen to lay before the Parliament of the United Kingdom of Great Britain and Northern Ireland a measure to amend the Constitution of Canada affecting federal-provincial relationships or the powers, rights or privileges granted or secured by the Constitution of Canada to the provinces, their legislatures or governments without first obtaining the agreement of the provinces?"

Answer by Martland, Ritchie, Dickson, Beetz, Chouinard and Lamer JJ.: Yes.

Answer by Laskin C.J.C., Estey and McIntyre JJ.: No.

"3. Is the agreement of the provinces of Canada constitutionally required for amendment to the Constitution of Canada where such amendment affects federal-provincial relationships or alters the powers, rights or privileges granted or secured by the Constitution of Canada to the provinces, their legislatures or governments?"

Answer by Laskin C.J.C., Dickson, Beetz, Estey, McIntyre, Chouinard and Lamer JJ.: No.

Answer by Martland and Ritchie JJ.: Yes.

A FURTHER QUESTION ON THE APPEAL FROM THE NEWFOUNDLAND COURT OF APPEAL

"4. If Part V of the proposed resolution referred to in question 1 is enacted and proclaimed into force could
(a) the Terms of Union, including terms 2 and 17 thereof contained in the Schedule to the British North America Act 1949 (12–13 George VI, c. 22 [U.K.]), or
(b) section 3 of the British North America Act, 1871 (34–35 Victoria, c. 28 [U.K.])
be amended directly or indirectly pursuant to Part V without the consent of the Government, Legislature or a majority of the people of the Province of Newfoundland voting in a referendum held pursuant to Part V?"

Answer by all members of the Court:

(1) By s. 3 of the *British North America Act, 1871*, Term 2 of the Terms of Union cannot now be changed without the consent of the Newfoundland Legislature.

(2) By s. 43 of the *"Constitution Act"*, as it now reads, none of the Terms of Union can be changed without the consent of the Newfoundland Legislative Assembly.

(3) Both of these sections can be changed by the amending formulae prescribed in s. 41 and the Terms of Union could then be changed without the consent of the Newfoundland Legislature.

(4) If the amending formula under s. 42 is utilized, both of these sections can be changed by a referendum held pursuant to the provisions of s. 42. In this event, the Terms of Union could then be changed without the consent of the Newfoundland Legislature, and without the consent of the majority of the Newfoundland people voting in a referendum.

ON THE APPEAL FROM THE QUEBEC COURT OF APPEAL

"A. If the Canada Act and the Constitution Act 1981 should

come into force and if they should be valid in all respects in Canada would they affect:

    (i) the legislative competence of the provincial legislatures in virtue of the Canadian Constitution?

    (ii) the status or role of the provincial legislatures or governments within the Canadian Federation?''

Answer by all members of the Court: Yes.

    ''B. Does the Canadian Constitution empower, whether by statute, convention or otherwise, the Senate and the House of Commons of Canada to cause the Canadian Constitution to be amended without the consent of the provinces and in spite of the objection of several of them, in such a manner as to affect:

    (i) the legislative competence of the provincial legislatures in virtue of the Canadian Constitution?

    (ii) the status or role of the provincial legislatures or governments within the Canadian Federation?''

Answer by Martland, Ritchie, Dickson, Beetz, Chouinard and Lamer JJ.: As a matter of convention, No.

Answer by Laskin C.J.C., Estey and McIntyre JJ.: As a matter of convention, Yes.

Answer by Laskin C.J.C., Dickson, Beetz, Estey, McIntyre, Chouinard and Lamer JJ.: As a matter of law, Yes.

Answer by Martland and Ritchie JJ.: As a matter of law, No.

On Question 1 from the Manitoba and Newfoundland References and Question A from the Quebec Reference

Per curiam: Under the terms of the enactments proposed in the Resolution, the legislative powers of the provincial Legislatures would be limited by the *Charter of Rights and Freedoms*. The limitations of the proposed *Charter of Rights and Freedoms* on legislative power apply both at the federal level and the provincial level. This does not, however, alter the fact that there is an intended suppression of provincial legislative power. Moreover, the enhancement of provincial legislative authority under some provisions of the proposed enactment, as, for example, in respect of resource control, including interprovincial export (albeit subject to federal paramountcy), and in respect of taxing power, does not alter the fact that there is an effect on existing federal-provincial relationships under these and other provisions of the draft statute intended for submission to enactment by the Parliament of the United Kingdom.

On Question 2 from the Manitoba and
Newfoundland References and the
Conventional Aspect of Question B
from the Quebec Reference

Per Martland, Ritchie, Dickson, Beetz, Chouinard and Lamer JJ.: A substantial part of the rules of the Canadian Constitution is written. They are contained not in a single document called a ''Constitution'' but in a great variety of statutes some of which have been enacted by the Parliament of Westminster, such as the

British North America Act, 1867, or by the Parliament of Canada, such as the *Alberta Act*, 1905 (Can.), c. 3, the *Saskatchewan Act*, 1905 (Can.), 42, and the *Senate and House of Commons Act*, R.S.C. 1970, c. S-8, or by the provincial Legislatures, such as the provincial electoral Acts. They are also to be found in Orders in Council like the Imperial Order in Council of May 16, 1871, admitting British Columbia into the Union, and Imperial Order in Council of June 26, 1873, admitting Prince Edward Island into the Union. Another part of the Constitution of Canada consists of the rules of the common law. These are rules which the Courts have developed over the centuries in the discharge of their judicial duties. An important portion of these rules concerns the prerogative of the Crown. Those parts of the Constitution of Canada that are composed of statutory rules and common law rules are generically referred to as the law of the Constitution. In cases of doubt or dispute it is the function of the Court to declare what the law is, and since the law is sometimes breached it is generally the function of the Courts to ascertain whether it has in fact been breached in specific instances and, if so, to apply such sanctions as are contemplated by the law, whether they be punitive sanctions or civil sanctions such as a declaration of nullity. Thus, when a federal or a provincial satute is found by the Court to be in excess of the legislative competence of the Legislature that has enacted it, it is declared null and void and the Courts refuse to give effect to it. In this sense it can be said that the law of the Constitution is administered or enforced by the Courts.

Many important parts of the Constitution of Canada, with which people are most familiar because they are directly involved when they exercise their right to vote at federal and provincial elections, are nowhere to be found in the law of the constitution. For instance, it is a fundamental requirement of the Constitution that if the Opposition obtains the majority at the polls the Government must tender its resignation forthwith. But fundamental as it is, this requirement of the Constitution does not form part of the law of the Constitution. Such essential rules of the Constitution are called conventions of the Constitution. They are the principles and rules of responsible government, which were developed in Great Britain by way of custom and precedent during the nineteenth century and were exported to such British colonies as were granted self-government. A federal constitution provides for the distribution of powers between various Legislatures and Governments and may also constitute a fertile ground for the growth of constitutional conventions between those Legislatures and Governments. It is conceivable for instance that usage and practice might give birth to conventions in Canada relating to the holding of federal-provincial conferences, the appointment of Lieutenant-Governors, the reservation and disallowance of provincial legislation. The main purpose of constitutional conventions is to ensure that the legal framework of the Constitution will be operated in accordance with the prevailing constitutional values or principles of the period. Being based on custom and precedent, constitutional conventions are usually unwritten rules. Some of them, however, may be reduced to writing and expressed in the proceedings and documents of Imperial conferences, or in the preamble of statutes such as the

Statute of Westminster, 1931 (U.K.), c. 4, or in the proceedings and documents of federal-provincial conferences. They are often referred to and recognized in statements made by members of Governments. The conventional rules of the Constitution present one striking peculiarity: in contradistinction to the laws of the Constitution, they are not enforced by the Courts. One reason for this situation is that, unlike common law rules, conventions are not Judge-made rules. They are not based on judicial precedents but on precedents established by the institutions of government themselves. Nor are they in the nature of statutory commands which it is the function and duty of the Courts to obey and enforce. Furthermore, to enforce them would mean to administer some formal sanction when they are breached. But the legal system from which they are distinct does not contemplate formal sanctions for their breach. The main reason that conventional rules cannot be enforced by the Courts is that they are generally in conflict with the legal rules that they postulate and the Courts are bound to enforce the legal rules. The conflict is not of a type that would entail the commission of any illegality. It results from the fact that legal rules create wide powers, discretions and rights which conventions prescribe should be exercised only in a certain limited manner, if at all. This conflict between convention and law which prevents the Courts from enforcing conventions also prevents conventions from crystallizing into laws, unless it be by statutory adoption. It is because the sanctions of convention rest with the institutions of government other than Courts, such as the Governor General or the Lieutenant-Governor, or the Houses of Parliament, or with public opinion and, ultimately, with the electorate that it is generally said that they are political. It should be borne in mind, however, that, while they are not laws, some conventions may be more important than some laws. Their importance depends on that of the value or principle which they are meant to safeguard. They form an integral part of the Constitution and of the constitutional system. That is why it is appropriate to say that to violate a convention is to do something which is unconstitutional although it entails no direct legal consequence. But the words "constitutional" and "unconstitutional" may also be used in a strict legal sense, for instance with respect to a statute that is found *ultra vires* or unconstitutional. All this may be summarized in an equation: constitutional conventions plus constitutional law equal the total Constitution of the country.

It was submitted by counsel for Canada, Ontario and New Brunswick that there is no constitutional convention that the House of Commons and Senate of Canada will not request the Queen to lay before the Parliament of Westminster a measure to amend the Constitution of Canada affecting federal-provincial relationships without first obtaining the agreement of the Provinces. It was submitted by counsel for Manitoba, Newfoundland, Quebec, Nova Scotia, British Columbia, Prince Edward Island and Alberta that the convention does exist, that it requires the agreement of all the Provinces and that the second question in the Manitoba and Newfoundland References should accordingly be answered in the affirmative. Counsel for Saskatchewan agreed that the question be answered in the affirmative but on a different

basis. He submitted that the convention exists and requires a measure of provincial agreement. Counsel for Saskatchewan further submitted that the Resolution before the Court has not received a sufficient measure of provincial consent. We agree with the submissions made on this issue by counsel for Saskatchewan.

In determining whether a convention has been established three questions must be asked: first, what are the precedents; secondly, did the actors in the precedents believe that they were bound by a rule; and thirdly, is there a reason for the rule? A single precedent with a good reason may be enough to establish the rule. A whole string of precedents without such a reason will be of no avail, unless it is perfectly certain that the persons concerned regarded themselves as bound by it. As far as the precedents are concerned, no amendment changing provincial legislative powers has been made since Confederation when agreement of a Province whose legislative powers would have been charged was withheld. The accumulation of these precedents does not of itself suffice in establishing the existence of the convention, but it points in its direction. If the precedents stood alone, it might be argued that unanimity is required. As far as the actors in the precedents are concerned there is a recognition that the requirement of provincial agreement is a constitutional rule. However, while the precedents taken alone point at unanimity, the unanimity principle cannot be said to have been accepted by all the actors in the precedents. In 1965 the White Paper on constitutional amendment stated that: "The nature and the degree of provincial participation in the amending process . . . have not lent themselves to easy definition." Nothing has occurred since then which would permit a more precise conclusion. Nor can it be said that this lack of precision is such as to prevent the principle from acquiring the constitutional status of a conventional rule. If a consensus had emerged on the measure of provincial agreement, an amending formula would quickly have been enacted. To demand as much precision as if this were the case and as if the rule were a legal one is tantamount to denying that this area of the Canadian Constitution is capable of being governed by conventional rules. It would not be appropriate for the Court to devise in the abstract a specific formula which would indicate in positive terms what measure of provincial agreement is required for the convention to be complied with. Conventions by their nature develop in the political field and it will be for the political actors, not the Court, to determine the degree of provincial consent required. It is sufficient for the Court to decide that at least a substantial measure of provincial consent is required and to decide further whether the situation before the Court meets with this requirement. The situation is one where Ontario and New Brunswick agree with the proposed amendments whereas the eight other provinces oppose it. By no conceivable standard could this situation be thought to pass muster. It does not disclose a sufficient measure of provincial agreement. The reason for the rule is the federal principle. Canada is a federal union. The federal principle cannot be reconciled with a state of affairs where the modification of provincial legislative powers could be obtained by the unilateral action of the federal authorities. The purpose of this conventional rule is to protect the federal character of the Canadian Constitution and prevent the anomaly that the House of Commons and Senate could obtain by simple resolutions what they could not validly accomplish by statute.

Per Laskin C.J.C., Estey and MacIntyre JJ.: The convention contended for by all objecting Provinces except Saskatchewan is a constitutional convention which requires that before the two Houses of the Canadian Parliament will request the Queen to lay before the Parliament of the United Kingdom a measure to amend the Constitution of Canada affecting federal-provincial reltionships, it will obtain agreement thereto from all the Provinces. An affirmative answer would involve a declaration that such a convention, requiring the consent of *all* the Provinces, exists while a negative answer would deny its existence. No other answers can be open to the Court for, on a reference of this nature, the Court may answer only the questions put and may not conjure up questions of its own which, in turn, would lead to uninvited answers.

While we are in agreement with much of what has been said by the majority, as to the general nature of conventions, we cannot agree with any suggestion that the non-observance of a convention can properly be termed unconstitutional in any strict or legal sense, or that its observance could be, in any sense, a constitutional requirement within the meaning of Question 3 of the Manitoba and Newfoundland References. In a federal State where the essential feature of the Constitution must be the distribution of powers between the two levels of Government, each supreme in its own legislative sphere, constitutionality and legality must be synonymous, and conventional rules will be accorded less significance than they may have in a unitary State such as the United Kingdom.

Can it be said that any convention having a clear definition and acceptance concerning provincial participation in the amendment of the Canadian Constitution has developed? The answer must be "no". The degree of provincial participation in constitutional amendments has been a subject of controversy in Canadian political life for generations. No view on this subject has become so clear and so broadly accepted as to constitute a constitutional convention. There is a fundamental difference between the convention in the Dicey concept and the convention for which some of the provinces contend. The Dicey convention relates to the functioning of individuals and institutions within a parliamentary democracy in unitary form. It does not qualify or limit the authority or sovereignty of Parliament or the Crown. The convention sought to be advanced here would truncate the functioning of the executive and legislative branches at the federal level. This would impose a limitation on the sovereign body itself within the Constitution. Such a convention would require for its recognition, even in the non-legal, political sphere, the clearest signal from the plenary unit intended to be bound, and not simply a plea from the majority of the beneficiaries of such a convention, the provincial plenary units. Since confederation Canada has grown from a group of four somewhat hesitant colonies into a modern, independent State, vastly increased in size, power and wealth, and having a social and governmental structure unimagined in 1867. Vast change has occurred in Dominion-Provincial relations over that period. Many factors have influenced this process and the amendments to the *British North America Act 1867*, have played a significant part. All must receive consideration in resolving this question. Only in four cases has full provincial consent been obtained and in many cases the federal Government has proceeded with amendments in the face of active provincial opposition. It is unrealistic to say that the convention has emerged.

ON QUESTION 3 FROM THE MANITOBA AND NEWFOUNDLAND REFERENCES AND THE LEGAL ASPECT OF QUESTION B FROM THE QUEBEC REFERENCE

Per Laskin C.J.C., Dickson, Beetz, McIntyre, Chouinard and Lamer JJ.: There are two broad aspects to the matter which divide into a number of separate issues: (1) the authority of the two federal Houses to proceed by Resolution where provincial powers and federal-provincial relationships are thereby affected, and (2) the role or authority of the Parliament of the United Kingdom to act on the Resolution. The first point concerns the need of legal power to initiate the process in Canada; the second concerns legal power or want of it in the Parliament of the United Kingdom to act on the Resolution when it does not carry the consent of the Provinces. The proposition was advanced on behalf of the Attorney-General of Manitoba that a convention may crystallize into law and that the requirement of provincial consent, although in origin political, has become a rule of law. This is not so. No instance of an explicit recognition of a convention as having matured into a rule of law was produced. The nature of a convention, as political in inception and as depending on a consistent course of political recognition by those for whose benefit and to whose detriment (if any) the convention developed over a considerable period of time, is inconsistent with its legal enforcement. There is no limit in law, either in Canada or in the United Kingdom (having regard to s. 18 of the *British North America Act, 1867*, as enacted by 1875 (U.K.), c. 38, s. 1, which ties the privileges, immunities and powers of the federal Houses to those of the British House of Commons), to the power of the Houses to pass resolutions. Under s. 18 the federal Parliament may by statute define those privileges, immunities and powers so long as they do not exceed those held and enjoyed the British House of Commons at the time of the passing of the federal statute. It is said, however, that where the Resolution touches provincial powers, there is a limitation on federal authority to pass it on to the Queen unless there is provincial consent. If there is such a limitation, it arises not from any limitation on the power to adopt resolutions but from an external limitation based on other considerations. The legal question is whether this Court can enact, by what would be judicial legislation, a formula of unanimity to initiate the amending process which would be binding not only in Canada but also on the Parliament of the United Kingdom with which amending authority would still remain. The *Statute of Westminster, 1931* is put forward not only as signifying an equality of status as between the Dominion and the Provinces vis-à-vis the United Kingdom Parliament, but also as attenuating the theretofore untrammelled legislative authority of that Parliament in relation to Canada where provincial interests are involved. What s. 7(1) of the *Statute of Westminster, 1931*, reinforced by s. 7(3), appeared to do was to maintain the *status quo ante*; that is, to leave any changes in the *British North America Act, 1867* (that is, such changes which, under its terms, could not be carried out by legislation of the Provinces or of the Dominion) to the prevailing situation, namely, with the legislative authority of the United Kingdom Parliament being left untouched. The "old machinery" remained in place as a result of the *Statute of Westminster, 1931*.

The challenge to the competency in law of the federal Houses to seek enactment by the Parliament of the United Kingdom of the statutes embodied in the Resolution is based on the recognized supremacy of provincial Legislatures in relation to the powers conferred upon them under the *British North America Act, 1867*, a supremacy vis-à-vis the federal Parliament. Reinforcement, or the foundation, of this supremacy is said to lie in the nature or character of Canadian federalism. What is put forward by the Provinces that oppose the forwarding of the address without provincial consent is that external relations with Great Britain in this respect must take account of the nature and character of Canadian federalism. It is contended that a legal underpinning of their position is to be found in the Canadian federal system, as reflected in historical antecedents, in the pronouncements of leading political figures and in the preamble to the *British North America Act, 1867*. The arguments from history do not lead to any consistent view or any single view of the nature of the *British North America Act, 1867*. History cannot alter the fact that in law there is a British statute to construe and apply in relation to a matter, fundamental as it is, that is not provided for by the statute. So too with pronouncements by political figures or persons in other branches of public life. What is stressed in the preamble to the *British North America Act, 1867* is the desire of the named Provinces "to be federally united . . . with a Constitution similar in principle to that of the United Kingdom". The preamble speaks also of union into "one Dominion" and of the establishment of the Union "by authority of Parliament", that is the United Kingdom Parliament. What, then, is to be drawn from the preamble as a matter of law? A preamble has no enacting force, but it can be called in aid to illuminate provisions of the statute in which it appears. Federal union "with a constitution similar in principle to that of the United Kingdom" may well embrace responsible government and some common law aspects of the United Kingdom's unitary constitutionalism, such as the rule of law and Crown prerogatives and immunities. There is an internal contradiction in speaking of federalism in the light of the invariable principle of British parliamentary supremacy. The resolution of this contradiction lies in the scheme of distribution of legislative power, but this owes nothing to the preamble, resting rather on its own exposition in the substantive terms of the *British North America Act, 1867*. It is the allocation of legislative power

as between the central Parliament and the provincial Legislatures that the Provinces rely on as precluding unilateral federal action to seek amendments to the *British North America Act, 1867* that affect, whether by limitation or extension, provincial legislative authority. The Attorney-General of Canada was forced to answer affirmatively the theoretical question whether in law the federal Government could procure an amendment to the *British North America Act, 1867* that would turn Canada into a unitary State. That is not what the present Resolution envisages because the essential federal character of the country is preserved under the enactments proposed by the Resolution. That, it is argued, is no reason for conceding unilateral federal authority to accomplish, through invocation of legislation by the United Kingdom Parliament, the purposes of the Resolution. There is here, however, an unprecedented situation in which the one constant since the enactment of the *British North America Act* in 1867 has been the legal authority of the United Kingdom Parliament to amend it. The law knows nothing of any requirement of provincial consent, either to a resolution of the federal Houses or as a condition of the exercise of United Kingdom legislative power.

Per Martland and Ritchie JJ.: We are not concerned with the matter of legality or illegality in the sense of determining whether or not the passage of the Resolution under consideration involves a breach of the law. The issue is as to the existence of power to do that which is proposed to be done. The question is whether it is *intra vires* of the Senate and the House of Commons to cause the proposed amendments to the *British North America Act, 1867* to be made by the Imperial Parliament in the absence of provincial agreement. This issue is unique because in the 114 years since Confederation the Senate and House of Commons of Canada have never sought, without the consent of the Provinces, to obtain such an amendment; nor has that possibility ever been contemplated. The enactment of the *British North America Act, 1867* created a federal constitution of Canada which confided the whole area of self-government within Canada to the Parliament of Canada and the provincial Legislatures, each being supreme within its own defined sphere and area. It can fairly be said, therefore, that the dominant principle of Canadian constitutional law is federalism. Neither level of government should be permitted to encroach on the other, either directly or indirectly. The political compromise achieved as a result of the Quebec and London Conferences preceding the passage of the *British North America Act, 1867* would be dissolved unless there were substantive and effective limits on unconstitutional action. The issue is whether the established incompetence of the federal Government to encroach on provincial powers can be avoided through the use of the resolution procedure to effect a constitutional amendment passed at the behest of the federal Government by the Parliament of the United Kingdom. In no instance in the past has an amendment to the *British North America Act, 1867* been enacted which directly affected federal-provincial relationships, in the sense of changing provincial legislative powers, in the absence of federal consultation with and the consent of all the Provinces. The history of amendments reveals the operation of constitutional constraints.

While the choice of the resolution procedure is itself a matter of internal parliamentary responsibility, the making of the addresses to the Sovereign falls into two areas. Resolutions concerning the federal juristic unit and federal powers were made without reference to any but the members of the federal Houses. Resolutions abridging provincial authority have never been passed without the concurrence of the Provinces. In other words, the normal constitutional principles recognizing the inviolability of separate and exclusive legislative powers were carried into, and considered an integral part of, the operation of the resolution procedure.

In order to pass the Resolution now under consideration the Senate and the House of Commons must purport to exercise a power. The source of that power must be found in s. 4(*a*) of the *Senate and House of Commons Act*, R.S.C. 1970, c. S-8, since there has been no legislation enacted to date, other than s. 4(*a*), which actually defines the privileges, immunities and powers of the two Houses of Parliament. The Resolution now before us was passed for the purpose of obtaining an amendment to the *British North America Act, 1867*, the admitted effect of which is to curtail provincial legislative powers under s. 92 of that Act. That power is not consistent with the *British North America Act, 1867* but is repugnant to it. It is a power which is out of harmony with the very basis of the Act. Therefore para. (*a*) of s. 4, because of the limitations which it contains, does not confer that power. The Senate and the House of Commons are purporting to exercise a power that they do not possess. The two Houses of Parliament lack legal authority, of their own motion, to obtain constitutional amendments which would strike at the very basis of the Canadian federal system, *i.e.*, the complete division of legislative powers between the Parliament of Canada and the provincial Legislatures. It is the duty of the Court to consider this assertion of rights with a view to the preservation of the Constitution. The federal Parliament is attempting to accomplish indirectly that which it is legally precluded from doing directly by perverting the recognized resolution method of obtaining constitutional amendments by the Imperial Parliament for an improper purpose. Since it is beyond the power of the federal Parliament to enact such an amendment, it is equally beyond the power of its two Houses to effect such an amendment through the agency of the Imperial Parliament.

On Question 4 from the Newfoundland Reference

Per curiam: The Attorney-General of Canada agrees with the conclusions of the Newfoundland Court of Appeal as set out in the first three parts of its answer to the question, and the Attorney-General of Newfoundland agrees with the Attorney-General of Canada that the Newfoundland Court of Appeal was in error in the fourth part of its answer to the question. It was wrong to say that in a referendum under s. 42 (as it then was) of the proposed statute (now s. 46) the approval of the majority of the people in each Province was required. The proper view was that only the approval of the majority of the people voting in a referendum in those Provinces, the approval of whose Legislatures would be required under the general amending formula, would be necessary.

[*Reference re Legislative Authority of Parliament to Alter or Replace the Senate* (1979), 102 D.L.R. (3d) 1, [1980] 1 S.C.R. 54 *sub nom. Re Authority of Parliament in Relation to the Upper House*, distd and refd to; *A.-G. Can. v. A.-G. Ont. et al., Reference re Weekly Rest in Industrial Undertakings Act*, [1936] 3 D.L.R. 673, [1936] S.C.R. 461; affd [1937] 1 D.L.R. 673, [1937] A.C. 326, [1937] 1 W.W.R. 299, [1937] W.N. 53; *British Coal Corp. et al. v. The King*, [1935] 3 D.L.R. 401, 64 C.C.C. 145, [1935] A.C. 500, [1935] 2 W.W.R. 564; *Attorney-General v. Jonathan Cape Ltd.*, [1976] 1 Q.B. 752; *Commercial Cable Co. v. Government of Newfoundland* (1916), 29 D.L.R. 7, [1916] 2 A.C. 610; *Alexander E. Hull & Co. v. M'Kenna*, [1926] 1 R. 402; *Copyright Owners v. E.M.I. Australia (Pty.) Ltd.* (1958), 100 C.L.R. 597; *Blackburn v. Attorney-General*, [1971] 2 All E.R. 1380; *Reference re Ownership of Off-Shore Mineral Rights* (1967), 65 D.L.R. (2d) 353, [1967] S.C.R. 792, 62 W.W.R. 21; *A.-G. N.S. et al. v. A.-G. Can. et al.*, [1950] 4 D.L.R. 369, [1951] S.C.R. 31, distd; *Re Water Powers' Reference*, [1929] 2 D.L.R. 481, [1929] S.C.R. 200 *sub nom. Reference re Waters and Water-Powers*; *Re Royal Prerogative of Mercy upon Deportation Proceedings*, [1933] 2 D.L.R. 348, 59 C.C.C. 301, [1933] S.C.R. 269; *Bonanza Creek Gold Mining Co. v. The King* (1916), 26 D.L.R. 273, [1916] 1 A.C. 566, 10 W.W.R. 391, 25 Que. K.B. 170, 114 L.T. 765; *Liquidators of Maritime Bank of Canada v. Receiver-General of New Brunswick*, [1892] A.C. 437; *A.-G. Ont. v. Mercer* (1883), 8 App. Cas. 767; *A.-G. B.C. v. A.-G. Can.* (1889), 14 App. Cas. 295; *R. v. A.-G. B.C.*, [1924] 3 D.L.R. 690, [1924] A.C. 213, [1923] 3 W.W.R. 1252; *Reference re Power of Disallowance and Power of Reservation*, [1938] 2 D.L.R. 8, [1938] S.C.R. 71; *Wilson v. E. & N. R. Co.* (1921), 61 D.L.R. 1, [1922] 1 A.C. 202, [1921] 3 W.W.R. 817, 28 C.R.C. 296; *Gallant v. The King*, [1949] 2 D.L.R. 425, 93 C.C.C. 237, 23 M.P.R. 48; *Stockdale v. Hansard* (1839), 9 Ad. & E. 1, 112 E.R. 1112; *Commonwealth v. Kreglinger & Fernau Ltd.* (1925), 37 C.L.R. 393; *Liversidge v. Anderson*, [1942] A.C. 206; *Carltona Ltd. v. Com'rs of Works*, [1943] 2 All E.R. 560; *Adegbenro v. Akintola*, [1963] A.C. 614; *Ibralebbe v. The Queen*, [1964] A.C. 900; *Arseneau v. The Queen* (1979), 95 D.L.R. (3d) 1, 45 C.C.C. (2d) 321, [1979] 2 S.C.R. 136, 25 N.B.R. (2d) 390, 26 N.R. 226; *A.-G. Que. v. Blaikie et al.* (1981), 123 D.L.R. (3d) 15; *Madzimbamuto v. Lardner-Burke et al.*, [1969] 1 A.C. 645; *Madden v. Nelson and Fort Sheppard R. Co.*, [1899] A.C. 626; *Ladore et al. v. Bennett et al.*, [1939] 3 D.L.R. 1, [1939] A.C. 468, [1939] 2 W.W.R. 566, 21 C.B.R. 1, [1939] 3 All E.R. 98, [1939] W.N. 194; *Hodge v. The Queen* (1883), 9 App. Cas. 117, refd to]

Appeals to the Supreme Court of Canada arising out of References made, respectively, to the Manitoba Court of Appeal, 117 D.L.R. (3d) 1, 7 Man. R. (2d) 269, [1981] 2 W.W.R. 193, the Newfoundland Court of Appeal, 118 D.L.R. (3d) 1, 29 Nfld. & P.E.I.R. 503, and the Quebec Court of Appeal, 120 D.L.R. (3d) 385, by the respective Governments of those three Provinces.

John J. Robinette, Q.C., *John A. Scollin*, Q.C., *Clyde K. Wells*, Q.C., *Barry L. Stayer*, Q.C., *Michel Robert*, *Barbara Reed*, *Raynold Langlois* and *Louis Reynolds*, for Attorney-General of Canada.

Ross W. Paisley, Q.C., and *Wm. Henkel*, Q.C., for Attorney-General of Alberta.

D. M. M. Goldie, Q.C., *E. R. A. Edwards* and *C. F. Willms*, for Attorney-General of British Columbia.

A. Kerr Twaddle, Q.C., *Douglas A.J. Schmeiser* and *Brian F. Squair*, for Attorney-General of Manitoba.

Alan D. Reid and *Alfred R. Landry*, Q.C., for Attorney-General of New Brunswick.

John J. O'Neill, Q.C., *John J. Ashley* and *James L. Thistle*, for Attorney-General of Newfoundland.

Gordon F. Coles, Q.C., *Reinhold M. Enders* and *Mollie Dunsmuir*, for Attorney-General of Nova Scotia.

R. Roy McMurtry, Q.C., *D.W. Mundell*, Q.C., *John Cavarzan*, Q.C., and *Lorraine E. Weinrib*, for Attorney-General of Ontario.

Ian W. H. Bailey, for Attorney-General of Prince Edward Island.

Colin K. Irving, *Georges Emery*, Q.C., *Lucien Bouchard* and *Peter S. Martin*, for Attorney-General of Quebec.

K. M. Lysyk, Q.C., *Darryl G. Bogdasavich* and *John D. Whyte*, for Attorney-General of Saskatchewan.

D'Arcy C. H. McCaffrey, Q.C., for Four Nations Confederacy.

LASKIN C.J.C., DICKSON, BEETZ, ESTEY, MCINTYRE, CHOUINARD AND LAMER, JJ.: —

I

Three appeals as of right are before this Court, concerning in the main common issues. They arise out of three References made, respectively, to the Manitoba Court of Appeal, to the Newfoundland Court of Appeal and to the Quebec Court of Appeal by the respective Governments of the three Provinces.

Three questions were posed in the Manitoba Reference, as follows:

1. If the amendments to the Constitution of Canada sought in the "Proposed Resolution for a Joint Address to Her Majesty the Queen respecting the Constitution of Canada", or any of them, were enacted, would federal-provincial relationships or the powers, rights or privileges granted or secured by the Constitution of Canada to the provinces, their legislatures or governments be affected and if so, in what respect or respects?

2. It is a constitutional convention that the House of Commons and Senate of Canada will not request Her Majesty the Queen to lay before the Parliament of the United Kingdom of Great Britain and Northern Ireland a measure to amend the Constitution of Canada affecting federal-provincial relationships or the powers, rights or privileges granted or secured by the Constitution of Canada to the provinces, their legislatures or governments without first obtaining the agreement of the provinces?

3. Is the agreement of the provinces of Canada constitutionally required for amendment to the Constitution of Canada where such amendment affects federal-provincial relationships or alters the powers, rights or privileges granted or secured by the Constitution of Canada to the provinces, their legislatures or governments?

The same three questions were asked in the Newfoundland Reference and, in addition, a fourth question was put in these terms:

4. If Part V of the proposed resolution referred to in question 1 is enacted and proclaimed into force could
    (a) the Terms of Union, including terms 2 and 17 thereof contained in the Schedule to the British North America Act 1949 (12–13 George VI, c. 22 [U.K.]), or
    (b) section 3 of the British North America Act, 1871 (34–35 Victoria, c. 28 [U.K.])
be amended directly or indirectly pursuant to Part V without the consent of the Government, Legislature or a majority of the people of the Province of Newfoundland voting in a referendum held pursuant to Part V?

In the Quebec Reference there was a different formulation, two questions being asked which read (translation):

A. If the Canada Act and the Constitution Act 1981 should come into force and if they should be valid in all respects in Canada would they affect:
    (i) the legislative competence of the provincial legislatures in virtue of the Canadian Constitution?
    (ii) the status or role of the provincial legislature or governments within the Canadian Federation?
B. Does the Canadian Constitution empower, whether by statute, convention or otherwise, the Senate and the House of Commons of Canada to cause the Canadian Constitution to be amended without the consent of the provinces and in spite of the objection of several of them, in such a manner as to affect:
    (i) the legislative competence of the provincial legislatures in virtue of the Canadian Constitution?
    (ii) the status or role of the provincial legislatures or governments within the Canadian Federation?

The answers given by the Judges of the Manitoba Court of Appeal, each of whom wrote reasons [117 D.L.R. (3d) 1, 7 Man. R. (2d) 269, [1981] 2 W.W.R. 193], are as follows:

Freedman C.J.M.:
   Question 1 —Not answered, because it is tentative and premature.
   Question 2 —No
   Question 3 —No

Hall J.A.:
   Question 1 —Not answered because it is not appropriate for judicial response, and, in any event, the question is speculative and premature.
   Question 2 —Not answered because it is not appropriate for judicial response.
   Question 3 —No, because there is no legal requirement of Provincial agreement to amendment of the Constitution as asserted in the question.

Matas J.A.:
   Question 1 —Not answered, because it is speculative and premature.
   Question 2 —No
   Question 3 —No

O'Sullivan J.A.:
   Question 1 —Yes, as set out in reasons.
   Question 2 —The constitutional convention referred to has not been established as a matter simply of precedent; it is, however, a constitutional principle binding in law that the House of Commons and Senate of Canada should not request Her Majesty the Queen to lay before the Parliament of the United Kingdom of Great Britain and Northern Ireland any measure to amend the Constitution of Canada affecting federal-provincial relationships or the powers, rights or privileges granted or secured by the Constitution of Canada to the provinces, their legislatures or governments without first obtaining the agreement of the provinces.
   Question 3 —Yes, as set out in reasons.

Huband J.A.:
   Question 1 —Yes
   Question 2 —No
   Question 3 —Yes

The Newfoundland Court of Appeal, in reasons of the Court concurred in by all three Judges who sat on the Reference, answered all three questions common to the Manitoba Reference in the affirmative. The Court answered the fourth question in this way [118 D.L.R. (3d) 1 at pp. 30–1, 29 Nfld. & P.E.I.R. 503]:

(1) By s. 3 of the *British North America Act, 1871, Term 2* of the Terms of Union cannot now be changed without the consent of the Newfoundland Legislature.
(2) By s. 43 of the *Constitution Act, 1981*, as it now reads, none of the Terms of Union can be changed without the consent of the Newfoundland Legislative Assembly.
(3) Both of these sections can be changed by the amending formulae prescribed in s. 41 and the Terms of Union could then be changed without the consent of the Newfoundland Legislature.
(4) If the amending formula under s. 42 is utilized, both of these sections can be changed by a referendum held pursuant to the provisions of s. 42. In this event, the Terms of Union could then be changed without the consent of the Newfoundland Legislature, but not without the consent of the majority of the Newfoundland people voting in a referendum.

The Quebec Court of Appeal, in reasons delivered by each of the five Judges who sat on the Reference [120 D.L.R. (3d) 385], answered the two questions submitted to it as follows (translation):

Question A	(i) yes	(unanimously)
	(ii) yes	(unanimously)
Question B	(i) yes	(Bisson J.A. dissenting) would answer no)
	(ii) yes	(Bisson J.A. dissenting) would answer no)

II

The References in question here were prompted by the opposition of six Provinces, later joined by two others, to a proposed Resolution which was published on October 2, 1980, and intended for submission to the House of Commons and as well to the Senate of Canada. It contained an address to be presented to Her Majesty the Queen in right of the United Kingdom respecting what may generally be referred to as the Constitution of Canada. The address laid before the House of Commons on October 6, 1980, was in these terms:

   To the Queen's Most Excellent Majesty:
   Most Gracious Sovereign:
   We, Your Majesty's loyal subjects, the Senate and the House of Commons of Canada in Parliament assembled, respectfully approach Your Majesty, requesting that you

may graciously be pleased to cause to be laid before the Parliament of the United Kingdom a measure containing the recitals and clauses hereinafter set forth:

An Act to amend the Constitution of Canada

Whereas Canada has requested and consented to the enactment of an Act of Parliament of the United Kingdom to give effect to the provisions hereinafter set forth and the Senate and the House of Commons of Canada in Parliament assembled have submitted an address to Her Majesty requesting that Her Majesty may graciously be pleased to cause a Bill to be laid before the Parliament of the United Kingdom for that purpose.

Be it therefore enacted by the Queen's Most Excellent Majesty, by and with the advice and consent of the Lords Spiritual and Temporal, and Commons, in this present Parliament assembled, and by the authority of the same, as follows:

1. The *Constitution Act, 1980* set out in Schedule B to this Act is hereby enacted for and shall have the force of law in Canada and shall come into force as provided in that Act.

2. No Act of the Parliament of the United Kingdom passed after the *Constitution Act, 1980* comes into force shall extend to Canada as part of its law.

3. So far as it is not contained in Schedule B, the French version of this Act is set out in Schedule A to this Act and has the same authority in Canada as the English version thereof.

4. This Act may be cited as the *Canada Act*.

It will be noticed that included in the terms of address are the words "cause to be laid before the Parliament of the United Kingdom" and that they are reflected in Question B put before the Quebec Court of Appeal. The proposed Resolution, as the terms of the address indicate, includes a statute which, in turn, has appended to it another statute providing for the patriation of the *British North America Act, 1867* (and a consequent change of name), with an amending procedure, and a *Charter of Rights and Freedoms* including a range of provisions (to be entrenched against legislative invasion) which it is unnecessary to enumerate. The proposed Resolution carried the approval of only two Provinces, Ontario and New Brunswick, expressed by their respective Governments. The opposition of the others, save Saskatchewan, was based on their assertion that both conventionally and legally the consent of all the Provinces was required for the address to go forward to Her Majesty with the appended statutes. Although there was general agreement on the desirability of patriation with an amending procedure, agreement could not be reached at conferences preceding the introduction of the proposed Resolution into the House of Commons,

either on the constituents of such a procedure or on the formula to be embodied therein, or on the inclusion of a *Charter of Rights*.

The References to the respective Courts of Appeal were made and the hearings on the questions asked were held before the proposed Resolution was adopted. This fact underlays the unwillingness of Judges in the Manitoba Court of Appeal to answer Question 1; changes might be made to the proposed Resolution in the course of debate and hence the assertion of prematurity.

The proposed Resolution, as adopted by the House of Commons on April 23, 1981, and by the Senate on April 24, 1981, achieved its final form (there were but a few amendments to the original proposal) almost on the eve of the hearings in this Court on the three appeals. Indeed, the opinions of the Courts in all three References were given and certified before the ultimate adoption of the proposed Resolution. The result of its adoption by the Senate and by the House of Commons was to change the position of the Attorney-General of Canada and of his two supporting intervenors on the propriety of answering Question 1 in the Manitoba and Newfoundland References. He abandoned his initial contention that the question should not be answered.

III

The Reference legislation under which the various questions were put to the three Courts of Appeal is in wide terms. The Manitoba legislation, "An Act for Expediting the Decision of Constitutional and Other Provincial Questions", R.S.M. 1970, c. C-180, provides in s. 2 that the Lieutenant-Governor in Council may refer to the Court of Queen's Bench or a Judge thereof or to the Court of Appeal or a Judge thereof for hearing or consideration "any matter which he thinks fit to refer". The Newfoundland *Judicature Act*, R.S.N. 1970, c. 187, s. 6, as amended [1972, c. 11, s. 2; c. 43, s. 2; 1974, c. 57, s. 4], similarly provides for a reference by the Lieutenant-Governor in Council to the Court of Appeal of "any matter which he thinks fit to refer". The *Court of Appeal Reference Act*, R.S.Q. 1977, c. R-23, s. 1, authorizes the Government of Quebec to refer to the Court of Appeal for hearing and consideration "any question which it deems expedient". The scope of the authority in each case is wide enough to saddle the respective Courts with the determination of questions which may not be justiciable and there is no doubt that those Courts, and this Court on appeal, have a discretion to refuse to answer such questions.

In the appeals now before this Court, it will have been noticed that three members of the Manitoba Court of

Appeal refused to answer the first question before that Court as being tentative and premature or speculative and premature, and one of those Judges, Hall J.A., refused to answer the second question as not being appropriate for judicial response. As has already been noted, the adoption of the proposed Resolution by the Senate and House of Commons changed the position of the Attorney-General of Canada who conceded in this Court that it was answerable. There is no doubt in this Court that since the first question in the Manitoba and Newfoundland References and Question A in the Quebec Reference concern the construction of a document, especially one said to be in its final form, a justiciable issue is raised.

There is equally no doubt that the third question in those two References and Question B in the Quebec Reference raise jusiciable issues and, clearly, they must be answered when they raise question of law. The different formulation of Question B in the Quebec Reference, addressed to the authority of the federal Houses by convention, statute or otherwise to cause the Constitution to be amended (as proposed by the Resolution) without the consent of the Provinces, combines issues raised separately in Questions 2 and 3 in the other References.

IV

A summary of the views expressed in the Courts below on the various questions before them may usefully be set out at this point.

In the Manitoba Court of Appeal, the Chief Justice, Hall and Matas JJ.A. declined to answer Question 1 because they felt the question was speculative and premature. O'Sullivan and Huband JJ.A. in dissent each answered Question 1 in the affirmative.

The Chief Justice, Matas and Huband JJ.A. answered Question 2 in the negative. The Chief Justice canvassed previous amendments, and on that basis decided that no convention of provincial consent existed. Huband J.A. concurred with the Chief Justice. Matas J.A. also concurred, and went on to point out the numerous undefined and uncertain aspects of the alleged convention. Hall J.A. declined to answer Question 2, being of the opinon that conventions were in the realm of politics and inappropriate for judicial consideration. O'Sullivan J.A., in dissent, declined to find any convention in precedent, but none the less stated that there was a "constitutional principle" requiring provincial consent.

Question 3 was answered in the negative by the Chief Justice, Hall and Matas JJ.A. Any "crystallization" of a convention was denied, as was the allegation of provincial "sovereignty". The Chief Justice analyzed and rejected

the "compact theory" as a source of legal obligation. He was further of the view that the "sovereignty" contended for by the Provinces did not flow from the legislative supremacy granted by s. 92 of the *British North America Act, 1867*, but rather from something in the nature of an inherent right flowing from the fact of union. As such, it bore a direct relationship to the "compact theory", and was untenable. Hall J.A. unequivocally rejected the "compact theory", also, and denied that provincial supremacy within s. 92 created a legal requirement of provincial consent to constitutional amendment. Matas J.A. noted that the *Statute of Westminster*, 1931 (U.K.), c. 4, gave the Provinces no new powers over amendment, and he also set out various limitations upon provincial legislative supremacy. O'Sullivan J.A. in dissent discussed and accepted the "compact theory", and futher held that provincial sovereignty within s. 92 made it illegal for anyone to interfere with that sovereignty without provincial consent. Huband J.A. agreed, without expressing any opinion on the 'compact theory". He was of the view that the Crown in these matters must rely on the advice of its provincial ministers. Further, he said that the United Kingdom Parliament is a "bare legislative trustee" for both the Provinces and the federal Parliament.

The Court of Appeal of Newfoundland began with Question 3. It stressed the *Statute of Westminster, 1931* and the discussions leading to its passage, found that the United Kingdom had renounced all legislative sovereignty over Canada, and acts as a "bare legislative trustee" of the provincial Legislatures and the federal Parliament. The Provinces, it said, were "autonomous communities", and the United Kingdom Parliament could not pass an amendment over their objections.

As to Question 2, the Court analyzed the precedents and various positions of political figures. Stress was placed upon the 1965 federal White Paper on "The Amendment of the Constitution of Canada", and on the few occasions when provincial consent was obtained. The Court concluded that the direction of constitutional thinking has been towards the recognition of the right of the Provinces to be consulted, and answered Question 2 in the affirmative.

Addressing Question 1 in broad terms, the Court concluded it clearly must be answered in the affirmative.

Question 4, particular to the Newfoundland Reference, concerned the exact effect of the proposed amending formula upon the Terms of Union on which Newfoundland entered Confederation. The Court gave a complex answer which has already been quoted.

The Quebec Court of Appeal was in general faced with the same questions that were before the other Courts although phrased in a different way. All five members of the Court delivered reasons.

The Court unanimously answered Question A in the affirmative. Four members of the Court answered Question B in the affirmative, Bisson J.A. dissenting. As to Question B, the Chief Justice of Quebec rejected any convention of provincial consent, and noted rather that any convention was in favour of the federal Parliament alone proceeding by joint resolution. The effect of the *Statute of Westminster, 1931* was simply to leave the legal power to amend the Constitution in the United Kingdom Parliament.

Owen J.A. stated that although the Resolution was not specifically authorized by statute, the inherent power of Parliament justified the action. He rejected the "sovereignty", convention and "compact theory" arguments by reference to the reasons of Turgeon J.A. He noted that the provincial argument was weakened by the fact that Canada is not "the theoretical ideal confederation contemplated by text-book writers".

Turgeon J.A. affirmed that the power to amend before 1931 was in the United Kingdom Parliament, and the *Statute of Westminster, 1931* changed nothing. He listed the various fetters on provincial legislative supremacy, and noted that only the federal Parliament could act extraterritorially. After a lengthy analysis of previous amendments, he denied the existence of any convention of provincial consent. He also held the "compact theory" to be without historical or legal support.

Bélanger J.A. doubted whether a resolution, as a matter of internal parliamentary procedure, was susceptible to review by a Court. None the less, he answered Question B in the affirmative, concurring with the Chief Justice and Turgeon J.A., and asking rhetorically whether it was the "essence of a federal union" that it remain stagnant and incapable of evolution in the face of perhaps only one provincial objection.

Bisson J.A. dissented on Question B, and characterized the Resolution as a "*quasi*-legislative" act. In upholding provincial 'sovereignty", he stressed the conferences and resolutions which preceded Confederation and which were given "legislative sanction" in the *British North America Act, 1867*. Canada, he held, was a "*quasi*-federation". Although provincial sovereignty was limited in some ways, none the less, the federal Parliament could not proceed alone. This, he said, was borne out by past practice.

V

The reasons which now follow deal with Questions 1 and 3 in the Manitoba and Newfoundland References, with Question 4 in the Newfoundland Reference, with Question

A in the Quebec Reference and with Question B in that Reference in its legal aspect. Question 2 in the Manitoba and Newfoundland References and Question B in the Quebec Reference in its comparable conventional aspect are dealt with in separate reasons.

VI

On the footing of the adopted Resolution, the Attorney-General of Canada agrees that Question 1 in the Manitoba and Newfoundland References and Question A in the Quebec Reference should be answered in the affirmative as is asserted by the Attorneys-General of Manitoba, Newfoundland and Quebec. Certainly, it is plain that under the terms of the enactments proposed in the Resolution, the legislative powers of the provincial Legislatures would be affected, indeed, limited by the *Charter of Rights and Freedoms.* The limitations of the proposed *Charter of Rights and Freedoms* on the legislative power apply both at the federal level and the provincial level. This does not, however, alter the fact that there is an intended suppression of provincial legislative power. Moreover, the enhancement of provincial legislative authority under some provisions of the proposed enactment, as for example, in respect of resource control, including interprovincial export (albeit subject to federal paramountcy), and in respect of taxing power does not alter the fact that there is an effect on existing federal-provincial relationships under these and other provisions of the draft statute intended for submission to enactment by the Parliament of the United Kingdom.

The simple answer "yes" to Question 1 and Question A answers both of them sufficiently, even though question 1 asks also "in what respect or respects" would federal-provincial relationships and provincial powers, rights or privileges be affected. Counsel were agreed that it would carry them and the Court into considerable exposition of detail if this aspect of Question 1 were to be explored; for the time being, an affirmative answer to the primary issue in question would satisfy all concerned.

VII

Coming now to Question 3 in the Manitoba and Newfoundland References and Question B (on its legal side) in the Quebec Reference. By reason of the use of the words "constitutionally required" in Question 3, the question imports both legal and conventional issues, and as the latter are dealt with in separate reasons, what follows is concerned only with the legal side of Question 3 in the Manitoba and Newfoundland References and Question B (on its legal side) in the Quebec Reference, which meets the submissions of all counsel on this issue.

There are two broad aspects to the matter under discussion which divide into a number of separate issues: (1) the authority of the two federal Houses to proceed by Resolution where provincial powers and federal-provincial relationships are thereby affected, and (2) the role or authority of the Parliament of the United Kingdom to act on the Resolution. The first point concerns the need of legal power to initiate the process in Canada; the second concerns legal power or want of it in the Parliament of the United Kingdom to act on the Resolution when it does not carry the consent of the Provinces.

The submission of the eight Provinces which invites this Court to consider the position of the British Parliament is based on the *Statute of Westminster, 1931* in its application to Canada. The submission is that the effect of the statute is to qualify the authority of the British Parliament to act on the federal Resolution without previous provincial consent where provincial powers and interests are therby affected, as they plainly are here. This issue will be examined later in these reasons.

Two observations are pertinent here. First, we have the anomaly that although Canada has international recognition as an independent, autonomous and self-governing State, as, for example, a founding member of the United Nations, and through membership in other international associations of sovereign States, yet it suffers from an internal deficiency in the absence of legal power to alter or amend the essential distributive arrangements under which legal authority is exercised in the country, whether at the federal or provincial level. When a country has been in existence as an operating federal State for more than a century, the task of introducing a legal mechanism that will thereafter remove the anomaly undoubtedly raises a profound problem. Secondly, the authority of the British Parliament or its practices and conventions are not matters upon which this Court would presume to pronounce.

The proposition was advanced on behalf of the Attorney-General of Manitoba that a convention may crystallize into law and that the requirement of provincial consent to the kind of Resolution that we have here, although in origin political, has become a rule of law. (No firm position was taken on whether the consent must be that of the Governments or that of the Legislatures.)

In our view, this is not so. No instance of an explicit recognition of a convention as having matured into a rule of law was produced. The very nature of a convention, as political in inception and as depending on a consistent course of political recognition by those for whose benefit and to whose detriment (if any) the convention developed over a considerable period of time is inconsistent with its legal enforcement.

The attempted assimilation of the growth of a convention to the growth of the common law is misconceived. The latter is the product of judicial effort, based on justiciable issues which have attained legal formulation and are subject to modification and even reversal by the Courts which gave them birth when acting within their role in the State in obedience to statutes or constitutional directives. No such parental role is played by the Courts with respect to conventions.

It was urged before us that a host of cases have given legal force to conventions. This is an overdrawn proposition. One case in which direct recognition and enforcement of a convention was sought is *Madzimbamuto v. Lardner-Burke et al.*, [1969] 1 A.C. 645. There the Privy Council rejected the assertion that a convention formally recognized by the United Kingdom as established, namely, that it would not legislate for Southern Rhodesia on matters within the competence of the latter's Legislature without its Government's consent, could not be overridden by British legislation made applicable to Southern Rhodesia after the unilateral declaration of independence by the latter's Govenment. Speaking for the Privy Council, Lord Reid pointed out that although the convention was a very important one, "it had no legal effect in limiting the legal power of Parliament" (at p. 723). And, again (at the same page):

> It is often said that it would be unconstitutional for the United Kingdom Parliament to do certain things, meaning that the moral, political and other reasons against doing them are so strong that most people would regard it as highly improper if Parliament did these things. But that does not mean that it is beyond the power of Parliament to do such things. If Parliament chose to do any of them the courts could not hold the Act of Parliament invalid. It may be that it would be unconstitutional to disregard this convention. But it may also be that the unilateral Declaration of Independence released the United Kingdom from any obligation to observe the convention. Their Lordships in declaring the law are not concerned with these matters. They are only concerned with the legal powers of Parliament.

Counsel for Manitoba sought to distinguish this case on the ground that the *Statute of Westminster, 1931* did not embrace Southern Rhodesia, a point to which the Privy Council adverted. The *Statute of Westminster, 1931* will be considered later in these reasons, but if it had been in force in Southern Rhodesia it would be only under its terms and not through any conventional rule *per se* that the Parliament of the United Kingdom would have desisted from legislating for Southern Rhodesia.

Quite a number of cases were cited on which counsel for Manitoba relied to support his contention of conventions crystallizing into law. The chief support put forward for the "crystallization into law" proposition was the opinion of Duff C.J.C. in *A.-G. Can. v. A.-G. Ont. et al., Reference re Weekly Rest in Industrial Undertakings Act,* [1936] 3 D.L.R. 673, [1936] S.C.R. 461, better known as the *Labour Conventions* case when appealed to the Privy Council, [1937] 1 D.L.R. 673, [1937] A.C. 326, [1937] 1 W.W.R. 299, which took a different view on the constitutional merits than did the equally divided Supreme Court of Canada. The issue, so far as it touched the matter under discussion here, concerned the alleged want of power of the Governor-General in Council, the federal executive, to enter into a treaty or accept an international obligation toward and with a foreign State, especially where the substance of the treaty or obligation related to matters which, legislatively within Canada, were within exclusive provincial competence.

The following portion of the reasons of Sir Lyman P. Duff contains the passage relied on, but extends it for more accurate context (at pp. 678–80 D.L.R., pp. 476–8 S.C.R.):

> With reference to the Report of the Conference of 1926, which in explicit terms recognizes treaties in the form of agreements between governments (to which His Majesty is not, in form, a party), it is said that since an Imperial Conference possesses no legislative power, its declarations do not operate to affect changes in the law, and it is emphatically affirmed that, in point of strict law, neither the Governor-General nor any other Canadian authority has received from the Crown power to exercise the prerogative.
>
> The argument is founded on the distinction it draws between constitutional convention and legal rule; and it is necessary to examine the contention that, in point of legal rule, as distinct from constitutional convention, the Governor-General in Council had no authority to become party by ratification to the convention with which we are concerned.
>
> There are various points of view from which this contention may be considered. First of all, constitutional law consists very largely of established constitutional usages recognized by the Courts as embodying a rule of law. An Imperial Conference, it is true, possesses no legislative authority. But there could hardly be more authoritative evidence as to constitutional usage than the declarations of such a Conference. The Conference of 1926 categorically recognizes treaties in the form of agreements between

> governments in which His Majesty does not formally appear, and in respect of which there has been no Royal intervention. It is the practice of the Dominion to conclude with foreign countries agreements in such form, and agreements even of a still more informal character — merely by an exchange of notes. Conventions under the auspices of the Labour Organization of the League of Nations invariably are ratified by the Government of the Dominion concerned. As a rule, the crystallization of constitutional usage into a rule of constitutional law to which the Courts will give effect is a slow process extending over a long period of time; but the Great War accelerated the pace of development in the region with which we are concerned, and it would seem that the usages to which I have referred, the practice, that is to say, under which Great Britain and the Dominions enter into agreements with foreign countries in the form of agreements between Governments and of a still more informal character, must be recognized by the Courts as having the force of law.
>
> Indeed, agreements between the Government of Canada and other Governments in the form of an agreement between Governments, to which His Majesty is not a party, have been recognized by the Judicial Committee of the Privy Council as adequate in international law to create an international obligation binding upon Canada (*Re Regulation & Control of Radio Communication, A.-G. Que. v. A.-G. Can.,* [1932] 2 D.L.R. 81, 39 C.R.C. 49).
>
> . . . . . .
>
> Ratification was the effective act which gave binding force to the convention. It was, as respects Canada, the act of the Government of Canada alone, and the decision mentioned appears, therefore, to negative decisively the contention that, in point of strict law, the Government of Canada is incompetent to enter into an international engagement.

What the learned Chief Justice was dealing with was an evolution which is characteristic of customary international law; the attainment by the Canadian federal executive of full and independent power to enter into international agreements. (Indeed, in speaking of "convention" in the last quoted paragraph, he was referring to an international agreement and, similarly, in the use of the word in the second last line of the second paragraph of the quotation and again in the middle of the third paragraph.) International law perforce has had to develop, if it was to exist at all, through commonly recognized political practices of States, there being no governing constitution, no legislating authority, no executive enforcement authority and no generally accepted judicial organ through which international law could be developed. The situation is entirely different in domestic law, in the position of a State having its own governing legislative, executive and judicial organs and, in most cases, an overarching written constitution.

Chief Justice Duff indicated his view of convention as allegedly maturing into law in a domestic setting in *Reference re Power of Disallowance and Power of Reservation,* [1938] 2 D.L.R. 8, [1938] S.C.R. 71. There it was urged that a certain portion of s. 90 of the *British North America Act, 1867* (incorporating, in respect of the Provinces, ss. 56 and 57, with some modification) had by reason of convention become spent and was suspended by the alleged convention. As to this, the Chief Justice said (at p. 13 D.L.R., p. 78 S.C.R.):

> We are not concerned with constitutional usage. We are concerned with questions of law which, we repeat, must be determined by reference to the enactments of the *B.N.A. Acts* of 1867 to 1930, the *Statute of Westminster* and, it might be, to relevant statutes of the Parliament of Canada if there were any.

> Section 90 which, with the changes therein specified, re-enacts ss. 55, 56 and 57 of the *B.N.A. Act,* is still subsisting. It has not been repealed or amended by the Imperial Parliament and it is quite clear that, by force of s-s. (1) of s. 7 of the *Statute of Westminster,* 1932 (Imp.), c. 4, the Dominion Parliament did not acquire by that statute, any authority to repeal, amend or alter the *B.N.A. Acts.* Whether or not, by force of s. 91(29) and s. 92(1) of the *B.N.A. Act,* the Dominion Parliament has authority to legislate in respect of reservation, it is not necessary to consider because no such legislation has been passed.

> The Powers are, therefore, subsisting. Are they subject to any limitation or restriction?

> Once more, we are not concerned with constitutional usage or constitutional practice.

There is nothing in the other judgments delivered in the *Labour Conventions* case, *supra,* either in the Supreme Court or in the Privy Council that takes the matter there beyond its international law setting or lends credence to the crystallization proposition urged by counsel for the Attorney-General of Manitoba and, it should be said, supported by other Provinces and by observations in the reasons of the Newfoundland Court of Appeal. Other cases cited for the proposition turn out, on examination, to be instances where the Courts proceeded on firm statutory or other legal principles. This is as true of the observation of Viscount Sankey L.C. on the position of the Privy Council in *British Coal Corp. et at. v. The King,* [1935] 3 D.L.R. 401 at p. 403, 64 C.C.C. 145, [1935] A.C. 500 at p. 510, as it is of the denial of injunctive relief in respect of disclosure of the Crossman diaries in *Attorney-General v. Jonathan Cape*

Ltd., [1976] 1 Q.B. 752. The Court pointed out in the latter case that it had the power to restrain breaches of confidence where demanded in the public interest, although the confidence stemmed from a convention respecting Cabinet deliberations. However, the need for restraint had gone because of the passage of time. The Court was applying its own legal principles as it might to any question of confidence, however it arose.

A close look at some other cases and issues raised on so-called crystallization reveals no support for the contention. Nothing need be said about Crown immunity or Crown prerogative, which rested firmly on common law principles and have long since been transformed by various statutes. Among cases put forward, were *Commercial Cable Co. v. Government of Newfoundland* (1916), 29 D.L.R. 7, [1916] 2 A.C. 610; *Alexander E. Hull & Co. v. M'Kenna,* [1926] 1 R. 402; *Copyright Owners v. E.M.I. (Australia) Pty. Ltd.* (1958), 100 C.L.R. 597; *Blackburn v. Attorney-General,* [1971] 2 All E.R. 1380, and the judgment of this Court in the *Senate Reference, Reference re Legislative Authority of Parliament to Alter or Replace the Senate* (1979), 102 D.L.R. (3d) 1, [1980] 1 S.C.R. 54 *sub nom. Re Authority of Parliament in Relation to the Upper House.*

In the *Commercial Cable Co.* case, a certain contract was held not to be binding on the Government of Newfoundland when it was not approved by a resolution of the House of Assembly as required by a rule of the House promulgated pursuant to statute. *Hull v. M'Kenna* was the first instance of an application for leave to appeal to the Privy Council from the Court of Appeal, the final Court of the Irish Free State, which had been recognized as a Dominion under a treaty with the United Kingdom. The question at issue was the application of Privy Council practice on petitions to it for leave to appeal. The legal issue, on which the case turned, was the manner in which the Privy Council exercised its discretion on such petitions.

The *Copyright Owners* case, somewhat involved in its facts, concerned the effect upon and in Australia of a British Act of 1928 and a subsequent Act of 1956. The latter Act repealed the *British Copyright Act* of 1911 which, pursuant to its terms had been brought into force in Australia by Commonwealth legislation. The British Act of 1911 expressly declared that it would not extend to a self-governing Dominion unless declared by the Legislature of that Dominion to be in force there, and with certain limited modifications if thought desirable. The 1956 Act, as a post-*Statute of Westminster Act, 1931* did not apply to Australia when there was no declaration that the Commonwealth had requested and consented to its application. Hence the

1911 British Act was left in force in Australia; indeed, it was so protected under the 1956 British Act, although as Dixon C.J. noted, it was perhaps unnecessary to say so in view of s. 4 of the *Statute of Westminster, 1931*.

The real issue concerned the British Act of 1928 which confirmed a Board of Trade order, resulting in the increase of the royalty payable for reproduction of musical works beyond that fixed by the act of 1911. There was provision in the 1911 Act for alteration of rates through an inquiry by the Board of Trade and the making of an order to be confirmed by statute. Although the *Statute of Westminster, 1931* was three years away, the High Court applied a rule of construction against any British legislative intention, even in 1928, to apply its legislation to Australia when it did not expressly say so. True, this took account of political practice but it was the Court's application of rules of interpretation which governed and the political practice would have counted for nothing if the British legislation of 1928 had been made expressly applicable to Australia. The following passage from the reasons of McTiernan J. is instructive (at p. 613):

> The rule of construction which found its source in the political and constitutional relations between the United Kingdom and the Commonwealth of Australia before the *Statute of Westminster* would raise a presumption that the Act of 1928 was not intended to operate of its own force in this country. Needless to say, it is a rule of construction which this Court would be expected to apply. The fact that the Parliament of the Commonwealth in adopting the *Copyright Act* 1911 (Imp.) made no special modifications in relation to s. 19(3) does not seem to me to afford any reason for our departing from that rule of construction by holding that the Act of 1928 has force and effect in the Commonwealth. I think that it would be fanciful to say that although the latter Act does not apply in Australia as a piece of Imperial legislation, nevertheless, it may operate as no more than a fulfilment of the conditions prescribed by s. 19(3) for altering the rates for the calculations of royalties.

An *obiter* of Lord Denning in the *Blackburn* case was urged before the Court to support the crystallization contention. The case itself arose through an attempt to stall negotiations for entry by the United Kingdom into the European Common Market on the ground that it would involve the surrender by the British Parliament of some at least of its traditional sovereignty. All three Judges in the case agreed that there was no doubt of the power of the United Kingdom executive to enter into treaties and that this was beyond judicial control. Lord Denning's *obiter* was as follows (at pp. 1382–3):

We have all been brought up to believe that, in legal theory, one Parliament cannot bind another and that no Act is irreversible. But legal theory does not always march alongside political reality. Take the Statute of Westminster 1931, which takes away the power of Parliament to legislate for the dominions. Can anyone imagine that Parliament could or would reverse that statute? Take the Acts which have granted independence to the dominions and territories overseas. Can anyone imagine that Parliament could or would reverse those laws and take away their independence? Most clearly not. Freedom once given cannot be taken away. Legal theory must give way to practical politics. . . . What are the realities here? If Her Majesty's Ministers sign this treaty and Parliament enacts provisions to implement it, I do not envisage that Parliament would afterwards go back on it and try to withdraw from it. But, if Parliament should do so, then I say we will consider that event when it happens. We will then say whether Parliament can lawfully do it or not.

Both sides referred us to the valuable article by Professor H W R Wade in the Cambridge Law Journal in which he said that "sovereignty is a political fact for which no purely legal authority can be constituted". That is true. We must wait to see what happens before we pronounce on sovereignty in the Common Market.

The relevance of this to the legal issues in the case is not clear. Certainly the other two Judges who sat in the case, Salmon and Stamp L.JJ., were of the view that the only concern of the Court is with the interpretation of legislation when enacted, not with the Crown's conduct in entering into treaties.

Finally, there was an appeal to the *Senate Reference* decision of this Court. It is baffling how it can be said that this Court recognized convention as having *per se* grown into law. What was involved was a proposed federal enactment sought to be justified mainly under s. 91(1) of the *British North America Act, 1867*. This Court held that the proposal, at least in its main features, was beyond federal competence. Although the Court referred to certain historical background for perspective on the position of the Senate as it was dealt with under the *British North America Act, 1867*, its fundamental duty was to examine the validity of a proposed federal measure sought to be justified under a grant of federal power under that Act.

As to all the cases cited, it must be said that there is no independent force to be found in selective quotations from a portion of the reasons unless regard is had to issues raised and the context in which the quotations are found.

We were invited to consider academic writings on the matter under discussion. There is no consensus among the author-scholars, but the better and prevailing view is that expressed in an article by Munro, "Laws and Conventions Distinguished", 91 Law Q. Rev. 218 (1975), where he says (at p. 228):

> The validity of conventions cannot be the subject of proceedings in a court of law. Reparation for breach of such rules will not be effected by any legal sanction. There are no cases which contradict these propositions. In fact, the idea of a court enforcing a mere convention is so strange that the question hardly arises.

Another passage from this article deserves mention, as follows (at p. 224):

> If in fact laws and conventions are different in kind, as is my argument, then an accurate and meaningful picture of the constitution may only be obtained if this distinction *is* made. If the distinction is blurred, analysis of the constitution is less complete; this is not only dangerous for the lawyer, but less than helpful to the political scientist.

There is no difference in approach whether the issue arises in a unitary State or in a federal State: see Hogg, *Constitutional Law of Canada* (1977), at pp. 7–11.

A contrary view relied on by the provincial appellants is that expressed by Professor W. R. Lederman in two published articles, one entitled "Process of Constitutional Amendment in Canada", 12 McGill L.J. 371 (1967), and the second entitled "Constitutional Amendment and Canadian Unity", Law Soc. U.C. Lectures 17 (1978). As a respected scholar, Professor Lederman's views deserve more than cursory consideration. He himself recognizes that there are contrary views, including those of an equally distinguished scholar, Professor F. R. Scott: see Scott, *Essays on the Constitution* (1977), pp. 144, 169, 204–5, 245, 370–1, 402. There is also the contrary view of Professor Hogg, already cited.

Professor Lederman relies in part on a line of cases that has already been considered, especially the reasons of Sir Lyman P. Duff in the *Labour Conventions* case. The leap from convention to law is explained almost as if there was a common law of constitutional law, but originating in political practice. That is simply not so. What is desirable as a political limitation does not translate into a legal limitation, without expression in imperative constitutional text or statute. The position advocated is all the more unacceptable when substantial provincial compliance or consent is by him said to be sufficient. Although Professor Lederman would not give a veto to Prince Edward Island, he would to Ontario or Quebec or British Columbia or Alberta. This is an impossible position for a Court to

manage. Further reference to this is made later in these reasons.

VIII

Turning now to the authority or power of the two federal Houses to proceed by Resolution to forward the address and appended draft statutes to Her Majesty the Queen for enactment by the Parliament of the United Kingdom. There is no limit anywhere in law, either in Canada or in the United Kingdom (having regard to s. 18 of the *British North America Act, 1867*, as enacted by 1875 (U.K.), c. 38, s. 1, which ties the privileges, immunities and powers of the federal Houses to those of the British House of Commons) to the power of the Houses to pass resolutions. Under s. 18 aforesaid, the federal Parliament may by statute define those privileges, immunities and powers, so long as they do not exceed those held and enjoyed by the British House of Commons at the time of the passing of the federal statute.

May, *Treatise on the Law, Privileges, Proceedings and Usages of Parliament*, 19th ed. (1976), a leading treatise on British parliamentary proceedings, states (at p. 382):

> Every question, when agreed to, assumes the form either of an order or of a resolution of the House. One or the other of these terms is applied in the records of the House to every motion which has been agreed to, and the application of the term is carefully regulated with reference to the content of the motion. By its orders the House directs its committees, its members, its officers, the order of its own proceedings and the acts of all persons whom they concern; by its resolutions the House declares its own opinions and purposes.

This passage is repeated almost verbatim in Beauchesne's *Parliamentary Rules and Forms*, 5th ed. (1978), at p. 150. The *Senate and House of Commons Act*, R.S.C. 1970, c. S-8, ss. 4 and 5, reinforces what is set out in s. 18 of the *British North America Act, 1867*, as amended in 1875.

How Houses of Parliament proceed, how a provincial Legislative Assembly proceeds is in either case a matter of self-definition, subject to any overriding constitutional or self-imposed statutory or indoor prescription. It is unnecessary here to embark on any historical review of the "court" aspect of Parliament and the immunity of its procedures from judicial review. Courts come into the picture when legislation is enacted and not before (unless references are made to them for their opinion on a Bill or a proposed enactment). It would be incompatible with the self-regulating — "inherent" is as apt a word — authority of Houses of Parliament to deny their capacity to pass any kind of resolution. Reference may appropriately be made to art. 9 of the *Bill of Rights*, 1689, 1 Will. & Mary, Sess. 2, c. 2, undoubtedly in force as part of the law of Canada, which provides that "proceedings in Parliament ought not to be impeached or questioned in any Court or place out of Parliament".

It is said, however, that where the Resolution touches provincial powers, as the one in question here does, there is a limitation on federal authority to pass it on to Her Majesty the Queen unless there is provincial consent. If there is such a limitation, it arises not from any limitation on the power to adopt Resolutions but from an external limitation based on other considerations which will shortly be considered.

Although the *British North America Act, 1867* itself is silent on the question of the power of the federal Houses to proceed by Resolution to procure an amendment to the Act by an address to Her Majesty, its silence gives positive support as much as it may reflect the negative. Quebec Question B suggests in its formulation that there is the necessity of affirmative proof of the power asserted, but it would be equally consistent with constitutional precedent to require disproof. Moreover, if the two federal Houses had the power to proceed by Resolution, how is it that they have lost it?

For the moment, it is relevent to point out that even in those cases where an amendment to the *British North America Act, 1867* was founded on a Resolution of the federal Houses after having received provincial consent, there is no instance, save in the *British North America Act, 1930* where such consent was recited in the Resolution. The matter remained, in short, a conventional one within Canada, without effect on the validity of the Resolution in respect of United Kingdom action. The point is underscored in relation to the very first amendment directly affecting provincial legislative power, that in 1940 which added "Unemployment Insurance" [1940 (U.K.), c. 36] to the catalogue of exclusive federal powers. Sir William Jowitt, then Solicitor-General, and later Lord Chancellor, was asked in the British House of Commons about provincial consent when the amendment was in course of passage. The question put to him and his answer are as follows (see 362 U.K. Parl. Deb., 5th Series, H.C., 1177–81);

> Mr. Mander . . . In this bill we are concerned only with the Parliament of Canada, but, as a matter of interest, I would be obliged if the Solicitor-General would say whether the Provincial Canadian Parliaments are in agreement with the proposals submitted by the Dominion Parliament . . . .

> Sir William Jowitt . . . One might think that the Canadian Parliament was in some way subservient to ours, which is not the fact. The true position is that at the request of Canada this old machinery still survives until something better is thought of, but we square the legal with the constitutional position by passing these Acts only in the form that the Canadian Parliament require and at the request of the Canadian Parliament.

> My justification to the House for this Bill — and it is important to observe this — is not on the merits of the proposal, which is a matter for the Canadian Parliament; if we were to embark upon that, we might trespass on what I conceive to be their constitutional position. The sole justification for this enactment is that we are doing in this way what the Parliament of Canada desires to do. . . .

> In reply to the hon. Member for East Wolverhampton (Mr. Mander), I do not know what the view of the Provincial Parliament is. I know, however, that when the matter was before the Privy Council some of the Provincial Parliaments supported the Dominion Parliament. It is a sufficient justification for the Bill that we are morally bound to act on the ground that we have here the request of the Dominion Parliament and that we must operate the old machinery which has been left over at their request in accordance with their wishes.

IX

This Court is being asked, in effect, to enshrine as a legal imperative a principle of unanimity for constitutional amendment to overcome the anomaly — more of an anomaly today than it was in 1867 — that the *British North America Act, 1867* contained no provision for effecting amendments by Canadian action alone. Although Saskatchewan has, alone of the eight Provinces opposing the federal package embodied in the Resolution, taken a less stringent position, eschewing unanimity but without quantifying the substantial support that it advocates, the Provinces, parties to the References and to the appeals here, are entitled to have this Court's primary consideration of their views.

The effect of those views, if they are correct in their legal position, is, of course, to leave at least the formal amending authority in the United Kingdom Parliament. Reference will be made later to the ingredients of the arguments on legality. The effect of the present Resolution is to terminate any need to resort to the United Kingdom Parliament in the future. In line with its rejection of unanimity, Saskatchewan asserted that it sees no violation of the principles of federalism in the Resolution so far as concerns the amending formula proposed thereby.

An important question was raised by the Saskatchewan position which invited this Court to take a severable view of the substance of the Resolution, namely, to hive off the *Charter of Rights and Freedoms* and perhaps other elements, save the amending formula and the patriation feature. This was not the position of the Attorney-General of Canada nor of any of the other provincial Attorneys-General; they were all of the view that it was the whole package that was involved in the legal issue posed by Question 3 and Question B. Indeed, the legal arguments pro and con do not engage the contents of the package, and it is impossible to qualify the issue of legality by considerations of fairness or equity or political acceptability or even judicial desirability.

The stark legal question is whether this Court can enact by what would be judicial legislation a formula of unanimity to initiate the amending process which would be binding not only in Canada but also on the Parliament of the United Kingdom with which amending authority would still remain. It would be anomalous indeed, overshadowing the anomaly of a Constitution which contains no provision for its amendment, for this Court to say retroactively that in law we have had an amending formula all along, even if we have not hitherto known it; or, to say, that we have had in law one amending formula, say from 1867 to 1931, and a second amending formula that has emerged after 1931. No one can gainsay the desirability of federal-provincial accord of acceptable compromise. That does not, however, go to legality. As Sir William Jowitt said, and quoted earlier, we must operate the old machinery perhaps one more time.

X

The provincial contentions asserted a legal incapacity in the federal Houses to proceed with the Resolution which is the subject of the References and of the appeals here. Joined to this assertion was a claim that the United Kingdom Parliament had, in effect, relinquished its legal power to act on a Resolution such as the one before this Court, and that it could only act in relation to Canada if a request was made by "the proper authorities". The federal Houses would be such authorities if provincial powers or interests would not be affected; if they would be, then the proper authorities would include the Provinces. It is not that the Provinces must be joined in the federal address to Her Majesty the Queen; that was not argued. Rather their consent (or, as in the Saskatchewan submission, substantial provincial compliance or approval) was required as a condition of the validity of the process by address and Resolution and, equally, as a condition of valid action thereon by the United Kingdom Parliament.

There are a number of interwoven strands in this position which must be separated for proper analysis and assessment. They include some dependence on the *Balfour Declaration*, arising out of the Imperial Conference of 1926, and also in the Imperial Conference of 1930, the last-mentioned Conference preceded by a meeting of experts in 1929 on the Operation of Dominion Legislation. Then there is a considerable emphasis on a particular view of the *Statute of Westminster, 1931* in respect of some of its terms, and especially ss. 4 and 7(1). Perhaps most important is a conjoint contention based on sovereignty (softened in reply by the Attorney-General of Manitoba) and on what are said to be basic presuppositions and constitutional underpinnings of Canadian federalism.

XI

The Court was invited to regard the *Balfour Declaration* of 1926 as embracing the Provinces of Canada (and, presumably, the States of the sister Dominion of Australia) in its reference to "autonomous communities". That well-known statement of principle, a political statement in the context of evolving independence of the Dominions in their relations with the United Kingdom, is as follows:

> They are autonomous Communities within the British Empire, equal in status, in no way subordinate one to another in any aspect of their domestic or external affairs, though united by a common allegiance to the Crown, and freely associated as members of the British Commonwealth of Nations.

It is impossible to seek nourishment for the provincial position in these appeals in this declaration. The Provinces did not come into the picture in the march to the *Statute of Westminster, 1931* until after the 1929 Conference on the Operation of Dominion Legislation, although to a degree before the Imperial Conference of 1930. They then made their views known on certain aspects of the looming statute, views which were canvassed in a Dominion-Provincial Conference in 1931. The main concern touched the proposed repeal of the *Colonial Laws Validity Act*, 1865 (U.K.), c. 63, and the effect that this might have on the amendment of the *British North America Act, 1867*, a matter to be considered later in these reasons.

Although the *Balfour Declaration* cannot, of itself, support the assertion of provincial autonomy in the wide sense contended for, it seems to have been regarded as retroactively having that effect by reason of the ultimate enactment of the *Statute of Westminster, 1931*. That statute is put forward not only as signifying an equality of status as between the Dominion and the Provinces vis-à-vis the

United Kingdom Parliament, but also as attenuating the theretofore untrammelled legislative authority of that Parliament in relation to Canada where provincial interests are involved. The germ of these consequences was said by the Newfoundland Court of Appeal to be in the *Balfour Declaration*, arising out of the Imperial Conference of 1926 and embodied in the Report of that Conference.

The following summarizing passage on Question 3 is contained in the reasons of the Newfoundland Court of Appeal [118 D.L.R. (3d) 1 at p. 18, 29 Nfld. & P.E.I.R. 503]:

> In our opinion, the constitutional status of the Provinces of Canada as autonomous communities was confirmed and perfected by: (a) the *Statute of Westminster, 1931* giving effect to the constitutional principle declared by the Imperial Conference that both the United Kingdom and the Dominions are autonomous communities equal in status, in no way subordinate one to another in any aspect of their domestic or external affairs; (b) the recognition by that Conference of the division of power among the constituent parts that make up the Dominion of Canada by which each is autonomous, in no way subordinate one to another; and (c) the surrender by the Imperial Parliament to the Provinces of its legislative sovereignty, over matters declared by the *British North America Act, 1867* to be within the exclusive legislative competence of the Provinces. The modification of that constitutional status was thereby withdrawn from future British parliamentary competence except with the consent of the Provinces.
>
> While the Parliament of Great Britain, in the absence of notice to the contrary, is constitutionally entitled to accept a Resolution passed by both Houses of the Canadian Parliament as a proper request for a constitutional amendment from the whole Canadian community, it is nonetheless precluded, for the reasons stated above, from enacting an amendment restricting the powers, rights and privileges granted the Provinces by the *British North America Act, 1867*, and enlarged by the *Statute of Westminster, 1931* over the objections of the Provinces.

If the significance attached to the *Statute of Westminster, 1931* is, indeed, what is asserted in the above-quoted passage and what has been urged by the Provinces in this Court, there is no need to resort to the *Balfour Declaration*, save possibly as a footnote. The course of events leading to the *Statute of Westminster, 1931* is detailed in numerous writings. It is sufficient to refer, in general, to the discussion in Wheare, *The Statute of Westminster and Dominion Status*, 5th ed. (1953), *passim*; and see, especially, c. VII, "The Statute and the Legal Status of Canada".

The submissions made on the *Statute of Westminster, 1931* by counsel who were before this Court engage

(1) the preamble to the statute; (2) s. 2(1) and (2); (3) s. 3; (4) s. 4 and (5) s. 7(1)(2)(3). These provisions are in the following terms:

> Whereas the delegates of His Majesty's Governments in the United Kingdom, the Dominion of Canada, the Commonwealth of Australia, the Dominion of New Zealand, the Union of South Africa, the Irish Free State and Newfoundland, at Imperial Conferences holden at Westminster in the years of our Lord nineteen hundred and twenty-six and nineteen hundred and thirty did concur in making the declarations and resolutions set forth in the Reports of the said Conferences:
>
> And whereas it is meet and proper to set out by way of preamble to this Act that, inasmuch as the Crown is the symbol of the free association of the members of the British Commonwealth of Nations, and as they are united by a common allegiance to the Crown, it would be in accord with the established constitutional position of all the members of the Commonwealth in relation to one another that any alteration in the law touching the Succession to the Throne or the Royal Style and Titles shall hereafter require the assent as well of the Parliaments of all the Dominions as of the Parliament of the United Kingdom:
>
> And whereas it is in accord with the established constitutional position that no law hereafter made by the Parliament of the United Kingdom shall extend to any of the said Dominions as part of the law of that Dominion otherwise than at the request and with the consent of that Dominion:
>
> And whereas it is necessary for the ratifying, confirming and establishing of certain of the said declarations and resolutions of the said Conferences that a law be made and enacted in due form by authority of the Parliament of the United Kingdom:
>
> And whereas the Dominion of Canada, the Commonwealth of Australia, the Dominion of New Zealand, the Union of South Africa, the Irish Free State and Newfoundland have severally requested and consented to the submission of a measure to the Parliament of the United Kingdom for making such provision with regard to the matters aforesaid as is hereafter in this Act contained:
>
> Now, therefore, be it enacted by the King's most Excellent Majesty by and with the advice and consent of the Lords Spiritual and Temporal, and Commons, in this present Parliament assembled, and by the authority of the same, as follows: —
>
> . . . . .
>
> 2(1) The Colonial Laws Validity Act, 1865, shall not apply to any law made after the commencement of this Act by the Parliament of a Dominion.
>
> (2) No law and no provision of any law made after the commencement of this Act by the Parliament of a

Dominion shall be void or inoperative on the ground that it is repugnant to the law of England, or to the provisions of any existing or future Act of Parliament of the United Kingdom, or to any order, rule or regulation made under any such Act, and the powers of the Parliament of a Dominion shall include the power to repeal or amend any such Act, order, rule or regulation in so far as the same is part of the law of the Dominion.

3. It is hereby declared and enacted that the Parliament of a Dominion has full power to make laws having extra-territorial operation.

4. No Act of Parliament of the United Kingdom passed after the commencement of this Act shall extend, or be deemed to extend, to a Dominion as part of the law of that Dominion, unless it is expressly declared in that Act that that Dominion has requested, and consented to, the enactment thereof.

. . . . .

7(1) Nothing in this Act shall be deemed to apply to the repeal, amendment or alteration of the British North America Acts, 1867 to 1930, or any order, rule or regulation made thereunder.

(2) The provisions of section two of this Act shall extend to laws made by any of the Provinces of Canada and to the powers of the legislatures of such Provinces.

(3) The powers conferred by this Act upon the Parliament of Canada or upon the legislatures of the Provinces shall be restricted to the enactment of laws in relation to matters within the competence of the Parliament of Canada or of any of the legislatures of the Provinces respectively.

There is nothing in the preamble that relates to the Provinces other than the reference to the Report of the Imperial Conference of 1930. What emerged prior to this Conference was an understandable provincial concern that the effect of the proposed repeal of the *Colonial Laws Validity Act* in favour of the Parliament of a Dominion and, in addition, the effect of what became s. 2(2) of the statute might enlarge federal power to alter, by its own legislation, provisions of the *British North America Act, 1867*. Thus it was that the Conference of 1930 placed on record (Cmd. 3717, pp. 17–8):

. . . that the sections of the Statute relating to the Colonial Laws Validity Act should be so drafted as not to extend to Canada unless the Statute was enacted in response to such requests as are appropriate to an amendment of the British North America Act. It also seemed desirable to place on record the view that the sections should not subsequently be extended to Canada except by an Act of the Parliament of the United Kingdom enacted in response to such requests as are appropriate to an amendment of the British North America Act.

The *Colonial Laws Validity Act* was intended to be a liberating statute, releasing colonial Legislatures from subservience to British common law (subject to Privy Council authority) and from subservience to British statute law unless such statute law applied expressly or by necessary implication to the colony. In the evolution of independence of the Dominions, it came to be recognized that the United Kingdom should no longer legislate at its own instance for any Dominion; and that the latter should be free to repeal any British legislation that was or would be made applicable to it. Hence, the statement in the preamble and hence ss. 2 and 4 in their application to a Dominion. Following the Imperial Conference of 1930 and as a result of the Dominion-Provincial Conference of 1931, the Provinces obtained an assurance that they too would benefit by the repeal of the *Colonial Laws Validity Act* and by being empowered to repeal any British legislation made applicable to them. This was achieved by s. 7(2) of the *Statute of Westminster, 1931*. There did not appear to be any need to include them in s. 4.

The most important issue was, however, the position of the Dominion vis-à-vis the *British North America Act, 1867*. What s. 7(1), reinforced by s. 7(3), appeared to do was to maintain the *status quo ante*; that is, to leave any changes in the *British North America Act, 1867* (that is, such changes which, under its terms, could not be carried out by legislation of the Provinces or of the Dominion) to the prevailing situation, namely, with the legislative authority of the United Kingdom Parliament being left untouched. As Sir William Jowitt put it, in the passage quoted earlier (in connection with the debate on the unemployment insurance amendment), ''the old machinery'' remained in place as a result of the *Statute of Westminster, 1931*. No other conclusion is supportable on any fair reading of the terms of the *Statute of Westminster, 1931*.

The Provinces, other than Ontario and New Brunswick, do not agree with this view of the *Statute of Westminster, 1931*. There were a number of positions taken by them. Much was made, especially in the submissions of counsel for the Attorney-General of Manitoba, of the use of the plural in the phrase ''such requests as are appropriate to an amendment of the British North America Act'' in the passage above-quoted from the Report of the 1930 Imperial Conference. The point taken from this was said to be a re-emphasis of that portion of the 1929 Conference on the Operation of Dominion Legislation which, in referring to the *British North America Act, 1867*, said that the question of the proper method of amending it should remain ''for future consideration by the appropriate Canadian authorities''. It was contended, certainly with justification, that the ''proper Canadian authorities'' were the Dominion and the Provinces and, presumably, it would be for them to decide whether it would be the respective Governments or Parliament and the Legislatures or both, and also what degree of agreement among the Provinces would be proper. It is, however, impossible to draw from this any legal rule of conduct because, ultimately, whatever political consensus might be achieved, there would still be the legal necessity of final United Kingdom legislative action.

The matter is not advanced by the follow-up Dominion-Provincial Conference of 1931. As the brief summary of the conference stated, its purpose was:

> . . . to give the Provinces an opportunity to express their views with regard to the Statute of Westminster and the proposed Section, numbered 7, which will be inserted to deal exclusively with the Canadian position. No objection was made to the principle of the proposed legislation, and a proposal that the provisions of the Statute relating to the repeal of the Colonial Laws Validity Act should extend to the Provinces was approved. The Canadian Section (7) was drafted and found satisfactory by all the Provinces, though Quebec asked for further time for consideration. Meanwhile, the approval of the Quebec Government has been received.

The Conference summary continued as follows:

> Certain other constitutional questions arose during the Conference. *Some Provinces desired that the question of powers and procedure in respect to constitutional amendment should be discussed together with the wider subject of constitutional relations between Dominions [sic] and Provinces.* This was found to be impossible at that meeting, but it was agreed that a constitutional conference should be summoned as soon as possible. It was the general opinion that at such a conference a method of amending the Canadian constitution by Canadian agencies might be discovered which would reconcile the two essential features of reasonable elasticity of change and the preservation of provincial rights.

The italicized sentence in the above-quoted Conference summary shows quite clearly that as of 1930, there was certainly no rule of law with respect to constitutional amendment. No change was effected in the legal position by the *Statute of Westminster, 1931*.

It was also urged upon this Court that s. 7(1), which in terms (''nothing in this Act shall be deemed to apply to . . . the British North America Acts, 1867 to 1930'') removes the *British North America Act, 1867* (at least as it then stood) from the application of any terms of the *Statute*

of Westminster, 1931, was addressed to ss. 2 and 3 and not to s. 4. The argument goes that s. 7(1) does not exclude the application of s. 4; that s. 4 must be read in its preclusive effect on a Dominion as having the Provinces in view; that the ''request and consent'' which must be declared in a British statute to make it applicable to Canada, is the request and consent of the Dominion and the Provinces if the statute is one affecting provincial interests or powers, for example, an amendment of the *British North America Act, 1867* as envisaged by the Resolution herein. The word ''Dominion'' in s. 4, it is said, must be read in what may be called a conjoint or collective sense as including both the Dominion and the Provinces; otherwise, it is submitted, the purpose of the *Statute of Westminster, 1931* would be defeated. A difference, said to be significant, is pointed up in the reference to ''Parliament of a Dominion'' in s. 3 and the bare word ''Dominion'' in s. 4.

Nothing in the language of the *Statute of Westminster, 1931* supports the provincial position yet it is on this interpretation that it is contended that the Parliament of the United Kingdom has relinquished or yielded its previous omnipotent legal authority in relation to the *British North America Act, 1867*, one of its own statutes. As an argument on Question 3 and Question B (in its legal aspect), it asserts a legal diminution of United Kingdom legislative supremacy. The short answer to this ramified submission is that it distorts both history and ordinary principles of statutory or constitutional interpretation. The plain fact is that s. 7(1) was enacted to obviate any inference of direct unilateral federal power to amend the *British North America Act, 1867* and that it is s. 7(3) that is addressed to s. 2 and not s. 7(1). It is for this reason that it was unnecessary to provide in respect of Canada what was provided by s. 9(3) in respect of Australia, namely, that in the application of the *Statute of Westminster, 1931* to the Commonwealth of Australia ''the request and consent referred to in section 4 shall mean the request and consent of the Parliament and Government of the Commonwealth''. There is, moreover, an interpretation section in the *Statute of Westminster, 1931*, being s. 1, and in it ''Dominion'' means any of the following Dominions, ''that is to say the Dominion of Canada, the Commonwealth of Australia, the Dominion of New Zealand, the Union of South Africa, the Irish Free State and Newfoundland''. The reference to ''Parliament of a Dominion'' in s. 3 and ''Dominion'' in s. 4 is easily explained by the context. The argument on the *Statute of Westminster, 1931* is untenable, but it leaves for more anxious consideration the effect of the removal of the *British North America Act, 1867* from the *Statute of*

Westminster, 1931 and the preservation by s. 7(3) of the existing distribution of legislative powers under the *British North America Act, 1867.*

XII

This leads to the submissions made on the sovereignty of the Provinces in respect of their powers under the *British North America Act, 1867,* the term "sovereignty" being modified in the course of argument to "supremacy". Allied to this was the contention that Canada cannot do indirectly what it cannot do directly; it could not by an enactment of its own accomplish that which is proposed by the Resolution. Such an enactment would be clearly *ultra vires* as to most of the provisions put forward by the Resolution, and it should not be able to improve its position in law by invoking the aid of the United Kingdom Parliament. Moreover, even if the Parliament of the United Kingdom retained its formal legal authority over the *British North America Act, 1867,* as one of its enactments, it was in the words used by the late and at the time, former Justice Rand, "a bare legislative trustee", subject as a matter of law to the direction of the beneficiaries, namely, the Dominion and the Provinces, in respect of the Resolution.

It will be convenient to deal at this point with the "direct-indirect" contention and with the notion of legislative trusteeship, before returning to the main submission on provincial legislative supremacy. That submission involves a consideration of the character of Canadian federalism and it must, of course, be carefully assessed.

The direct-indirect contention, taken by itself, amounts to this: that whether or not the federal Houses can seek to obtain enactment of the draft statute appended to the Resolution, it would, in any event, be illegal to invoke United Kingdom authority to do for Canada what it cannot do itself. The maxim "you cannot do indirectly what you cannot do directly" is a much abused one. It was used to invalidate provincial legislation in *Madden v. Nelson and Fort Sheppard R. Co.*, [1889] A.C. 626. It is a pithy way of describing colourable legislation: see *Ladore et al. v. Bennett et al.*, [1939] 3 D.L.R. 1 at p. 7, [1939] A.C. 468 at p. 482, [1939] 2 W.W.R. 566. However, it does not preclude a limited Legislature from achieving directly under one head of legislative power what it could not do directly under another head. The question, of course, remains whether the two federal Houses may alone initiate and carry through the process to invoke the competence of the United Kingdom Parliament.

At least with regard to the amending formula the process in question here concerns not the amendment of a complete constitution but rather the completion of an incomplete constitution.

We are involved here with a finishing operation, with fitting a piece into the constitutional edifice; it is idle to expect to find anything in the *British North America Act, 1867* that regulates the process that has been initiated in this case. Were it otherwise, there would be no need to resort to the Resolution procedure invoked here, a procedure which takes account of the intergovernmental and international link between Canada and Great Britain. There is no comparable link that engages the Provinces with Great Britain. Moreover, it is to confuse the issue of process, which is the basic question here, with the legal competence of the British Parliament when resort is had to the direct-indirect argument. The legal competence of that Parliament, for the reasons already given, remains unimpaired, and it is for it alone to determine if and how it will act.

The late Justice Rand used the words "a bare legislative trustee" in the Holmes Lecture delivered at Harvard Law School under the title "Some Aspects of Canadian Constitutionalism" and reproduced in 38 Can. Bar Rev. 135 (1960). His use of the phrase came in the course of his discussion of the effect of the *Statute of Westminster, 1931.* He said this (at p. 145):

> Legislatively, a unique situation has been created. The British Parliament has in effect become a bare legislative trustee for the Dominion; the constitutional organ for altering the provisions of the Canadian constitution contained in the Act of 1867 remains so far the British Parliament; but the political direction resides in the Parliament of the Dominion; the former has conceded its residue of legislative power vis-à-vis Canada, to be no more than means for effecting the will of Canada. It might happen, although it is most unlikely, that the British Parliament should demur to a request for a legislative amendment, as, for example, involving important legislative effects not concurred in by one or more of the provinces; but that amounts to no more than saying that the Canadian people would not yet have agreed on the mode of modifying their internal constitutional relations. Once that means has been agreed upon, legislative independence, not only in substance but in form, will have been attained.

The Newfoundland Court of Appeal adopted the phrase but decided that Justice Rand should not have limited the suggested trusteeship as being for the Dominion of Canada alone. Moreover, the Court overlooked a central point in the Rand lecture that "the political direction resides in the Parliament of the Dominion". Thus the Court said [118 D.L.R. (3d) 1 at p. 17, 29 Nfld. & P.E.I.R. 503]:

> We adopt that statement fully with the important addi-

tion that the Parliament of Great Britain is a "bare legislative trustee" for *both* the federal Parliament and the provincial Legislatures in relation to the matters within their respective legislative competence. Any amendment enacted by the Parliament of Great Britain affecting the legislative competence of either of the parties, without that party's consent, would not only be contrary to the intendment of the *Statute of Westminster*, 1931 but it could defeat the whole scheme of the Canadian federal Constitution.

It is enough to counter this assessment of the Newfoundland Court of Appeal by referring to what Gérin-Lajoie said in his seminal text *Constitutional Amendment in Canada* (1950), at p. 138:

> While the Parliament of the United Kingdom is precluded from enacting any constitutional amendment without a proper request from Canada the only competent voice of Canada for this purpose is that of the federal power. The provincial authorities — either executive or legislative — have no *locus standi* to move the British Parliament or Government with a view to securing an amendment to the federal Constitution.

It is obvious that any change in the legislative power of either Parliament or the provincial Legislatures would directly affect the other. The thrust of the Newfoundland Court of Appeal's remarks just quoted goes more properly to the submissions and contentions on the nature of Canadian federalism than to any intendment of the *Statute of Westminster, 1931*. Whatever the statute may import as to intra-Canadian conventional procedures, there is nothing in it or in the proceedings leading up to it that casts any doubt in law as to the undiminished authority of the Parliament of the United Kingdom over the *British North America Act, 1867*.

XIII

At bottom, the challenge to the competency in law of the federal Houses to seek enactment by the Parliament of the United Kingdom of the statutes embodied in the Resolution is based on the recognized supremacy of provincial Legislatures in relation to the powers conferred upon them under the *British North America Act, 1867*, a supremacy vis-à-vis the federal Parliament. Reinforcement, or perhaps the foundation of this supremacy is said to lie in the nature or character of Canadian federalism.

The supremacy position, taken alone, needs no further justification than that found in the respective formulations of the powers of Parliament and the provincial Legislatures in ss. 91 and 92 of the *British North America Act, 1867*. Federal paramountcy is, however, the general rule in the actual exercise of these powers. This notwithstanding, the exclusiveness of the provincial powers (another way of expressing supremacy and more consonant with the terms of the *British North America Act, 1867*) cannot be gainsaid. The long list of judicial decisions, beginning with *Hodge v. The Queen* (1883), 9 App. Cas. 117, and carrying through such cases as *Liquidators of Maritime Bank of Canada v. Receiver-General of New Brunswick*, [1892] A.C. 437, and the *Labour Conventions* case where the Privy Council expressed its "water-tight compartment view" of legislative power (see [1937] 1 D.L.R. 673 at p. 684, [1937] A.C. 326 at p. 354) provide adequate support for the principle of exclusiveness or supremacy but, of course, within the limits of the *British North America Act, 1867*.

Although there are what have been called unitary features in the *British North America Act, 1867*, involving overriding powers (to be distinguished from paramountcy of legislation) in the federal Parliament and Government, their modification of exclusive provincial authority does not detract from that authority to any substantial degree. Thus, the federal declaratory power under s. 92(10)(*c*) has a limited operation; reservation and disallowance of provincial legislation, although in law still open, have, to all intents and purposes, fallen into disuse. The fact of appointment of the Lieutenant-Governors of the Provinces by the central Government does not, as a practical matter, have any significance for provincial powers when, under the law, the Lieutenant-Governor is as much the personal representative of the Crown as is the Governor-General. In each case, the representation is, of course, in respect of the powers respectively assigned to Parliament and the Legislatures. Moreover, since there is an international, a foreign relations aspect involved in the relationship of Canada and Great Britain, any formal communication between a Province and its Lieutenant-Governor with the United Kingdom Government or with the Queen, must be through the federal Government or through the Governor-General.

It is important in this connection to emphasize that the Government of Canada had, by 1923, obtained recognition internationally of its independent power to enter into external obligations when it negotiated the Halibut Treaty with the United States. Great Britain understood this by that time as did the United States. The subsequent Imperial Conferences added confirmation, sanctified by the *Statute of Westminster, 1931* which also put internal independence from Great Britain on a legal foundation. The remaining badge of subservience, the need to resort to the British Parliament to amend the *British North America Act, 1867*, although preserved by the *Statute of Westminster, 1931*, did not carry any diminution of Canada's legal right in international law, and as a matter of Canadian constitutional law, to assert its independence in external relations, be they with Great Britain or other countries. The matter is emphasized by the judgment of this Court in *Reference re Ownership of Off-Shore Mineral Rights* (1967), 65 D.L.R. (2d) 353 at p. 375, [1967] S.C.R. 792 at p. 816, 62 W.W.R. 21. This is a relevant consideration in the appeals which are before this Court.

What is put forward by the Provinces which oppose the forwarding of the address without provincial consent is that external relations with Great Britain in this respect must take account of the nature and character of Canadian federalism. It is contended that a legal underpinning of their position is to be found in the Canadian federal system as reflected in historical antecedents, in the pronouncements of leading political figures and in the preamble to the *British North America Act, 1867.*

The arguments from history do not lead to any consistent view or any single view of the nature of the *British North America Act, 1867*; selective interpretations are open and have been made: see Report of the Royal Commission on Dominion-Provincial Relations (1940), Book 1, pp. 29 *ff.* History cannot alter the fact that in law there is a British statute to construe and apply in relation to a matter, fundamental as it is, that is not provided for by the statute. Practices which took account of evolving Canadian independence, did, of course, develop. They had both intra-Canadian and extra-Canadian aspects in relation to British legislative authority. The former have already been canvassed, both in the reasons on Question 2 and Question B and, to a degree, in these reasons. Theories, whether of a full compact theory (which, even factually, cannot be sustained, having regard to federal power to create new Provinces out of federal territories, which was exercised in the creation of Alberta and Saskatchewan) or of a modified compact theory, as urged by some of the Provinces, operate in the political realm, in political science studies. They do not engage the law, save as they might have some peripheral relevance to actual provisions of the *British North America Act, 1867* and its interpretation and application. Thus it is, to take one example, that in the *Nova Scotia Interdelegation* case, *A.-G. N.S. et al. v. A.-G. Can. et al.,* [1950] 4 D.L.R. 369 at p. 371, [1951] S.C.R. 31 at p. 34, Rinfret C.J.C. said:

> The constitution of Canada does not belong either to Parliament, or to the Legislatures; it belongs to the country and it is there that the citizens of the country will find the protection of the rights to which they are entitled. It

is part of that protection that Parliament can legislate only on the subject-matters referred to it by s. 91 and that each Province can legislate exclusively on the subject-matters referred to it by s. 92.

This was said, however, in the context of an issue raised under the terms of the *British North America Act, 1867*, the issue being whether there could be interdelegation between the Parliament of Canada and the provincial Legislatures of their respective legislative powers which, as to each level of authority, were conferred as exclusive powers. In the Court below, the Nova Scotia Supreme Court *en banc*, Chief Justice Chisholm remarked that the *British North America Act, 1867* is not a counter for the exchange of constitutional wares: see [1948] 4 D.L.R. 1 at p. 6, 22 M.P.R. 83, *sub nom. Re Bill 136 in the Nova Scotia Legislature, 1947, Re Delegation of Legislative Jurisdiction.*

The statement, above-quoted, of Chief Justice Rinfret carries no independent legal consequence; it simply underscores the imperative character of the distribution of legislative power. In short, as in the attempt to argue crystallization of convention into law, there is nothing in the reference to theories of federalism reflected in some case law that goes beyond their use as an aid to a justiciable question raised apart from them.

So too, with pronouncements by political figures or persons in other branches of public life. There is little profit in parading them.

Support for a legal requirement of provincial consent to the Resolution that is before this Court, consent which is also alleged to condition United Kingdom response to the Resolution, is, finally, asserted to lie in the preamble of the *British North America Act, 1867* itself, and in the reflection, in the substantive terms of the Act, of what are said to be fundamental presuppositions in the preamble as to the nature of Canadian federalism. The preamble recites (and the whole of it is reproduced) the following:

> Whereas the Provinces of Canada, Nova Scotia, and New Brunswick have expressed their Desire to be federally united into One Dominion under the Crown of the United Kingdom of Great Britain and Ireland, with a Constitution similar in Principle to that of the United Kingdom:
>
> And whereas such a Union would conduce to the Welfare of the Provinces and promote the Interest of the British Empire:
>
> And whereas on the Establishment of the Union by Authority of Parliament it is expedient, not only that the Constitution of the Legislative Authority in the Dominion be provided for, but also that the Nature of the Executive Government therein be declared:

And whereas it is expedient that Provision be made for the eventual Admission into the Union of other Parts of the British North America:

What is stressed is the desire of the named Provinces "to be federally united . . . with a Constitution similar in principle to that of the United Kingdom". The preamble speaks also of union into "one Dominion" and of the establishment of the Union "by authority of Parliament", that is the United Kingdom Parliament. What, then, is to be drawn from the preamble as a matter of law? A preamble, needless to say, has no enacting force but, certainly, it can be called in aid to illuminate provisions of the statute in which it appears. Federal union "with a constitution similar in principle to that of the United Kingdom" may well embrace responsible government and some common law aspects of the United Kingdom's unitary constitutionalism, such as the rule of law and Crown prerogatives and immunities. The "rule of law" is a highly textured expression, importing many things which are beyond the need of these reasons to explore but conveying, for example, a sense of orderliness, of subjection to known legal rules and of executive accountability to legal authority. Legislative changes may alter common law prescriptions, as has happened with respect to Crown prerogatives and immunities. There is also an internal contradiction in speaking of federalism in the light of the invariable principle of British parliamentary supremacy. Of course, the resolution of this contradiction lies in the scheme of distribution of legislative power, but this owes nothing to the preamble, resting rather on its own exposition in the substantive terms of the *British North America Act, 1867.*

There is not and cannot be any standardized federal system from which particular conclusions must necessarily be drawn. Reference was made earlier to what were called unitary features of Canadian federalism and they operate to distinguish Canadian federalism from that of Australia and that of the United States. Allocations of legislative power differ as do the institutional arrangements through which power is exercised. This Court is being asked by the Provinces which object to the so-called federal "package" to say that the internal distribution of legislative power must be projected externally, as a matter of law, although there is no legal warrant for this assertion and, indeed, what legal authority exists (as in s. 3 of the *Statute of Westminster, 1931*) denies this provincial position.

At bottom, it is this distribution, it is the allocation of legislative power as between the central Parliament and the provincial Legislatures that the Provinces rely on as precluding unilateral federal action to seek amendments

to the *British North America Act, 1867* that affect, whether by limitation or extension, provincial legislative authority. The Attorney-General of Canada was pushed to the extreme by being forced to answer affirmatively the theoretical question whether in law the federal Government could procure an amendment to the *British North America Act, 1867* what would turn Canada into a unitary State. That is not what the present Resolution envisages because the essential federal character of the country is preserved under the enactments proposed by the Resolution.

That, it is argued, is no reason for conceding unilateral federal authority to accomplish, through invocation of legislation by the United Kingdom Parliament, the purposes of the Resolution. There is here, however, an unprecedented situation in which the one constant since the enactment of the *British North America Act* in 1867 has been the legal authority of the United Kingdom Parliament to amend it. The law knows nothing of any requirement of provincial consent, either to a resolution of the federal Houses or as a condition of the exercise of United Kingdom legislative power.

In the result, the third question in the Manitoba and Newfoundland cases should, as a matter of law, be answered in the negative and Question B should, in its legal aspect, be answered in the affirmative.

XIV

There remains for consideration Question 4 in the Newfoundland Reference. The question, in effect, asks if the matters therein raised could happen under the amending formula in the draft statute appended to the Resolution proposed for adoption by the two federal Houses. There were, as previously noted, some changes in the draft statute prior to its adoption by the federal Houses and a change as well in the numbering of some of the sections relevant to Question 4. However, it is unnecessary to go into these number changes because the Attorney-General of Canada agrees with the conclusions of the Newfoundland Court of Appeal as set out in the first three parts of its answer to the question, and the Attorney-General of Newfoundland agrees with the Attorney-General of Canada that the Newfoundland Court of Appeal was in error in the fourth part of its answer to the question. It was wrong to say that in a referendum under s. 42 (as it then was) of the proposed statute (now s. 46) the approval of the majority of the people in each Province was required. The proper view was that only the approval of the majority of the people voting in a referendum in those Provinces, the approval of whose Legislatures would be required under the general amending formula, would be necessary.

The Attorney-General of Canada agreed with the Newfoundland Court of Appeal that an unqualified answer to Question 4 might be misleading and he submitted what he considered to be better answers to Question 4. Since there was substantial agreement before this Court by the Attorney-General of Canada and the Attorney-General of Newfoundland as to the proper answer to Question 4, it is unnecessary to dwell on its details here. Moreover, it involves an assessment of the substantive terms of the draft statute proposed for enactment by the United Kingdom Parliament, and, in that respect, it is an example of the specifics which were sought in the answer to Question 1 and which, it was agreed by counsel, need not be elaborated. It is hence unnecessary to say more on Question 4, in the recognition also that this Court is not concerned here with the wisdom of the proposed enactment.

XV

Nothing said in these reasons is to be construed as either favouring or disapproving the proposed amending formula or the *Charter of Rights and Freedoms* or any of the other provisions of which enactment is sought. The questions put to this Court do not ask for its approval or disapproval of the contents of the so-called ''package''.

What is central here is the untrammelled authority at law of the two federal Houses to proceed as they wish in the management of their own procedures and hence to adopt the Resolution which is intended for submission to Her Majesty for action thereon by the United Kingdom Parliament. The *British North America Act, 1867* does not, either in terms or by implication, control this authority or require that it be subordinated to provincial assent. Nor does the *Statute of Westminster, 1931* interpose any requirement of such assent. If anything, it leaves the position as it was before its enactment. Developments subsequent thereto do not affect the legal position.

In summary, the answers to Questions 1 and 3 common to the Manitoba and Newfoundland References, should be as follows:

Question 1:   Yes

Question 3:   As a matter of law, no.

The answer to Question 4 in the Newfoundland Reference should be as expressed in the reasons of the Newfoundland Court of Appeal, subject to the correction made in the reasons herein.

The answers to the questions in the Quebec Reference should be as follows:

Question A(i):   Yes.

(ii):   Yes.

Question B(i):   As a matter of law, yes.

(ii):   As a matter of law, yes.

There will be, of course, no order as to costs.

MARTLAND AND RITCHIE JJ.: — These are three appeals from the opinions of the Courts of Appeal of Manitoba, Newfoundland and Quebec pronounced in respect of three References to those Courts concerning the constitutional propriety and lawfulness of a proposed Resolution now before the Senate and House of Commons of Canada.

The Lieutenant-Governor in Council of Manitoba referred three questions to the Manitoba Court of Appeal for hearing and consideration by Order in Council dated October 24, 1980; the questions were:

1. If the amendments to the Constitution of Canada sought in the ''Proposed Resolution for a Joint Address to Her Majesty the Queen respecting the Constitution of Canada'', or any of them, were enacted, would federal-provincial relationships or the powers, rights or privileges granted or secured by the Constitution of Canada to the provinces, their legislatures or governments be affected and if so, in what respect or respects?

2. Is it a constitutional convention that the House of Commons and Senate of Canada will not request Her Majesty the Queen to lay before the Parliament of the United Kingdom of Great Britain and Northern Ireland a measure to amend the Constitution of Canada affecting federal-provincial relationships or the powers, rights or privileges granted or secured by the Constitution of Canada to the provinces, their legislatures or governments without first obtaining the agreement of the provinces?

3. Is the agreement of the provinces of Canada constitutionally required for amendment to the Constitution of Canada where such amendment affects federal-provincial relationships or alters the powers, rights or privileges granted or secured by the Constitution of Canada to the provinces, their legislatures or governments?

The reasons for judgment were delivered by the Manitoba Court of Appeal on February 3, 1981: 117 D.L.R. (3d) 1, 7 Man. R. (2d) 269, [1981] 2 W.W.R. 193. A majority of the Court refused to answer Question 1. Freedman C.J.M. and Matas J.A. held that the question was at that time tentative and premature. Hall J.A. held that Question 1 was not appropriate for a judicial response, and in any event was speculative and premature. Huband and O'Sullivan JJ.A. both held that the question should have been answered in the affirmative.

Freedman C.J.M., Matas, O'Sullivan and Huband JJ.A. answered Question 2 in the negative. Hall J.A. held that Question 2 was not appropriate for a judicial response.

Question 3 was answered in the negative by Freedman C.J.M., Hall and Matas JJ.A. O'Sullivan and Huband JJ.A. would have answered Question 3 in the affirmative.

By Order in Council dated December 5, 1980, the Lieutenant-Governor in Council of Newfoundland referred four questions to the Newfoundland Court of Appeal for hearing and consideration. The first three questions asked were the same as those in the Manitoba Reference. Question 4 was as follows:

4. If Part V of the proposed resolution referred to in question 1 is enacted and proclaimed into force could

(a) the Terms of Union, including terms 2 and 17 thereof contained in the Schedule to the British North America Act 1949 (12–13 George VI, c. 22 [U.K.], or

(b) section 3 of the British North America Act, 1871 (34–35 Victoria, c. 28 [U.K.])

be amended directly or indirectly pursuant to Part V without the consent of the Government, Legislature or a majority of the people of the Province of Newfoundland voting in a referendum held pursuant to Part V?

The judgment of the unanimous Court was delivered on March 31, 1981: 118 D.L.R. (3d) 1, 29 Nfld. & P.E.I.R. 503. In a joint opinion, Mifflin C.J.N., Morgan and Gushue JJ.A. answered Questions 1, 2 and 3 in the affirmative. Question 4 was answered in the following terms [at pp. 30–1]:

(1) By s. 3 of the *British North America Act, 1871, Term 2* of the Terms of Union cannot now be changed without the consent of the Newfoundland Legislature.

(2) By s. 43 of the *Constitution Act, 1981*, as it now reads, none of the Terms of Union can be changed without the consent of the Newfoundland Legislative Assembly.

(3) Both of these sections can be changed by the amending formulae prescribed in s. 41 and the Terms of Union could then be changed without the consent of the Newfoundland Legislature.

(4) If the amending formula under s. 42 is utilized, both of these sections can be changed by a referendum held pursuant to the provisions of s. 42. In this event, the Terms of Union could then be changed without the consent of the Newfoundland Legislature, but not without the consent of the majority of the Newfoundland people voting in a referendum.

By Order in Council dated December 17, 1980, the Government of Quebec submitted to the Quebec Court of Appeal two questions, each containing two sub-questions. The following is the English translation of the questions submitted:

A. If the Canada Act and the Constitution Act 1981 should come into force and if they should be valid in all respects in Canada would they affect:

(i) the legislative competence of the provincial legislatures in virtue of the Canadian Constitution?

(ii) the status or role of the provincial legislatures or governments within the Canadian Federation?

B. Does the Canadian Constitution empower, whether by statute, convention or otherwise, the Senate and the House of Commons of Canada to cause the Canadian Constitution to be amended without the consent of the provinces and in spite of the objection of several of them, in such a manner as to affect:

(i) the legislative competence of the provincial legislatures in virtue of the Canadian Constitution?

(ii) the status or role of the provincial legislatures or governments within the Canadian Federation?

The judgment of the Quebec Court of Appeal was delivered on April 15, 1981 [120 D.L.R. (3d) 385]. Crête C.J.Q., Owen, Turgeon and Belanger JJ.A. answered both questions in the affirmative. Bisson J.A., dissenting, would have answered Question A in the affirmative and Question B in the negative.

Each of these judgments was appealed to this Court as of right. Argument was heard in this Court from the Attorneys-General of all ten Provinces, the Attorney-General of Canada, and the Four Nations Confederacy Inc. Argument was heard on each appeal, but the appeals were heard consecutively.

The *Canada Act* and the *Constitution Act, 1981*, referred to in the Quebec Reference, are the subjects of a Resolution now before the Senate and House of Commons of Canada. That Resolution states:

THAT, WHEREAS in the past certain amendments to the Constitution of Canada have been made by the Parliament of the United Kingdom at the request and with the consent of Canada;

AND WHEREAS it is in accord with the status of Canada as an independent state that Canadians are able to amend their Constitution in Canada in all respects;

AND WHEREAS it is also desirable to provide in the Constitution of Canada for the recognition of certain fundamental rights and freedoms and to make other amendments to that Constitution;

A respectful address be presented to Her Majesty the Queen in the following words:

To the Queen's Most Excellent Majesty:
Most Gracious Sovereign:

We, Your Majesty's loyal subjects, the House of Commons of Canada in Parliament assembled, respectfully approach Your Majesty, requesting that you may graciously be pleased to cause to be laid before the Parliament of the United Kingdom a measure containing the recitals and clauses hereinafter set forth:

The recitals and clauses referred to in the Resolution set forth the *Canada Act* and the *Constitution Act, 1981*. The *Canada Act* recites the request and consent of the Senate and House of Commons to the measure, enacts the *Constitution Act, 1981*, and declares that no Act of the Parliament of the United Kingdom passed after the *Constitution Act, 1981*, shall form part of the laws of Canada.

The *Constitution Act, 1981*, if validly enacted, would effect two major changes to the existing Constitution of Canada. Part I of the Act contains a *Charter of Rights and Freedoms* which would bind both the provincial and federal Legislatures. Parts IV and V of the Act contain elaborate provisions for all future amendments to the Canadian Constitution.

It is now conceded that the answer to the first question in the Manitoba and Newfoundland References and to Questions A(i) and (ii) of the Quebec Reference should be in the affirmative. The second question in the Manitoba and Newfoundland References has been dealt with in a separate judgment to which we are parties. We agree with the disposition of the fourth question in the Newfoundland Reference proposed in the reasons for judgment of the other members of the Court which deal with that matter.

The third question in the Manitoba and the Newfoundland References asks whether the agreement of the Provinces of Canada is "constitutionally required" for amendment to the Constitution of Canada where such amendment affects federal-provincial relationships or alters the powers, rights or privileges granted or secured by the Constitution of Canada to the Provinces, their Legislatures or Governments. If the second question is answered in the affirmative, then it is recognized that a constitutional convention exists that the House of Commons and the Senate will not request an amendment of the *British North America Act, 1867* of the kind contemplated in Question 2 without first obtaining the agreement of the Provinces. If that is so, then the agreement of the Provinces is constitutionally required for such an amendment and the answer to Question 3 should be in the affirmative and, in our opinion, that answer should be given.

However, there is a further issue which requires consideration in that in the Courts below and in the arguments submitted by counsel before this Court, the answer to

Question 3 was debated as though the words "constitutionally required" were to be considered as meaning "legally required".

In the Quebec Reference the question is phrased differently in Question B. What is asked is whether the Senate and the House of Commons are empowered by the Canadian Constitution, whether by statute, convention or otherwise, to cause the Canadian Constitution to be amended without the consent of the Provinces, and in spite of the objection of several of them, in such a manner as to affect the legislative competence of provincial Legislatures, or the status or role or provincial Legislatures or Governments within the Canadian Federation.

We were not referred to any statute which confers such a power. The answer to Question 2, if answered in the affirmative, denies that such a power exists by convention. The remaining issue is whether such a power has been conferred on the two Houses otherwise than by statute or convention.

We think Question B of the Quebec Reference more clearly raises the legal issue than does Question 3 in the other two References and we shall deal with that issue in these reasons.

At the outset, we would point out that we are not concerned with the matter of legality or illegality in the sense of determining whether or not the passage of the Resolution under consideration involves a breach of the law. The issue is as to the existence of a power to do that which is proposed to be done. The question is whether it is *intra vires* of the Senate and the House of Commons to cause the proposed amendments to the *British North America Act, 1867* to be made by the Imperial Parliament by means of the Resolution now before the Court, in the absence of provincial agreement.

This issue is unique because in the 114 years since Confederation the Senate and House of Commons of Canada have never sought, without the consent of the Provinces, to obtain such an amendment nor, apparently, has that possibility ever been contemplated.

The *British North America Act, 1867* (herein the *B.N.A. Act*) commences with the following significant recitals:

Whereas the Provinces of Canada, Nova Scotia, and New Brunswick have expressed their Desire to be federally united into One Dominion under the Crown of the United Kingdom of Great Britain and Ireland, with a Constitution similar in Principle to that of the United Kingdom:

And whereas such a Union should conduce to the Welfare of the Provinces and promote the Interests of the British Empire:

And whereas on the Establishment of the Union by

Authority of Parliament it is expedient, not only that the Constitution of the Legislative Authority in the Dominion be provided for, but also that the Nature of the Executive Government therein be declared:

And whereas it is expedient that Provision be made for the eventual Admission into the Union of other Parts of British North America:

The first recital makes it clear that this statute was passed at the behest of the named Provinces and that what was sought was a federal union. The second recital states that such union would "conduce to the Welfare of the Provinces".

Parts I–V of the *B.N.A. Act* provide for the establishment of the Union by the Proclamation, and for the vesting of executive and legislative authority in Her Majesty the Queen and Her representatives, and in the Parliament of Canada and the Legislatures of the Provinces. Part VI deals with the distribution of legislative powers. The opening words of s. 91 and s. 92 bear reproduction; they provide:

> 91. It shall be lawful for the Queen, by and with the Advice and Consent of the Senate and House of Commons, to make Laws for the Peace, Order and good Government of Canada, in relation to all Matters not coming within the Classes of Subjects by this Act assigned exclusively to the Legislatures of the Provinces; and for greater Certainty, but not so as to restrict the Generality of the foregoing Terms of this Section, it is hereby declared that (notwithstanding anything in this Act) the exclusive Legislative Authority of the Parliament of Canada extends to all Matters coming within the Classes of Subjects next hereinafter enumerated; that is to say, —
>
> . . . . . .
>
> 92. In each Province the Legislature may exclusively make Laws in relation to Matters coming within the Classes of Subjects next hereinafter enumerated; that is to suggest, —

Section 93 gave exclusive power to the Provinces to make laws in relation to education, subject to certain protective provisions in respect of denominational and separate schools.

Section 95 gave concurrent legislative power to the provincial Legislatures and to the Parliament of Canada with respect to agriculture and immigration, but provincial legislation was to be effective only so long as it was not repugnant to an Act of the Canadian Parliament.

Part VII of the *B.N.A. Act* dealt with judicature.

Part VIII dealt with revenues, debts and taxation. Section 109 provided that all lands, mines, minerals and royalties belonging to the several Provinces of Canada, Nova Scotia and New Brunswick should belong to the several Provinces of Ontario, Quebec, Nova Scotia and New Brunswick in which the same were situate.

Part IX is entitled "Miscellaneous Provisions". Section 129 continued all laws in effect in Canada, Nova Scotia and New Brunswick in effect at the Union, subject, except as to Acts of the Parliament of Great Britain, to repeal, abolition or alteration by the Parliament of Canada or a provincial Legislature according to their authority under the *B.N.A. Act*.

Part X dealt with the intercolonial railway.

Part XI is concerned with the admission of other colonies. Section 146 provided:

> 146. It shall be lawful for the Queen, by and with the Advice of Her Majesty's Most Honourable Privy Council, on Addresses from the Houses of the Parliament of Canada, and from the Houses of the respective Legislatures of the Colonies or Provinces of Newfoundland, Prince Edward Island, and British Columbia, to admit those Colonies or Provinces, or any of them, into the Union, and on Address from the Houses of the Parliament of Canada to admit Rupert's Land and the Northwestern Territory, or either of them, into the Union, on such Terms and Conditions in each Case as are in the Addresses expressed and as the Queen thinks fit to approve, subject to the Provisions of this Act; and the Provisions of any Order in Council in that Behalf shall have effect as if they had been enacted by the Parliament of the United Kingdom of Great Britain and Ireland.

This Act became the Constitution of Canada. It created a federal union of Provinces and it carefully defined the respective spheres of the Canadian Parliament and the provincial Legislatures in matters of legislative jurisdiction and property rights.

The status of the Provinces under the Constitution was determined by the Privy Council in two important cases which arose not long after the enactment of the *B.N.A. Act*.

It was contended in *Hodge v. The Queen* (1883), 9 App. Cas. 117, that a provincial Legislature could not delegate its legislative powers to License Commissioners, for it was itself merely a delegate of the Imperial Parliament. The Judicial Committee of the Privy Council rejected this argument in the following terms, at p. 132:

> It appears to their Lordships, however, that the objection thus raised by the appellants is founded on an entire misconception of the true character and position of the provincial legislatures. They are in no sense delegates of or acting under any mandate from the Imperial Parliament. When the British North America Act enacted that there should be a legislature for Ontario, and that its legislative

assembly should have exclusive authority to make laws for the Province and for provincial purposes in relation to the matters enumerated in sect. 92, it conferred powers not in any sense to be exercised by delegation from or as agents of the Imperial Parliament, but authority as plenary and as ample within the limits prescribed by sect. 92 as the Imperial Parliament in the plenitude of its power possessed and could bestow. Within these limits of subjects and area the local legislature is supreme, and has the same authority as the Imperial Parliament, or the Parliament of the Dominion, would have had under like circumstances to confide to a municipal institution or body of its own creation authority to make by-laws or resolutions as to subjects specified in the enactment, and with the object of carrying the enactment into operation and effect.

In *Liquidators of Maritime Bank of Canada v. Receiver-General of New Brunswick*, [1892] A.C. 437, it was argued that the Province enjoyed no part of the Crown prerogative, and accordingly the Province of New Brunswick could not claim priority in respect of the bank's assets for a debt owed to the Province. The argument also involved the proposition that the federal Government did not share this constitutional incompetence. At p. 438, counsel contended:

> The prerogative rights of the Crown cannot be invoked and exercised by the provincial government, as distinguished from the Dominion Government. There is no section in the British North America Act of 1867 which gives this Crown right to the province. Accordingly, if the province possesses that right it must be on the general principle that the Lieutenant-Governor is entitled to exercise the prerogative of the Crown. But the effect of the Act of 1867 is that the Dominion Government represents the four provinces existing at the time of the Union and other provinces which were thereafter to be constituted; and, consequently, the direct connection between the Crown and the provinces has ceased. The Governor-General of Canada is the real representative of the Crown as the Dominion is at present constituted; and the Lieutenant-Governor of each province is not. Certain portions of prerogative are given to the Lieutenant-Governors, and that is inconsistent with their representing the Crown entirely. Otherwise, if the Dominion and the provinces both possess full prerogative rights you might have the Crown as representing the one contending with the Crown as representing the other.

Lord Watson spoke for the Judicial Committee and, at pp. 441-2, had this to say:

> . . . they maintained that the effect of the statute has been to sever all connection between the Crown and the provinces; to make the government of the Dominion the only government of Her Majesty in North America; and to reduce the provinces to the rank of independent municipal institutions. For these propositions, which contain the sum and substance of the arguments addressed to them in support of this appeal, their Lordships have been unable to find either principle or authority.
>
> Their Lordships do not think it necessary to examine, in minute detail, the provisions of the Act of 1867, which nowhere profess to curtail in any respect the rights and privileges of the Crown, or to disturb the relations then subsisting between the Sovereign and the provinces. The object of the Act was neither to weld the provinces into one, nor to subordinate provincial governments to a central authority, but to create a federal government in which they should all be represented, entrusted with the exclusive administration of affairs in which they had a common interest, each province retaining its independence and autonomy. That object was accomplished by distributing, between the Dominion and the provinces, all powers executive and legislative, and all public property and revenues which had previously belonged to the provinces; so that the Dominion Government should be vested with such of these powers, property, and revenues as were necessary for the due performance of its constitutional functions, and that the remainder should be retained by the provinces for the purposes of provincial government. But, in so far as regards those matters which, by sect. 92, are specially reserved for provincial legislation, the legislation of each province continues to be free from the control of the Dominion, and as supreme as it was before the passing of the Act.

After quoting from the *Hodge* case, *supra*, included in the passage cited above, he continued at pp. 442–3:

> It is clear, therefore, that the provincial legislature of New Brunswick does not occupy the subordinate position which was ascribed to it in the argument of the appellants. It derives no authority from the Government of Canada, and its status is in no way analogous to that of a municipal institution, which is an authority constituted for purposes of local administration. It possesses powers, not of administration merely, but of legislation, in the strictest sense of that word; and, within the limits assigned by sect. 92 of the Act of 1867, these powers are exclusive and supreme. It would require very express language, such as is not to be found in the Act of 1867, to warrant the inference that the Imperial Legislature meant to vest in the provinces of Canada the right of exercising supreme Legislative powers in which the British Sovereign was to have no share.

It was later established that the federal distribution of powers embraces not only legislative but also executive powers: *Bonanza Creek Gold Mining Co. v. The King* (1916),

26 D.L.R. 273 at p. 281, [1916] 1 A.C. 566 at p. 580, 10 W.W.R. 391, *per* Viscount Haldane L.C. At p. 281 D.L.R., p. 581 A.C., he said, referring to the *Maritime Bank* case, *supra:*

> It was there laid down that "the act of the Governor-General and his Council, in making the appointments is, within the meaning of the statute, the act of the Crown; and a Lieutenant-Governor, when appointed, is as much the representative of Her Majesty for all purposes of provincial government, as the Governor-General himself is for all purposes of Dominion government."

The assignment of powers by the Act to the Parliament of Canada and to the provincial Legislatures covered the whole area of self-government. This was recognized by the Privy Council in *A.-G. Ont. et al. v. A.-G. Can. et al.* (1912), 3 D.L.R. 509 at p. 511, [1912] A.C. 571 at p. 581, 81 L.J.P.C. 210:

> In 1867 the desire of Canada for a definite Constitution embracing the entire Dominion was embodied in the British North America Act. Now, there can be no doubt that under this organic instrument the powers distributed between the Dominion on the one hand and the provinces on the other hand cover the whole area of self-government within the whole area of Canada. It would be subversive of the entire scheme and policy of the Act to assume that any point of internal self-government was withheld from Canada.

In *Murphy v. C.P.R. Co. et al.* (1958), 15 D.L.R. (2d) 145 at p. 153, [1958] S.C.R. 626 at p. 643, 77 C.R.T.C. 322, Rand J. stated:

> It has become a truism that the totality of effective legislative power is conferred by the Act of 1867, subject always to the express or necessarily implied limitation of the Act itself . . .

The foregoing review shows that the enactment of the *B.N.A. Act* created a federal Constitution of Canada which confided the whole area of self-government within Canada to the Parliament of Canada and the provincial Legislatures each being supreme within its own defined sphere and area. It can fairly be said, therefore, that the dominant principle of Canadian constitutional law is federalism. The implications of that principle are clear. Each level of Government should not be permitted to encroach on the other, either directly or indirectly. The political compromise achieved as a result of the Quebec and London Conferences preceding the passage of the *B.N.A. Act* would be dissolved unless there were substantive and effective limits on unconstitutional action.

The *B.N.A. Act* did not make any specific provision as

to the means of determining the constitutionality of any federal or provincial legislation. That task has been assumed and performed by the Courts, with supreme authority initially resting with the Judicial Committee of the Privy Council and, since, 1949, with this Court.

In performing this function, the Courts, in addition to dealing with cases involving alleged excesses of legislative jurisdiction, have had occasion to develop legal principles based on the necessity of preserving the integrity of the federal structure. We will be dealing with these later in this judgment. We will, however, at this point cite one instance of the performance of this task in the following case by the Privy Council.

In *A.-G. Can. v. A.-G. Ont. et al., Reference re Weekly Rest in Industrial Undertakings Act,* [1937] 1 D.L.R. 673, [1937] A.C. 326, [1937] 1 W.W.R. 299 (the *Labour Conventions* case) [affg [1936] 3 D.L.R. 673, [1936] S.C.R. 461], the issue was as to the constitutional validity of three federal statutes enacted in 1935 dealing with labour matters, such as weekly rest in industrial undertakings, hours of work and minimum wages. In substance, they gave effect to draft conventions adopted by the International Labour Organization of the League of Nations in accordance with the Labour Pact of the Treaty of Versailles, 1919, ratified by Canada. For the Attorney-General for Canada it was argued that the legislation was valid because it was for the purpose of performing Canadian treaty obligations. For the Province it was contended that the statutes related to property and civil rights in the Province.

The argument made on behalf of the Attorney-General for Canada, as reported at p. 330 [A.C.], was very similar to the submissions made for the Attorney-General of Canada in this case:

> By the transference of the treaty-making power to the Dominion executive, and correlative power to legislate to carry out the obligations, nothing is taken from the Provinces.
>
> [Lord Atkin. The Dominion has not got unlimited powers of legislation.]
>
> The residuary clause of s. 91 of the British North America Act is capable of the construction, which is not inconsistent with decided cases, that where Canada has properly incurred an international obligation with respect to any matter whatsoever, that within whatever classes in ss. 91 and 92 it may be described as coming under other circumstances, once the matter has assumed the aspect of an international bargain it is no longer to be treated as belonging to any one of the enumerated classes.
>
> [Lord Atkin. That is a very far-reaching doctrine: it means that Canada could make an agreement with any State which would seriously affect Provincial rights.]

It is a power which cannot be exercised by Canada alone; some other country must be found which is willing to enter into a bargain. This matter must not be looked at as though Canada is going to look about the world to find some one with whom to make an agreement for the purpose of robbing the Provinces of their constitutional rights. But, logically, it must be admitted that whatever Canada and such other country agree to can be effected by Canada.

This argument was rejected not only on the basis that there was no support for it in the constitution itself, but also because of its incompatability with the federal structure of Government in Canada. At pp. 681–3 D.L.R., pp. 351–2 A.C., Lord Atkin said:

> For the purposes of ss. 91 and 92, *i.e.*, the distribution of legislative powers between the Dominion and the Provinces, there is no such thing as treaty legislation as such. The distribution is based on classes of subjects: and as a treaty deals with a particular class of subjects so will the legislative power of performing it be ascertained. No one can doubt that this distribution is one of the most essential conditions, probably the most essential condition, in the inter-provincial compact to which the B.N.A. Act gives effect. If the position of Lower Canada, now Quebec, alone were considered, the existence of her separate jurisprudence as to both property and civil rights might be said to depend upon loyal adherence to her constitutional right to the exclusive competence of her own Legislature in these matters. Nor is it of less importance for the other Provinces, though their law may be based on English jurisprudence, to preserve their own right to legislate for themselves in respect of local conditions which may vary by as great a distance as separates the Atlantic from the Pacific. It would be remarkable that while the Dominion could not initiate legislation however desirable which affected civil rights in the Provinces, yet its Government not responsible to the Provinces nor controlled by provincial Parliaments need only agree with a foreign country to enact such legislation: and its Parliament would be forthwith clothed with authority to affect provincial rights to the full extent of such agreement. Such a result would appear to undermine the constitutional safeguards of provincial constitutional autonomy.

> It follows from what has been said that no further legislative competence is obtained by the Dominion from its accession to international status, and the consequent increase in the scope of its executive functions. It is true, as pointed out in the judgment of the Chief Justice, that as the executive is now clothed with the powers of making treaties so the Parliament of Canada, to which the executive is responsible, has imposed upon it responsibilities in connection with such treaties, for if it were to disapprove of them they would either not be made or the

Ministers would meet their constitutional fate. But this is true of all executive functions in their relation to Parliament. There is no existing constitutional ground for stretching the competence of the Dominion Parliament so that it becomes enlarged to keep pace with enlarged functions of the Dominion executive. If the new functions affect the classes of subjects enumerated in s. 92 legislation to support the new functions is in the competence of the provincial Legislatures only. If they do not, the competence of the Dominion Legislature is declared by s. 91 and existed *ab origine*. In other words the Dominion cannot merely by making promises to foreign countries clothe itself with legislative authority inconsistent with the constitution which gave it birth.

There are several features of the *Labour Conventions* case which require emphasis. The federal Government was in that case asserting the right to enact legislation which was within provincial authority in order to carry out the treaty obligations which it had assumed. No question was raised as to the validity of the federal Government's authority to negotiate and ratify international treaties. What was held unconstitutional by the Privy Council was the use of that lawful procedure to legislate indirectly beyond the powers invested in the federal Parliament by s. 91 of the *B.N.A. Act*.

In these appeals this Court is equally concerned with the exercise of a valid power, namely, the power of the federal Houses of Parliament to pass resolutions requesting amendments to the *B.N.A. Act*. That power has historic foundation, but we note that it has never before been exercised for the purpose of curtailing provincial legislative authority without provincial consent. In the context of the *Labour Conventions* case, the issue in these appeals is whether the established incompetence of the federal Government to encroach on provincial powers can be avoided through the use of the resolution procedure to effect a constitutional amendment passed at the behest of the federal Government by the Parliament of the United Kingdom.

The only provisions of the *B.N.A. Act* dealing with amendments to the Constitution are as follows. Head 1 of s. 92 empowered a provincial Legislature to make laws in relation to:

1. The Amendment from Time to Time, notwithstanding anything in this Act, of the Constitution of the Province, except as regards the Office of Lieutenant Governor.

Section 146, already cited, made provision for the admission of other colonies and territories into the Union.

By an amendment made in 1949 to s. 91 of the *B.N.A. Act* [1949 (2) (U.K.), c. 81, s. 1], a limited power of amendment was given to the federal Parliament. Head 1 of s. 91 enabled it to legislate in relation to:

> 1. The amendment from time to time of the Constitution of Canada, except as regards matters coming within the classes of subjects by this Act assigned exclusively to the Legislatures of the provinces, or as regards rights or privileges by this or any other Constitutional Act granted or secured to the Legislature or the Government of a province, or to any class of persons with respect to schools or as regards the use of the English or the French language or as regards the requirements that there shall be a session of the Parliament of Canada at least once each year, and that no House of Commons shall continue for more than five years from the day of the return of the Writs for choosing the House: Provided, however, that a House of Commons may in time of real or apprehended war, invasion or insurrection be continued by the Parliament of Canada if such continuation is not opposed by the votes of more than one-third of the members of such House.

This provision specifically excepted from its operation, *inter alia*, matters coming within the classes of subjects assigned exclusively to the Provinces. The scope of s. 91(1) was considered by this Court in *Reference re Legislative Authority of Parliament to Alter or Replace the Senate* (1979), 102 D.L.R. (3d) 1, [1980] 1 S.C.R. 54 *sub nom. Re Authority of Parliament in Relation to the Upper House* (herein the *Senate Reference*). In that case, this Court unanimously held that the federal Government could not, acting under s. 91(1), abolish the Senate. The term "Constitution of Canada" found in s. 91(1) was held in its context to refer only to the federal juristic unit. It is significant that when, as recently as 1949, the Houses of Parliament sought and obtained a provision permitting the federal Parliament to amend the Constitution by legislation, specific provision was made to ensure that this power was not capable of implying any right to interfere with those powers assigned to the Provinces by the *B.N.A. Act*.

Because the Canadian Constitution was created by the *B.N.A. Act* in the form of an Imperial statute, it followed that in the absence of a provision for amendment within it, its amendment could only be effected by the enactment of an Imperial statute. Over the years many amendments have occurred in this way. The practice has developed, since 1895, to have the formal approach to the Imperial Parliament made by means of a joint address of both Houses of Parliament. This form of procedure had been followed earlier in respect of amendments to the *Union Act*, 1840 (U.K.), c. 35. It is also the procedure spelled out in s. 146 of the *B.N.A. Act* as the means of approach to the Queen,

acting on the advice of her Privy Council for the admission of existing colonies, or territories, into the Union.

The record of constitutional amendments passed since 1867 by the Imperial Parliament is contained in the Favreau White Paper of 1965, issued by the federal Government, and approved by the provincial Governments. It was cited by this Court in the *Senate Reference*. Many of these amendments concerned mere formalities, such as the postponement of redistribution of seats in the House of Commons in 1916 and 1943 to await the cessation of hostilities. Those amendments which were important in relation to the proper procedure for amendment were discussed in that Paper, and we think they bear repetition in full:

(1) *The British North America Act of 1871* — (Establishment of new provinces and administration of territories)

Because this was the first attempt by Canada to have the Constitution amended, there were no precedents for the government of the day to follow. It requested the amendment from the British Parliament without reference to the Parliament of Canada, and the latter took strong exception. The opposition in Parliament condemned the government for its failure to secure prior approval of Canada's legislative authority. The government agreed that such matters should be referred to Parliament, and the House of Commons unanimously adopted a resolution stating that ". . . no changes in the provisions of the British North America (would) be sought by the Executive Government without the previous assent of the Parliament of this Dominion". A few days later, the government brought down a joint Address, which was concurred in by both Houses of Parliament, and which formed the basis upon which the amendment was finally passed by the British Parliament.

(2) *The Parliament of Canada Act, 1875* — (Privileges, immunities and powers of the House of Parliament)

Notwithstanding the principle it had pressed for, and had had unanimously adopted by Parliament four years earlier when it was in opposition, the Canadian government of the day requested this amendment without "previous assent" or formal Address by Parliament. Objections again were raised in the House of Commons and a resolution similar to that of 1871 was introduced. After debate, the government conceded the propriety of the principle it had originally espoused: of referring proposed constitutional amendments to Parliament. The new resolution was withdrawn when the government agreed that a joint Address by both Houses of Parliament was the only appropriate way of securing amendments to the Constitution.

(3) *The British North America Act of 1886 —*
(Representation of territories in Parliament)

The Canadian government submitted its request for this amendment to Westminster on the basis of a formal Address by both Houses of Parliament. With one exception, this principle has been followed by every Canadian government since that time. The exception was the enactment in 1895 by the United Kingdom Parliament of the Canadian Speaker (Appointment of Deputy) Act, which was allowed without protest by the Canadian Parliament because of particular circumstances.

(4) *The British North America Act of 1907 —*
(Subsidies to provinces)

This was the first occasion on which the federal government consulted with the provinces before seeking a constitutional amendment. In this case, all nine of the provinces in existence were directly concerned with the amendment. All were consulted and eight of the nine provincial governments agreed to the federal proposal. One province opposed the proposal, both in Canada and in Great Britain. The British government made minor changes in the text of the draft bill, and the amendment was enacted.

(5) *The British North America Act of 1915 —*
(Redefinition of divisions of the Senate)

This amendment was passed without consultation with the provinces and without provincial government representations concerning its enactment. This amendment is important to Canadian constitutional development in that it was put forward in the form of a Canadian draft bill, embodied in the Address to the Crown and enactment without modification by the British Parliament.

(6) *The British North America Act of 1930 —*
(Jurisdiction of Western provinces over their natural resources)

This was the first application for a constitutional amendment relating to a provincial field that did not directly concern all provinces. It was obtained by the federal government after consultation with only those provinces directly affected except in one province where a resolution was adopted by the legislature after the Premier had already expressed the consent of his government to the amendment.

(7) *The British North America Act of 1940 —*
(Unemployment Insurance)

This was the first amendment to change the distribution of legislative powers between Parliament and the provinces, as provided in the 1867 Constitution. It transferred the authority to legislate on unemployment insurance from provincial to federal jurisdiction. Before seeking this amendment, the federal government obtained the consent of all provincial governments. In this, as in

previous cases of provincial concurrence, there was no reference of the question by any government to its legislature.

(8) *The British North America Act of 1943 —*
(Postponement of redistribution of seats in the House of Commons)

The federal government did not consult the provinces prior to seeking this amendment, and notwithstanding the protest of one provincial government, the Parliament of the United Kingdom granted it. The position of the federal government was that this amendment concerned only the Government of Canada, since it did not affect provincial governments or legislatures.

(9) *The British North America Act of 1946 —*
(Readjustment of representation in the House of Commons)

The federal government sought this amendment on the same basis as that of 1943 — that is, without provincial consultations — and for the same reasons.

(10) *The British North America Act of 1949 —*
(Entry of Newfoundland into Confederation)

A resolution was moved in the House of Commons urging that this amendment not be proceeded with until after consultation with the provincial governments. What the resolution meant by "consultation" was not clear. However, the amendment was enacted without such consultation and without any of the provincial governments formally objecting to its enactment, though one or two provincial governments stated publicly that consultation should have taken place.

(11) *The British North America Act of 1949(2) —*
(Authority of Parliament to amend certain aspects of the Constitution of Canada)

This amendment was obtained without consultation or formal consent of provincial governments, the federal government maintaining the position taken in connection with the 1943 and 1946 amendments. At a federal-provincial constitutional conference the following year, however, the federal government indicated that, in the event of agreement on an overall procedure for amending the Constitution of Canada, it would be prepared to reconsider the broad provisions of this amendment.

(12) *The British North America Act of 1951 —*
(Old Age Pensions)

This amendment was enacted after the federal government secured the agreement of all provinces. In the case of the provinces of Quebec, Saskatchewan and Manitoba, the matter was referred to the legislature, which authorized the governments of those provinces to agree to the amendment. Other provincial governments gave concurrence on their own authority.

(13) *The British North America Act of 1960* —
(Tenure of office of certain Judges)

The federal government sought this amendment only after obtaining the agreement of all provinces, since the amendment provided for the compulsory retirement at age 75 of judges of provincial courts. In this instance again Quebec placed the matter before its legislature before agreeing.

(14) *The British North America Act of 1964* —
(Supplementary benefits to Old Age Pensions)

This amendment was enacted after agreement of all provincial governments, with, in the case of Quebec, the concurrence of the Legislative Assembly. It involved a modification of section 94A created by the 1951 amendment on which prior agreement of all provinces had been obtained.

The Favreau White Paper goes on to say:

There have been five instances — in 1907, 1940, 1951, 1960 and 1964 — of federal consultation with all provinces on matters of direct concern to all of them. There has been only one instance up to the present time in which an amendment was sought after consultation with only those provinces directly affected by it. This was the amendment of 1930, which transferred to the Western provinces natural resources that had been under the control of the federal government since their admission to Confederation. There have been ten instances [in 1871, 1875, 1886, 1895, 1915, 1916, 1943, 1946, 1949 and 1949(2)] of amendments to the Constitution without prior consultation with the provinces on matters that the federal government considered were of exclusive federal concern. In the last four of these, one or two provinces protested that federal-provincial consultations should have taken place prior to action by Parliament.

In no instance has an amendment to the *B.N.A. Act* been enacted which directly affected federal-provincial relationships in the sense of changing provincial legislative powers, in the absence of federal consultation with and the consent of all the Provinces. Notably, this procedure continued to be followed in the four instances which occurred after the enactment of the *Statute of Westminster, 1931* (U.K.), c. 4 (herein the *Statute of Westminster, 1931*).

This history of amendments reveals the operation of constitutional constraints. While the choice of the resolution procedure is itself a matter of internal parliamentary responsibility, the making of the addresses to the Sovereign falls into two areas. Resolutions concerning the federal juristic unit and federal powers were made without reference to any but the members of the federal Houses. Resolutions abridging provincial authority have never been

passed without the concurrence of the Provinces. In other words, the normal constitutional principles recognizing the inviolability of separate and exclusive legislative powers were carried into and considered an integral part of the operation of the resolution procedure.

The history of constitutional amendments also parallels the development of Canadian sovereignty. The *B.N.A. Act* did not have among its purposes the severance of Canada from the British Commonwealth. However, the vital role of Canadian consent as an expression of Canadian sovereignty is revealed in the fact that no constitutional amendment has been passed without that consent.

The *Statute of Westminster, 1931* was enacted following two Imperial Conferences held in 1926 and 1930, attended by representatives of the United Kingdom, Canada, Australia, New Zealand, South Africa, the Irish Free State and Newfoundland. At the earlier conference, the established constitutional position was stated in a form which has come to be called the *Balfour Declaration:*

They are autonomous communities within the British Empire, equal in status, in no way subordinate one to another in any aspect of their domestic or external affairs, though united by a common allegiance to the Crown, and freely associated as members of the British Commonwealth.

The *Statute of Westminster, 1931* was enacted to give effect in the law of the United Kingdom to the established fact of sovereign status of the communities within the British Empire.

The following provisions of the statute were referred to in argument before us:

2(1) The Colonial Laws Validity Act, 1865, shall not apply to any law made after the commencement of this Act by the Parliament of a Dominion.

(2) No law and no provision of any law made after the commencement of this Act by the Parliament of a Dominion shall be void or inoperative on the ground that it is repugnant to the law of England, or to the provisions of any existing or future Act of Parliament of the United Kingdom, or to any order, rule, or regulation made under any such Act, and the powers of the Parliament of a Dominion shall include the power to repeal or amend any such Act, order, rule or regulation in so far as the same is part of the law of the Dominion.

3. It is hereby declared and enacted that the Parliament of a Dominion has full power to make laws having extra-territorial operation.

4. No Act of Parliament of the United Kingdom passed after the commencement of this Act shall extend, or be deemed to extend, to a Dominion as part of the law of that Dominion, unless it is expressly declared in that

Act that that Dominion has requested, and consented to, the enactment thereof.

. . . . .

7(1) Nothing in this Act shall be deemed to apply to the repeal, amendment or alteration of the British North America Acts, 1867 to 1930, or any order, rule or regulation made thereunder.

(2) The provisions of section two of this Act shall extend to laws made by any of the Provinces of Canada and to the powers of the legislatures of such Provinces.

(3) The powers conferred by this Act upon the Parliament of Canada or upon the legislatures of the Provinces shall be restricted to the enactment of laws in relation to matters within the competence of the Parliament of Canada or of any of the legislatures of the Provinces respectively.

We do not regard s. 4 as having any real impact on the matter in issue in these appeals. The section uses the word "extend" and we therefore regard the section as meaning that a United Kingdom statute would not, in the absence of the declaration referred to in the section, be a part of the law of any Dominion. It is, however, of interest that each of the amendments made after the *Statute of Westminster, 1931* took effect contains a declaration that the enactment had been requested and consented to by Canada.

Of the Dominions to which the *Statute of Westminster, 1931* applied, all were unitary States except Canada and Australia, and the Australian constitution already contained provision for its amendment.

In relation to Canada, the possible impact of s. 2 was a cause of concern to the Provinces because it could be construed as enabling the federal Parliament to repeal or amend the *B.N.A. Act*. The origin of s. 7 was the result of that concern. The Favreau White Paper at pp. 18-9 deals with the history of this section:

On June 30th, 1931, the Right Honourable R. B. Bennett, Prime Minister of Canada, introduced in the House of Commons a resolution for an Address to His Majesty requesting the enactment of the Statute of Westminster. The preamble to the resolution said:

"And whereas consideration has been given by the proper authorities in Canada as to whether and to what extent the principles enbodied in the proposed act of the parliament of the United Kingdom should be applied to provincial legislation; and, at a dominion-provincial conference, held at Ottawa on the seventh and eighth days of April, in the year of Our Lord one thousand nine hundred and thirty-one, a clause was approved by the delegates of His Majesty's government in Canada and of the governments of all of the provinces of Canada, for insertion in the proposed act for the purpose of providing that the provisions of the pro-posed act relating to the Colonial Laws Validity Act should extend to laws made by the provinces of Canada and to the powers of the legislatures of the provinces; and also for the purpose of providing that nothing in the proposed act should be deemed to apply to the repeal, amendment or alteration of the British North America Acts of 1867 to 1930; or any order, rule or regulation made thereunder; and also for the purpose of providing that the powers conferred by the proposed act on the parliament of Canada and upon the legislatures of the provinces should be restricted to the enactment of laws in relation to matters within the competence of the parliament of Canada or any of the legislatures of the provinces respectively."

The Prime Minister explained that the Dominion-Provincial Conference referred to in the preamble had been convened in response to representations by Ontario, subsequently supported by the other provinces. He referred to the apprehension of some of the provinces that under provisions as broad as those to be inserted in the Statute of Westminster, a dominion parliament might encroach upon the jurisdiction of a provincial legislature and exercise powers beyond its competence. He pointed out that ". . . lest it be concluded by inference that the rights of the provinces as defined by the British North America Act had been by reason of this Statute curtailed, lessened, modified or repealed", a section of the Statute of special application to Canada declared, with the unanimous concurrence of the provinces, that such was not the case.

The *Statute of Westminster, 1931* was passed on December 11, 1931. Earlier that year, Mr. Louis St. Laurent, then President of the Canadian Bar Association, and a distinguished constitutional lawyer, referred in his "Presidential Address", reported in 9 Can. Bar Rev. 525 (1931), to the Resolutions of the House of Commons and the Senate requesting the enactment of the statute. This speech was not delivered in a political context. At that time he did not hold any political office. It was some years later that he became a Member of the House of Commons and a Minister of the Crown. The following passage from that speech is relevant to the issue now before the Court:

Now, it may be that while both the Dominion and the Provinces remained subject to the legislative jurisdiction of His Majesty's Parliament of the United Kingdom, that Parliament had, in theory, full power to vary the distribution of legislative jurisdiction between them. But after the declaration of 1926 that both the United Kingdom and the Dominions are autonomous communities equal in status, in no way subordinate one to another in any aspect of their domestic or external affairs, it would hardly seem probable that the Parliament of the United Kingdom would undertake to legislate for the territory of any one of those Dominions, unless it be expressly declared in the Act that the Dominion had requested and consented to the enactment for the proposed legislation. And if the United Kingdom and the Dominions are equal in status and in no way subordinate one to another in any aspect of their domestic or external affairs, does not the provision of section 92 of the Act of 1867, that in each province the legislature may exclusively make laws in relation to the amendment from time to time of its constitution, except as regards the office of Lieutenant-Governor, seem to indicate that the Houses of the Dominion Parliament would have no jurisdiction to request or to consent to enactments that might extend or abridge Provincial legislative autonomy? It is true that one of the proposed subsections of the Statute of Westminster is to declare that nothing in that Statute shall be deemed to apply to the repeal, amendment or alteration of the British North America Acts, 1867 to 1930, or any order, rule or regulation made thereunder; but the declaration of the Imperial Conference purports to be a statement of the established constitutional position, and if it is so in fact, is anything further required to make it clear that the constitution of the provinces can be amended or affected only by the provinces themselves?

Section 92 excludes federal jurisdiction over them, and the declaration of 1926 does seem to state a constitutional position that precluded interference with them by any other Parliament to which they are said to be in no way subordinate.

The *Statute of Westminster, 1931* gave statutory recognition to the independent sovereign status of Canada as a nation. However, while Canada, as a nation, was recognized as being sovereign, the Government of the nation remained federal in character and the federal Parliament did not acquire sole control of the exercise of that sovereignty. Section 2 of the *Statute of Westminster, 1931*, standing alone, could be construed as giving that control to the federal Parliament, but the enactment of s. 7, at the instance of the Provinces, was intended to preclude that exercise of power by the federal Parliament. Subsection 7(3) in particular gave explicit recognition to the continuation of the division of powers created by the *B.N.A. Act*. The powers conferred on the Parliament of Canada by the *Statute of Westminster, 1931* were restricted to the enactment of laws in relation to matters within the competence of the Parliament of Canada.

The effect of s. 7(1) was to preserve the Imperial Parliament as the legal instrument for enacting amendments to the *B.N.A. Acts*, 1867–1930. This clearly had no effect on the existing procedure which had been used to obtain the amendment of the *B.N.A. Act*. The resolution procedure, which, after 1895, had produced all the constitutional

amendments until 1931, has been followed in respect of all the constitutional amendments passed since 1931.

The Attorney-General of Canada presented a deceptively simple argument in support of the legality of the Resolution at issue in these appeals. It was argued that the Resolution is not a law, and therefore not a proper subject for judicial consideration and, further, that the two Houses can legally pass any resolution which they desire. The Imperial Parliament has full legal authority to amend the *B.N.A. Act* by enacting a statute, and its power to do so cannot be questioned. If, therefore, the Imperial Parliament enacts such a statute in response to a resolution of the Senate and the House of Commons, there can be no question of illegality.

However, it was also submitted that while the Imperial Parliament has full legal authority to amend the *B.N.A. Act*, there exists a "firm and unbending" convention that such an amendment will only be enacted in response to a resolution of the two Houses requesting it, and, futher, that it will enact any amendent to the *B.N.A. Act* which is so requested.

In the result, if this process is examined from the point of view of substance rather than of form, what is being asserted is the existence of a power in the Senate and the House of Commons to cause any amendment to the *B.N.A. Act* which they desire to be enacted, even though that amendment subtracts, without provincial consent, from the legislative powers of the Provinces granted to them by the *B.N.A. Act*.

In support of the proposition that resolutions are questions of internal parliamentary procedure and are not proper subjects of judicial consideration, reference was made to two British authors. In his *Introduction to the Study of the Law of the Constitution*, 10th ed., Dicey states at pp. 54–5 that the resolution of neither House is law and each House has complete control over its own proceedings. May's *Parliamentary Practice*, 18th ed., at p. 195, affirms the rule that each House has exclusive jurisdiction over its own internal proceedings.

The English authorities, such as Dicey and May, respecting the power of the Houses of Parliament to pass resolutions, and as to their effect, are related to resolutions of the Houses of Parliament in a unitary State. Under the British Constitution, the only limitation on the power of Parliament is that its authority must be expressed in legislation. Any "constitutional amendment" under the British Constitution can be passed by normal legislation. Accordingly, these authorities are of no help in determining the limitations, if any, on the authority of one level of government in a federal State, respecting the use of an accepted amending procedure for the purpose of abridging the powers of the other legislative level. The Resolution under consideration is not a matter of internal procedure. A resolution of the Senate and the House of Commons has become recognized as the means whereby a request is made to the Imperial Parliament for legislation to effect a constitutional amendment.

The power of the Senate and the House of Commons to pass resolutions of any kind, and to use such resolutions for any purpose, was stated by the Attorney-General to have been recognized in s. 18 of the *B.N.A. Act* and s. 4 of the *Senate and House of Commons Act*, R.S.C. 1970, c. S-8. Section 18 of the *B.N.A. Act* provides:

> 18. The privileges, immunities, and powers to be held, enjoyed, and exercised by the Senate and by the House of Commons, and by the members thereof respectively, shall be such as are from time to time defined by Act of the Parliament of Canada, but so that any Act of the Parliament of Canada defining such privileges, immunities, and powers shall not confer any privileges, immunities, or powers exceeding those at the passing of such Act held, enjoyed, and exercised by the Commons House of Parliament of the United Kingdom of Great Britain and Ireland, and by the members thereof.

Section 18 in its present form was enacted by the *Parliament of Canada Act*, 1875 (U.K.), c. 38, to replace s. 18 of the *B.N.A. Act, 1867*. The difference in phraseology of the two sections is not relevant to the matter in issue in these appeals.

Section 18 did not, in itself, create or recognize the existence of the privileges, immunities and powers of the Senate and the House of Commons. It provided that their privileges, immunities and powers should be such as are, from time to time, defined by Act of the Parliament of Canada, subject to the limitation that Parliament could not by statute, give to the Senate or the House of Commons any privileges, immunities or powers which exceeded those enjoyed by the House of Commons of the United Kingdom Parliament. Parliament could not grant legislative powers to its two Houses. Furthermore, because, unlike the Parliament of the United Kingdom, Parliament's power to legislate was limited in extent, it could not grant to the Senate and the House of Commons powers which it did not itself possess.

In the exercise of the power granted to it by s. 18 of the *B.N.A. Act*, the Parliament of Canada, in 1868, passed "An Act to define the privileges, immunities and powers of the Senate and House of Commons, and to give summary protection to persons employed in the publication of Parliamentary Papers", 1868 (Can.), c. 23. Sections 1 and 2 of that Act provided as follows:

> 1. The Senate and the House of Commons respectively, and the Members thereof respectively, shall hold, enjoy and exercise such and the like privileges, immunities and powers as, at the time of the passing of the British North America Act, 1867, were held, enjoyed and exercised by the Commons House of Parliament of the United Kingdom of Great Britain and Ireland, and by the Members thereof, so far as the same are consistent with and not repugnant to the said Act.

> 2. Such privileges, immunities and powers shall be deemed to be and shall be part of the General and Public Law of Canada, and it shall not be necessary to plead the same, but the same shall in all Courts in Canada and by and before all Judges be taken notice of judicially.

The essential provisions of these two sections were repeated in subsequent legislation. They now appear in ss. 4 and 5 of the *Senate and House of Commons Act* as follows:

> 4. The Senate and the Houses of Commons respectively, and the members thereof respectively, hold, enjoy and exercise,
>
> (*a*) such and the like privileges, immunities and powers as, at the time of the passing of the *British North America Act, 1867*, were held, enjoyed and exercised by the Commons House of Parliament of the United Kingdom, and by the members thereof, so far as the same are consistent with and not repugnant to that Act; and
>
> (*b*) such privileges, immunities and powers as are from time to time defined by Act of the Parliament of Canada, not exceeding those at the time of the passing of such Act held, enjoyed and exercised by the Commons House of Parliament of the United Kingdom and by the members thereof respectively.

> 5. Such privileges, immunities and powers are part of the general and public law of Canada, and it is not necessary to plead the same, but the same shall, in all courts in Canada, and by and before all judges, to be taken notice of judicially.

Parliament did not confer upon the Senate and the House of Commons all of the privileges, immunities and powers held, enjoyed and exercised by the House of Commons of the United Kingdom, but only conferred them "so far as the same are consistent with and not repugnant to that Act", *i.e.*, the *B.N.A. Act, 1867*. It thus recognized that some powers enjoyed by the House of Commons of the United Kingdom might not be consistent with the provisions of the *B.N.A. Act*.

In our opinion this very important proviso took into account the fact that, whereas the House of Commons in the United Kingdom was one of the Houses in the Parliament of a unitary State, the Canadian Senate and House of Commons were Houses in a Parliament in a federal State, whose powers were not all embracing, but were specifically limited by the Act which created it.

In order to pass the Resolution now under consideration the Senate and the House of Commons must purport to exercise a power. The source of that power must be found in para. 4(*a*) of the *Senate and House of Commons Act*, since there has been no legislation enacted to date, other than para. 4(*a*) which actually defines the privileges, immunities and powers upon the two Houses of Parliament. The Resolution now before us was passed for the purpose of obtaining an amendment to the *B.N.A. Act*, the admitted effect of which is to curtail provincial legislative powers under s. 92 of the *B.N.A. Act*. In our opinion that power is not consistent with the *B.N.A. Act* but is repugnant to it. It is a power which is out of harmony with the very basis of the *B.N.A. Act*. Therefore para. (*a*) of s. 4, because of the limitations which it contains, does not confer that power. The Senate and the House of Commons are purporting to exercise a power which they do not possess.

The effect of the position taken by the Attorney-General of Canada is that the two Houses of Parliament have unfettered control of a triggering mechanism by means of which they can cause the *B.N.A. Act* to be amended in any way they desire. It was frankly conceded in argument that there were no limits of any kind upon the type of amendment that could be made in this fashion. In our opinion, this argument in essence maintains that the Provinces have since, at the latest 1931, owed their continued existence not to their constitutional powers expressed in the *B.N.A. Act*, but to the federal Parliament's sufferance. While the federal Parliament was throughout this period incompetent to legislate in respect of matters assigned to the Provinces by s. 92, its two Houses could at any time have done so by means of a Resolution to the Imperial Parliament, procuring an amendment to the *B.N.A. Act*.

The Attorney-General of Canada, in substance, is asserting the existence of a power in the two Houses of Parliament to obtain amendments to the *B.N.A. Act* which could disturb and even destroy the federal system of constitutional government in Canada. We are not aware of any possible legal source for such a power. The House of Commons and the Senate are part of the Parliament of Canada. Section 17 of the *B.N.A. Act* states that there "shall be one Parliament for Canada, consisting of the

Queen, an Upper House styled the Senate and the House of Commons". Laws under s. 91 of the *B.N.A. Act* are enacted by the Queen, with the advice and consent of the Senate and House of Commons. These two constituents of Parliament cannot by themselves enact legislation, nor could Parliament clothe them with powers beyond those possessed by Parliament itself.

The Attorney-General of Canada contends that because s-s. 7(1) of the statute left the repeal, amendment or alteration of the *British North America Acts*, 1867 to 1930 in the hands of the Imperial Parliament, there is nothing to prevent the two Houses of Parliament from requesting that an amendment be made in whatever form they submit. This submission means that the two Houses of Parliament can accomplish, indirectly, through the intervention of the Imperial Parliament, that which the Parliament of Canada itself is unable to do. In our opinion, the two Houses lack legal authority, of their own motion, to obtain constitutional amendments which would strike at the very basis of the Canadian federal system, *i.e.*, the complete division of legislative powers between the Parliament of Canada and the provincial Legislatures. It is the duty of this Court to consider this assertion of rights with a view to the preservation of the Constitution.

This Court, since its inception, has been active in reviewing the constitutionality of both federal and provincial legislation. This role has generally been concerned with the interpretation of the express terms of the *B.N.A. Act*. However, on occasions, this Court has had to consider issues for which the *B.N.A. Act* offered no answer. In each case, this Court denied the assertion of any power which would offend against the basic principles of the Constitution.

In *Amax Potash Ltd. et al. v. Government of Saskatchewan* (1976), 71 D.L.R. (3d) 1, [1977] 2 S.C.R. 576, [1976] 6 W.W.R. 61, the plaintiff sued for a declaration that certain sections of the *Mineral Taxation Act*, R.S.S. 1965, c. 64, and certain Regulations made pursuant to that Act, were *ultra vires* and sought the recovery of moneys paid by way of tax under the Regulations. The Government of Saskatchewan disputed the contention that these provisions were *ultra vires*, but also contended that no cause of action was disclosed because s-s. 5(7) of the *Proceedings against the Crown Act*, R.S.S. 1965, c. 87, was a bar to the recovery of moneys paid to the Crown. The relevant part of s-s. 5(7) provided:

> 5(7) No proceedings lie against the Crown under this or any other section of this Act in respect of anything heretofore or hereafter done or omitted and purporting

to have been done or omitted in the exercise of a power or authority under a statute or a statutory provision purporting to confer or to have conferred on the Crown such power or authority, which statute or statutory provision is or was or may be beyond the legislative jurisdiction of the Legislature . . .

In the course of his reasons, Dickson J., who delivered the judgment of the Court, said at p. 10 D.L.R., p. 590 S.C.R.:

A State, it is said, is sovereign and it is not for the Courts to pass upon the policy or wisdom of legislative will. As a broad statement of principle that is undoubtedly correct, but the general principle must yield to the requisites of the constitution in a federal State. By it the bounds of sovereignty are defined and supremacy circumscribed. The Courts will not question the wisdom of enactments which, by the terms of the Canadian Constitution, are within the competence of the Legislatures, but it is the high duty of this Court to insure that the Legislatures do not transgress the limits of their constitutional mandate and engage in the illegal exercise of power. Both Saskatchewan and Alberta inform the Court that justice and equity are irrelevant in this case. If injustice results, it is the electorate which must administer a rebuke, and not the Courts. The two Provinces apparently find nothing inconsistent or repellent in the contention that a subject can be barred from recovery of sums paid to the Crown under protest, in response to the compulsion of the legislature later found to be *ultra vires*.

Section 5(7) of the *Proceedings Against the Crown Act*, in my opinion, has much broader implications than mere Crown immunity. In the present context, it directly concerns the right to tax. It affects, therefore, the division of powers under the *British North Ameirca Act, 1867*. It also brings into question the right of a Province, or the federal Parliament for that matter, to act in violation of the Canadian Constitution. Since it is manifest that if either the federal Parliament or a provincial Legislature can tax beyond the limit of its powers, and by prior or *ex post facto* legislation give itself immunity from such illegal act, it could readily place itself in the same position as if the act had been done within proper constitutional limits. To allow moneys collected under compulsion, pursuant to an *ultra vires* statute, to be retained would be tantamount to allowing the provincial Legislature to do indirectly what it could not do directly, and by covert means to impose illegal burdens.

In *B.C. Power Corp. Ltd. v. B.C. Electric Co. Ltd. et al.* (1962), 34 D.L.R. (2d) 196, [1962] S.C.R. 642, 38 W.W.R. 701, this Court had to decide whether a receivership order could be made to preserve assets pending a decision as to the constitutionality of certain legislation in British Columbia which litigation would determine whether the Crown had title to the common shares of British Columbia Electric Company Limited which the legislation gave to the Crown.

It was contended that a receivership order could not be made by virtue of the Crown's perogative of immunity. Chief Justice Kerwin, who delivered the judgment of the Court, said at pp. 275–6 D.L.R., pp. 644–5 S.C.R.:

In a Federal system, where legislative authority is divided, as are also the perogatives of the Crown, as between the Dominion and the Provinces, it is my view that it is not open to the Crown, either in right of Canada or of a Province, to claim a Crown immunity based upon an interest in certain property, where its very interest in that property depends completely and solely on the validity of the legislation which it has itself passed, if there is a reasonable doubt as to whether such legislation is constitutionally valid. To permit it to do so would be to enable it, by the assertion of rights claimed under legislation which is beyond its powers, to achieve the same results as if the legislation were valid. In a Federal system it appears to me that, in such circumstances, the Court has the same jurisdiction to preserve assets whose title is dependent on the validity of the legislation as it has to determine the validity of the legislation itself.

In *A.-G. N.S. et al. v. A.-G. Can. et al.*, [1950] 4 D.L.R. 369, [1951] S.C.R. 3, the Court had to consider the validity of legislation which contemplated a delegation of legislative powers by the provincial Legislature to the Parliament of Canada, and by Parliament to the provincial Legislature. Chief Justice Rinfret said, at pp. 371–2 D.L.R., p. 34 S.C.R.:

The constitution of Canada does not belong either to Parliament, or to the Legislatures; it belongs to the country and it is there that the citizens of the country will find the protection of the rights to which they are entitled. It is part of that protection that Parliament can legislate only on the subject-matters referred to it by s. 91 and that each Province can legislate exclusively on the subject-matters referred to it by s. 92. The country is entitled to insist that legislation adopted under s. 91 should be passed exclusively by the Parliament of Canada in the same way as the people of each Province are entitled to insist that legislation concerning the matters enumerated in s. 92 should come exclusively from their respective Legislatures. In each case the Members elected to Parliament or to the Legislatures are the only ones entrusted with the power and the duty to legislate concerning the subjects exclusively distributed by the constitutional Act to each of them.

No power of delegation is expressed either in s. 91 or

in s. 92, nor, indeed, is there to be found the power of accepting delegation from one body to the other; and I have no doubt that if it had been the intention to give such powers it would have been expressed in clear and unequivocal language. Under the scheme of the *B.N.A. Act* there were to be, in the words of Lord Atkin in *Reference re Weekly Rest in Industrial Undertakings Act*, [1937] 1 D.L.R. 673 at p. 648, A.C. 326, "water-tight compartments which are an essential part of the original structure".

Neither legislative bodies, federal or provincial, possess any portion of the powers respectively vested in the other and they cannot receive it by delegation. In that connection the word "exclusively" used both in s. 91 and in s. 92 indicates a settled line of demarcation and it does not belong to either Parliament, or the Legislatures, to confer powers upon the other . . .

In *Reference re Alberta Legislation*, [1938] 2 D.L.R. 81, [1938] S.C.R. 100 [affd [1938] 4 D.L.R. 433, [1939] A.C. 117, [1938] 3 W.W.R. 337 (P.C.)], the Court considered, *inter alia*, the constitutional validity of the *Accurate News and Information Act* which imposed certain duties of publication upon newspapers published in Alberta. Chief Justice Duff (Davis J. concurring) referred to the right of public discussion and the authority of Parliament to protect that right and said at pp. 107–8 D.L.R., pp. 133–4 S.C.R.:

That authority rests upon the principle that the powers requisite for the protection of the constitution itself arise by necessary implication from *B.N.A. Act* as a whole (*Fort Frances Pulp & Paper Co. Ltd. v. Manitoba Free Press Co.*, [1923] 3 D.L.R. 629, [1923] A.C. 695); and since the subject-matter in relation to which the power is exercised is not exclusively a provincial matter, it is necessarily vested in Parliament.

It may be noted that the above instances of judicially developed legal principles and doctrines share several characteristics. *First*, none is to be found in express provisions of the *British North America Acts* or other constitutional enactments. *Second*, all have been perceived to represent constitutional requirements that are derived from the federal character of Canada's Constitution. *Third*, they have been accorded full legal force in the sense of being employed to strike down legislative enactments. *Fourth*, each was judicially developed in response to a particular legislative initiative in respect of which it might have been observed, as it was by Dickson J. in the *Amax* case, *supra*, at p. 10 D.L.R., p. 591 S.C.R., that: "There are no Canadian constitutional law predecents addressed directly to the present issue . . .".

The cases just considered were all decisions of this Court.

We have already referred to the judgment of the Privy Council in the *Labour Conventions* case, which, in our opinion, by analogy, is of considerable assistance in determining the issue before the Court. In that case, the Attorney-General of Canada argued that the federal Government's power to enter into treaties on behalf of a sovereign Canada enabled the federal Parliament to legislate pursuant to any treaty obligation. That submission was rejected by the Privy Council which held that the federal Parliament did not derive further legislative competence because of the accession by Canada to sovereign status. The federal Parliament was not clothed with additional legislative authority in consequence of the commitments it had made under an international treaty.

The contention of the Attorney-General of Canada in the present proceedings is that only the federal Parliament can speak for Canada as a sovereign State. It is the Houses of Parliament which, alone, under the practice developed in the obtaining of amendments to the *B.N.A. Act*, can submit a request to the Imperial Parliament to amend the *B.N.A. Act*, and the Imperial Parliament by a firm and unbending convention must comply with such a request. There is, therefore, it is contended, nothing which lawfully precludes the submission to the Imperial Parliament by resolution of both Houses of a request for an amendment to the *B.N.A. Act* which affects the basic division of legislative powers enshrined in the *B.N.A. Act*.

In our opinion the accession of Canada to sovereign international status did not enable the federal Parliament, whose legislative authority is limited to the matters defined in s. 91 of the *B.N.A. Act* unilaterally by means of a resolution of its two Houses, to effect an amendment to the *B.N.A. Act* which would offend against the basic principle of the division of powers created by that Act. The assertion of such a right, which has never before been attempted, is not contrary to the federal system created by the *B.N.A. Act*, but also runs counter to the objective sought to be achieved by s. 7 of the *Statute of Westminster, 1931*.

The federal position in these appeals can be summarized in these terms. While the federal Parliament lacks legal authority to achieve the objectives set out in the Resolution by the enactment of its own legislation, that limitation upon its authority can be evaded by having the legislation enacted by the Imperial Parliament at the behest of a resolution of the two Houses of the federal Parliament. This is an attempt by the federal Parliament to accomplish indirectly that which it is legally precluded from doing directly by perverting the recognized resolution method of obtaining constitutional amendments by the Imperial

Parliament for an improper purpose. In our opinion, since it is beyond the power of the federal Parliament to enact such an amendment, it is equally beyond the power of its two Houses to effect such an amendment through the agency of the Imperial Parliament.

We would adopt the views expressed by the Right Honourable Louis St. Laurent, then Prime Minister of Canada, on January 31, 1949, when in the debate on the address he said:

> With respect to all matters given by the constitution to the provincial governments, nothing this House could do could take anything away from them. We have no jurisdiction over what has been assigned exclusively to the provinces. We cannot ask that what is not within our jurisdiction be changed. We have jurisdiction over the matters assigned to us and we can ask that the manner of dealing with those matters be changed.

(House of Commons Debates, 1949, vol. 1, at p. 85.)

This passage clearly defines the scope of the power of the federal Parliament to request, on its own motion, amendments to the *B.N.A. Act*. It is limited to matters which are assigned to the federal Parliament by the *B.N.A. Act*.

Conclusions

The *B.N.A. Act* created a federal union. It was of the very essence of the federal nature of the Constitution that the Parliament of Canada and the provincial Legislatures should have distinct and separate legislative powers. The nature of the legislative powers of the Provinces under s. 92 and the status of the provincial Legislatures was declared by the Privy Council in the *Hodge* case, *supra*, and in the *Maritime Bank* case, *supra*. We repeat the statement of Lord Watson in the latter case at pp. 441–2:

> The object of the Act was neither to weld the provinces into one, nor to subordinate provincial governments to a central authority, but to create a federal government in which they should all be represented, entrusted with the exclusive administration of affairs in which they had a common interest, each province retaining its independence and autonomy.

The continuation of that basic division of legislative powers was recognized in s-s. 7(3) of the *Statute of Westminster, 1931*. The Parliament of Canada has no power to trespass on the area of legislative powers given to the provincial Legislatures. Section 7 of the statute was intended to safeguard provincial legislative powers from possible encroachment by the federal Parliament as a result of the powers being conferred upon the Parliament of Canada by the statute.

The fact that the status of Canada became recognized as a sovereign State did not alter its federal nature. It is a sovereign State, but its Government is federal in character with a clear division of legislative powers. The Resolution at issue in these appeals could only be an effective expression of Canadian sovereignty if it had the support of both levels of government.

The two Houses of the Canadian Parliament claim the power unilaterally to effect an amendment to the *B.N.A. Act* which they desire, including the curtailment of provincial legislative powers. This strikes at the basis of the whole federal system. It asserts a right by one part of the Canadian governmental system to curtail, without agreement, the powers of the other part.

There is no statutory basis for the exercise of such a power. On the contrary, the powers of the Senate and the House of Commons, given to them by para. 4(*a*) of the *Senate and House of Commons Act*, excluded the power to do anything inconsistent with the *B.N.A. Act*. The exercise of such a power has no support in constitutional convention. The constitutional convention is entirely to the contrary. We see no other basis for the recognition of the existence of such a power. This being so, it is the proper function of this Court, in its role of protecting and preserving the Canadian Constitution, to declare that no such power exists. We are, therefore, of the opinion that the Canadian Constitution does not empower the Senate and the House of Commons to cause the Canadian Constitution to be amended in respect of provincial legislative powers without the consent of the Provinces.

Question B in the Quebec Reference raises the issue as to the power of the Senate and the House of Commons of Canada to cause the Canadian Constitution to be amended "without the consent of the provinces and in spite of the objection of several of them". The Attorney-General of Saskatchewan when dealing with Question 3 in the Manitoba and Newfoundland References submitted that it was not necessary in these proceedings for the Court to pronounce on the necessity for the unanimous consent of all the Provinces to the constitutional amendments proposed in the Resolution. It was sufficient, in order to answer the question, to note the opposition of eight of the Provinces which contained a majority of the population of Canada.

We would answer Question B in the negative. We would answer Question 3 of the Manitoba and Newfoundland References in the affirmative without deciding, at this time, whether the agreement referred to in that question must be unanimous.

MARTLAND, RITCHIE, DICKSON, BEETZ, CHOUINARD AND LAMER JJ.: — The second question in the Manitoba Reference (*Reference re Amendment of the Constitution of Canada* (1981), 117 D.L.R. (3d) 1, 7 Man. R. (2d) 269, [1981] 2 W.W.R. 193) and Newfoundland Reference (*Reference re Amendment of the Constitution of Canada (No. 2)* (1981), 118 D.L.R. (3d) 1, 29 Nfld. & P.E.I.R. 503) is the same:

> 2. Is it a constitutional convention that the House of Commons and Senate of Canada will not request Her Majesty the Queen to lay before the Parliament of the United Kingdom of Great Britain and Northern Ireland a measure to amend the Constitution of Canada affecting federal-provincial relationships or the powers, rights or privileges granted or secured by the Constitution of Canada to the provinces, their legislatures or governments without first obtaining the agreement of the provinces?

As for Question B in the Quebec Reference (*Reference re Amendment of the Constitution of Canada (No. 3)* (1981), 120 D.L.R. (3d) 385), it reads in part as follows (translation):

> B. Does the Canadian Constitution empower . . . by . . . convention . . . the Senate and the House of Commons of Canada to cause the Canadian Constitution to be amended without the consent of the provinces and in spite of the objection of several of them, in such a manner as to affect:
> (i) the legislative competence of the provincial legislatures in virtue of the Canadian Constitution?
> (ii) the status or role of the provincial legislatures or governments within the Canadian Federation?

In these questions, the phrases "Constitution of Canada" and "Canadian Constitution" do not refer to matters of interest only to the federal Government or federal juristic unit. They are clearly meant in a broader sense and embrace the global system of rules and principles which govern the exercise of constitutional authority in the whole and in every part of the Canadian State. They will be used in the same broad sense in these reasons.

The meaning of the second question in the Manitoba and Newfoundland References calls for futher observations.

As will be seen later, counsel for several Provinces strenuously argued that the convention exists and requires the agreement of all the Provinces. However, we did not understand any of them to have taken the position that the second question in the Manitoba and Newfoundland References should be dealt with and answered as if the last part of the question read ". . . without obtaining the agreement of *all* the provinces?"

Be that as it may, the question should not in our view be so read.

It would have been easy to insert the words "all" into the question had it been intended to narrow its meaning. But we do not think it was so intended. The issue raised by the question is esentially whether there is a constitutional convention that the House of Commons and Senate of Canada will not proceed alone. The thrust of the question is accordingly on whether or not there is a conventional requirement for provincial agreement, not on whether the agreement should be unanimous assuming that it is required. Furthermore, this manner of reading the question is more in keeping with the wording of Question B in the Quebec Reference which refers to something less than unanimity when it says: ". . . without the consent of the provinces and in spite of the objection of several of them . . .".

If the questions are thought to be ambiguous, this Court should not, in a constitutional reference, be in a worse position than that of a witness in a trial and feel compelled simply to answer yes or no. Should it find that a question might be misleading, or should it simply wish to avoid the risk of misunderstanding, the Court is free either to interpret the question as in *Reference re Legislative Authority of Parliament to Alter or Replace the Senate* (1979), 102 D.L.R. (3d) 1 at p. 4, [1980] 1 S.C.R. 54 (*sub nom. Re Authority of Parliament in Relation to the Upper House*) at p. 59 (the *Senate Reference*), or it may qualify both the question and the answer as in *Re Water Powers' Reference*, [1929] 2 D.L.R. 481, [1929] S.C.R. 200 *sub nom. Reference re Waters and Water Powers*.

I — THE NATURE OF CONSTITUTIONAL CONVENTIONS

A substantial part of the rules of the Canadian Constitution are written. They are contained not in a single document called a Constitution but in a great variety of statutes some of which have been enacted by the Parliament of Westminster, such as the *British North America Act, 1867*, 30 & 31 Vict. c. 3 (U.K.) (the *B.N.A. Act*), or by the Parliament of Canada, such as the *Alberta Act*, 1905, 4-5 Edw. VII, c. 3 (Can.); the *Saskatchewan Act*, 1905, 4-5 Edw. VII, c. 42 (Can.); the *Senate and House of Commons Act*, R.S.C. 1970, c. S-8, or by the provincial Legislatures, such as the provincial electoral Acts. They are also to be found in Orders in Council like the Imperial Order in Council of May 16, 1871, admitting British Columbia into the Union, and the Imperial Order in Council of June 26, 1873, admitting Prince Edward Island into the Union.

Another part of the Constitution of Canada consists of the rules of the common law. These are rules which the Courts have developed over the centuries in the discharge of their judicial duties. An important portion of these rules concerns the prerogative of the Crown. Sections 9 and 15 of the *B.N.A. Act* provide:

> 9. The Executive Government and authority of and over Canada is hereby declared to continue and be vested in the Queen.
>
> . . . . .
>
> 15. The Comander-in-Chief of the Land and Naval Militia, and of all Naval and Military Forces, of and in Canada, is hereby declared to continue and be vested in the Queen.

But the Act does not otherwise say very much with respect to the elements of "Executive Government and authority" and one must look at the common law to find out what they are, apart from authority delegated to the Executive by statute.

The common law provides that the authority of the Crown includes for instance the prerogative of mercy or clemency (*Re Royal Prerogative of Mercy upon Deportation Proceedings*, [1933] 2 D.L.R. 348, [1933] S.C.R. 269, 59 C.C.C. 301) and the power to incorporate by charter so as to confer a general capacity analogous to that of a natural person (*Bonanza Creek Gold Mining Co. v. The King* (1916), 26 D.L.R. 273, [1916] 1 A.C. 566, 10 W.W.R. 391). The royal prerogative puts the Crown in a preferred position as a creditor (*Liquidators of Maritime Bank of Canada v. Receiver-Gereral of New Brunswick*, [1892] A.C. 437) or with respect to the inheritance of lands for defect of heirs (*A.-G. Ont. v. Mercer* (1883), 8 App. Cas. 767) or in relation to the ownership of precious metals (*A.-G. B.C. v. A.-G. Can.* (1889), 14 App. Cas. 295) and *bona vacantia* (*R. v. A.-G. B.C.*, [1924] 3 D.L.R. 690, [1924] A.C. 213, [1923] 3 W.W.R. 1252). It is also under the prerogative and the common law that the Crown appoints and receives ambassadors, declares war, concludes treaties and it is in the name of the Queen that passports are issued.

Those parts of the Constitution of Canada which are composed of statutory rules and common law rules are generically referred to as the law of the Constitution. In cases of doubt or dispute, it is the function of the Courts to declare what the law is and since the law is sometimes breached, it is generally the function of the Courts to ascer-tain whether it has in fact been breached in specific instances and, if so, to apply such sanctions as are contemplated by the law, whether they be punitive sanctions or civil sanctions such as a declaration of nullity. Thus, when a federal or a provincial statute is found by the Courts to be in excess of the legislative competence of the Legislature which has enacted it, it is declared null and void and the Courts refuse to give effect to it. In this sense it can be said that the law of the Constitution is administered or enforced by the Courts.

But many Canadians would perhaps be surprised to learn that important parts of the Constitution of Canada, with which they are the most familiar because they are directly involved when they exercise their right to vote at federal and provincial elections, are nowhere to be found in the law of the Constitution. For instance it is a fundamental requirement of the Constitution that if the Opposition obtains the majority at the polls, the Government must tender its resignation forthwith. But fundamental as it is, this requirement of the Constitution does not form part of the law of the Constitution.

It is also a constitutional requirement that the person who is appointed Prime Minister or Premier by the Crown and who is the effective head of Government should have the support of the elected branch of the Legislature; in practice this means in most cases the leader of the political party which has won a majority of seats at a general election. Other ministers are appointed by the Crown on the advice of the Prime Minister or Premier when he forms or reshuffles his cabinet. Ministers must continuously have the confidence of the elected branch of the Legislature, individually and collectively. Should they lose it, they must either resign or ask the Crown for a dissolution of the Legislature and the holding of a general election. Most of the powers of the Crown under the prerogative are exercised only upon the advice of the Prime Minister or the Cabinet which means that they are effectively exercised by the latter, together with the innumerable statutory powers delegated to the Crown in council.

Yet none of these essential rules of the Constitution can be said to be a law of the Constitution. It was apparently Dicey who, in the first edition of his *Law of the Constitution*, in 1885, called them "the conventions of the constitution" (W. S. Holdsworth, "The Conventions of the Eighteenth Century Constitution, 17 Iowa Law Rev. 161 (1932)), an expression which quickly became current. What Dicey described under these terms are the principles and rules of responsible government, several of which are stated above and which regulate the relations between the Crown, the Prime Minister, the Cabinet and the two

Houses of Parliament. These rules developed in Great Britain by way of custom and precedent during the nineteenth century and were exported to such British colonies as were granted self-government.

Dicey first gave the impression that constitutional conventions are a peculiarly British and modern phenomenon. But he recognized in later editions that different conventions are found in other constitutions. As Sir William Holdsworth wrote (W. S. Holdsworth, *op. cit.*, p. 162):

> In fact conventions must grow up at all times and in all places where the powers of government are vested in different persons or bodies—where in other words there is a mixed constitution. "The constituent parts of a state," said Burje, [French Revolution, 28] "are we obliged to hold their public faith with each other, and with all those who derive any serious interest under their engagements, as much as the whole state is bound to keep its faith with separate communities." Necessarily conventional rules spring up to regulate the working of the various parts of the constitution, their relations to one another, and to the subject.

Within the British Empire, powers of government were vested in different bodies which provided a fertile ground for the growth of new constitutional conventions unknown to Dicey whereby self-governing colonies acquired equal and independent status within the Commonwealth. Many of these culminated in the *Statute of Westminster*, 1931, 22 Geo. V, c. 4 (U.K.).

The federal constitution provides for the distribution of powers between various Legislatures and Governments and may also constitute a fertile ground for the growth of constitutional conventions between those Legislatures and Governments. It is conceivable for instance that usage and practice might give birth to conventions in Canada relating to the holding of federal-provincial conferences, the appointment of Lieutenant-Governors, the reservation and disallowance of provincial legislation. It was to this possibility that Duff C.J.C. alluded when he referred to "constitutional usage or constitutional practice" in *Reference re Power of Disallowance and Power of Reservation*, [1938] 2 D.L.R. 8 at p. 13, [1938] S.C.R. 71 at p. 78. He had previously called them "recognized constitutional conventions" in *Wilson v. E. & N. R. Co.* (1921), 61 D.L.R. 1 at p. 6, [1922] 1 A.C. 202 at p. 210, [1921] 3 W.W.R. 817.

The main purpose of constitutional conventions is to ensure that the legal framework of the Constitution will be operated in accordance with the prevailing constitutional values or principles of the period. For example, the constitutional value which is the pivot of the conventions stated above and relating to responsible government is the democratic principle: the powers of the State must be exercised in accordance with the wishes of the electorate; and the constitutional value or principle which anchors the conventions regulating the relationship between the members of the Commonwealth is the independence of the former British colonies.

Being based on custom and precedent, constitutional conventions are usually unwritten rules. Some of them, however, may be reduced to writing and expressed in the proceedings and documents of Imperial conferences, or in the preamble of statutes such as the *Statute of Westminster, 1931*, or in the proceedings and documents of federal-provincial conferences. They are often referred to and recognized in statements made by members of governments.

The conventional rules of the Constitution present one striking peculiarity. In contradistinction to the laws of the Constitution, they are not enforced by the courts. One reason for this situation is that, unlike common law rules, conventions are not judge-made rules. They are not based on judicial precedents but on precedents established by the institutions of government themselves. Nor are they in the nature of statutory commands which it is the function and duty of the Courts to obey and enforce. Furthermore, to enforce them would mean to administer some formal sanction when they are breached. But the legal system from which they are distinct does not contemplate formal sanctions for their breach.

Perhaps the main reason why conventional rules cannot be enforced by the Courts is that they are generally in conflict with the legal rules which they postulate and the Courts are bound to enforce the legal rules. The conflict is not of a type which would entail the commission of any illegality. It results from the fact that legal rules create wide powers, discretions and rights which conventions prescribe should be exercised only in a certain limited manner, if at all.

Some examples will illustrate this point.

As a matter of law, the Queen, or the Governor General or the Lieutenant-Governor could refuse assent to every bill passed by both Houses of Parliament or by a Legislative Assembly as the case may be. But by convention they cannot of their own motion refuse to assent to any such bill on any ground, for instance because they disapprove of the policy of the bill. We have here a conflict between a legal rule which creates a complete discretion and a conventional rule which completely neutralizes it. But conventions, like laws, are sometimes violated. And if this particular convention were violated and assent were improperly withheld, the Courts would be bound to enforce the law, not the convention. They would refuse to recognize the validity of a vetoed bill. This is what happened in *Gallant v. The King*, [1949] 2 D.L.R. 425, 93 C.C.C. 237, 23 M.P.R. 48 (see also for a comment on the situation by K.M. Martin in 24 Can. Bar Rev. 434 (1946)), a case in keeping with the classic case of *Stockdale v. Hansard* (1839), 9 Ad. & E. 1, 112 E.R. 1112, where the English Court of Queen's Bench held that only the Queen and both Houses of Parliament could make or unmake laws. The Lieutenant-Governor who had withheld assent in *Gallant* apparently did so towards the end of his term of office. Had it been otherwise, it is not inconceivable that his withholding of assent might have produced a political crisis leading to his removal from office which shows that if the remedy for a breach of convention does not lie with the Courts, still the breach is not necessarily without a remedy. The remedy lies with some other institutions of Government; furthermore, it is not a formal remedy and it may be administered with less certainty or regularity than it would be by a Court.

Another example of the conflict between law and convention is provided by a fundamental convention already stated above: if after a general election where the Opposition obtained the majority at the polls the Government refused to resign and clung to office, it would thereby commit a fundamental breach of conventions, one so serious indeed that it could be regarded as tantamount to a *coup d'état*. The remedy in this case would lie with the Governor General or the Lieutenant Governor as the case might be who would be justified in dismissing the Ministry and in calling on the Opposition to form the Government. But should the Crown be slow in taking this course, there is nothing the Courts could do about it except at the risk of creating a state of legal discontinuity, that is a form of revolution. An order or a regulation passed by a Minister under statutory authority and otherwise valid could not be invalidated on the ground that, by convention, the Minister ought no longer to be a Minister. A writ of *quo warranto* aimed at Ministers, assuming that *quo warranto* lies against a Minister of the Crown, which is very doubtful, would be of no avail to remove them from office. Required to say by what warrant they occupy their ministerial office, they would answer that they occupy it by the pleasure of the Crown under a commission issued by the Crown and this answer would be a complete one at law for at law, the Government is in office by the pleasure of the Crown although by convention it is there by the will of the people.

This conflict between convention and law which prevents the Courts from enforcing conventions also prevents conventions from crystallizing into laws, unless it be by statutory adoption.

It is because the sanctions of convention rest with institutions of government other than Courts, such as the Governor General or the Lieutenant-Governor, or the Houses of Parliament, or with public opinion and ultimately, with the electorate that it is generally said that they are political.

We respectfully adopt the definition of a convention given by the learned Chief Justice of Manitoba, Freedman C.J.M., in the Manitoba Reference at pp. 13–4:

> What is a constitutional convention? There is a fairly lengthy literature on the subject. Although there may be shades of difference among the constitutional lawyers, political scientists and Judges who have contributed to that literature, the essential features of a convention may be set forth with some degree of confidence. Thus there is general agreement that a convention occupies a position somewhere in between a usage or custom on the one hand and a constitutional law on the other. There is general agreement that if one sought to fix that position with greater precision he would place convention nearer to law than to usage or custom. There is also general agreement that ''a convention is a rule which is regarded as obligatory by the officials to whom it applies''. Hogg, *Constitutional Law of Canada* (1977), p. 9. There is, if not general agreement, at least weighty authority, that the sanction for breach of a convention will be political rather than legal.

It should be borne in mind, however, that, while they are not laws, some conventions may be more important than some laws. Their importance depends on that of the value or principle which they are meant to safeguard. Also they form an integral part of the Constitution and of the constitutional system. They come within the meaning of the word ''Constitution'' in the preamble of the *British North America Act, 1867*:

> Whereas the Provinces of Canada, Nova Scotia, and New Brunswick have expressed their Desire to be federally united . . . with a Constitution similar in principle to that of the United Kingdom:

That is why it is perfectly appropriate to say that to violate a convention is to do something which is unconstitutional although it entails no direct legal consequence. But the words ''constitutional'' and ''unconstitutional'' may also be used in a strict legal sense, for instance with respect to a statute which is found *ultra vires* or unconstitutional. The foregoing may perhaps be summarized in an equation: constitutional conventions plus constitutional law equal the total Constitution of the country.

II — WHETHER THE QUESTIONS SHOULD BE ANSWERED

It was submitted by counsel for Canada and for Ontario that the second question in the Manitoba and Newfoundland References and the conventional part of Question B in the Quebec Reference ought not be answered because they do not raise a justiciable issue and are accordingly not appropriate for a Court. It was contended that the issue whether a particular convention exists or not is a purely political one. The existence of a definite convention is always unclear and a matter of debate. Furthermore, conventions are flexible, somewhat imprecise and unsuitable for judicial determination.

The same submission was made in substance to the three Courts below and, in our respectful opinion, rightfully dismissed by all three of them, Hall J.A. dissenting in the Manitoba Court of Appeal.

We agree with what Freedman C.J.M. wrote on this subject in the Manitoba Reference at p. 13:

> In my view, this submission goes too far. Its characterization of Question 2 as "purely political" overstates the case. That there is a political element embodied in the question, arising from the contents of the joint address, may well be the case. But that does not end the matter. If Question 2, even if in part political, possesses a constitutional feature, it would legitimately call for our reply.
>
> In my view, the request for a decision by this Court on whether there is a constitutional convention, in the circumstances described, that the Dominion will not act without the agreement of the Provinces poses a question that is, at least in part, constitutional in character. It therefore calls for an answer, and I propose to answer it.

Question 2 is not confined to an issue of pure legality but it has to do with a fundamental issue of constitutionality and legitimacy. Given the broad statutory basis upon which the Governments of Manitoba, Newfoundland and Quebec are empowered to put questions to their three respective Courts of Appeal, they are in our view entitled to an answer to a question of this type.

Furthermore, one of the main points made by Manitoba with respect to Question 3 was that the constitutional convention referred to in Question 2 had become crystallized into a rule of law. Question 3 is admitted by all to raise a question of law. We agree with Matas J.A. of the Manitoba Court of Appeal that it would be difficult to answer Question 3 without an analysis of the points raised in Question 2. It is accordingly incumbent on us to answer Question 2.

Finally, we are not asked to hold that a convention has in effect repealed a provision of the *B.N.A. Act*, as was the case in the *Reference re Disallowance, supra*. Nor are we asked to enforce a convention. We are asked to recognize it if it exists. Courts have done this very thing many times in England and the Commonwealth to provide aid for a background to constitutional or statutory construction. Several such cases are mentioned in the reasons of the majority of this Court relating to the question whether constitutional conventions are capable of crystallizing into law. There are many others, among them: *Commonwealth v. Kreglinger & Fernau Ltd.* (1925), 37 C.L.R. 393; *Liversidge v. Anderson*, [1942] A.C. 206; *Carltona Ltd. v. Com'rs of Works*, [1943] 2 All E.R. 560; *Adegbenro v. Akintola*, [1963] A.C. 614; *Ibralebbe v. The Queen*, [1964] A.C. 900. This Court did the same in the recent case of *Arseneau v. The Queen* (1979), 95 D.L.R. (3d) 1 at pp. 5–6, [1979] 2 S.C.R. 136 at p. 149, 45 C.C.C. (2d) 321, and in the still unreported judgment rendered on April 6, 1981 [now reported 123 D.L.R. (3d) 15], after the rehearing of *A.-G. Que. v. Blaikie et al.* (1979), 101 D.L.R. (3d) 394, 49 C.C.C. (2d) 359, [1979] 2 S.C.R. 1016.

In so recognizing conventional rules, the Courts have described them, sometimes commented upon them and given them such precision as is derived from the written form of a judgment. They did not shrink from doing so on account of the political aspects of conventions, nor because of their supposed vagueness, uncertainty or flexibility.

In our view, we should not, in a constitutional reference, decline to accomplish a type of exercise that Courts have been doing of their own motion for years.

III — WHETHER THE CONVENTION EXISTS

It was submitted by counsel for Canada, Ontario and New Brunswick that there is no constitutional convention that the House of Commons and Senate of Canada will not request Her Majesty the Queen to lay before the Parliament of Westminster a measure to amend the Constitution of Canada affecting federal-provincial relationships, etc., without first obtaining the agreement of the Provinces.

It was submitted by counsel for Manitoba, Newfoundland, Quebec, Nova Scotia, British Columbia, Prince Edward Island and Alberta that the convention does exist, that it requires the agreement of all the Provinces and that the second question in the Manitoba and Newfoundland References should accordingly be answered in the affirmative.

Counsel for Saskatchewan agreed that the question be answered in the affirmative but on a different basis. He submitted that the convention does exist and requires a measure of provincial agreement. Counsel for Saskatchewan further submitted that the Resolution before the Court has not received a sufficient measure of provincial consent.

We wish to indicate at the outset that we find ourselves in agreement with the submissions made on this issue by counsel for Saskatchewan.

1. The class of constitutional amendments contemplated by the question

Constitutional amendments fall into three categories: (1) amendments which may be made by a provincial Legislature acting alone under s. 92(1) of the *B.N.A. Act*; (2) amendments which may be made by the Parliament of Canada acting alone under s. 91(1) of the *B.N.A. Act*; (3) all other amendments.

The first two categories are irrelevant for the purposes of these References. While the wording of the second and third questions of the Manitoba and Newfoundland References may be broad enough to embrace all amendments in the third category, it is not necessary for us to consider those amendments which affect federal-provincial relationships only indirectly. In a sense, most amendments of the third category are susceptible of affecting federal-provincial relationships to some extent. But we should restrict ourselves to the consideration of amendments which ". . . directly affect federal-provincial relationships in the sense of changing federal and provincial legislative powers. . ." (the *Senate Reference, supra*, at pp. 8–9 D.L.R., p. 65 S.C.R.).

The reason for this is that the second and third questions of the Manitoba and Newfoundland References must be read in the light of the first question. They must be meant to contemplate the same specific class of constitutional amendments as the ones which are sought in the "Proposed Resolution for a Joint Address to Her Majesty the Queen respecting the Constitution of Canada". More particularly, they must be meant to address the same type of amendments as the *Charter of Rights*, which abridges federal and provincial legislative powers, and the amending formula, which would provide for the amendment of the Constitution including the distribution of legislative powers.

These proposed amendments present one essential characteristic: they directly affect federal-provincial relationships in changing legislative powers and in providing for a formula to effect such change.

Therefore, in essence although not in terms, the issue raised by the second question in the Manitoba and Newfoundland References is whether there is a constitutional convention for agreement of the Provinces to amendments which change legislative powers and provide for a method of effecting such change. The same issue is raised by Question B of the Quebec Reference, above-quoted in part.

2. Requirements for establishing a convention

The requirements for establishing a convention bear some resemblance with those which apply to customary law. Precedents and usage are necessary but do not suffice. They must be normative. We adopt the following passage of Sir W. Ivor Jennings in *The Law and the Constitution*, 5th ed. (1959), p. 136:

> We have to ask ourselves three questions: first, what are the precedents; secondly, did the actors in the precedents believe that they were bound by a rule; and thirdly, is there a reason for the rule? A single precedent with a good reason may be enough to establish the rule. A whole string of precedents without such a reason will be of no avail, unless it is perfectly certain that the persons concerned regarded them as bound by it.

(i) The precedents

An account of the statutes enacted by the Parliament of Westminster to modify the Constitution of Canada is found in a White Paper published in 1965 under the authority of the Honourable Guy Favreau, then Minister of Justice for Canada, under the title of "The Amendment of the Constitution of Canada" (the White Paper). This account is quoted in the *Senate Reference, supra*, but we find it necessary to reproduce it here for convenience:

> (1) *The Rupert's Land Act, 1868* authorized the acceptance by Canada of the rights of the Hudson's Bay Company over Rupert's Land and the North-Western Territory. It also provided that, on Address from the Houses of Parliament of Canada, the Crown could declare this territory part of Canada and the Parliament of Canada could make laws for its peace, order and good government.
>
> (2) *The British North America Act of 1871* ratified the Manitoba Act passed by the Parliament of Canada in 1870, creating the province of Manitoba and giving it a provincial constitution similar to those of the other provinces. The British North America Act of 1871 also empowered the Parliament of Canada to establish new provinces out of any Canadian territory not then included in a province; to alter the boundaries of any territory not then included in a province; to alter the boundaries of any province (with the consent of its legislature), and to provide for the administration, peace and good government of any territory not included in a province.
>
> (3) *The Parliament of Canada Act of 1875* amended sec-

tion 18 of the British North America Act, 1867, which set forth the privileges, immunities and powers of each of the Houses of Parliament.

(4) *The British North America Act of 1886* authorized the Parliament of Canada to provide for the representation in the Senate and the House of Commons of any territories not included in any province.

*(5) *The Statute Law Revision Act, 1893* repealed some obsolete provisions of the British North America Act of 1867.

(6) *The Canadian Speaker (Appointment of Deputy) Act, 1895* confirmed an Act of the Parliament of Canada which provided for the appointment of a Deputy-Speaker for the Senate.

(7) *The British North America Act, 1907* established a new scale of financial subsidies to the provinces in lieu of those set forth in section 118 of the British North America Act of 1867. While not expressly repealing the original section, it made its provisions obsolete.

(8) *The British North America Act, 1915* re-defined the Senatorial Divisions of Canada to take into account the provinces of Manitoba, British Columbia, Saskatchewan and Alberta. Although this statute did not expressly amend the text of the original section 22, it did alter its effect.

(9) *The British North America Act, 1916* provided for the extension of the life of the current Parliament of Canada beyond the normal period of five years.

*(10) *The Statute Law Revision Act, 1927* repealed additional spent or obsolete provisions in the United Kingdom statutes, including two provisions of the British North America Acts.

(11) *The British North America Act, 1930* confirmed the natural resources agreements between the Government of Canada and the Governments of Manitoba, British Columbia, Alberta and Saskatchewan, giving the agreements the force of law notwithstanding anything in the British North America Acts.

(12) *The Statute of Westminster, 1931*, while not directly amending the British North America Acts, did alter some of their provisions. Thus, the Parliament of Canada was given the power to make laws having extra-territorial effect. Also, Parliament and the provincial legislatures were given the authority, within their powers under the British North America Acts, to repeal any United Kingdom statute that formed part of the law of Canada. This authority, however, expressly excluded the British North America Act itself.

(13) *The British North America Act, 1940* gave the Parliament of Canada the exclusive jurisdiction to make laws in relation to Unemployment Insurance.

(14) *The British North America Act, 1943* provided for the postponement of redistribution of the seats in the House of Commons until the first session of Parliament after the cessation of hostilities.

(15) *The British North America Act, 1946* replaced section 51 of the British North America Act, 1867, and altered the provisions for the readjustment of representation in the House of Commons.

(16) *The British North America Act, 1949* confirmed the Terms of Union between Canada and Newfoundland.

(17) *The British North America Act (No. 2), 1949* gave the Parliament of Canada authority to amend the Constitution of Canada with certain exceptions.

*(18) *The Statute Law Revision Act, 1950* repealed an obsolete section of the British North America Act, 1867.

(19) *The British North America Act, 1951* gave the Parliament of Canada concurrent jurisdiction with the provinces to make laws in relation to Old Age Pensions.

(20) *The British North America Act, 1960* amended section 99 and altered the tenure of office of superior court judges.

(21) *The British North America Act, 1964* amended the authority conferred upon the Parliament of Canada by the British North America Act, 1951, in relation to benefits supplementary to Old Age Pensions.

(22) *Amendment by Order in Council*

Section 146 of the British North America Act, 1867 provided for the admission of other British North American territories by Order in Council and stipulated that the provisions of any such Order in Council would have the same effect as if enacted by the Parliament of the United Kingdom. Under this section, Rupert's Land and the North-Western Territory were admitted by Order in Council on June 23rd, 1870; British Columbia by Order in Council on May 16, 1871; Prince Edward Island by Order in Council on June 26th, 1873. Because all of these Orders in Council contained provisions of a constitutional character — adapting the provisions of the British North America Act to the new provinces, but with some modifications in each case — they may therefore be regarded as constitutional amendments.

*The amendments appear to have been done by the Parliament of Westminster on its own initiative and not in response to a joint resolution of the Senate and House of Commons.

For reasons already stated, these precedents must be considered selectively. They must also be considered in positive as well as in negative terms.

Of these twenty-two amendments or groups of amendments, five directly affected federal-provincial relationships in the sense of changing provincial legislative powers: they are the amendment of 1930, the *Statute of Westminster, 1931*, and the amendments of 1940, 1951 and 1964.

Under the agreements confirmed by the 1930 amendment, the western Provinces were granted ownership and administrative control of their natural resources so as to place these Provinces in the same position vis-à-vis natural resources as the original confederating colonies. The western Provinces, however, received these natural resources subject to some limits on their power to make laws relating to hunting and fishing rights of Indians. Furthermore, the agreements did provide a very substantial object for the provincial power to make laws relating to "The Management and Sale of Public Lands belonging to the Province and the Timber and Wood thereon" under s. 92(5) of the *B.N.A. Act*. The long title reads as follows [1930, 20–21 Geo. V. c. 26 (U.K.)]:

> An Act to confirm and give effect to certain agreements entered into between the Government of the Dominion of Canada and the Government of the Provinces of Manitoba, British Columbia, Alberta and Saskatchewan respectively

The preamble of the Act recites that "each of the said agreements has been duly approved by the Parliament of Canada and by the Legislature of the Province to which it relates". The other Provinces lost no power, right or privilege in consequence. In any event, the proposed transfer of natural resources to the western Provinces had been discussed at the 1927 Dominion-Provincial Conference and had met with general approval: Paul Gérin-Lajoie, *Constitutional Amendment in Canada* (1950, University of Toronto Press), pp. 91–2.

All the Provinces agreed to the passing of the *Statute of Westminster, 1931*. It changed legislative powers: Parliament and the Legislatures were given the authority, within their powers, to repeal any United Kingdom statute that formed part of the law of Canada; Parliament was also given the power to make laws having extra-territorial effect.

The 1940 amendment is of special interest in that it transferred an exclusive legislative power from the provincial Legislatures to the Parliament of Canada.

In 1938, the Speech from the Throne stated:

> The co-operation of the provinces has been sought with a view to an amendment of the British North America Act, which would empower the parliament of Canada to enact forthwith a national scheme of unemployment insurance. My ministers hope the proposal may meet with early approval, in order that unemployment insurance legislation may be enacted during the present session of parliament.

(Commons Debates, 1938, p. 2.)

In November, 1937, the Government of Canada had communicated with the Provinces and asked for their views in principle. A draft amendment was later circulated. By March, 1938, five of the nine Provinces had approved the draft amendment. Ontario had agreed in principle, but Alberta, New Brunswick and Quebec had declined to join in. The proposed amendment was not proceeded with until June, 1940, when Prime Minister King announced to the House of Commons that all nine Provinces had assented to the proposed amendment. (Paul Gérin-Lajoie (*op. cit.*) p. 106.)

The 1951 and 1964 amendments changed the legislative powers: areas of exclusive provincial competence became areas of concurrent legislative competence. They were agreed upon by all the Provinces.

These five amendments are the only ones which can be viewed as positive precedents whereby federal-provincial relationships were directly affected in the sense of changing legislative powers.

Every one of these five amendments was agreed upon by each Province whose legislative authority was affected.

In negative terms, no amendments changing provincial legislative powers has been made since Confederation when agreement of a Province whose legislative powers would have been changed was withheld.

There are no exceptions.

Furthermore, in even more telling negative terms, in 1951, an amendment was proposed to give the Provinces a limited power of indirect taxation. Ontario and Quebec did not agree and the amendment was not proceeded with. (Common Debates, 1951, pp. 2682 and 2726 to 2743.)

The Constitutional Conference of 1960 devised a formula for the amendment of the Constitution of Canada. Under this formula, the distribution of legislative powers could have been modified. The great majority of the participants found the formula acceptable but some differences remained and the proposed amendment was not proceeded with. (The White Paper, p. 29.)

In 1964, a conference of first ministers unanimously agreed on an amending formula that would have permitted the modification of legislative powers. Quebec subsequently withdrew its agreement and the proposed amendment was not proceeded with. (Senate House of Commons Special Joint Committees on Constitution of Canada, issue No. 5, August 23, 1978, p. 14, Professor Lederman.)

Finally, in 1971, proposed amendments which included

an amending formula were agreed upon by the federal Government and eight of the ten provincial Governments. Quebec disagreed and Saskatchewan which had a new Government did not take a position because it was believed the disagreement of Quebec rendered the question academic. The proposed amendments were not proceeded with. (Gérald A. Beaudoin, *Le partage des pouvoirs*, Editions de L'Université d'Ottawa, Ottawa, 1980, p. 349.)

The accumulation of these precedents, positive and negative, concurrent and without exception, does not of itself suffice in establishing the existence of the convention; but it unmistakedly points in its direction. Indeed, if the precedents stood alone, it might be argued that unanimity is required.

In the *Senate Reference, supra*, this Court went a considerable distance in recognizing the significance of some of these precedents when it wrote at pp. 7–8 D.L.R., pp. 63–5 S.C.R.:

> The amendments of 1940, 1951, 1960 and 1964, respecting unemployment insurance, old age pensions, the compulsory retirement of Judges and adding supplementary benefits to old age pensions all had the unanimous consent of the Provinces.

. . . . .

> The apparent intention of the 1949 amendment to the Act which enacted s. 91(1) was to obviate the necessity for the enactment of a statute of the British Parliament to effect amendments to the Act which theretofore had been obtained through a joint resolution of both Houses of Parliament and without provincial consent. Legislation enacted since 1949 pursuant to s. 91(1) has not, to quote the White Paper, "affected federal-provincial relationships". The following statutes have been enacted by the Parliament of Canada . . .

The Court then enumerated the five amendments enacted by the Parliament of Canada pursuant to s. 91(1) of the *B.N.A. Act* and continued [at p. 8 D.L.R., p. 65 S.C.R.]:

> All of these measures dealt with what might be described as federal "housekeeping" matters which, according to the practice existing before 1949, would have been referred to the British Parliament by way of a joint resolution of both Houses of Parliament, and without the consent of the Provinces.

In our respectful opinion, the majority of the Quebec Court of Appeal fell into error in this issue in failing to differentiate between various types of constitutional amendments. The Quebec Court of Appeal put all or practically all constitutional amendments since 1867 on the same footing and, as could then be expected, concluded not only that the convention requiring provincial consent did not exist but that there even appeared to be a convention to the contrary. (See the reasons of Crête C.J.Q. and Turgeon J.A. at pp. 92 and 124 of the case in the Quebec Reference [120 D.L.R. (3d) 385 at pp. 389–410, pp. 418–41]. Owen J.A. agreed with Turgeon J.A. on this issue, and Bélanger J.A. with both Crête C.J.Q. and Turgeon J.A.)

The Manitoba Court of Appeal was similarly misled, in our respectful opinion, but to a lesser extent, which perhaps explains that Freedman C.J.M wrote at p. 21 of the Manitoba Reference [117 D.L.R. (3d) 1], speaking for himself, Matas and Huband JJ.A. on this point: "That we may be moving towards such a convention is certainly a tenable view. But we have not yet arrived there."

We do not think it is necessary to deal with classes of constitutional amendments other than those which change legislative powers or provide for a method to effect such change. But we will briefly comment on two amendments about which much has been made to support the argument against the existence of the convention. These are the amendment of 1907 increasing the scale of financial subsidies to the Provinces and the amendments of 1949 confirming the Terms of Union between Canada and Newfoundland.

It was contended that British Columbia objected to the 1907 amendment which had been agreed upon by all the other Provinces.

Even if it were so, this precedent would at best constitute an argument against the unanimity rule.

But the fact is that British Columbia did agree in principle with the increase of financial subsidies to the Provinces. It wanted more and objected to the proposed finality of the increase. The finality aspect was deleted from the amendment by the United Kingdom authorities. Mr. Winston Churchill, Under Secretary of State for the Colonies, made the following comment in the House of Commons: "In deference to the representations of British Columbia the words 'final and unalterable' applying to the revised scale, have been omitted from the Bill." (Commons Debates (U.K.), June 13, 1907, p. 1617.)

In the end, the Premier of British Columbia did not refuse to agree to the Act being passed. (A.B. Keith, *The Constitutional Law of the British Dominions* (1933), p. 109.)

With respect to the 1949 amendment, it was observed by Turgeon J.A. in the Quebec Reference that, without Quebec's consent, this amendment confirmed the Quebec-Labrador Boundary as delimited in the report delivered by the Judicial Committee of the Privy Council on March 1, 1927.

The entry of Newfoundland into Confederation was contemplated from the beginning by s. 146 of the *B.N.A. Act*. It was at the request of Quebec in 1904 that the dispute relating to the boundary was ultimately submitted to the Judicial Committee. (Minute of Privy Council (Canada), P.C. 82 of M. April 18, 1904.) Quebec participated in the litigation, being represented by counsel appointed and paid by the Province, although the Province did not intervene separately from Canada. When the 1949 amendment was passed, the Premier of Quebec is reported to have stated at a press conference simply that the Province should have been "consulted" or "advised" as a matter of "courtesy". He is not reported as having said that the consent of the Province was required. See Luce Patenaude, *Le Labrador à l'heure de la contestation* (1972, Presses de l'Université de Montréal), pp. 6, 7, 13, 14, 193 and 194. The Premier of Nova Scotia spoke to the same effect. Neither Premier made any formal demand or protest. (Paul Gérin-Lajoie (*op. cit.*), p. 129.)

We fail to see how this precedent can affect the convention.

It was also observed by Turgeon J.A. in the Quebec Reference that the *Charter of Rights* annexed to the proposed Resolution for a Joint Address does not alter the distribution of powers between the Parliament of Canada and the provincial Legislatures.

This observation may be meant as an argument to the effect that the five positive precedents mentioned above should be distinguished and ought not to govern the situation before the Court since in those five cases the distribution of legislative powers was altered.

To this argument we would reply that if provincial consent was required in those five cases, it would be *a fortiori* required in the case at bar.

Each of those five constitutional amendments effected a limited change in legislative powers, effecting one head of legislative competence such as unemployment insurance. Whereas if the proposed *Charter of Rights* became law, every head of provincial (and federal) legislative authority could be affected. Furthermore, the *Charter of Rights* would operate retrospectively as well as prospectively with the result that laws enacted in the future as well as in the past, even before Confederation, would be exposed to attack if inconsistent with the provisions of the *Charter of Rights*. This Charter would thus abridge provincial legislative authority on a scale exceeding the effect of any previous constitutional amendment for which provincial consent was sought and obtained.

Finally, it was noted in the course of argument that in the case of four of the five amendments mentioned above

where provincial consent effectively had been obtained, the statutes enacted by the Parliament of Westminster did not refer to this consent. This does not alter the fact that consent was obtained.

(ii) *The actors treating the rule as binding*

In the White Paper, one finds this passage at pp. 10–11:

PROCEDURES FOLLOWED IN THE PAST
IN SECURING AMENDMENTS TO THE BRITISH NORTH
AMERICA ACT

The procedures for amending a constitution are normally a fundamental part of the laws and conventions by which a country is governed. This is particularly true if the constitution is embodied in a formal document as is the case in such federal states as Australia, the United States and Switzerland. In these countries, the amending process forms an important part of their constitutional law.

In this respect, Canada has been in a unique constitutional position. Not only did the British North America Act not provide for its amendment by Canadian legislative authority, except to the extent outlined at the beginning of this chapter, but it also left Canada without any clearly defined procedure for securing constitutional amendments from the British Parliament. As a result, procedures have varied from time to time, with recurring controversies and doubts over the conditions under which various provisions of the Constitution should be amended.

Certain rules and principles relating to amending procedures have nevertheless developed over the years. They have emerged from the practices and procedures employed in securing various amendments to the British North America Act since 1867. Though not constitutionally binding in any strict sense, they have come to be recognized and accepted in practice as part of the amendment process in Canada.

In order to trace and describe the manner in which these rules and principles have developed, the approaches used to secure amendments through the Parliament of the United Kingdom over the past 96 years are described in the following paragraphs. Not all the amendments are included in this review, but only those that have contributed to the development of accepted constitutional rules and principles.

There follows a list of fourteen constitutional amendments thought to "have contributed to the development of accepted constitutional rules and principles". The White Paper then goes on to state these principles, at p. 15:

The first general principle that emerges in the foregoing résumé is that although an enactment by the United Kingdom is necessary to amend the British North America Act, such action is taken only upon formal request from Canada. No Act of the United Kingdom Parliament affecting Canada is therefore passed unless it is requested and consented to by Canada. Conversely, every amendment requested by Canada in the past has been enacted.

The second general principle is that the sanction of Parliament is required for a request to the British Parliament for an amendment to the British North America Act. This principle was established early in the history of Canada's constitutional amendments, and has not been violated since 1895. The procedure invariably is to seek amendments by a joint Address of the Canadian House of Commons and Senate to the Crown.

The third general principle is that no amendment to Canada's Constitution will be made by the British Parliament merely upon the request of a Canadian province. A number of attempts to secure such amendments have been made, but none has been successful. The first such attempt was made as early as 1868, by a province which was at that time dissatisfied with the terms of Confederation. This was followed by other attempts in 1869, 1874 and 1887. The British Government refused in all cases to act on provincial government representations on the grounds that it should not intervene in the affairs of Canada except at the request of the federal government representing all of Canada.

The fourth general principle is that the Canadian Parliament will not request an amendment directly affecting federal-provincial relationships without prior consultation and agreement with the provinces. This principle did not emerge as early as others but since 1907, and particularly since 1930, has gained increasing recognition and acceptance. The nature and the degree of provincial participation in the amending process, however, have not lent themselves to easy definition.

The text which precedes the four general principles makes it clear that it deals with conventions. It refers to the laws and conventions by which a country is governed and to constitutional rules which are not binding in any strict sense (that is in a legal sense) but which have come to be recognized and accepted in practice as part of the amendment process in Canada. The first three general principles are statements of well-known constitutional conventions governing the relationships between Canada and the United Kingdom with respect to constitutional amendments.

In our view, the fourth general principle equally and unmistakedly states and recognizes as a rule of the Canadian Constitution the convention referred to in the second question of the Manitoba and Newfoundland References as well as in Question B of the Quebec Reference, namely,

that there is a requirement for provincial agreement to amendments which change provincial legislative powers.

This statement is not a casual utterance. It is contained in a carefully drafted document which had been circulated to all the Provinces prior to its publication and been found satisfactory by all of them. (Commons Debates, 1965, p. 11574; Background Paper published by the Government of Canada, "The Role of the United Kingdom in the Amendment of the Canadian Constitution" (March, 1981) at p. 30.) It was published as a White Paper, that is as an official statement of Government policy, under the authority of the federal Minister of Justice as member of a Government responsible to Parliament neither House of which, so far as we know, has taken issue with it. This statement is a recognition by all the actors in the precedents that the requirement of provincial agreement is a constitutional rule.

In the Manitoba Reference, Freedman C.J.M. took the view that the third sentence in the fourth general principle stated in the White Paper contradicted, and therefore negated, the first sentence.

With the greatest respect, this interpretation is erroneous. The first sentence is concerned with the existence of the convention, and the third sentence, not with its existence, but with the measure of provincial agreement which is necessary with respect to this class of constitutional amendment. It seems clear that while the precedents taken alone point at unanimity, the unanimity principle cannot be said to have been accepted by all the actors in the precedents.

This distinction is illustrated by statements made by Prime Minister King in the House of Commons in 1938 and 1940 with respect to the unemployment insurance amendment.

In 1938, some Provinces had not yet assented to the unemployment insurance amendment and one finds the following exchange in the Commons Debates:

> Right Hon. R. B. BENNETT (Leader of the Opposition): Perhaps the Prime Minister would not object to a supplementary question: Does he conceive it necessary or desirable that all the provinces should agree before action is taken?
>
> Mr. MACKENZIE KING: I do not think this is the moment to answer that question. We had better wait and see what replies we get in the first instance.

(Commons Debates, 1938, p. 1747.)

In 1940, Mr. J. T. Thorson, not then a member of the Government, took issue with the contention that it was necessary to obtain the consent of the Provinces before an application is made to amend the *B.N.A. Act*. Mr. Lapointe replied:

> May I tell my hon. friend that neither the Prime Minister nor I have said it is necessary, but it may be desirable.

(Commons Debates, 1940, p. 1122.)

But what the Prime Minister had said in fact was this:

> We have avoided anything in the nature of coercion of any of the provinces. Moreover we have avoided the raising of a very critical constitutional question, namely, whether or not in amending the British North America Act it is absolutely necessary to secure the consent of all the provinces, or whether the consent of a certain number of provinces would of itself be sufficient. That question may come up but not in reference to unemployment insurance at some time later on.

(Commons Debates, 1940, p. 1117.)

This statement expressed some uncertainty as to whether unanimity is a necessity, but none as to whether substantial provincial support is required.

As for Mr. Lapointe's reply, it is non-committal and must be qualified by several other statements he made indicating the necessity of provincial consent. (For instance: Commons Debates, 1924, p. 520; Commons Debates, 1925, p. 298; Commons Debates, 1940, p. 1110; Commons Debates, 1951, pp. 1477–8.)

Prime Minister Bennett had expressed a similar concern with respect to the unanimity rule during the Dominion-Provincial Conference of 1931. He is reported to have said:

> As to the requirement of unanimity for change in the British North America Act this would mean that one Province, say Prince Edward Island, might absolutely prevent any change. No state at present required unanimity. Australia does not; nor does South Africa, a bi-lingual country. From one point of view he (Mr. Bennett) could recognize that unanimity might be desirable, but from another it seems to be wholly out of keeping with present political developments in the British Empire and indeed in the world. There must, of course, be safeguards for minorities but there must be no absolute rigidity as regards change.

(Report of Dominion-Provincial Conference, 1931, pp. 8–9.)

We were referred to an abundance of declarations made by Canadian politicians on this issue. A few are unfavourable to the provincial position but they were generally made by politicians such as Mr. J. T. Thorson who were not ministers in office and could not be considered as "actors in the precedents".

Most declarations made by statesmen favour the conventional requirements of provincial consent. We will quote only two such declarations.

In discussing the 1943 amendment, Mr. St. Laurent argued that the amendment did not alter the allocation of federal and provincial powers. He said:

> The Honourable L. S. St. Laurent (Minister of Justice) . . . I would readily concede to hon. members that if there were to be any suggested amendment to change the allocation of legislative or administrative jurisdiction as between the provinces, on the one hand, and the federal parliament, on the other, it could not properly be done without the consent of the organism that was set up by the constitution to have powers that would assumedly be taken from that organism. . . .
>
> I submit that it would have been quite improper to take away from the provinces without their consent anything that they had by the constitution.

(Commons Debates, 1943, p. 4366.)

The statement is addressed at constitutional propriety which is the terminology ordinarily used for conventions.

In 1960, it was suggested to Prime Minister Diefenbaker that his proposed *Canadian Bill of Rights* be entrenched in the Constitution and made binding on the Provinces as would be the *Charter of Rights* annexed to the proposed Resolution for a Joint Address. Here is how he dealt with this suggestion:

> They say, if you want to make this effective it has to cover the provinces too. Any one advocating that must realize the fact that there is no chance of securing the consent of all the provinces.
>
> . . . . .
>
> As far as constitutional amendment is concerned, it is impossible of attainment at this time.
>
> Mr. Winch: Why?
>
> Mr. Diefenbaker: Simply because of the fact that the consent of the provinces to any interference with property and civil rights cannot be secured.
>
> . . . . .
>
> I also want to add that if at any time the provinces are prepared to give their consent to a constitutional amendment embodying a bill of rights comprising these freedoms, there will be immediate co-operation from this government. We will forthwith introduce a constitutional amendment covering not only the federal, but the provincial jurisdictions when and if there is consent by the provinces everywhere in this country.

(Commons Debates, 1960, pp. 5648–9.)

Prime Minister Diefenbaker was clearly of the view that the *Canadian Bill of Rights* could not be entrenched in the Constitution and made to apply to the Provinces without the consent of all of them. We have also indicated that while the precedents point at unanimity, it does not appear that all the actors in the precedents have accepted the unanimity rule as a binding one.

In 1965, the White Paper had stated that: "The nature and the degree of provincial participation in the amending process . . . have not lent themselves to easy definition."

Nothing has occurred since then which would permit us to conclude in a more precise manner.

Nor can it be said that this lack of precision is such as to prevent the principle from acquiring the constitutional *status* of a conventional rule. If a consensus had emerged on the measure of provincial agreement, an amending formula would quickly have been enacted and we would no longer be in the realm of conventions. To demand as much precision as if this were the case and as if the rule were a legal one is tantamount to denying that this area of the Canadian Constitution is capable of being governed by conventional rules.

Furthermore, the Government of Canada and the Governments of the Provinces have attempted to reach a consensus on a constitutional amending formula in the course of ten federal-provincial conferences held in 1927, 1931, 1935, 1950, 1960, 1964, 1971, 1978, 1979 and 1980. (Gérald A. Beaudoin, *op. cit.*, at p. 346.) A major issue at these conferences was the quantification of provincial consent. No consensus was reached on this issue. But the discussion of this very issue for more than fifty years postulates a clear recognition by all the Governments concerned of the principle that a substantial degree of provincial consent is required.

It would not be appropriate for the Court to devise in the abstract a specific formula which would indicate in positive terms what measure of provincial agreement is required for the convention to be complied with. Conventions by their nature develop in the political field and it will be for the political actors, not this Court, to determine the degree of provincial consent required.

It is sufficient for the Court to decide that at least a substantial measure of provincial consent is required and to decide further whether the situation before the Court meets with this requirement. The situation is one where Ontario and New Brunswick agree with the proposed amendments whereas the eight other Provinces oppose it. By no conceivable standard could this situation be thought to pass muster. It clearly does not disclose a sufficient mea-sure of provincial agreement. Nothing more should be said about this.

(iii) *A reason for the rule*

The reason for the rule is the federal principle. Canada is a federal union. The preamble of the *B.N.A. Act* states that "the Provinces of Canada, Nova Scotia, and New Brunswick have expressed their Desire to be federally united . . .".

The federal character of the Canadian Constitution was recognized in innumerable judicial pronouncements. We will quote only one, that of Lord Watson in *Liquidators of Maritime Bank v. Receiver-General of New Brunswick, supra,* at pp. 441–2:

> The object of the Act was neither to weld the provinces into one, nor to subordinate provincial governments to a central authority, but to create a federal government in which they should all be represented, entrusted with the exclusive administration of affairs in which they had a common interest, each province retaining its independence and autonomy.

The federal principle cannot be reconciled with a state of affairs where the modification of provincial legislative powers could be obtained by the unilateral action of the federal authorities. It would indeed offend the federal principle that "a radical change to [the] constitution [be] taken at the request of a bare majority of the members of the Canadian House of Commons and Senate". (Report of Dominion-Provincial Conference, 1931, p. 3.)

This is an essential requirement of the federal principle which was clearly recognized by the Dominion-Provincial Conference of 1931. This conference had been convened to consider the proposed Statute of Westminster as well as a draft of s. 7 which dealt exclusively with the Canadian position.

At the opening of the Conference, Prime Minister Bennett said:

> It should be noted that nothing in the Statute confers on the Parliament of Canada the power to alter the constitution.
>
> The position remained that nothing in the future could be done to amend the British North America Act except as the result of appropriate action taken in Canada and in London. In the past such appropriate action had been an address by both Houses of the Canadian Parliament to the Parliament of Westminster. It was recognized, however, that this might result in a radical change to our constitution taken at the request of a bare majority of the members of the Canadian House of Commons and Senate.

The original draft of the Statute appeared, in the opinion of some provincial authorities, to sanction such a procedure, but in the draft before the conference this was clearly not the case.

(Report of Dominion-Provincial Conference, 1931, pp. 3–4.)

This did not satisfy Premier Taschereau of Quebec who, the next day, said:

> Do we wish the British North America Act to be amended at the request of the Dominion only, without the consent of the Provinces? Do we wish it to be amended by the Parliament of Canada? Quebec could not accept either of these suggestions. She was not prepared to agree that the British North America Act might be amended without the consent of the Provinces.

(Report of Dominion-Provincial Conference, 1931, p. 12.)

Mr. Geoffrion, of the Quebec Delegation, suggested an amendment to s. 7(1) of the draft statute, in order to meet the difficulty.

Prime Minister Bennett replied:

> Our purpose is to leave things as they are and we are definitely trying not to do what Mr. Taschereau suggests may be done.

(Report of Dominion-Provincial Conference, 1931, p. 18.)

The following day, the Conference had before it another draft of s. 7 the first paragraph of which was the one which was ultimately adopted. Premier Taschereau was not yet reassured:

> Mr. Taschereau said that so far as the repeal of the Colonial Laws Validity Act was concerned he had no objection to make. Further, the new draft of Section 7 struck him favourably, but more time was necessary for its consideration. However, the Statute, both in its preamble and in Section 4 still, by implication, gave the Dominion the sole right to request an amendment of the British North America Act. It put in black and white what had been the practice of the past. Can we be assured, he asked, that the Government of the Dominion will make no request for an amendment of the British North America Act at Westminster without the consent of the Provinces?

(Report of Dominion-Provincial Conference, 1931, p. 18.)

Prime Minister Bennett replied:

> Mr. Bennett felt that Mr. Taschereau's fears concerning the amendment of the constitution by the Dominion action alone were dealt with by Sub-section 1 of the new Section 7. Mr. Taschereau replied that he realised that the power in respect to amendment was not altered by the Statute, but that the practice in that connection had been put down in black and white, and that practice, which left out the Provinces, was not satisfactory.

> Mr. Bennett did not feel that the statute went so far. It was his opinion that in minor amendments such as a change in the quorum of the House of Commons there was no reason for consulting the Provinces, but that in more important amendments, such as the distribution of legislative power, the Provinces should of course, be consulted.

>   . . . . .

> Previous amendments to the British North America Act had been non-controversial, but Mr. Taschereau could assure his colleagues that there would be no amendment to the constitution of Canada in its federal aspect without consulting the Provinces which, it must be remembered had the same powers within their domain that the Dominion has within hers.

(Report of Dominion-Provincial Conference, 1931, pp. 19–20.)

Several other Premiers shared the concern of Premier Taschereau. It was to meet this concern that s. 7(1) of the *Statute of Westminster, 1931* was re-drafted. What the re-drafting accomplished as a matter of law is an issue which arises under the third question of the Manitoba and Newfoundland References. But the fact that an attempt was made to do something about it as a matter of law carries all the more weight on the conventional plane.

It is true also that Prime Minister Bennett spoke of consultation of the Provinces rather than of their consent but this must be understood in the light of his previously quoted statement expressing his reluctance to accept the unanimity principle.

Furthermore, as was stated in the fourth general principle of the White Paper, the requirement of provincial consent did not emerge as early as other principles, but it has gained increasing recognition and acceptance since 1907 and particularly since 1930. This is clearly demonstrated by the proceedings of the Dominion-Provincial Conference of 1931.

Then followed the positive precedents of 1940, 1951 and 1964 as well as the abortive ones of 1951, 1960 and 1964, all discussed above. By 1965, the rule had become recognized as a binding constitutional one formulated in the fourth general principle of the White Paper already quoted reading in part as follows:

> *The fourth general principle* is that the Canadian Parliament will not request an amendment directly affecting federal-provincial relationships without prior consultation and agreement with the provinces.

The purpose of this conventional rule is to protect the federal character of the Canadian Constitution and prevent the anomaly that the House of Commons and Senate could obtain by simple resolutions what they could not validly accomplish by statute.

It was contended by counsel for Canada, Ontario and New Brunswick that the proposed amendments would not offend the federal principle and that, if they became law, Canada would remain a federation. The federal principle would even be reinforced, it was said, since the Provinces would as a matter of law be given an important role in the amending formula.

It is true that Canada would remain a federation if the proposed amendments became law. But it would be a different federation made different at the instance of a majority in the Houses of the federal Parliament acting alone. It is this process itself which offends the federal principle.

It was suggested by counsel for Saskatchewan that the proposed amendments were perhaps severable; that the proposed *Charter of Rights* offended the federal principle in that it would unilaterally alter legislative powers whereas the proposed amending formula did not offend the federal principle.

To this suggestion we cannot accede. Counsel for Canada (as well as counsel for other parties and all intervenors) took the firm position that the proposed amendment formed an unseverable package. Furthermore, and to repeat, whatever the result, the process offends the federal principle. It was to guard against this process that the constitutional convention came about.

IV — CONCLUSION

We have reached the conclusion that the agreement of the Provinces of Canada, no views being expressed as to its quantification, is constitutionally required for the passing of the "Proposed Resolution for a Joint Address to Her Majesty respecting the Constitution of Canada" and that the passing of this Resolution without such agreement would be unconstitutional in the conventional sense.

We would, subject to these reasons, answer Question 2 of the Manitoba and Newfoundland References and that part of Question B in the Quebec Reference which relates to conventions as follows:

2. Is it a constitutional convention that the House of Commons and Senate of Canada will not request Her Majesty the Queen to lay before the Parliament of the United Kingdom of Great Britain and Northern Ireland a measure to amend the Constitution of Canada affect-ing federal-provincial relationships or the powers, rights or privileges granted or secured by the Constitution of Canada to the provinces, their legislatures or governments without first obtaining the agreement of the provinces?

YES.

B. Does the Canadian Constitution empower . . . by . . . convention . . . the Senate and the House of Commons of Canada to cause the Canadian Constitution to be amended without the consent of the provinces and in spite of the objection of several of them, in such a manner as to affect:

(i) the legislative competence of the provincial legislatures in virtue of the Canadian Constitution?
(ii) the status or role of the provincial legislatures or governments within the Canadian Federation?

NO.

LASKIN C.J.C., ESTEY AND McINTYRE JJ.: — These reasons are addressed solely to Question 2 in the Manitoba and Newfoundland References and the conventional segment of Question B in the Quebec Reference. Our views upon the other questions raised in the three References are expressed in another judgment. As will be pointed out later, no legal question is raised in the questions under consideration in these reasons and, ordinarily, the Court would not undertake to answer them for it is not the function of the Court to go beyond legal determinations. Because of the unusual nature of these References and because the issue raised in the questions now before us were argued at some length before the Court and have become the subject of the reasons of the majority, with which, with the utmost deference, we cannot agree, we feel obliged to answer the questions notwithstanding their extra-legal nature.

Question 2 in the Manitoba and Newfoundland References is in the form set out hereunder:

2. Is it a constitutional convention that the House of Commons and Senate of Canada will not request Her Majesty the Queen to lay before the Parliament of the United Kingdom of Great Britain and Northern Ireland a measure to amend the Constitution of Canada affect-ing federal-provincial relationships or the powers, rights or privileges granted or secured by the Constitution of Canada to the provinces, their legislatures or governments without first obtaining the agreement of the provinces?

The same question arises from the wording of Question B in the Quebec Reference which asks (translation):

B. Does the Canadian Constitution empower, whether by statute, convention or otherwise, the Senate and the House of Commons of Canada to cause the Canadian Constitution to be amended without the consent of the provinces and in spite of the objection of several of them, in such a manner as to affect:

    (i) the legislative competence of the provincial legislatures in virtue of the Canadian Constitution?

    (ii) the status or role of the provincial legislatures or governments within the Canadian Federation?

At the outset it should be observed that the convention referred to in the above questions, and contended for by all objecting Provinces except Saskatchewan, is a constitutional convention which requires that before the two Houses of the Canadian Parliament will request Her Majesty the Queen to lay before the Parliament of the United Kingdom a measure to amend the Constitution of Canada, affecting federal-provincial relationships, it will obtain agreement thereto from the Provinces. From the wording of the questions and from the course of argument it is clear that the questions meant the consent of *all* the Provinces. This then is the question which must be answered on this part of the References. An affirmative answer would involve a declaration that such a convention, requiring the consent of *all* the Provinces, exists, while a negative answer would, of course, deny its existence. No other answers can be open to the Court for, on a reference of this nature, the Court may answer only the questions put and may not conjure up questions of its own which, in turn, would lead to uninvited answers: see *Reference re Jurisdiction of the Magistrate's Court (Que.)* (1965), 55 D.L.R. (2d) 701 at pp. 706–7, [1965] S.C.R. 722 at pp. 779–80; *Lord's Day Alliance v. A.-G. Man. et al.*, [1925] 1 D.L.R. 561, [1925] A.C. 384, 43 C.C.C. 185; *A.-G. Ont. v. A.-G. Can. et al.* (1912), 3 D.L.R. 509, [1912] A.C. 571, 81 L.J.P.C. 210; and *Re Water Powers' Reference*, [1929] 2 D.L.R. 481, [1929] S.C.R. 200 *sub nom. Reference re Waters and Water-Powers*.

The position was expressed succinctly in the *Lord's Day Alliance* case by Lord Blanesburgh, at pp. 562–3 D.L.R., pp. 388–9 A.C. He said:

It will be observed that each of these questions is concerned with a state of things resulting from the new Act being duly brought into force. The Lieutenant-Governor-in-Council expresses a desire to be informed as to the legality of the excursions to which he refers only on the assumption that that Act has been made operative, and no question as to their legality apart from the Act is propounded. Their Lordships were, however, strongly urged by the appellants to deal with and dispose of the view that such excursions were lawful in Manitoba inde-

pendently of the Act altogether — a view expressed by some of the learned Judges of the Court of Appeal in this case . . . and foreshadowed in an earlier decision of the same Court . . .

Their Lordships will refrain from taking this course, for one compelling reason, which they name out of several which would justify reserve in this matter.

Statutes empowering the executive Government, whether of the Dominion of Canada or of a Canadian Province, to obtain by direct request from the Court answers to questions both of fact and law, although *intra vires* of the respective Legislatures, impose a novel duty to be discharged, but not enlarged by the Court. See *Att'y-Gen'l for Ontario v. Att'y-Gen'l for Canada* (1912), 3 D.L.R. 509, [1912] A.C. 571. It is more than ordinarily expedient in the case of such references that a Court should refrain from dealing with questions other than those which on excessive responsibility are in express terms referred to it, and their Lordships will here act upon that view.

Where there is ambiguity, or where questions are phrased in such general terms that a precise answer is difficult or impossible to give, the Court may qualify the answers, answer in general terms, or refuse to answer: see *Reference re Waters and Water-Powers, supra*. No such considerations apply here. There is no ambiguity in the questions before the Court. Question 2 in the Manitoba and Newfoundland References refers without qualification to the "agreement of the provinces". Question B in the Quebec Reference uses the words "the consent of the provinces", also without qualification. The expressions "of the provinces" or "of the provinces of Canada" in this context and in general usage mean in plain English *all* of the Provinces of Canada, and our consideration of the questions must be upon this basis. The Court, in our view, would not be justified in editing the questions to develop a meaning not clearly expressed. These expressions in ordinary usage mean *each* of the Provinces. This, in turn, connotes all of the Provinces. This is so because the question assumes that all Provinces are equal regarding their respective constitutional positions. Where the expression "Houses of Parliament" is used in many instances in the record before this Court on these appeals it could hardly be argued that the expression could mean either or one of the Houses of Parliament; that is to say, if the consent of the Houses of Parliament were required by statute, the provision could not be read as including the possibility that the consent of one of the Houses of Parliament would be sufficient. So it is with the questions before us.

What are conventions and, particularly, what are constitutional conventions? While our answers to Question 2 in the Manitoba and Newfoundland References and the conventional segment of Question B in the Quebec Reference will differ from those of the majority of the Court, we are in agreement with much of what has been said as to the general nature of constitutional conventions in the reasons for judgment by the majority, which we have had the advantage of reading. We are in agreement, as well, with the words of Freedman C.J.M. in his reasons for judgment in the Manitoba Reference, referred to with approval and quoted by the majority. We cannot, however, agree with any suggestion that the non-observance of a convention can properly be termed unconstitutional in any strict or legal sense, or that its observance could be, in any sense, a constitutional requirement within the meaning of Question 3 of the Manitoba and Newfoundland References. In a federal State where the essential feature of the Constitution must be the distribution of powers between the two levels of government, each supreme in its own legislative sphere, constitutionality and legality must be synonymous, and conventional rules will be accorded less significance than they may have in a unitary State such as the United Kingdom. At the risk of undue repetition, the point must again be made that constitutionalism in a unitary State and practices in the national and regional political units of a federal State must be differentiated from constitutional law in a federal State. Such law cannot be ascribed to informal or customary origins, but must be found in a formal document which is the source of authority, legal authority, through which the central and regional units function and exercise their powers.

The Constitution of Canada, as has been pointed out by the majority, is only in part written, i.e., contained in statutes which have the force of law and which include, in addition to the *British North America Act, 1867* (hereinafter called the *B.N.A. Act*), the various other enactments which are listed in the reasons of the majority. Another, and indeed highly important, part of the Constitution has taken the form of custom and usage, adopting in large part the practices of the Parliament of the United Kingdom and adapting them to the federal nature of this country. These have evolved with time to form with the statutes referred to above and certain rules of the common law a Constitution for Canada. This Constitution depends then on statutes and common law rules which declare the law and have the force of law, and upon customs, usages and conventions developed in political science which, while not having the force of law in the sense that there is a legal enforcement process or sanction available for their breach, form a vital part of the Constitution without which it would be incomplete and unable to serve its purpose.

As has been pointed out by the majority, a fundamental difference between the legal, that is the statutory and common law rules of the Constitution, and the conventional rules is that, while a breach of the legal rules, whether of statutory or common law nature, has a legal consequence in that it will be restrained by the Courts, no such sanction exists for breach or non-observance of the conventional rules. The observance of constitutional conventions depends upon the acceptance of the obligation of conformance by the actors deemed to be bound thereby. When this consideration is insufficient to compel observance no Court may enforce the convention by legal action. The sanction for non-observance of a convention is political in that disregard of a convention may lead to political defeat, to loss of office, or to other political consequences, but it will not engage the attention of the Courts which are limited to matters of law alone. Courts, however, may recognize the existence of conventions and that is what is asked of us in answering the questions. The answer, whether affirmative or negative, however, can have no legal effect, and acts performed or done in conformance with the law, even though in direct contradiction of well-established conventions, will not be enjoined or set aside by the Courts. For one of many examples of the application of this principle see: *Madzimbamuto v. Lardner-Burke et al.*, [1969] 1 A.C. 645. Simple convention cannot create such a power in either level of government. A Canadian convention could only be of negative effect, that is, to limit the exercise of such power. However, no limitative practice can have the effect of giving away such power where it exists in law.

There are different kinds of conventions and usages, but we are concerned here with what may be termed "constitutional" conventions or rules of the Constitution. They were described by Professor Dicey in the tenth edition of his *Law of the Constitution*, at pp. 23–4, in the following passage:

> The one set of rules are in the strictest sense "laws", since they are rules which (whether written or unwritten, whether enacted by statute or derived from the mass of custom, tradition, or judge-made maxims known as the common law) are enforced by the courts; these rules constitute "constitutional law" in the proper sense of that term, and may for the sake of distinction be called collectively "the law of the constitution".
>
> The other set of rules consist of conventions, understandings, habits, or practices which, though they may regulate the conduct of the several members of the sovereign power, of the Ministry, or of other officials, are not in reality laws at all since they are not enforced by the courts. This portion of constitutional law may, for the

sake of distinction, be termed the "conventions of the constitution", or constitutional morality.

Later, at p. 27, after discussing examples from English practice, he said:

> Under the English constitution they have one point in common: they are none of them "laws" in the true sense of that word, for if any or all of them were broken, no court would take notice of their violation.

And further, at pp. 30–1, he added:

> With conventions or understandings he [the lawyer and law teacher] has no direct concern. They vary from generation to generation, almost from year to year. Whether a Ministry defeated at the polling booths ought to retire on the day when the result of the election is known, or may more properly retain office until after a defeat in Parliament, is or may be a question of practical importance. The opinions on this point which prevail to-day differ (it is said) from the opinions or understandings which prevailed thirty years back, and are possibly different from the opinions or understandings which may prevail ten years hence. Weighty precedents and high authority are cited on either side of this knotty question; the dicta or practice of Russell and Peel may be balanced off against the dicta or practice of Beaconsfield and Gladstone. The subject, however, is not one of law but of politics, and need trouble no lawyer or the class of any professor of law. If he is concerned with it at all, he is so only in so far as he may be called upon to show what is the connection (if any there be) between the conventions of the constitution and the law of the constitution.

This view has been adopted by Canadian writers, *e.g.*, Professor Peter W. Hogg in *Constitutional Law of Canada* (1977), dealt with the matter in these terms, at p. 7:

> Conventions are rules of the constitution which are not enforced by the law courts. Because they are not enforced by the law courts they are best regarded as non-legal rules, but because they do not in fact regulate the working of the constitution they are an important concern of the constitutional lawyer. What conventions do is to prescribe the way in which legal powers shall be exercised. Some conventions have the effect of transferring effective power from the legal holder to another official or institution. Other conventions limit an apparently broad legal power, or even prescribe that a legal power shall not be exercised at all.

At p. 8, he said:

> If a convention is disobeyed by an official, then it is common, especially in the United Kingdom, to describe the official's act or omission as "unconstitutional". But

this use of the term unconstitutional must be carefully distinguished from the case where a legal rule of the constitution has been disobeyed. Where unconstitutionality springs from a breach of law, the purported act is normally a nullity and there is a remedy available in the courts. But where "unconstitutionality" springs merely from a breach off convention, no breach of the law has occurred and no legal remedy will be available. If a court did give a remedy for a breach of convention, for example, by declaring invalid a statute enacted for Canada by the United Kingdom Parliament without Canada's request or consent, or by ordering an unwilling Governor General to give his assent to a bill enacted by both houses of Parliament, then we would have to change our language and describe the rule which used to be thought of as a convention as a rule of the common law. In other words a judicial decision could have the effect of transforming a conventional rule into a legal rule. A convention may also be transformed into law by being enacted as a statute.

It will be noted that Professor Hogg, in the quotation immediately above, has expressed the view that a judicial decision could have the effect of transforming a conventional rule into a legal rule, as could the enactment of a convention in statutory form. There can be no doubt that a statute, by enacting the terms of a convention, could create positive law, but it is our view that it is not for the Courts to raise a convention to the status of a legal principle. As pointed out above, Courts may recognize the existence of conventions in their proper sphere. That is all that may be properly sought from the Court in answering Question 2 in the Manitoba and Newfoundland References and the conventional part of Question B in the Quebec Reference: an answer by the Court recognizing the existence of the convention or denying its existence. For the Court to postulate some other convention requiring less than unanimous provincial consent to constitutional amendments would be to go beyond the terms of the References and in so doing to answer a question not posed in the References. It would amount, in effect, to an attempt by judicial pronouncement to create an amending formula for the Canadian Constitution which, in addition to being beyond the Court's power to declare, not being raised in a question posed in any of the References before the Court, would be incomplete for failure to specify the degree or percentage of provincial consent required. Furthermore, all the Provinces, with the exception of Saskatchewan, oppose such a step. Those favouring the position of the federal Parliament, Ontario and New Brunswick, do so because they say no convention exists and those attacking the federal position, Quebec, Nova Scotia, Prince Edward Island, Manitoba, Alberta and British Columbia, do so because they say provincial participation is already fixed by what may be called "the rule of unanimity".

Conventions, while frequently unwritten, may none the less be reduced to writing. They may be reached by specific agreement between the parties to be bound, or they may more commonly arise from practice and usage. It is true, as well, that conventions can become law but this, in our view, would require some formal legal step such as enactment in statutory form. The *Statute of Westminster*, 1931 (U.K.), c. 4, affords an example of the enactment of conventions concerning constitutional relations between the United Kingdom and the various Dominions. However a convention may arise or be created, the essential condition for its recognition must be that the parties concerned regard it as binding upon them. While a convention, by its very nature, will often lack the precision and clearness of expression of a law, it must be recognized, known and understood with sufficient clarity that conformance is possible and a breach of conformance immediately discernible. It must play as well a necessary constitutional role.

There are many such conventions of the Canadian Constitution and while at different periods they may have taken different forms, and while change and development have been observable and are, no doubt, continuing processes, they have been recognized none the less as rules or conventions of the Canadian Constitution, known and observed at any given time in Canadian affairs. As the reasons of the majority point out, there are many examples. The general rule that the Governor General will act only according to the advice of the Prime Minister is purely conventional and is not to be found in any legal enactment. In the same category is the rule that after a general election the Governor General will call upon the leader of the party with the greatest number of seats to form a government. The rule of responsible government that a government losing the confidence of the House of Commons must itself resign, or obtain a dissolution, the general principles of majority rule and responsible government underlying the daily workings of the institutions of the executive and legislative branches of each level of government, and a variety of other such conventional arrangements, serve as further illustrations. These rules have an historical origin and bind, and have bound, the actors in constitutional matters in Canada for generations. No one can doubt their operative force or the reality of their existence as an effective part of the Canadian Constitution. They are, none the less, conventional and, therefore, distinct from purely legal rules. They are observed without demur because all parties concerned recognize their existence and accept the obligation of observance, considering themselves to be bound. Even though it may be, as the majority of the Court has said, a matter of some surprise to many Canadians, these conventions have no legal force. They are, in short, the product of political experience, the adoption of which allows the political process to function in a way acceptable to the community.

These then are recognized conventions, they are definite, understandable and understood. They have the unquestioned acceptance not only of the actors in political affairs but of the public at large. Can it be said that any convention having such clear definition and acceptance concerning provincial participation in the amendment of the Canadian Constitution has developed? It is in the light of this comparison that the existence of any supposed constitutional convention must be considered. It is abundantly clear, in our view, that the answer must be No. The degree of provincial participation in constitutional amendments has been a subject of lasting controversy in Canadian political life for generations. It cannot be asserted, in our opinion, that any view on this subject has become so clear and so broadly accepted as to constitute a constitutional convention. It should be observed that there is a fundamental difference between the convention in the Dicey concept and the convention for which some of the Provinces here contend. The Dicey convention relates to the functioning of individuals and institutions within a parliamentary democracy in unitary form. It does not qualify or limit the authority or sovereignty of Parliament or the Crown. The convention sought to be advanced here would truncate the functioning of the executive and legislative branches at the federal level. This would impose a limitation on the sovereign body itself within the Constitution. Surely such a convention would require for its recognition, even in the non-legal, political sphere, the clearest signal from the plenary unit intended to be bound, and not simply a plea from the majority of the beneficiaries of such a convention, the provincial plenary units.

An examination of the Canadian experience since Confederation will, bearing in mind the considerations above described, serve to support our conclusion on this question. It may be observed here that it was not suggested in argument before this Court that there was any procedure for amendment now available other than by the addresses of both Houses of Parliament to Her Majesty the Queen. It was argued, however, that this was a procedural step only and that before it could be undertaken by Parliament the consent of the Provinces would be required. It is with the frequency with which provincial consents were obtained or omitted, with the circumstances under which consent was or was not sought, with the nature of the amendments involved, and with provincial attitudes towards them that we must concern ourselves. As has been pointed out in other judgments on these References, here and in the other Courts, there have been since Confederation some twenty-two amendments to the *B.N.A. Act.* Brief particulars of each amendment taken from the Government paper entitled, "The Amendment of the Constitution of Canada", published in 1965 under the authority of The Hon. Guy Favreau, the federal Minister of Justice, hereinafter referred to as the White Paper, are set out below for convenience of reference:

(1) *The Rupert's Land Act, 1868* authorized the acceptance by Canada of the rights of the Hudson's Bay Company over Rupert's Land and the North-Western Territory. It also provided that, on Address from the Houses of Parliament of Canada, the Crown could declare this territory part of Canada and the Parliament of Canada could make laws for its peace, order and good government.

(2) *The British North America Act of 1871* ratified the Manitoba Act passed by the Parliament of Canada in 1870, creating the province of Manitoba and giving it a provincial constitution similar to those of the other provinces. The British North America Act of 1871 also empowered the Parliament of Canada to establish new provinces out of any Canadian territory not then included in a province; to alter the boundaries of any province (with the consent of its legislature), and to provide for the administration, peace and good government of any territory not included in a province.

(3) *The Parliament of Canada Act of 1875* amended section 18 of the British North America Act, 1867, which set forth the privileges, immunities and powers of each of the Houses of Parliament.

(4) *The British North America Act of 1886* authorized the Parliament of Canada to provide for the representation in the Senate and the House of Commons of any territories not included in any province.

(5) *The Statute Law Revision Act, 1893* repealed some obsolete provisions of the British North America Act of 1867.

(6) *The Canadian Speaker (Appointment of Deputy) Act, 1895* confirmed an Act of Parliament of Canada which provided for the appointment of a Deputy-Speaker for the Senate.

(7) *The British North America Act, 1907* established a new scale of financial subsidies to the provinces in lieu of those set forth in section 118 of the British North America Act of 1867. While not expressly repealing the original section, it made its provisions obsolete.

(8) *The British North America Act, 1915* re-defined the Senatorial Divisions of Canada to take into account the provinces of Manitoba, British Columbia, Saskatchewan and Alberta. Although this statute did not expressly amend the text of the original section 22, it did alter its effect.

(9) *The British North America Act, 1916* provided for the extension of the life of the current Parliament of Canada beyond the normal period of five years.

(10) *The Senate Law Revision Act, 1927* repealed additional spent or obsolete provisions in the United Kingdom statutes, including two provisions of the British North America Acts.

(11) *The British North America Act, 1930* confirmed the natural resources agreements between the Government of Canada and the Governments of Manitoba, British Columbia, Alberta and Saskatchewan, giving the agreements the force of law notwithstanding anything in the British North America Acts.

(12) *The Statute of Westminster, 1931*, while not directly amending the British North America Acts, did alter some of their provisions. Thus, the Parliament of Canada was given the power to make laws having extraterritorial effect. Also, Parliament and the provincial legislatures were given the authority, within their powers under the British North America Acts, to repeal any United Kingdom statute that formed part of the law of Canada. This authority, however, expressly excluded the British North America Act itself.

(13) *The British North America Act, 1940* gave the Parliament of Canada the exclusive jurisdiction to make laws in relation to Unemployment Insurance.

(14) *The British North America Act, 1943* provided for the postponement of redistribution of the seats in the House of Commons until the first session of Parliament after the cessation of hostilities.

(15) *The British North America Act, 1946* replaced section 51 of the British North America Act, 1867, and altered the provisions for the readjustment of representation in the House of Commons.

(16) *The British North America Act, 1949* confirmed the Terms of Union between Canada and Newfoundland.

(17) *The British North America Act (No. 2), 1949* gave the Parliament of Canada authority to amend the Constitution of Canada with certain exceptions.

(18) *The Statute Law Revision Act, 1950* repealed an obsolete section of the British North America Act, 1867.

(19) *The British North America Act, 1951* gave the Parliament of Canada concurrent jurisdiction with the provinces to make laws in relation to Old Age Pensions.

(20) *The British North America Act, 1960* amended sec-

tion 99 and altered the tenure of office of superior court judges.

(21) *The British North America Act, 1964* amended the authority conferred upon the Parliament of Canada by the British North America Act, 1951, in relation to benefits supplementary to Old Age Pensions.

(22) *Amendment by Order in Council*

Section 146 of the British North America Act, 1867 provided for the admission of other British North American territories by Order in Council and stipulated that the provisions of any such Order in Council would have the same effect as if enacted by the Parliament of the United Kingdom. Under this section, Rupert's Land and the North-Western Territory were admitted by Order in Council on June 23rd, 1870; British Columbia by Order in Council on May 16th, 1871; Prince Edward Island by Order in Council on June 26th, 1873. Because all of these Orders in Council contained provisions of a constitutional character — adapting the provisions of the British North America Act to the new provinces, but with some modifications in each case — they may therefore be regarded as constitutional amendments.

In examining these amendments it must be borne in mind that all do not possess the same relevance or force for the purpose of this inquiry. Question 2 of the Manitoba and Newfoundland References and the conventional segment of Question B in the Quebec Reference raise the issue of the propriety of non-consensual amendments which affect federal-provincial relationships and the powers, rights and privileges of the Provinces. The questions do not limit consideration to those amendments which affected the distribution of legislative powers between the federal Parliament and the provincial Legislatures. Since the distribution of powers is the very essence of a federal system, amendments affecting such distribution will be of especial concern to the Provinces. Precedents found in such amendments will be entitled to serious consideration. It does not follow, however, that other amendments which affected federal-provincial relationships without altering the distribution of powers should be disregarded in this inquiry. Consideration must be given in according weight to the various amendments, to the reaction they provoked from the Provinces. This is surely the real test of relevance in this discussion. On many occasions Provinces considered that amendments not affecting the distribution of legislative power were sufficiently undesirable to call for strenuous opposition. The test of whether the convention exists, or has existed, is to be found by examining the results of such opposition. Professor William S. Livingston in *Fed-*

eralism and Constitutional Change (1956, Oxford University Press), made this comment, at p. 62, when considering the 1943 amendment which did not affect the distribution of powers, and the 1940 amendment which did:

> The important difference between the two amendments lies, of course, in the fact that that of 1940 clearly and significantly altered the distribution of powers, a part of the constitution which, it has been argued, is especially deserving of the protection afforded by the principle of unanimous consent. But the facts themselves demonstrate that at least one of the provinces considered the alteration of 1943 sufficiently important to call for long and bitter protests at the disdainful attitude of the Dominion Government. If unanimity is for the protection of provinces, whether singly or collectively, it is reasonable to think that the provinces should be the ones to judge when it should be invoked. By the very operation of the principle, a province will not protest unless it considers the matter at hand worth protesting about.

The true test of the importance of the various amendments for our purpose is a consideration of the degree of provincial opposition they aroused, for whatever reason, the consideration that such opposition received, and the influence it had on the course of the amendment proceedings.

Prior to the amendment effected by the *B.N.A. Act* of 1930 there were at least three amendments, those of 1886, 1907 and 1915, which substantially affected the Provinces and which were procured without the consent of all the Provinces. The amendment of 1886 gave power to Parliament to provide for parliamentary representation in the Senate and House of Commons for territories not forming part of any Province, and therefore altered the provincial balance of representation. That of 1907 changed the basis of federal subsidies payable to the Provinces and thus directly affected the provincial interests. That of 1915 redefined territorial divisions for senatorial representation, and therefore had a potential for altering the provincial balance. Those of 1886 and 1915 were passed without provincial consultation or consent, and that of 1907 had the consent of all Provinces save British Columbia, which actively opposed its passage both in Canada and in the United Kingdom. The amendment was passed with minor changes. These precedents, it may be said, should by themselves have only a modest influence in the consideration of the question before the Court. It is clear, however, that no support whatever for the convention may be found on an examination of the amendments made up to 1930. None had full provincial approval.

The *B.N.A. Act* of 1930 provided for the transfer of natural resources within the provincial territories to the

Provinces of Manitoba, Saskatchewan and Alberta. It also provided for the reconveyance of certain railway lands to British Columbia. In effecting this amendment the consent of the Provinces directly concerned, *i.e.*, the four western Provinces only, was obtained, although the arrangement had received the general approval of the other Provinces as expressed at a conference in 1927. This is a precedent of modest weight, but it is worthy of note that despite the fact that the interests of all non-involved Provinces were affected by the alienation of the assets formerly under federal control, it was not considered necessary to procure any formal consent from them. It is of more than passing interest to note that in the amending procedure provided for in the 1930 *British North America Act, 1867* amendment [1930 (U.K.), c. 26] there is no requirement for consent or participation by any of the other five Provinces (as they then were) although their indirect interest in federal resources might be affected.

The amendments of 1943, 1946, 1949, 1949(2), 1950 and 1960 were not considered of great significance on this issue by the parties and little comment was made upon them but all, save that of 1960, were achieved without full provincial consent. This, subject to what is later said concerning the 1943 amendment, leaves for consideration the *Statute of Westminster, 1931* and the amendments of 1940, 1951 and 1964. The *Statute of Westminster, 1931* and the amendments of 1940, 1951 and 1964 affected the Provinces directly. Canadian participation in the settlement of the provisions of the statute and the said amendments had the consent of all Provinces. These examples were heavily relied upon by the objecting Provinces to support an affirmative answer to Question 2 of the Manitoba and Newfoundland References and the negative answer to the conventional part of Question B of the Quebec Reference. As to the *Statute of Westminster, 1931*, it freed federal and provincial legislation from the restrictions imposed by the *Colonial Laws Validity Act*, 1865 (U.K.), c. 63, and gave statutory recognition to certain conventions which had grown up with the development of self-government in the former colonies. The pre-existing division of legislative power between federal and provincial legislatures in Canada was not, however, in any way affected and it did not recognize or give statutory form to any convention requiring provincial consent to the amendment of the *B.N.A. Act*. In fact, it specifically excepted the question of *B.N.A. Act* amendments from its purview in s. 7(1).

The amendment of 1940 transferring legislative power over unemployment insurance to the federal Parliament also had full provincial consent. It must be observed here, however, that when questioned in the House of Commons on this point Mr. Mackenzie King, then Prime Minister, while acknowledging that consents had been obtained, specifically stated that this course had been followed to avoid any constitutional issue on this point and he disclaimed any necessity for such consent. The following interchange is recorded in the House of Commons Debates, 1940, pp. 1117 and 1122:

> *Mr. Mackenzie King*: . . . We have avoided anything in the nature of coercion of any of the provinces. Moreover we have avoided the raising of a very critical constitutional question, namely, whether or not in amending the British North America Act it is absolutely necessary to secure the consent of all the provinces, or whether the consent of a certain number of provinces would of itself be sufficient. That question may come up but not in reference to unemployment insurance at some time later on.
>
> . . . . .
>
> *Mr. J.T. Thorson* (Selkirk): I shall be only a few moments in my advocacy of this resolution. Unemployment insurance is a very important part of the programme of national reform upon which this country must embark. I wish, however, to dispute the contention that it is necessary to obtain the consent of the provinces before an application is made to amend the British North America Act. In my opinion there is no such necessity. On the other hand, it is the course of wisdom to advance as advances may be properly made, and I am sure that every hon. member is very glad that all the provinces of Canada have agreed to this measure. But I would not wish this debate to conclude with an acceptance, either direct or implied, of the doctrine that it is necessary to obtain the consent of the provinces before an application is made to amend the British North America Act. Fortunately, this is an academic question at this time.
>
> *Mr. Lapointe* (Quebec East): May I tell my hon. friend that neither the Prime Minister nor I have said it is necessary but it may be desirable.
>
> *Mr. Thorson*: The Prime Minister (Mr. Mackenzie King) has made it perfectly clear that the question does not enter into this discussion, in view of the fact that all the provinces have signified their willingness that this amendment should be requested.

It appears from the foregoing that the then Prime Minister recognized the existence of a question on this point. It cannot be said, however, that his words support the view that he considered that there was any convention requiring provincial consent in existence. It is clear, we suggest, that he procured the consent of the Provinces on that occasion in order to avoid raising any question on the subject and as a measure of good politics rather than as a constitutional requirement. It is surely obvious that the federal Government would always prefer to have, as a political matter, provincial approval, but the position of the federal authorities as expressed in the foregoing parliamentary exchange does not support the proposition that they considered that they were bound by any convention.

We are aware, of course, that other declarations have been made upon this subject by persons of high political rank as well as academics of high standing. Many such pronouncements were cited in argument before us. We do not propose to deal with them in detail. It is sufficient to say that many favour the existence of the convention; many deny its existence. Some of the authors of such statements have contradicted themselves on the point at different times in their careers. The debate on this question has been active and long drawn out but, in our view, has never been resolved in favour of the existence of the convention. The continuation of controversy on the subject among political and academic figures only adds additional weight to the contention that no convention of provincial consent has achieved constitutional recognition to this day.

The amendment of 1951 had full approval from the Provinces, as did that of 1964. The 1951 amendment gave power relating to old age pensions to the federal Parliament and the 1964 amendment was merely a supplementary tidying-up of the original 1951 provisions. In our view, they dealt with the same matter and can stand as only one precedent favouring the existence of the convention.

After examining the amendments made since Confederation, and after observing that out of the twenty-two amendments listed above only in the case of four was unanimous provincial consent sought or obtained and, even after according special weight to those amendments relied on by the Provinces, we cannot agree that history justifies a conclusion that the convention contended for by the Provinces has emerged.

Great weight was put upon the 1940 *Unemployment Insurance Act* amendment (1940 (Can.), c. 44) as a precedent favouring the existence of the convention. Despite the obtaining of provincial consent for the 1940 amendment, the federal Government proceeded three years later to the completion of the amendment of 1943 [1943-44 (Can.), c. 41] without provincial consent and in the face of the strong protests of the Province of Quebec. This amendment did not touch provincial powers. It dealt with the postponement of redistribution of seats in the House of Commons. Nevertheless, it was deemed of sufficient importance by Quebec because its interest was particularly affected to arouse active opposition which was overborne by the federal Government in procuring the amendment.

Livingston, in discussing this amendment in his text, referred to above, said, at p. 61:

> But though the treatment of the 1940 Act came dangerously near acceptance of the principle of unanimous consent, the procedure followed in 1943 destroyed all hope that the question had been settled. The 1943 amendment was for the purpose of postponing the redistribution of seats in the House of Commons until after the war. The redistribution was prescribed by the constitution (Sec. 51) and it therefore required an Act of the British Parliament to postpone it. Quebec, whose population had increased more than that of other provinces, was to benefit considerably from the reassignment of seats and was loath to postpone it. But the inconvenience and injustice of reorganizing the basis of representation in wartime impelled the Government to push its proposal through the House. It was introduced and defended by Mr. St. Laurent, then Minister of Justice, and was supported by both Opposition parties; the issue in the House was never in serious doubt. There was no effort on the part of the Dominion Government to consult the provinces, and this action evoked no protest except on the part of Quebec. This province, however, objected strongly to the Government's treatment of the matter and protests were voiced both at Quebec and at Ottawa. The provincial legislature passed a resolution of protest which the Government was requested to transmit to the British Government. Mackenzie King refused, however, replying that the matter concerned only the Dominion Parliament and not the provincial legislatures; that the compact theory was indefensible both in theory and in law; and that the British could not take cognizance of such a communication, since it was bound by the address of the Dominion Parliament. In the House bitter complaints were heard that the Government was simply ignoring the official protest of the Quebec legislature and that such high-handedness abused the constitution and violated the rights of the provinces. But the Government, secure in the support of the Opposition, pressed the matter to a vote without even replying to these protestations.

In summary, we observe that in one hundred and fourteen years since confederation Canada has grown from a group of four somewhat hesitant colonies into a modern, independent State, vastly increased in size, power and wealth, and having a social and governmental structure unimagined in 1867. It cannot be denied that vast change has occurred in Dominion-Provincial relations over that period. Many factors have influenced this process and the amendments to the *B.N.A. Act* — all the amendments — have played a significant part and all must receive consideration in resolving this question. Only in four cases has full provincial consent been obtained and in many cases the federal Government has proceeded with amendments in the face of active provincial opposition. In our view, it is unrealistic in the extreme to say that the convention has emerged.

As a further support for the convention argument, the White Paper referred to above was cited and relied upon. It was asserted that the statement of principles set out, at p. 15, being an authoritative Government pronouncement, was decisive on the point. The summary of principles is set out hereunder.

> *The first general principle* that emerges in the foregoing resumé is that although an enactment by the United Kingdom is necessary to amend the British North America Act, such action is taken only upon formal request from Canada. No Act of the United Kingdom Parliament affecting Canada is therefore passed unless it is requested and consented to by Canada. Conversely, every amendment requested by Canada in the past has been enacted.

> *The second general principle* is that the sanction of Parliament is required for a request to the British Parliament for an amendment to the British North America Act. This principle was established early in the history of Canada's constitutional amendments, and has not been violated since 1865. The procedure invariably is to seek amendments by a joint Address of the Canadian House of Commons and Senate to the Crown.

> *The third general principle* is that no amendment to Canada's Constitution will be made by the British Parliament merely upon the request of a Canadian province. A number of attempts to secure such amendments have been made, but none has been successful. The first such attempt was made as early as 1868, by a province which was at that time dissatisfied with the terms of Confederation. This was followed by other attempts in 1869, 1874 and 1887. The British Government refused in all cases to act on provincial government representations on the grounds that it should not intervene in the affairs of Canada except at the request of the federal government representing all of Canada.

> *The fourth general principle* is that the Canadian Parliament will not request an amendment directly affecting federal-provincial relationships without prior consultation and agreement with the provinces. This principle did not emerge as early as others but since 1907, and particularly since 1930, has gained increasing recognition and acceptance. The nature and the degree of provincial participation in the amending process, however, have not lent themselves to easy definition.

It is the fourth principle which is stressed by the objecting Provinces. In our view, they have attributed too much significance to this statement of the four principles. The author of the White Paper was at pains to say, at p. 11:

> Certain rules and principles relating to amending procedures have nevertheless developed over the years. They have emerged from the practices and procedures employed in securing various amendments to the British North America Act since 1867. *Though not constitutionally binding in any strict sense*, they have come to be recognized and accepted in practice as part of the amendment process in Canada.

(Emphasis added.) It would not appear that he was satisfied that the principles had become so well-established that they had acquired strict constitutional force. Furthermore, we are unable to accord to the fourth principle the significance given to it by the objecting Provinces. The first sentence pronounces strongly in favour of the existence of the convention. If it stopped there, subject to what the author had said earlier, it would constitute a statement of great weight. However, the third sentence contradicts the first and, in fact, cancels it out. By suggesting the possibility of a requirement of partial provincial consent it answers Question 2 in the Manitoba and Newfoundland References and the conventional segment of Question B in the Quebec Reference against the Provinces. "Increasing recognition", that is "partial" but not "complete" recognition, is all that is claimed by the author of the White Paper. A convention requires universal recognition by the actors in a scheme and this is certainly so where, as here, acceptance of a convention involves the surrender of a power by a sovereign body said to be a party to the convention. Furthermore, in recognizing uncertainty in specifying the degree of provincial participation, it denies the existence of any convention including that suggested by the Province of Saskatchewan. If there is difficulty in defining the degee of provincial participation, which there surely is, it cannot be said that any convention on the subject has been settled and recognized as a constitutional condition for the making of an amendment. It is the very difficulty of fixing the degree of provincial participation which, while it remains unresolved, prevents the formation or recognition of any convention. It robs any supposed convention of that degree of definition which is necessary to allow for its operation, for its binding effect upon the persons deemed to be bound, and it renders difficult if not impossible any clear discernment of a breach of the convention. In our view, then the fourth principle enunciated in the White Paper does not advance the provincial argument.

It was also argued that Canada was formed as a federal

union and that the existence of a legal power of the central Government to unilaterally change the Constitution was inimical to the concept of federalism. The convention then, it was argued, arose out of the necessity to restrain such unilateral conduct and preserve the federal nature of Canada. In this connection, it must be acknowledged at once that, in a federal union, the powers and rights of each of the two levels of government must be protected from the assault of the other. The whole history of constitutional law and constitutional litigation in Canada since Confederation has been concerned with this vital question. We are asked to say whether the need for the preservation of the principles of Canadian federalism dictates the necessity for a convention, requiring consent from the Provinces as a condition of the exercise by the federal Government of its legal powers, to procure amendment to the Canadian Constitution. If the convention requires only partial consent, as is contended by Saskatchewan, it is difficult to see how the federal concept is thereby protected for, while those Provinces favouring amendment would be pleased, those refusing consent could claim coercion. If unanimous consent is required (as contended by the other objecting Provinces), while it may be said that in general terms the concept of federalism would be protected it would only be by over-looking the special nature of Canadian federalism that this protection would be achieved. The *B.N.A. Act* has not created a perfect or ideal federal State. Its provisions have accorded a measure of paramountcy to the federal Parliament. Certainly this has been done in a more marked degree in Canada than in many other federal States. For example, one need only look to the power of reservation and disallowance of provincial enactments; the power to declare works in a Province to be for the benefit of all Canada and to place them under federal regulatory control; the wide powers to legislate generally for the peace, order and good government of Canada as a whole; the power to enact the criminal law of the entire country; the power to create and admit Provinces out of existing territories and, as well, the paramountcy accorded federal legislation. It is this special nature of Canadian federalism which deprives the federalism argument described above of its force. This is particularly true when it involves the final settlement of Canadian constitutional affairs with an external government, the federal authority being the sole conduit for communication between Canada and the Sovereign and Canada alone having the power to deal in external matters. We therefore reject the argument that the preservation of the principles of Canadian federalism requires the recognition of the convention asserted before us.

While it may not be necessary to do so in dealing with Question 2, we feel obliged to make a further comment related to the federalism argument. It was argued that the federal authorities were assuming a power to act without restraint in disregard of provincial wishes which could go so far as to convert Canada into a unitary State by means of a majority vote in the Houses of Parliament. A few words will suffice to lay that argument at rest. What is before the Court is the task of answering the questions posed in three references. As has been pointed out, the Court can do no more than that. The questions all deal with the constitutional validity of precise proposals for constitutional amendment and they form the complete subject-matter of the Court's inquiry and our comments must be made with reference to them. It is not for the Court to express views on the wisdom or lack of wisdom of these proposals. We are concerned solely with their constitutionality. In view of the fact that the unitary argument has been raised, however, it should be noted, in our view, that the federal constitutional proposals, which preserve a federal State without disturbing the distribution or balance of power, would create an amending formula which would enshrine provincial rights on the question of amendments on a secure, legal and constitutional footing, and would extinguish, as well, any presently existing power on the part of the federal Parliament to act unilaterally in constitutional matters. In so doing, it may be said that the parliamentary Resolution here under examination does not, save for the enactment of the *Charter of Rights*, which circumscribes the legislative powers of both the federal and provincial Legislatures, truly amend the Canadian Constitution. Its effect is to complete the formation of an incomplete constitution by supplying its present deficiency, *i.e.,* an amending formula, which will enable the Constitution to be amended in Canada as befits a sovereign State. We are not here faced with an action which in any way has the effect of transforming this federal union into a unitary State. The *in terrorem* argument raising the spectre of a unitary State has no validity.

For the above reasons we answer the questions posed in the three References as follows:

Manitoba and Newfoundland References:
Question 2: No

Quebec Reference:
Question B (i): Yes
           (ii): Yes

48. Federal-Provincial First Ministers' Conference, Ottawa, Ontario, November 2–5, 1981

(a) First Ministers' Agreement on the Constitution, November 5, 1981

Document: 800-15/021

In an effort to reach an acceptable consensus on the constitutional issue which meets the concerns of the federal government and a substantial number of provincial governments, the undersigned governments have agreed to the following:

(1) Patriation

(2) Amending Formula:
  — Acceptance of the April Accord Amending Formula with the deletion of Section 3 which provides for fiscal compensation to a province which opts out of a constitutional amendment.
  — The Delegation of Legislative Authority from the April Accord is deleted.

(3) Charter of Rights and Freedoms:
  — The entrenchment of the full Charter of Rights and Freedoms now before Parliament with the following changes:
  (*a*) With respect to Mobility Rights the inclusion of the right of a province to undertake affirmative action programs for socially and economically disadvantaged individuals as long as a province's employment rate was below the National average.
  (*b*) A "notwithstanding" clause covering sections dealing with Fundamental Freedoms, Legal Rights and Equality Rights. Each "notwithstanding" provision would require reenactment not less frequently than once every five years.
  (*c*) We have agreed that the provisions of Section 23 in respect of Minority Language Education Rights will apply to our provinces.

(4) The provisions of the Act now before Parliament relating to Equalization and Regional Disparities, and Non Renewable Natural Resources, Forestry Resources and Electrical Energy would be included.

(5) A constitutional conference as provided for in clause 36 of the Resolution, including in its agenda an item respecting constitutional matters that directly affect the Aboriginal peoples of Canada, including the identification and definition of the rights of those peoples to be included in the Constitution of Canada, shall be provided for in the Resolution. The Prime Minister of Canada shall invite representatives of the Aboriginal peoples of Canada to participate in the discussion of that item.

Dated at Ottawa this 5th day of November, 1981.

CANADA/POUR LE CANADA
Pierre Elliott Trudeau, Prime Minister of Canada/Premier ministre du Canada

ONTARIO/POUR L'ONTARIO
William G. Davis, Premier/Premier ministre

NOVA SCOTIA/POUR LA NOUVELLE-ECOSSE
[*illegible*] for John M. Buchanan, Premier/Premier ministre

NEW BRUNSWICK/POUR LE NOUVEAU-BRUNSWICK
Richard B. Hatfield, Premier/Premier ministre

MANITOBA/POUR LE MANITOBA
(*subject to approval of section 3(c) by the Legislative Assembly of Manitoba*) [*illegible*] for Sterling R. Lyon, Premier/Premier ministre

BRITISH COLUMBIA/POUR LA COLOMBIE-BRITANNIQUE
William R. Bennett, Premier/Premier ministre

PRINCE EDWARD ISLAND/POUR L'ILE-DU-PRINCE-EDOUARD
J. Angus MacLean, Premier/Premier ministre

SASKATCHEWAN/POUR LA SASKATCHEWAN
Allan E. Blakeney, Premier/Premier ministre

ALBERTA/POUR L'ALBERTA
Peter Lougheed, Premier/Premier ministre

NEWFOUNDLAND/POUR TERRE-NEUVE
A. Brian Peckford, Premier/Premier ministre

(b) Fact Sheet: The Notwithstanding or Override Clause as Applied to the Charter of Rights and Freedoms

Document: 800-15/022

A notwithstanding clause is one which enables a legislative body (federal and provincial) to enact expressly that a particular provision of an Act will be valid, notwithstanding the fact that it conflicts with a specific provision of the Charter of Rights and Freedoms. The notwithstanding principle has been recognized and is contained in a number of bills of rights, including the Canadian Bill of Rights (1960), the Alberta Bill of Rights (1972), The Quebec Charter of Rights and Freedoms (1975), the Saskatchewan Human Rights Code (1979), and Ontario's Bill 7 to Amend its Human Rights Code (1981).

How it would be applied

Any enactment overriding any specific provisions of the Charter would contain a clause expressly declaring that a specific provision of the proposed enactment shall operate, notwithstanding a specific provision of the Charter of Rights and Freedoms.

Any notwithstanding enactment would have to be reviewed and renewed every five years by the enacting legislature if it were to remain in force.

49. House of Commons and Senate Debates, November–December, 1981

(a) Proposed Resolution for a Joint Address to Her Majesty the Queen Respecting the Constitution of Canada, as Altered by the November 5, 1981, First Ministers' Agreement on the Constitution, from the *House of Commons Journals*, Issue 260, November 20, 1981

The following Notice of Motion, having been called, was transferred to Government Orders for consideration later this day or at the next sitting of the House pursuant to Standing Order 21(2):

> THAT, WHEREAS in the past certain amendments to the Constitution of Canada have been made by the Parliament of the United Kingdom at the request and with the consent of Canada:
>
> AND WHEREAS it is in accord with the status of Canada as independent state that Canadians be able to amend their Constitution in Canada in all respects;
>
> AND WHEREAS it is also desirable to provide in the Constitution of Canada for the recognition of certain fundamental rights and freedoms and to make other amendments to that Constitution:
>
> A respectful address be presented to Her Majesty the Queen in the following words:

> To the Queen's Most Excellent Majesty:
> Most Gracious Sovereign:

> We, Your Majesty's loyal subjects, the House of Commons of Canada in Parliament assembled, respectfully approach Your Majesty, requesting that you may graciously be pleased to cause to be laid before the Parliament of the United Kingdom a measure containing the recitals and clauses hereinafter set forth:

ANNEXE A—SCHEDULE A

An Act to give effect to a request by the Senate and House of Commons of Canada

Whereas Canada has requested and consented to the enactment of an Act of the Parliament of the United Kingdom to give effect to the provisions hereinafter set forth and the Senate and the House of Commons

Loi donnant suite à une demande du Sénat et de la Chambre des communes du Canada

Sa Très Excellente Majesté la Reine, considérant :

qu'à la demande et avec le consentement du Canada, le Parlement du Royaume-

of Canada in Parliament assembled have submitted an address to Her Majesty requesting that Her Majesty may graciously be pleased to cause a Bill to be laid before the Parliament of the United Kingdom for that purpose.

Be it therefore enacted by the Queen's Most Excellent Majesty, by and with the advice and consent of the Lords Spiritual and Temporal, and Commons, in this present Parliament assembled, and by the authority of the same, as follows:

Constitution Act 1981 enacted

1. The *Constitution Act, 1981* set out in Schedule B to this Act is hereby enacted for and shall have the force of law in Canada and shall come into force as provided in that Act.

Termination of power to legislate for Canada

2. No Act of the Parliament of the United Kingdom passed after the *Constitution Act, 1981* comes into force shall extend to Canada as part of its law.

French version

3. So far as it is not contained in Schedule B, the French version of this Act is set out in Schedule A to this Act and has the same authority in Canada as the English version thereof.

Short title

4. This Act may be cited as the *Canada Act.*

Uni est invité à adopter une loi visant à donner effet aux dispositions énoncées ci-après et que le Sénat et la Chambre des communes du Canada réunis en Parlement ont présenté une adresse demandant à Sa Très Gracieuse Majesté de bien vouloir faire déposer devant le Parlement du Royaume-Uni un projet de loi à cette fin,

sur l'avis et du consentement des Lords spirituels et temporels et des Communes réunis en parlement, et par l'autorité de celui-ci, édicte :

1. La *Loi constitutionnelle de 1981*, énoncée à l'annexe B, est édictée pour le Canada et y a force de loi. Elle entre en vigueur conformément à ses dispositions.

Adoption de la Loi constitutionnelle de 1981

2. Les lois adoptées par le Parlement du Royaume-Uni après l'entrée en vigueur de la *Loi constitutionnelle de 1981* ne font pas partie du droit du Canada.

Cessation du pouvoir de légiférer pour le Canada

3. La partie de la version française de la présente loi qui figure à l'annexe A a force de loi au Canada au même titre que la version anglaise correspondante.

Version française

4. Titre abrégé de la présente loi : *Loi sur le Canada.*

Titre abrégé

SCHEDULE B

CONSTITUTION ACT, 1981

PART I

CANADIAN CHARTER OF RIGHTS AND FREEDOMS

Whereas Canada is founded upon principles that recognize the supremacy of God and the rule of law:

Guarantee of Rights and Freedoms

Rights and freedoms in Canada

1. The *Canadian Charter of Rights and Freedoms* guarantees the rights and freedoms set out in it subject only to such reasonable limits prescribed by law as can be demonstrably justified in a free and democratic society.

Fundamental Freedoms

Fundamental freedoms

2. Everyone has the following fundamental freedoms:

(*a*) freedom of conscience and religion;

(*b*) freedom of thought, belief, opinion and expression, including freedom of the press and other media of communication;

(*c*) freedom of peaceful assembly; and

(*d*) freedom of association.

Democratic Rights

Democratic rights of citizens

3. Every citizen of Canada has the right to vote in an election of members of the House of Commons or of a legislative assembly and to be qualified for membership therein.

Maximum duration of legislative bodies

4. (1) No House of Commons and no legislative assembly shall continue for longer than five years from the date fixed for the return of the writs at a general election of its members.

Continuation in special circumstances

(2) In time of real or apprehended war, invasion or insurrection, a House of Commons may be continued by Parliament and a legislative assembly may be continued by the legislature beyond five years if such continuation is not opposed by the votes of more than one-third of the members of the House of Commons or the legislative assembly, as the case may be.

Annual sitting of legislative bodies

5. There shall be a sitting of Parliament and of each legislature at least once every twelve months.

Mobility Rights

Mobility of citizens

6. (1) Every citizen of Canada has the right to enter, remain in and leave Canada.

Rights to move and gain livelihood

(2) Every citizen of Canada and every person who has the status of a permanent resident of Canada has the right

(*a*) to move to and take up residence in any province; and

(*b*) to pursue the gaining of a livelihood in any province.

Limitation

(3) The rights specified in subsection (2) are subject to

(*a*) any laws or practices of general application in force in a province other than those that discriminate among persons primarily on the basis of present or previous residence; and

(*b*) any laws providing for reasonable residency requirements as a qualification for the receipt of publicly provided social services.

Affirmative action programs

(4) Subsections (2) and (3) do not preclude any law, program or activity that has as its object the amelioration in a province of conditions of individuals in that province who are socially or economically disadvantaged if the rate of employment in that province is below the rate of employment in Canada.

Legal Rights

Life, liberty and security of person

7. Everyone has the right to life, liberty and security of the person and the right not to be deprived thereof except in accordance with the principles of fundamental justice.

Search or seizure

8. Everyone has the right to be secure against unreasonable search or seizure.

Detention or imprisonment

9. Everyone has the right not to be arbitrarily detained or imprisoned.

Arrest or detention

10. Everyone has the right on arrest or detention

(*a*) to be informed promptly of the reasons therefor;

(*b*) to retain and instruct counsel without delay and to be informed of that right; and

(*c*) to have the validity of the detention determined by way of *habeas corpus* and to be released if the detention is not lawful.

Proceedings in criminal and penal matters

11. Any person charged with an offence has the right

(*a*) to be informed without unreasonable delay of the specific offence;

(*b*) to be tried within a reasonable time;

(*c*) not to be compelled to be a witness in proceedings against that person in respect of the offence;

(*d*) to be presumed innocent until proven guilty according to law in a fair and public hearing by an independent and impartial tribunal;

(*e*) not to be denied reasonable bail without just cause;

(*f*) except in the case of an offence under military law tried before a military tribunal, to the benefit of trial by jury where the maximum punishment for the offence is imprisonment for five years or a more severe punishment;

(*g*) not to be found guilty on account of any act or omission unless, at the time of the act or omission, it constituted an offence under Canadian or international law or was criminal according to the general principles of law recognized by the community of nations;

(*h*) if finally acquitted of the offence, not to be tried for it again and, if finally found guilty and punished for the offence, not to be tried or punished for it again; and

(*i*) if found guilty of the offence and if the punishment for the offence has been varied between the time of commission and the time of sentencing, to the benefit of the lesser punishment.

Treatment or punishment

12. Everyone has the right not to be subjected to any cruel and unusual treatment or punishment.

Self-crimination

13. A witness who testifies in any proceedings has the right not to have any incriminating evidence so given used to incriminate that witness in any other proceedings, except in a prosecution for perjury or for the giving of contradictory evidence.

Interpreter

14. A party or witness in any proceedings who does not understand or speak the language in which the proceedings are conducted or who is deaf has the right to the assistance of an interpreter.

Equality Rights

Equality before and under law and equal protection and benefit of law

15. (1) Every individual is equal before and under the law and has the right to the equal protection and equal benefit of the law without discrimination and, in particular, without discrimination based on race, national or ethnic origin, colour, religion, sex, age or mental or physical disability.

Affirmative action programs

(2) Subsection (1) does not preclude any law, program or activity that has as its object the amelioration of conditions of disadvantaged individuals or groups including those that are disadvantaged because of race, national or ethnic origin, colour, religion, sex, age or mental or physical disability.

Official Languages of Canada

Official languages of Canada

16. (1) English and French are the official languages of Canada and have equality of status and equal rights and privileges as to their use in all institutions of the Parliament and government of Canada.

Official languages of New Brunswick

(2) English and French are the official languages of New Brunswick and have equality of status and equal rights and privileges as to their use in all institutions of the legislature and government of New Brunswick.

Advancement of status and use

(3) Nothing in this Charter limits the authority of Parliament or a legislature to advance the equality of status or use of English and French.

Proceedings of Parliament

17. (1) Everyone has the right to use English or French in any debates and other proceedings of Parliament.

Proceedings of New Brunswick legislature

(2) Everyone has the right to use English or French in any debates and other proceedings of the legislature of New Brunswick.

Parliamentary statutes and records

18. (1) The statutes, records and journals of Parliament shall be printed and published in English and French and both language versions are equally authoritative.

New Brunswick statutes and records

(2) The statutes, records and journals of the legislature of New Brunswick shall be printed and published in English and French and both language versions are equally authoritative.

Proceedings in courts established by Parliament

19. (1) Either English or French may be used by any person in, or in any pleading in or process issuing from, any court established by Parliament.

Proceedings in New Brunswick courts

(2) Either English or French may be used by any person in, or in any pleading in or process issuing from, any court of New Brunswick.

Communications by public with federal institutions

20. (1) Any member of the public in Canada has the right to communicate with, and to receive available services from, any head or central office of an institution of the Parliament or government of Canada in English or French, and has the same right with respect to any other office of any such institution where

(a) there is a significant demand for communications with and services from that office in such language; or

(b) due to the nature of the office, it is reasonable that communications with and services from that office be available in both English and French.

Communications by public with New Brunswick institutions

(2) Any member of the public in New Brunswick has the right to communicate with, and to receive available services from, any office of an institution of the legislature or government of New Brunswick in English or French.

Continuation of existing constitutional provisions

21. Nothing in sections 16 to 20 abrogates or derogates from any right, privilege or obligation with respect to the English and French languages, or either of them, that exists or is continued by virtue of any other provision of the Constitution of Canada.

Rights and privileges preserved

22. Nothing in sections 16 to 20 abrogates or derogates from any legal or customary right or privilege acquired or enjoyed either before or after the coming into force of this Charter with respect to any language that is not English or French.

Minority Language Educational Rights

Language of instruction

23. (1) Citizens of Canada

(a) whose first language learned and still understood is that of the English or French linguistic minority population of the province in which they reside, or (*b*) who have received their primary school instruction in Canada in English or French and reside in a province where the language in which they received that instruction is the language of the English or French linguistic minority population of the province,

have the right to have their children receive primary and secondary school instruction in that language in that province.

Continuity of language instruction

(2) Citizens of Canada of whom any child has received or is receiving primary or secondary school instruction in English or French in Canada, have the right to have all their children receive primary and secondary school instruction in the same language.

Application where numbers warrant

(3) The right of citizens of Canada under subsections (1) and (2) to have their children receive primary and secondary school instruction in the language of the English or French linguistic minority population of a province

(*a*) applies wherever in the province the number of children of citizens who have such a right is sufficient to warrant the provision to them out of public funds of minority language instruction; and

(*b*) includes, where the number of those children so warrants, the right to have them receive that instruction in minority language educational facilities provided out of public funds.

Enforcement

Enforcement of guaranteed rights and freedoms

24. (1) Anyone whose rights or freedoms, as guaranteed by this Charter, have been infringed or denied may apply to a court of competent jurisdiction to obtain such remedy as the court considers appropriate and just in the circumstances.

Exclusion of evidence bringing administration of justice into disrepute

(2) Where, in proceedings under subsection (1), a court concludes that evidence was obtained in a manner that infringed or denied any rights or freedoms guaranteed by this Charter, the evidence shall be excluded if it is established that, having regard to all the circumstances, the admission of it in the proceedings would bring the administration of justice into disrepute.

General

Aboriginal rights and freedoms not affected by Charter

25. The guarantee in this Charter of certain rights and freedoms shall not be construed so as to abrogate or derogate from any aboriginal, treaty or other rights or freedoms that pertain to the aboriginal peoples of Canada including

(*a*) any rights or freedoms that have been recognized by the Royal Proclamation of October 7, 1763; and

(*b*) any rights or freedoms that may be acquired by the aboriginal peoples of Canada by way of land claims settlement.

Other rights and freedoms not affected by Charter

26. The guarantee in this Charter of certain rights and freedoms shall not be construed as denying the existence of any other rights or freedoms that exist in Canada.

Multicultural heritage

27. This Charter shall be interpreted in a manner consistent with the preservation and enhancement of the multicultural heritage of Canadians.

Rights guaranteed equally to both sexes

28. Notwithstanding anything in this Charter except section 33, the rights and freedoms referred to in it are guaranteed equally to male and female persons.

Rights respecting certain schools preserved

29. Nothing in this Charter abrogates or derogates from any rights or privileges guaranteed by or under the Constitution of Canada in respect of denominational, separate or dissentient schools.

Application to territories and
territorial authorities

30. A reference in this Charter to a province or to the legislative assembly
or legislature of a province shall be deemed to include a reference to the Yukon
Territory and the Northwest Territories, or to the appropriate legislative
authority thereof, as the case may be.

Legislative powers not extended

31. Nothing in this Charter extends the legislative powers of any body or
authority.

Application of Charter

Application of Charter

32. (1) This Charter applies

(*a*) to the Parliament and government of Canada in respect of all matters
within the authority of Parliament including all matters relating to the
Yukon Territory and Northwest Territories; and

(*b*) to the legislature and government of each province in respect of all
matters within the authority of the legislature of each province.

Exception

(2) Notwithstanding subsection (1), section 15 shall not have effect until
three years after this section comes into force.

Exception where express declaration

33. (1) Parliament or the legislature of a province may expressly declare in
an Act of Parliament or of the legislature, as the case may be, that the Act or a
provision thereof shall operate notwithstanding a provision included in section
2 or sections 7 to 15 of this Charter, or section 28 of this Charter in its
application to discrimination based on sex referred to in section 15.

Operation of exception

(2) An Act or a provision of an Act in respect of which a declaration made
under this section is in effect shall have such operation as it would have but for
the provision of this Charter referred to in the declaration.

Five year limitation

(3) A declaration made under subsection (1) shall cease to have effect five
years after it comes into force or on such earlier date as may be specified in the
declaration.

Re-enactment

(4) Parliament or a legislature of a province may re-enact a declaration made
under subsection (1).

Five year limitation

(5) Subsection (3) applies in respect of a re-enactment made under
subsection (4).

Citation

Citation

34. This Part may be cited as the *Canadian Charter of Rights and Freedoms*.

PART II

EQUALIZATION AND REGIONAL DISPARITIES

Commitment to promote equal
opportunities

35. (1) Without altering the legislative authority of Parliament or of the
provincial legislatures, or the rights of any of them with respect to the
exercise of their legislative authority, Parliament and the legislatures, together
with the government of Canada and the provincial governments, are
committed to

(*a*) promoting equal opportunities for the well-being of Canadians;

(*b*) furthering economic development to reduce disparity in opportunities;
and

(*c*) providing essential public services of reasonable quality to all Canadians.

Commitment respecting public
services

(2) Parliament and the government of Canada are committed to the
principle of making equalization payments to ensure that provincial
governments have sufficient revenues to provide reasonably comparable levels
of public services at reasonably comparable levels of taxation.

PART III

CONSTITUTIONAL CONFERENCE

Constitutional conference

36. (1) A constitutional conference composed of the Prime Minister of Canada and the first ministers of the provinces shall be convened by the Prime Minister of Canada within one year after this Part comes into force.

Participation of aboriginal peoples

(2) The conference convened under subsection (1) shall have included in its agenda an item respecting constitutional matters that directly affect the aboriginal peoples of Canada, including the identification and definition of the rights of those peoples to be included in the Constitution of Canada, and the Prime Minister of Canada shall invite representatives of those peoples to participate in the discussions on that item.

Participation of territories

(3) The Prime Minister of Canada shall invite elected representatives of the governments of the Yukon Territory and the Northwest Territories to participate in the discussions on any item on the agenda of the conference convened under subsection (1) that, in the opinion of the Prime Minister, directly affects the Yukon Territory and the Northwest Territories.

PART IV

PROCEDURE FOR AMENDING CONSTITUTION OF CANADA

General procedure for amending Constitution of Canada

37. (1) An amendment to the Constitution of Canada may be made by proclamation issued by the Governor General under the Great Seal of Canada where so authorized by

(*a*) resolutions of the Senate and House of Commons; and

(*b*) resolutions of the legislative assemblies of at least two-thirds of the provinces that have, in the aggregate, according to the then latest general census, at least fifty per cent of the population of all the provinces.

Majority of members

(2) An amendment made under subsection (1) that derogates from the legislative powers, the proprietary rights or any other rights or privileges of the legislature or government of a province shall require a resolution supported by a majority of the members of each of the Senate, the House of Commons and the legislative assemblies required under subsection (1).

Expression of dissent

(3) An amendment referred to in subsection (2) shall not have effect in a province the legislative assembly of which has expressed its dissent thereto by resolution supported by a majority of its members prior to the issue of the proclamation to which the amendment relates unless that legislative assembly, subsequently, by resolution supported by a majority of its members, revokes its dissent and authorizes the amendment.

Revocation of dissent

(4) A resolution of dissent made for the purposes of subsection (3) may be revoked at any time before or after the issue of the proclamation to which it relates.

Restriction on proclamation

38. (1) A proclamation shall not be issued under subsection 37(1) before the expiration of one year from the adoption of the resolution initiating the amendment procedure thereunder, unless the legislative assembly of each province has previously adopted a resolution of assent or dissent.

Idem

(2) A proclamation shall not be issued under subsection 37(1) after the expiration of three years from the adoption of the resolution initiating the amendment procedure thereunder.

Compensation

39. Where an amendment is made under subsection 37(1) that transfers provincial legislative powers relating to education or other cultural matters from provincial legislatures to Parliament, Canada shall provide reasonable compensation to any province to which the amendment does not apply.

Amendment by unanimous consent

40. An amendment to the Constitution of Canada in relation to the following matters may be made by proclamation issued by the Governor General under the Great Seal of Canada only where authorized by resolutions of the Senate and House of Commons and of the legislative assembly of each province:

(*a*) the office of the Queen, the Governor General and the Lieutenant Governor of a province;

(*b*) the right of a province to a number of members in the House of Commons not less than the number of Senators by which the province is entitled to be represented at the time this Part comes into force;

(*c*) subject to section 42, the use of the English or the French language;

(*d*) the composition of the Supreme Court of Canada; and

(*e*) an amendment to this Part.

Amendment by general procedure

41. (1) An amendment to the Constitution of Canada in relation to the following matters may be made only in accordance with subsection 37(1):

(*a*) the principle of proportionate representation of the provinces in the House of Commons prescribed by the Constitution of Canada;

(*b*) the powers of the Senate and the method of selecting Senators;

(*c*) the number of members by which a province is entitled to be represented in the Senate and the residence qualifications of Senators;

(*d*) subject to paragraph 40(*d*), the Supreme Court of Canada;

(*e*) the extension of existing provinces into the territories; and

(*f*) notwithstanding any other law or practice, the establishment of new provinces.

Exception

(2) Subsections 37(2) to (4) do not apply in respect of amendments in relation to matters referred to in subsection (1).

Amendment of provisions relating to some but not all provinces

42. An amendment to the Constitution of Canada in relation to any provision that applies to one or more, but not all, provinces, including

(*a*) any alteration to boundaries between provinces, and

(*b*) any amendment to any provision that relates to the use of the English or the French language within a province,

may be made by proclamation issued by the Governor General under the Great Seal of Canada only where so authorized by resolutions of the Senate and House of Commons and of the legislative assembly of each province to which the amendment applies.

Amendments by Parliament

43. Subject to sections 40 and 41, Parliament may exclusively make laws amending the Constitution of Canada in relation to the executive government of Canada or the Senate and House of Commons.

Amendments by provincial legislatures

44. Subject to section 40, the legislature of each province may exclusively make laws amending the constitution of the province.

Initiation of amendment procedures

45. (1) The procedures for amendment under sections 37, 40, 41 and 42 may be initiated either by the Senate or the House of Commons or by the legislative assembly of a province.

Revocation of authorization

(2) A resolution of assent made for the purposes of this Part may be revoked at any time before the issue of a proclamation authorized by it.

Amendments without Senate resolution

46. (1) An amendment to the Constitution of Canada made by proclamation under section 37, 40, 41 or 42 may be made without a resolution of the Senate authorizing the issue of the proclamation if, within one hundred and eighty days after the adoption by the House of Commons of a resolution authorizing its issue, the Senate has not adopted such a resolution and if, at any time after the expiration of that period, the House of Commons again adopts the resolution.

Computation of period

(2) Any period when Parliament is prorogued or dissolved shall not be counted in computing the one hundred and eighty day period referred to in subsection (1).

Advice to issue proclamation

47. The Queen's Privy Council for Canada shall advise the Governor General to issue a proclamation under this Part forthwith on the adoption of the resolutions required for an amendment made by proclamation under this Part.

Constitutional conference

48. A constitutional conference composed of the Prime Minister of Canada and the first ministers of the provinces shall be convened by the Prime Minister of Canada within fifteen years after this Part comes into force to review the provisions of this Part.

PART V

AMENDMENT TO THE CONSTITUTION ACT, 1867

Amendment to *Constitution Act, 1867*

49. The *Constitution Act, 1867* (formerly named the *British North America Act, 1867*) is amended by adding thereto, immediately after section 92 thereof, the following heading and section:

"Non-Renewable Natural Resources, Forestry Resources and Electrical Energy

Laws respecting non-renewable natural resources, forestry resources and electrical energy

92A. (1) In each province, the legislature may exclusively make laws in relation to

(*a*) exploration for non-renewable natural resources in the province;

(*b*) development, conservation and management of non-renewable natural resources and forestry resources in the province, including laws in relation to the rate of primary production therefrom; and

(*c*) development, conservation and management of sites and facilities in the province for the generation and production of electrical energy.

Export from provinces of resources

(2) In each province, the legislature may make laws in relation to the export from the province to another part of Canada of the primary production from non-renewable natural resources and forestry resources in the province and the production from facilities in the province for the generation of electrical energy, but such laws may not authorize or provide for discrimination in prices or in supplies exported to another part of Canada.

Authority of Parliament

(3) Nothing in subsection (2) derogates from the authority of Parliament to enact laws in relation to the matters referred to in that subsection and, where such a law of Parliament and a law of a province conflict, the law of Parliament prevails to the extent of the conflict.

Taxation of resources

(4) In each province, the legislature may make laws in relation to the raising of money by any mode or system of taxation in respect of

(*a*) non-renewable natural resources and forestry resources in the province and the primary production therefrom, and

(*b*) sites and facilities in the province for the generation of electrical energy and the production therefrom,

whether or not such production is exported in whole or in part from the province, but such laws may not authorize or provide for taxation that differentiates between production exported to another part of Canada and production not exported from the province.

"Primary production"

(5) The expression "primary production" has the meaning assigned by the Sixth Schedule.

Existing powers or rights

(6) Nothing in subsections (1) to (5) derogates from any powers or rights that a legislature or government of a province had immediately before the coming into force of this section.''

Idem

50. The said Act is further amended by adding thereto the following Schedule:

"THE SIXTH SCHEDULE

Primary Production from Non-Renewable Natural Resources and Forestry Resources

1. For the purposes of section 92A of this Act,

(*a*) production from a non-renewable natural resource is primary production therefrom if

(i) it is in the form in which it exists upon its recovery or severance from its natural state, or

(ii) it is a product resulting from processing or refining the resource, and is not a manufactured product or a product resulting from refining crude oil, refining upgraded heavy crude oil, refining gases or liquids derived from coal or refining a synthetic equivalent of crude oil; and

(*b*) production from a forestry resource is primary production therefrom if it consists of sawlogs, poles, lumber, wood chips, sawdust or any other primary wood product, or wood pulp, and is not a product manufactured from wood.''

PART VI

GENERAL

Primacy of Constitution of Canada

51. (1) The Constitution of Canada is the supreme law of Canada, and any law that is inconsistent with the provisions of the Constitution is, to the extent of the inconsistency, of no force or effect.

Constitution of Canada

(2) The Constitution of Canada includes

(*a*) the *Canada Act*, including this Act;

(*b*) the Acts and orders referred to in Schedule I; and

(*c*) any amendment to any Act or order referred to in paragraph (*a*) or (*b*).

Amendments to Constitution of Canada

(3) Amendments to the Constitution of Canada shall be made only in accordance with the authority contained in the Constitution of Canada.

Repeals and new names

52. (1) The enactments referred to in Column I of Schedule I are hereby repealed or amended to the extent indicated in Column II thereof and, unless repealed, shall continue as law in Canada under the names set out in Column III thereof.

Consequential amendments

(2) Every enactment, except the *Canada Act*, that refers to an enactment referred to in Schedule I by the name in Column I thereof is hereby amended by substituting for that name the corresponding name in Column III thereof, and any British North America Act not referred to in Schedule I may be cited as the *Constitution Act* followed by the year and number, if any, of its enactment.

Repeal and consequential amendments

53. Part III is repealed on the day that is one year after this Part comes into force and this section may be repealed and this Act renumbered, consequential upon the repeal of Part III and this section, by proclamation issued by the Governor General under the Great Seal of Canada.

French version of Constitution of Canada

54. A French version of the portions of the Constitution of Canada referred to in Schedule I shall be prepared by the Minister of Justice of Canada as expeditiously as possible and, when any portion thereof sufficient to warrant action being taken has been so prepared, it shall be put forward for enactment by proclamation issued by the Governor General under the Great Seal of Canada pursuant to the procedure then applicable to an amendment of the same provisions of the Constitution of Canada.

English and French versions of certain constitutional texts

55. Where any portion of the Constitution of Canada has been or is enacted in English and French or where a French version of any portion of the Constitution is enacted pursuant to section 54, the English and French versions of that portion of the Constitution are equally authoritative.

English and French versions of this Act

56. The English and French versions of this Act are equally authoritative.

Commencement

57. Subject to section 58, this Act shall come into force on a day to be fixed by proclamation issued by the Queen or the Governor General under the Great Seal of Canada.

Commencement of paragraph 23(1)(*a*) in respect of Quebec

58. (1) Paragraph 23(1)(*a*) shall come into force in respect of Quebec on a day to be fixed by proclamation issued by the Queen or the Governor General under the Great Seal of Canada.

Authorization of Quebec

(2) A proclamation under subsection (1) shall be issued only where authorized by the legislative assembly or government of Quebec.

Repeal of this section

(3) This section may be repealed on the day paragraph 23(1)(*a*) comes into force in respect of Quebec and this Act amended and renumbered, consequential upon the repeal of this section, by proclamation issued by the Queen or the Governor General under the Great Seal of Canada.

Short title and citations

59. This Act may be cited as the *Constitution Act, 1981*, and the Constitution Acts 1867 to 1975 (No. 2) and this Act may be cited together as the *Constitution Acts, 1867 to 1981*.

SCHEDULE I TO THE CONSTITUTION ACT, 1981
MODERNIZATION OF THE CONSTITUTION

Item	Column I Act Affected	Column II Amendment	Column III New Name
1.	British North America Act, 1867, 30-31 Vict., c. 3 (U.K.)	(1) Section 1 is repealed and the following substituted therefor: "1. This Act may be cited as the *Constitution Act, 1867*." (2) Section 20 is repealed. (3) Class 1 of section 91 is repealed. (4) Class 1 of section 92 is repealed.	Constitution Act, 1867

Item	Act Affected	Amendment	New Name
2.	An Act to amend and continue the Act 32-33 Victoria chapter 3; and to establish and provide for the Government of the Province of Manitoba, 1870, 33 Vict., c. 3 (Can.)	(1) The long title is repealed and the following substituted therefor: "*Manitoba Act, 1870.*" (2) Section 20 is repealed.	Manitoba Act, 1870
3.	Order of Her Majesty in Council admitting Rupert's Land and the North-Western Territory into the union, dated the 23rd day of June, 1870		Rupert's Land and North-Western Territory Order
4.	Order of Her Majesty in Council admitting British Columbia into the Union, dated the 16th day of May, 1871		British Columbia Terms of Union
5.	British North America Act, 1871, 34-35 Vict., c. 28 (U.K.)	Section 1 is repealed and the following substituted therefor: "1. This Act may be cited as the *Constitution Act, 1871.*"	Constitution Act, 1871
6.	Order of Her Majesty in Council admitting Prince Edward Island into the Union, dated the 26th day of June, 1873		Prince Edward Island Terms of Union
7.	Parliament of Canada Act, 1875, 38-39 Vict., c. 38 (U.K.)		Parliament of Canada Act, 1875
8.	Order of Her Majesty in Council admitting all British possessions and Territories in North America and islands adjacent thereto into the Union, dated the 31st day of July, 1880		Adjacent Territories Order
9.	British North America Act, 1886, 49-50 Vict., c. 35 (U.K.)	Section 3 is repealed and the following substituted therefor: "3. This Act may be cited as the *Constitution Act, 1886.*"	Constitution Act, 1886
10.	Canada (Ontario Boundary) Act, 1889, 52-53 Vict., c. 28 (U.K.)		Canada (Ontario Boundary) Act, 1889
11.	Canadian Speaker (Appointment of Deputy) Act, 1895, 2nd Sess., 59 Vict., c. 3 (U.K.)	The Act is repealed.	

Item	Act Affected	Amendment	New Name
12.	The Alberta Act, 1905, 4-5 Edw. VII, c. 3 (Can.)		Alberta Act
13.	The Saskatchewan Act, 1905, 4-5 Edw. VII, c. 42 (Can.)		Saskatchewan Act
14.	British North America Act, 1907, 7 Edw. VII, c. 11 (U.K.)	Section 2 is repealed and the following substituted therefor: "2. This Act may be cited as the *Constitution Act, 1907*."	Constitution Act, 1907
15.	British North America Act, 1915, 5-6 Geo. V, c. 45 (U.K.)	Section 3 is repealed and the following substituted therefor: "3. This Act may be cited as the *Constitution Act, 1915*."	Constitution Act, 1915
16.	British North America Act, 1930, 20-21 Geo. V, c. 26 (U.K.)	Section 3 is repealed and the following substituted therefor: "3. This Act may be cited as the *Constitution Act, 1930*."	Constitution Act, 1930
17.	Statute of Westminster, 1931, 22 Geo. V, c. 4 (U.K.)	In so far as they apply to Canada, (*a*) section 4 is repealed; and (*b*) subsection 7(1) is repealed.	Statute of Westminster, 1931
18.	British North America Act, 1940, 3-4 Geo. VI, c. 36 (U.K.)	Section 2 is repealed and the following substituted therefor: "2. This Act may be cited as the *Constitution Act, 1940*."	Constitution Act, 1940
19.	British North America Act, 1943, 6-7 Geo. VI, c. 30 (U.K.)	The Act is repealed.	
20.	British North America Act, 1946, 9-10 Geo. VI, c. 63 (U.K.)	The Act is repealed.	
21.	British North America Act, 1949, 12-13 Geo. VI, c. 81 (U.K.)	Section 3 is repealed and the following substituted therefor: "3. This Act may be cited as the *Newfoundland Act*."	Newfoundland Act
22.	British North America (No. 2) Act, 1949, 13 Geo. VI, c. 81 (U.K.)	The Act is repealed.	
23.	British North America Act, 1951, 14-15 Geo. VI, c. 32 (U.K.)	The Act is repealed.	

Item	Act Affected	Amendment	New Name
24.	British North America Act, 1952, 1 Eliz. II, c. 15 (Can.)	The Act is repealed.	
25.	British North America Act, 1960, 9 Eliz. II, c. 2 (U.K.)	Section 2 is repealed and the following substituted therefor: "2. This Act may be cited as the *Constitution Act, 1960*."	Constitution Act, 1960
26.	British North America Act, 1964, 12-13 Eliz. II, c. 73 (U.K.)	Section 2 is repealed and the following substituted therefor: "2. This Act may be cited as the *Constitution Act, 1964*."	Constitution Act, 1964
27.	British North America Act, 1965, 14 Eliz. II, c. 4, Part I (Can.)	Section 2 is repealed and the following substituted therefor: "2. This Part may be cited as the *Constitution Act, 1965*."	Constitution Act, 1965
28.	British North America Act, 1974, 23 Eliz. II, c. 13, Part I (Can.)	Section 3, as amended by 25-26 Eliz. II, c. 28, s. 38(1) (Can.) is repealed and the following substituted therefor: "3. This Part may be cited as the *Constitution Act, 1974*."	Constitution Act, 1974
29.	British North America Act, 1975, 23-24 Eliz. II, c. 28, Part I (Can.)	Section 3, as amended by 25-26 Eliz. II, c. 28, s. 31 (Can.) is repealed and the following substituted therefor: "3. This Part may be cited as the *Constitution Act (No. 1), 1975*."	Constitution Act (No. 1), 1975
30.	British North America Act (No. 2), 1975, 23-24 Eliz. II, c. 53 (Can.)	Section 3 is repealed and the following substituted therefor: "3. This Act may be cited as the *Constitution Act (No. 2), 1975*."	Constitution Act (No. 2), 1975

(b) Amendments to the Proposed Resolution for a Joint Address to Her Majesty the Queen Respecting the Constitution of Canada (as Altered by the November 5, 1981, First Ministers' Agreement on the Constitution and Tabled in the House of Commons, November 20, 1981, and as Amended Subsequently from Time to Time in the Course of the Debates)*

HOUSE OF COMMONS

Debates, Monday, November 23, 1981

Madam Speaker ruled the proposed amendment receivable.

Whereupon, *Mr. Clark* (Yellowhead), seconded by Miss MacDonald, moved in amendment thereto, — That the proposed *Constitution Act 1981* be amended

(*a*) by striking out Clause 28 and substituting the following:

28. Notwithstanding anything in this Charter, the rights and freedoms referred to in it are guaranteed equally to male and female persons.

(*b*) by striking out subclause 33(1) and substituting the following:

33.(1) Parliament or the legislature of a province may expressly declare in an Act of Parliament or of the legislature, as the case may be, that the Act or a provision thereof shall operate notwithstanding a provision included in section 2 or sections 7 to 15 of this Charter.   p. 13082

November 24, 1981

After further debate, the question being put on the amendment, it was agreed to on the following division: (Yeas, 222;   Nays, 0)   p. 13200

Debates, Tuesday, November 24, 1981

Mr. Munro (Hamilton East), seconded by Mr. Gingras, moved in amendment thereto, — That the proposed *Constitution Act 1981* contained in the motion in the name of the Minister of Justice (Government Business, Government Motion No. 56), as printed in the *Order Paper* of Monday, November 23, 1981, be amended

(*a*) by adding, immediately after line 19 on page 24 of the *Order Paper*, the following:

"PART II

RIGHTS OF THE ABORIGINAL PEOPLES
OF CANADA

35. (1) The existing aboriginal and treaty rights of the aboriginal peoples of Canada are hereby recognized and affirmed.

(2) In this Act, "aboriginal peoples of Canada" includes the Indian, Inuit and Métis peoples of Canada."

(*b*) by renumbering the subsequent parts and clauses accordingly.   p. 13200

See Mr. Munro's amendment Nov. 26, 1981.

Debates, Wednesday, November 25, 1981

By unanimous consent, it was ordered, — That the motion of the Minister of Indian Affairs and Northern Development in amendment to the motion of the Minister of Justice be amended in the French version to read as follows:

"*a*) insertion, après la ligne 19, parge 24 du *Feuilleton*, de ce qui suit:

«PARTIE II

DROITS DES PEUPLES AUTOCHTONES DU
CANADA

35. (1) Les droits existants — ancestraux ou issus de traités — des peuples autochtones du Canada sont reconnus et confirmés.

(2) Dans la présente loi, «peuples autochtones du Canada» s'entend notamment des Indiens, des Inuit et des Métis du Canada.»,

---

* Compiled by Janet Brooks, Bibliographies and Compilations Section, Information and Reference Branch, Library of Parliament, Ottawa.

b) les changements de numéros de partie et d'article qui en découlent.''   p. 13292

Debates, Thursday, November 26, 1981

And on the motion, *as amended in the French version*, of *Mr. Munro* (Hamilton East), seconded by Mr. Gingras, in amendment thereto, — That the proposed *Constitution Act 1981* contained in the motion in the name of the Minister of Justice (Government Business, Government Motion No. 56), as printed in the *Order Paper* of Monday, November 23, 1981, be amended

(*a*) by adding, immediately after line 19 on page 24 of the *Order Paper*, the following:

''PART II

RIGHTS OF THE ABORIGINAL PEOPLES OF CANADA

35. (1) The existing aboriginal and treaty rights of the aboriginal peoples of Canada are hereby recognized and affirmed.

(2) In this Act, ''aboriginal peoples of Canada'' includes the Indian, Inuit and Métis peoples of Canada.''

(*b*) by renumbering the subsequent parts and clauses accordingly.

After further debate, the question being put on the amendment, as amended in the French version, it was agreed to on the following division:
(Yeas, 222;   Nays, 0)   p. 13345

Debates, Tuesday, November 24, 1981

Mr. Fulton, seconded by Mr. Broadbent, moved in amendment to the amendment, — That the amendment be amended by deleting the word ''existing''.   p. 13219

November 25, 1981

After further debate, the question being put on the amendment to the amendment, it was negatived on the following division:
(Yeas, 32;   Nays, 179)   p. 13292

Debates, Thursday, November 26, 1981

Mr. Nielsen, seconded by Mr. Baker (Nepean — Carleton), moved in amendment thereto, — That the proposed *Constitution Act 1981* be amended by striking out paragraphs (*e*) and (*f*) of subsection 41(1).   p. 13346

November 27, 1981

After further debate, the question being put on the amendment, it was negatived on the following division:
(Yeas, 85;   Nays, 117)   p. 13435

Debates, Friday, November 27, 1981

Mr. Crombie, seconded by Mr. McGrath, moved in amendment thereto, — That the proposed *Constitution Act 1981* be amended by adding immediately after clause 31 of Part I the following new clause: p. 13436

''32. Nothing in this Charter affects the authority of Parliament to legislate in respect of abortion.''

The House divided on the amendment (Mr. Crombie) which was negatived on the following division:
(Yeas, 60;   Nays, 129)   p. 13442

Debates, Monday, November 30, 1981

Mr. Epp, seconded by Miss MacDonald, moved in amendment thereto, — That the proposed *Constitution Act 1981* be amended by striking out Section 40 and substituting the following therefor:

''40. In the event that a province dissents from an amendment conferring legislative jurisdiction on Parliament, the Government of Canada shall provide reasonable compensation to the government of that province, taking into account the *per capita* costs to exercise that jurisdiction in the provinces which have approved the amendment.''   p. 13492

December 2, 1981

it was negatived on the following division:
(Yeas, 87;   Nays, 174)   p. 13661

Debates, Monday, November 30, 1981

Mr. Broadbent, seconded by Mr. Deans, moved in amendment to the amendment, — That the amendment be amended by striking out, in the first line, the words ''a province'' and substituting the words ''the province of Québec.''   p. 13497

December 2, 1981

it was negatived on the following division:
(Yeas, 34;   Nays, 235)   p. 13660

Debates, Tuesday, December 1, 1981

Pursuant to Order made Friday, November 27, 1981, the following amendment was deemed to have been moved in the name of *Mr. Manly*, seconded by Mr. Fulton:

That the proposed *Constitution Act 1981* be amended
(*a*) by adding immediately after section 47 the following new section:

''48. An amendment to the Constitution of Canada in relation to the rights of the aboriginal peoples of Canada set out in Part II may be made by proclamation issued by the Governor General under the Great Seal of Canada only in accordance with the following procedure:

(*a*) in the Yukon and Northwest Territories, when so authorized by resolution of a two-thirds majority vote in the Senate and House of Commons and with the consent of a majority of each of the aboriginal peoples so affected;

(*b*) in the provinces, when so authorized in accordance with section 42 and with the consent of a majority of each of the aboriginal peoples so affected; and

(*c*) for the purposes referred to in this section, consent of the aboriginal peoples shall be obtained by a procedure determined by the Government of Canada and the aboriginal peoples of Canada.''; and

(*b*) by renumbering the subsequent sections accordingly.

p. 13616

December 2, 1981

it was negatived on the following division:
(Yeas, 33; Nays, 236)   p. 13662

SENATE

Debates, Thursday, December 3, 1981

In amendment, the *Honourable Senator Roblin*, P.C., moved, seconded by the Honourable Senator Tremblay:

That the proposed Constitution Act 1981 be amended by striking out Section 40 and substituting the following therefor:

"40. In the event that a province dissents from an amendment conferring legislative jurisdiction on Parliament, the Government of Canada shall provide reasonable compensation to the government of that province, taking into account the *per capita* costs to exercise that jurisdiction in the provinces which have approved the amendment.''   p. 3157

After debate,

Pursuant to the Order adopted by the Senate on 2nd December, 1981, a recorded division on the motion in amendment was deferred.

December 8, 1981

The Senate divided and the names being called they were taken down
(Yeas, 29; Nays, 51)   p. 3394

So it was resolved in the negative.

Debates, Thursday, December 3, 1981

In amendment, the *Honourable Senator Walker*, P.C., moved, seconded by the Honourable Senator Macquarrie:

That the proposed Constitution Act 1981 be amended by deleting therefrom Section 47 and making the appropriate changes by re-numbering the remaining Sections accordingly.

Pursuant to the Order adopted by the Senate on 2nd December, 1981, a recorded division on the motion in amendment was deferred.   p. 3175

December 8, 1981

It was —

Resolved in the negative, on division.   p. 3395

Debates, Friday, December 4, 1981

In amendment, the *Honourable Senator Sullivan* moved, seconded by the Honourable Senator Macdonald:

That Section 7 of the proposed Constitution Act 1981 be amended to read as follows:

"7. Everyone, including the unborn child, has the right to life, which life begins at conception and which right is assertable from the moment of conception. Everyone has the right to liberty and security of the person and the right not to be deprived thereof except in accordance with the principles of fundamental justice.''   p. 3218

Pursuant to the Order adopted by the Senate on 2nd December, 1981, a recorded division on the motion in amendment was deferred.

December 8, 1981

The Senate divided and the names being called they were taken down
(Yeas, 16; Nays, 60)   p. 3395

So it was resolved in the negative.

Debates, Friday, December 4, 1981

In amendment, the *Honourable Senator Tremblay* moved, seconded by the Honourable Senator Flynn, P.C.:

That Section 59 of the proposed Constitution Act 1981 be amended as follows:

(a) by substituting, in the first line of subsection (1), the words "Paragraphs 23(1)(*a*), 23(1)(*b*) and subsections 23(2) and 23(3)'' for the words "Paragraph 23(1)(*a*)'';

(b) by substituting, in the second line of subsection (3), the words "paragraph 23(1)(*a*) or 23(1)(*b*) or subsection 23(3) or 23(3)'' for the words "paragraph 23(1)(*a*)''.

After debate,   p. 3225
Pursuant to the Order adopted by the Senate on 2nd December, 1981, a recorded division on the motion in amendment was deferred.

December 8, 1981

The Senate divided and the names being called they were taken down
(Yeas, 27; Nays, 53) p. 3396
So it was resolved in the negative.

Debates, Monday, December 7, 1981

In amendment, the *Honourable Senator Macquarrie* moved, seconded by the Honourable Senator Nurgitz:

That the proposed Constitution Act 1981 be amended by striking out paragraphs (*e*) and (*f*) of subsection 42(1).
After debate,   p. 3270
Pursuant to the Order adopted by the Senate on 2nd December, 1981, a recorded division on the motion in amendment was deferred.

December 8, 1981

The Senate divided and the names being called they were taken down
(Yeas, 26; Nays, 55) p. 3397
So it was resolved in the negative.

Debates, Monday, December 7, 1981

In amendment, the *Honourable Senator Bell* moved, seconded by the Honourable Senator Deschatelets, P.C.:

That the proposed Constitution Act 1981 be amended as follows:

(a) by deleting therefrom Parts I, II, III, IV and VI and Sections 54 and 59 of Part VII;

(b) by deleting the first line of Section 58 and replacing it with the following:

"This Act shall"; and

(c) by renumbering the remaining Parts and Sections accordingly.   p. 3311
Pursuant to the Order adopted by the Senate on 2nd December, 1981, a recorded division on the motion in amendment was deferred.

December 8, 1981

The Senate divided and the names being called they were taken down
(Yeas, 26; Nays, 52) p. 3398
So it was resolved in the negative.

Debates, Tuesday, December 8, 1981

In amendment, the *Honourable Senator Haidasz*, P.C., moved, seconded by the Honourable Senator McGrand:

That the proposed Constitution Act 1981 be amended by

(a) adding after Section 31 the following new Section:

"32. Nothing in this Charter precludes Parliament from legislating on the rights of unborn children"; and

(b) renumbering the subsequent Sections accordingly.
After debate,   p. 3372
Pursuant to the Order adopted by the Senate on 2nd December, 1981, a recorded division on the motion in amendment was deferred.

The Senate divided and the names being called they were taken down
(Yeas, 28; Nays, 50) p. 3398
So it was resolved in the negative.

(c) Text of the Resolution Respecting the Constitution of Canada Adopted by the House of Commons on December 2, 1981 and by the Senate on December 8, 1981

Catalogue no. CP45-22/1981

THAT, WHEREAS in the past certain amendments to the Constitution of Canada have been made by Parliament of the United Kingdom at the request and with the consent of Canada;

AND WHEREAS it is in accord with the status of Canada as an independent state that Canadians be able to amend their Constitution in Canada in all respects;

AND WHEREAS it is also desirable to provide in the Constitution of Canada for the recognition of certain fundamental rights and freedoms and to make other amendments to that Constitution;

A respectful address be presented to Her Majesty the Queen in the following words:

To the Queen's Most Excellent Majesty:
Most Gracious Sovereign:

We, Your Majesty's loyal subjects, the House of Commons of Canada in Parliament assembled, respectfully approach Your Majesty, requesting that you may graciously be pleased to cause to be laid before the Parliament of the United Kingdom a measure containing the recitals and clauses hereinafter set forth:

An Act to give effect to a request by the Senate and House of Commons of Canada	ANNEXE A — SCHEDULE A Loi donnant suite à une demande du Sénat et de la Chambre des communes du Canada
Whereas Canada has requested and consented to the enactment of an Act of the Parliament of the United Kingdom to give effect to the provisions hereinafter set forth and the Senate and the House of Commons of Canada in Parliament assembled have submitted an address to Her Majesty requesting that Her Majesty may graciously be pleased to cause a Bill to be laid before the Parliament of the United Kingdom for that purpose.	Sa Très Excellente Majesté la Reine, considérant : qu'à la demande et avec le consentement du Canada, le Parlement du Royaume-Uni est invité à adopter une loi visant à donner effet aux dispositions énoncées ci-après et que le Sénat et la Chambre des communes du Canada réunis en Parlement ont présenté une adresse demandant à Sa Très Gracieuse Majesté de bien vouloir faire déposer devant le Parlement du Royaume-Uni un projet de loi à cette fin,
Be it therefore enacted by the Queen's Most Excellent Majesty, by and with the advice and consent of the Lords Spiritual and Temporal, and Commons, in this present Parliament assembled, and by the authority of the same, as follows:	sur l'avis et du consentement des Lords spirituels et temporels et des Communes réunis en Parlement, et par l'autorité de celui-ci, édicte :

Constitution Act 1981 enacted

1. The *Constitution Act, 1981* set out in Schedule B to this Act is hereby enacted for and shall have the force of law in Canada and shall come into force as provided in that Act.

1. La *Loi constitutionnelle de 1981*, énoncée à l'annexe B, est édictée pour le Canada et y a force de loi. Elle entre en vigueur conformément à ses dispositions.

Adoption de la *Loi constitutionnelle de 1981*

Termination of power to legislate for Canada

2. No Act of the Parliament of the United Kingdom passed after the *Constitution Act, 1981* comes into force shall extend to Canada as part of its law.

2. Les lois adoptées par le Parlement du Royaume-Uni après l'entrée en vigueur de la *Loi constitutionnelle de 1981* ne font pas partie du droit du Canada.

Cessation du pouvoir de légiférer pour le Canada

French version   **3.** So far as it is not contained in Schedule B, the French version of this Act is set out in Schedule A to this Act and has the same authority in Canada as the English version thereof.

3. La partie de la version française de la présente loi qui figure à l'annexe A a force de loi au Canada au même titre que la version anglaise correspondante.   Version française

Short title   **4.** This Act may be cited as the *Canada Act*.

4. Titre abrégé de la présente loi : *Loi sur le Canada*.   Titre abrégé

SCHEDULE B

CONSTITUTION ACT, 1981

PART I

CANADIAN CHARTER OF RIGHTS AND FREEDOMS

Whereas Canada is founded upon principles that recognize the supremacy of God and the rule of law:

Guarantee of Rights and Freedoms

Rights and freedoms in Canada   **1.** The *Canadian Charter of Rights and Freedoms* guarantees the rights and freedoms set out in it subject only to such reasonable limits prescribed by law as can be demonstrably justified in a free and democratic society.

Fundamental Freedoms

Fundamental freedoms   **2.** Everyone has the following fundamental freedoms:
(*a*) freedom of conscience and religion;
(*b*) freedom of thought, belief, opinion and expression, including freedom of the press and other media of communication;
(*c*) freedom of peaceful assembly; and
(*d*) freedom of association.

Democratic Rights

Democratic rights of citizens   **3.** Every citizen of Canada has the right to vote in an election of members of the House of Commons or of a legislative assembly and to be qualified for membership therein.

Maximum duration of legislative bodies   **4.** (1) No House of Commons and no legislative assembly shall continue for longer than five years from the date fixed for the return of the writs at a general election of its members.

Continuation in special circumstances   (2) In time of real or apprehended war, invasion or insurrection, a House of Commons may be continued by Parliament and a legislative assembly may be continued by the legislature beyond five years if such continuation is not opposed by the votes of more than one-third of the members of the House of Commons or the legislative assembly, as the case may be.

Annual sitting of legislative bodies   **5.** There shall be a sitting of Parliament and of each legislature at least once every twelve months.

Mobility Rights

Mobility of citizens

6. (1) Every citizen of Canada has the right to enter, remain in and leave Canada.

Rights to move and gain livelihood

(2) Every citizen of Canada and every person who has the status of a permanent resident of Canada has the right

(*a*) to move to and take up residence in any province; and

(*b*) to pursue the gaining of a livelihood in any province.

Limitation

(3) The rights specified in subsection (2) are subject to

(*a*) any laws or practices of general application in force in a province other than those that discriminate among persons primarily on the basis of province of present or previous residence; and

(*b*) any laws providing for reasonable residency requirements as a qualification for the receipt of publicly provided social services.

Affirmative action programs

(4) Subsections (2) and (3) do not preclude any law, program or activity that has as its object the amelioration in a province of conditions of individuals in that province who are socially or economically disadvantaged if the rate of employment in that province is below the rate of employment in Canada.

Legal Rights

Life, liberty and security of person

7. Everyone has the right to life, liberty and security of the person and the right not to be deprived thereof except in accordance with the principles of fundamental justice.

Search or seizure

8. Everyone has the right to be secure against unreasonable search or seizure.

Detention or imprisonment

9. Everyone has the right not to be arbitrarily detained or imprisoned.

Arrest or detention

10. Everyone has the right on arrest or detention

(*a*) to be informed promptly of the reasons therefor;

(*b*) to retain and instruct counsel without delay and to be informed of that right; and

(*c*) to have the validity of the detention determined by way of *habeas corpus* and to be released if the detention is not lawful.

Proceedings in criminal and penal matters

11. Any person charged with an offence has the right

(*a*) to be informed without unreasonable delay of the specific offence;

(*b*) to be tried within a reasonable time;

(*c*) not to be compelled to be a witness in proceedings against that person in respect of the offence;

(*d*) to be presumed innocent until proven guilty according to law in a fair and public hearing by an independent and impartial tribunal;

(*e*) not to be denied reasonable bail without just cause;

(*f*) except in the case of an offence under military law tried before a military tribunal, to the benefit of trial by jury where the maximum punishment for the offence is imprisonment for five years or a more severe punishment;

(*g*) not to be found guilty on account of any act or omission unless, at the time of the act or omission, it constituted an offence under Canadian or international law or was criminal according to the general principles of law recognized by the community of nations;

(*h*) if finally acquitted of the offence, not to be tried for it again and, if finally found guilty and punished for the offence, not to be tried or punished for it again; and

(*i*) if found guilty of the offence and if the punishment for the offence has been varied between the time of commission and the time of sentencing, to the benefit of the lesser punishment.

Treatment or punishement

12. Everyone has the right not to be subjected to any cruel and unusual treatment or punishment.

Self-crimination

13. A witness who testifies in any proceedings has the right not to have any incriminating evidence so given used to incriminate that witness in any other proceedings, except in a prosecution for perjury or for the giving of contradictory evidence.

Interpreter

14. A party or witness in any proceedings who does not understand or speak the language in which the proceedings are conducted or who is deaf has the right to the assistance of an interpreter.

Equality Rights

Equality before and under law and equal protection and benefit of law

15. (1) Every individual is equal before and under the law and has the right to the equal protection and equal benefit of the law without discrimination and, in particular, without discrimination based on race, national or ethnic origin, colour, religion, sex, age or mental or physical disability.

Affirmative action programs

(2) Subsection (1) does not preclude any law, program or activity that has as its object the amelioration of conditions of disadvantaged individuals or groups including those that are disadvantaged because of race, national or ethnic origin, colour, religion, sex, age or mental or physical disability.

Official Languages of Canada

Official languages of Canada

16. (1) English and French are the official languages of Canada and have equality of status and equal rights and privileges as to their use in all institutions of the Parliament and government of Canada.

Official languages of New Brunswick

(2) English and French are the official languages of New Brunswick and have equality of status and equal rights and privileges as to their use in all institutions of the legislature and government of New Brunswick.

Advancement of status and use

(3) Nothing in this Charter limits the authority of Parliament or a legislature to advance the equality of status or use of English and French.

Proceedings of Parliament

17. (1) Everyone has the right to use English or French in any debates and other proceedings of Parliament.

Proceedings of New Brunswick legislature

(2) Everyone has the right to use English or French in any debates and other proceedings of the legislature of New Brunswick.

Parliamentary statutes and records

18. (1) The statutes, records and journals of Parliament shall be printed and published in English and French and both language versions are equally authoritative.

New Brunswick statues and records

(2) The statutes, records and journals of the legislature of New Brunswick shall be printed and published in English and French and both language versions are equally authoritative.

Proceedings in courts established by Parliament

19. (1) Either English or French may be used by any person in, or in any pleading in or process issuing from, any court established by Parliament.

Proceedings in New Brunswick courts

Communications by public with federal institutions

(2) Either English or French may be used by any person in, or in any pleading in or process issuing from, any court of New Brunswick.

20. (1) Any member of the public in Canada has the right to communicate with, and to receive available services from, any head or central office of an institution of the Parliament or government of Canada in English or French, and has the same right with respect to any other office of any such institution where

(*a*) there is a significant demand for communications with and services from that office in such language; or

(*b*) due to the nature of the office, it is reasonable that communications with and services from that office be available in both English and French.

Communications by public with New Brunswick institutions

(2) Any member of the public in New Brunswick has the right to communicate with, and to receive available services from, any office of an institution of the legislature or government of New Brunswick in English or French.

Continuation of existing constitutional provisions

21. Nothing in sections 16 to 20 abrogates or derogates from any right, privilege or obligation with respect to the English and French languages, or either of them, that exists or is continued by virtue of any other provision of the Constitution of Canada.

Rights and privileges preserved

22. Nothing in sections 16 to 20 abrogates or derogates from any legal or customary right or privilege acquired or enjoyed either before or after the coming into force of this Charter with respect to any language that is not English or French.

Minority Language Educational Rights

Language of instruction

23. (1) Citizens of Canada

(*a*) whose first language learned and still understood is that of the English or French linguistic minority population of the province in which they reside, or

(*b*) who have received their primary school instruction in Canada in English or French and reside in a province where the language in which they received that instruction is the language of the English or French linguistic minority population of the province,

have the right to have their children receive primary and secondary school instruction in that language in that province.

Continuity of language instruction

(2) Citizens of Canada of whom any child has received or is receiving primary or secondary school instruction in English or French in Canada, have the right to have all their children receive primary and secondary school instruction in the same language.

Application where numbers warrant

(3) The right of citizens of Canada under subsections (1) and (2) to have their children receive primary and secondary school instruction in the language of the English or French linguistic minority population of a province

(*a*) applies wherever in the province the number of children of citizens who have such a right is sufficient to warrant the provision to them out of public funds of minority language instruction; and

(*b*) includes, where the number of those children so warrants, the right to have them receive that instruction in minority language educational facilities provided out of public funds.

Enforcement

Enforcement of guaranteed rights and freedoms

24. (1) Anyone whose rights or freedoms, as guaranteed by this Charter, have been infringed or denied may apply to a court of competent jurisdiction to obtain such remedy as the court considers appropriate and just in the circumstances.

Exclusion of evidence bringing administration of justice into disrepute

(2) Where, in proceedings under subsection (1), a court concludes that evidence was obtained in a manner that infringed or denied any rights or freedoms guaranteed by this Charter, the evidence shall be excluded if it is established that, having regard to all the circumstances, the admission of it in the proceedings would bring the administration of justice into disrepute.

General

Aboriginal rights and freedoms not affected by Charter

25. The guarantee in this Charter of certain rights and freedoms shall not be construed so as to abrogate or derogate from any aboriginal, treaty or other rights or freedoms that pertain to the aboriginal peoples of Canada including

(*a*) any rights or freedoms that have been recognized by the Royal Proclamation of October 7, 1763; and

(*b*) any rights or freedoms that may be acquired by the aboriginal peoples of Canada by way of land claims settlement.

Other rights and freedoms not affected by Charter

26. The guarantee in this Charter of certain rights and freedoms shall not be construed as denying the existence of any other rights or freedoms that exist in Canada.

Multicultural heritage

27. This Charter shall be interpreted in a manner consistent with the preservation and enhancement of the multicultural heritage of Canadians.

Rights guaranteed equally to both sexes

28. Notwithstanding anything in this Charter, the rights and freedoms referred to in it are guaranteed equally to male and female persons.

Rights respecting certain schools preserved

29. Nothing in this Charter abrogates or derogates from any rights or privileges guaranteed by or under the Constitution of Canada in respect of denominational, separate or dissentient schools.

Application to territories and territorial authorities

30. A reference in this Charter to a province or to the legislative assembly or legislature of a province shall be deemed to include a reference to the Yukon Territory and the Northwest Territories, or to the appropriate legislative authority thereof, as the case may be.

Legislative powers not extended

31. Nothing in this Charter extends the legislative powers of any body or authority.

Application of Charter

Application of Charter

32. (1) This Charter applies

(*a*) to the Parliament and government of Canada in respect of all matters within the authority of Parliament including all matters relating to the Yukon Territory and Northwest Territories; and

(*b*) to the legislature and government of each province in respect of all matters within the authority of the legislature of each province.

Exception

(2) Notwithstanding subsection (1), section 15 shall not have effect until three years after this section comes into force.

Exception where express declaration

33. (1) Parliament or the legislature of a province may expressly declare in an Act of Parliament or of the legislature, as the case may be, that the Act or a provision thereof shall operate notwithstanding a provision included in section 2 or sections 7 to 15 of this Charter.

Operation of exception

(2) An Act or a provision of an Act in respect of which a declaration made under this section is in effect shall have such operation as it would have but for the provision of this Charter referred to in the declaration.

Five year limitation

(3) A declaration made under subsection (1) shall cease to have effect five years after it comes into force or on such earlier date as may be specified in the declaration.

Re-enactment

(4) Parliament or a legislature or a province may re-enact a declaration made under subsection (1).

Five year limitation

(5) Subsection (2) applies in respect of a re-enactment made under subsection (4).

Citation

Citation

34. This Part may be cited as the *Canadian Charter of Rights and Freedoms*.

PART II

RIGHTS OF THE ABORIGINAL PEOPLES OF CANADA

Recognition of existing aboriginal and treaty rights

35. (1) The existing aboriginal and treaty rights of the aboriginal peoples of Canada are hereby recognized and affirmed.

Definition of "aboriginal peoples of Canada"

(2) In this Act, "aboriginal peoples of Canada" includes the Indian, Inuit and Métis peoples of Canada.

PART III

EQUALIZATION AND REGIONAL DISPARITIES

Commitment to promote equal opportunities

36. (1) Without altering the legislative authority of Parliament or of the provincial legislatures, or the rights of any of them with respect to the exercise of their legislative authority, Parliament and the legislatures, together with the government of Canada and the provincial governments, are committed to

(*a*) promoting equal opportunities for the well-being of Canadians;

(*b*) furthering economic development to reduce disparity in opportunities; and

(*c*) providing essential public services of reasonable quality to all Canadians.

Commitment respecting public services

(2) Parliament and the government of Canada are committed to the principle of making equalization payments to ensure that provincial governments have sufficient revenues to provide reasonably comparable levels of public services at reasonably comparable levels of taxation.

PART IV

CONSTITUTIONAL CONFERENCE

Constitutional conference

37. (1) A constitutional conference composed of the Prime Minister of Canada and the first ministers of the provinces shall be convened by the Prime Minister of Canada within one year after this Part comes into force.

Participation of aboriginal peoples

(2) The conference convened under subsection (1) shall have included in its agenda an item respecting constitutional matters that directly affect the

aboriginal peoples of Canada, including the identification and definition of the rights of those peoples to be included in the Constitution of Canada, and the Prime Minister of Canada shall invite representatives of those peoples to participate in the discussions on that item.

Participation of territories

(3) The Prime Minister of Canada shall invite elected representatives of the governments of the Yukon Territory and the Northwest Territories to participate in the discussions on any item on the agenda of the conference convened under subsection (1) that, in the opinion of the Prime Minister, directly affects the Yukon Territory and the Northwest Territories.

PART V

PROCEDURE FOR AMENDING CONSTITUTION OF CANADA

General procedure for amending Constitution of Canada

38. (1) An amendment to the Constitution of Canada may be made by proclamation issued by the Governor General under the Great Seal of Canada where so authorized by

(*a*) resolutions of the Senate and House of Commons; and

(*b*) resolutions of the legislative assemblies of at least two-thirds of the provinces that have, in the aggregate, according to the then latest general census, at least fifty per cent of the population of all the provinces.

Majority of members

(2) An amendment made under subsection (1) that derogates from the legislative powers, the proprietary rights or any other rights or privileges of the legislature or government of a province shall require a resolution supported by a majority of the members of each of the Senate, the House of Commons and the legislative assemblies required under subsection (1).

Expression of dissent

(3) An amendment referred to in subsection (2) shall not have effect in a province the legislative assembly of which has expressed its dissent thereto by resolution supported by a majority of its members prior to the issue of the proclamation to which the amendment relates unless that legislative assembly, subsequently, by resolutions supported by a majority of its members, revokes its dissent and authorizes the amendment.

Revocation of dissent

(4) A resolution of dissent made for the purposes of subsection (3) may be revoked at any time before or after the issue of the proclamation to which it relates.

Restriction on proclamation

39. (1) A proclamation shall not be issued under subsection 38(1) before the expiration of one year from the adoption of the resolution initiating the amendment procedure thereunder, unless the legislative assembly of each province has previously adopted a resolution of assent or dissent.

Idem

(2) A proclamation shall not be issued under subsection 38(1) after the expiration of three years from the adoption of the resolution initiating the amendment procedure thereunder.

Compensation

40. Where an amendment is made under subsection 38(1) that transfers provincial legislative powers relating to education or other cultural matters from provincial legislatures to Parliament, Canada shall provide reasonable compensation to any province to which the amendment does not apply.

Amendment by unanimous consent

41. An amendment to the Constitution of Canada in relation to the following matters may be made by proclamation issued by the Governor General under the Great Seal of Canada only where authorized by resolutions of the Senate and House of Commons and of the legislative assembly of each province:

(*a*) the office of the Queen, the Governor General and the Lieutenant Governor of a province;

(*b*) the right of a province to a number of members in the House of Commons not less than the number of Senators by which the province is entitled to be represented at the time this Part come into force;

(*c*) subject to section 43, the use of the English or the French language;

(*d*) the composition of the Supreme Court of Canada; and

(*e*) an amendment to this Part.

Amendment by general procedure

42. (1) An amendment to the Constitution of Canada in relation to to the following matters may be made only in accordance with subsection 38(1):

(*a*) the principle of proportionate representation of the provinces in the House of Commons prescribed by the Constitution of Canada;

(*b*) the powers of the Senate and the method of selecting Senators;

(*c*) the number of members by which a province is entitled to be represented in the Senate and the residence qualifications of Senators;

(*d*) subject to paragraph 41(*d*), the Supreme Court of Canada;

(*e*) the extension of exising provinces into the territories; and

(*f*) notwithstanding any other law or practice, the establishment of new provinces.

Exception

(2) Subsections 38(2) to (4) do not apply in respect of amendments in relation to matters referred to in subsection (1).

Amendment of provisions relating to some but not all provinces

43. An amendment to the Constitution of Canada in relation to any provision that applies to one or more, but not all, provinces, including

(*a*) any alteration to boundaries between provinces, and

(*b*) any amendment to any provision that relates to the use of the English or the French language within a province,

may be made by proclamation issued by the Governor General under the Great Seal of Canada only where so authorized by resolution of the Senate and House of Commons and of the legislative assembly of each province to which the amendment applies.

Amendments by Parliament

44. Subject to sections 41 and 42, Parliament may exclusively make laws amending the Constitution of Canada in relation to the executive government of Canada or the Senate or House of Commons.

Amendments by provincial legislatures

45. Subject to section 41, the legislature of each province may exclusively make laws amending the constitution of the province.

Initiation of amendment procedures

46. (1) The procedures for amendment under sections 38, 41, 42 and 43 may be initiated either by the Senate or the House of Commons or by the legislative assembly of a province.

Revocation of authorization

(2) A resolution of assent made for the purpose of this Part may be revoked at any time before the issue of a proclamation authorized by it.

Amendments without Senate resolution

47. (1) An amendment to the Constitution of Canada made by proclamation under section 38, 41, 42 or 43 may be made without a resolution of the Senate authorizing the issue of the proclamation if, within one hundred and eighty days after the adoption by the House of Commons of a resolution authorizing its issue, the Senate has not adopted such a resolution and if, at any time after the expiration of that period, the House of Commons again adopts the resolution.

Computation of period

(2) Any period when Parliament is prorogued or dissolved shall not be counted in computing the one hundred and eighty day period referred to in subsection (1).

Advice to issue proclamation

48. The Queen's Privy Council for Canada shall advise the Governor General to issue a proclamation under this Part forthwith on the adoption of the resolutions required for an amendment made by proclamation under this Part.

Constitutional conference

49. A constitutional conference composed of the Prime Minister of Canada and the first ministers of the provinces shall be convened by the Prime Minister of Canada within fifteen years after this Part comes into force to review the provisions of this Part.

PART VI

AMENDMENT TO THE CONSTITUTION ACT, 1867

Amendment to *Constitution Act, 1867*

50. The *Constitution Act, 1867* (formerly named the *British North America Act, 1867*) is amended by adding thereto, immediately after section 92 thereof, the following heading and section:

"Non-Renewable Natural Resources, Forestry Resources and Electrical Energy

Laws respecting non-renewable natural resources, forestry resources and electrical energy

92A. (1) In each province, the legislature may exclusively make laws in relation to

(*a*) exploration for non-renewable natural resources in the province;

(*b*) development, conservation and management of non-renewable natural resources and forestry resources in the province, including laws in relation to the rate of primary production therefrom; and

(*c*) development, conservation and management of sites and facilities in the province for the generation and production of electrical energy.

Export from provinces of resources

(2) In each province, the legislature may make laws in relation to the export from the province to another part of Canada of the primary production from non-renewable natural resources and forestry resources in the province and the production from facilities in the province for the generation of electrical energy, but such laws may not authorize or provide for discrimination in prices or in supplies exported to another part of Canada.

Authority of Parliament

(3) Nothing in subsection (2) derogates from the authority of Parliament to enact laws in relation to the matters referred to in that subsection and, where such a law of Parliament and a law of a province conflict, the law of Parliament prevails to the extent of the conflict.

Taxation of resources

(4) In each province, the legislature may make laws in relation to the raising of money by any mode or system or taxation in respect of

(*a*) non-renewable natural resources and forestry resources in the province and the primary production therefrom, and

(*b*) sites and facilities in the province for the generation of electrical energy and the production therefrom,

whether or not such production is exported in whole or in part from the province, but such laws may not authorize or provide for taxation that differentiates between production exported to another part of Canada and production not exported from the province.

"Primary production"

"Existing powers or rights"

Idem

(5) The expression "primary production" has the meaning assigned by the Sixth Schedule.

(6) Nothing in subsections (1) to (5) derogates from any powers or rights that a legislature or government of a province had immediately before the coming into force of this section."

51. The said Act is further amended by adding thereto the following Schedule:

"THE SIXTH SCHEDULE

Primary Production from Non-Renewable Natural Resources and Forestry Resources

1. For the purposes of section 92A of this Act,

(*a*) production from a non-renewable natural resource is primary production therefrom if

(i) it is in the form in which it exists upon its recovery or severance from its natural state, or

(ii) it is a product resulting from processing or refining the resources, and is not a manufactured product or a product resulting from refining crude oil, refining upgraded heavy crude oil, refining gases or liquids derived from coal or refining a synthetic equivalent of crude oil; and

(*b*) production from a forestry resource is primary production therefrom if it consists of sawlogs, poles, lumber, wood chips, sawdust or any other primary wood product, or wood pulp, and is not a product manufactured from wood."

PART VII

GENERAL

Primacy of Constitution of Canada

52. (1) The Constitution of Canada is the supreme law of Canada, and any law that is inconsistent with the provisions of the Constitution is, to the extent of the inconsistency, of no force or effect.

Constitution of Canada

(2) The Constitution of Canada includes

(*a*) the *Canada Act*, including this Act;

(*b*) the Acts and orders referred to in Schedule I; and

(*c*) any amendment to any Act or order referred to in paragraph (*a*) or (*b*).

Amendments to Constitution of Canada

(3) Amendments to the Constitution of Canada shall be made only in accordance with the authority contained in the Constitution of Canada.

Repeals and new names

53. (1) The enactments referred to in Column I of Schedule I are hereby repealed or amended to the extent indicated in Column II thereof and, unless repealed, shall continue as law in Canada under the names set out in Column III thereof.

Consequential amendments

(2) Every enactment, except the *Canada Act*, that refers to an enactment referred to in Schedule I by the name in Column I thereof is hereby amended by substituting for that name the corresponding name in Column III thereof, and any British North America Act not referred to in Schedule I may be cited as the *Constitution Act* followed by the year and number, if any, of its enactment.

Repeal and consequential amendments

54. Part IV is repealed on the day that is one year after this Part comes into force and this section may be repealed and this Act renumbered, consequential upon the repeal of Part IV and this section, by proclamation issued by the Governor General under the Great Seal of Canada.

French version of Constitution of Canada

55. A French version of the portions of the Constitution of Canada referred to in Schedule I shall be prepared by the Minister of Justice of Canada as expeditiously as possible and, when any portion thereof sufficient to warrant action being taken has been so prepared, it shall be put forward for enactment by proclamation issued by the Governor General under the Great Seal of Canada pursuant to the procedure then applicable to an amendment of the same provisions of the Constitution of Canada.

English and French versions of certain constitutional texts

56. Where any portion of the Constitution of Canada has been or is enacted in English and French or where a French version of any portion of the Constitution is enacted pursuant to section 55, the English and French versions of that portion of the Constitution are equally authoritative.

English and French versions of this Act

57. The English and French versions of this Act are equally authoritative.

Commencement

58. Subject to section 59, this Act shall come into force on a day to be fixed by proclamation issued by the Queen or the Governor General under the Great Seal of Canada.

Commencement of paragraph 23(1)(*a*) in respect of Quebec

59. (1) Paragraph 23(1)(*a*) shall come into force in respect of Quebec on a day to be fixed by proclamation issued by the Queen or the Governor General under the Great Seal of Canada.

Authorization of Quebec

(2) A proclamation under subsection (1) shall be issued only where authorized by the legislative assembly or government of Quebec.

Repeal of this section

(3) This section may be repealed on the day paragraph 23(1)(*a*) comes into force in respect of Quebec and this Act amended and renumbered, consequential upon the repeal of this section, by proclamation issued by the Queen or the Governor General under the Great Seal of Canada.

Short title and citations

60. This Act may be cited as the *Constitution Act, 1981*, and the Constitution Acts 1867 to 1975 (No. 2) and this Act may be cited together as the *Constitution Acts, 1867 to 1981*.

SCHEDULE I TO THE CONSTITUTION ACT, 1981
MODERNIZATION OF THE CONSTITUTION

Item	Column I Act Affected	Column II Amendment	Column III New Name
1.	British North America Act, 1867, 30-31 Vict., c. 3 (U.K.)	(1) Section 1 is repealed and the following substituted therefor: "1. This Act may be cited as the *Constitution Act, 1867*." (2) Section 20 is repealed. (3) Class 1 of section 91 is repealed. (4) Class 1 of section 92 is repealed.	Constitution Act, 1867

Item	Act Affected	Amendment	New Name
2.	An Act to amend and continue the Act 32-33 Victoria chapter 3; and to establish and provide for the Government of the Province of Manitoba, 1870, 33 Vict., c. 3 (Can.)	(1) The long title is repealed and the following substituted therefor: "*Manitoba Act, 1870.*" (2) Section 20 is repealed.	Manitoba Act, 1870
3.	Order of Her Majesty in Council admitting Rupert's Land and the North-Western Territory into the union, dated the 23rd day of June, 1870		Rupert's Land and North-Western Territory Order
4.	Order of Her Majesty in Council admitting British Columbia into the Union, dated the 16th day of May, 1871		British Columbia Terms of Union
5.	British North America Act, 1871, 34-35 Vict., c. 28 (U.K.)	Section 1 is repealed and the following substituted therefor: "1. This Act may be cited as the *Constitution Act, 1871.*"	Constitution Act, 1871
6.	Order of Her Majesty in Council admitting Prince Edward Island into the Union, dated the 26th day of June, 1873		Prince Edward Island Terms of Union
7.	Parliament of Canada Act, 1875, 38-39 Vict., c. 38 (U.K.)		Parliament of Canada Act, 1875
8.	Order of Her Majesty in Council admitting all British possessions and Territories in North America and islands adjacent thereto into the Union, dated the 31st day of July, 1880		Adjacent Territories Order
9.	British North America Act, 1886, 49-50 Vict., c. 35 (U.K.)	Section 3 is repealed and the following substituted therefor: "3. This Act may be cited as the *Constitution Act, 1886.*"	Constitution Act, 1886
10.	Canada (Ontario Boundary) Act, 1889, 52-53 Vict., c. 28 (U.K.)		Canada (Ontario Boundary) Act, 1889

Item	Act Affected	Amendment	New Name
11.	Canadian Speaker (Appointment of Deputy) Act, 1895, 2nd Sess., 59 Vict., c. 3 (U.K.)	The Act is repealed.	
12.	The Alberta Act, 1905, 4-5 Edw. VII, c. 3 (Can.)		Alberta Act
13.	The Saskatchewan Act, 1905, 4-5 Edw. VII, c. 42 (Can.)		Saskatchewan Act
14.	British North America Act, 1907, 7 Edw. VII, c. 11 (U.K.)	Section 2 is repealed and the following substituted therefor: "2. This Act may be cited as the *Constitution Act, 1907*."	Constitution Act, 1907
15.	British North America Act, 1915, 5-6 Geo. V, c. 45 (U.K.)	Section 3 is repealed and the following substituted therefor: "3. This Act may be cited as the *Constitution Act, 1915*."	Constitution Act, 1915
16.	British North America Act, 1930, 20-21 Geo. V, c. 26 (U.K.)	Section 3 is repealed and the following substituted therefor: "3. This Act may be cited as the *Constitution Act, 1930*."	Constitution Act, 1930
17.	Statute of Westminster, 1931, 22 Geo. V, c. 4 (U.K.)	In so far as they apply to Canada, (*a*) section 4 is repealed; and (*b*) subsection 7(1) is repealed.	Statute of Westminster, 1931
18.	British North America Act, 1940, 3-4 Geo. VI, c. 36 (U.K.)	Section 2 is repealed and the following substituted therefor: "2. This Act may be cited as the *Constitution Act, 1940*."	Constitution Act, 1940
19.	British North America Act, 1943, 6-7 Geo. VI, c. 30 (U.K.)	The Act is repealed.	
20.	British North Amercia Act, 1946, 9-10 Geo. VI, c. 63 (U.K.)	The Act is repealed.	
21.	British North America Act, 1949, 12-13 Geo. VI, c. 22 (U.K.)	Section 3 is repealed and the following substituted therefor: "3. This Act may be cited as the *Newfoundland Act*."	Newfoundland Act

Item	Act Affected	Amendment	New Name
22.	British North America (No. 2) Act, 1949, 12 Geo. VI, c. 81 (U.K.)	The Act is repealed.	
23.	British North America Act, 1951, 14-15 Geo. VI, c. 32 (U.K.)	The Act is repealed.	
24.	British North America Act, 1952, 1 Eliz. II, c. 15 (Can.)	The Act is repealed.	
25.	British North America Act, 1960, 9 Eliz. II, c. 2 (U.K.)	Section 2 is repealed and the following substituted therefor: "2. This Act may be cited as the *Constitution Act, 1960.*"	Constitution Act, 1960
26.	British North America Act, 1964, 12-13 Eliz. II, c. 73 (U.K.)	Section 2 is repealed and the following substituted therefor: "2. This Act may be cited as the *Constitution Act, 1964.*"	Constitution Act, 1964
27.	British North America Act, 1965, 14 Eliz. II, c. 4, Part I (Can.)	Section 2 is repealed and the following substituted therefor: "2. This Part may be cited as the *Constitution Act, 1965.*"	Constitution Act, 1965
28.	British North America Act, 1974, 23 Eliz. II, c. 13, Part I (Can.)	Section 3, as amended by 25-26 Eliz. II, c. 28, s. 38(1) (Can.), is repealed and the following substituted therefor: "3. This Part may be cited as the *Constitution Act, 1974.*"	Constitution Act, 1974
29.	British North America Act, 1975, 23-24 Eliz. II, c. 28, Part I (Can.)	Section 3, as amended by 25-26 Eliz. II, c. 28, s. 31 (Can.), is repealed and the following substituted therefor: "3. This Part may be cited as the *Constitution Act (No. 1), 1975.*"	Constitution Act (No. 1), 1975
30.	British North America Act (No. 2), 1975, 23-24 Eliz. II, c. 53 (Can.)	Section 3 is repealed and the following substituted therefor: "3. This Act may be cited as the *Constitution Act (No. 2), 1975.*"	Constitution Act (No. 2), 1975

50. Events Following the Adoption of the Resolution by the House of Commons and the Senate, Chronology to April 17, 1982

The resolution was transmitted by the Governor General to the United Kingdom for action by Parliament.

House of Commons (U.K.)

December 22, 1981:   Bill presented, and read the first time.

February 17, 1982:   Second reading.

February 23, 1982:   The British Commons (Committee of the Whole) began a clause-by-clause study of the Bill. Twenty-six amendments were accepted for debate. Only one amendment was voted on — to delete the word "existing" from the phrase existing native rights in the rights charter. It was defeated.

March 3, 1982:   Third day of debate. Only one amendment was called to a vote — it would give native organizations the power to approve any changes to the constitution affecting their rights. The amendment was defeated.

March 8, 1982:   Third reading.

House of Lords (U.K.)

March 9, 1982:   Bill presented and read the first time.

March 18, 1982:   Second reading.

March 23, 1982:   Committee of the Whole study is completed.

March 25, 1982:   Third reading.

March 29, 1982:   Royal Assent given by Queen Elizabeth II.

April 17, 1982:   Proclaimed in force by Queen Elizabeth II (in Ottawa).

51. First Ministers' Conference on Aboriginal Constitutional Matters, Ottawa, Ontario, March 15–16, 1983

1983 Constitutional Accord on Aboriginal Rights

Document: 800-17/041 (revised)

Whereas pursuant to section 37 of the *Constitution Act, 1982*, a constitutional conference composed of the Prime Minister of Canada and the first ministers of the provinces was held on March 15 and 16, 1983, to which representatives of the aboriginal peoples of Canada and elected representatives of the governments of the Yukon Territory and the Northwest Territories were invited;

And whereas it was agreed at that conference that certain amendments to the *Constitution Act, 1982* would be sought in accordance with section 38 of that Act;

And whereas that conference had included in its agenda the following matters that directly affect the aboriginal peoples of Canada:

Agenda

1. Charter of Rights of the Aboriginal Peoples (Expanded Part II) Including:
   — Preamble
   — Removal of "Existing", and Expansion of Section 35 to Include Recognition of Modern Treaties, Treaties signed Outside Canada and Before Confederation, and Specific Mention of "Aboriginal Title" Including the Rights of Aboriginal Peoples of Canada to a Land and Water Base (including Land base for the Métis)
   — Statement of the Particular Rights of Aboriginal Peoples
   — Equality
   — Enforcement
   — Interpretation
2. Amending Formula Revisions, Including:
   — Amendments on Aboriginal Matters not to be Subject to Provincial Opting Out (Section 42)
   — Consent Clause
3. Self-Government
4. Repeal of Section 42(1) (*e*) and (*f*)

5. Amendments to Part III, Including:
   — Equalization   )
   — Cost-Sharing   ) Resourcing of
   — Service Delivery   ) Aboriginal Governments
6. Ongoing Process, Including Further First Ministers Conferences and the Entrenchment of Necessary Mechanisms to Implement Rights.

And whereas that conference was unable to complete its full consideration of all the agenda items;

And whereas it was agreed at that conference that future conferences be held at which those agenda items and other constitutional matters that directly affect the aboriginal peoples of Canada will be discussed;

NOW THEREFORE the Government of Canada and the provincial governments hereby agree as follows:

1. A constitutional conference composed of the Prime Minister of Canada and the first ministers of the provinces will be convened by the Prime Minister within one year after the completion of the constitutional conference held on March 15 and 16, 1983.
2. The conference convened under subsection (1) shall have included in its agenda those items that were not fully considered at the conference held on March 15 and 16, 1983, and the Prime Minister of Canada shall invite representatives of the aboriginal peoples of Canada to participate in the discussions on those items.
3. The Prime Minister of Canada shall invite elected representatives of the governments of the Yukon Territory and the Northwest Territories to participate in the discussions on any item on the agenda of the conference convened under subsection (1) that, in the opinion of the Prime Minister, directly affects the Yukon Territory and the Northwest Territories.
4. The Prime Minister of Canada will lay or cause to be laid before the Senate and House of Commons, and the

first ministers of the provinces will lay or cause to be laid before their legislative assemblies, prior to December 31, 1983, a resolution in the form set out in the Schedule to authorize a proclamation issued by the Governor General under the Great Seal of Canada to amend the *Constitution Act, 1982.*

5. In preparation for the constitutional conferences contemplated by this Accord, meetings composed of ministers of the governments of Canada and the provinces, together with representatives of the aboriginal peoples of Canada and elected representatives of the governments of the Yukon Territory and the Northwest Territories shall be convened at least annually by the government of Canada.

6. Nothing in this Accord is intended to preclude, or substitute for, any bilateral or other discussions or agreements between governments and the various aboriginal peoples and, in particular, having regard to the authority of Parliament under Class 24 of section 91 of the *Constitution Act, 1867,* and to the special relationship that has existed and continues to exist between the Parliament and government of Canada and the peoples referred to in that Class, this Accord is made without prejudice to any bilateral process that has been or may be established between the government of Canada and those peoples.

7. Nothing in this Accord shall be construed so as to affect the interpretation of the Constitution of Canada.

Signed at Ottawa the 16th day of March, 1983 by [representatives of the following governments: Canada, Ontario, British Columbia, Prince Edward Island, Nova Scotia, Saskatchewan, New Brunswick, Alberta, Manitoba, and Newfoundland, "with the participation of" representatives of the Assembly of First Nations, Inuit Committee on National Issues, Métis National Council, Native Council of Canada, Yukon Territory, and Northwest Territories.]

SCHEDULE

[Proclaimed by Her Excellency the Governor General, June 21, 1984.]

Motion for a Resolution to authorize His Excellency the Governor General to issue a proclamation respecting amendments to the Constitution of Canada

Whereas the *Constitution Act, 1982* provides that an amendment to the Constitution of Canada may be made

by proclamation issued by the Governor General under the Great Seal of Canada where so authorized by resolutions of the Senate and House of Commons and resolutions of the legislative assemblies as provided for in sections 38 and 41 thereof;

And Whereas the Constitution of Canada, reflecting the country and Canadian society, continues to develop and strengthen the rights and freedoms that it guarantees;

And Whereas, after a gradual transition of Canada from colonial status to the status of an independent and sovereign state, Canadians have, as of April 17, 1982, full authority to amend their Constitution in Canada;

And Whereas historically and equitably it is fitting that the early exercise of that full authority should relate to the rights and freedoms of the first inhabitants of Canada, the aboriginal peoples;

Now Therefore the (Senate) (House of Commons) (legislative assembly) resolves that His Excellency the Governor General be authorized to issue a proclamation under the Great Seal of Canada amending the Constitution of Canada as follows:

Proclamation Amending the Constitution of Canada

Amendment to the Constitution of Canada

1. Paragraph 25(*b*) of the *Constitution Act, 1982* is repealed and the following substituted therefor:

"(*b*) any rights or freedoms that now exist by way of land claims agreements or may be so acquired."

2. Section 35 of the *Constitution Act, 1982* is amended by adding thereto the following subsections:

Land claims agreements

"(3) For greater certainty, in subsection (1) "treaty rights" includes rights that now exist by way of land claims agreements or may be so acquired.

Aboriginal and treaty rights are guaranteed equally to both sexes

(4) Notwithstanding any other provision of this Act, the aboriginal and treaty rights referred to in subsection (1) are guaranteed equally to male and female persons."

3. The said Act is further amended by adding thereto, immediately after section 35 thereof, the following section:

*Commitment to
participation in
constitutional
conference*

"**35.1** The government of Canada and the provincial governments are committed to the principle that, before any amendment is made to Class 24 of section 91 of the *Constitution Act, 1867*, to section 25 of this Act or to this Part,

(*a*) a constitutional conference that includes in its agenda an item relating to the proposed amendment, composed of the Prime Minister of Canada and the first ministers of the provinces, will be convened by the Prime Minister of Canada; and

(*b*) the Prime Minister of Canada will invite representatives of the aboriginal peoples of Canada to participate in the discussions on that item."

4. The said Act is further amended by adding thereto, immediately after section 37 thereof, the following Part:

"PART IV.1
CONSTITUTIONAL CONFERENCES

*Constitutional
conferences*

37.1 (1) In addition to the conferences convened in March 1983, at least two constitutional conferences composed of the Prime Minister of Canada and the first ministers of the provinces shall be convened by the Prime Minister of Canada, the first within three years after April 17, 1982 and the second within five years after that date.

*Participation
of aboriginal
peoples*

(2) Each conference convened under subsection (1) shall have included in its agenda constitutional matters that directly affect the aboriginal peoples of Canada, and the Prime Minister of Canada shall invite representatives of those peoples to participate in the discussions on those matters.

*Participation
of territories*

(3) The Prime Minister of Canada shall invite elected representatives of the governments of the Yukon Territory and the Northwest Territories to participate in the discussion on any item on the agenda of a conference convened under subsection (1) that, in the opinion of the Prime Minister, directly affects the Yukon Territory and the Northwest Territories.

*Subsection 35(1)
not affected*

(4) Nothing in this section shall be construed so as to derogate from subsection 35(1)."

5. The said Act is further amended by adding thereto, immediately after section 54 thereof, the following section:

*Repeal of
Part IV.1
and this
section*

"**54.1** Part IV.1 and this section are repealed on April 18, 1987."

6. The said Act is further amended by adding thereto the following section:

References

"**61.** A reference to the *Constitution Acts, 1867 to 1982* shall be deemed to include a reference to the *Constitution Amendment Proclamation, 1983*."

Citation

7. This Proclamation may be cited as the *Constitution Amendment Proclamation, 1983*.

52. "Rebuilding the Relationship: Quebec and Its Confederation Partners," Seminar Held at Mont-Gabriel, Quebec, May 9, 1986

Speech by Gil Rémillard, Quebec Minister of Intergovernmental Affairs, May 9, 1986

"Nothing less than Quebec's dignity is at stake in future constitutional discussions."

(Mastering the Future, p. 49)

To begin with I would like to thank the Institute of Intergovernmental Relations and the Ecole de l'Administration Publique for having invited me to this seminar and for having given me the opportunity to participate in your work. It is certainly promising to see the Institute of Intergovernmental Relations of Queen's University at Kingston and the Ecole de l'Administration Publique of Quebec associate to organize such a seminar. This association is entirely to the credit of these two teaching and research establishments and I congratulate their respective directors, Mr. Peter Leslie and Mr. Jocelyn Jacques.

The theme of the seminar "Rebuilding the Relationship: Quebec and Its Confederation Partners" could not be more apt. As constitutional talks resume between Quebec, Ottawa, and the other provinces, this type of forum can prove very useful. Therefore, I am pleased as minister responsible for constitutional matters to share with you the overall orientation the Quebec government intends to promote in its talks with its partners in the Canadian federation.

April 17, 1982 is a historic date for Canada. It was on this day that Elizabeth II, Queen of Canada, proclaimed the *Constitution Act of 1982* on Parliament Hill in Ottawa. After more than 55 years of difficult discussions which, on some occasions, even plunged Canadian federalism into profound crises, Canada cut its last colonial tie with London. It also took advantage of the opportunity to substantially amend its constitution by adding a Charter of Rights and Freedoms, an amending formula, aboriginal peoples' rights, an equalization principle, and a modification in the distribution of power in matters concerning natural resources.

Little remains to be said on the fact that the *Constitution Act of 1982* marked the end of the last vestige of Canada's colonial status. Canada has been a sovereign country since the Statute of Westminster of 1931. However, since the British North America Act of 1867 did not include an amending formula and since, at the time, Ottawa and the nine provinces disagreed about how to fill this very important gap, it was agreed that London would act as trustee for certain parts of the Canadian constitution. As we know, this role was really very much a matter of form. Westminster always acted at the request and according to the specifications of Canada. This role was also temporary since the provinces and Ottawa anticipated soon agreeing on an amending formula.

Many Canadians would certainly be surprised to learn that, from a strictly legal point of view, London could renege on its decision and once again make Canada a colony by amending the Statute of Westminster of 1931 and the "Canada Bill" of 1982. However, as Lord Denning put it in his famous obiter dictum in the Blackburn affair, "Legal theory does not always coincide with political reality". This is clearly a utopian consideration which is nevertheless possible in law strictly construed since a choice was made to proceed via Westminster rather than acting by Canadian proclamation.

As we know, nothing obliged Canada to ask Westminster to put an end to the last vestige of its colonial status. The Canadian Parliament and the provinces could have unilaterally proclaimed their independence and the changes they intended to make sovereignly to the compromise of 1867. Resorting one last time to the old colonial mechanism, facilitated the possibility of Ottawa acting without the provinces' agreement since the Canadian Parliament had the power to act alone to amend the Canadian constitution legally, if not legitimately, as clarified by the

Supreme Court of Canada in its famous September 28, 1981 Patriation Reference.

We should also mention that resorting to the old colonial mechanism made it all the easier for Ottawa and the other nine provinces to disregard Quebec despite its refusal to accept these fundamental changes to the Canadian constitution. This refusal has no judicial consequence since the constitution was patriated legally. The *Constitution Act of 1982* applies to Quebec despite its disagreement; however, the political consequences are very real. Since it does not accept the *Constitution Act of 1982*, Quebec refuses to vote on any constitutional amendment. For instance, we refuse to vote on any amendment proposal dealing with the senate, entrenching property rights in the charter, or making changes to the rights of aboriginal peoples, with whom we sympathize greatly.

Clearly, Quebec does not object to the fact that Canada recovered full jurisdiction over its own constitution from London. What we do object to is that patriation was used as a pretext for substantially modifying the Canadian constitution without taking Quebec's historic rights into consideration.

Four years after the proclamation of the *Constitution Act of 1982*, Quebec, headed by a new government, still does not adhere to this act. No Quebec government, regardless of its political tendencies, could sign the *Constitution Act of 1982* in its present form. However, if certain modifications were made, it could be acceptable to Quebec.

The Quebec government therefore hopes that constitutional talks will be resumed. However, conditions have not been satisfied for beginning serious, formal constitutional negotiations. Certain points must be clarified first. For instance, Ottawa must indicate what, in its words, might be meant by signing a constitutional agreement "with honor and enthusiasm", as stated by the Prime Minister of Canada, Mr. Mulroney.

It should be stressed that it is not only up to Quebec to act. Our federal partners must not sit back idly; we expect concrete action on their part, action that is likely to steer the talks in the right direction. The ball is not only in Quebec's court but also in that of the federation that isolated one of the main partners that created it in 1867. We wish to talk with partners, who must begin by showing concrete proof of their desire to make good the injustice that the *Constitution Act of 1982* represents for Quebec.

This is not the time for listing the errors committed by one side or the other. Instead, it is time for cooperation and understanding. Quebec will tackle these constitutional talks determinedly and firmly but also with an open mind, as dictated by the higher interests of Quebec and Canada.

However, you will agree with me that Quebec's isolation cannot continue much longer without jeopardizing the very foundation of true federalism.

Nor is it time for giving a backhand sweep and starting all over again. Absolutely not. Not everything contained in the *Constitution Act of 1982* is negative. After four years of being interpreted by our courts, the Charter of Rights and Freedoms, for instance, is, on the whole, a document which we, as Quebecers and Canadians, can be proud of. Its greatest merit no doubt lies in gradually giving us a new outlook on the respect of human rights. This is why our first decision as the new government last December was to stop systematically using, as the former government had done, the "notwithstanding" clause in Quebec statutes, to depart from sections 2 and 7 to 15 of the Canadian charter. We want the fundamental rights of Quebecers to be as well protected as those of other Canadians.

The only valid reason for systematically using the departure clause could be as a symbol, a symbol of Quebec's disputing the *Constitution Act of 1982*. We feel that this symbol is empty of meaning. We do not have the right to take Quebecers hostage for the purposes of constitutional talks. As Quebec's government, we refuse to deprive our people of such fundamental constitutional rights as: the right to life, liberty and security of the person, the right to a just, fair trial and equality rights. Without in any manner accepting the *Constitution Act of 1982*, we wanted to be fair to Quebecers, who are also full-fledged Canadians.

If the Canadian charter poses few problems for being acceptable to Quebec, the same is not true for other aspects of the *Constitution Act of 1982* which, in many respects, opposes Quebec's historic rights.

On December 2, 1985, the population of Quebec clearly gave us the mandate of carrying out our electoral program, which states the main conditions that could persuade Quebec to support the *Constitution Act of 1982*. These conditions are:
— explicit recognition of Quebec as a distinct society;
— guarantee of increased powers in matters of immigration;
— limitation of the federal spending power;
— recognition of a right of veto;
— Quebec's participation in appointing judges to the Supreme Court of Canada.

As far as we are concerned, recognition of Quebec's specificity is a pre-requisite to any talks likely to persuade Quebec to support the *Constitution Act of 1982*.

Quebec's identity is the culmination of a slow social and political evolution. At the time of the conquest of 1760, a unique francophone community existed with its own customs, mentality, lifestyle and civil, religious and military institutions. These were the true Canadians whereas the conquerors were Englishmen. The Quebec Act of 1774 and the Constitution Act of 1791, which created Lower Canada, confirm the French-Canadians' unique character by giving them their first legal bases of existence and expression by permitting them to conserve their civil law and their religion and by establishing a parliamentary system. Then came the Act of Union of 1840, which followed the Durham Report drafted after the unrest of 1837–1838. In guise of retaliation, this act united Upper and Lower Canada into a single political entity. This was the birth of the two designations, "French Canadians" and "English Canadians", that the British North America Act sanctioned in 1867 both in letter and in spirit.

More than a century would go by before a national Quebec character emerged from this French Canadian people. During the one hundred years of federation, Quebecers would increasingly become aware of their identity in terms of their provincial government and in terms of a common good which was increasingly identified with their society.

This identity must not in any way be jeopardized. We must therefore be assured that the Canadian constitution will explicitly recognize the unique character of Quebec society and guarantee us the means necessary to ensure its full development within the framework of Canadian federalism.

Recognition of the unique nature of Quebec gives rise to the need for obtaining real guarantees for our cultural safety. This safety is translated notably by the sole power to plan our immigration, in order to maintain our francophone character by countering or even reversing demographic trends that forecast a decrease in Quebec's relative size within Canada.

Cultural safety and security also signifies the possibility of Quebec acting alone in its fields of jurisdiction without interference from the federal government through its spending power. You are no doubt aware that this power allows Ottawa to spend sums of money in any area it wishes whether it falls under federal jurisdiction or not. This situation has become intolerable. For all provinces it has become a type of "sword of Damocles" hanging menacingly over all planned policies of social, cultural or economic development. Bill C-96 dealing with the financing of health and post-secondary education, which is before the Canadian Parliament, is a good example of this situation. This bill is clearly unjust and discriminatory as far as Quebec is concerned. It represents a lack of earning totalling $82,000,000 in 1986–1987. It would be desirable for the federal government to remove itself from the areas which are not within its jurisdiction. However, it would be unacceptable for the federal government not to consequently give these financial resources to the provinces. It appears increasingly necessary to subject the exercise of the spending power to the provinces' approval. Doing so would contribute greatly to improving the functioning of the present federal system. Should Bill C-96 be passed by the Canadian Parliament, the result would certainly have a severe impact on the progress of constitutional talks.

Spending power related to the principle of equalization is much more acceptable. However, once again, the current situation is completely unfair to Quebec. My colleague, the Minister of Finance, Mr. Gerard D. Levesque, was right in denouncing Ottawa's attitude in his recent budget. Ottawa unilaterally changed the rules for applying equalization. It is unacceptable for Ottawa to have acted unilaterally to change the rules for the application of the principle of equalization, which is entrenched in section 36 of the *Constitution Act of 1982*. The general parameters for applying this principle, which is fundamental to our federal system, must be written into the constitution. In this way, modifying these parameters would mean resorting to the amending formula. This provides a further reason for demanding revision of the amending formula hereby protecting Quebec from any changes likely to affect its rights.

The current amending formula is unacceptable to Quebec because it does not make provision for financial compensation in case of withdrawal, and because it permits changing federal institutions or accepting a new province into the federation despite Quebec's objection. We therefore demand a right of veto able to protect us adquately against any constitutional amendment which goes against Quebec's interests.

The constitution is not always changed formally using the amending formula. The Supreme Court of Canada, the highest court in the land, can, for all intents and purposes, impose constitutional amendments upon us through its interpretation of the constitution.

The role of our Supreme Court is also significant for the respect of certain values that are essential to Quebec's specificity such as: civil law and, from certain points of view, fundamental rights and freedoms. We must therefore be entitled to participate in the process of selecting and appointing the Supreme Court judges.

We also wish to point out a very important question left hanging since the proclamation of the *Constitution Act of 1982*, namely, since sections 41 and 42 refer to the Supreme Court, is the latter, by this very fact, constitutionalized?

The question is important since, if the answer is positive, the composition of the Supreme Court is constitutionalized and unanimity is required to change it. In this way, Quebec sees itself ensuring the fact that 3 Supreme Court judges must come from the Quebec bar or magistrature. We consider this the required minimum. However, if the answer is negative, this guarantee no longer exists and the federal government remains the sole master of our Supreme Court in general. This is clearly unacceptable in a federation like ours, given the essential role played by the Supreme Court in its very evolution.

In short, our stipulations for supporting the *Constitution Act of 1982* are based on three main objectives: making the act acceptable to Quebec, improving it to the benefit of the entire Canadian federation and improving the situation of francophones living outside the province of Quebec.

This last point is especially important to us. In fact, the situation of francophones outside of Quebec will be one of our major concerns during the upcoming constitutional talks. Their situation could be greatly improved, for example, by specifying in paragraph 3B of section 23 that the expression "minority-language educational facilities" includes the right to management. There has already been a ruling to this effect by the Ontario Court of Appeal. However, the case, which was a reference for an opinion by the Ontario government, did not go to the Supreme Court.

Why not take advantage of these constitutional talks to clarify this point which is so important for the survival of francophones outside Quebec? It would perhaps also be timely to question the well-known concept of "where numbers warrant". Is limiting the right to instruction in its mother tongue for one of the two national minorities always appropriate? We want to discuss these issues and many others with the federal government and the other provinces in an attempt to improve the situation of francophones outside Quebec.

Furthermore, these improvements to section 23 could only benefit Quebec's anglophone minority. Clearly, the problems encountered by francophones outside Quebec and anglophones within Quebec are not identical. However, we wish to ensure Quebec's anglophones of their language rights. These rights must naturally fall within the context of Quebec's society's francophone character and the government's firm desire to ensure its full development.

Quebec's future is within Canada. This is the heartfelt conviction of the huge majority of Quebecers just as it is the prime, fundamental commitment of this government. We believe in Canadian federalism because, within the federal system, Quebec can be faithful to its history and its unique identity while enjoying favorable conditions for its full economic, social and cultural development.

Stating our full, complete belonging to Quebec and to Canada involves stating as significantly as possible our keen regret and feeling of helplessness about what occurred at the time of the patriation of the constitution.

As Quebecers and as Canadians, we cannot accept the fact that important amendments to our country's constitution were made without us and, in some respects, contrary to Quebec's historic rights. This is why Quebec's new government and the population of Quebec, in the interests of Quebec and Canada, would like matters to be corrected. Mention has been made of signing "with honor". Certainly, since what we are asking for is the respect of the dignity and pride of the people of Quebec and respect of the province's historic rights. "With enthusiasm — this too is possible if Quebec is once again made the major partner in the Canadian federation that it had always been.

The election of a Liberal government in Quebec last December signifies a new era for federal-provincial and interprovincial relations. Faithful to our federalist commitment, we want to guarantee Quebec its rights as a distinct society and major partner in the Canadian federation.

Quebec nationalism is not dead, far from it. It is thriving more than ever but in a different form. It is no longer synonymous with "isolationism" or "xenophobia" but rather with "excellence".

More than ever, we, Quebecers, we, French Canadians, must recall our history and remember that we owe our survival to the dangers that aroused the sense of daring and excellence in our ancestors.

Our existence as a people and our belonging to the Canadian federation is a challenge to history. Faithful to our history and confident in our future, Quebec intends to devote its efforts to continuing to meet this challenge and, within Canada, make Quebec a modern, just and dynamic society. We must remember that our present is a token of our future.

53. The 27th Annual Premiers' Conference, Edmonton, Alberta, August 10–12, 1986

The Edmonton Declaration, August 12, 1986

The Premiers unanimously agreed that their top constitutional priority is to embark immediately upon a federal-provincial process, using Quebec's five proposals as a basis for discussion, to bring about Quebec's full and active participation in the Canadian federation.

There was a consensus among the Premiers that then they will pursue further constitutional discussions on matters raised by some provinces which will include, amongst other items, Senate reform, fisheries, property rights, etc.

54. Annual Conference of First Ministers, Vancouver, British Columbia, November 20–21, 1986

Quebec Constitutional Issue, November 21, 1986

The First Ministers, on the occasion of their Annual Conference in Vancouver, expressed their satisfaction with the process followed to date on the constitutional issue and noted that important progress towards a better understanding of Quebec's five proposals has been achieved since the Edmonton Declaration.

The First Ministers are threfore of the view that the discussions now in progress should continue. Consequently, contacts already established at the political and officials' level among the federal government, the government of Quebec and the governments of the other provinces will be intensified and expanded in order to evaluate more fully the chances of success of eventual formal negotiations based on Quebec's five proposals.

During the coming months, First Ministers hope to conclude an agreement that will enable Quebec to become again a full partner in the Canadian federation, and to undertake later another stage in constitutional reform on matters that will include, amongst other items, Senate reform, fisheries, property rights, etc.

55. First Ministers' Meeting on the Constitution, Meech Lake, Quebec, April 30, 1987

(a) Background Information on Quebec's Conditions, Produced by the Prime Minister's Office, April 28, 1987

QUEBEC'S DISTINCT SOCIETY

When Canada's Constitution was "patriated" in 1982, most of the basic values Canadians share and the special characteristics that make Canada unique were recognized and protected in the fundamental law of the land. The Canadian Charter of Rights and Freedoms was entrenched in the Constitution. For the most part, the Charter guarantees individual rights. However, the rights of the aboriginal peoples of Canada were recognized and affirmed in the *Constitution Act, 1982*. Provision was made for the Charter to be interpreted in a manner consistent with the preservation and enhancement of the multicultural heritage of Canadians. The commitment of Parliament and the legislatures to promote and build on the regional strength of Canada was affirmed.

The *Constitution Act, 1982* is thus more than a constitutional document. It is, in large measure, a statement of many of Canada's fundamental characteristics. Nowhere, however, does the Constitution recognize Quebec's distinct society or the existence of French-speaking Canada, centred — but not exclusively so — in Quebec, and of English-speaking Canada concentrated in the rest of the country but present also in Quebec. Yet, without acknowledging these central facts, how can the language provisions of the Charter or Quebec's special system of civil law be explained or understood?

IMMIGRATION

Under section 95 of the *Constitution Act, 1867*, Parliament and the provincial legislature have concurrent legislative authority over immigration, with federal paramountcy in the event of conflicting laws. In practice, most of the legislative activity in this area has been undertaken by Parliament, primarily through the *Immigration Act*.

Over the years, however, the federal government has concluded administrative agreements respecting immigration with seven provinces to take into account their special concerns. The most comprehensive of these agreements was concluded in 1978 with the province of Quebec and is often referred to as the "Cullen-Couture Agreement". Under this agreement, Quebec exercises considerable powers, according to its own selection criteria, over the selection of immigrants from abroad. The federal government, however, retains control over the national standards and objectives of immigration policy, primarily through its ability to establish classes of immigrants and admission criteria, to determine overall levels of immigration and to prescribe categories of inadmissible persons.

THE SUPREME COURT

Since 1949, the Supreme Court of Canada has been the final court of appeal for Canada. Among other responsibilities, the Court has the last word on constitutional challenges respecting federal and provincial jurisdiction and on cases involving the Canadian Charter of Rights and Freedoms.

The Supreme Court has a very important role in maintaining and interpreting the Constitution. Yet, section 101 of the *Constitution Act, 1867* merely states that Parliament may provide for "the constitution, maintenance and organization of a general court of appeal for Canada". The Supreme Court was established, in 1875, by Act of Parliament.

The Supreme Court is a national institution of fundamental importance, whose existence should clearly be provided for in the Constitution. As a vital institution of the federation, the appointment of its members should conform with the spirit of federalism. Once the Court has been entrenched, section 42(1)(d) of the *Constitution Act, 1982* will require the support of Parliament and at least two-thirds of the provinces, representing at least 50 per-cent of the population, for any future changes to the entrenched provisions (except for the Court's composition, which is subject to unanimity).

THE SPENDING POWER OF PARLIAMENT

The courts have long held that, under the Constitution, Parliament can not only raise money by any mode or sys-tem of taxation, but can also spend money for any purpose. Thus, in addition to spending money on programs and activities that fall under its own legislative jurisdiction, Parliament can also spend for purposes to which its legis-lative authority does not extend. The federal spending power, however, is being contested before the courts. It is generally agreed that Parliament's use of the spending power cannot amount in fact to regulation of activities beyond federal authority.

The provinces also have a general spending power which they have used, for example, to establish missions abroad, even though the legislative assemblies cannot legislate to regulate international trade or international relations. Only the spending power of Parliament, however, is at issue under the terms of Quebec's conditions.

THE AMENDING FORMULA

The main purposes of a Constitution are to minimize the possibility of arbitrariness on the part of governments, and to prevent uncertainty and caprice from entering the relations between government institutions and between those institutions and the public. For these reasons, con-stitutional stability is of great importance. Such stability can be achieved by ensuring the Constitution is more difficult to amend than are ordinary laws.

The procedures for amending the Canadian Constitution are set out in Part V of the *Constitution Act, 1982* (sections 38 to 49). The consent of Parliament and at least two-thirds of the provinces, representing at least 50 per cent of the total provincial population, is required for most major constitutional amendments, including those respecting the distribution of powers.

However, this formula provides for the right to "opt out" of any amendment that transfers legislative jurisdiction to Parliament if the legislative assembly of a province has expressed its dissent through a resolution supported by a majority of its members.

Under such circumstances, the amendment does not apply to the dissenting province. If the amendment concerns education or other cultural matters, Canada is to provide reasonable compensation to the province to which the amendment does not apply.

As for national institutions — where it is not possible to "opt out" of amendments — there are two procedures:
—Unanimous consent is required for amendments on the following matters (section 41):
   the office of the Queen, the Governor General and the Lieutenant Governor of a province;
   the right of a province to a number of members in the House of Commons not less than the number of Senators by which the province was represented in 1982;
   the provisions concerning the use of English or French that apply to Parliament, the Government of Canada and all the provinces;
   the composition of the Supreme Court of Canada; and
   the amending formula itself.
—The consent of Parliament and at least two-thirds of the provinces, representing at least 50 per cent of the popu-lation, is required for constitutional amendments on the following matters (section 42):
   the principle of proportionate representation of the provinces in the House of Commons;
   the powers of the Senate and the method of selecting Senators;
   the number of Senators for each province and their residence qualifications;
   the Supreme Court of Canada (except its composition);
   the extension of existing provinces into the territories; and
   the establishment of new provinces.

If a provision of the Constitution applies to one or more, but not all provinces, there is a special amending procedure, which requires the consent of Parliament and the legislative assembly of each province to which the amendment applies. Alterations to the boundary between two provinces would be covered by this procedure.

THE SECOND ROUND

As testimony of their desire that Quebec become once again a full and active participant in Canada's constitutional evolution, the Premiers unanimously agreed at Edmonton in August 1986 that working towards this goal on the basis of Quebec's conditions constituted "their top constitutional priority".

A number of other constitutional objectives, such as Senate reform, entrenched property rights or revised fisheries jurisdiction, interest some provinces; they have agreed to defer action on these issues until the Quebec question has been addressed. They seek assurances, however, that once the Quebec round has been completed, a second round of constitutional discussions will indeed occur and that their own interests will then be addressed.

(b) Meech Lake Communiqué, April 30, 1987

At their meeting today at Meech Lake, the Prime Minister and the ten Premiers agreed to ask officials to transform into a constitutional text the agreement in principle found in the attached document.

First Ministers also agreed to hold a constitutional conference within weeks to approve a formal text intended to allow Quebec to resume its place as a full participant in Canada's constitutional development.

QUEBEC'S DISTINCT SOCIETY

(1) The Constitution of Canada shall be interpreted in a manner consistent with
  a) the recognition that the existence of French-speaking Canada, centred in but not limited to Quebec, and English-speaking Canada, concentrated outside Quebec but also present in Quebec, constitutes a fundamental characteristic of Canada; and
  b) the recognition that Quebec constitutes within Canada a distinct society.
(2) Parliament and the provincial legislatures, in the exercise of their respective powers, are committed to preserving the fundamental characteristics of Canada referred to in paragraph (1)(*a*).
(3) The role of the legislature and Government of Quebec to preserve and promote the distinct identity of Quebec referred to in paragraph (1)(*b*) is affirmed.

IMMIGRATION

—Provide under the Constitution that the Government of Canada shall negotiate an immigration agreement appropriate to the needs and circumstances of a province that so requests and that, once concluded, the agreement may be entrenched at the request of the province;
—such agreements must recognize the federal government's power to set national standards and objectives relating to immigration, such as the ability to determine general categories of immigrants, to establish overall levels of immigration and prescribe categories of inadmissible persons;
—under the foregoing provisions, conclude in the first instance an agreement with Quebec that would:
incorporate the principles of the Cullen-Couture agreement on the selection abroad and in Canada of independent immigrants, visitors for medical treatment, students and temporary workers, and on the selection of refugees abroad and economic criteria for family reunification and assisted relatives;
guarantee that Quebec will receive a number of immigrants, including refugees, within the annual total established by the federal government for all of Canada proportionate to its share of the population of Canada, with the right to exceed that figure by 5% for demographic reasons; and
provide an undertaking by Canada to withdraw services (except citizenship services) for the reception and integration (including linguistic and cultural) of all foreign nationals wishing to settle in Quebec where services are to be provided by Quebec, with such withdrawal to be accompanied by reasonable compensation;
—nothing in the foregoing should be construed as preventing the negotiation of similar agreements with other provinces.

SUPREME COURT OF CANADA

—Entrench the Supreme Court and the requirement that at least three of the nine justices appointed be from the civil bar;

—provide that, where there is a vacancy on the Supreme Court, the federal government shall appoint a person from a list of candidates proposed by the provinces and who is acceptable to the federal government.

SPENDING POWER

—Stipulate that Canada must provide reasonable compensation to any province that does not participate in a future national shared-cost program in an area of exclusive provincial jurisdiction if that province undertakes its own initiative or programs compatible with national objectives.

AMENDING FORMULA

—Maintain the current general amending formula set out in section 38, which requires the consent of Parliament and at least two-thirds of the provinces representing at least fifty percent of the population;
—guarantee reasonable compensation in all cases where a province opts out of an amendment transferring provincial jurisdiction to Parliament;
—because opting out of constitutional amendments to matters set out in section 42 of the *Constitution Act, 1982* is

not possible, require the consent of Parliament and all the provinces for such amendments.

SECOND ROUND

—Require that a First Ministers' Conference on the Constitution be held not less than once per year and that the first be held within twelve months of proclamation of this amendment but not later than the end of 1988;
—entrench in the Constitution the following items on the agenda:
1) Senate reform including:
    —the functions and role of the Senate;
    —the powers of the Senate;
    —the method of selection of Senators;
    —the distribution of Senate seats;
2) fisheries roles and responsibilities; and
3) other agreed upon matters;
—entrench in the Constitution the annual First Ministers' Conference on the Economy now held under the terms of the February 1985 Memorandum of Agreement;
—until constitutional amendments regarding the Senate are accomplished the federal government shall appoint persons from lists of candidates provided by provinces where vacancies occur and who are acceptable to the federal government.

56. 1987 Constitutional Accord, June 3, 1987*

(a) 1987 Constitutional Accord

WHEREAS first ministers, assembled in Ottawa, have arrived at a unanimous accord on constitutional amendments that would bring about the full and active participation of Quebec in Canada's constitutional evolution, would recognize the principle of equality of all the provinces, would provide new arrangements to foster greater harmony and cooperation between the Government of Canada and the governments of the provinces and would require that annual first ministers' conferences on the state of the Canadian economy and such other matters as may be appropriate be convened and that annual constitutional conferences composed of first ministers be convened commencing not later than December 31, 1988;

AND WHEREAS first ministers have also reached unanimous agreement on certain additional commitments in relation to some of those amendments;

NOW THEREFORE the Prime Minister of Canada and the first ministers of the provinces commit themselves and the governments they represent to the following:

1. The Prime Minister of Canada will lay or cause to be laid before the Senate and House of Commons, and the first ministers of the provinces will lay or cause to be laid before their legislative assemblies, as soon as possible, a resolution, in the form appended hereto, to authorize a proclamation to be issued by the Governor General under the Great Seal of Canada to amend the Constitution of Canada.

2. The Government of Canada will, as soon as possible, conclude an agreement with the Government of Quebec that would

(a) incorporate the principles of the Cullen-Couture agreement on the selection abroad and in Canada of independent immigrants, visitors for medical treatment, students and temporary workers, and on the selection of refugees abroad and economic criteria for family reunification and assisted relatives,

(b) guarantee that Quebec will receive a number of immigrants, including refugees, within the annual total established by the federal government for all of Canada proportionate to its share of the population of Canada, with the right to exceed that figure by five percent for demographic reasons, and

(c) provide an undertaking by Canada to withdraw services (except citizenship services) for the reception and integration (including linguistic and cultural) of all foreign nationals wishing to settle in Quebec where services are to be provided by Quebec, with such withdrawal to be accompanied by reasonable compensation,

and the Government of Canada and the Government of Quebec will take the necessary steps to give the agreement the force of law under the proposed amendment relating to such agreements.

3. Nothing in this Accord should be construed as preventing the negotiation of similar agreements with other provinces relating to immigration and the temporary admission of aliens.

4. Until the proposed amendment relating to appointments to the Senate comes into force, any person summoned to fill a vacancy in the Senate shall be chosen from among persons whose names have been submitted by the government of the province to which the vacancy relates and must be acceptable to the Queen's Privy Council for Canada.

Motion for a Resolution to authorize an amendment to the Constitution of Canada

WHEREAS the *Constitution Act, 1982* came into force on April 17, 1982, following an agreement between Canada and all the provinces except Quebec;

AND WHEREAS the Government of Quebec has established a set of five proposals for constitutional change and

---

* At the time of publication this Constitutional Accord has not become law. In order to do so a resolution authorizing a proclamation to be issued by the Governor General to amend the Constitution of Canada as set out in the Accord must be passed by both Houses of Parliament and all provincial Legislative Assemblies within three years from the adoption of the resolution initiating the amendment procedure (in this case: June 23, 1987 — the date the resolution was adopted by the Quebec National Assembly).

has stated that amendments to give effect to those proposals would enable Quebec to resume a full role in the constitutional councils of Canada;

AND WHEREAS the amendment proposed in the schedule hereto sets out the basis on which Quebec's five constitutional proposals may be met;

AND WHEREAS the amendment proposed in the schedule hereto also recognizes the principle of the equality of all the provinces, provides new arrangements to foster greater harmony and cooperation between the Government of Canada and the governments of the provinces and requires that conferences be convened to consider important constitutional, economic and other issues;

AND WHEREAS certain portions of the amendment proposed in the schedule hereto relate to matters referred to in section 41 of the *Constitution Act, 1982*;

AND WHEREAS section 41 of the *Constitution Act, 1982* provides that an amendment to the Constitution of Canada may be made by proclamation issued by the Governor General under the Great Seal of Canada where so authorized by resolutions of the Senate and the House of Commons and of the legislative assembly of each province;

NOW THEREFORE the (Senate) (House of Commons) (legislative assembly) resolves that an amendment to the Constitution of Canada be authorized to be made by proclamation issued by Her Excellency the Governor General under the Great Seal of Canada in accordance with the schedule hereto.

SCHEDULE

CONSTITUTION AMENDMENT, 1987

Constitution Act, 1867

1. The *Constitution Act, 1867* is amended by adding thereto, immediately after section 1 thereof, the following section:

Interpretation

"2.(1) The Constitution of Canada shall be interpreted in a manner consistent with

(*a*) the recognition that the existence of French-speaking Canadians, centred in Quebec but also present elsewhere in Canada, and English-speaking Canadians, concentrated outside Quebec but also present in Quebec, constitutes a fundamental characteristic of Canada; and

(*b*) the recognition that Quebec constitutes within Canada a distinct society.

Role of Parliament and legislatures

(2) The role of the Parliament of Canada and the provincial legislature to preserve the fundamental characteristic of Canada referred to in paragraph (1)(*a*) is affirmed.

Role of legislature and Government of Quebec

(3) The role of the legislature and Government of Quebec to preserve and promote the distinct identity of Quebec referred to in paragraph (1)(*b*) is affirmed.

Rights of legislatures and governments preserved

(4) Nothing in this section derogates from the powers, rights or privileges of Parliament or the Government of Canada, or of the legislatures or governments of the provinces, including any powers, rights or privileges relating to language."

2. The said Act is further amended by adding thereto, immediately after section 24 thereof, the following section:

Names to be submitted

"25.(1) Where a vacancy occurs in the Senate, the government of the province to which the vacancy relates may, in relation to that vacancy, submit to the Queen's Privy Council for Canada the names of persons who may be summoned to the Senate.

Choice of Senators from names submitted

(2) Until an amendment to the Constitution of Canada is made in relation to the Senate pursuant to section 41 of the *Constitution Act, 1982*, the person summoned to fill a vacancy in the Senate shall be chosen from among persons whose names have been submitted under subsection (1) by the government of the province to which the vacancy relates and must be acceptable to the Queen's Privy Council for Canada.''

3. The said Act is further amended by adding thereto, immediately after section 95 thereof, the following heading and sections:

"Agreements on Immigration and Aliens

Commitment to negotiate

95A. The Government of Canada shall, at the request of the government of any province, negotiate with the government of that province for the purpose of concluding an agreement relating to immigration or the temporary admission of aliens into that province that is appropriate to the needs and circumstances of that province.

Agreements

95B.(1) Any agreement concluded between Canada and a province in relation to immigration or the temporary admission of aliens into that province has the force of law from the time it is declared to do so in accordance with subsection 95C(1) and shall from that time have effect notwithstanding class 25 of section 91 or section 95.

Limitation

(2) An agreement that has the force of law under subsection (1) shall have effect only so long and so far as it is not repugnant to any provision of an Act of the Parliament of Canada that sets national standards and objectives relating to immigration or aliens, including any provision that establishes general classes of immigrants or relates to levels of immigration for Canada or that prescribes classes of individuals who are inadmissible into Canada.

Application of Charter

(3) The *Canadian Charter of Rights and Freedoms* applies in respect of any agreement that has the force of law under subsection (1) and in respect of anything done by the Parliament or Government of Canada, or the legislature or government of a province, pursuant to any such agreement.

Proclamation relating to agreements

95C.(1) A declaration that an agreement referred to in subsection 95B(1) has the force of law may be made by proclamation issued by the Governor General under the Great Seal of Canada only where so authorized by resolutions of the Senate and House of Commons and of the legislative assembly of the province that is a party to the agreement.

Amendment of agreements

(2) An amendment to an agreement referred to in subsection 95(B)(1) may be made by proclamation issued by the Governor General under the Great Seal of Canada only where so authorized

(*a*) by resolutions of the Senate and House of Commons and of the legislative assembly of the province that is a party to the agreement;

(*b*) in such other manner as is set out in the agreement.

Application of sections 46 to 48 of *Constitution Act, 1982*

95D. Sections 46 to 48 of the *Constitution Act, 1982* apply, with such modifications as the circumstances require, in respect of any declaration made pursuant to subsection 95C(1), any amendment to an agreement made pursuant to subsection 95C(2) or any amendment made pursuant to section 95E.

Amendments to sections 95A to 95D or this section

95E. An amendment to sections 95A to 95D or this section may be made in accordance with the procedure set out in subsection 38(1) of the *Constitution Act, 1982*, but only if the amendment is authorized by resolutions of the legislative assemblies of all the provinces that are, at the time of the amendment, parties to an agreement that has the force of law under subsection 95B(1).''

4. The said Act is further amended by adding thereto, immediately preceding section 96 thereof, the following heading:

''*General*''

5. The said Act is further amended by adding thereto, immediately preceding section 101 thereof, the following heading:

''*Courts Established by the Parliament of Canada*''

6. The said Act is further amended by adding thereto, immediately after section 101 thereof, the following heading and sections:

''*Supreme Court of Canada*

Supreme Court continued

101A.(1) The court existing under the name of the Supreme Court of Canada is hereby continued as the general court of appeal for Canada, and as an additional court for the better administration of the laws of Canada, and shall continue to be a superior court of record.

Constitution of court

(2) The Supreme Court of Canada shall consist of a chief justice to be called the Chief Justice of Canada and eight other judges, who shall be appointed by the Governor General in Council by letters patent under the Great Seal.

Who may be appointed judges

101B.(1) Any person may be appointed a judge of the Supreme Court of Canada who, after having been admitted to the bar of any province or territory, has, for a total of at least ten years, been a judge of any court in Canada or a member of the bar of any province or territory.

Three judges from Quebec

(2) At least three judges of the Supreme Court of Canada shall be appointed from among persons who, after having been admitted to the bar of Quebec, have, for a total of at least ten years, been judges of any court of Quebec or of any court established by the Parliament of Canada, or members of the bar of Quebec.

Names may be submitted

101C.(1) Where a vacancy occurs in the Supreme Court of Canada, the government of each province may, in relation to that vacancy, submit to the Minister of Justice of Canada the names of any of the persons who have been admitted to the bar of that province and are qualified under section 101B for appointment to that court.

Appointment from names submitted

(2) Where an appointment is made to the Supreme Court of Canada, the Governor General in Council shall, except where the Chief Justice is appointed from among members of the Court, appoint a person whose name has been submitted under subsection (1) and who is acceptable to the Queen's Privy Council for Canada.

Appointment from Quebec

(3) Where an appointment is made in accordance with subsection (2) of any of the three judges necessary to meet the requirement set out in subsection 101B(2), the Government General in Council shall appoint a person whose name has been submitted by the Government of Quebec.

Appointment from other provinces

(4) Where an appointment is made in accordance with subsection (2) otherwise than as required under subsection (3), the Governor General in Council shall appoint a person whose name has been submitted by the government of a province other than Quebec.

Tenure, salaries, etc. of judges

101D. Sections 99 and 100 apply in respect of the judges of the Supreme Court of Canada.

Relationship to section 101

101E.(1) Sections 101A to 101D shall not be construed as abrogating or derogating from the powers of the Parliament of Canada to make laws under section 101 except to the extent that such laws are inconsistent with those sections.

References to the Supreme Court of Canada

(2) For greater certainty, section 101A shall not be construed as abrogating or derogating from the powers of the Parliament of Canada to make laws relating to the reference of questions of law or fact, or any other matters, to the Supreme Court of Canada.''

7. The said Act is further amended by adding thereto, immediately after section 106 thereof, the following section:

Shared-cost program

''106A.(1) The Government of Canada shall provide reasonable compensation to the government of a province that chooses not to participate in a national shared-cost program that is established by the Government of Canada after the coming into force of this section, in an area of exclusive provincial jurisdiction, if the province carries on a program or initiative that is compatible with the national objectives.

Legislative power not extended

(2) Nothing in this section extends the legislative powers of the Parliament of Canada or of the legislatures of the provinces.''

8. The said Act is further amended by adding thereto the following heading and sections:

''XII — *Conferences on the Economy and Other Matters*

Conferences on the economy and other matters

148. A conference composed of the Prime Minister of Canada and the first ministers of the provinces shall be convened by the Prime Minister of Canada at least once each year to discuss the state of the Canadian economy and such other matters as may be appropriate.

XIII — *References*

Reference includes amendments

149. A reference to this Act shall be deemed to include a reference to any amendments thereto.''

Constitution Act, 1982

9. Sections 40 to 42 of the *Constitution Act, 1982* are repealed and the following substituted therefor:

Compensation

"40. Where an amendment is made under subsection 38(1) that transfers legislative powers from provincial legislatures to Parliament, Canada shall provide reasonable compensation to any province to which the amendment does not apply.

Amendment by unanimous consent

41. An amendment to the Constitution of Canada in relation to the following matters may be made by proclamation issued by the Governor General under the Great Seal of Canada only where authorized by resolutions of the Senate and House of Commons and of the legislative assembly of each province:

(*a*) the office of the Queen, the Governor General and the Lieutenant Governor of a province;

(*b*) the powers of the Senate and the method of selecting Senators;

(*c*) the number of members by which a province is entitled to be represented in the Senate and the residence qualifications of Senators;

(*d*) the right of a province to a number of members in the House of Commons not less than the number of Senators by which the province *was* entitled to be represented on *April 17, 1982*;

(*e*) the principle of proportionate representation of the provinces in the House of Commons prescribed by the Constitution of Canada;

(*f*) subject to section 43, the use of the English or the French language;

(*g*) the Supreme Court of Canada;

(*h*) the extension of existing provinces into the territories;

(*i*) notwithstanding any other law or practice, the establishment of new provinces; and

(*j*) an amendment to this Part."

10. Section 44 of the said Act is repealed and the following substituted therefor:

Amendments by Parliament

"44. Subject to section 41, Parliament may exclusively make laws amending the Constitution of Canada in relation to the executive government of Canada or the Senate and House of Commons."

11. Subsection 46(1) of the said Act is repealed and the following substituted therefor:

Initiation of amendment procedures

"46.(1) The procedures for amendment under sections 38, 41 and 43 may be initiated either by the Senate or the House of Commons or by the legislative assembly of a province."

12. Subsection 47(1) of the said Act is repealed and the following substituted therefor:

Amendments without Senate resolution

"47.(1) An amendment to the Constitution of Canada made by proclamation under section 38, 41 or 43 may be made without a resolution of the Senate authorizing the issue of the proclamation if, within one hundred and eighty days after the adoption by the House of Commons of a resolution authorizing its issue, the Senate has not adopted such a resolution and if, at any time after the expiration of that period, the House of Commons again adopts the resolution."

13. Part VI of the said Act is repealed and the following substituted therefor:

"PART VI
Constitutional Conferences

Constitutional conference

50(1). A constitutional conference composed of the Prime Minister of Canada and the first ministers of the provinces shall be convened by the Prime Minister of Canada at least once each year, commencing in 1988.

Agenda

(2) The conferences convened under subsection (1) shall have included on their agenda the following matters:

(*a*) Senate reform, including the role and functions of the Senate, its powers, the method of selecting Senators and representation in the Senate;

(*b*) roles and responsibilities in relation to fisheries; and

(*c*) such other matters as are agreed upon."

14. Subsection 52(2) of the said Act is amended by striking out the word "and" at the end of paragraph (b) thereof, by adding the word "and" at the end of paragraph (c) thereof and by adding thereto the following paragraph:

"(*d*) any other amendment to the Constitution of Canada."

15. Section 61 of the said Act is repealed and the following substituted therefor:

References

"61. *A reference to the Constitution Act 1982, or* a reference to the *Constitution Acts 1867 to 1982*, shall be deemed to include a reference to *any amendments thereto.*"

General

Multicultural heritage and aboriginal peoples

16. Nothing in section 2 of the *Constitution Act, 1867* affects section 25 or 27 of the *Canadian Charter of Rights and Freedoms*, section 35 of the *Constitution Act, 1982* or class 24 of section 91 of the *Constitution Act, 1867.*

Citation

Citation

17. This amendment may be cited as the *Constitution Amendment, 1987.*

Signed at Ottawa, June 3, 1987/*Fait à Ottawa le 3 juin 1987*:

Brian Mulroney/Canada

David Peterson/Ontario

Robert Bourassa/Quebec

John Buchanan/Nova Scotia/*Nouvelle-Écosse*

Richard B. Hatfield/New Brunswick/*Nouveau Brunswick*

Howard Pawley/Manitoba

Bill Vander Zalm/British Columbia/*Colombie-Britannique*

Joseph A. Ghiz/Prince Edward Island/*Ile-du-Prince-Édouard*

Grant Devine/Saskatchewan

Donald R. Getty/Alberta

A. Brian Peckford/Newfoundland/*Terre-Neuve*

(b) A Guide to the Constitutional Accord of June 3, 1987, Produced by the Prime Minister's Office

INTRODUCTION

On April 30, 1987, First Ministers met at Meech Lake, Quebec, to consider proposals intended to bring about Quebec's full participation in Canada's constitutional evolution and to lead governments to begin a "second round" of discussions on further constitutional change. At that meeting, First Ministers reached unanimous agreement on six major elements of constitutional change, which were set out in what has become known as the Meech Lake agreement. On the basis of that document, officials were instructed to draft constitutional amendments. The proposed amendments were reviewed and unanimously approved by First Ministers at their meeting in Ottawa on June 2 and 3, 1987, together with a companion political accord.

The purpose of this document is to highlight briefly the principal features of (a) the political accord, (b) the constitutional resolution which will be submitted to Parliament and the legislatures, and (c) the text of the proposed amendments.

CANADA'S CONSTITUTION AND ITS AMENDMENT

In proceeding with these amendments, all First Ministers have been mindful of their role as modern Fathers of Confederation. Patriation of the Constitution on April 17, 1982 was an historic milestone in Canada's constitutional history, which ensured Canadians could effect changes necessary to the development of their modern federation without reference to the British Parliament. It also provided Canadians with a Charter of Rights and Freedoms. Nevertheless, the achievement of patriation was flawed because Quebec, which represents over a quarter of the Canadian population, did not agree to the constitutional accord of November 5, 1981.

The constitutional resolution agreed to by First Ministers on June 3, once approved by the Senate, House of Commons and the legislative assembly of each province,

and proclaimed in force by the Governor General, will give constitutional expression to the principles of the Meech Lake agreement. These amendments will be the first that have been supported by all provinces, including Quebec, since patriation and proclamation of the *Constitution Act, 1982*.

Proclamation of the amendments agreed to on June 3 will ensure that Quebec participates fully once again in the constitutional councils of Canada. It will also set in motion an agenda for constitutional discussions in the years ahead.

THE MEECH LAKE AGREEMENT AND THE 1987 CONSTITUTIONAL RESOLUTION

The Meech Lake agreement expressed First Ministers' commitment to proceed with constitutional amendments in six areas: Quebec's distinct society, immigration, the Supreme Court, the spending power of Parliament, the amending formula and a second round of constitutional discussions (the last item also covered conferences of the economy and Senate appointments).

In developing the legal text for the amendments, First Ministers further agreed that the spirit and wording of the Meech Lake agreement should be respected as much as possible and that all Meech Lake commitments be honoured. This has been accomplished, in part, through the political accord and, for the most part, in the text of the proposed amendments appended to the resolution.

There are, then, three documents:
—the *political accord* sets out First Ministers' commitment to proceed expeditiously with the constitutional amendments and certain other related undertakings that would be inappropriate in the Constitution itself;
—the *motion for a resolution* provides the means for seeking authorization by the two Houses of Parliament and the provincial legislative assemblies of a constitutional proclamation by the Governor General of the amendments set out in the schedule to the resolution;
—in the *schedule* to the resolution are found the actual *texts*

of the proposed amendments to the Constitution.

The schedule, entitled the *Constitution Amendment, 1987* will have a life of its own after proclamation. But since most of its clauses will amend either the *Constitution Act, 1867* or the *Constitution Act, 1982*, little will remain in it after the amendments have been consolidated with the Acts to which they refer.

Let us then look at the three documents.

1. THE 1987 CONSTITUTIONAL ACCORD

The Accord sets out the commitment by all First Ministers and the governments they represent to take early action on the constitutional amendment resolution, as well as three other commitments arising out of the Meech Lake agreement that are not reflected in the amendments.

The "preamble" to the Accord reflects the intention of the Meech Lake agreement: that is, to bring about Quebec's full and active participation in Canada's constitutional evolution, to foster greater harmony among governments through new arrangements and to hold annual constitutional conferences, the first of which must be held before the end of 1988. The agenda of those conferences will include Senate reform, fisheries roles and responsibilities and other agreed upon matters. The Accord then goes on to state four commitments:

—the first is to lay or cause to be laid before the Senate and House of Commons and the provincial legislative assemblies the resolution as soon as possible;

—the second provides that, prior to proclamation of these amendments, an immigration agreement shall be concluded between Canada and Quebec which will subsequently receive constitutional protection in accordance with the procedure provided by the new constitutional provisions respecting immigration;

—the third confirms that immigration agreements with other provinces can also be negotiated;

—the final commitment ensures that the new nomination procedure for Senators (described below) is to take effect forthwith upon signature of the Accord and prior to the proclamation of the amendments.

2. THE MOTION FOR A RESOLUTION

This is the formal instrument which, once approved by the Senate, the House of Commons and the provincial legislative assemblies, will authorize the Governor General of Canada to proclaim the amendments. Once proclaimed, these amendments will become part of the Constitution and could not be changed except in accordance with the appropriate amending formula in the Constitution.

The first three recitals (the paragraphs beginning with "whereas") in the motion merely state that Quebec did not consent to the November 5, 1981 agreement to patriate the Constitution; that it set out five constitutional proposals upon which action would enable it to resume a full role in the constitutional councils of Canada; and that those proposals provide the basis of these amendments. The fourth recital notes the amendments will provide for new cooperative arrangements among governments and for a "second round" of constitutional deliberations. The fifth and sixth recitals make clear that unanimous consent will be necessary for the proclamation. The seventh paragraph is the resolution itself.

3. SCHEDULE: CONSTITUTION AMENDMENT, 1987

The schedule to the resolution provides the legal amendment text based on the Meech Lake agreement. It comprises amendments to certain provisions of the *Constitution Act, 1867* and the *Constitution Act, 1982*, as well as certain provisions that will remain in the *Constitution Amendment, 1987*.

QUEBEC'S DISTINCT SOCIETY

The wording of this section (found in clause 1 of the *Constitution Amendment, 1987*) is taken from the Meech Lake agreement and reflects First Ministers' intention to recognize that the existence of English-speaking Canadians and French-speaking Canadians, both present in all parts of the country, but the latter concentrated within and the former outside Quebec, constitutes a fundamental characteristic of Canada. It would also recognize that Quebec constitutes a distinct society within Canada.

The section also affirms the role of Parliament and all legislatures to preserve the fundamental characteristic of Canada recognized above, and the role of the government and legislature of Quebec to preserve and promote its distinct identity.

However, it is made clear that nothing in the section derogates from the existing powers, rights or privileges of either order of government, including those relating to language.

This section will become a new section 2 of the *Constitution Act, 1867*. Clause 16 of the *Constitution Amendment, 1987* ensures that nothing in it affects the provisions of the Constitution respecting the aboriginal peoples or the multicultural heritage of Canadians.

SENATE APPOINTMENTS

The second clause of the *Constitution Amendment, 1987* will add a new section 25 to the *Constitution Act, 1867* respecting the procedure for summoning persons to the Senate. When a vacancy occurs in relation to a province, the provincial government will submit names of persons to fill the seat, but the person ultimately chosen for appointment must be named by (and thus be acceptable to) the Government of Canada. Technically, the Queen's Privy Council for Canada (i.e., the federal Cabinet) recommends that the Governor General "summon" the nominee it finds acceptable to sit in the Senate.

IMMIGRATION

The third clause of the *Constitution Amendment, 1987* will add sections 95A to 95E to the *Constitution Act, 1867*. Section 95 of that Act provides that immigration is a concurrent power with federal paramountcy.

Section 95A commits Canada to negotiate an immigration agreement with any province that so requests. Such an agreement, once concluded, could receive constitutional protection under procedures set out in sections 95B and 95C, and could not be unilaterally changed by either party subsequently.

These sections are based on the Meech Lake agreement and would allow constitutional protection for arrangements agreed upon by the federal government and a provincial government respecting immigration and the temporary admission of aliens into Canada.

Subsection 95B(2) of the constitutional amendment will ensure the federal government retains control over the national standards and objectives of immigration policy, primarily through its ability to establish classes of immigrants and admission criteria, to determine overall levels of immigration and to prescribe categories of inadmissible persons.

Furthermore, whatever immigration agreements with the provinces are eventually entrenched in the Constitution, the mobility rights of Canadian citizens and permanent residents protected by section 6 of the *Canadian Charter of Rights and Freedoms* will apply, as will all the other provisions of the Charter.

Sections 95B and C are, in effect, constitutional amend-ment procedures. Sections 95D and E set out special amending procedures for the amendment of 95B and C. Among other things, they seek to ensure that the constitutional foundation of an immigration agreement could not be abrogated without the consent of the province directly concerned.

SUPREME COURT OF CANADA

The sixth clause would add sections 101A to 101E to the *Constitution Act, 1867*. Their effect would be to entrench the Supreme Court, as agreed at Meech Lake, as well as the requirement that at least three of the nine Justices be appointed from the Quebec Bar (this reflects the existing requirement of the *Supreme Court Act*). Quebec, of course, is the only province with a civil code system.

Section 101C provides for a nomination process for appointments to the Supreme Court whereby a person acceptable to the federal government would be chosen from names proposed by the provinces. Only Quebec may propose persons for the three appointments representing its system of civil law and only the other provinces may propose persons to fill vacancies for the six positions which represent the common law tradition.

THE SPENDING POWER

The seventh clause of the 1987 Amendment will add section 106A to the *Constitution Act, 1867*. The purpose of this provision is not to define or extend the spending power of Parliament, but rather to require that the Government of Canada provide reasonable compensation to the government of a province that chooses not to participate in new national shared-cost programs in areas of exclusive provincial jurisdiction, but only if the province carries on a program or initiative compatible with the national objectives.

CONFERENCES ON THE ECONOMY AND OTHER MATTERS

The eighth clause of the 1987 Amendment adds a new part XII to the *Constitution Act, 1867*, which would require the Prime Minister to convene once a year a First Ministers' Conference on the Canadian economy and such other matters as may be appropriate.

THE AMENDING FORMULA

The ninth clause of the 1987 Amendment will amend section 40 of the *Constitution Act, 1982* to require reasonable compensation in all cases where a province exercises its right to opt out of an amendment transferring provincial legislative jurisdiction to Parliament, rather than, as at present, restricting such compensation to transfers related to education and other cultural matters.

The ninth clause will also combine sections 41 and 42 of the *Constitution Act, 1982*. Section 41 requires unanimous consent for changes to some national institutions and the amending formula, while section 42 requires the support of Parliament and at least two-thirds of the provinces representing at least 50 per cent of the population of all the provinces for other amendments to certain national institutions and the creation of new provinces.

Now one rule — unanimity — will apply to all of these matters. The deletion of section 42 from the *Constitution Act, 1982* will require a number of consequential changes.

CONSTITUTIONAL CONFERENCES

The thirteenth clause of the 1987 Amendment will provide a new Part VI on Constitutional Conferences in the *Constitution Act, 1982*. It will require that the Prime Minister convene a First Ministers' Constitutional Conference at least once a year, beginning in 1988. The agenda will include Senate reform, fisheries roles and responsibilities and such other matters as may be agreed upon.

THE NEXT STEPS

Each First Minister has agreed to take steps as soon as possible to introduce the resolution in Parliament or the provincial legislature, as the case may be. Once the resolution has been adopted, the Speaker will send a certified copy of the resolution as adopted to the Clerk of the Privy Council (the Secretary to Cabinet) in Ottawa.

When the Clerk of the Privy Council has ascertained that all of the resolutions have been adopted in proper form and that the necessary conditions to authorize a proclamation by the Governor General have been met, he so informs the Queen's Privy Council for Canada (the Cabinet) which, in turn, advises the Governor General to issue a proclamation forthwith.

When Her Excellency the Governor General proclaims the *Constitution Amendment, 1987*, an important but flawed chapter in Canada's constitutional development will come to an end. Governments, with new arrangements favouring greater harmony and cooperation, and Canadian citizens, will then be able to set their sights on the future and work towards a constitutional renewal that will enhance national identity, strengthen federal institutions in the service of the people, and further ensure a tolerant and open society.

Appendices

Appendix 1: Canadian Bill of Rights, S.C. 1960, c. 44

An Act for the Recognition and Protection of Human Rights and Fundamental Freedoms

8-9 Elizabeth II, c. 44 (Canada)

(Assented to 10th August 1960)

Preamble

The Parliament of Canada, affirming that the Canadian Nation is founded upon principles that acknowledge the supremacy of God, the dignity and worth of the human person and the position of the family in a society of free men and free institutions;

Affirming also that men and institutions remain free only when freedom is founded upon respect for moral and spiritual values and the rule of law;

And being desirous of enshrining these principles and the human rights and fundamental freedoms derived from them, in a Bill of Rights which shall reflect the respect of Parliament for its constitutional authority and which shall ensure the protection of these rights and freedoms in Canada:

Therefore Her Majesty, by and with the advice and consent of the Senate and House of Commons of Canada, enacts as follows:

PART I

BILL OF RIGHTS

Recognition and declaration of rights and freedoms

1. It is hereby recognized and declared that in Canada there have existed and shall continue to exist without discrimination by reason of race, national origin, colour, religion or sex, the following human rights and fundamental freedoms, namely,

(a) the right of the individual to life, liberty, security of the person and enjoyment of property, and the right not to be deprived thereof except by due process of law;

(b) the right of the individual to equality before the law and the protection of the law;

(c) freedom of religion;

(d) freedom of speech;

(e) freedom of assembly and association; and

(f) freedom of the press.

Construction of law

2. Every law of Canada shall, unless it is expressly declared by an Act of the Parliament of Canada that it shall operate notwithstanding the *Canadian Bill of*

Rights, be so construed and applied as not to abrogate, abridge or infringe or to authorize the abrogation, abridgment or infringement of any of the rights or freedoms herein recognized and declared, and in particular, no law of Canada shall be construed or applied so as to

(*a*) authorize or effect the arbitrary detention, imprisonment or exile of any person;

(*b*) impose or authorize the imposition of cruel and unusual treatment or punishment;

(*c*) deprive a person who has been arrested or detained

(i) of the right to be informed promptly of the reason for his arrest or detention,

(ii) of the right to retain and instruct counsel without delay, or

(iii) of the remedy by way of *habeas corpus* for the determination of the validity of his detention and for his release if the detention is not lawful;

(*d*) authorize a court, tribunal, commission, board or other authority to compel a person to give evidence if he is denied counsel, protection against self crimination or other constitutional safeguards;

(*e*) deprive a person of the right to a fair hearing in accordance with the principles of fundamental justice for the determination of his rights and obligations;

(*f*) deprive a person charged with a criminal offence of the right to be presumed innocent until proved guilty according to law in a fair and public hearing by an independent and impartial tribunal, or of the right to reasonable bail without just cause; or

(*g*) deprive a person of the right to the assistance of an interpreter in any proceedings in which he is involved or in which he is a party or a witness, before a court, commission, board or other tribunal, if he does not understand or speak the language in which such proceedings are conducted.

Duties of Minister of Justice

3. The Minister of Justice shall, in accordance with such regulations as may be prescribed by the Governor in Council, examine every proposed regulation submitted in draft form to the Clerk of the Privy Council pursuant to the *Regulations Act* and every Bill introduced in or presented to the House of Commons, in order to ascertain whether any of the provisions thereof are inconsistent with the purposes and provisions of this Part and he shall report any such inconsistency to the House of Commons at the first convenient opportunity.

Short title

4. The provisions of this Part shall be known as the *Canadian Bill of Rights*.

PART II

Savings

5. (1) Nothing in Part I shall be construed to abrogate or abridge any human right or fundamental freedom not enumerated therein that may have existed in Canada at the commencement of this Act.

"Law of Canada" defined

(2) The expression "law of Canada" in Part I means an Act of the Parliament of Canada enacted before or after the coming into force of this Act, any order, rule or regulation thereunder, and any law in force in Canada or in any part of Canada at the commencement of this Act that is subject to be repealed, abolished or altered by the Parliament of Canada.

Jurisdiction of Parliament

(3) The provisions of Part I shall be construed as extending only to matters coming within the legislative authority of the Parliament of Canada.

Appendix 2: *Re Attorney General of Quebec and Attorney General of Canada* (1982), 140 D.L.R. (3d) 385 (S.C.C.)

Supreme Court of Canada, Laskin C.J.C., Ritchie, Dickson, Beetz, Estey, McIntyre, Chouinard, Lamer and Wilson JJ. December 6, 1982.

Constitutional law — Amendment — Constitutional convention — Whether agreement of Quebec required for amendments to Constitution of Canada affecting legislative authority of its Legislature and status or role of its Legislature and Government.

Pursuant to the *Court of Appeal Reference Act*, R.S.Q. 1977, c. R-23, the Government of Quebec submitted the following question to the Quebec Court of Appeal:

"Is the consent of the Province of Quebec constitutionally required, by convention, for the adoption by the Senate and the House of Commons of Canada of a resolution the purpose of which is to cause the Canadian Constitution to be amended in such a manner as to affect:

i) the legislative competence of the Legislature of the Province of Quebec in virtue of the Canadian Constitution;

ii) the status or role of the Legislature or Government of the Province of Quebec within the Canadian federation;

and does the objection of the Province of Quebec render the adoption of such resolution unconstitutional in the conventional sense?"

The Quebec Court of Appeal answered the question in the negative. The Attorney-General of Quebec appealed to the Supreme Court of Canada. *Held*, the appeal should be dismissed.

The appellant made two submissions, the first claiming a conventional rule of unanimity and the second a conventional power of veto. While the submissions seek the same answer to the constitutional question, they are alternative ones as they actually contradict one another. The rule of unanimity is predicated on the fundamental equality of all the provinces as it would give a power of veto to each of them. An exclusive power of veto for Quebec negates the rule of unanimity as well as the principle of fundamental equality.

The main purpose of constitutional conventions is to ensure that the legal framework of the Constitution will be operated in accordance with generally accepted principles. Conventional rules, although quite distinct from legal rules, are nevertheless to be distinguished from rules of morality, rules of expediency and subjective rules. Like legal rules, they are positive rules the existence of which has to be ascertained by reference to objective standards. In being asked to answer the question whether the convention did or did not exist, the court is called upon to say

whether or not the objective requirements for establishing a convention have been met. But it is not called upon to say whether it is desirable that the convention should or should not exist. There are three requirements for establishing a conventional rule: there must be precedents recognizing the rule; there must be a reason for the rule; and the actors in the precedents must believe that they are bound by the rule.

(1) *Whether there exists a conventional rule of unanimity*

In an earlier reference the court was unanimous in rejecting the conventional rule of unanimity. In the opinion of the majority, one essential requirement was missing: acceptance of the rule of unanimity by all the actors in the precedents. The appellant advanced no compelling reasons why this opinion should be modified. That some of the actors in the precedents had accepted the rule of unanimity is not enough. Other important actors declined to accept the unanimity rule. The opinion expressed in the first reference that there existed no conventional rule of unanimity should be reaffirmed.

(2) *Whether Quebec has a conventional power of veto*

The reasons advanced by the appellant for the existence of such a conventional rule is the principle of duality, the principle being understood in the special sense of viewing Quebec as a distinct society within the Canadian federation. However, the appellant failed to demonstrate compliance with the most important requirement for establishing a convention, that is, acceptance or recognition by the actors in the precedents. The federal authorities had not recognized either explicitly or by necessary implication that Quebec had a conventional power of veto over certain types of constitutional amendments. Nor was there any statement by the actors in any of the other provinces acknowledging such a convention. Recognition by the actors in the precedents is not only an essential element of conventions. It is the most important element since it is the normative one, the formal one which enables one unmistakably to distinguish a constitutional rule from a rule of convenience or from political expediency.

[*Reference re Amendment of the Constitution of Canada (Nos. 1, 2 and 3)* (1981), 125 D.L.R. (3d) 1, [1981] 1 S.C.R. 753, 11 Man. R. (2d) 1, 34 Nfld. & P.E.I.R. 1, [1981] 6 W.W.R. 1, 34 N.R. 1, folld]

Constitutional law — Reference — Constitutional convention — Political question — Question referred should be answered by court if, although having political element, it also has constitutional feature.

[*Reference re Amendment of the Constitution of Canada (Nos. 1, 2 and 3)* (1981), 125 D.L.R. (3d) 1, [1981] 1 S.C.R. 753, 11 Man. R. (2d) 1, 34 Nfld. & P.E.I.R. 1, [1981] 6 W.W.R. 1, 34 N.R. 1, folld]

Constitutional law — Reference — Constitutional convention — Moot question — Consent of Quebec to substantial amendments to Constitution — Quebec Court of Appeal giving opinion on reference just before proclamation of Constitution Act, 1982 — Appeal to Supreme Court of Canada as of right — Discretion in Supreme Court not to entertain appeal where issue moot — Importance of constitutional issue — Discretion exercised in favour of hearing appeal.

APPEAL by the Attorney-General of Quebec from a judgment of the Quebec Court of Appeal, 134 D.L.R. (3d) 719, on a reference of a constitutional question to the court pursuant to the *Court of Appeal Reference Act* (Que.).

Jean K. Samson, Henri Brun, Robert Décary and *Odette Laverdière*, for appellant.

Raynold Langlois, Michel Robert, Edward Goldenberg, Louis Reynolds, Louise Cadieux, Luc Martineau and *Claude Joli-Coeur*, for respondent.

Emile Colas, Q.C., for intervenant, Association canadienne-francaise de l'Ontario.

James O'Reilly, for intervenant, Grand Council of the Crees (of Quebec).

BY THE COURT: —

I — *The Facts*

This is an appeal from the opinion pronounced on April 7, 1982, by the Quebec Court of Appeal on a question referred to it by the Government of Quebec regarding the resolution to amend the Constitution.

This appeal is brought as of right pursuant to s. 37 of the *Supreme Court Act*, R.S.C. 1970, c. S-19, and to s. 1 of an *Act respecting a reference to the Court of Appeal*, 1981 (Que.), c. 17.

The reference is the second one on this subject. The first reference also gave rise to an appeal to this court in which judgment was delivered on September 28, 1981, at the same time as in two other appeals arising from a reference by the Government of Manitoba and a reference by the Government of Newfoundland: *Reference re Amendment of the Constitution of Canada (Nos. 1, 2 and 3)*, 125

D.L.R. (3d) 1, [1981] 1 S.C.R. 753, 11 Man. R. (2d) 1, 34 Nfld. & P.E.I.R. 1, hereinafter referred to as the *First Reference*.

Following the judgment in the *First Reference*, the Government of Canada and the governments of the ten provinces held a Constitutional Conference, on November 2 to 5, 1981, to seek agreement on the patriation of the Constitution together with a charter of rights and an amending formula. On November 5, 1981, Canada and nine of the ten provinces signed an agreement to this effect. Quebec was the dissenting province.

By the agreement of November 5, 1981, in essence, the Government of Canada and the Governments of Ontario and New Brunswick accepted, with some amendments, a procedure for amending the Constitution of Canada, the so-called Vancouver formula, which had been agreed upon on April 16, 1981, by the eight other provinces. Nova Scotia, Manitoba, British Columbia, Prince Edward Island, Alberta, Saskatchewan and Newfoundland also accepted, with some amendments, the entrenchment of a *Canadian Charter of Rights and Freedoms*, binding on Parliament and the provincial legislatures, already agreed upon by the Government of Canada and the Governments of Ontario and New Brunswick.

On November 18, 1981, the Minister of Justice of Canada laid before the House of Commons a resolution which contained a joint address of the Senate and the House of Commons to be presented to Her Majesty the Queen in right of the United Kingdom. While in substance the joint address reflected the agreement of November 5, 1981, it was similar in form to the one quoted in the *First Reference*, at p. 15 D.L.R., p. 766 S.C.R. It included a draft United Kingdom statute the short title of which was the *Canada Act* which, in turn, had appended to it another draft statute entitled the *Constitution Act, 1981*, later designated as the *Constitution Act, 1982*. The latter statute provided for the entrenchment of a *Canadian Charter of Rights and Freedoms* and it contained the new procedure for amending the Constitution of Canada. The *Constitution Act, 1982* also contained a range of other provisions which it is unnecessary to enumerate.

Section 2 of the *Canada Act* constituted the so-called abdication clause, reading as follows:

2. No Act of the Parliament of the United Kingdom passed after the *Constitution Act, 1981* comes into force shall extend to Canada as part of its law.

On November 25, 1981, the Government of Quebec expressed its formal opposition to the proposed resolution in Decree No. 3214-81 (translation:)

DECREE

GOVERNMENT OF QUEBEC

CONCERNING the objection by Quebec
to the proposed patriation and amendment
of the Constitution of Canada;

WHEREAS on November 18, 1981 the federal government tabled in the House of Commons a motion regarding the patriation and amendment of the Constitution of Canada;

WHEREAS if implemented, this motion would have the effect of substantially reducing the powers and rights of Quebec and of its National Assembly without its consent;

WHEREAS it has always been recognized that no change of this kind could be made without the consent of Quebec.

BE IT RESOLVED, on the motion of the Premier:

THAT Quebec formally vetoes the resolution tabled in the House of Commons on November 18, 1981 by the federal Minister of Justice.

THAT this objection be officially communicated to the federal government and the governments of the other provinces.

AUTHENTIC COPY
DEPUTY CLERK OF THE
EXECUTIVE COUNCIL
Jean Pierre Vaillancourt

On the same date, the Government of Quebec ordered the present reference in Decree No. 3215-81. It is unnecessary to quote this decree, however, as it was superseded by Decree No. 3367-81, the text of which is quoted below, adopted on December 9, 1981, and drafted in almost identical terms as Decree No. 3215-81, except for two minor corrections in the preamble which made allowance for the fact that by then, the joint address had already been voted.

The joint address was adopted by the House of Commons on December 2, 1981, and by the Senate on December 8, 1981. It included further amendments agreed upon by Canada and all the provinces except Quebec.

On December 8, 1981, the Governor General of Canada received the text of the joint address and, pursuant to the advice of Her Majesty's Privy Council for Canada, transmitted it to Her Majesty on December 9, 1981.

On the same date, the Government of Quebec reordered the present reference in Decree No. 3367-81 (translation):

WHEREAS the Senate and House of Commons of Canada adopted a Resolution regarding the Constitution of Canada;

WHEREAS this Resolution requests the introduction in the Parliament of the United Kingdom of a bill entitled the Canada Act which, if adopted by the Parliament of the United Kingdom, will most notably have the effect of enacting for Canada the Constitution Act, 1981;

WHEREAS the proposed legislation has the effect of making significant changes in the status and role of Quebec within the Canadian federal system;

WHEREAS Quebec forms a distinct society within the Canadian federation;

WHEREAS the Supreme Court of Canada stated on September 28, 1981 that the consent of the provinces is constitutionally necessary for the adoption of this proposal;

WHEREAS Quebec has not agreed and has objected to the proposed changes;

WHEREAS no change of a similar significance to that proposed in this Resolution has to date been made without the consent and over the objection of Quebec;

WHEREAS it is expedient to submit to the Court of Appeal for hearing and consideration, pursuant to the Court of Appeal Reference Act the question herein below set out.

ACCORDINGLY, it is ordered, upon the proposal of the Minister of Justice, that the following question be submitted to the Court of Appeal for hearing and consideration:

Is the consent of the Province of Quebec consitutionally required, by convention, for the adoption by the Senate and the House of Commons of Canada of a resolution the purpose of which is to cause the Canadian Constitution to be amended in such a manner as to affect:

    i) the legislative competence of the Legislature of the Province of Quebec in virtue of the Canadian Constitution;

    ii) the status or role of the Legislature or Government of the Province of Quebec within the Canadian federation;

and, does the objection of the Province of Quebec render the adoption of such resolution unconstitutional in the conventional sense?

On December 22, 1981, the Government of the United Kingdom introduced in the Parliament of Westminster a bill known as "A Bill to Give Effect to a Request of the Senate and House of Commons of Canada" which was to become the *Canada Act*, 1982 (U.K.), c. 11.

The Quebec Court of Appeal heard counsel in argument on the reference on March 15, 16 and 17, 1982.

The bill introduced at Westminster was passed on March 29, 1982 and received royal assent on March 29, 1982. The *Canada Act, 1982* came into force on this date.

On April 7, 1982, the Quebec Court of Appeal rendered its unanimous opinion answering in the negative the question referred to it [134 D.L.R. (3d) 719].

On April 13, 1982, the Attorney-General of Quebec appealed to this court and on April 15, 1982, at the request of the appellant, Lamer J. stated a constitutional question pursuant to Rule 17 of this court. The terms of this question are identical to those of the question referred to the Quebec Court of Appeal.

On April 17, 1982, the *Constitution Act, 1982* was proclaimed in force by the Queen under the Great Seal of Canada and has been in force since that date.

II — *The opinion of the Court of Appeal*

The unanimous opinion of the Quebec Court of Appeal, answering the question in the negative, is a collective one. It has been signed as a multiple-author opinion by the five judges who participated in the reference, Crête, C.J.Q. and Montgomery, Turgeon, Monet and Jacques JJ.A.

The Court of Appeal first observed that at the time of the hearing, on March 15, 16 and 17, 1982, the process of constitutional amendment had not yet been completed. Although it had been conceded by counsel for the Attorney-General for Quebec that an affirmative answer to the question could have political consequences but no legal ones, the Court of Appeal took the view that, given the broad terms of the *Court of Appeal Reference Act*, R.S.Q. 1977, c. R-23, it should answer a question which had to do with the ''legitimacy'' if not the ''legality'' of the patriation process.

The Court of Appeal was asked by the Attorney-General of Quebec to answer the question in the affirmative on the basis of two alternative submissions. According to the first submission, there was a convention requiring the unanimous consent of the ten provinces to any constitutional amendment of the type in issue. According to the second submission, because of the principle of duality, Quebec had by convention a power of veto over any constitutional amendment affecting the legislative competence of the province or the status or role of its legislature or government within the Canadian federation.

The Court of Appeal rejected the first submission as it found that this court had already ruled it out in the *First Reference*. It rejected the second submission on the following grounds: at law, all the provinces are fundamentally equal and the Attorney-General of Quebec had failed to establish that either the Government of Canada or the other provinces had conventionally recognized in Quebec any special power of veto over constitutional amendment not possessed by the other provinces.

The Court of Appeal further held that at the Constitutional Conference of November 2 to 5, 1981, the degree of provincial consent required had been determined and achieved by the political actors, in accordance with the judgment of this court in the *First Reference*.

III — *The positions of the parties*

Before coming to the submissions made by the parties, it should be said at the outset that the Attorney-General of Canada conceded that the *Canadian Charter of Rights and Freedoms* contained in the *Constitution Act, 1982* affects the legislative competence of all the provinces including Quebec.

To the question whether the status or role of the Legislature or Government of the Province of Quebec within the Canadian federation is affected by the *Constitution Act, 1982*, the factum of the Attorney-General of Canada makes the following answer:

> As for the role and status of Quebec within the Canadian federation, this Act provides Quebec a constitutionally guaranteed right to participate in the amendment of the constitution and to opt out of amendments that derogate from its legislative powers, its proprietary rights or any other rights or privileges of its legislature or government (section 38(2)) under reserve of its constitutionally guaranteed right to financial compensation when the amendment involves a transfer of provincial legislative competence to Parliament in relation to education or other cultural matters (section 40).

This answer is a qualified admission, but an admission none the less, that the role and status of Quebec within the Canadian federation are modified by the procedure for amending the Constitution.

The *Canadian Charter of Rights and Freedoms* is not identical to the *Charter of Rights and Freedoms* referred to in the *First Reference* and the procedure for amending the Constitution of Canada differs substantially from the amending procedure also referred to in the *First Reference*. But it is unnecessary to review these differences. It is sufficient to note that in spite of these differences and on the whole, the *Constitution Act, 1982* directly affects federal-provincial relationships to the same relevant extent as the proposed constitutional legislation discussed in the *First Reference*.

The position of the appellant was that the appeal should be allowed and the constitutional question answered in the affirmative on the basis of the same two submissions which he had made to the Court of Appeal, the first relating to a conventional rule of unanimity and the second to a conventional power of veto said to have been held by Quebec. (Actually, the submission relating to unanimity was made in the second place, but it will be dealt with first, as was done in the Court of Appeal.)

While both submissions seek the same answer to the constitutional question, they are alternative ones, as they have to be, for not only are they quite distinct from each other, they actually contradict one another: the rule of unanimity is predicated on the fundamental equality of all the provinces as it would give a power of veto to each of them whereas an exclusive power of veto for Quebec negates the rule of unanimity as well as the principle of fundamental equality. Also, and as will be seen below, the reason which is said to anchor the conventional rule is a different one in each submission.

In the *First Reference*, there was no substantial disagreement between the majority opinion on convention (hereinafter referred to as the majority opinion), and the dissenting opinion on convention (hereinafter referred to as the dissenting opinion), with respect to the nature of constitutional conventions and the requirements for establishing a convention.

The majority opinion as well as the dissenting opinion both approved, at pp. 110 and 86 D.L.R., pp. 852 and 883 S.C.R., the definition of a convention given by Freedman C.J.M. in the Manitoba Reference [117 D.L.R. (3d) 1 at pp. 13–4, 7 Man. R. (2d) 269, [1981] 2 W.W.R. 193] and quoted at pp. 86–7 D.L.R., p. 883 S.C.R., of the *First Reference*:

> "What is a constitutional convention? There is a fairly lengthy literature on the subject. Although there may be shades of difference among the constitutional lawyers, political scientists, and Judges who have contributed to that literature, the essential features of a convention may be set forth with some degree of confidence. Thus there is general agreement that a convention occupies a position somewhere in between a usage or custom on the one hand and a constitutional law on the other. There is general agreement that if one sought to fix that position with greater precision he would place convention nearer to law than to usage or custom. There is also general agreement that 'a convention is a rule which is regarded as obligatory by the officials to whom it applies'. Hogg, *Constitutional Law of Canada* (1977), p. 9. There is, if not general agreement, at least weighty authority, that the sanction for breach of a convention will be political rather than legal."

At p. 90 D.L.R., p. 888 S.C.R., of the *First Reference*, the majority opinion adopted the following passage of Sir W. Ivor Jennings, *The Law and the Constitution*, 5th ed. (1959), at p. 136:

> "We have to ask ourselves three questions: first, what are the precedents; secondly, did the actors in the precedents believe that they were bound by a rule; and thirdly,

is there a reason for the rule? A single precedent with a good reason may be enough to establish the rule. A whole string of precedents without such a reason will be of no avail, unless it is perfectly certain that the persons concerned regarded them as bound by it."

The main purpose of constitutional conventions is to ensure that the legal framework of the constitution will be operated in accordance with generally accepted principles. It should be borne in mind, however, that conventional rules, although quite distinct from legal ones, are nevertheless to be distinguished from rules of morality, rules of expediency and subjective rules. Like legal rules, they are positive rules the existence of which has to be ascertained by reference to objective standards. In being asked to answer the question whether the convention did or did not exist, we are called upon to say whether or not the objective requirements for establishing a convention had been met. But we are in no way called upon to say whether it was desirable that the convention should or should not exist and no view is expressed on the matter.

Subject to an important qualification which will be dealt with in due course, appellant accepted the above-stated requirements for establishing conventions and made his two submissions within the framework defined by this court in the *First Reference*.

With respect to the precedents, positive and negative, the appellant invoked for the purposes of his two submissions the same precedents as had been relied upon by the majority opinion in the *First Reference*, at pp. 93–5 D.L.R., pp. 891–4 S.C.R.

The positive precedents are the constitutional amendments leading to the *Constitution Act, 1930*, the *Statute of Westminster, 1931*, the *Constitution Act, 1940*, the *British North America Act, 1951* and the *Constitution Act, 1964*, all of which directly affected federal-provincial relationships in the sense of changing legislative powers and each of which was agreed upon by each province whose legislative authority was affected.

The negative precedents are the failure of a proposed amendment relating to indirect taxation in 1951 and the failure of the Constitutional Conferences of 1960, 1964 and 1971. The precedents also comprise, in negative terms, the fact that no amendment changing provincial legislative powers had been made when agreement of a province whose legislative power would have been changed was withheld.

It was further pointed out by the appellant that no relevant constitutional amendment had been passed without the consent of Quebec and that with respect to one of them, the *Constitution Act, 1964*, Quebec alone had delayed the amendment already agreed upon by the nine other provinces as early as 1962. Quebec finally gave its consent in 1964 and the amendment was passed.

The appellant also underlined that the *Constitution Act, 1940* had been delayed because three provinces, Quebec, New Brunswick and Alberta had not yet consented to it; that the lack of agreement of two provinces, Ontario and Quebec, had prevented a proposed constitutional amendment relating to indirect taxation in 1951; and that the lack of agreement of the sole Province of Quebec had caused the failure of the Constitutional Conference of 1964, relating to the Fulton-Favreau formula as well, in practice, as the failure of the Constitutional Conference of 1971 relating to the Victoria Charter, although in the latter case, Saskatchewan did not make its position known.

It was recognized by the appellant that there must be a reason for the alleged conventional rule.

The reason for the unanimity role, he argued, was the federal principle within the meaning given to this principle by the majority opinion in the *First Reference*.

The reason for the conventional rule giving to Quebec a power of veto was said to be the principle of duality, the meaning and nature of which will be discussed in more detail below.

Finally, as to the requirement that the actors in the precedents believe that they were bound by the rule, the appellant submitted that it had been met. But his counsel substantially qualified this submission by pleading in his factum and in oral argument that the precedents and the reason for the rule suffice to establish a constitutional convention and, accordingly, that the recognition of the actors in the precedents is not required or, alternatively, that recognition can be tacit and inferred from the precedents.

The respondent submitted that the court should refuse to answer the question. He also submitted that if the court should answer the question it should answer in the negative on the basis of the *First Reference*. He submitted alternatively that, if the court should answer the question, it should answer that the political leaders had complied with the convention recognized by this court in the *First Reference*.

The interveners generally supported the position of the appellant.

IV — *Whether the question should be answered*

The respondent advanced two reasons why the court should refuse to answer the question: it was a purely political question and it had become academic.

The first objection had also been raised in the *First Reference* and dismissed in the majority opinion as well as in the dissenting opinion. The majority opinion adopted the view of Freedman C.J.M. [Manitoba Reference, at p. 13] on this point, at pp. 87–8 D.L.R., p. 884 S.C.R.:

> "In my view, this submission goes too far. Its characterization of Question 2 as 'purely political' overstates the case. That there is a political element embodied in the question, arising from the contents of the joint address, may well be the case. But that does not end the matter. If Question 2, even if in part political, possesses a constitutional feature, it would legitimately call for our reply.
>
> "In my view, the request for a decision by this Court on whether there is a constitutional convention, in the circumstances described, that the Dominion will not act without the agreement of the Provinces poses a question that is, at least in part, constitutional in character. It therefore calls for an answer, and I propose to answer it."

This view is still vivid and ought to prevail in the case at bar.

On the other hand, counsel for the respondent is right in asserting that the constitutional question has become moot. The *Constitution Act, 1982* is now in force. Its legality is neither challenged nor assailable. It contains a new procedure for amending the Constitution of Canada which entirely replaces the old one in its legal as well as in its conventional aspects. Even assuming therefore that there was a conventional requirement for the consent of Quebec under the old system, it would no longer have any object or force.

However, when the reference was ordered, when it was argued before the Court of Appeal and when the Court of Appeal delivered its certified opinion on April 7, 1982, it could not be said that the question was moot since the process of constitutional amendment had not been completed, the *Constitution Act, 1982* having not yet been proclaimed.

This opinion of the Court of Appeal is now standing. Under an *Act respecting a reference to the Court of Appeal, supra*, this opinion is deemed to be a judgment of the Court of Appeal which may be appealed to this court as a judgment in an action. In such a case, an appeal to this court lies as of right under s. 37 of the *Supreme Court Act*:

> 37. An appeal lies to the Supreme Court from an opinion pronounced by the highest court of final resort in a province on any matter referred to it for hearing and consideration by the lieutenant governor in council of that province whenever it has been by the statutes of that province declared that such opinion is to be deemed a judgment of the highest court of final resort and that an appeal lies therefrom as from a judgment in an action.

While this court retains its discretion to entertain or not to entertain an appeal as of right where the issue has become moot, it may, in the exercise of its discretion, take into consideration the importance of the constitutional issue determined by a court of appeal judgment which would remain unreviewed by this court.

In the circumstances of this case, it appears desirable that the constitutional question be answered in order to dispel any doubt over it and it accordingly will be answered.

V — *Whether there exists a conventional rule of unanimity*

It was the appellant's contention that the majority opinion in the *First Reference* has left open the question whether there existed a conventional rule of unanimity. His main argument for so contending was that the majority opinion did not limit the meaning of the questions relating to convention solely to determining whether there existed a convention which required the unanimous consent of the provinces.

It is quite true that the majority opinion in the *First Reference* gave to the constitutional questions a wider scope than did the dissenting opinion, but this enabled the majority to consider all arguments, including the one relating to unanimity, which it clearly rejected.

The majority opinion in the *First Reference* indicated the position of the majority at the outset, after having stated the submissions of the provinces. Contrary to the provinces which had submitted that the convention did exist, that it required the agreement of all the provinces and that the second question in the Manitoba and Newfoundland [118 D.L.R. (3d) 1, 29 Nfld. & P.E.I.R. 503] References should be answered in the affirmative, counsel for Saskatchewan had also submitted that the question be answered in the affirmative, but on a different basis:

> He submitted that the convention does exist and requires a measure of provincial agreement. Counsel for Saskatchewan further submitted that the Resolution before the Court has not received a sufficient measure of provincial consent.
>
> We wish to indicate at the outset that we find ourselves in agreement with the submissions made on this issue by counsel for Saskatchewan.

(*First Reference*, at p. 89 D.L.R., p. 886 S.C.R.)

At pp. 90–1 D.L.R., p. 888 S.C.R., the majority opinion held that precedents and usage did not suffice to establish a convention, that they had to be normative and be founded on acceptance by the actors in the precedents. The majority went on to make the following statements. At p. 95 D.L.R., p. 894 S.C.R.:

> Indeed, if the precedents stood alone, it might be argued that unanimity is required.

At p. 100 D.L.R., p. 901 S.C.R.:

> It seems clear that while the precedents taken alone point at unanimity, the unanimity principle cannot be said to have been accepted by all the actors in the precedents.

At p. 102 D.L.R., p. 904 S.C.R.:

> We have also indicated that while the precedents point at unanimity, it does not appear that all the actors in the precedents have accepted the unanimity rule as a binding one.

It necessarily follows that, in the opinion of the majority, one essential requirement for establishing a conventional rule of unanimity was missing. This requirement was acceptance by all the actors in the precedents. Accordingly, there existed no such convention.

At p. 103 D.L.R., p. 905 S.C.R., of the *First Reference*, the majority decided that "a substantial measure of provincial consent" was required. A "substantial measure of provincial consent" means less than unanimity. This is what the dissenting judges understood that the majority was deciding: the dissenting opinion contains the following statement at p. 113 D.L.R., p. 856 S.C.R.:

> For the Court to postulate some other convention requiring less than unanimous provincial consent to constitutional amendments would be to go beyond the terms of the References and in so doing to answer a question not posed by the References.

The dissenting opinion was based on the understanding of the dissenting judges that the constitutional questions relating to conventions meant the consent of all the provinces. The dissenting judges held that there existed no convention requiring any such consent.

This court was therefore unanimous in the *First Reference* in rejecting the conventional rule of unanimity.

The appellant advanced no compelling reason why this unanimous opinion should be modified.

The appellant did quote a passage from the notes released to the press for a speech delivered by the Minister of Justice, the Honourable Guy Favreau, on November 20, 1964. The notes have been published under the title "Constitutional Amendment in a Canadian Canada", 12 McGill L.J. 384 (1966-67). The passage is to be found at pp. 388–9:

> . . . the procedure does not impose any legal constraint that thwarts the traditional forces of constitutional change; on the contrary, it mirrors these forces with utter realism. In the past, Ottawa has never amended the Constitution

on matters touching essential provincial rights (as defined in clause 2 of the formula) without the consent of all the provinces. Given the current — and I think, fruitful — resurgence of provincial initiative, a change in this convention becomes inconceivable. However much some people may regret this convention, it remains an undeniable political reality. The formula does not invent that reality; it merely acknowledges it.

The appellant also quoted the following passage of the *White Paper* published in February, 1965, under the authority of Minister Favreau, entitled ''The Amendment of the Constitution of Canada'' (the *White Paper*), at pp. 46–7:

> It may be argued that a requirement of unanimity is too inflexible to be applied to the distribution of legislative powers, but this distribution is basic to the Canadian federation. In fact, in the 97 years that have elapsed since Confederation, no amendment has altered the powers of provincial legislatures under section 92 of the British North America Act without the consent of all the provinces.
>
> This clearly reflects a basic and historic fact in Canadian constitutional affairs. The Constitution cannot be changed in a way that might deprive provinces of their legislative powers unless they consent. The law has not said so, but the facts of national life have imposed the unanimity requirement, and experience since Confederation has established it as a convention that a government or Parliament would disregard at its peril. This experience is reflected in the formula worked out in 1960–61 and now proposed.

In the *First Reference*, counsel had not relied on these extracts which, in appellant's submission, none the less amounted to a recognition of a conventional rule of unanimity.

This is not the case, in our view.

The above-quoted statements of Minister Favreau must be read in context. The passage of the *White Paper* is to be found in c. V entitled ''The Amending Formula: An Appraisal'', under a sub-title which reads ''Stability versus Flexibility''.

Chapter V is preceded by c. II entitled ''History of Constitutional Amendment in Canada'' the fourth sub-title of which reads ''Procedures Followed in the Past in Securing Amendments to the British North America Act''. Substantial parts of the text written under this last sub-title were quoted, analysed and relied upon by the majority opinion in the *First Reference*, at pp. 98–9 D.L.R., pp. 989–9 S.C.R. They include the following at pp. 10–11 of the *White Paper*:

> ''The procedures for amending a constitution are normally a fundamental part of the laws and conventions by which a country is governed. This is particularly true if the constitution is embodied in a formal document as is the case in such federal states as Australia, the United States and Switzerland. In these countries, the amending process forms an important part of their constitutional law.
>
> ''In this respect, Canada has been in a unique constitutional position. Not only did the British North America Act not provide for its amendment by Canadian legislative authority, except to the extent outlined at the beginning of this chapter, but it also left Canada without clearly defined procedure for securing constitutional amendments from the British Parliament. As a result, procedures have varied from time to time, with recurring controversies and doubts over the conditions under which various provisions of the Constitution should be amended.
>
> ''Certain rules and principles relating to amending procedures have nevertheless developed over the years. They have emerged from the practices and procedures employed in securing various amendments to the British North America Act since 1867. Though not constitutionally binding in any strict sense, they have come to be recognized and accepted in practice as part of the amendment process in Canada.
>
> ''In order to trace and describe the manner in which these rules and principles have developed, the approaches used to secure amendments through the Parliament of the United Kingdom over the past 97 years are described in the following paragraphs. Not all the amendments are included in this review, but only those that have contributed to the development of accepted constitutional rules and principles.''

There follows a list of fourteen constitutional amendments thought to ''have contributed to the development of accepted constitutional rules and principles''. The *White Paper* then goes on to state these principles, at p. 15, in the form of a code composed of four conventional rules the fourth of which is the only relevant one:

> ''*The fourth general principle* is that the Canadian Parliament will not request an amendment directly affecting federal-provincial relationships without prior consultation and agreement with the provinces. This principle did not emerge as early as others but since 1907, and particularly since 1930, has gained increasing recognition and acceptance. The nature and the degree of provincial participation in the amending process, however, have not lent themselves to easy definition.''

The statement written at p. 47 of the *White Paper* to the effect that

> . . . the facts of national life have imposed the unanimity requirement, and experience since Confederation has established it as a convention . . .

cannot be reconciled with the last sentence of the fourth general principle:

> The nature and the degree of provincial participation in the amending process, however, have not lent themselves to easy definition.

If unanimity had been established as a convention, the nature and degree of provincial participation in the amending process would have been fully defined.

In our view, the fourth general principle is to be preferred as an accurate statement of the rule. It is expressed as a part of a conventional code in a chapter which constitutes a detached analysis of historical precedents.

By contrast, the statement made at pp. 46–7 of the *White Paper* is an apology or a plea in favour of an amending formula which had come under attack as being too rigid. It is not an authoritative statement of the rule. The same can be said of the above-quoted statement made by Minister Favreau on November 20, 1964, which, incidentally, is part of a chapter entitled "The Formula Defended".

That some of the actors in the precedents had accepted the rule of unanimity is not doubted and was recognized by this court in the majority opinion at p. 102 D.L.R., p. 904 S.C.R., of the *First Reference*. But this is not enough. Other important actors declined to accept the unanimity rule, as indicated in the majority opinion at p. 101 D.L.R., p. 902 S.C.R., of the *First Reference*.

The opinion expressed in the *First Reference* that there existed no conventional rule of unanimity should be reaffirmed.

VI — *Whether Quebec has a conventional power of veto*

It has already been indicated, with respect to the precedents which are said to establish the conventional rule of a power of veto for Quebec, that the appellant relied upon those which had been invoked by the majority opinion in the *First Reference*, at pp. 93–5 D.L.R., pp. 891–4 S.C.R.

The reason advanced by the appellant for the existence of a conventional rule of a power of veto for Quebec is the principle of duality, this principle being however understood in a special sense.

The expression "Canadian duality" is frequently used to refer to the two larger linguistic groups in Canada and to the constitutional protection afforded to the official languages by provisions such as s. 133 of the *Constitution Act, 1867* and s. 23 of the *Manitoba Act, 1870*.

Counsel for the appellant characterized this aspect of the Canadian duality as the "federal" aspect and recognized that the central government had a role to play in this respect within the framework of federal institutions as well as outside Quebec. But he also made it clear that what he meant by the principle of duality embraced much more than linguistic or cultural differences. What was meant by the principle of duality was what counsel called its "Quebec" aspect which he defined more precisely in his factum at pp. 8 and 16 (translation):

> In the context of this reference, *the word "duality" covers all the circumstances that have contributed to making Quebec a distinct society, since the foundation of Canada and long before, and the range of guarantees that were made to Quebec in 1867, as a province which the Task Force on Canadian Unity has described as "the stronghold of the French-Canadian people" and the "living heart of the French presence in North America."* These circumstances and these guarantees extend far beyond matters of language and culture alone: the protection of the *British North America Act* was extended to all aspects of Quebec society — language, certainly, but also the society's values, its law, religion, education, territory, natural resources, government and the sovereignty of its legislative assembly over everything which was at the time of a "local" nature.

. . . . .

> In 1867, the French Canadian minority became a majority within the Quebec Legislature. This is what accounts for the special nature of this province, and it is the reason underlying the convention that the powers of its Legislature cannot be reduced without consent.

One finds another expression of the principle of duality understood in this sense in the preamble of the above-quoted Decree No. 3367-81, dated December 9, 1981, the fourth paragraph of which states in concise terms (translation):

> WHEREAS Quebec forms a distinct society within the Canadian federation;

Another more elaborate expression of the principle of duality understood in the special sense urged by counsel for the appellant is to be found in a resolution passed by the Quebec National Assembly on December 1, 1981, and more particularly in condition No. 1 of the resolution (translation):

> that the National Assembly of Quebec, having in mind the right of the people of Quebec to self-determination and exercising its historical right to be a party to and approve any change in the Constitution of Canada which might affect the rights and powers of Quebec, states that it cannot approve the proposal to patriate the constitution unless it includes the following conditions:
>
> 1. It shall be recognized that the two founding people of Canada are fundamentally equal, and that

within the Canadian federation Quebec forms a society distinct by its language, culture and institutions, one which possesses all the attributes of a distinct national community;

   2. The constitutional amending formula:

    a) shall either preserve Quebec's right of veto, or

    b) shall be the one approved in the constitutional agreement signed by Quebec on April 16, 1981, affirming the right of Quebec not to have imposed on it any change which would reduce its powers or rights, and if such a reduction were to take place, to be given reasonable compensation as a matter of right.

   3. . . .

   4. . . .

These then are the precedents and the reason for the rule, according to counsel for the appellant.

It will not be necessary in our view to look further into these matters because this submission must in any event be rejected, the appellant having failed completely to demonstrate compliance with the most important requirement for establishing a convention, that is, acceptance or recognition by the actors in the precedents.

We have been referred to an abundance of material, speeches made in the course of parliamentary debates, reports of royal commissions, opinions of historians, political scientists, constitutional experts which endorse in one way or another the principle of duality within the meaning assigned to it by the appellant, and there can be no doubt that many Canadian statesmen, politicians and experts favoured this principle.

But neither in his factum nor in oral argument did counsel for the appellant quote a single statement made by any representative of the federal authorities recognizing either explicitly or by necessary implication that Quebec had a conventional power of veto over certain types of constitutional amendments. The statement made by Minister Favreau on November 20, 1964, and the passage to be found at pp. 46–7 of the *White Paper* have been quoted twice in the appellant's factum, as if they supported the veto rule as well as the unanimity one, but they refer only to unanimity and have been above dealt with in this respect.

Furthermore, a convention such as the one now asserted by Quebec would have to be recognized by other provinces. We have not been referred to and we are not aware of any statement by the actors in any of the other provinces acknowledging such a convention. Not only have we not been given any evidence of the acquiescence of other provinces but in the *First Reference*, three of them, Manitoba, Prince Edward Island and Alberta, explicitly pleaded in favour of the unanimity rule in their factums, a position compatible only with the principle of equality among the provinces and incompatible with a special power of veto for Quebec. It should also be noted that in the *First Reference*, Ontario and New Brunswick had taken the position that the constitutional amending process was not regulated by conventions involving the provinces.

In order to make up for these fundamental flaws in his submission, counsel for the appellant argued as follows in his factum (translation):

> In the opinion of the Attorney General, custom and a reason suffice by themselves to establish the normative nature of the rule.

Counsel for the appellant also referred to Sir Ivor Jennings' test, adopted by this court in the *First Reference*, and more particularly to the last part of this test:

> A single precedent with a good reason may be enough to establish the rule. A whole string of precedents without such a reason will be of no avail, unless it is perfectly certain that the persons concerned regarded them as bound by them.

As we understand it, the contention was that recognition by the actors in the precedents is not an absolutely essential requirement for establishing a convention and that the last part of Jennings' test is an authority for that proposition.

This contention is based on two sentences taken out of context and is an over-simplified and erroneous view of Jennings' test. In these two sentences, Jennings is merely expanding on what he said in the sentence immediately preceding them about the three requirements and illustrating the interrelation between them. He is not doing away with the requirement that the actors in the precedents believe that they were bound by a rule. Indeed Jennings insists in several passages of his book, *The Law and the Constitution, supra,* that recognition or acquiescence is an essential ingredient of constitutional conventions. Thus he writes, at p. 81:

> "Conventions" imply some form of agreement, whether expressed or implied . . .

And at p. 117:

> The conventions are like most fundamental rules of any constitution in that they rest essentially upon general acquiescence.

And at p. 135:

> . . . if the authority itself and those connected with it believe that they ought to do so, then the convention exists. This is the ordinary rule applied to customary law. Practice alone is not enough. It must be normative.

In the *First Reference*, at pp. 110, 114 and 86–7 D.L.R., pp. 852, 857 and 883 S.C.R., these views were approved by all the members of this court who adopted the definition of convention given by Freedman, C.J.M. in the Manitoba Reference, including, at p. 87 D.L.R., p. 883 S.C.R., the following quotation of Hogg, *Constitutional Law of Canada*, (1977), p. 9:

> "a convention is a rule which is regarded as obligatory by the officials to whom it applies".

Recognition by the actors in the precedents is not only an essential element of conventions. In our opinion, it is the most important element since it is the normative one, the formal one which enables us unmistakably to distinguish a constitutional rule from a rule of convenience or from political expediency.

Counsel for the appellant also contended in reply that recognition by the actors in the precedents need not be explicit, and this contention appears to be supported by the following statement of Jennings already quoted above: " 'Conventions' imply some form of agreement, whether expressed or implied . . .".

Again, Jennings' assertion must be qualified. Some conventions have been formulated in writing, for instance in the Reports of Imperial conferences or in the preamble of the *Statute of Westminster, 1931*. Such conventions can be said to have been expressly agreed upon in authoritative or official form.

The majority of constitutional conventions, however, have not so been reduced to writing. Does this mean that they are based on implied agreements strictly so-called in that they have never been the object of any form of utterance? We do not think so.

Conventions are commonly asserted or claimed by some political actors in more or less informal statements, while the other actors similarly acknowledge them in principle if not always in their application to particular facts. Conventions are analyzed, dissected, commented upon and sometimes criticized albeit not to the point of rejection. But, in our view, a convention could not have remained wholly inarticulate, except perhaps at the inchoate stage when it has not yet been accepted as a binding rule. There is no example that we know of of a convention being born while remaining completely unspoken, and none was cited to us. It seems to us that the contention of appellant's counsel to the effect that conventions need not be explicitly accepted is impossible to distinguish in practice from a denial of the requirement of acceptance by the actors in the precedents. It is precisely through reported statements by numerous actors that a convention could be identified in the *First Reference*. Such statements provide the only true test of recognition, and, once again, unmistakably to distinguish a constitutional rule from a rule of convenience or from political expediency.

In our view, the Quebec Court of Appeal was correct in holding that the appellant had failed to establish that Quebec had a conventional power of veto over constitutional amendments such as those in issue in the present reference.

VII — *Conclusion*

For these reasons, we would answer "No" to the constitutional question, and we would dismiss the appeal. There should be no order as to costs.

Appeal dismissed.

INDEX